D0858276

METHODS IN ENVIRONMENTAL AND BEHAVIORAL RESEARCH

METHODS IN ENVIRONMENTAL AND BEHAVIORAL RESEARCH

EDITED BY

Robert B. Bechtel
Robert W. Marans
William Michelson

VAN NOSTRAND REINHOLD COMPANY
New York

Library of Congress Catalog Card Number 86-13130
ISBN 0-442-21157-0

Printed in the United States of America

Van Nostrand Reinhold Company Inc.
115 Fifth Avenue
New York, New York 10003

Van Nostrand Reinhold Company Limited
Molly Millars Lane
Wokingham, Berkshire RG11 2PY, England

Van Nostrand Reinhold
480 La Trobe Street
Melbourne, Victoria 3000, Australia

Macmillan of Canada
Division of Canada Publishing Corporation
164 Commander Boulevard
Agincourt, Ontario M1S 3C7, Canada

16 15 14 13 12 11 10 9 8 7 6 5 4 3 2 1

Library of Congress Cataloging-in-Publication Data

Methods in environmental and behavioral research.

Includes index.
1. Environmental psychology—Research—Methodology.
I. Bechtel, Robert B. II. Marans, Robert W.
III. Michelson, William M., 1940-
BF353.M48 1986 155.9 86-13130
ISBN 0-442-21157-0

CONTENTS

INTRODUCTION: ENVIRONMENTAL DESIGN RESEARCH

Robert B. Bechtel
Robert W. Marans
and William Michelson

In the PBS television series *Shock of the New* (BBC, 1970), three dramatic environmental failures were presented, the dynamiting of Pruitt Igoe (the St. Louis housing project), and the inadequate living conditions of Brasília in Brazil and Chandigarh in India. The total cost of these failures is uncounted but in the hundreds of millions of dollars. At the very least, the television series pointed out, a new basis is necessary for designing, researching, and even thinking about new buildings and new cities. The complexities are too many to be encompassed by one kind of person or professional acting alone. What is needed is a new way to collect and use information to take into account many of the complex modern requirements of human life.

This book deals with research methods in environmental design that will help to alleviate some of these seemingly overwhelming problems and bring into focus the kinds of knowledge needed for their solutions. While this first chapter will provide an expected introduction to the chapters that follow, it also examines the larger context that this book addresses. We shall discuss successively the scope of environmental design research, why special concentration on methodology within this context is necessary and desirable, the developments reflected in this book, and, by no means least, the content and organization of the chapters that follow.

This book is intended to succeed another in which the present editors previously collaborated (Michelson 1975). Why is an almost entirely new book needed at this time? The reason is that the field of environment-behavior research has advanced at such a pace that a new text is long overdue. Old methods have become outmoded and new methods have been refined. It is time to take stock of these changes and record current practice. Further, the field has now diversified, making it much harder to gain a knowledge of all its methods from one source.

THE SCOPE OF DESIGN RESEARCH

Environmental design means many things to many people. Architects do it when creating rooms and buildings. Landscape architects do it to outdoor spaces, space planners do it in offices and factories. City and regional planners do it, too, when working with the content, layout, and movements of neighborhoods, cities, and regions. Engineers increasingly deal with all these considerations, as well as aspects of infrastructure such as transportation that are necessary elements in the planning.

What design professionals have in common is that they deal with aspects of the physical environment, man-made and natural, in conjunction with the human functions that their designs are intended to facilitate. They diverge, nonetheless, along several dimensions. The research that helps inform environmental design, in providing the factual basis for making the optimal match of any physical arrangement to its human purposes, would vary along similar lines.

One obvious dimension of variation in environmental design and research is scale. Environments may vary from extremely small ones, of very tangible qualities, to environments greater than can be viewed from one location. The latter macroenvironments may lack the same visual qualities as smaller design objects, but their organization and spatial arrangements are no less relevant to human functioning and movement.

Environments whose attributes are keyed to human implications can also be arrayed on a continuum from man-made to natural. Buildings and their interior spaces are usually at the former extreme. Wilderness areas, maintained and managed to preserve their natural values and accommodate human use, are at the latter extreme. In between lie different degrees of combinations, including neighborhoods, which often include natural elements, and parks, which require man-made infrastructure to go with the natural elements.

Another dimension lies in the design process itself. This has at least five stages, each of which involves unique informational needs. A very preliminary stage requires the determination of the kind of design initiative that should be taken. At this stage priorities must be determined—which neighborhood needs intervention, which department needs new furnishings and equipment, which sector of wilderness or watershed is to be protected. Research in this instance is often of a structural, economic, or cultural nature. Once priorities are set, the next step in the design process, called programming, is to identify the needs and behaviors of the eventual users of an environment, the factors that will be a central focus for later, more detailed design work. Often a detailed study is made of what people generally do, what they want, and what they typically lack in existing settings, in order to provide some idea of the organizational and dynamic requirements of the newly designed environment. The stage of detailed design, where drawings and plans are made, requires knowledge of just what is known to happen in response to particular features that may be incorporated into a plan. Here, knowledge of the effects and implications of previously created spaces or plans becomes useful, as is experimental work aimed at stimulating and testing the proposals. When a design or plan has been created but not yet implemented, the use of feedback on it from directly and indirectly affected persons is a helpful, often essential corrective step. Public opinion and subjectively deep approaches are often helpful toward that end. Finally, once something has been built or otherwise implemented, it is critical to evaluate how well it works and otherwise succeeds in order to accumulate knowledge about suitable design. Approaches that allow assessment at both individual and aggregate levels contribute to such evaluations. More active participation by citizens and users can enter at every stage too. Clearly, a large variety of research approaches and methodologies responds to needs for information that vary at different stages of the design process.

All environments are not for all people on the same terms. People other than the elderly play a role in a nursing home; such an environment must fit the exacting requirements of an aging population, as well as those of the people who care for and visit them. Schools must fit the needs of children of the appropriate ages, which are not necessarily the same as those of a cross-section of the population; yet schools should be appropriate for uses by others as well. Environments that are explicitly shared, such as transportation systems, public spaces, and government buildings, need designs that take the needs and abilities of widely different population subgroups into consideration; targeting just some adult, affluent, able-bodied groups effectively excludes those not fitting such characteristics from comfortable use of such places, indeed sometimes forcing separate facilities for the latter or nonparticipation in desired activities. Research for design therefore considers the needs of special populations and how these interact with the physical environment; and methodological approaches vary according to the subpopulation involved (Zimring et al. 1986).

Finally, a spectrum of social science perspectives and theories are brought to bear on design questions. To some extent, these will vary according to the stage of the design process to which they are applied. Nonetheless, even at a single stage, particularly that of explicit design work, more than one will almost certainly have to be considered.

Dealing with the social science perspectives necessary for a given design solution is not like buying a loaf of bread. When you buy bread, you may have to choose from a wide variety of ryes, wheats, and oats, but you still walk out with a loaf of bread that satisfies your needs. Dealing with social science and design is more like jumping hurdles. Once you have cleared one hurdle, others still lie in your way, until you have disposed of them one by one in a satisfactory manner.

The hurdles represent different perspectives on human life. Many social scientists specialize in only one or possibly two of them, since the pursuit of these perspectives usually involves different interests and skills. All perspectives, nonetheless, are drawn from the single context of people's use of designed environments; hence a satisfactory design framework takes account of people in considering different and complementary perspectives. You do not finish the race, let alone win it, until you have cleared all the hurdles. And this is the kind of race where you do not run fastest to win, but run in the most methodical manner possible.

One such perspective, a vital, imperative first consideration, is whether people have the physical opportunity to perform that which is intended in the designed environment. Are the desired movements and activities actually permitted by the environment? Or does the design really make them more difficult or even impossible? Too many buildings and communities, in fact, present the wrong answer to these questions.

Behavior that occurs in a given physical setting can be both desirable and undesirable. Although environment is designed for the most part to accommodate certain explicit and implicit types of behavior, careful planning may be necessary to eliminate the possibility of certain kinds of undesired behavior. Oscar Newman (1972) expounded this theme in describing his attempt to redesign high-density residential settings so as to lessen the possibility of criminal activity.

On a micro scale, behavioral needs to be accommodated in housing are frequently referred to by the term *user needs*. Although research in user needs is not particularly well developed at the lower level of the scale, it is nonetheless applied as well, though in less tangible terms, to larger-scale environments, such as concern the city planner. Large-scale entities are the setting for frequent, regular, and important activities that are more or less difficult to facilitate through environmental design. Recreational, commercial, and travel patterns are but the tip of the iceberg in this regard; a whole complex of life-styles is either fostered or stifled in the macro-level milieu.

If we ask specifically what occurs in designed environments, the most immediate answer is behavior. Hence a first question to ask of any potential or recently completed environment is how it provides the opportunity for specific types of human behavior. Obviously, then, concepts to discuss and methods to assess behavior itself are required of social scientists by environmental research.

Once the opportunity for behavior has been taken into consideration, however, it does not necessarily follow that the desired behavior will, in fact, ensue. Other perspectives come into play at this time. Perceptual phenomena, for example, are highly important—the opportunity for a given behavior has to be perceived before it can be acted upon. A whole different line of investigation is then necessary to see what types of symbolic representation people identify with as preconditions for their own behavior. Spaces, for example, can favor conviviality or solitude depending on an array of symbolic properties, including color, furniture, and decorative touches such as bookcases or bars, crosses or cartoons. Most societies or subcultures have conventions concerning the way phenomena are arrayed and how people perceive them. These conventions must be observed; creative activity on the part of the designer starts with these as a basis, for ignoring them in the pursuit of fancy leads to the functional collapse of the product, however imaginative.

Even when the hurdles of perception and opportunity are cleared, however, we are not home free, although these may be preconditions for a successful design. The norms governing people's activities in particular environments must still be taken into account. Edward Hall in *The Hidden Dimension* (1966) refers to the fact that in any culture the rules guiding how people deal with one another (with strong social sanctions guarding against violation of the rules) have a strong spatial dimension. Certain activities, ranging from extreme intimacy to public demagoguery, contain implicit but nonetheless real standards of separation between the participants. Notions of privacy differ from culture to culture, but imply identifiable standards within a given setting. Within this normative perspective, Sommer (1969) has contributed considerable work on institutional settings, through his handling of the environmental implications of interpersonal, spatial norms in such settings as classrooms, libraries, and mental hospitals.

Whether at a micro or macro level, studies relevant to the normative perspective may focus, on the one hand, on what people actually do in particular spatial settings and, on the other hand, on what they consider right or correct (for people like themselves) regarding environmental design.

In short, any project that truly accounts for relevant social science considerations will have explored at least to some degree whatever behavioral, perceptual-symbolic, and normative implications may be lodged in its design. This is the joint task of social scientists and designers. Even at the solution and evaluation stages of the design process, it is no wonder that we find leading methodological approaches to be diverse in character and representative of different social science perspectives.

SPECIAL METHODOLOGICAL CONSIDERATIONS IN ENVIRONMENTAL DESIGN

The wide-ranging scope of environmental design and the research pertinent to it makes clear that the approaches taken to research and the methodologies utilized will be diverse. Besides diversity, what special emphases might be required by research in environment and behavior?

In the previous section we noted that despite enormous differences in approach, the different design professions share informational needs on the interface of physical environment with human functioning. This is not a trivial point, because the presence of the physical environment as an integral part of environmental design research represents a major point of departure from the more general social science research, with implications for research design and procedure.

Research that ties together the environmental and the behavioral is relatively recent, but individual studies and substantive texts have advanced far more explicitly than have works focusing on method. Moreover, on the practicum side of design, the research and development process has been sadly neglected, largely as a consequence of unfamiliarity and perceived lack of salience. Thus, explicit attention to research methods in this area serves to demonstrate how the disparate factors in environmental design research can be made to meet.

In the process of examining the methodological requirements of working in the context of physical settings, it becomes apparent that some methods, such as the time budget and simulation, which are not widely known or frequently used in the social sciences generally, are of strategic value within environmental design research because they join context to behavior. Furthermore, other methods—the social survey, for example—have particular uses and demands made upon them when applied to questions of environmental design. Their adaptation to design research requires knowledge of a number of special considerations such as sampling and questionnaire construction that are not apparent from more general practice.

The emphasis on environment has several direct and far-reaching implications—and hence, requirements for research that differ from customary practice. First, there is the question as to who or what is the basic unit of analysis. In most social science research, it is the person, group, or societal aggregate. In environmental research, it is as much, if not more, the space or place than the person or agglomeration. Most such physical entities involve more than one person, often great numbers. Thus, attention must be focused on this collectivity, which will often consist of persons with dissimilar characteristics and needs (from sex and age at the most micro level to socioeconomic and subcultural differences at macro levels). Yet such settings are utilized by individuals whose motivations and cognitive processes are of essential relevance to explanation and decision making. As a result, researchers in this area are forced to direct their attention back and forth between individuals and collectivities. And their methods must be sufficient to address this shifting need (see Lindberg and Hellberg 1975).

Social scientists typically sample individuals, not environments. When areas are picked, such as in cluster sampling, it is for the purpose of shrinking the territory that interviewers need to cover, while attempting to ensure representativeness. In design research, one will often choose territories as a principal sampling unit because they are an intrinsic (often independent) variable in the research question. As Robert Marans points out in chapter 2, design research involving cluster sampling has the advantage of simultaneously selecting individuals and the territory associated with them.

Research design thus becomes of particular concern in much of environmental design. Unlike much experimental work in psychology, the crucial stimulus or variable may lie in the environment, which can be simulated in a laboratory or selected from among existing environments outside the lab. Few guidelines in the general research design literature help this form of application.

Environmental design research is applied and is relevant to future decisions and plans. Even when research is not attached to an ongoing design project, the researchers almost always have an intended application in their minds. When dealing with real-world phenomena, researchers have to consider the relevance of diverse groups. In this era of large-scale economic organization and governments, those who initiate and manage matters of design and planning are often bureaucrats one or two steps, at the least, removed from those who will primarily use the environments. There are other groups that will be indirectly affected by such environments. Researchers working in this area have to be aware of who the pertinently affected populations will be and how to reach them, a task not, for the most part, addressed in normal survey or experimental work.

Furthermore, all these considerations suggest the need for the use of a number of methods at the same time. This is being increasingly accepted in the social sciences, where three or more methods are considered useful to enhance the validity of results. Nonetheless, in environmental design research, multiple methods are essential if only to cover adequately the many different considerations that flow from a need to concentrate on environment, individuals, and groups, different kinds of individuals and groups, and more, in addition to the need for validity.

Therefore, we were convinced in 1975 and are even more convinced ten years later of the need to examine environmental design research on its own terms and in greater depth.

RECENT DEVELOPMENTS IN DESIGN RESEARCH

The past decade has seen many innovations in environmental design research. Advances that have been made in the techniques discussed in the earlier book (Michelson 1975) require expanded coverage and the updating of illustrations. Simulation, an approach that was not included in the first book, has reached a stage of development that makes coverage important at this time. Observational and behavior setting research, combined in the earlier volume, now require separate treatment.

Work over the years on certain major target groups in the population has expanded to the point where these deserve explicit treatment, not least because each involves unique methodological considerations. Of particular importance are methods for the study of children and of the elderly, which are considered in separate chapters.

Since research is becoming more common both as part of architectural programming and after environments are put into use, applications chapters have been added on programming and post-occupancy evaluation.

During the past ten years, geography has begun to receive the attention of psychologists and sociologists interested in environmental perception, who are applying this and related research perspectives to a realm that geographers were first to recognize—the macro, outdoor environment. Because of increased interest in this design area, we included a chapter devoted entirely to natural environments.

Despite the continued use of our previous volume, as indicated by course adoptions, we have felt an obligation to produce a virtually new work, to reflect the diversification of the field and the many advances that have occurred in it.

CONTENTS OF THE PRESENT VOLUME

Encompassing both methods and applications, this book focuses in the first half on discrete methods, while the second half turns to a variety of applications that use different methods in combination.

An unobtrusive method, observation, is examined by Robert Bechtel and John Zeisel in chapter 1. Much can be learned in relatively micro environments when the eye of the observer is trained and systematic.

Marans looks at survey research in chapter 2. He has added a number of examples showing the practical application of surveys in evaluations of built environments ranging from micro to macro in scale, though survey research remains the chief method for the latter type of project.

In chapter 3, Bechtel details the use of standardized tests and scales, their applications, and their increasing popularity. A controversy that has developed in this field over the use of self-report techniques is also explored.

A highly formal approach is exemplified in Ira Robinson's chapter on urban gaming. This method allows alternatives of urban structure and process, with which people are not necessarily in contact but whose priority or implications are in question, to be presented and manipulated in hypothetical but engrossing forms.

Chapter 5, contributed by Peter Bosselmann and Kenneth H. Craik, looks at simulation methods that provide either a visual view of how those environments could be and/or a functional view of what it would be like to do things within them. As these two objectives suggest, simulation can be miniaturized and then enlarged for the visual experience or presented full-scale, for hands-on experience.

Methods for the identification of specific micro places outside the home in which culturally customary behavior occurs—that is, behavior settings—form the basis of chapter 6, by Bechtel. The methodology has recently been condensed and improved, and it is now time and cost competitive. Research projects utilizing it in isolated communities have produced results that have justified some important design decisions.

William Michelson's chapter shifts the focus to the larger scale, measuring macroenvironment and behavior through the application of the time-budget and time-geography approaches. Though less tangible in many respects than microenvironments, communities, cities, and regions nonetheless have temporal and spatial dimensions that carry the potential for constraining or liberating effects in daily life. These require exploration with methods that can cope with both the complexity and collectivities applicable at higher levels of scale.

In the second part of the book, we turn to particular applications. In chapter 8, Kent Spreckelmeyer focuses on an early stage in the design process—programming, the systematic listing of needs a design must fill. Programming is the critical point at which all previous knowledge, gained by the methods described, is brought to bear. Programming has now achieved the status of a separate profession, a specialty often supplied by independent firms of architects and researchers. Spreckelmeyer goes into the methods involved in this aspect of the design process.

Craig Zimring in chapter 9 discusses methods for the other end of the process—post-occupancy evaluation. This chapter provides a particularly clear illustration of the nature and value of using combinations of methods for the most meaningful and fruitful results.

In chapter 10, Suzanne Ziegler and Howard Andrews examine in considerable depth what it means to do research on youthful users of the environment. They show, among other considerations, how critical a child's stage of development is not only to what environments are utilized but to how these can be studied.

Turning to another major demographic group, chapter 11, by M. Powell Lawton, investigates approaches to studying the elderly and their environments. Much activity and many resources are being directed to the growing sector of the population comprising the elderly, whose environmental needs and methodological requirements are in many ways unlike those of other groups. Demographically speaking, they are the fastest growing population segment in the developed countries.

Natural environments differ from the others in the degree to which they are manipulable, and they are also typically of a larger scale. Research relevant to their management and control involves particular attention. In chapter 12, Jonathan Taylor,

Ervin Zube, and James Sell examine methods for assessing landscapes, emphasizing perceptual methods.

Finally, in the conclusions, the editors return to present an overview of the lessons presented. In addition, this discussion allows for the choice of combinations of methods in terms of mutual compatibility for particular design (or evaluation needs). It also shows once again the range of applications of individual research methods.

Although we have expanded our coverage of established areas and introduced important new developments, our approach was inevitably selective. We have attempted to present a broad introduction to a field that is increasingly diversified and continues to experience rapid change. Readers are encouraged to consult specialized sources that go into greater depth on both the specific methods we describe and their applications to various aspects of design research. The references in each chapter help facilitate this purpose.

No amount of reading, however, can duplicate the experience of trying methods in the field, and it would be a mistake merely to read this volume without attempting to apply its methods. Only by application of these approaches to real problems can the text realize the full range of our intentions.

REFERENCES

BBC. 1970. *Shock of the New.* Series of 8 segments filmed for PBS.

Hall, E. 1966. *The Hidden Dimension.* New York: Doubleday.

Lindberg, G., and J. Hellberg. 1975. Strategic decisions in research design. In *Behavioral Research Methods in Environmental Design,* ed. W. Michelson. Stroudsburg, Pa.: Dowden, Hutchinson & Ross.

Michelson, W., ed. 1975. *Behavioral Research Methods in Environmental Design.* Stroudsburg, Pa.: Dowden, Hutchinson & Ross.

Newman, O. 1972. *Defensible Space.* New York: Macmillan.

Sommer, R. 1969. *Personal Space.* Englewood Cliffs, N.J.: Prentice-Hall.

Zimring, C., et al. 1986. Design for special populations. In *Handbook of Environmental Psychology,* ed. I. Altman and D. Stokols. New York: Wiley.

PART I

METHODS

CHAPTER 1

OBSERVATION: THE WORLD UNDER A GLASS

Robert B. Bechtel
and
John Zeisel

Observation is the most fun of any of the methods in environment behavior research. This is because every person enjoys watching other humans and then, to compound the enjoyment, delights as much or more in telling someone else about it. Yet it is an expectation of enjoyment that can sometimes stand in the way of getting useful results. A long observation can become boring. The fact that observation has become a high-technology method can increase or decrease the enjoyment, depending on one's viewpoint.

Everyone watches and therefore ''knows'' what people do at the beach on a Sunday afternoon. But what about funerals? How do people sit, stand, move about, and otherwise behave at a funeral? Most people are too emotionally involved in the funerals they attend to watch the behavior of others or feel self-conscious about observing the bereaved. Yet the answer to this question is vital to the design of churches and funeral parlors.

And what about the everyday behavior that nobody bothers to watch? How do people sit on buses, work in offices, live in houses, throw money away at gambling casinos, or wait in line at shopping centers? All these are important questions to answer in the behavior–environment equation, but people tend not to observe the commonplace. The observer, then, becomes the poet laureate of the ordinary. A good observer not only records what people do in these everyday circumstances, but presents the findings in such a way as to help people understand their behavior in situations they would not ordinarily think about.

Observation has developed into a highly technological field, yet it remains the one method that people can use with minimal training. Some sort of training, however, must take place before observation can be useful in research. It is useful to describe observation as having five dimensions: the behavior, the environment, the time, the observer, and the record of observation. These five dimensions will be explored and the issues and specialized methods of observation will be described.

BEHAVIOR

What one watches other people do is referred to loosely as *behavior*. People cannot stop ''behaving'' unless they are dead. Behavior is what an organism is doing at any moment. The words we use to describe behavior may be simple, like "standing," "sitting," "talking," or "sleeping." In environment behavior research, however, another element is introduced: the behavior must always be seen within an environmental context. People sleep in beds or on the floor. They converse in restaurants or on sidewalks. In the same sense that people cannot stop behaving, they cannot get away from the environment. There is always a surrounding environment and thus always a behavior–environment relationship.

The span of behavior goes from *molar,* or global, to molecular. Molar behavior consists of the larger units of behavior. These do not include very large numbers of people, however, because an observer cannot watch very many people at once. Instead, molar units of behavior refer to more complex activities, such as going to the store or working in an office. *Molecular* units are smaller in the sense that they involve quantitatively less behavior. The distinction is relative, however. What is a molar unit to one researcher may seem like a molecular one to another. Birdwhistell (1970) watches minute facial gestures, but these may be too small to be mentioned by Barker (1968), who describes behavior settings, which are units of behavior containing several people and many molecular units. The divisions of behavior, then, are on a continuum and are arbitrarily designated by the observer.

Most environment behavior research deals with molar behavior, while the molecular is more often given to *human factors* research (McCormick and Sanders 1982). Human factors research most often deals with man–machine interactions or person–furniture units. These involve finer distinctions than most environment and behavior research. The observer must clearly define the kind of units of behavior being observed so that someone else using the same unit can *count* them. Ultimately, it is the goal of observation to record units of behavior. Yet, to insist that this is the only goal of behavioral observation is to miss a significant amount of what observation can accomplish. For example, observation can serve as *orientation.* When first encountering an environment or a new design, the observer may want to walk around the environment and/or watch others in a casual fashion.

For example, smelling the air in an office building gives a researcher an indication of air quality. Looking at windows from different places in a room at different times of the day gives a researcher a sense of how much glare users of the space experience. Listening to conversations and noise gives a researcher a picture of the acoustic environment. Sensing the dryness or humidity in the air gives a researcher an idea of how users of a space experience the atmosphere. And eating the food in a building's cafeteria can provide a perspective on what it is like to eat there on a daily basis. Observation, therefore, can mean using all of one's senses.

By such informal sampling of the environment and its related behavior, the observer can derive several hypotheses about what environmental factors may influence behavior. However, the same observations may serve merely to orient one to the general structure of the environment, to identify actors, count rooms, experience the size and shape of the buildings, and establish reference points. This orientation should really precede any other form of observation, for the observer must always have at least a superficial familiarity with any environment before beginning observation.

The ultimate goal of observational methods in environment behavior research is primarily to gain insight into research questions and problems. This may, in fact, be the purpose of using any or all research methods. To probe a research question in an actual research setting means focusing on the problem, the question, and the setting, rather than on the definition of the method itself. In other words, if a researcher has overly much concern for defining and circumscribing the method too early in the study, it is possible to overlook the ultimate goal.

An example of gaining insight in a research situation will clarify what this can mean to a research project. Zeisel and Drake (1984) were writing a guidebook on how to evaluate emergency departments for the Department of Health and Welfare, Canada, first, in order to help the department determine where redesign of particular emergency departments should be of priority, and second, to develop a knowledge base of design and management decision to help achieve the results desired by hospital staff, administrators, and patients. The project began with the researchers analyzing available methods—both observational and interviewing—and determining for each method what data could be gathered. Interviews can assess users' attitudes and perceptions, inventories can be taken of wear and tear on materials in the department, behavior maps can be accumulated to describe where people spend time, photographs can record instances of effective and ineffective design, and so on. But rather than begin the research project with a case study in which to test this methodological outline, the researchers decided to spend some time observing several emergency departments that had not been part of the research plan. The first department observed was three years old. There it was found that an entire observation room had been redesigned since the facility opened. It also appeared the methods would be quite useful in discovering the data expected. In the second emergency department, only one year old, it was found that other major physical redesigns were being planned for. In both these hospitals, administrators and staff explained that they had difficulties in planning for the emergency department because, contrary to the prevailing policy, the emergency rooms were a convenient place to tell emergency patients to return for check-ups rather than send them to outpatient departments. In both of the case study hospitals it was also found that major changes had been made or planned, but that the problem of confusion between emergency and outpatient use was not a problem. In one of the case study hospitals, the staff sometimes answered the telephone "Emergency Department" and sometimes "Outpatient Department." Signs in one facility said "Emergency Department," while staff and the rest of the hospital often directed potential patients to the "Outpatient Department" at the same location, where they found no signs indicating such a department. The insight gained from these planned observations was that change was an essential and ongoing part of the life of an emergency department but, more importantly, that the medical and local culture in which a hospital finds itself determines the nature of treatment and the service boundaries in any emergency department. In some areas, casual walk-in patients to the emergency department are considered to be legitimate users and these departments are set up to handle them. In other hospitals, the distinction between outpatient and emergency patients is much more distinct and any confusion between the two is seen as an administrative problem. These general insights helped to frame the evaluation methods guidebook in a way that enabled local authorities to tailor the way they should use particular research methods to reflect the culture and the definition of an emergency department in their own hospitals. In concrete terms, the most visible evidence of this was that a description of the relationship between emergency and outpatient cases was seen as a given variable, defining the situation within which the emergency department was to be evaluated, rather than an evaluative variable where a greater outpatient-to-emergency patient ratio was assumed to be negative.

This lesson gained from an unstructured observation reveals the *behavior–environment paradox.* This paradox takes the form of a misperception of the "true" environment–behavior relationship. In many cases the research problem is presented to the researcher as a need for a physical change, when a little observation can reveal that the change is not necessarily needed if behavior (a cheaper and less permanent commodity) is changed. The paradox is the assumption of environmental dominance over behavior. In simple terms: ''The environment makes us behave this way, therefore, if the environment is changed a certain way, our behavior will change accordingly.''

The behavior-environment paradox underlies the ''common sense'' thinking of many designers and their clients. Observation can often reveal mistaken assumptions and prevent the research from getting off on a false start.

Defining the Problem

The loosest use of observation comes about when one simply wants to know what is happening in an environment. This can happen when a designer asks, ''How does my building work?'' or when a designer or social scientist wants to know what it is like to live in a certain place.

To answer such a question, the observer uses his or her full range of abilities and tries to cover the widest range of behavior in an environment. Sights, sounds, smells, temperature, lighting, subjective moods, objective actions. All these are noticed—but not necessarily recorded—and processed into a slowly forming impression of what is happening.

In a local county office Bechtel observed the activities in the reception room. One secretary acted as receptionist in a large space also used by staff for coffee breaks and as a gathering place. At the same time it served as a waiting room for clients. The staff-client conflict was immediately obvious. Clients could overhear staff talking about other clients. In addition, clients sometimes brought children who had to be supervised by a second secretary in an adjoining room. At such times chaos was at a maximum. The lack of order created a less than businesslike image of the office and created doubts in both staff and clients. It did not take much observation to recognize that a clear separation of spaces was needed as a first step. Here, several methods of observation—visual, aural, and participatory—were required, but the observer did not need to record specific categories because a more general familiarization was first necessary.

Gans (1970) moved to a suburban development to find out what it was like to live there. Whyte (1980) walked down Manhattan streets to find out what was happening. Many designers enter buildings to observe ''how they work.'' In these circumstances the observer is looking for some way to organize the chaos of activity so that it can be understood. A variety of concepts may be tried and abandoned. An observation may lead to puzzlement—why is everybody hurrying? And this may lead the observer to ask a passing pedestrian that question. Thus, the most open form of observation is a constant seeking to comprehend what is being observed. This may lead to many questions and to many more observations.

And sometimes observation can also answer more specific questions that interviews and questionnaires cannot reveal. In the Arrowhead project (Dumouchel 1971) broken windows were a serious economic problem but questioning did not reveal the source. Residents attributed these acts to ''outsiders.'' Observation revealed, however, that children in the residences (and some adults) would often get locked outside and break the windows to get in. The cold of the Cleveland winter was a highly motivating force. Therefore, the problem was not one of outside ''invaders,'' but of lack of control over one's own living space. This illustrates an observation followed by a query through other methods, followed by more observations—that is, the observation ''sandwich'' design.

Interviews and questionnaires are the most frequent methods used, with observation in the middle of the sandwich. The first layer of the sandwich is made by conducting enough observation to get the question or questions properly formulated for application to other methods. For example, the Arrowhead project revealed that while the elderly constituted 10 percent of the population, they were only 1 percent of the observed population out of doors. Interviews were then designed to solicit reasons why the elderly did not leave their apartments. Several reasons became apparent. The elderly found it difficult to move about the grounds when there was ice and snow. Furthermore, they feared exploitation from younger people who often robbed older people while on the street or who would sometimes push open the doors while they were entering and rob their homes. Later observation of street activity showed these reports to be accurate. Thus, the first layer of the sandwich poses the question from observation data. The second layer attempts to answer by more causal methods, while the final layer of the sandwich confirms the answer by additional observation.

THE ENVIRONMENT

The environmental end of the behavior–environment equation does recognize that an environmental context provides cues to the proper behavior expected. Often, the environment will determine the kind of observation that takes place. A setting that is too dark may prevent photography, or, with increasing technology, require either a high-speed film or infrared nightscopes for observation. Similarly, some environments allow an observer to become unobtrusive because of sheer numbers, while in other environments, lack of numbers makes the observer conspicuous.

Perhaps the most frequent observation that assumes the environment is a prime variable is that which measures environmental change.

Testing for Change

One of the most frequent kinds of studies done in environmental behavior research is to test for an expected difference in behavior that design or a change in environment is assumed to have produced. An astute reader will recognize that this is a direct test of the environment–behavior paradox: hence, the need to understand how the original behavior was related to the change. This observation may be an attempt to measure a change by comparing measures after construction with measures taken before a building was built; it may be an attempt to determine the form a design should take *before* a building is produced, or it may be an attempt to measure whether a change in behavior was successful *after* a building has been lived in. In all these cases observation is a critical tool because it can document how people respond naturally to environmental changes.

Trites et al. (1970) observed the amount of walking nurses did in three kinds of hospital designs and demonstrated that the least amount of walking occurred in a radial design. These data led to the popular radial design of intensive care units that has become a standard.

Howroyd (discussed in Bechtel, Ledbetter, and Cummings 1976) studied traditional and modern middle eastern desert communities and observed how important a wall was in defining the separation of community from the harsh environment. The wall served both as a psychological comfort and as a physical provider of shade. This led Howroyd to select a townsite for his community that was naturally surrounded by hills on three sides. Research showed that the residents of the town felt safer and more protected from the environment by the hills. The original hypothesis was confirmed.

Much of the observational testing for change follows a pre-post-measure model, where the effect of design is determined by the observed difference in behavior in the post design observation. A classical

POE paradigm (see chapter 9) occurs when the designer works from data in the pre-measure; this is *not* an experimental design. Many maintain that it should really involve a control group that does not experience the new design. Nevertheless, studies continue to involve the simpler pre-post-measures in an attempt to determine whether a design has had the effect intended. One might dub these kinds of studies the *design-change paradigm.* What is important is to obtain comparable observations between the pre-post-measurement periods. For example, if one wants to measure the effect of a renovation in a cafeteria, the most *obvious* observation periods are mealtimes before and after the design period.

In a follow-up to the Arrowhead study (Dumouchel 1971), the observation of children's play before and after the installation of new playgrounds showed that the children's play had changed from solitary and fragmented to healthier group play centered around the playgrounds.

THE TIME

It should be perfectly obvious that any observation covers a slice in time and can never cover the full life history of an environment. The time scale of observation ranges from one year in the classical ecological psychology studies (see chapter 6) to a few minutes in a classical time-motion study of human factors. The best framework to use in approaching the time-sampling dilemma is to ask: What is the time frame surrounding the behavior as it naturally occurs in the environment? Does the behavior begin repeating itself every twenty-four-hour period? Or, does the behavior take a weekly cycle? Unfortunately (in the sense of time sampling), many environments show marked differences in seasons critical for indoor environments when requirements change from heating to cooling or from wet to dry.

Strictly speaking, if it is thought that seasons will make a critical difference, observation should be made on a time period representative of each season—for example, periods in May, July, October, and February. In practical terms, this is almost never done because few clients are willing to wait a year for results. More often, the most critical season is chosen for observation and the other seasons are asked about in a retrospective questionnaire.

Deciding on a critical season is not always easy, however. For example, in a cold regions study (Bechtel and Ledbetter 1976), it first seemed obvious that winter would be the most critical season in Alaska. Yet, observations in summer demonstrated that the constant daylight had as much of a disruptive effect as the extremes of winter. Some people were unable to sleep for days at a time. Blackout curtains were a necessity for many homes. Children were especially susceptible to the interruption of diurnal rhythms. Thus, had there been no measures taken during the summer, important design information would have been missed.

It is becoming obvious that any time measure of less than a year incurs the danger of missing critical information. Therefore, although it must be recognized that very few studies will collect annual data, an attempt must be made to try to compensate by gathering detailed information about seasonal differences.

Within the season chosen various times must be sampled, to give a representative picture of behavior. An important question is, what takes place at night? Does the place being studied close down? If so, does some kind of activity such as cleaning or maintenance take place?

Another major question is whether to study weekends. Can it be assumed that weekdays are the same as weekends? Or do weekends see a complete absence of behavior? For public places, weekends become the prime time for behavior observation, while for factories, weekends may hold a complete absence of behavior.

Within each day the time sample becomes more precise. Does one observe during the entire day? Wright (Barker and Wright 1955) discovered that intense observation tires the observer within about twenty minutes. Should observation therefore be spaced so as to increase observer accuracy? The answer is that most observation is adapted to a time interval schedule to allow the observer to rest.

Observation can take place every five minutes or ten minutes, but the intervals cannot be purely arbitrary. Time intervals must be pre-tested to determine whether they miss a significant amount of data. This is usually done by having one team do intensive observation simultaneously with a second team that records only at the selected time interval.

In summary, the process of deciding on time intervals is a continuous narrowing of focus from seasonal to weekly, to daily, and, finally, to a selection of an appropriate time interval between observations.

THE OBSERVER

So far little has been said about the observer. The most obvious requirement is that the observer always appear to blend with the crowd, since an observer who is observed performing this task becomes an obtrusive presence. A matching of dress and demeanor is therefore a first necessity. In other respects the observer has a wide choice of approaches to making observations.

The Naive Observer

The simplest, and yet probably the most difficult stance to take, is that of naive observer. Ideally, this kind of observer comes as if from a distant planet and knows absolutely nothing about the customs and practices of the human race. The value of such a stance is that it makes no assumptions about behavior and reports behavior as literally as possible. The disadvantage is that it is difficult to take on this degree of naivete and free oneself of assumptions about behavior. Yet, like any other skill, it can be learned. The advantage of using a naive observer is that often persons living in a particular culture are the last to realize obvious facts about themselves.

A naive observer stance is especially effective in observing children, the elderly, or the handicapped because these groups offer a rich field of discovery for the uninitiated. The inability of arthritic patients to use common doorknobs, or the inability of children to see over adult-height barriers can open up new vistas to the naive observer. After just a short period of exposure, the naive observer can see that the normal world is filled with barriers to wheelchair access, how some door jambs can be insurmountable, how wrinkled carpets and soft deep carpets become an obstacle course, and how the strewn objects of a child's room can help account for many home accidents.

Participant Observation

The most common of all observation roles, and the one that has the longest history, is participant observation (Jacobs 1970). This technique, which is the principal method of anthropology, has been used for over a hundred years. With this method, a single observer becomes a member of a society or group and attempts to observe and record every aspect of behavior in that culture. Typically an anthropologist becomes a member of the society for several years and then writes up the observation in book-length format. Primary data are a daily journal and conversations with *informants.* Informants are natives of the culture who become teachers and interpreters of what the observer sees. Informants are necessary to provide a cultural perspective on what is observed. The goal of participant observation is to become familiar with the culture or the rules of behavior of the entire group rather than to study the behavior of any individual.

Long-term participant observation has several distinct problems relating to the acceptance by the people observed, the feelings of the observer, and entry and exit from the place of observation. The first task of a participant observer is to be accepted by the people who will be observed. The observer has a "cover" story, for example: "I am an anthropologist, and I want to learn your ways." Sometimes the observer does not reveal his/her true identity because this would interfere with the behavior to be observed. For example, when Caudill (1958) went to a mental hospital to observe patients, he pretended to be a patient or attendant. If the patients had learned his true identity they would very likely not have behaved "naturally" in his presence. This kind of deception raises ethical issues. Does the investigator have the right to observe under false pretenses, given the need for behavioral data (Redlich and Brody 1955)?

Since no single participant observer is able to participate in all roles in a society, any observation is somewhat biased by being limited to the points of view obtained in the roles penetrated. Thus, for example, Bechtel (1965) pointed out that a participant observer in a mental hospital would have very different reports on behavior depending on whether the observer was posing as an attendant, a patient, or an accountant. While every good observer will attempt to report on all roles in a given society or situation, it is not possible to participate in all roles. Liebow (1970) also raises the point that a participant observer is never fully a part of the society being observed.

Anthropologists have developed techniques for being accepted in societies. One of these is the withdrawal-and-return method. First the anthropologist arrives, sets up housekeeping, and goes about his or her business. People are suspicious, not eager to converse and shy with the stranger. After a time the anthropologist leaves. In a week or so, he or she returns. Now the neighbors, fellow shoppers, or passers-by have a reason to talk. "Oh," they say, "you've been away." Conversation naturally follows, and with it, acceptance into the group.

Not so easily handled is the entry-exit problem. This involves an internal adjustment on the part of the observer. Being a member of another culture, the observer brings values, beliefs, and behaviors that are out of place in the new society. Holding those values and customs in abeyance may require a severe personal adjustment. Neophyte anthropologists have been known to leave the field because of the emotional difficulties this situation presents. These problems can range from severe depression and loneliness to identity crises. And even when the entry adjustment is made and the observer can feel comfortable in the new society, the same problems can arise all over again when the observer leaves. In some cases, adjustment to an American lifestyle after living among peasants can be just as severe. Overcoming these emotional and value conflicts is a major part of learning to make accurate observations. Liebow (1970, 273) concludes: "In retrospect, it seems as if the degree to which one becomes a participant is as much a matter of perceiving oneself as a participant as it is being accepted as a participant by others."

For most environment behavior research, the observation attempted will not be as long and intensive as an anthropological study, but with increasing international involvement, the need for cross-cultural data on environment behavioral issues is becoming more imperative. Thus, much existing anthropological data are used as background material to prepare for observation and questionnaire combinations or for shorter-term participant observation. For example, in studies of mental hospitals in Peru (Bechtel and Gonzales 1971) and housing in Iran (Tadjer, Cohen, Shefferman, and Bigelson, Inc. 1975), anthropological observations were very helpful in identifying the particular behaviors on which to concentrate observations. In Peru the interaction between doctor and patient was closer and far more paternal than in the United States. In Iran, larger spaces for visiting were a critical design factor in supporting the extended families that were the primary basis of Iranian culture.

Participant observation as it is practiced in most environment behavior studies today will typically be a short-term observation of particular places or life-styles to determine both the global patterns of behavior–environment linkages and some easily observable specifics. Participant observation is also useful as a method of acquainting designer and researcher with the lifestyles of the people for whom a design is intended. A good example of the unexpected things observation can turn up is provided in the Arrowhead (Dumouchel 1971) project, where it was found that a number of salespeople and visitors could not find their way around the housing estate. This led to recommendations for a more comprehensible pathway system.

The Hidden Observer

Many times when it is necessary to observe behavior in a naturalistic setting, it becomes imperative that the behavior not be influenced in any way by the knowledge that there is an observer about. This is often true in public places where one wants to observe the embarrassment and awkwardness of getting lost, or in mother-child interactions where one wants to see whether parents will take part in child's play in public or private, and in many other circumstances where it is especially important to keep observation secret.

The most common laboratory form of secret observation is through the one-way mirror—a large half-silvered glass that prevents subjects seeing anything but their own reflection while the observer can see everything the subjects do through the glass.

In the field, hidden observation is most often achieved by moving away from the subjects and viewing from a nearby building with a vantage point above eye level. Here the observer can observe with the naked eye, with a telescope or field glasses, or with a photographic long lens without being detected by the subjects. A possible problem with increased distance from the subjects is the loss of detail, but with modern optics the lenses can often reveal more detail than would be available to the naked eye even at close range.

With secret observation there is again an ethical issue—does the observation constitute an invasion of privacy? It is commonly accepted that behavior in public can be observed secretly as long as anonymity is preserved, but if pictures are to be published, either written permission must be obtained or the faces of the subjects must be blocked out.

The Professional Observer

The role most often played in observing is that of the professional, armed with social science knowledge and techniques, knowing that information on time and behavior must be categorized and recorded before it can be turned into useful data. Experience as a professional observer cuts down the time needed for defining problems and deriving hypotheses and enables the researcher to develop and test categories more quickly. After taking part in a number of observational studies, an observer learns how and where to look to define critical behavior in relation to designs. The professional role is largely one of developing and using the categories in the section that follows.

RECORDING OBSERVATION

Categories of Observation

Several methods have been developed for working out the behavioral and time categories necessary before observation can take place for data gathering. Up to this point most of the observation described has been relatively loose and impressionistic. This is fine for the definition of problems or for participant observation, but when scientific data are needed, a category system must be developed that deals simultaneously with behavior and time categories. These techniques range from the most global, like *behavior specimen recording,* to the most specific, like Bale's *interaction process analysis,* which is a fully developed instrument.

Developing categories involves a stage of reconnaissance similar to the problem definition stage, followed by a trial of categories, or a pre-test, then a reliability testing stage, followed by data collection and analysis.

Behavioral Specimen Records

A particular global method of observation developed by Wright (1967) originally involved watching children. Wright's technique is to have an observer write down every behavior in common-sense language. Traditionally this observation lasts a full day (Barker and Wright 1951), but more often it involves much shorter periods.

The behavior specimen record is written by the observer, typically by hand on a lined 8½- by 11-inch tablet on a clip board with a stop watch attached. The observer writes down the behavior as it occurs and marks the time in a margin at specified intervals. Since this form of recording is very exhausting, a team of observers is used so that each one observes for only fifteen or twenty minutes.

An alternative to the constant writing is to record the observation by speaking into a microphone. If one is close to the person being observed, however, the sound of the voice will be very obtrusive. This particular form of obtrusiveness can be overcome by the use of a device called a *steno mask* (fig. 1-1), which is placed over the face and spoken

1-1. Steno mask being used by observer.

into. The rubber surrounding the face successfully masks the sound of the voice. Unfortunately, since the device resembles a gas mask, it is itself obtrusive when used in public! It is only appropriate when the observer can be well hidden. It must also be remembered that tape recordings relieve the observer from the need to record in writing but involve added expense and time for transcription.

Behavior specimen records become primary data that are scored into *episodes*—actions that have a beginning and an end. Two or more observers mark episodes and must reach a reliable agreement on their definition and scoring (fig. 1-2) (from Barker and Wright 1955, 237).

At this point we pause in our review to consider

Erratum

William Michelson is a professor of sociology at the University of Toronto and an Associate of the Centre for Urban and Community Studies there.

searcher defines an episode for this type of observation by deciding how inclusive he or she wants it to be. Looking at figure 1-2, it could be decided that the whole observation from beginning to end would be one episode called "coming into the house." It began with the decision to come in and ended with getting the last wrap off and settling into a new activity. Or, still being molar, but on a lower scale, one could call it three episodes: going inside, taking off wraps, and putting wraps away. The decision is purely arbitrary and depends on the purposes served by recording the episodes. For example, one could use the three smaller episodes to demonstrate the need for a closet near the doorway to allow coats to be put away most conveniently. An interesting question that could be answered by observations would be: Do children in houses with closets near the door put their clothes away more often than children in houses with closets further from the door, and how do parental admonitions affect the situation?

BEHAVIOR MAPPING

A behavioral map is actually an observational tool. The researcher takes a drawn-to-scale map of an environment and then notes behavior as it occurs in its true location on the map. Usually the notation is made in some code with a specific time frame adhered to. For example, *the number of times* people speak to each other may be noted on the map *every two minutes.* Often the maps indicate one-square-foot grids on the floor. An example of behavioral categories is given in figure 1-3, which breaks down patient behaviors observed in a hospice, a special home for terminally ill cancer patients (Koff et al. 1980). Figure 1-3 shows the same categories parcelled into an observation format. A critical point in behavioral mapping is to decide on the categories of behavior needed and to pre-test these in an actual environment.

Going Inside

7:32 The father called good-naturedly, "Come on, Chuck. Come along, boy."
Chuck jumped down easily and quickly.
He trotted a few steps ahead of his father.
Mr. Thurston caught up at the back door of the house. There he said briskly, as he opened the door, "Come on; let's get inside."
Chuck bounded into the house.
He walked quickly through the kitchen and dining room into the living room, where his mother sat resting on a couch.

Taking off Wraps

He started to peel off his jacket.

Commenting on Cold

At the same time, he remarked companionably to his mother, "It's cold outside. It's really cold out there."
He said this in a very adult way.
Only smiling pleasantly, his mother seemed to take it that way.

7:33 Chuck pulled his jacket down from his shoulders; but it stayed on because the sleeves jammed against the bulky gloves he was wearing.

Getting Mittens Off

Chuck demanded of no one in particular, "Mittens off!"
His mother said nothing and made no move to help.
Chuck resolutely walked over to his mother.
Standing before her with his coat sagging, he soberly held out his hands.
The mother reached over toward him.
Then, while he helped by pulling back a little, she tugged off his gloves.

Chuck wriggled on out of his coat, letting it drop where he stood.

Putting Wraps Away

His mother said firmly, "Chuck, put your hat and coat away."
He just stood there.
His mother repeated her command, this time very firmly.
Chuck asked, looking impish, "Shall I get the ruler, Mommie?"
Earlier in the day Chuck had refused to put away his wraps, whereupon his mother had said threateningly, "Now, where is my ruler?" So, in asking now if he should get the ruler, Chuck evidently was just beating his mother to the draw.
Chuck did not press the question about the ruler. Before his mother could answer it, he picked up his hat and coat.
Then he carried the wraps into the bedroom. He was smiling.
He returned to the living room at once.

1–2. Episodes in behavior specimen recording. Reprinted with permission from* Midwest and Its Children *by Roger G. Barker.

Behavioral mapping was developed by Ittelson et al. (1970) to record behavior as it occurred in the design. In this way design features and behavior were linked in both time and space. It is usually used on a microscale for an environment such as a room because it is a convenient space for one person to observe. It can, however, be used on a wider scale with proper techniques for observation.

Ittelson claims behavioral mapping has five elements:

1. *Professional duty without patient*—any actions necessary for the completion of a staff member's professional duty, including: charting, punching in, medication preparation, deliveries, preparations for parties that do not involve food, adjusting equipment, cleaning, clerical, Xeroxing.
2. *Professional duty with patient*—caring for and assisting patient, except in feeding, including: bathing, applying equipment, sitting with patient so patient can smoke, giving medicine, wheeling patient in wheelchair, physical therapy, hygiene.
3. *Meeting*—formal, more than two individuals, congregating in same location for a specific purpose, exclusive of special activities; examples: report, family conferences, administrative/staff meetings.
4. *Smoking*—a sole personal activity, all other categories take precedence except postural categories.
5. *Talking*—more than one person necessary, speaking with another, no particular location is necessary, talking takes precedence over smoking, sitting, standing, pacing, T.V., radio, traffic, lying in bed.
6. *Eating and drinking*—sole activity, consumption, personal activity, does not include food preparation that involves other person helping the patient eat, no certain location necessary.
7. *Food preparation*—includes anything to do with food, except personal eating and drinking; examples: storage, distribution, clean up, encouragement, cooking, setting up for parties (displaying food).
8. *Hygiene*—personal body care; examples: makeup, hair, teeth, fingernails, shaving, grooming, toileting, done by or to oneself.
9. *Telephone*—using the telephone.
10. *Lying in bed*—patient activity, all other categories take precedence.
11. *Sitting*—independent of location, postural category, all other categories take precedence except lying in bed and standing.
12. *Standing*—postural category, all other categories take precedence except for sitting and lying in bed.
13. *Pacing*—undirected walking, back and forth, takes precedence over no other category.
14. *T.V./radio*—the act of viewing or listening, takes precedence over postural categories, talking, and smoking.
15. *Reading and writing*—if an individual is being read to, the reader is performing a professional duty; if person is reading or writing and listening to radio, the observable behavior (reading or writing) is chosen.
16. *Recreation*—play activities, arts and crafts, group or individual, not T.V./radio, reading or writing, or special events.
17. *Traffic*—movement from one place to another, all other categories take precedence; includes: moving of equipment without patient being involved.
18. *Interaction*—communication between two individuals.

1–3. Categories for behavioral mapping of hospice patients.

1. A *graphic* rendering of the area(s) observed
2. A clear *definition* of the human behaviors observed, counted, described, or diagrammed
3. A *schedule* of repeated times during which the observation and recording take place
4. A *systematic procedure* followed in observing
5. A *coding* and *counting* system, which minimizes the effort required in recording observations.

In other words, to do behavioral mapping it is necessary to obtain an accurate scale map of the area to be observed, to decide clearly on the behaviors to be observed, schedule specific times for observation, agree on a system for recording the behavior, and then analyze the data in relation to how it has accumulated on the map. The purpose of behavioral mapping is to locate behavior on the map itself, to identify kinds and frequencies of behavior, and to demonstrate their association with a particular design feature. By associating the behavior with a design feature it is then possible to both ask questions and draw conclusions about the

Observer ______________ Day ________ Date ________ time begun am pm

time completed am pm

KITCHEN	ZONE 1					KITCHEN					MEDICAL RECORDS					PUBLIC BATH-ROOMS					STORAGE				
	P	V	Ch	S	V1	P	V	Ch	S	V1	P	V	Ch	S	V1	P	V	Ch	S	V1	P	V	Ch	S	V1
1. prof duty w/o ptnt																									
2. prof duty with ptnt																									
3. meeting																									
4. smoking																									
5. talking																									
6. eating & drinking																									
7. food prep																									
8. hygiene																									
9. telephone																									
10. lying in bed																									
11. sitting																									
12. standing																									
13. pacing																									
14. TV-radio																									
15. reading & writing																									
16. recreation																									
17. traffic																									
Interaction																									
Patient wheelchair																									
sitting																									
standing																									

1–4. Recording format for hospice patients' behaviors.

behavior and its relationship to design. For example, in a mental hospital it was possible to show how patients' standing behaviors related to the nurse's office and how social conversation related to the TV area. Lack of activities was associated with poorly planned lounges. See figure 1-4 for an illustration of categories and mapping (in this case a map was not used).

Behavioral mapping was used in the post-occupancy evaluation of a hospice, a nonhospital institution whose purpose is to make terminally ill patients feel comfortable in their last hours. It minimizes institutional requirements and emphasizes the comfort of the patient. The purpose of the design was to make the environment feel more homelike. The behavioral mapping was carried out by recording categories of patient and staff behavior at five-minute intervals over a twenty-four-hour period. The researchers discovered (1) that patients spent 84 percent of their time in the rooms, making the room the most important design feature from that standpoint, and (2) that auxiliary rooms such as the chapel and viewing room for deceased patients were used very little. This latter finding did not mean that these features were useless, however, because questionnaire and interview data showed that these rooms served an important purpose in affirming that the hospice was not a hospital.

For behavioral mapping to be useful, procedures and categories must be standardized for each specific location to establish the reliability of observers.

Behavioral mapping is also used with other methods such as interviews and questionnaires. Once the behavior has been associated with a design feature, people are questioned in order to confirm or disprove the initial finding.

PRESELECTED CATEGORY SCALES

Once it becomes necessary to select units of behavior that are below the molar level, one has a choice of trying to find an instrument with pretested categories, which is difficult, or developing one's own categories, which is also difficult. An example of a scale that has been used extensively is the Bales Interaction Process. While this scale was developed to score the social behavior of interaction, it has obvious relevance as a measure of how the environment, or specific variables, influence social interaction. It can be used to study the design process as it unfolds in a design team, or the effects of environmental variables on board meetings, discussions, and so on. The interaction process analysis, which was developed over thirty years ago (Bales 1950), has since been modernized (Bales and Cohen 1979). Both versions can be used depending on researcher preference. An example of the older scale is given in figure 1-5 (from Bales 1950, 18). Note the twelve categories on which subjects are scored: ''shows solidarity,'' ''shows tension release,'' and so on. Note also that a partial explanation of each category is given on the chart itself so that the observer does not always have to rely on memory.

Observation with the Bales scale requires a period of practice with a trained observer until a high degree of reliability is obtained. The modernized version, called SYMLOG, is shown in figure 1-6 (from Bales and Cohen 1979, 413). Note that the categories have increased to twenty-six, and are given in abbreviated form. Much more training is required to learn these categories, but more detailed data are obtained.

FROM PROXEMICS TO KINESICS

One of the earliest types of observation in environment behavior research came from Edward Hall's (1960) studies of the social distances people try to maintain in different cultures. Hall observed that these distances often relate to the senses: whether we can smell the other person, feel body heat, reach out and touch, or see facial features. The distances

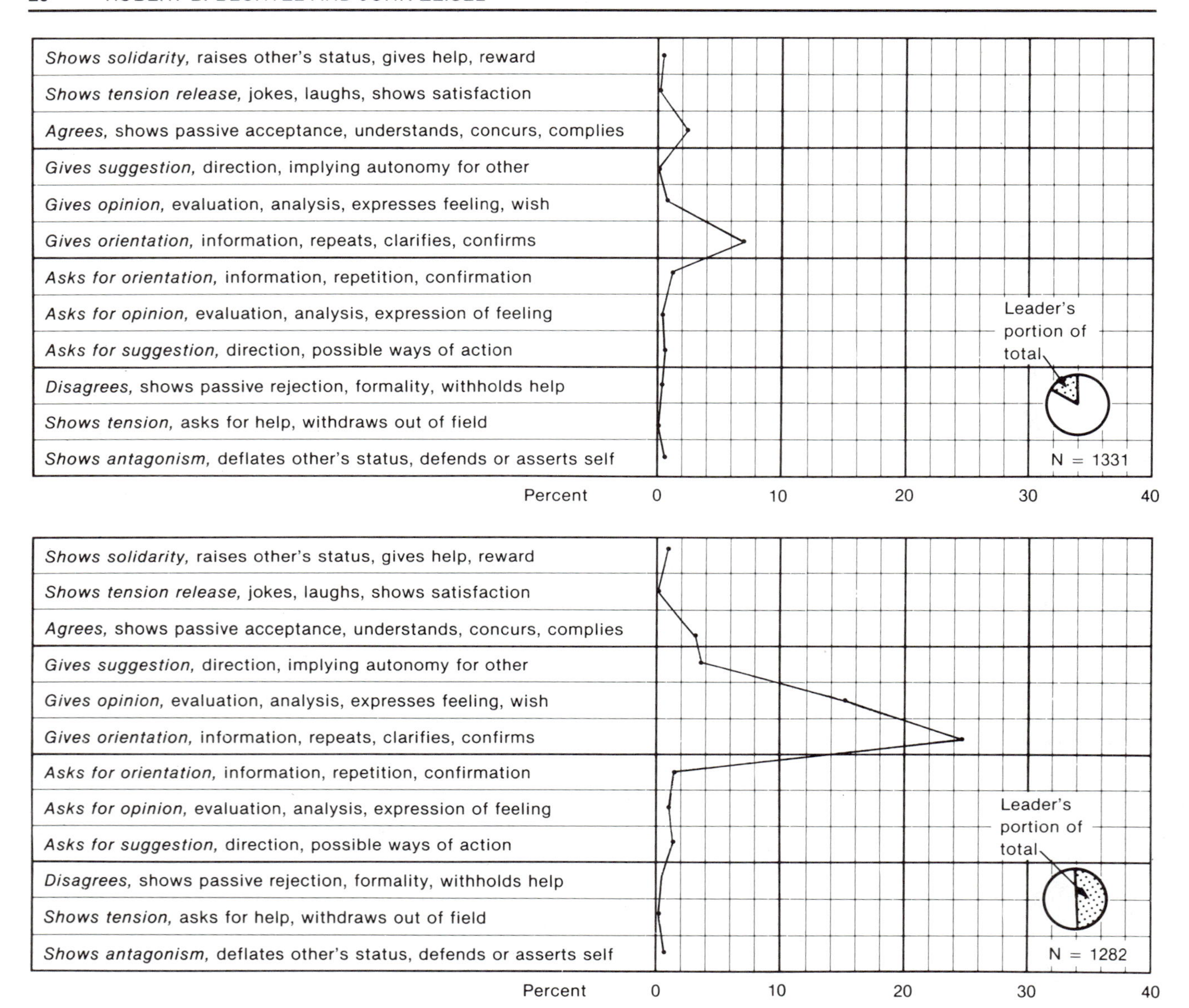

1–5. Older Bales' interaction scale. Reprinted with permission from **Interaction Process Analysis** *by R. F. Bales (Chicago: University of Chicago Press, 1950).*

also vary according to social situations—friends stand closer in conversation than do strangers. Hall called the study of these distances *proxemics.* "Proxemic patterns" are the spatial patterns that constitute the norm for a culture in specific types of situations. Hall's manual (1974) has a series of proxetic codes for recording behavior. Figure 1-7 shows examples of proxetic codes for posture, body orientation, and lateral displacement of bodies (from Hall 1974, 57).

Your name ____________________

Of what group: ____________________ Present date ____________________

From what date: ____________________ to what date: ____________________ Page ________ of ________

What method: ____________________ Whose perceptions: ____________________ What level: ____________________

Who, or What Image → Direction ↓						
U						
UP						
UPF						
UF						
UNF						
UN						
UNB						
UB						
UPB						
P						
PF						
F						
NF						
N						
NB						
B						
PB						
DP						
DPF						
DF						
DNF						
DN						
DNB						
DB						
DPB						
D						
TOTAL						
U						
D						
P						
N						
F						
B						

1–6. Modernized Bales' interaction scale called SYMLOG. Reprinted with permission from **SYMLOG: A System for the Multiple Level Observation of Groups** *by R. F. Bales and S. Cohen (New York: The Free Press, 1979).*

INSTRUCTIONS	*CODE*		
	Column No.	***Variable***	***Description***
62 *Posture* See Coding Scale opposite.	62	Posture	0 1 2 standing 3 leaning 4 sitting 5 squatting 6 prone 7 8 9
63 *Body orientation* This scale describes the orientation of the subjects' bodies to each other, beginning with back-to-back orientation (0) and opening out through side-by-side (5) and right-angle (7) to face-to-face orientation (9). The shoulders are the reference points to observe in deciding orientation. The most common positions for interacting are 5 through 9, although two persons standing "in line" (4) or backed up to each other (0) in crowds will also be aware of and interact with each other to some extent. Be sure that both subjects in an interaction are rated the same on this scale. (See Coding Scale opposite.)	63	Body orientation	0 1 2 3 4 5 6 7 8 9
64 *Lateral displacement of bodies* Refers to the amount of displacement on the body orientation scale (63). Records the degree to which the subjects are removed from the base positions. The displacement spectrum is amplified by adding increments of space to the basic displacement of the subjects; this space is indicated by the "plus" in the coding scale opposite.	64	Lateral displacement of bodies	0 (two arms extended—plus) 1 (two arms extended) 2 (one arm extended—plus) 3 (one arm extended) 4 (two elbows extended)

1-7. Examples of proxetic codes. Reprinted with permission from **Handbook for Proxemic Research** *by Edward T. Hall (Philadelphia: Society for the Anthropology of Visual Communication, 1974).*

INSTRUCTIONS	CODE		
	Column No.	Variable	Description
			5 (one elbow extended—plus)
			6 (one elbow extended)
			7 (line up of opposite shoulders)
			8 (shoulders overlap)
			9 (facing directly)

Figure 1–7 continued

Proxemics continues to be a viable method in cross-cultural studies. Sussman and Rosenfeld (1982), for example, found that bilingual people use different distances when speaking different languages. They "jump back" to speak English and move closer together to speak Spanish. De Long (1976) found that proxemic distances were maintained when he asked subjects to simulate behavior with dolls in a one-twelfth-scale model building.

Kinesics is undoubtedly the most minute of all the observational categories. Developed by Albert Scheflen, Jacques van Vlack and Ray Birdwhistell at the Eastern Pennsylvania Psychiatric Institute (but chiefly by Birdwhistell), this system of observation concentrates on the nonverbal motions of the body as a language. Symbols are used called kinographs (fig. 1–8, from Birdwhistell 1970, 260). Macrokinesic (larger categories) and microkinesic (smaller categories) are recorded, usually from films. It is much more difficult to record from "live" observation because of the large number of kinesic activities going on. Birdwhistell is fond of saying that "a lot goes on in twenty seconds." While this system has had its widest application in the field of psychotherapy, it has obvious uses as a measure of discomfort under various environmental conditions. Le Compte (1981) used a kinesic observation of gestures to rate discomfort under crowded conditions in Turkey. He observed that despite its potential, kinesics has been applied very little in environmental studies.

PHOTOGRAPHIC TECHNIQUES AND SOUND RECORDING

A particularly useful method for observing molar behavior has been developed in film (Cook and Miles 1978). Time-lapse photography offers a way of speeding up time in motion picture filming by shooting a single frame every thirty seconds or so. When the film is played at normal speeds, the action is time-compressed—a day's behavior can be seen in fifteen or twenty minutes of viewing. This method is especially effective for outdoor spaces

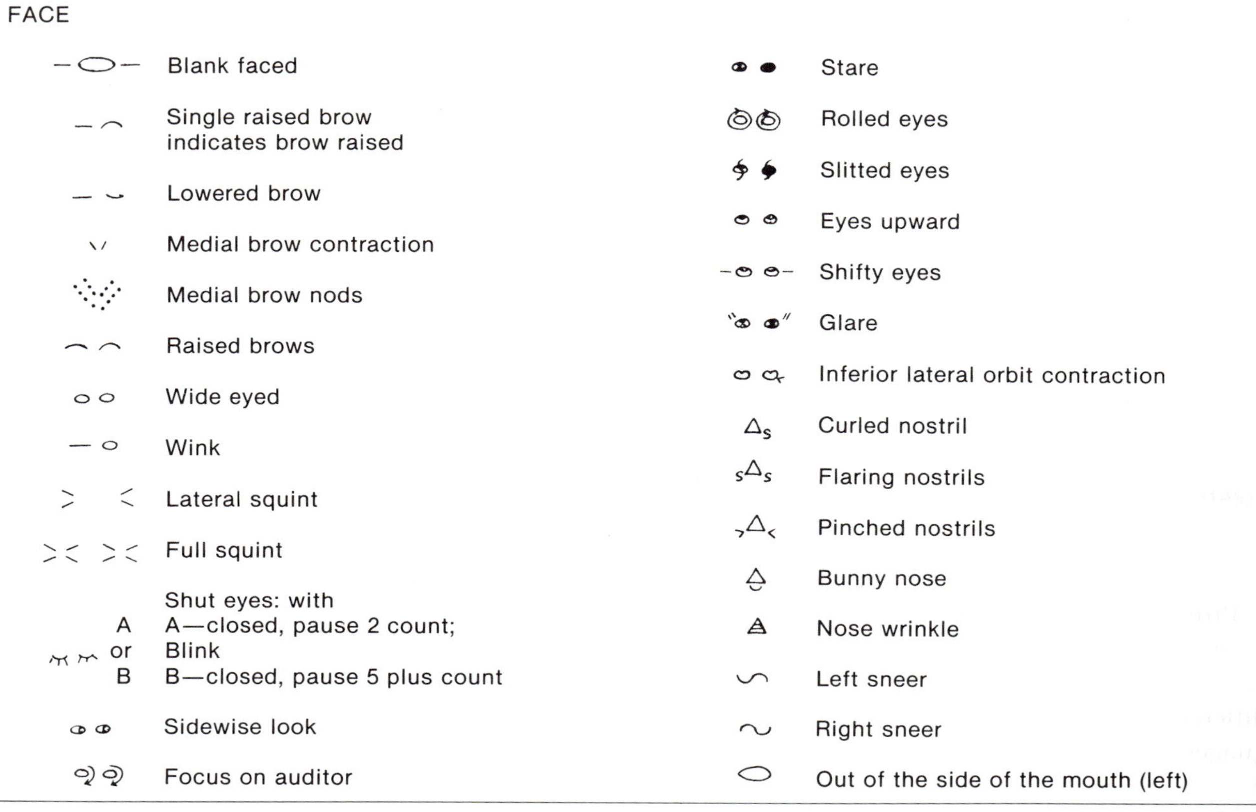

1–8. Kinographs.

such as plazas, patios, shopping malls, and even indoor areas, where crowd activity can be effectively condensed into a short viewing period. New high-speed film makes indoor and night photography practical.

The film itself can act as an educator and salesman. Projects for Public Spaces, Inc., a research organization, has very effectively sold social science to businessmen merely on the basis of their viewing such films. It becomes immediately obvious that the behavior fits or does not fit the environment. It is easy to identify, for example, the places where no one sits or where crowds gather and obstruct traffic. Indeed, many design research projects for public spaces can be effectively accomplished by filming activity on a busy weekend.

Time-lapse filming can also be used as a primary data source in the following ways. Slowed down, it can score particular behaviors for peak periods. (Photographing a clock in the corner of each frame counted provides a record of the time period.) Not only can numbers of people be counted but sexes can be differentiated and children counted separately from adults; and unlike "live" observation, the film can be run again and again to check reliability of observation. Categories of observation can be defined and observed with a precision that is not possible with live observation. The time-lapse

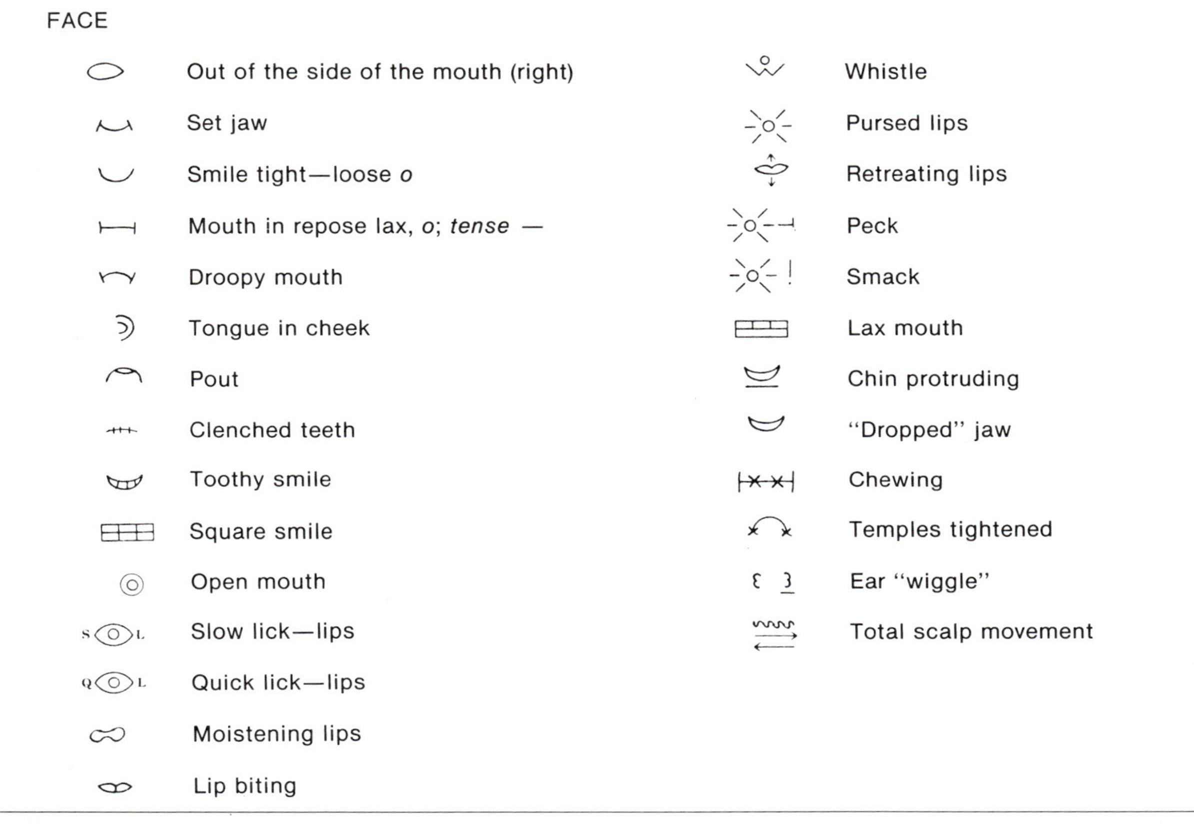

Figure 1–8 continued

technique has become an outstandingly successful method for studying behavior in public spaces.

Photography, video tapes, and sound tape recordings of behavior are new and rapidly developing techniques that are fast becoming a part of established observation methodology. The lure of gadgetry, however, often leads to inappropriate use and disappointment with results. The time-lapse camera is useful for molar behavior but progressively more limited as scale is reduced. *Molecular* behavioral categories such as facial expressions are often not discernible in the normal format used for studying a public area. Graininess of film presents a problem, especially with video, because one often cannot see the direction of a subject's glance or discern nuances of expression without an obtrusive close-up of the face.

Sound tapes are another tempting approach, as a substitute for taking notes. With tapes one expects to obtain the same clarity of speech we find in motion pictures and on television. As every filmmaker knows, however, clarity of sound is often achieved by "dubbing over" the visual film in the studio where the sound can be completely controlled. The actor gets in a sound booth and tries to match voice to the lip movements in the film. In "live" recording, several people often speak simultaneously, producing an unintelligible garble, and background noises may overwhelm the words. People who are not trained actors may speak too softly to be heard or they may not pronounce words very well and depend on hand gestures instead of words to express ideas. It is normal for at least 10 to 20 percent of the words spoken in everyday conversation to be lost in a recorded conversation, and in a meeting with several people present the percentage may go much higher. In meetings where all spoken words are needed as data, researchers have found that employing court recorders with stenographic machines is necessary to insure accuracy (Conway 1973).

RECORDING TRACES

When researchers want to know how people behave or have behaved in places they cannot observe, we enter the realm of reconstruction. Behavior that has taken place in the past leaves many kinds of traces behind. From these, researchers reconstruct the behaviors that produced them.

Archeology

Anthropologists in archeology were the first to recognize that ancient traces are a useful source of data about human behavior (Rathje 1979). Archeology, which is the science of inferring human behavior from such traces, has become very sophisticated with carbon, argon, and tree-ring dating, pollen analysis, and even the diagnosis of diseases in fossil skeletons and mummies. Few give a thought, however, to the fact that the fossils of tomorrow are the garbage dumps of today. The *Project du Garbage* (Rathje and Hughes 1978; Rathje and Ritenbaugh 1984) counted, dated, cataloged, and weighed the garbage of urban America to explore what the material traces in garbage can reveal about human behavior. The study demonstrated that the United States has undergone a significant dietary change between 1981 and 1985, eating less meat and more fruits and vegetables. In addition, the garbage studies documented increased waste of sugar and beef during wartime sugar and beef shortages (Rathje 1977).

Other Surface Recordings

Zeisel (1981) has described traces as they are more commonly used in environment behavior research. He divides traces into four categories: by-products of use, adaptations of use, displays of self, and public messages. *By-products* are created by erosion of surfaces, leftovers, and missing traces.

Erosion is a relative term. Trained Indian scouts of pioneer days regarded a broken blade of grass as evidence that a person had passed by. For the average observer, however, erosions must be more obvious. Worn pathways in the grass are an indication of traffic. More subtle are the worn control surfaces in an automobile or airplane cockpit that indicate frequency of use of those controls. Another example of traces occurs in institutions for the handicapped, where areas that are difficult to traverse are heavily marked by bumps from wheelchairs. Evidence of erosion may be seen everywhere, but great caution must be taken in interpreting it. In judging that a pathway through the grass indicates that a cement sidewalk should have been placed there, one may have failed to consider how the particular environment is managed. The buildings and grounds managers may prefer the appearance of the dirt path to a gleaming white sidewalk that would conflict with the landscape design. Another approach is to allow pathways to form first as a guide to where sidewalks should be placed.

Erosions can be used to uncover hidden pathways and unexpected uses. In the Arrowhead study (Dumouchel 1971), tracks in snow were an effective erosion measure because they indicated how a centrally located playground acted as a barrier to neighborhood traffic.

Leftovers are the most ubiquitous kind of traces, most often constituting what we commonly call "trash"—paper cups, beer cans, cigarette butts. Several researchers have used photographs of trash scatter to measure effectiveness of anti-litter campaigns (Geller et al. 1982). Others have randomly sampled and weighed trash. A good observation training exercise is to reconstruct a party from its leftovers. How many people smoked? How much liquor was consumed? Where did most of the party take place? Did the party stay together as a group or split up into subgroups? What were the favorite places? In a more systematic study, researchers would establish traces to observe by watching several parties first and recording traces as they occurred to build up a statistical basis for later behavioral inferences. For example, how many cups per person are normal use, how many napkins, and so on.

Missing traces indicate a lack of use in areas where erosion and leftovers are expected but do not occur. Lawton (1968) discovered that many social areas in high-rise buildings were not used. Very frequently outdoor places are not used; these are the "nondefensible spaces" described by Newman (1972) (nondefensible in that they are claimed by no one). The cues that Newman used to determine this were a failure to clean up the area and the fact that no one watched the space informally. Also significant are the many balconies that show lack of use in the United States compared to similar spaces in other countries. It is possible to count physical traces of use on balconies by viewing the side of a building. A series of photographs can document use over a year.

Zeisel's *adaptations for use* (1981) are clear indications that a change has been made in the environment because it did not serve its original intention. These would include all additions to buildings, renovations, redecorating, and "improvements." It is hard to detect adaptations when they were intended to fit into an existing structure but others like solar units and windmills are easily recognized. *Repairs* as a general class are sometimes easy to detect, often not. Zeisel calls many additions (such as solar units) *props*. He also looks for deliberate barriers, which he calls *separations*. Newman (1972) recommends separations as a way of creating defensible space. Arches over entryways, railings, fences, and other forms of separation act to keep intruders out and to convey the message that the separated area is someone's property. *Connections*, according to Zeisel, are created by occupants between two spaces when the design intended a separation that should have been a connection. Figure 1–9 shows a "connection" made through a basketball court fence at Project Arrowhead because it blocked a well-used pathway.

1–9. Broken fence indicates blockage of a pathway.

Zeisel's category *displays of self,* similar to what biologists call territorial marking, conveys a message of ownership. Decorative lettering on mailboxes, name plates on doorways, and the display of personal possessions are examples. Such displays become important for families and individuals who move often from place to place because the mementos seem to symbolize home. For older people, mementos represent ties with the past. The mantelpiece or the top of a bureau or coffee table is made into the shrine of the house, where the pictures of family and souvenirs of trips are displayed.

Zeisel defines *personalization* as a further step in identifying a place as belonging to a specific person. A desktop is adorned by pictures of family and by trophies or awards. Office walls contain personal photos or mementos. The child's room has souvenirs of special occasions, school, and travel. The college dormitory room displays posters that express the personal taste of the student. Personalization seems to be a basic need of workers. When the Lever Brothers building in New York City was first constructed, it had been designed to eliminate all personalization. Management forbade the hanging of any personal pictures or display of personal objects because they would conflict with the integrity of the design. The workers rebelled by vandalizing the building so severely that management relented and allowed personalization. When observing management policy, which either allows or tries to discourage personalization, it should be treated as a separate variable, unrelated to whether the design itself seems to encourage or make personalization difficult.

In the Cold Regions study (Bechtel and Ledbetter 1976) airmen at remote airbases preferred older barracks to new ones because the older ones were so run down that it did not matter how highly they were personalized. The new buildings had fancy vinyl wall coverings in which one was forbidden to place nails or tacks. Thus, how the design provides for the display of personal items is extremely critical to personalization. Figure 1-10 shows a single narrow shelf provided for each house in new housing for Iranians. It is loaded nearly to the bursting point. Ironically, nearby housing was being demolished that had provided countless niches in the walls for displays.

Clare Cooper-Marcus (1970) claims that each house is to some extent an expression of self, both in its selection and the way it is arranged. An environmental inventory of display is suggested to analyze the quality of self-presentation.

So important is furniture and other living room objects that Laumann and House (1970) and Davis (1955) created living room scales to measure social class. While these scales are now outdated, they can be brought up to date by inclusion of VCRs, home computers, and other devices.

Zeisel also uses *identification* and *group membership* as definite messages in the environment. Marking articles with one's name is identification, while group membership is often expressed in bumper stickers and jacket and sweatshirt labels.

Public messages are another form of traces. These range from official signs to public bulletin boards to graffiti. The PBS film *Style Wars* (Silver and

1-10. Narrow shelf in room of government (pre-Khomeini) housing in Iran, piled with possessions.

Chalfant 1983) chronicled the state of high art to which graffiti has been carried in the New York City subways. The film takes a cinema verité tour of the graffiti gangs as they go about "writing" on subway cars and buildings. Their pride in their work is an unintended satire on more highbrow art forms. The young artists show a concern for the mortality of their work and its artistic excellence and keep scrapbooks filled with photos of their best work. In New York graffiti became a vehicle for artistic competition. In other cities (Suttles 1968) graffiti serves as a territorial marking for neighborhood gangs.

Whatever classification one applies to personalized traces, it is important to attempt to understand the purpose of the trace and its potential conflict or blending with the surrounding environment. A high degree of personalization indicates a corresponding degree of ease with the environment but not necessarily comfort. The prevalence of graffiti can signal areas of social conflict.

Archives

Official records of various kinds constitute another category of traces. They differ from the types discussed thus far in that they are formal, organized, and stored in archives.

Census data and other public records are an important resource. The U.S. Bureau of the Census began counting citizens in 1790 and has continued to do so every ten years since. As the country grew, so did the number of questions asked. In addition, state and local governments as well as branches of the federal government began to collect their own data. Marriages, births, property exchanges, tax records, service and employment records, and credit records have become part of the enormous data banks that exist today and are readily available to researchers. Census and early military records are stored at the national archives in Washington, D.C. Federal employment records are stored in a warehouse in St. Louis, Missouri. Most of these records are microfilmed for preservation and ease of use.

Institutional records are also useful but more difficult to obtain. If a researcher is asked to study an organization, he or she quickly finds out that the records of organizations and businesses tend to be widely scattered and incomplete. Records of meetings and sales transactions are kept locally, but many other sets of data may be systematically destroyed or kept in separate locations.

Individual records comprise another category of traces. Each individual carries an increasing array of credit cards, a social security number and voter registration card, cards for membership in organizations and auto clubs, a driver's license, and I.D. for place of employment and leaves a trail of records of purchases, rents and mortgages paid, debts, contributions, traffic tickets, library books borrowed, bank deposits, checks written, taxes paid at various levels, hospital and doctor visits, dental records, and school grades. These constitute an endless source of data for an equally endless number of purposes.

Health records are an important source for studies relating physical aspects of the environment to physical and mental health (Wilner et al. 1962; Faris and Dunham 1939; Kaplan 1971). At one time it was believed that providing a clean, physically attractive environment would improve health. Now it is recognized that the causal chain to health is influenced by many more variables. Nevertheless, the many health archives are useful in ascertaining environmental relationships.

Condon (1983) used health records to show a critical link between illness and seasonal changes among the Copper Eskimos. Those uninitiated to cold climate studies would expect health to be linked closely to the cold. Actually, the disorienting effects of constant daylight in summer are greater than the constant dark and cold of winter. Yet, the greatest number of sick calls is in January because of the pressures of interrupted diurnal rhythms and the relatively crowded conditions of the settlement. The Eskimos disperse for hunting in the summer and are less likely to communicate diseases. Local archives of this kind are an invaluable source for determining environment–behavior interactions. In earlier studies it was revealed that merely gathering the population into a settlement increased the incidence of tuberculosis, and measures were needed to curb the further spread of the disease.

Crime statistics are a form of archival data that are used for a variety of purposes. Wilkinson and Bechtel (1970) were able to reconstruct the Kansas City riot of 1968 from police calls. Evidence from this study showed many areas of spontaneous activity as opposed to the unsupported concept of a single group of leaders. Many studies have been done with crime data to discover whether there is any truth to the popular belief that the moon influences criminal behavior (Campbell and Beets 1978). So far, although the debate continues (Garzino 1982; Campbell 1982) there does not seem to be much evidence for such an influence.

The theory that weather influences crime and violence, however, does seem to have some support (Harries and Stadler 1983; De Fronzo 1984; Atlas 1984), and the builders of prisons are well advised to consider frequent showers and air-conditioning as useful preventatives of violence.

The use of archival data is increasing and the view of what constitutes archival data is increasing as well. A popular new form of recycling data from old studies is called *meta analysis.* This form of analysis takes a series of studies done on a given subject and re-analyzes the data from a new viewpoint. For example, Mullen (1983) examined studies on helping behavior to determine effects of group size. While there is some debate about the various conclusions drawn from meta analysis, it seems to be a new form of archival use that is well established (Glass, McGaw, and Smith 1981).

Personal documents are a resource that may be overlooked. Many people have been moved by *The Diary of Anne Frank* (Frank 1952), yet do not readily see the diary as a valid document for historical and environmental research. Its historical value as a document of Nazi persecution during World War II is obvious, but it also documents an attempt to remain civilized in extremely close quarters and during a very tense time. Descriptions of how toilet and bathtub use had to be scheduled and how noise and eating were carefully controlled are important data on the basic requirements for living under such environmentally constrained circumstances. Diaries, letters, and other personal documents are important sources for obtaining data concerning how people reacted to and felt about observational conditions. A good example of diary use is Zube's (1982) compilation of how Arizona pioneers responded to the landscape of the nineteenth century. The diaries and letters of pioneers contain comments on their observations of the landscape as they encountered and lived with it. These observations can be compared with contemporary responses using present-day research methods to measure historical change.

Post-occupancy evaluations (POEs) are an important archival source for both designers and researchers (see chapter 6). Since relatively few of these are being published, it becomes a challenge to accumulate a sufficient personal archive. A good designer will want to acquire as many POEs as possible in his or her own specialty areas and this may mean personally conducting POEs. In many cases POEs are done by students as class exercises, theses or dissertations. Governmental agencies such as the General Services Administration have a number of unpublished studies on office buildings. To find out about these POEs, one must establish an extensive network of colleagues that will share information. The Environmental Design Research Associates maintain such a network with a list of researchers and practitioners interested in POEs.

The POE study on housing conducted by Bechtel and Srivastava in 1978 uncovered over 1,300 POE studies; many more have been performed since then. However, the quality of many of these studies is a problem. Of the original 1,300 less than 300 reported enough information to determine what methods they used. Many simply did not report "data" as such but gave impressionistic opinions. Thus, the discerning collector of POE information has to exercise a great deal of judgment in selecting those that provide the most useful information. Despite these difficulties in uniformity, reporting, and accessibility, POEs remain the largest source of information on how completed buildings and design projects actually function. In fact, they comprise the largest archive of environment behavior research.

ISSUES

How Not to Obtrude

The classic study on how being studied affects behavior is the famous Hawthorne project (Roethlisberger and Dickson 1939). The original purpose of the Hawthorne studies was to improve production at an electronics plant by increasing available lighting. It was discovered, however, that the control group, which was not exposed to the new lighting (and, in fact, where lighting decreased) also improved in production. Thus, the finding of the control group improvement became more famous than the original study because it illustrated that just being studied may make people feel special and stimulate a desire to please the experimenter or observer, in this case, by producing more. Since that time, the Hawthorne study has become a classic example of observer and experimenter effects on subjects.

Of course, not all observer effects are attempts to please the observer. Often the effect is to avoid or eject the observer from the scene. The question of how much an observation influences what is observed is a problem that pervades all scientific measurement. Heisenberg's uncertainty principle (Price and Chissick 1977) is a dictum that says that nothing in nature can be measured without interfering with it in some way. Thus, the attempt to measure itself introduces an irreducible error. Although no less an authority than Einstein could not accept Heisenberg's principle, it is commonly accepted today.

Translated into social science methodology and observation as a specific method, Heisenberg's uncertainty principle means that behavior will be influenced if the subjects know they are being watched. In short, the Hawthorne effect is social science's counterpart of the uncertainty principle. How can this be overcome? There are at least two somewhat polarized responses to this important question. One answer is never to let the subjects of a study know they are being observed. The other and opposite extreme is to require the informed consent of any subjects being observed. The objection to the first extreme is that it violates the privacy and civil rights of people if they are observed without their knowledge. The "informed consent" alternative is objected to because it maximizes the Hawthorne effect and negates the very purpose of studying "natural" behavior. Evidence for this effect abounds. Bechtel (1967) found that when visitors to a museum knew they were in an experiment, they spent three times the amount of time in a room looking at prints as the uninformed visitors (220 versus 71 seconds).

Thus, the ethical dilemma of observation is whether to gain consent and thus risk invalidation of the behavior to be observed. Most researchers solve this dilemma by assuming that any public behavior observed is not a violation of privacy and do not ask for consent. When it comes to observation in a school or institution, however, or a clearly private situation such as therapy, consent is obtained. Observation must be made for a time to determine whether researcher effects occur, and the principal measurement is made once effects seem to wear off. Also, if any pictures are to be published of people in public settings, consent must be obtained. While this solution may not meet the approval of all researchers, it is consistent with published ethical procedures.

Reliability of Categories

Perhaps the most critical issue in the use of observation is obtaining proper reliability among judges when recording categories. Since it is seldom that all behavior is observed, the selection of categories of behavior is critical to the success of observation, yet without reliability, the data become useless. A few scales, such as Bales (1950 and Bales and Cohen 1979), have high reliability, but most have to establish reliability among judges before they are used. This is a difficult task that is often overlooked in the desire to obtain quick results. Every research project should report reliability of judges as being .90 or better to elicit confidence in the data.

Inference of Causality

The main issue, once observation has taken place and reliability has been established, is the problem of determining why the observed behavior occurs and what it means. In participant observation this is overcome by asking informants about purpose and meaning and by living with the behaviors as a participant. In briefer methods of observation, other means such as interviewing, questionnaires, and archives are used independently to verify interpretations. Even when interviews or questionnaires are used to ask subjects directly about observed behavior, it is not a simple two-step process. Both observations and questionnaires need to be pre-tested so that both are found to be reliable and valid before the main data collecting in the field. Most often a third method is employed to obtain three sets of data, converging on the findings related to causality (Campbell and Fiske 1959).

REFERENCES

Atlas, R. 1984. Violence in prison: Environmental influences. *Environment and Behavior* 16:275–306.

Bales, R. 1950. *Interaction Process Analysis: A Method for the Study of Small Groups.* Reading, Mass.: Addison-Wesley.

Bales, R., and S. Cohen. 1979. *SYMLOG: A System for the Multiple Level Observation of Groups.* New York: Free Press.

Barker, R., and H. Wright. 1951. *One Boy's Day.* New York: Harper Brothers.

———. 1955. *Midwest and Its Children.* Evanston, Ill.: Row, Peterson.

Bechtel, R. 1965. Participation and observation in the mental hospital. *Kansas Journal of Sociology* 1:166–74.

———. 1967. Hodometer research in museums. *Museum News,* March 1967, pp. 23–25.

Bechtel, R., and A. Gonzales. 1971. A comparison of treatment environments between North American and Peruvian mental hospitals. *Archives of General Psychiatry* 25:64–68.

Bechtel, R., and C. B. Ledbetter. 1976. *The Temporary Environment.* Hanover, N.H.: U.S. Army Cold Regions Research and Engineering Laboratory.

Bechtel, R., C. B. Ledbetter, and N. Cummings. 1980. *Post-occupancy Evaluation of a Remote Australian Community: Shay Gap, Australia.* Hanover, N.H.: U.S. Army Cold Regions Research and Engineering Laboratory.

Bechtel, R., and R. Srivastava. 1978. *Post-occupancy Evaluation of Housing.* Washington, D.C.: Dept. of Housing and Urban Development.

Birdwhistell, R. 1970. *Kinesics in Context: Essays on Body Motion Communication.* Philadelphia: Univ. of Pennsylvania Press.

Campbell, D. 1982. Lunar-lunacy research: When enough is enough. *Environment and Behavior* 14:418–24.

Campbell, D., and J. Beets. 1978. Lunacy and the moon. *Psychological Bulletin* 85:1123–29.

Campbell, D., and D. Fiske. 1959. Convergent and discriminant validation by the multi-trait-multi-method matrix. *Psychological Bulletin* 56:81–105.

Caudill, W. 1958. *A Psychiatric Hospital as a Small Society.* Cambridge, Mass.: Harvard Univ. Press.

Chapin, F. 1974. *Human Activity Patterns in the City.* New York: Wiley.

Condon, R. 1983. *Inuit Behavior and Seasonal Change in the Canadian Arctic.* Ann Arbor: UMI Research Press.

Conway, D. 1973. *Social Science and Design: A Process Model for Architect and Social Scientist Collaboration.* Washington, D.C.: American Institute of Architects.

Cook, R., and D. Miles. 1978. *Plazas for People: Seattle Federal Building Plaza: A Case Study.* New York: Project for Public Spaces, Inc.

Cooper-Marcus, C. 1974. The house as symbol of the self. In *Designing for Human Behavior,* ed. J. Lang, C. Burnette, W. Moleski, and D. Vachon. Stroudsburg, Pa.: Dowden, Hutchinson and Ross.

Davis, J. 1955. Living Rooms as Symbols of Status: A Study in Social Judgment. Ph.D. diss., Harvard University.

De Fronzo, J. 1984. Climate and crime: Tests of an FBI assumption. *Environment and Behavior* 16:185–210.

De Long, A. 1976. Architectural research and design: The art and architecture building project. *Free Flow* 1:1–11.

Dumouchel, J. R. 1971. *Arrowhead: Final Recommendations.* Kansas City, Mo.: Environmental Research and Development Foundation.

Faris, R., and H. W. Dunham. 1939. *Mental Disorders in Urban Areas.* Chicago: Univ. of Chicago Press.

Frank, O. 1952. *Anne Frank: Diary of a Young Girl.* New York: Doubleday.

Gans, H. 1970. *The Levittowners.* New York: Pantheon.

Garzino, S. 1982. Lunar effects on mental behavior: A defense of the empirical research. *Environment and Behavior* 14:395–417.

Geller, S., R. Winette, and P. Everett. 1982. *Preserving the Environment.* Elmsford, N.Y.: Pergamon.

Glass, G., B. McGaw, and M. Smith. 1981. *Meta-Analysis in Social Research.* Beverly Hills, Cal.: Sage.

Guetzgow, H. 1950. Unitizing and categorizing problems in coding qualitative data. *Journal of Clinical Psychology* 6:47–58.

Hall, E. 1960. *The Hidden Dimension.* New York: Doubleday.

———. 1974. *Handbook for Proxemic Research.* Philadelphia: Society for the Anthropology of Visual Communication.

Harries, K., and S. Stadler. 1983. Determinism revisited: Assault and heat stress in Dallas, 1980. *Environment and Behavior* 15:235–56.

Ittelson, W., L. Rivlin, and H. Proshansky. 1970. The use of behavioral maps in environmental psychology. In *Environmental Psychology,* ed. H. Proshansky, W. Ittelson, and L. Rivlin. New York: Holt, Rinehart & Winston.

Jacobs, G. 1970. *The Participant Observer.* New York: Braziller.

Kaplan, B. 1971. *Psychiatric Disorder and the Urban Environment.* New York: Behavioral Publications.

Koff, T., W. Ittelson, R. Bechtel, D. Monahan, D. Lupu, K. Bursal, and E. Gerrity. 1980. *A Post Occupancy Evaluation of Hillhaven Hospice.* Tucson, Ariz.: Long Term Care Gerontology Center.

Laumann, E., and J. House. 1970. Living room styles and social attributes: The patterning of material artifacts in a modern urban community. *Sociology and Social Research* 54:321–42.

Lawton, M. P. 1968. Social and Medical Services in Housing for the Aged. Philadelphia: Philadelphia Geriatric Center. Mimeo.

Le Compte, A. 1981. The ecology of anxiety: Situational stress and the rate of self stimulation in Turkey. *Journal of Personality and Social Psychology* 40:712–21.

Liebow, E. 1970. A field experience in retrospect. In *The Participant Observer,* ed. G. Jacobs, 260–73. New York: Braziller.

McCormick, E., and M. Sanders. 1982. *Human Factors in Engineering.* New York: McGraw-Hill.

Mullen, B. 1983. Operationalizing the effect of the group on the individual: A self-attention perspective. *Journal of Experimental Social Psychology* 19:295–322.

Newman, O. 1972. *Defensible Space.* New York: Macmillan.

Price, S., and S. Chissick, eds. 1977. *The Uncertainty Principle and Foundation of Quantum Mechanics: A Fifty Years' Survey.* New York: Wiley.

Rathje, W. 1977. In praise of archeology. In *Historic Archeology and the Importance of Material Things,* ed. L. G. Ferguson. Columbia, S.C.: Society for Historical Archeology.

———. 1979. Trace measures. *New Directions for Methodology of Behavioral Science* 1.

Rathje, W., and W. Hughes. 1978. *Final Report, Project du Garbage.* Washington, D.C.: National Science Foundation.

Rathje, W., and C. Rittenbaugh. 1984. Household refuse analysis. *American Behavioral Scientist* 28 (special issue).

Redlich, R., and E. Brody. 1955. Emotional problems of interdisciplinary research in psychiatry. *Psychiatry* 18:233–39.

Roethlisberger, F., and W. Dickson. 1939. *Management and the Worker.* Cambridge, Mass.: Harvard University Press.

Rosenfeld, H. 1960. Instrumental affiliative functions of facial and gestural expressions. *Journal of Personality and Social Psychology* 4:65–72.

Silver, T., and H. Chalfant. 1983. *Style Wars.* New York: Public Art Films, Inc.

Sussman, N., and H. Rosenfeld. 1982. Influence of culture, language, and sex on conversational distance. *Journal of Personality and Social Psychology* 42:66–74.

Suttles, G. 1968. *The Social Order of the Slum.* Chicago: Univ. of Chicago Press.

Tadjer, Cohen, Shefferman, & Bigelson, Inc. 1975. *Studies and Planning Services to Develop and Apply Performance Specifications in Procurement and Evaluation of Housing.*

Trites, D., F. Galbraith, M. Sturdavant, and J. Leckwart. 1970. Influence of nursing unit design on the activities and subjective feelings of nursing personnel. *Environment and Behavior* 3:303–34.

Wilkinson, C., and R. Bechtel. 1970. *The Social History of a Riot.* Washington, D.C.: National Institutes of Mental Health, Metropolitan Mental Health Problems Division.

Whyte, W. 1980. *The Social Life of Small Urban Spaces.* Washington, D.C.: The Conservation Foundation.

Wilner, D., R. Walkley, R. Pinkerton, and M. Tayback. 1962. *The Housing Environment and Family Life.* Baltimore: Johns Hopkins Univ. Press.

Wright, H. 1967. *Recording and Analyzing Child Behavior.* New York: Harper & Row.

Zeisel, J. 1981. *Inquiry by Design.* Monterey, Cal.: Brooks/Cole.

Zeisel, J., and P. Drake. 1984. Post-Occupancy Evaluation Methodology for Emergency Departments. A report prepared by Building Diagnostics, Inc., for the Department of Health and Welfare, Health Facilities Design Division, Ottawa.

Zube, E. 1982. An exploration of landscape images. *Landscape Journal* 1:31–40.

CHAPTER 2
SURVEY RESEARCH

Robert W. Marans

Social surveys have gained wide acceptance among architects, planners, and other environmental designers over the past decade. Although this statement may still be questioned, there is little doubt that surveys, or at least components of the survey process, have found their way into the designer's world since an earlier version of this chapter was written. During the past ten years, community needs assessments, user studies for architectural programs, post-occupancy evaluations, and environment and behavior research have proliferated, exposing both design students and practitioners to methods of the social sciences such as questionnaires, sample designs, systematic observations, and statistical analysis of quantitative data. During the same period, the social survey has been called upon by governmental officials and policy makers when judging the effectiveness of public programs, including many that deal with the physical environment. For a number of environmental designers and planners, the social survey has altered the process whereby design decisions are made and, although it may be difficult to demonstrate, the changes in decision making have probably resulted in environmental designs of higher quality.

The decade has also seen numerous methodological advances in survey research. Most notable are improvements in questionnaire design, data collection techniques, coding, and analytic procedures. Many of these advances are reported in scholarly journals, monographs, and technical reports to clients (Cannell et al. 1981; Groves and Kahn 1979; Alwin 1977; Schuman and Presser 1981; Frey 1984). Some are discussed later in this chapter. The appropriateness of social surveys or survey research for the environmental design professions is first considered, however. First, the question of how surveys are used by design professionals and researchers is addressed. Next, because environmental design operates at several scales ranging from interior spaces to buildings and regions, a discussion of the geographic breadth of surveys is presented. In order to give the reader an expanded view of the potential of surveys, several survey designs are then considered. This is followed by an overview of the major steps in the survey process. Particular attention is given to the design of samples and alternative data collection techniques. The chapter concludes with an example of the application of surveys to research on a built environment.

WHAT IS SURVEY RESEARCH?

Survey research, as discussed in this chapter, has four definitional characteristics. First, it involves the systematic collection of information from a population using standardized questionnaires. Second, the information is about the population and the environment it occupies. As we shall see momentarily, the information can cover a wide range of topics. Third, the information is collected from every person in the population, or from a sample of the population. Finally, most of the information is obtained by either face-to-face personal interviews, telephone interviews, or through self-administered questionnaires.

Surveys have other characteristics as well. In principle, they are relatively objective. They offer a formal way of obtaining information that is more or less free from the biases, values, and predispositions of the designer or researcher. At the same time, surveys are quantitative in that numerical values are assigned to people's attitudes, behaviors, and environmental conditions in ways that enable the researcher to uniformly analyze, interpret, and report the information. Another characteristic of surveys is that they can be replicated. Other researchers using identical procedures and methods for studying a population occupying the same environment should obtain essentially the same results supporting the validity of the initial study findings. Surveys are also generalizable. That is, it is possible to make generalizations about a large number of people and their surroundings by selecting and studying a subset of the group. Finally, surveys can overcome problems associated with using secondary sources of information. Instead of relying on data that are often out of date, surveys produce information about people and their environments that is contemporary.

This array of characteristics would suggest that survey research is an attractive and powerful tool for design practitioners and researchers. Yet there is the inherent danger with any new tool or technique that when first introduced without guidance or instruction, it tends to be used indiscriminately. For the environmental designer or researcher, using surveys too freely or without the benefits of other complementary techniques can be costly and time consuming and can result in information that is irrelevant or incomplete. As two pioneers in survey research have suggested, it requires great restraint to use surveys only when they are most appropriate (Lansing and Morgan 1971).

SOME APPROPRIATE USES OF SURVEYS

Surveys can be used by environmental designers and researchers in several ways. From the practitioner's perspective, surveys can provide objective and timely information about people and their environments during the initial stages of the planning and design process. At a general level, survey data can inform decisions on matters of design policy. During the deliberations that often take place over the drawing board or in the conference room, the survey is the vehicle through which designers and other decision makers can become aware of the feelings, actions, expectations, and levels of awareness of the population that will be affected by their decisions. The information can be used in discussions that revolve around a particular issue or problem, such as where to locate a new park, whether high-rise or low-rise buildings are more suitable for housing older persons, or whether the placement of furniture in an office is likely to have any bearing on the way workers respond to word-processing equipment.

It is important to note that because there are so many factors that collectively influence such decisions, the survey should not be thought of as the only source of information to be used in establishing policy. What the survey does is to sensitize decision makers to another important set of factors that needs to be considered, namely the different views, interests, and activities of a substantial number and representative group of people associated with an environment.

A second use of surveys during the early period of planning and design is in the development of programs for new environments. For example, survey results have been used in establishing design goals and in setting priorities for housing projects (Sanoff 1977), in identifying and understanding the complexities of office organizations (Moleski 1974), and in developing design guidelines for patient rooms, signage, and outdoor spaces in a hospital (Reizenstein and Grant 1982).

Closely related to the use of surveys and survey data for programming is their use in evaluating built environments and environmentally related programs. There are numerous examples of surveys undertaken as part of post-occupancy evaluations aimed at understanding the degree to which a particular built environment is satisfying user needs (Zeisel and Griffin 1975; Elder and Tibbett 1981; Van der Ryn and Silverstein 1967; Marans and Spreckelmeyer 1981).

Surveys have also been used as an evaluative tool in identifying salient issues in prisons that warrant further study (Farbstein and Wener 1982), in evaluations designed to generate data suitable for proposing housing designs and management strategies (Reynolds and Nicholson 1972; Cooper 1975; Marans 1978; Weidemann et al. 1982), and in the evaluation of specific programs related to housing (Burby and Weiss 1976; Francescato et al. 1979; Peroff et al. 1979), environmental education (Marans et al. 1972), and energy conservation (McClelland and Cook 1980).

Evaluations using multiple surveys can be an effective means of determining the degree of success of a built environment or program in fulfilling its intended goals. When the same survey instrument is used prior to introducing a change in a program or physical setting, and then again afterwards, the survey results can show the degree to which specific objectives have been achieved. They can also demonstrate how far off the mark the designers are in achieving program and design objectives. It is possible, for instance, to use a survey to assess how residents feel about a local playground prior to improvements, and, using the same survey instrument, to measure their feelings after improvements have been made.

In addition to the use of surveys by practitioners early in the planning and design process and as a tool for evaluating built environments and programs, surveys can be used by researchers in describing something about a population or the environment it occupies. For example, surveys can produce data estimating the number of neighborhood residents who are bothered by local traffic or the proportion of workers leaving their offices during the noon hour. They can indicate how many households have home computers or they can yield up-to-date figures on residents in a housing estate over sixty-five years of age having a balcony or other private outdoor space. Such information usually is not available to the designer, planner, or environmental researcher, nor is it easily attainable through other methods of inquiry.

Survey data can be used to explain the sentiments and actions of populations. For instance, it may be important to know why certain people are bothered by local traffic while others are not. And for residents who are bothered, why some are more vociferous in their complaints than others. The degree to which traffic is viewed as problematic could be influenced by a number of factors including where residents have previously lived, the amount of time they spend at home, or where within the neighborhood their homes are located vis-à-vis streets, intersections, or wooded areas. The analysis of survey data can help in identifying factors that explain why people respond as they do.

Surveys can also be helpful to the environmental designer or researcher in substantiating hunches about a problem, including its severity, causes, and geographic distribution. When the designer-researcher thinks about a particular problem, why it exists, or where within the environment it is focused, the survey can yield appropriate data that will enable a test of these assumptions.

Finally, surveys can be used in establishing priorities by determining the relative importance of several factors that may affect what people do or how they feel. If, for instance, the designer-researcher wants to know which of several environmental conditions is most likely to influence or explain the actions of a group of people, the answer in part can be determined through a multivariate analysis of survey data.

In sum, surveys can be useful during the initial stages of planning and design and after environments and programs have been established. Data derived from surveys can inform current decisions as well as test the assumptions underlying past decisions by describing, explaining, and predicting situations involving people, what they do and how they feel, and the environments in which they operate.

USEFUL INFORMATION FROM SURVEYS

What specific kinds of survey data can be used by designers and other environmental decision makers? As suggested earlier, there are numerous topics that surveys can cover in relation to people, their environments, and the interrelationships among them.

Unlike other methodologies, surveys about people can answer questions about "who," "how," and "what." The "who" questions are usually designed to provide factual information about a particular population, such as its average age, its marital status, the number of children at home, the monthly rent payments, or the job classification of office personnel. These factual data can be used in three ways. First, they make it possible to describe the population under investigation in very precise terms—to specify the proportion that is married, the number of secretaries in an organization, the differences in electrical bills among tenants, and so on. Second, the data can help explain why there may be variations among the reported behaviors or feelings of a population—for example, relating the extent to which workers eat lunch in the building to job classification, and finding that secretaries do so less frequently, on average, then supervisors. Finally, "who" data can show how a study population differs from or is similar to other populations such as the residents in the community at large, people in another neighborhood receiving the same services, or the occupants of other office buildings of comparable size.

The "how" and "what" questions deal with people's thoughts and feelings, their behaviors, and their understanding and awareness of situations and places. Surveys can be used to find out what goes on in people's minds in terms of how they feel about a particular environment they use or know. Survey questions can also tap people's thoughts about a hypothetical environment, such as a design proposal for a new housing complex. Prospective residents may be asked to evaluate the proposal and indicate what they like and dislike about it. For the most part, expressions of approval and disapproval, statements of preference, likes and dislikes, and positive and negative evaluations, as well as the rationale for these sentiments can contribute to our understanding of why people behave as they do, how strongly they will support a new idea, or how they might react to a proposed environment still on the drawing board.

Another set of "how" and "what" questions deals with people's behaviors or, more generally, with how they use their time. Questions about what people do in an environment or what they do *to* an environment can be asked in surveys (Zeisel 1982). Survey-based studies have reported how often and in what ways children use nearby recreation areas (Cooper 1975; Francescato et al. 1979; van Vliet 1980), what kinds of tasks are performed by office personnel (Harris 1980), or how often residents use public transportation, visit a nearby shopping center, or attend a neighborhood meeting (Lansing et al. 1970).

Surveys can also be used to determine whether employees have personalized their workspaces, whether residents have remodeled their homes, or whether teachers have rearranged the furniture in their classrooms. Such information can cover past as well as current behaviors. Survey questions can address whether or not a person had previously engaged in a particular activity during a predetermined time period (Have you been to the neighborhood park during the past year?) or they can determine whether a person participates in an activity on a regular, ongoing basis (How often do you visit the park—never, once or twice a week, or more often?). The latter type of question assumes that the response—the number of park visits—reflects current behavior even though the activity is reported after the fact and does not say anything about whether the respondent will continue to engage in the activity in the future.

Anticipated or expected behaviors can also be explored through survey questions: Will you be visiting the park this summer? or Do you plan to move during the next twelve months? When questions such as these are asked as part of a panel study (see "Types of Survey Designs," below), it is possible to find out the extent to which people's expectations or anticipated behaviors have been fulfilled. For example, Duncan and Newman (1976) asked a national household sample about their intentions to move, and using data from a follow-up survey of the same households, determined the proportion of the original sample that had actually changed their residence.

Whereas these behavioral questions are likely to be asked of individuals, the reported behaviors need not be limited to those of the respondent. It is possible, for example, to ask an individual about past, current, and in many instances, future behaviors of others with whom the respondent is familiar—his employees, family, or spouse.

A third set of "how" and "what" questions asked as part of surveys covers how much people know and, relatedly, what their level of understanding is about a place, situation, or event. Surveys have been used to test students' knowledge of ecological principles and environmental issues (Marans et al. 1972), to examine people's awareness of the layout of a city or buildings (Orleans 1973; Wiseman 1981; Hunt 1984), and to explore people's understanding of conditions in particular environments. For instance, studies have considered residents' perceptions and awareness of neighborhood crime (Greenberg et al. 1981), the water quality of inland lakes (Marans and Wellman 1978), and the safety and upkeep of an urban park (Kaplan 1980). To a large extent, questions of understanding are aimed at identifying what people see or perceive in their surroundings.

In addition to data about people and how they feel about, use, and perceive the environment, surveys can produce information about the objective environment. The objective environment, which refers to the environment as it actually is, may be described in physical, sociocultural, or organizational terms. It is possible, for instance, to quantify several physical dimensions of a neighborhood, including the size of dwellings or yards, the degree to which the latter are enclosed, the amount and kinds of open space in the neighborhood, the volume of traffic on streets, and the density of development. In the work setting, data on the physical environment can cover the amount of space assigned to workers, the intensity and direction of lighting, noise levels, colors of the workspace, distance between workers, or distances from workers to fire exits and coffee machines.

The sociocultural environment of the residential setting can include the income, ethnic, and racial composition of the resident population; the prevalence of neighborhood organizations such as church groups, parent-teacher associations, and improvement associations; or various indicators of crime (reported robberies) and health (incidences of tuberculosis, school absences, and so on).

Whereas environmental characteristics for a particular physical setting can be described in much the same way as characteristics of individuals or occupants of that setting, the true value of environmental data is in their analysis vis-à-vis data covering the feelings and behaviors of the people associated with that setting. It is possible, for example, to use environmental data collected as part of a survey to determine the extent to which various lighting levels throughout a building correspond to people's complaints about its being too bright or too dark to work satisfactorily; or using data from a survey of neighborhoods, to determine which of several environmental conditions is most likely to contribute to the residents' use or nonuse of outdoor recreation facilities (Marans and Fly 1981).

To examine relationships between objective environmental conditions and people's objective responses and reported behaviors requires the collection of environmental data for each unit (person) in the population or in the sample. For instance, the individuals whose personal characteristics, attitudes, and behaviors are being examined represent the units for which environmental data are collected. In a sample of occupants of dwellings throughout a housing complex, environmental data covering attributes of their dwellings—size, amount of outdoor space, distance to the bus stop, and so forth—are gathered for each person in the sample and incorporated in the data file along with attitudinal and behavioral information. The means of gathering these environmental data may include the direct questioning of each occupant ("How many rooms do you have?"), observations by interviewers trained to estimate sizes and distances, or to judge environmental states ("Is there a carpet or piece of furniture within three feet of the respondent's fireplace?"), or secondary sources such as maps, floor plans, or aerial photographs.

GEOGRAPHIC SCOPE OF SURVEYS

Surveys can be used to examine a population occupying any geographic area or place. Most familiar to environmental researchers and designers are surveys of people associated with relatively small areas such as buildings, parks, housing projects, or neighborhoods. Ideally, the survey conducted in a particular place is one of several sources of information about the population and the manner in which it interacts with the physical environment. The early work on married student housing by Festinger et al. (1950) and the later studies of Gans (1962, 1967), Cooper (1975), and Sundstrom et al. (1982) typify field investigations of specific places that combine the survey methodology with other data-gathering techniques.

Although the survey in combination with other methods can provide valuable information about a particular place, it is important to recognize that the information reflects the responses of a single group of people at a single point in time. For example, it may be useful for architects to know how employees in a corporate office building feel about their present work situation when planning new corporate headquarters. But it would be unwise for these or other architects to infer from employee responses the reactions of workers in other organizations to their work settings. In other words, it is inappropriate to generalize from the results of a survey conducted at one location to other locations and even to the same location at a later time.

Generalizing from survey findings to other settings may be possible when the populations associated with several comparable sites are studied simultaneously. For instance, Zube et al. (1976) conducted interviews with users at twelve national park visitor centers, and based on survey results, made a number of statements about visitor center users including who they were, their reasons for going to centers, and the first place they went after entering the buildings. Others have conducted interviews with residents of public housing projects (Francescato et al. 1979; Lawton et al. 1975), retirement communities (Walkley et al. 1966), new towns (Burby and Weiss 1976) and with workers in offices (Harris 1978), and within these types of settings, have described a wide range of person–environment interactions.

If the sites where surveys were conducted were located within the same geographic area, the findings could be used to describe the population for that area. For instance, surveys could be designed to study residents in a sample of neighborhoods throughout a city or users of regional parks. Survey designs such as these would enable the researcher to make generalizations about residents of that city or about regional park visitors. The designs would also permit comparisons between populations at the different sites: for example, findings that residents of Neighborhood A are more satisfied with public services than residents of other neighborhoods; Park B is more popular among recreationists than other regional parks; and so forth.

Comparisons of people in different places can also be made using data from surveys conducted nationally. Sample surveys of U.S. households, which represent the other end of the geographic spectrum, typically are conducted by large polling organizations (Harris, Gallup), university research centers (such as the Social Research Center at Michigan or the National Opinion Research Center at Chicago), or the federal government (U.S. Bureau of the Census). Working with data from these national surveys, it is not uncommon for researchers to compare populations in different regions of the country or in communities that differ in size (large urban, suburban, small town, rural farm). For example, Annual Housing Survey data have been used to show those types of communities where neighborhood conditions are most problematic (Marans 1978). They have also been used to examine the effects of race on opinions about neighborhood quality (Casey 1980), and in studying mobility patterns among households living in metropolitan and nonmetropolitan areas (Chi 1979).

National survey data can be used by planners and designers as bench marks for comparing data obtained from a survey conducted in a small geographic area or place. For instance, if questions about neighborhood quality used in the Annual Housing Survey were asked by local planners in a community or neighborhood survey, the national data covering people's ratings of neighborhoods would represent a yardstick against which neighborhood ratings by local residents could be analyzed and interpreted. In a similar vein, questions asked in a national survey of office workers were used in a survey conducted as part of an evaluation of an office building (Marans and Spreckelmeyer 1981). An analysis of the two sets of responses added credence to the conclusion that environmental conditions within the building were poor.

National surveys, because of the large number of respondents, offer the potential for differentiating between various population subgroups within the country. For example, data from a 1972 national quality-of-life survey were examined to determine the differences, if any, in housing assessments among blacks and whites, older single people and families with children, and household heads with varying income and educational levels (Campbell et al. 1976). Similarly, the Harris national office worker surveys (1978, 1980) compared questionnaire responses from personnel in different types of jobs (executive, manager, and secretary) and at different job levels (senior manager, supervisor, and regular worker).

Thus far, our discussion of the scope of surveys has focused on geography or the size of places within which surveys can be conducted. Clearly, surveys can be used to study populations associated with areas of any size. For the designer-researcher, the challenge in planning a survey is simultaneously to define the population to be studied and its geographic scope.

It is less clear that surveys can be designed to examine populations distinguished by a common characteristic, experience, or behavior. There have been surveys of college graduates, children and teenagers, prison officials, recent home-buyers, the elderly, public-transit riders, visitors to wilderness areas, and other equally specialized populations. Samples of these populations have been selected because they have special significance in relation to the objectives of the study. For example, in an attempt to learn about the residential search process of young families, Michelson (1977) studied a sample of households moving to single family homes and high-rise apartments in suburban and central Toronto. In this instance, the selection of intended movers was more important to the study design than the selection of the particular settings in which destination housing was located.

TYPES OF SURVEY DESIGNS

Whenever surveys are contemplated, a decision must be made about the overall study design, which in turn guides sampling and data collection procedures. This decision takes into account several factors, including the kinds of data deemed necessary, the hypotheses to be tested, the relationships to be explored, and the amount of the survey budget. There are three survey designs worthy of consideration by environmental researchers: cross-sectional surveys, longitudinal surveys, and contrasting sample surveys.

Cross-sectional Surveys

This survey design is used most often because it is relatively simple to plan and inexpensive to execute. Cross-sectional surveys are designed to collect data at a single point in time from a population or a sample of that population. That is, the data are intended to describe or explain something about the population at the time the survey is conducted.

Much of the data emanating from cross-sectional surveys are presented as percentage distributions. These data can inform the researcher or environmental designer about the responses of a particular population to some environmental phenomena. Distributional data can also convey information about people's behavior. For instance, the contention that neighborhood parks are not used extensively by children has been supported in part by distributional data from national and local area surveys. Findings from a national survey indicate that over two-thirds of all children between two and nine years of age play at home in their yards. An additional 15 percent play in the street or on the sidewalk near home, while only 5 percent visit the local or neighborhood park (Mandell and Marans 1972). Data from a metropolitan area survey show that older children (five to twelve years) are more willing to venture beyond their homes. Survey results show that over half play in their yards, whereas roughly one in ten most often use the local park or playground (Marans and Fly 1981). When distance between the home and the nearest recreational facility was considered in both studies, playground/park use by youth increased but not as much as one might suspect. Children living within a few minutes of a park or playground were somewhat more likely to use these facilities than those living beyond three minutes. The implications of these findings pose a number of important questions for recreation planners and researchers with respect to the distribution of urban parks and the degree to which they are serving the needs of young people.

Data from cross-sectional surveys can be used to examine possible differences in the attitudes and behaviors among subgroups of a population. For example, Weidemann et al. (1982) found significant differences in attitudes toward environmental attributes of a public housing project among youth, adults, and elderly residents. Although the findings reflect the sentiments of each subgroup at the time the survey was conducted, they say nothing about the attitudes of these groups at an earlier point in time nor how attitudes might change in the future. A subsequent survey could find that relationships between attitudes and population characteristics (for example, age) differ or no longer exist.

Longitudinal Surveys

This survey design permits the collection and analysis of data over a period of time enabling the researcher to report changes in the characteristics of a population and its behavioral and attitudinal responses. Two types of longitudinal designs are of interest and potential value to environmental designers. One involves the study of samples drawn from a population at different points of time (trend studies). The second design involves the collection of data at different times from the same people who make up a population or a sample of that population (panel studies).

Trend Studies. It is possible to consider change by studying different samples of the same population at different times. Essentially, changes or trends can be examined using data from repeated cross-sectional surveys. Whereas different persons are interviewed in each survey, the population from which each sample of respondents is selected is identical. For example, political polls conducted over the course of an election year represent a trend study in that samples of voters taken from the same population in the same geographic area are interviewed periodically to determine candidate preference. (Although the possibility exists for individual voters to be selected in more than one of the samples, it would be a chance occurrence.)

An example of a trend study dealing with the physical environment involves repeated surveys of workers in a large office building during the course of a major retrofit project. As a way of monitoring worker responses to environmental conditions as they change, questionnaires would be administered to a subset of, say, one hundred workers every month during the period in which energy conservation measures were being implemented. The data from these questionnaires would show the extent to which office workers, as a group, were more or less comfortable or distracted as a result of the construction activity taking place around them.

Panel Studies. Although repeated cross-sectional surveys can be used to identify changes that may be taking place among a population, they do not permit the researcher to identify the individuals within that population whose attitudes or behaviors have changed. Nor can the researcher examine individual or environmental factors that may affect change with data from repeated cross-sectional surveys. In the office building example, it is impossible to tell precisely which workers were being affected by changing environmental conditions or where within the building they worked. If a panel design were employed initially, the researcher would be able to address these issues.

Panel studies are a type of longitudinal survey involving the collection of data over time from the same respondents, referred to as panel members. In our example, the office workers selected initially would make up the panel and would be reinterviewed every month throughout the period of study. The data collected each month would enable the researcher to identify office workers whose views on environmental comfort had changed. The data would also permit the researcher to examine factors that might be associated with attitudinal change, such as where within the building the respondents were located.

Panel studies also have the advantage, compared to single cross-sectional surveys, of reducing errors in responses that may be attributed to faulty memory. Some surveys have been justifiably criticized on the grounds that certain variables are difficult to measure retrospectively. For instance, a respondent may not remember with any degree of accuracy the duration and frequency of coffee breaks taken prior to his moving into a new work setting. Nor could he reliably report on the condition of the dwelling he lived in, say, five years earlier. In both instances, a panel design allowing for two interviews with the same respondent would improve the quality of the data covering both points in time.

The number of surveys conducted as part of a panel design and the period between each can vary depending on the purposes of the research and the time and money available for conducting the study. For instance, a national study of income dynamics designed to discern patterns of poverty in the United States collected data annually from a panel of respondents over a fifteen-year period (Duncan 1984). Most panel designs, however, involve two or three data collections that typically occur prior to and following critical events such as an election, a change in residence, or the introduction of a program or service. Other panel designs may rely on more frequent data collections. In his seminal study of residential choice, Michelson (1977) collected information from his respondents at four different times in order to assess interim change. Initial contact with panel members was made just prior to their move to a new dwelling while the second point of contact, two months later, was designed to assess the immediate effects of the move. A third wave of interviews was conducted with the same respondents one year after the second interview, while the final wave, to assess long-term effects, was launched four years later.

Although panel designs are potentially valuable to environmental researchers and designers interested in the effects of changing environmental circumstances, they are not without problems. One difficulty is attrition, or the loss of respondents from the panel, which may occur in later waves of interviewing. Persons contacted during the initial survey may be unwilling or unable to be interviewed in a subsequent survey—they may refuse to participate or simply disappear from the scene. If a significant number of original respondents do not participate in subsequent surveys, the advantage of the panel design in being able to follow the same people over time is greatly diminished.

Another problem with panel designs is the expense of executing them. There are the additional costs of finding and interviewing people, particularly when they change their residence or workplace between surveys, and higher costs for coding and editing, managing the data, and administrative record keeping. Finally, there may be costs in maintaining the panel, such as remunerating respondents as an incentive for their continued participation in the study, for notifying the researchers as to their whereabouts, or for simply allowing their names or other identification to be maintained in computer files for an extended period of time.

A final difficulty in working with panel designs deals with the complexities of data analysis. Not only does the number of variables used by the researcher increase in proportion to the number of waves of data that are being collected, but additional variables are needed to measure differences in scores between the same questionnaire items collected at any two points in time.

In general, these problems have inhibited the use of panel designs in survey research. Nonetheless, it is possible that surveys using panels of respondents could become more important as the need to consider the environmental context of behavioral change is recognized and as the resources required to conduct longitudinal research become available. In the meantime, cross-sectional surveys will continue to be the most frequently used survey design and will contain, among other things, questions aimed at identifying prior situations and actions of respondents.

Contrasting Sample Designs

If we were interested in examining the effects of a particular environmental attribute or set of attributes on a population, studying two or more populations that contrast with respect to the attributes would be an appropriate survey design. For example, a hypothetical study might determine whether the introduction of supersonic aircraft produces stress among residents of communities surrounding airports scheduled to receive the aircraft. To test this hypothesis, samples from the populations in several cities located within ten miles of airports could be interviewed. Samples would also be interviewed in cities comparable to the airport cities in geographical, industrial, socioeconomic and other characteristics, but located more than ten miles distant from an airport. In other words, the cities would be selected so that the populations within them would be similar in every respect except their proximity to airports.

In two studies designed to measure the impact of planned communities on the quality of life of residents (Lansing et al. 1970; Burby and Weiss 1976), samples from contrasting communities were selected that differed in the extent to which they were planned. Degree of planning was associated with a number of environmental attributes including the layout of roads, the land-use mix, the amount of open space, and the number of recreational facilities. In order to determine whether living in a planned residential environment affected the quality of life of residents, highly planned communities and less planned residential environments in the same region housing families of the same socioeconomic level and composition were selected. Within each community, interviews were then conducted with samples of residents. In both studies, the researchers were able to demonstrate the effects of a set of environmental attributes by selecting places having extremes with respect to those attributes.

THE SURVEY PROCESS—A BRIEF OVERVIEW

Conducting a survey involves several steps, many of which occur simultaneously. The actual number and the time duration of each depends upon several factors: the complexity and number of issues the researcher intends to address vis-à-vis the survey, the size of the study population, and the characteristics of the environment occupied by the population. For example, a survey of fifty workers in a small plant purported to have poor indoor air quality would take less time and involve fewer steps than a survey designed to tap employee reactions to a full range of environmental conditions in, say, the World Trade Center.

Irrespective of the complexity of the problem, the size of the study population, or the scale of the environment, all surveys involve four sets of activities. These include the planning of the survey, the design and use of data-gathering instruments, the compilation and analysis of data, and the interpretation and reporting of survey findings. Quite often, surveys require another set of activities—the design and selection of a sample. These sets of activities and their interrelationships are shown in figure 2-1.

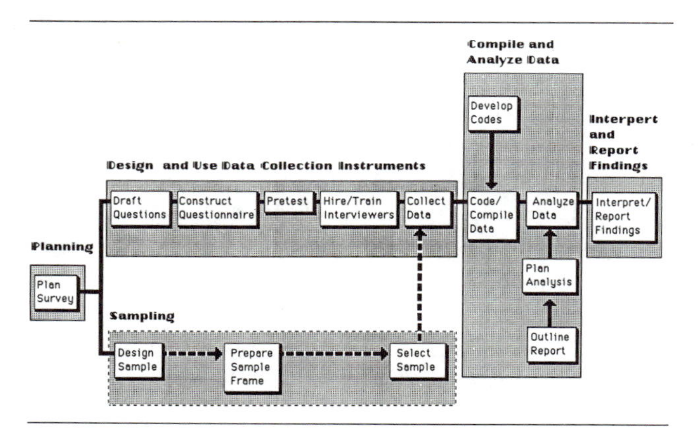

2–1. Activities in the survey process.

Survey Planning

As in the case of any research or design project, the planning of a survey requires considerable thought prior to collecting data or putting pencil to paper. The planning phase usually begins by spelling out the rationale or the general purposes for doing the survey. Often the general purpose relates to a problem or set of problems that make the survey necessary. These problems may be posed as questions. For example: Are there environmental conditions in the workplace that affect employee performance differentially? What factors contribute to dissatisfaction in the neighborhood? Why do some seventh graders in the same school learn more than others? In essence, these questions define the general contents of the survey and are translated into specific research questions and hypotheses. Additionally, they begin to identify the variables that are needed so that research questions can be addressed and hypotheses tested.

In surveys, variables can deal with the environment as well as with people. As the term variable implies, the characteristics of environments and the people who operate within them can take on different values. Even in the same office setting, there are attributes that will differ or vary in degree. For instance, variability may exist in the amount of light available to individual workers, the square footage allocated to each person, and the distance between work stations and windows, fire exits and washrooms.

Workers within the setting can vary as well. Variability can exist in terms of who the people are (their gender, age, or length of employment), how they feel, and what they do. The specification of these variables dealing with people and environments, as well as the manner in which they might relate to one another (the hypotheses), begins during the planning phase of the survey.

Paralleling the definition and specification of research questions, variables, and hypothesized relationships, efforts are typically made to obtain background information about the topic or issues under investigation. It is rare indeed that, when a survey is proposed, there is no prior information about the topic, either from within the environment under study or from another source. Inevitably, there is a literature search to be performed by the researcher that will enable him to understand the problems and issues to be addressed by the survey. There is also information about the setting that requires exploration. These background activities take place during the planning phase.

Design and Use of Data Collection Instruments

As part of the planning and design of a survey, consideration is given to the setting within which the survey will be conducted, the definition of the study population and the respondents from whom information will be obtained, and the means of gathering the information. Optional methods of data collection include personal interviewing and the use of self-administered questionnaires. Personal interviews can be conducted face to face or by telephone, whereas self-administered questionnaires can be distributed by mail or administered to individuals in groups—for instance, to students in classrooms. A more complete discussion of these options is presented later in the chapter.

The selection of a particular data collection method will depend upon several factors: the type of questions the researcher intends to ask, the number and spatial distribution of people who will be asked the questions, and the size of the budget allocated to data gathering. Once the method is determined, and the researcher has some idea about what he intends to ask, the process of writing questions can begin.

Drafting questions for surveys is more difficult than one might expect. Monographs and chapters in textbooks have been devoted to the topic (Kahn and Cannell 1967; Oppenheim 1966; Payne 1951; Labaw 1980), while systematic research aimed at understanding the effects of different forms of attitude questions on responses has been reported (Bishop et al. 1978; Schuman and Presser 1981). Suffice it to say that writing survey questions requires considerable care if the researcher expects to satisfy study objectives fully.

Once questions are drafted, the next task is to arrange them in a logically sequenced and easily understood set of inquiries. The construction or design of a questionnaire is in many ways an art blending the creative talents of the researcher with principles of good questionnaire design. The questionnaire is the means whereby ideas are communicated in a clear, interesting, and purposeful manner. The clarity of the questionnaire is important to both the respondents and the interviewers, who must know precisely what to do during the interchange. The questionnaire must also be sufficiently interesting so as to sustain the active involvement of the respondents. Finally, the questionnaire must reflect the purposes of the survey. That is, it is the channel through which theoretical issues and the interests of the researcher are converted into straightforward questions and answers that the average person can understand.

Good questionnaire design takes into account other factors besides the wording and sequencing of questions. It involves the layout of words and graphics on pages, the writing of clear and concise instructions for respondents and interviewers, the design of response categories, and a numerical system for responses that facilitates their coding and analysis. The reader who seeks a more in-depth understanding of questionnaire design is referred to one of several excellent references covering the topic (Backstrom and Hursh-Cesar 1981; Labaw 1980; Payne 1951).

Questionnaires that appear logically sequenced and carefully worded to the researcher may be difficult for respondents to follow and understand. Hence, pre-tests are conducted to detect both questionnaire and question weaknesses. Ideally, the draft of a questionnaire is tried out on a small group of, say, ten to twenty-five people who share many of the same characteristics as the study population. For instance, if we intend to survey residents of a local public housing project, we may want to pre-test our questionnaire on a small number of residents in a public housing project living in a nearby community or elsewhere in our city. The pre-test can reveal flaws in wording, illogical sequencing of questions, the range of responses that can be expected, and several other factors that can influence the quality of the survey. These factors include the length of time required to conduct the interview, the appropriateness of the introduction, and the extent to which respondents refuse to answer particular questions.

Following the pre-test interviewing, interviewers typically meet with the researcher staff to share experiences. This debriefing informs the study designers about the workability of the questionnaire, identifies wording problems, and clarifies other aspects of the interviewing experience. The questionnaire is then modified; if major revisions or additions have been made and time permits, a second pre-test is undertaken.

Pre-testing is crucial, irrespective of whether questionnaires are administered by trained interviewers or self-administered. With a self-administered questionnaire, it is useful to find people who are similar to those of the study population and seek out their cooperation in participating in the pretest. The draft questionnaires would be administered to these volunteers: afterward they would be asked if they had difficulties with questions, response categories, instructions, and so forth. At the same time, the completed questionnaires would be reviewed by the researchers to determine patterns of responses among specific questions. For example, if all pre-test respondents answered a question in exactly the same way, consideration should be given to dropping that question, particularly if the concept it is intended to measure is not central to the study.

Unless the researcher is associated with a large commercial polling organization or a private or university-based research center where a professional interviewing staff is available, new interviewers will have to be selected and trained. Although one typically expects to pay interviewers for their time and travel expenses, it may be possible to rely on volunteers or, if the survey is being conducted as part of a class project, on students.

Some who volunteer will have interviewing experience while others will not. With very few exceptions, volunteers should have considerable interest in the study and be highly motivated to carry out the work. Some volunteers may be overly motivated, having particularly strong feelings about the topics addressed in the survey. Using such interviewers could result in a biased interview.

Students may or may not be interested in the subject of the survey and therefore their motivation for performing well will vary. Some will want to learn more about the subject while others will be motivated by a desire for high grades. All will need training and will have time constraints placed on them by other classes.

If the survey budget can handle it, hiring and training an interviewing staff has the advantage, as against using volunteers and students, of allowing the researcher greater control over who the interviewers are and what they actually do. They are working for pay and therefore accountable to the researcher. They should be able to work the hours necessary to finish the job within a designated period of time; and as professionals, they should be committed to the objectives of the study.

There is a perception among some researchers that the closer the interviewers come to having similar characteristics to those of the study population, the better the chances of their establishing rapport with respondents and producing successful interviews. That is, interviewers should be matched with respondents of comparable age, gender, and race. Yet there is no research demonstrating that matching of interviewers and respondents improves response rates or yields more reliable answers to questions. If there is a general rule, it is that common sense should be used in hiring interviewers for a particular study. Clearly, it would be inappropriate to select interviewers without a Spanish language proficiency in a study of neighborhoods in Puerto Rico.

Once interviewers are lined up for the survey, they must be trained. Interviewer training means learning principles of good and bad interviewing, learning about the particular study they'll be working on, and learning about the questionnaire that will be administered as part of the study. With respect to the questionnaire, the interviewer must be able to deal with any number of problems that arise during the course of the interview. For example, the interviewer should know how to handle questions asked by the respondent in response to each survey question. At a more general level, the interviewer should be able to deal with refusals, uncooperative respondents, and abrupt terminations of the interview.

The interviewer must also know about methods

of selecting the designated respondents, the editing of questionnaires following the interview, and the actual procedures for administering interviews in the field, for editing them, and for transmitting completed copies to the researcher. Finally, the interviewer must understand that participating in interviews is completely voluntary and that the privacy and anonymity of the respondent must be guaranteed and protected.[1]

Procedures and techniques for training interviewers and carrying out interviews in person and over the telephone have been documented elsewhere (Guenzel et al. 1983). In self-administered questionnaires, no interviewers are available to ask the questions or guide respondents through unclear waters. The introductory letter and the wording and layout of the questionnaire must provide thorough explanations and instructions that make everything clear and unambiguous for the respondent. When a self-administered questionnaire is handed out to a group such as a class or workers at a job site, it is of course possible for an interviewer to add verbal instructions.

Compiling and Analyzing Data

Once questionnaires have been completed and returned to the researchers, responses must be converted to numerical values so that they can be tabulated and analyzed. This process, which is called coding, begins with the assignment of numbers to all possible answers to each survey question, irrespective of whether it is designed to yield a fixed response or an open-ended free response. These codes are usually recorded in a manual that is used to guide a coding staff in the actual coding of questionnaires. Working with the manual, coders review each questionnaire, assign the appropriate numerical value to question responses, and record them directly on coding sheets. In many surveys, however, precoded questionnaires are used, thus eliminating the need for a coding staff.

Once questionnaire responses have been translated into numerical data, the data must be assembled or compiled into a format that makes them suitable for analysis. Although it is possible to compile data manually, computers have simplified the task, making it less prone to human error.

The primary means of transmitting data from coding sheets or precoded questionnaires to computer files is through punch cards. Machine-readable cards are keypunched to reflect the code values for all questionnaire responses. Various accuracy checks are made to identify and correct errors in coding and keypunching. Next a computer file is created to facilitate data tabulation and analysis.

Increasingly, direct data entry (DDE) is being used to speed the coding and file-building process. DDE allows the coder working with a video display terminal (VDT) to enter numerical values for questionnaire responses and simultaneously build a computer file suitable for analysis.

The first step in the analysis process is tabulating data, which involves counting the number of times particular answers to each question are given by survey respondents. The counts are displayed as a set of frequency tables showing not only the number of persons associated with each response code but the percentage distribution of these numbers. As noted earlier in the chapter, these distributional data convey basic information about the people under study, including what they do, how they feel, and who they are.

Analyzing survey data is an interactive process in which, initially, distributional data covering survey questions are reviewed. Subsequently, hypothesized relationships between study variables are examined. Beyond this point, however, the direction of the analysis can vary depending on the preliminary analysis and what it uncovers. Nonetheless, future directions for analysis can be guided by a plan outlining the key dependent variables or outcome measures in the study, the independent variables of interest, and the manner in which these variables might be related to each other. Often, hypothesized relationships are presented in the form of a conceptual model developed as part of the research proposal or during the planning stage of the survey. For instance, we may be interested in descriptive data showing the proportion of elderly in the community who intend to move from their homes and those who plan to remain indefinitely. But we may also want to examine our data to determine which of several characteristics of the dwelling are associated with moving intentions. A diagrammatic model showing possible relationships among these variables could be used to guide the analysis.

Designing and executing data analysis have been aided by the availability of widely used and well-tested computer software packages such as BMDP, SAS, SPSS, and OSIRIS, as well as numerous statistical techniques. It is not the purpose of this chapter to describe or review these packages and techniques: much has been written about approaches to survey data analysis (Davis 1971; O'Muircheartaigh and Payne 1977) and the appropriate use of various statistical tests of significance (Andrews et al. 1981). Furthermore, examples of data analysis abound in *Environment and Behavior* and other journals covering environmental research. It is sufficient to remind the reader that converting questionnaire responses into quantitative data and then analyzing them so as to satisfy survey objectives are major activities in the survey process.

Interpreting and Reporting Data

The analysis of survey data involves more than tabulating responses to questions, examining relationships between study variables, and conducting statistical tests of significance. It also means interpreting the findings, knowing the limitations of the data, and being able to specify additional research questions not considered in the original survey design. Interpreting data requires insights and sound judgment often gained from experience in survey research and prior studies on the topic addressed by the survey.

Even with good data that have been thoroughly analyzed, it is possible to misinterpret survey findings and consequently draw incorrect conclusions. For example, suggesting causality between two related variables is an error often made when interpreting survey findings. Because noise levels in a factory are associated with workers' feelings about the job does not necessarily mean that the noisy equipment "causes" machine operators to express job dissatisfaction.

Generalizing from small samples is another problem in interpreting survey data. Suppose that in a survey of students at a large university, about half expressed a preference for post-modern architecture. If three-quarters of the sample of students from the architecture school favored post-modernism, does that mean that design students are inclined to be more avant-garde in their views about buildings than nondesigners? Probably not, since there were only twelve architectural students in the overall sample.

Still another problem in interpretation is extrapolating survey findings to populations that are different from the one that was studied. For instance, it would be unwise to make generalizations about the impact of CRTs on secretaries using the results of a survey conducted in a single office building. Similarly, we should not predict the number of community households that will move using only the expressed plans of people living in rental housing units. These are but a few of the pitfalls that need to be guarded against when interpreting and reporting data.

The issue of what to report and when to report

it requires careful consideration prior to entering the final phase of the survey process. In surveys dealing with environmental matters, we would expect the findings to be understandable and useful to designers and other environmental decision makers. That is, we conduct surveys so as to inform the design process about human behavior in different settings. In order to accomplish this goal, we must clearly present the survey results and explain their meaning. In surveys intended to help identify problems that require immediate resolution, findings and conclusions should be followed by recommendations for alternative courses of action.

Generally, survey findings are reported as a series of tables and accompanying text. The tables cover the statistical data in considerable detail so as to justify the conclusions that eventually are drawn. The text highlights the data shown in the tables. In principle, each table should stand on its own. That is, it should be self-explanatory in terms of what information is being conveyed, the meaning of the numbers, and the size and composition of the groups that are represented by the numbers. But often, readers of survey reports are not interested in numbers and only read the text to find out what the data mean and what conclusions have been drawn from the study. Thus, the text should be written with both the action-oriented person and the research-based individual in mind.

The question of when findings from a survey should be reported is particularly important in environmental research. Some surveys have been criticized because their results are published many months after the final tabulations have been completed. By that time, the problem may have been resolved or new issues requiring attention may have emerged. In many instances, however, the results are usually in the hands of study sponsors and users well in advance of their being officially released. In fact, preliminary findings are often presented to designers and sponsors with the expectation that their reactions may guide subsequent data analysis. Ideally, the analysis and reporting process is an interactive one in which the researcher and members of user groups jointly examine the data as they are being produced, deliberate on their meaning, and determine the next steps in the analysis. Clearly, the reporting and use of research findings is an integral part of the survey process.

Earlier, we noted that the survey process frequently involves another set of activities—the design and selection of a sample. In the following section, we examine sampling in some detail. We do so in the belief that its importance for environmental designers transcends its use in surveys. Whether it is in the testing of building materials, in examining plant specimens, or in measuring energy consumption, environmental designers will inevitably confront sampling at some time in their professional lives.

FUNDAMENTALS OF SAMPLING

In the definition of survey research presented earlier, we mentioned that information is collected from a population or a sample of a population. By population, we mean the totality of elements for which the survey results are to apply. Elements are also referred to as units of the population. In most sample surveys, the population consists of all people making up a particular group (tenants at a public housing site, workers in a factory); the individuals are the units of that population. Sample surveys are designed to obtain information from a selection of these "units" so that statements can be made about the entire population. These statements are usually expressed as statistical estimates: for example, 10 percent of the residents are dissatisfied with their housing; more than half the workers left the building during lunch; the typical graduate student is twenty-six years of age. If surveys were designed to obtain information from all units in the population, the statistics would no longer be estimates but true values describing characteristics of the population.

In surveys, units need not be limited to individuals. Nor in sampling terminology does "population" necessarily refer to people. We can have populations of organizations such as business establishments and universities. Environmental researchers might consider populations of places—parks, neighborhoods, census tracts, buildings, or floors in a building. Finally, populations of events (football games from a schedule) and time periods (hours in a workday, lunch periods during the week) might also be examined in environmental research.

In a study of the economic impacts of retirement communities on their surroundings, data could be collected from the entire "population" of retirement communities in the nation or data could be gathered from a "sample" of these communities. In either approach, the units of analysis would be the retirement communities. If, however, we wanted to study the leisure activities of retirement community residents, the units of analysis would be the residents. We would have the option of interviewing every resident in the selected communities, or we could interview a sample of those residents. If one of the sampled communities housed only a few dozen residents, we would probably interview each resident. If, on the other hand, our sample of communities contained large developments with several hundred residents, a sample from these large communities would be selected and interviewed. Thus, the decision as to whether to collect data from an entire population or from a sample of a population depends largely on the size of the population under study. That decision is also influenced by the level of funding available to conduct the research and the nature of the research objectives.

Unless the population is very small, or unlimited funds are available for data collection, surveys most likely will be based on samples. The prime advantage of sampling as opposed to obtaining complete coverage of a population should be obvious—it saves money.

The saving of labor and time is another advantage to sampling. The staff needed to carry out a sample survey is smaller than that needed to take a census or a complete enumeration of all units in the population. Additionally, fewer people are needed for coding and keypunching data. The time saved in gathering data from a sample of three hundred families rather than from all three thousand families in a neighborhood no doubt would produce results more speedily. In cases where the results are needed for making an impending decision affecting that neighborhood, a sample of the families is clearly advantageous.

Finally, observations or measurements can frequently be made more accurately on the basis of a sample of cases rather than an entire population. If information were needed about business establishments forced to relocate because of street widenings, the population of such establishments in the city could number in the thousands. Even if the information were abstracted from governmental records (rather than interviews), total coverage would entail constant supervision and painstaking verification of the work. Undetected clerical errors and failure to locate records that temporarily were missing from files could result in inaccuracies and biases greater than those associated with estimates derived from a sample.

When a sample of a population is contemplated, a decision must be made as to the most appropriate sampling procedure to follow. Although numerous approaches to sampling could be taken in any particular study, all procedures fall into one of two classifications—probability or nonprobability sampling.

Probability Sampling

Probability samples are designed to provide population estimates that are free from the personal judgments and biases of the researcher. The method of selection is such that every unit in the population has a known nonzero chance of being chosen as part of the sample. That is, the units that fall into a sample are selected by chance, rather than being judged as representative by the researcher. Biases in selecting the sample are therefore avoided.

With probability sampling, it is possible to measure the precision in the population estimates derived from survey results. For example, a sample survey of two hundred Columbia, Maryland residents selected by probability methods found that an estimated 21 percent of the adult population rode a bicycle for other than recreational purposes (Lansing et al. 1970). Because a probability sample design was used, the precision of this estimate could be measured. The precision is referred to as the sampling error, a measure of the difference between the sampling statistic (21 percent) and the corresponding true value that would occur had a full census been taken.

In addition to the level of precision, survey findings typically report the level of confidence. For the sampling of adult bike riders, the sampling error was 6.5 percent at the 95 percent confidence interval. This means that if repeated samples of 200 adults were taken, 95 out of 100 of them would yield a proportion within the interval from 15.5 percent to 27.5 percent. In other words, we can be 95 percent confident that the true proportion of adult bike riders in the community is somewhere between 15.5 percent and 27.5 percent.

If the sample size had been larger, say 800 persons, the sampling error would have been reduced to 3.4 percent, and the range for the true value would be 17.6 percent and 24.4 percent (21 ± 3.4). On the other hand, a smaller sample size of say 50, produces a larger sampling error of 13 percent, and the range of the true value of adult bike riders would be between 7 and 34 percent. This illustration demonstrates that, as the size of the sample increases, the precision of the estimates as measured by the sampling error will improve. This generalized relationship between sample size and sampling error is shown in figure 2–2.

The figure also reveals that the precision of sample estimates becomes numerically greater with increases in the sample size. Under the circumstances, a researcher's decision to increase the size of the sample in order to gain greater precision in the estimates must be weighed against the additional costs of collecting data from more respondents (units). The researcher is often faced with this dilemma and in making a decision, must take into account the resources available for conducting the research and the degree of precision that is acceptable for the study results.

In probability sampling, one often begins by obtaining a list containing all the elements in the population under investigation. This list is referred to

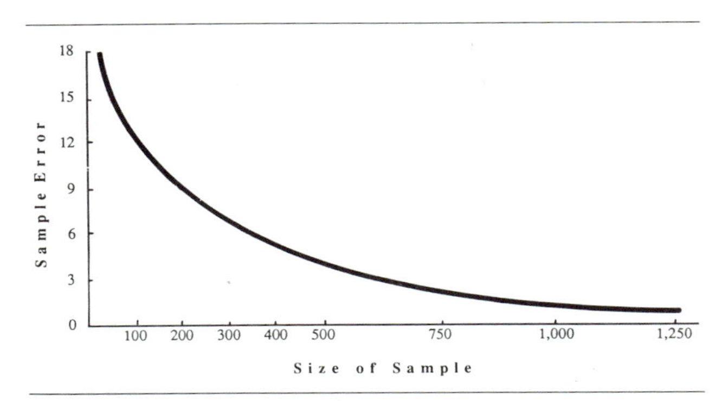

2–2. Approximate sampling error.

as the sampling frame and is used by the researcher in selecting the sample. Using a frame that is incomplete, out of date, or has duplicates among the population elements can result in a biased sample. Therefore, care should be taken to address these problems before proceeding with the sample selection.

When there is no list of population elements or it is difficult or costly to assemble one, another procedure known as area sampling may be followed. In area sampling, each element of a population is associated with a particular geographic area or place: city residents are associated with the residential blocks on which they live, office workers are associated with floors or bays in a building and so forth. In preparing an area sample, a list of the geographic areas (blocks, floors, or bays) is first compiled. A sample of these areas is then selected. The next step involves either the selection of a sample of elements or units from the selected geographic areas and collecting information from each of them, or a complete census of all units in the selected areas.

There are different types of probability sampling designs from which the researcher can choose. The choice will depend on several factors including the quality of the sampling frame, the study objectives, the precision of the estimates that would be acceptable, and the time and financial resources available to perform the work. A thorough discussion of the range of probability sample designs cannot adequately be covered in this chapter. Instead, we offer an introduction to several designs that are relevant to the work of environmental researchers. The reader seeking additional information is referred to one of the many texts on survey research and survey sampling procedures (Kish 1965; Lansing and Morgan 1971; Moser and Kalton 1971; Kalton 1983; Backstrom and Hursh-Cesar 1981).

Simple random sampling (SRS) is the basis for all probability sample designs. In SRS, every unit in the population has an equal and independent chance of being selected. Suppose an organization wanted additional space to house its employees and hires an architect to study the space requirements and work patterns of individual workers. As an initial step, the architect decides to interview 100 employees. There are a total of 1,200 people in the organization. The mechanics for selecting the 100 employees to ensure organizational representativeness while being able to measure the precision of the resulting survey estimates are as follows. First, each name on a complete list of employees would be numbered consecutively from 1 to 1,200. Second, using a table of random numbers found in most statistics textbooks, 100 different numbers within the range from 1 to 1,200 would be selected, ignoring duplicate numbers that have already been selected. Finally, the names associated with the selected numbers would represent the sample of employees from whom information would be obtained.

As noted above, one problem with this procedure occurs when the list of employees is incomplete or out of date or names appear on the list more than once. It would certainly be possible to go through the list to eliminate all repetitions and add missing names prior to making selections. However, this task would be tedious and costly and would not guarantee a complete list free of duplicates. One way of reducing the magnitude of this work and at the same time insuring that the selected cases are spread throughout the organization is to divide the list of workers by some known characteristic such as their departmental affiliation, "clean" the separate lists of duplicates and out-of-date entries, and draw a separate sample from each one. This approach is called stratification.

Stratified sampling, as the name implies, involves the a priori division of the population into homogeneous groups (strata) according to some known characteristic and the selection of a separate sample from within each stratum. For instance, we might know that the company occupying a building undergoing a diagnostic is organized by departments. In order to insure that information is obtained from a sufficient number of employees in each department, a separate sample would be selected from a list of names compiled by department. The benefits of stratification in this instance derive from the fact that the number of people contacted in each department is under the control of the researcher; if a simple random sample of all building employees were selected, the possibility exists that some departments would not be represented in the sample. Other known population characteristics that might be used in stratification include the job class of workers, the racial composition of neighborhoods, or the size classification of city parks. In each case, every unit (person, neighborhood, or park) in the population is placed within one and only one stratum before the sample selection is made. If there were an adequate-sized sample in each stratum, separate estimates of the population characteristics could be computed by stratum; the strata estimates when combined would constitute estimates for the entire population.

Besides the advantage of assured representativeness, stratification offers, first, greater precision in the sample estimates for a given sample size—conversely, stratification can yield the same precision as SRS with a smaller sample size. Second, there are opportunities to use different selection procedures within each stratum. Third, estimates of some stated precision can be specified for the subpopulation of each stratum as well as for the entire population (Hess et al. 1975).

Unfortunately, there are disadvantages in using stratified sample designs. First of all, it entails the same practical difficulties associated with a simple random sample, since SRS is used to select units from each stratum. Secondly, prior knowledge is required about the relationship of the variable of interest and those available for stratification. And unless there are large differences among the strata with respect to the key variables under investigation, the precision gained by using stratified sampling rather than simple random sampling is slight. Finally, a stratified sample constructed to estimate one variable with increased precision may result in less precise estimates for other variables in the study.

Drawing a simple random sample and preparing a stratified sample design involve considerable clerical work. In the above example, an alternative to numbering each employee in the organization and using random numbers to select the sample is to take an *interval* or *systematic sample*. This design involves selecting every *k*th individual from the list of employees after a random start equal to or less than *k*, but greater than zero. Since we want a sample of 100 employees from a total population of 1200, the sampling interval *k* would be 1200/100 or 120. A random number from 1 to 120 would be selected as would every 120th individual thereafter. For instance, if the initial random number selected were 35, the sampled employees would be those numbered 35, 155, 275, 395, and so on.

The main advantage of systematic sampling is that only one random number needs to be selected from a table of random numbers. Time and costs associated with the sample selection are therefore reduced. The main limitation of systematic sampling lies in working with a population list that is ordered cyclically, thereby possibly biasing the selection of elements. For instance, if an employee list is ordered by room numbers in a building and every manager has a corner office, it is conceivable that a systematic sample could result in the selection of a disproportionate number of managers. Suppose that the last two digits of room numbers for corner offices on each floor were 00 or 50. If the selection interval were 25, and there were four managers per floor, half of the sample would consist of managers in corner offices. That is, if the selection interval coincides with the cycle of room numbers, a biased sample will result. If, on the other hand, the interval were some number other than 25, the systematic sample would be appropriate.

When the list is an extremely long one, such as a list of all households in a city or all park visitors during a season, systematic sampling can become a tedious and time-consuming chore. When this occurs, still another sample design can be used to overcome these difficulties.

Cluster sampling involves the selection of population units in groups or clusters. To illustrate, instead of counting through a list of all households in a city to select a systematic sample of families, we can first select a sample of city blocks, and then include all or a fraction of households located within those blocks. The selection of blocks from a list of all city blocks could be made by systematic sampling. This selection of clusters represents the first stage of multi-stage sampling. The households selected within the sampled blocks represent a second stage.

Cluster sampling can also be used in buildings. For instance, the first stage could involve the selection of floors in a high-rise building and then from within the sampled floors, a sample of offices, structural bays, workstations, or workers could be selected.

One advantage of cluster sampling in community surveys using face-to-face interviewing is the savings in travel time and associated interviewer costs. If there is no one at home in one of the households within the sample cluster, the interviewer can simply try to obtain an interview from another cluster household. If the sample of households were not clustered but dispersed throughout the community, interviewers would be traveling greater distances in efforts to complete their interview assignments.

Cluster sampling in community surveys also has the advantage of reducing costs of measuring objective environmental conditions. For instance, if we wanted to know if households within the sample were within one-quarter mile of a bus stop, we could measure on maps the distance from the geographic center of each cluster to the nearest bus stop. For each cluster, we could then assign that measure to all households. Similarly, a density measure could be calculated for the cluster, the value of which would be assigned to all cluster households. If the sampled households were dispersed rather than clustered, more distance and density measurements would have to be made.

The question of *sample size* periodically arises in the planning and design of any probability sample. That is, how many units should be selected from the population so that generalizations can be made about that population and its subgroups? Prior to discussing nonprobability sampling, we will review several factors that contribute to the decision about how large a sample is needed.

The decision about sample size is based on several factors including the degree to which the population is homogeneous, the type of probability sample to be used, the number of subgroups to be examined, the precision of the estimates that the researcher wishes to achieve, and the time and money available for conducting the study.[2]

Homogeneous populations generally warrant smaller samples than populations that are dissimilar. For example, a behavioral study of an office setting occupied by a few hundred secretaries performing identical tasks would require a fairly small sample. Logically, a few secretaries could report on working conditions for the entire group. However, the likelihood of finding this situation is small. That same setting would probably be occupied by a group of two hundred comprised of secretaries, computer programmers, clerks, and managers: a much larger sample size would be required in order to understand the activities and sentiments of each group.

The type of probability sample also has a bearing on the size of the sample. As noted above, an advantage of using a stratified sample design as opposed to simple random sampling is that one can achieve the same level of precision with a smaller sample size. On the other hand, a larger sample size would be required for achieving comparable precision if cluster sampling were used.

A third factor influencing the sample size is the number of subgroups of the population the researcher intends to examine. As a general rule, the more subgroups for which information is needed, the larger the sample size. To illustrate, if we wanted to know how different subcategories of park visitors felt about recreational facilities, we would need a sample size large enough to make distinctions between the different groups. Before embarking on our research, we might decide to examine the sentiments of the following park users: young unmarried people, families with children, teenagers, middle-aged couples, and elderly people. If, for statistical purposes, we felt that a minimum of 30 people were needed in each subgroup, a sample size of at least 150 people would be required. If further analysis of these subgroups were anticipated for men and women, the sample size would have to be enlarged to 300.

Throughout our discussion of probability sampling, we have noted that sample size is related to accuracy, or the precision in the estimates derived from the survey. As the size of a sample increases, greater precision in the estimates is achieved through a reduction in sampling errors. Therefore an important determinant of sample size is the precision of the information the researcher wants or is willing to accept in the survey results.

For example, if we were interested in how neighborhood residents felt about a proposed park, we might not need a very precise estimate of the proportion of park proponents. A rough approximation would suffice. On the other hand, if we were planning a campaign for a bond millage for parks, we probably would want a fairly accurate estimate of the actual number of supporters. In the first instance, we might accept an estimate from our survey having a large sampling error of, say, plus or minus 10 percent. In the second illustration, a more precise estimate within 4 percent of the true proportion favoring the millage would be better, since the strategy for planning the campaign might be guided by our results.

To estimate the appropriate sample size in both cases, a formula linking sampling error to sample size for simple random sampling can be used. This formula states that the sampling error of a proportion $SE(p)$ is equal to $\sqrt{pq/n}$ where p is the sample proportion, q is equal to 100 percent $-p$, and n is the estimate of the sample size. If we set p equal to 50 percent, $SE(p)$—the desired level of precision—at 10 percent, and solve the equation for n, we would find the required sample to be 48 residents. If we suspected that 75 percent of the residents favored the park proposal, then a sample size of roughly 20 people would be needed to achieve a sampling error of plus or minus 10 percent. In the survey to determine the number of bond millage supporters, in which greater precision (4 percent) is desired, a sample of about 160 residents would be needed.

A related factor influencing sample size is the level of confidence we expect to have in our survey results. It is one thing to be able to specify the error we are willing to tolerate when planning a survey; it is another to say with a degree of certainty that the true value of the population characteristic is really within the limits established by the sampling error. It is possible, for instance, that despite the care given to designing the sample of residents in the bond millage survey, there is a chance that the sample of residents selected will not be a good one, and the sampling error will be greater than the 4 percent specified. We therefore need a statement, expressed in probabilistic terms, indicating how much confidence we have in our survey results. This statement is referred to as the confidence interval and in most surveys, it is taken at 95 percent. That is, the researcher wants to be 95 percent certain that the true value for the population characteristic is within the interval established by the sampling error bounding the sample estimate. In order to accomplish this degree of confidence, the formula for the sampling error must be modified so that

$$SE = 1.96 \sqrt{pq/n}.^{3}$$

As the perceptive reader will notice, the higher level of confidence has the effect of nearly doubling the size of the sample. In the case of the bond millage survey, we would need a sample size of about 310 residents if we wanted to be 95 percent certain that the actual number of supporters is within the 4 percent interval bounding the survey estimate.

A practical consideration in determining sample size is the amount of time and money available for conducting the survey. We may want a great deal of precision in the survey results but because our resources are limited, we cannot collect data from a sample large enough to gain that precision. Consequently, we often must sacrifice precision by selecting a smaller sample in order to perform the survey within time and budgetary constraints.

The trade-off between precision and sample size is not as much of a problem in surveys involving self-administered questionnaires. Whereas most of the cost of doing personal interviews is associated with interviewer salaries, the major costs for self-administered questionnaires are postage or other distribution and collection charges. Unless interviewers are participating in the survey voluntarily, alternatives to personal interviews are usually considered when the budget is limited and precision is deemed desirable.

Nonprobability Sampling

One way of saving money in surveys is through the use of nonprobability samples. Whereas in probability sampling, every member of the population has an equal chance of being selected, nonprobability sample designs rely heavily on human judgment. As noted earlier, the condition of equal probability of selection is necessary for measuring the precision of the estimates of population characteristics. In nonprobability sampling, the researcher is unable to determine the precision of the estimates. Furthermore, there is no definable population to which the estimates can be generalized with nonprobability samples.

The reliance on human judgment in nonprobability sampling is its most distinguishing feature. The judgments can be made either by the researchers or by the individuals gathering data (interviewers). In either case, the selection process is likely to be biased. Nonetheless, this approach to sampling is appropriately used in surveys where the population is extremely small, where issues are being explored in a preliminary manner, or where there is no need to generalize or estimate the precision of the findings.

There are several types of nonprobability samples. Judgmental or purposive sampling involves the deliberate selection of persons presumed to be "good" respondents or informants. For instance, in efforts to establish a research agenda for interior lighting, a telephone survey was conducted with a small sample of illuminating engineers, interior architects and designers, facility managers, and utility company representatives (Marans 1983). The number of people selected from each group was small, and each person was judged to be an expert who could offer insights deemed important to the purposes of the study. Purposive samples such as these are often used when background information is needed as a basis for designing a larger survey. For these samples, the judgment of the researcher or sponsor is used in selecting the respondents.

Surveys using quota samples rely on the judgment of the interviewers in selecting respondents. The selection is guided by a predetermined plan for obtaining a designated number of interviews (a quota) with respondents who are categorized according to gender, age, race, and/or some other identifiable characteristic. For example, in a statewide study of off-road vehicle owners, the first step might involve the selection of a sample of state parks and campgrounds where such vehicles are found. This selection could be made by using probability techniques. At each of the selected sites, interviewers would be instructed to find and conduct interviews with, say, 30 users in the morning and 30 in the afternoon. Furthermore, the assignment might specify that half the users during each period should be under the age of 30 and half should be over 30. The sample of vehicle owners would thus be left to the discretion of the interviewers. There is uncertainty in this procedure with respect to knowing exactly what was done at the sites. Additionally, there is no assurance that the vehicle owners selected will be representative of all off-road vehicle owners in the state.

If there is no great disadvantage in having biased estimates, or if the objective of the study is to obtain interviews without concern as to how and from whom they are obtained, quota sampling is an appropriate method of selection. Clearly, quota samples are economical to use because they reduce interviewer time and travel and, in household surveys, the need for making call backs to a predetermined respondent. They are also easy to administer since they involve little record keeping or clerical work.

It is important to recognize that using nonprobability methods of selection means that the estimates derived from the survey lack precision—that is, it is not possible to measure estimates. Quota samples therefore sometimes yield misleading results. As environment behavior research matures and as environmental designers become more sophisticated in the use of probability sampling techniques, nonprobability samples will become less justifiable in studies other than those of an exploratory nature.

ALTERNATIVE METHODS OF DATA COLLECTION

In the definition of survey research presented earlier in the chapter, we indicated that virtually all information about people is obtained through face-to-face personal interviews, telephone interviews, or self-administered questionnaires. The specific data collection mode or modes selected by the researcher will depend on the objectives of the study, the types of questions the researcher intends to ask, the size and spatial distribution of the sample, and the budget allocated to data collection. In most of the examples discussed earlier, face-to-face interviews conducted in the respondents' homes have been the principal means of gathering information. Given the settings in which environmentally related surveys are likely to be conducted in the future (for example, buildings, neighborhoods, and parks), face-to-face interviews along with self-administered questionnaires will probably remain the primary tools of data collection. Nevertheless, advances in telephone interviewing over the past decade suggest that its potential for use in surveys covering environmental issues is great. In this section of the chapter, we discuss some of the advantages and disadvantages of these three approaches to gathering survey data.

Telephone Interviewing

There are several factors contributing to the increased use of telephones in survey research over the past decade. First, very few households are without telephones. According to the 1981 census, nearly 98 percent of the households in the United States have at least one telephone. Of course telephone coverage is not the same in all parts of the country. Households in the central cities and in impoverished rural areas are most likely to be without telephones (Frey 1984). Second, the ability to obtain face-to-face interviews in national surveys has eroded over time. Whereas it was not uncommon to find national surveys in the early 1970s yielding response rates in the 75 percent to 80 percent range, we frequently find surveys today with response rates of 70 percent or lower. In part, people are more wary of opening their homes to strangers, even those having impeccable credentials. Third, telephones have become more attractive to survey researchers as interviewer and supervisory salaries as well as travel costs have increased. Finally, advances in telephone technology (e.g., push-button telephones, WATS lines) and the development of computer-assisted telephone interviewing techniques (CATI) have simplified many of the tasks associated with telephone interviewing.

There are other factors that make telephone interviewing an attractive alternative to face-to-face interviewing and mail questionnaires. Unlike other modes of data collection, interviewing by telephone is not as constrained by time. In mail questionnaires, the researcher has to deal with the time it takes to get questionnaires to the respondents, waiting a reasonable period before returns come in, and then spending additional time in following up nonrespondents in efforts to improve the response rate. Similarly in face-to-face interviewing, there is the additional time needed to track down nonresponses, to locate households where addresses are incorrectly recorded, and find the sampled dwellings in neighborhoods where streets or household numbers are difficult to locate. In telephone interviewing, little time is wasted when there is no one at home; the interviewer simply calls the next number on the list (Backstrom and Hursh-Cesar 1981). It is also possible, using CATI, to have the sampled telephone numbers dialed automatically and to tabulate question responses as the data are generated.

Research has demonstrated that when information is needed from special populations such as executives, politicians, or other elites, the telephone is more likely than self-administered questionnaires to yield responses and in-depth answers to specific questions. Yet telephones are not as appropriate for elite interviews as those conducted face to face (Becker and Meyers 1974).

Another advantage of telephone interviewing (and face-to-face interviewing) over mail and other self-administered questionnaires is in obtaining responses to open-ended questions. In self-administered questionnaires, time and care are needed to write out a response, and most people lack the patience and motivation to do so. However, respondents will freely offer opinions when a verbal response is expected of them.

From the researcher's point of view, the main disadvantage to telephone interviewing is that visual cues cannot be used. That is, it is impossible to use drawings, photographs, or other visual aids to elicit answers to survey questions. This could seriously handicap environmental research aimed at determining preferences for physical entities such as landscapes, architectural styles, or housing types.

Telephone interviewing is obviously an inappropriate means of data collection in areas where telephones are nonexistent, limited in number, or inaccessible to the study population. For example, studies of people in rooming houses, veterans hospitals, summer camps, or remote villages in a developing country should use personal interviews or, depending on the population's literacy rate, group-administered questionnaires. Other disadvantages associated with telephone interviewing are the relatively higher rates of nonresponse to sensitive questions such as those dealing with income (Groves and Kahn 1979), greater suspicion of an interviewer whom the respondent cannot see, and the need to have accurate and up-to-date lists of telephone numbers for those in the study population (Frey 1984).

If telephone interviewing is contemplated, a decision must be made about selecting a sample of numbers. Two choices are available to the researcher. A sample of telephone numbers can be selected from a list or directory such as a phone book, membership list, or employee directory; or random digit dialing (RDD) can be employed.

As noted earlier in the chapter, lists or sampling frames that are incomplete, out-of-date, or have duplicates among the elements can result in biased samples. Whereas telephone directories appear to be appropriate frames from which to select samples of household telephone numbers, they suffer from the same disadvantages. For one thing, not all households have their telephone numbers listed. Unlisted numbers have become quite common in large metropolitan areas, accounting for more than 20 percent of the households in some places (Rich 1977). At the same time, households having two or more listed telephones have an increased probability of falling into the sample. In addition, telephone directories become out-of-date rather quickly. They are usually published annually and in the interim, new families move to town while others leave, change telephone numbers, or go on extended vacations. Finally, telephone directories often include exchanges for geographic areas not covered by the survey. For instance, it is likely that a directory for a medium-sized city would contain telephone numbers of people living in the surrounding unincorporated townships and villages. If a survey dealt with attitudes toward municipal services, the use of the directory in drawing a sample of residents would be inappropriate.

Lists and directories for organizations present similar problems. New employees can arrive on the scene immediately after the roster is printed. Workers change offices, leave their jobs, or may even have incorrectly listed telephone numbers. Some may share a telephone with one or more coworkers, while others will not have access to any telephone. Often, organizations are slow in updating their employee lists except in the case of payroll information, which is unlikely to be listed with telephone numbers.

When a list or directory is "dirty" or known to suffer from many of the above problems, efforts should be made to "clean" it before using it to draw the sample.[4] However, cleaning is costly and time-consuming and many researchers do not feel the effort is justified, particularly when the frame is judged to be adequate given the nature of the research problem or characteristics of the population. The use of a dirty frame in a community survey will be discussed in the next section.

Many of the problems associated with the use of telephone directories have been overcome with random digit dailing (RDD), a technique for selecting numbers with the aid of a random number generator. The technique requires the researcher to determine beforehand the area code, the working three-digit prefix (the exchange) and the last four digits of all working telephones in the geographic area or areas under investigation. This information is available from the local telephone company. From these numbers, the computer can be used to generate a list of all possible first eight-digit combinations as sampling units; the computer randomly adds two digits to each and the telephone number is available to interviewers. With CATI, phone numbers can be dialed automatically for interviewers working at a video display terminal (Groves 1984). If the number called is a commercial establishment, the eight-digit sampling unit is dropped because the telephone companies assign commercial numbers to special blocks, and all other numbers in that eight-digit sequence are likely to be commercial numbers (Backstrom and Hursh-Cesar 1981).

The major advantage of RDD is that unlisted numbers will show up in the sample in the same proportion as they exist in the telephone exchange. Its disadvantages lie in its relatively high costs and the need for sampling expertise to generate the sample. Often the effort is not justified when the size of the sample is small, when a reasonably clean list of numbers is available from other sources, and when the study area is limited in scope.

Self-administered Questionnaires

Of the various methods for distributing self-administered questionnaires, using the mails is the most popular approach. Mail questionnaires are considered when the survey budget is limited and the population is dispersed over a large geographic area. For a given sample size, they are considerably cheaper to administer than telephone or face-to-face interviewing, since a much smaller staff is needed for data collection. The cost saving is therefore the major advantage of mail questionnaires. Another advantage is that the survey does not suffer from interviewer bias or from the reluctance of respondents to admit interviewers into their homes.

Mail questionnaires can also be useful when information is required from several members of a household. For example, if the researcher wants to know about swimming pool usage in different neighborhoods of a community, or more specifically, the total number of household members to use the facility, the mail questionnaire affords household members the opportunity to discuss or consult with one another prior to completing and returning the questionnaire. There is also the potential advantage that certain questions—perhaps those of a personal or embarrassing nature—will be answered more willingly and more accurately in a mail questionnaire than if they are asked as part of a personal interview.

The major disadvantage of using mail questionnaires is nonresponse. Whereas telephone and face-to-face interviewing generally yield response rates of 70 percent or more, a 10 percent response is not uncommon for a general population sample survey. Some researchers are therefore content with mail returns representing about one-third of the questionnaires sent out. The critical problem is not so much the small proportion of the original sample of questionnaires that is returned; it is the uncertainty about the nonrespondents and whether they are significantly different from the respondents in terms of who they are, how they feel, and what they do. It is quite likely that the estimates derived from the respondents may be greatly biased.

Three factors can affect the response rate of mail questionnaires and it is important for the researcher to determine how each will influence the returns. These factors are the organization sponsoring the study, the salience of the topic for the respondent, and the particular population that is being investigated.

In general, mail questionnaires sent to the general public having official government backing are likely to yield a higher response rate than those originating from a university or private organization. The best results are obtained when the organization conducting the survey has some direct link with the population—for example, a survey of its members by the American Institute of Architects. If the topic is of sufficient interest and importance to the respondents, the response rate will be higher than if it is viewed as irrelevant or lacking in interest. A questionnaire asking how residents feel about a proposed park adjacent to their neighborhood will certainly generate more interest and concomitantly more returns than one asking how people feel about United States involvement in Central America. Similarly, the educational level of the population will determine the response rate for mail questionnaires, with more educated respondents tending to complete and return them more often than others.

Other disadvantages associated with mail questionnaires include the inability to deal with "floating" populations such as the homeless or migrant workers, the requirements that the questionnaires be relatively short and the questions fairly simple and straightforward (mostly fixed response), and—because there is no interviewer involved in data collection—the inability to obtain spontaneous answers, probe when more information or clarification is needed, and gather data about the respondents' physical setting through observation.

It is also possible to distribute self-administered questionnaires to individuals who are members of groups and who occupy a particular space. For example, questionnaires may be administered to students in a classroom, neighborhood block-club members attending a meeting, or workers at a factory. In the first two cases, virtually everyone will complete the questionnaire, so that information on the total population in attendance will be obtained. When questionnaires are distributed to factory workers at their workstations, most are likely to respond, assuming permission and time are given to complete the questionnaire and workers have clear and precise instructions. When the respondents' workplaces are known, it is possible to measure the physical attributes at each place independent of the questionnaire and analyze those data vis-à-vis workers' responses. This approach was taken in the case study presented in the next part of the chapter.

Face-to-face Interviews

As might be expected, several of the limitations noted above can be overcome by combining mail questionnaires with telephone interviews or interviews conducted in person (Dillman 1978). It may be useful, for instance, to send questionnaires to people at their homes and later have them picked up by an interviewer, who can clarify difficulties, check answers, ask additional or more complex questions, and measure selected environmental conditions at the site. Or, conversely, visits may be made to people's homes to drop off questionnaires with instructions for completing and returning them by mail. While at the site, the staff person can collect environmental data and conduct a brief interview asking more complex questions.

Despite its relatively high costs, the face-to-face interview has been the most widely used data-gathering technique in surveys. One of its principle advantages lies in the amount of information that can be obtained—the interview can easily continue for an hour and some may last considerably longer. A second advantage of the face-to-face interview concerns the nature of the questions that can be asked. That is, the questions can be complex and open-ended, and the interviewer can probe if the responses are vague or incomplete. In other words, there are greater opportunities to obtain "rich" information about respondents using face-to-face interviews. While such interviews are usually conducted within the confines of the respondent's dwelling, they may also take place in an office, at a campground, on the street, or in a shopping center.

The mere presence of an interviewer can lead to a higher level of cooperation from the respondent—an advantage compared to surveys using mail questionnaires or telephone interviews. Cooperation is very often obtained despite the complexity of questions and the greater time demand on the respondent. And unlike other forms of data collection, the face-to-face interview enables the interviewer to gather information about the physical setting while he or she is at the site. Such information can deal with the interior as well as the exterior environment.

As in the case of self-administered questionnaires, face-to-face interviews permit the use of visual stimuli such as photographs and drawings. It is easier, however, in interviews to give a more complex set of instructions, such as asking respondents to choose elements in pictures of buildings that they find attractive and then to elaborate on their choices. Other visual stimuli such as "show cards" containing verbal response categories to selected questions can also be used in personal interviewing.

Higher data collection costs are the major disadvantage of face-to-face interviewing. Similarly, personnel requirements are greater—more interviewers and supervisors are needed, particularly when the study covers a large geographic area such as a state. The interviewers generally require a higher level of training, and they must have social skills in dealing with all kinds of people. They must also have an automobile. Other disadvantages in face-to-face interviewing include a greater likelihood of obtaining socially desirable answers (Groves and Kahn 1979) and the longer time often required to complete all assigned interviews.

USING SURVEYS IN A BUILDING EVALUATION

In the past decade, there has been a significant increase in the number of evaluations of built environments and environmentally related programs. Characteristic of these evaluations has been the extensive use of personal interviews and self-administered questionnaires in gathering information about users of environments and the populations targeted by programs (Zeisel and Griffin 1975; Francescato et al. 1979; Peroff et al. 1979; Elder and Tibbett 1981). One recently completed evaluation used both modes of data collection and applied other concepts and techniques from survey research as well (Marans and Spreckelmeyer 1981). In this part of the chapter, we review that study and discuss in some detail its methods of data collection, sampling procedures, and selected findings.

Background

The study, conducted under the sponsorship of the National Bureau of Standards, had two major objectives. The first was to develop a systematic approach for designing and implementing evaluations of built environments ranging in scale from individual buildings to large communities such as housing estates and new towns. The second objective was to apply or test that approach by evaluating a particular environment—a new federal office building. The approach is reflected in the development of two models: one covering a process and the other showing a set of hypothesized relationships used to guide the analysis of data collected as part of an evaluation. It had been suggested that in prior evaluations, little thought had been given during the planning phase as to the manner in which environmental conditions and user responses would be analyzed with respect to each other (Marans 1984).

Early in the federal building study, it was decided to conduct the evaluation from a single perspective—that of the building users. The major users were identified as the federal employees who worked in the building. Community residents represented a second group of users. The decision to focus the evaluation on users was made following a series of meetings with individuals involved in the inception, design, and management of the building. Included in this group were the architects, the interior designer, the facility manager, representatives from the municipality and the General Services Administration, and supervisors of the agencies occupying the building. As part of these meetings, the research team was told about the history of the building, the rationale behind the site selection, alleged problems, and the specific objectives government officials and their architects intended to achieve through site planning and building design. By understanding these objectives, the research team was able to focus on the most salient issues and ultimately to draw conclusions about the degree to which the building was successful. The major objectives of the building gleaned from the meetings and written documents were:

1. The building should be an integral part of the downtown area. It should be in visual harmony with the scale of the area and be a catalyst for new downtown development.
2. Interaction between the building occupants and patrons and, more generally, members of the downtown community should be fostered. The building should be functionally a part of the downtown area and should be used extensively by the public.
3. The building should exemplify good architectural design and aesthetic quality without being a dominating or imposing structure.
4. The work spaces within the building should allow for flexibility and change both within agencies and throughout the entire building. At the same time, there should be opportunities for employees to store personal belongings and personalize their work spaces according to individual tastes and interests.
5. Employees should take pride in and find satisfaction in their work environment.

Working from the list of objectives, the insights gained at the meetings, and from visits to the building, four sets of evaluative issues were identified: relationships between the building and the downtown area, transportation and parking, people's assessments of the building and the work environment, and relationships between the work environment and performance. In order to explore these issues and determine the extent to which the objectives had been fulfilled, specific information about the building and several of its user groups would be needed.

Information about the building would deal with ambient environmental conditions, the allocation of space for agencies and workers, the proximity of workstations to doors, windows, and light wells, and the arrangements and styles of furniture. Information about federal workers would cover their feelings and activities vis-à-vis the building. For example, employee attitudes toward individual work stations, agency spaces, the overall building, and the ease of travel to and from the site would be measured. Similarly, the nature of their work and the employees' uses of the building and the downtown area would be examined. Outside users would be queried in order to determine how much they knew about and used the building and whether or not they felt the building was worthy of its many architectural awards.

Information covering the user groups would be derived largely from questionnaires. Physical measures and visual inspections of the building and observations of people's behavior within its interiors would provide additional information.

Sources of Information

As noted, questionnaires were the primary sources of information about users. With limitations in research funds and time constraints imposed by the work schedule of building occupants, it was decided to distribute self-administered questionnaires to each of the estimated 270 federal workers. At the same time, personal interviews would be conducted with two outside user groups. Telephone interviewing would be the vehicle for obtaining information from community residents, whereas face-to-face interviews would be conducted with on-site visitors.

The self-administered questionnaires were designed to yield information that would enable the research team to examine specific issues and objectives, test hypotheses, and describe in considerable detail who the employees were, how they felt about the building, and what they did within it. It was also decided that, if possible, questions used in other office surveys would be asked so that comparisons of survey findings could be made against some benchmark or yardstick. Accordingly, several survey questions designed to tap workers' attitudes toward their offices and specific environmental attributes were drawn from a national office worker survey (Harris 1978).

Prior to administering the questionnaire to the office workers, two pre-tests were conducted. The first involved five former employees of agencies occupying the building. Members of the research team knew these individuals, who willingly agreed to complete the questionnaire and discuss its contents. Following substantial questionnaire revisions, a second pre-test was administered to twenty workers in another federal office building of comparable age located in a nearby city. Further revisions were made following a review of the completed questionnaires.

In addition to the pre-tests, two other steps were taken prior to actually administering the employee questionnaire. First, letters were distributed to everyone in the building describing the study and the forthcoming questionnaire. Workers were informed that their participation in the study would be voluntary and that their responses would remain anonymous; only the researchers would see the completed questionnaires and know the meaning of the identification number linking the respondent to a particular workstation. Workers were also told that their responses would be tabulated along with others in their agency and that the results would be made available to anyone expressing interest in the study. The letter attempted to motivate employees to participate.

During the period of pre-testing, drafts of the questionnaire were reviewed with agency supervisors, who expressed concern about questions that might be sensitive or inappropriate to ask in their respective organizations. As a result of these reviews, further modifications were made to the questionnaire.

On a prearranged Monday, members of the research team distributed copies of the final version of the questionnaire to employees at their desks and workstations. Workers who were out of the office (ill or on assignment) were given questionnaires later in the week. The instructions on the questionnaire briefly recapped the points made in the earlier letter and asked respondents to place their completed forms in a collection box located at each agency's main entrance. These boxes were clearly marked and under the watchful eye of a receptionist. The questionnaires were collected from the boxes at the end of each day. By the end of the week, 239 questionnaires had been returned, representing a response rate of 89 percent.

For the other two user groups—community residents and on-site visitors—nearly identical questionnaires were developed and pre-tested. Both were designed to find out how often people went to the building, the purpose of their visits, difficulties encountered in finding specific places within the building, how people rated the building architecturally, what they liked and disliked about it, and the degree to which respondents thought the building fit into the downtown area. One important difference between the two questionnaires was the initial line of inquiry; in the case of the telephone survey, interviewers had first to determine if respondents knew about the building and where it was located prior to asking evaluative and use questions. The size of the community's population and the number of visitors to the building necessitated the collection of data from samples of the two populations. For the community residents, a probability sample of 216 numbers was selected from the telephone directory with the expectation of obtaining about one hundred household interviews. It was acknowledged that the directory represented a poor list or frame from which to select a resident sample. Yet it was recognized that the costs associated with developing a more complete and up-to-date list or selecting a sample of telephone numbers using an RDD approach would be prohibitive. Furthermore, it was felt that people with unlisted telephone numbers were no different than those listed in the directory in their use of the building and the way they felt about it.

In determining the number of interviews, consideration was given to the level of precision in the estimates that the research team would find acceptable. It was decided that sampling estimates for the survey findings need not be very precise; sampling errors in the 10 to 15 percent range would be acceptable. Similarly, the number of hours scheduled for interviewing would allow for no more than 150 to 200 telephone calls. Accordingly, a systematic sample of 216 lines was selected from the telephone directory, of which 174 were residential numbers. When called, 36 of these numbers were disconnected. Of the remainder, 23 resulted in refusals or no one at home after four callbacks, while 113 produced completed interviews with an adult household member.

Face-to-face interviews were conducted at the building with a quota sample of visitors. Members of the research team were instructed to obtain interviews from people leaving the building at each of four entrances. When an individual was approached, the first question was whether he or she worked in the building. If the person responded affirmatively, the interviewer politely broke off contact, approached someone else, and repeated the process until a visitor was found.

The interviews were taken on two randomly selected days of the week within predetermined time periods. The interviewers assigned to each of the four entrances were expected to complete sixteen interviews, half of them with men and half with women. Furthermore, the sample was to be divided equally between men and women judged to be less than thirty, between thirty and sixty, and over sixty years of age. Thus, 64 visitors who varied in gender, age, and the time they entered the building represented the third group of users.

Independent of the questionnaires distributed to building occupants, environmental information about workstations was also collected. Two approaches to gathering the information were taken. One consisted of measuring environmental attributes using working drawings and floor plans showing furniture arrangements. The measurements were recorded on forms that were prenumbered to correspond to the questionnaires administered at the employees' workstations. These "indirect" measures included the square footage devoted to the workstation, the type of workstation, work space density, and distances to agency entrances, windows, and light wells.

More direct measures of ambient environmental conditions associated with each workstation were also made. On another set of prenumbered forms, noise levels, temperature, relative humidity, light levels, and glare conditions were recorded at two different times over a period of one month. Thus, for each workstation, a wide range of environmental data was available and could be used systematically to describe work environments throughout the building. These environmental data could also be analyzed vis-à-vis the responses of the people using the workstations.

In addition to the systematic collection of survey data and objective information about the work environment, visual inspections of the building were made and the activities of the user groups were observed. The initial effort at behavioral observation focused on the public areas, including the building's entrances.

Because it was known that the heaviest entrance use would occur during the early morning hours and late in the day, when employees came to and left work, full hourly counts were made between 7:30 and 8:30 A.M. on two mornings during a one-week period and between 3:30 and 4:30 P.M. on two different afternoons of the week. Similarly, because public use of the building was expected to be high during the lunch period, hourly counts were also made from noon to 1:00 P.M. on two other days. A sample of half-hour time periods was the basis for subsequent counts of building entrance use during the remaining daytime hours of the week. Observers counted persons at the four entrances during each of ten half-hour periods. Systematic counts were also made of the number of people who talked to the security guard at the information desk and the number who used the lounge area outside the coffee shop on the second floor of the building.

Finally, observations of a more impressionistic nature were made in the major agencies of the building in order to obtain a better understanding of furniture arrangements, the use of equipment, the interactions among workers, and the degree of contact between workers and building patrons.

An Overview of Major Findings

Among the study conclusions, it was shown that the federal building was successful in one major respect—it had become an integral part of the downtown area and had contributed to the attractiveness and economic vitality of that area. It was readily identifiable and used by the general public. Most community residents considered it attractive, worthy of its many awards for design excellence, and conveniently located. For the most part, the federal workers liked the location and took advantage of nearby shopping, restaurants, and other downtown amenities.

On the other hand, the building did not live up to the expectations that it would provide a high-quality work environment for all its occupants. The majority of employees rated their agency settings as only fair or poor, while a substantial number expressed dissatisfaction with the workspace assigned to them.

These conclusions were reached after examining and interpreting the results of the three surveys. Findings related to the objectives of the sponsors and the designers were given special attention. For example, eight out of ten community residents knew where the building was located and three-quarters had visited it at one time or another. Most (72 percent) said it fit into its surroundings, whereas a higher proportion of the on-site visitors (81 percent) believed the building was in scale with neighboring structures.

Survey findings also revealed that significant numbers of the visitors worked or conducted personal business in the downtown area. A third had walked to the building and a comparable proportion used the plaza on sunny days. The public was most likely to visit the post office and, to a lesser extent, the offices of the Social Security Administration. Other agencies were rarely visited, however. Neither the public nor agency personnel used the coffee shop or the public lounge extensively.

In terms of its architectural quality, three out of four members of the general public thought the building was attractive and worthy of its architectural honors. A somewhat smaller proportion liked its interior spaces. Building occupants, on the other hand, were likely to give it low marks on architectural quality and as a place to work.

Opportunities for changing furniture arrangements were found to be limited in the smaller agencies housed in conventional offices. Rearranging furniture, however, occurred with ease and regularity in the open offices characteristic of the larger agencies. Yet the flexibility inherent in the open-plan offices was not without costs. One-fourth of the workers in the open offices and a third in pool offices reported that the movement of furniture was bothersome and hindered their work.

With respect to the goal of creating a satisfying work setting for employees, the designers were only partially successful. While most workers expressed some level of satisfaction with the workspace available to them and the overall ambience of their agencies, many were dissatisfied with their physical surroundings. A third were unhappy with their immediate workplace and gave poor ratings to both the appearance and the spatial arrangement of their agency. Dissatisfaction was most prevalent among workers in the open and pool offices.

Specific Findings and Applications

Whereas the main purpose of the research was to develop an approach for designing and implementing evaluations, a secondary objective was to test that approach by actually performing an evaluation. The evaluation of the federal building produced several findings that pointed to possible guidelines for programming, designing, and managing federal buildings and office environments in other settings.

To illustrate, a major part of the evaluation focused on the workplace. In particular, interest centered on the manner in which individual workers rated their workstations and a number of specific workstation attributes. Relatedly, efforts were made to determine the relative importance of various attributes in understanding the workers' overall ratings. The evaluation showed that in both absolute and relative terms, building occupants had mixed feelings about their workspaces. Some liked them while others did not. Of the employees who responded, more than one-third (36 percent) expressed some level of dissatisfaction with the particular place in which they worked. Additionally, four in ten said their workstation was worse than what they had had prior to moving into the building (fig. 2-3). To a large extent, dissatisfaction was associated with limited space, lack of privacy, poor views, temperature variability, and distractions caused by noise from other agencies in the building. Similar responses were noted when workers were asked why their working conditions were worse.

	All Agencies	*Agency Responding Most Positively*	*Agency Responding Most Negatively*
Overall, how satisfied are you with your workstation?			
Very satisfied	6%	15%	—0—
Fairly satisfied	58%	69%	42%
Not very satisfied	28%	8%	37%
Not at all satisfied	8%	8%	21%
	100%	100%	100%
Compared to where you worked before coming to the Federal Building, is your present workstation:			
Better	30%	35%	15%
Worse	42%	27%	64%
Same	23%	34%	15%
Better in some ways, worse in others	5%	4%	6%
	100%	100%	100%
Number of respondents	235	26	48

2-3. Satisfaction with workstations among individuals in selected agencies.

The analysis of attitudinal data together with objective data covering workstation attributes indicated that while the latter were related to overall workstation satisfaction, so too were employees' assessments of these attributes. At a global level, it was suggested that designers and programmers who wish to create satisfying work settings take into account the opinions and activities of workers who will occupy those settings as well as objective design criteria. More specifically, the data analysis showed the nature and level of responses that might be expected from people who work at different densities, who have varying amounts of space, and who occupy different types of offices (see figs. 2-4, 2-5, and 2-6).

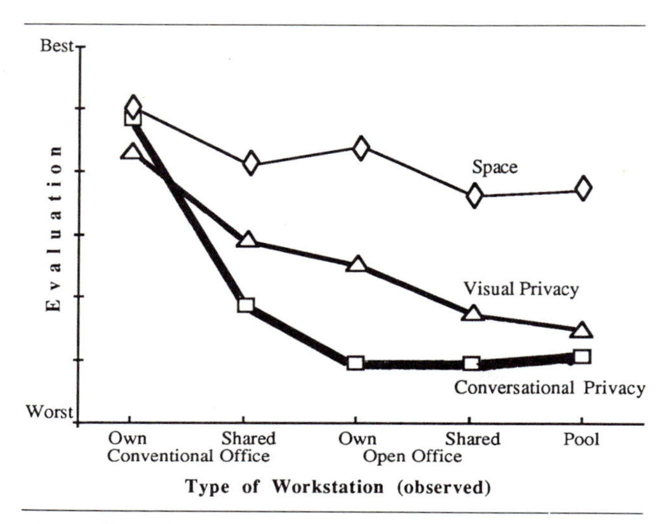

2-4. Relationships between type of workstation and evaluations of space, conversational privacy, and visual privacy.

The analysis of survey data also indicated that people's feelings about the ambience of the agency within which they work and the architecture of the building are colored by their reactions to their immediate workspace. Under the circumstances, designers who want their work appreciated by building occupants need to concentrate on details of the workspace as well as the larger-scale environment (Marans and Spreckelmeyer 1982).

SUMMARY

This chapter began with the assertion that during the 1970s, survey research or at least components

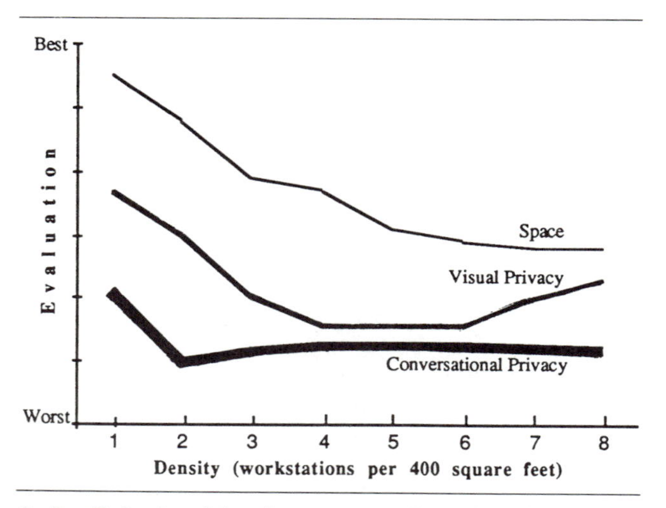

2-5. Relationships between workstation density and evaluations of space, conversational privacy, and visual privacy.

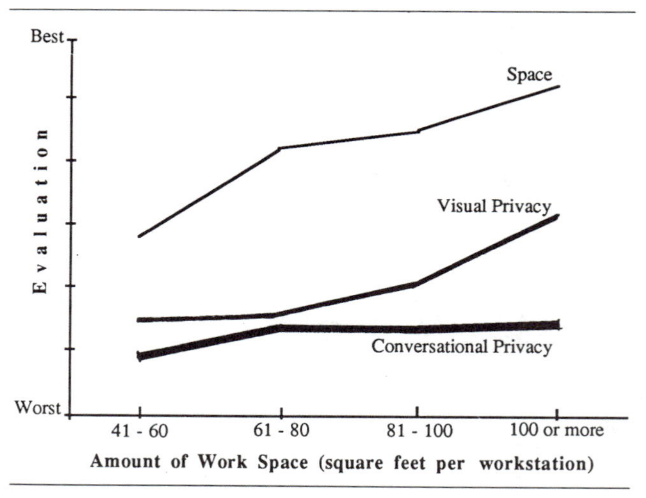

2-6. Relationships among amount of work space and evaluations of space, conversational privacy, and visual privacy.

of the survey process became an accepted part of the activities of many in the environmental design professions. With the onslaught of behavioral studies, community needs assessments, user studies, and post-occupancy evaluations, practitioners and students have been exposed to social science research methods including questionnaire design, sampling, and quantitative data analysis. The thrust of this chapter has been to demonstrate that surveys have significantly contributed to our understanding of how people interact with and respond to their environments. We have done this in several ways. First, the uses of survey research for environmental design practitioners and researchers were considered. These uses range from producing information that can inform design decisions to programming for new environments and evaluating those which are used. The nature of the information derived from surveys was then discussed. Next, because environmental designers operate at scales ranging from interiors to regions and nations, a discussion of the geographic breadth of survey work was presented. While specific geographic areas will continue to be the focus of most surveys, we suggested that surveys of specific populations are also important sources of information about person–environment interactions, irrespective of the settings within which the surveys take place. Following a description of three types of survey designs, we presented a brief overview of the major steps in the survey process. These steps include survey planning, the design and use of data collection instruments, the compiling and analysis of data, and the interpretation and reporting of survey findings. Since surveys are often conducted with representative samples of populations, a primer on sampling was presented. Special consideration was also given to three methods of data collection—telephone interviewing, self-administered questionnaires, and face-to-face interviewing. The chapter concluded with a capsule description of a research project, the purposes of which were to design and test a process for evaluating built environments. The evaluation of a federal office building, conducted as part of the research, used three surveys as the principal source of information. Selected findings from the evaluation were presented, and guidelines for future designs and the management of office buildings were then discussed.

NOTES

1. The matter of protecting the privacy of respondents and obtaining their informed consent before they participate in the study stems largely from past abuses in conducting survey research. For a succinct discussion of these abuses and specific efforts to deal with them, see Backstrom and Hursh-Cesar (1981, 46–50).
2. Other factors that often influence sample size include the type of prior information about the population that is available, the extent to which the population is geographically dispersed or concentrated, and the number of response categories for the questions to be answered. For a complete discussion of the determinants of sample size, see Kalton (1983) and Backstrom and Hursh-Cesar (1981).
3. The 1.96 indicates that 95 percent of the area under the normal distribution curve falls within 1.96 standard deviations around the distribution's mean. Suppose that in the above illustration, 56 percent of the 310 residents who fell into the sample said they supported the bond millage and would vote for it. We could say that we are 95 percent confident that the interval between 52 percent and 60 percent contains the actual proportion of neighborhood residents who favor the bond millage. With the sample of only 160 residents, our confidence level would be greatly reduced—the standard deviation from the mean is 1, and the area under the curve is only 65 percent. Thus we would have to say that if repeated samples of 160

residents were drawn, the results would be within the range of 52 percent to 60 percent in 68 times out of 100. For a thorough discussion of confidence intervals and sampling errors, see Kish (1965) and Moser and Kalton (1981).

4. Various methods of cleaning lists and techniques for selecting samples of telephone numbers are discussed in Frey (1984).

REFERENCES

Alwin, D. F. 1977. *Survey Design and Analysis.* Sage contemporary social science issues, vol. 46. Beverly Hills, Cal.: Sage.

Andrews, F. M., L. Klem, T. Davidson, P. O'Malley, and W. L. Rodgers. 1981. *A Guide for Selecting Techniques for Analysing Social Science Data.* Ann Arbor: Institute for Social Research, Univ. of Michigan.

Backstrom, C. H., and G. Hursh-Cesar. 1981. *Survey Research.* 2d ed. New York: Wiley.

Becker, T. M., and P. R. Meyers. 1974. Empathy and bravado: Interviewing reluctant bureaucrats. *Public Opinion Quarterly* 38:605–13.

Bishop, G. F., K. W. Oldendide, and A. J. Tuchfarber. 1978. Effects of question wording and format on political attitude consistency. *Public Opinion Quarterly* 42:81–92.

BMDP. 1983. *BMDP Statistical Software.* Rev., ed. W. J. Dixon. Berkeley, Cal.: Univ. of California Press.

Burby, R., and S. Weiss. 1976. *New Communities U.S.A.* Lexington, Mass.: Lexington.

Campbell, A., P. Converse, and W. L. Rodgers. 1976. *The Quality of American Life.* New York: Russell Sage Foundation.

Cannell, C. F., P. V. Miller, and L. Oksenberg. 1981. Research on interviewing techniques. In *Sociological Methodology.* San Francisco: Jossey-Bass.

Casey, S. 1980. *The Effects of Race upon Opinions of Structure and Neighborhood Quality.* Annual Housing Survey Study no. 5. Washington, D.C.: Department of Housing and Urban Development.

Chi, P. 1979. *Population Redistribution and Changes in Housing Tenant Status in the United States.* Annual Housing Survey Study no. 4. Washington, D.C.: Department of Housing and Urban Development.

Cooper, C. C. 1975. *Easter Hill Village.* New York: Free Press.

Davis, J. A. 1971. *Elementary Survey Analysis.* Englewood Cliffs, N.J.: Prentice-Hall.

Dillman, D. A. 1978. *Mail and Telephone Surveys: The Total Design Method.* New York: Wiley.

Duncan, G. J. 1984. *Years of Poverty, Years of Plenty.* Ann Arbor: Institute for Social Research, Univ. of Michigan.

Duncan, G. J., and S. J. Newman. 1976. Expected and actual residential mobility. *Journal of the American Institute of Planners,* April.

Elder, J., and R. L. Tibbett. 1981. *User Acceptance of an Energy Efficient Office Building—A Study of the Norris Cotton Federal Office Building.* Washington, D.C.: National Bureau of Standards.

Farbstein, J., and R. L. Wener. 1982. Evaluation of correctional facilities. *Environment and Behavior* 14 (6).

Festinger, L. S., S. Schacter, and K. Back. 1950. *Social Pressures in Informal Groups.* New York: Harper & Row.

Francescato, G., S. Weidemann, J. R. Anderson, and R. Chenoweth. 1979. *Residential Satisfaction in HUD-assisted Housing: Design and Management Factors.* Washington, D.C.: Department of Housing and Urban Development.

Frey, J. H. 1984. *Survey Research by Telephone.* Beverly Hills, Cal.: Sage.

Fried, M., and P. Gleicher. 1961. Some sources of residential satisfaction in an urban slum. *Journal of the American Institute of Planners* 4 (November).

Furguson, G. S., and G. D. Wiseman. 1986. Alternative approaches to the assessments of employee satisfaction with the office environment. In *Behav-*

ioral Issues in Office Design, ed. J. Wineman. New York: Van Nostrand Reinhold.

Gans, H. J. 1962. *The Urban Villagers.* New York: Free Press.

———. 1967. *The Levittowners.* New York: Pantheon.

Greenberg, S., W. Rohe, and J. R. Williams. 1981. *Safe and Secure Neighborhoods: Physical Characteristics and Informal Territorial Control in High and Low Crime Neighborhoods.* Triangle Park, N.C.: Research Triangle Institute.

Groves, R. M. 1984. Implications of CATI: Costs, errors and organization of survey research. *Sociological Methods and Research* 12(2):199–215.

Groves, R. M., and R. L. Kahn. 1979. *Surveys by Telephone: A National Comparison with Personal Interviews.* New York: Academic Press.

Guenzel, P. J., T. R. Berckmans, and C. F. Cannell. 1983. *General Interviewing Techniques: A Self-instructional Workbook for Telephone and Personal Interviewer Training.* Ann Arbor: Institute for Social Research, Univ. of Michigan.

Harris, L., and Associates. 1978. *The Steelcase National Survey of Office Environments: Do They Work?* Grand Rapids, Mich.: Steelcase, Inc.

Harris, L., and Associates. 1980. *The Steelcase National Study of Office Environments, no. 11: Comfort and Productivity in the Office of the 80s.* Grand Rapids, Mich.: Steelcase, Inc.

Hess, I., D. C. Reidel, and T. B. Fitzpatrick. 1975. *Probability Sampling of Hospitals and Patients.* Ann Arbor: Health Administration Press.

Hunt, M. 1984. Environmental learning without being there. *Environment and Behavior* 13:307–34.

Kahn, R. L., and C. F. Cannell. 1967. *The Dynamics of Interviewing.* New York: Wiley.

Kalton, G. 1983. *Introduction to Survey Sampling.* Beverly Hills, Cal.: Sage.

Kaplan, R. 1980. Citizen participation in the design and evaluation of a park. *Environment and Behavior* 12(4).

Keller, S. 1978. *Design and the Quality of Life in a New Community,* ed. J. M. Yinger and S. J. Cutler, 277–89. New York: Free Press.

Kish, L. 1965. *Survey Sampling.* New York: Wiley.

Labaw, P. J. 1980. *Advanced Questionnaire Design.* Cambridge, Mass.: Abt Assoc.

Lansing, J. B., R. W. Marans, and R. B. Zehner. 1970. *Planned Residential Environments.* Ann Arbor: Institute for Social Research, Univ. of Michigan.

Lansing, J. B., and J. N. Morgan. 1971. *Survey Research Methods.* Ann Arbor: Institute for Social Research. Univ. of Michigan.

Lawton, M. P., L. Nahemow, and J. Teaff. 1975. Environmental characteristics and the well-being of elderly tenants in federally-assisted housing. *Journal of Gerontology* 30:601–7.

McClelland, L., and S. Cook. 1980. Energy conservation in buildings: Encouraging and evaluating reductions in occupants' electricity use. *Evaluation Review* 4(1).

Mandell, L., and R. W. Marans. 1972. *Participation in Outdoor Recreation: A National Perspective.* Ann Arbor: Institute for Social Research, Univ. of Michigan.

Marans, R. W. 1978. Kiryat Gat: An experimental new town. In *The Role of Housing in Promoting Social Integration.* New York: United Nations.

———. 1983. *Perspectives on Lighting: Thoughts and Experiences of Selected Consumer and Supplier Groups.* New York: Lighting Research Institute.

———. 1984. Evaluation in architecture. In *Architectural Research,* ed. J. Snyder. New York: Van Nostrand Reinhold.

Marans, R. W., B. L. Driver, and J. C. Scott. 1972. *Youth and the Environment: An Evaluation of the 1971 Youth Conservation Corps.* Ann Arbor: Institute for Social Research, Univ. of Michigan.

Marans, R. W., and J. M. Fly. 1981. *Recreation and the Quality of Urban Life: Recreation Resources, Behaviors, and Evaluations of People in the Detroit Region.* Ann Arbor: Institute for Social Research, Univ. of Michigan.

Marans, R. W., and K. Spreckelmeyer. 1981. *Evaluating Built Environments: A Behavioral Approach.* Ann Arbor: Institute for Social Research and Architectural Research Laboratory, Univ. of Michigan.

———. 1982. Evaluating open and conventional office design. *Environment and Behavior,* May.

Marans, R. W., and J. D. Wellman. 1978. *The Quality of Nonmetropolitan Living: Evaluations, Behaviors and Expectations of Northern Michigan Residents.* Ann Arbor: Institute for Social Research, Univ. of Michigan.

Michelson, W. 1977. *Environmental Choice, Human Behavior, and Residential Satisfaction.* New York: Oxford Univ. Press.

Moos, R. H., and S. Lemke. 1980. Assessing the physical and architectural features of sheltered care settings. *Journal of Gerontology* 35(4):571–83.

Moleski, W. 1974. Behavioral analysis and environmental programming for offices. In *Designing for Human Behavior,* ed. J. Lang, C. Burnette, W. Moleski, and D. Vachon. Stroudsburg, Pa.: Dowden, Hutchinson & Ross.

Moser, C. A., and G. Kalton. 1981. *Survey Methods in Social Investigation,* 2d ed. London: Heinemann Educational.

O'Muircheartaigh, C., and C. Payne, eds. 1977. *The Analysis of Survey Data.* Vols. 1 and 2. New York: Wiley.

Oppenheim, A. N. 1966. *Questionnaire Design and Attitude Measurement.* New York: Basic Books.

Orleans, P. 1973. Differential cognition of urban residents: Effects of social scale on mapping. In *Images and Environments: Cognitive Mapping and Social Behavior,* ed. R. M. Downs and D. Stea. Chicago: Aldine.

OSIRIS Survey Research Center Support Group. 1982. *OSIRIS IV User's Manual.* 7th ed., rev. Ann Arbor: Institute for Social Research, Univ. of Michigan.

Payne, J. D. 1951. *The Art of Asking Questions.* Princeton: Princeton Univ. Press.

Peroff, K., C. Smith, R. Jones, R. Curtin, and R. W. Marans. 1979. *Gautreaux Housing Demonstration: An Evaluation of Its Impact on Participating Households.* Washington, D.C.: U.S. Department of Housing and Urban Development.

Reizenstein, J., and M. Grant. 1982. *From Hospital Research to Hospital Design.* Ann Arbor: Office of Hospital Planning and Research and Development.

Reynolds, I., and C. Nicholson. 1972. *The Estate Outside the Dwelling: Reactions of Residents to Aspects of Housing Layout.* London: Her Majesty's Stationary Office.

Rich, C. L. 1977. Is random digit dialing really necessary? *Journal of Marketing Research* 14:300–305.

Sanoff, H. 1977. *Methods of Architectural Programming.* Stroudsburg, Pa.: Dowden, Hutchinson & Ross.

SAS Institute, Inc. 1982. *SAS User's Guide: Basics.* 1982 ed. Raleigh, N.C.: SAS Institute.

Schuman, H., and S. Presser. 1981. *Questions and Answers in Attitude Surveys.* New York: Academic Press.

SPSS Inc. 1983. *SPSSx User's Guide.* New York: McGraw-Hill.

Sudman, S., and N. Bradburn. 1982. *Asking Questions: A Practical Guide to Questionnaire Design.* San Francisco: Jossey-Bass.

Sundstrom, E., R. K. Herbert, and D. W. Brown. 1982. Privacy and communication in an open-plan office: A case study. *Environment and Behavior* 14(3).

U.S. Bureau of the Census. 1981. *Statistical Abstract of the United States—1980.* Washington, D.C.: U.S. Department of Commerce.

Van der Ryn, S., and M. Silverstein. 1967. *Dorms at Berkeley: An Environmental Analysis.* New York: Educational Facilities Laboratories.

Van Vliet, W. 1980. Use, Evaluation, and Knowledge of City and Suburban Environments by Children of Employed and Nonemployed Mothers. Ph.D. diss., University of Toronto.

Walkley, R. P., W. R. Mangum, S. Sherman, S. Dodds, and D. M. Wilner. 1966. The California survey of retirement housing. *Gerontologist* 6:28–34.

Weidemann, S., J. R. Anderson, D. I. Butterfield, and P. M. O'Donnell. 1982. Residents' perceptions of satisfaction and safety: A basis for change in multifamily housing. *Environment and Behavior* 14(6).

Wiseman, J. 1981. Evaluating architectural legibility: Wayfinding in the built environment. *Environment and Behavior* 13:189–204.

Zeisel, J. 1982. *Inquiry by Design*. Monterey, Cal.: Brooks/Cole.

Zeisel, J., and M. Griffin. 1975. *Charlesview Housing: A Diagnostic Evaluation*. Cambridge, Mass.: Architectural Research Office, Harvard Graduate School of Design.

Zube, E. H., J. H. Crystal, and J. F. Palmer. 1976. *Visitor Center Design Evaluation*. Amherst: Institute for Man and Environment, Univ. of Massachusetts.

CHAPTER 3

THE UBIQUITOUS WORLD OF PAPER AND PENCIL TESTS

Robert B. Bechtel

Environment and behavior research is roughly divided into two broad areas: searching out responses to environments across people and searching out responses to environments *within* people. The first tries to measure universal responses to particular kinds of environments like forests or apartment houses, regardless of human differences, while the second tries to measure common responses that people bring to environments. This second kind of study tries to measure something within the person but which is also shared by a group of similar persons. Instruments for such measures have been the prime directive of psychology for many years under the heading of *paper and pencil tests.* Actually, these are not usually tests, although some are, in the literal sense. The principal idea is that one can measure an internal state by having someone sit down and fill out a printed form.

Paper and pencil instruments have been used for so long that the practices in constructing them have become quite sophisticated. A paper and pencil instrument that has been pre-tested on a representative population, has established its reliability and validity, and has normative scores for given populations, is said to be *standardized.* Standardized, printed tests are listed in a test-listing book like *Tests in Print* (Mitchell 1983) and reviewed in weighty tomes like the *Mental Measurements Yearbook* (Mitchell 1985). These are standard references for looking up psychological tests to learn their proper uses and the populations to which they can be applied.

The standardization process, which is complicated and costly, involves two dimensions: items and population. The usual procedure is to begin with a long list of questions (items) that seem to measure or relate to the central concept of the test—for example, intelligence or attitudes toward the environment. This list of questions is submitted to a representative population—that is, one that is thought to be typical of the population for whom the final version is applicable. For measures of attitudes toward commonly experienced environments, a proper sample could represent the entire United States or even the world. However, the world is too costly to consider and a representative sample of the United States could cost over $100,000.

The first answers are factor-analyzed to measure which items relate most closely to the central factor. A *pure* test has every item loading highly on the central factor, eliminating any items that do not load beyond a certain weight. Sometimes more than one factor may be considered. For example, intelligence has been found to have two factors: verbal and mathematical. Attitudes toward the environment may have many factors. The semantic differential has been found to have three factors: evaluation, power, and activity. Items within each factor can be added together to produce a total score.

Items are measured for reliability and validity. A given population is tested on particular items over a period of time, to measure consistency of response, which is termed *reliability. Validity* measures the ability of the test to measure what it is supposed to measure. For example, does an attitude-toward-environment test really measure attitudes toward the environment, or does it measure only what the respondents want the researcher to believe? One can have highly reliable tests that are invalid, but one can never have valid tests that are unreliable, because validity must always be consistent.

Because of the large costs involved, few tests are standardized for large populations. Unfortunately, too many are administered to college and school students with the hope that the results will be comparable to the larger population. Test scores for the population are reported as *norms*. For example, the normative score for an intelligence test is given as 100. This does not mean that most people score 100, but that the average score across the population is 100. Norms are important for comparison purposes, because they provide a means of determining whether the population used in research differs from the normative population.

In addition to the more formal standardized tests, many more informal instruments are developed that have not been standardized. These are experimental instruments that have not been tested on large populations and that may or may not have established reliability and validity. Of course, there is an overlap between many questionnaires and psychological tests. In a sense, every psychological test is really a questionnaire, but most questionnaires do not approach being tests.

GENERAL GUIDES TO FOLLOW AND PITFALLS TO AVOID

Before embarking on the hazardous and sometimes rewarding pathway of paper and pencil instruments, the reader who is unfamiliar with methods and theory in test development will need to take a short course on the primary obstacles to overcome. This short course is little more than a series of signposts, however, and the reader must realize that there is a depth of material to be eventually mastered behind each signpost. Psychological instruments must be approached with great skepticism and trepidation. The course is not unlike finding one's way through a minefield.

Hunting for Concepts—Deciding What Will Be Measured

Each instrument was developed to measure some concept, such as intelligence, attitude toward the environment, satisfaction with housing, or aesthetic appreciation. These are all concepts that someone has attempted to measure by developing a measuring instrument administered by having respondents make marks on a piece of paper. The dream is almost utopian—that we can extract from the mind of the ordinary person information on concepts that will help decide important or urgent questions. The concepts are all very slippery. Everyone seems to have their own definition, almost as though there were a conspiracy against the researcher who comes forth with his or her own crystal clear definitions!

Each instrument is itself evidence confirming the slipperiness of concepts. If one wants to measure tolerance, for example, Mitchell's *Tests in Print, III* or *The Ninth Mental Measurements Yearbook* are consulted, but since these are already outdated, a search of *Psychology Abstracts, Sociology Abstracts,* and *Environment and Behavior* would reveal many more recent measures used. And with luck, Kelman's *Tolerance for Ambiguity* scale, for example, would be uncovered. But this may be too specialized if the desired focus is tolerance in general. All the tests, however, measure tolerance for some specific thing like race, ambiguity, and so on. Concepts tend to be general while scales and tests tend to be more specific, and it pays to understand that in selecting any scale or measurement, you are dealing with a product that has already gone through a passage from general concept to more specific measure. Intelligence tests began with the purpose of testing intelligence as though it were a unitary, universal phenomenon. It was then discovered that intelligence could be broken down into at least two areas: verbal and quantitative. And now it is accepted that there are several aspects influenced by culture (Eysenck and Kamin 1981). Nearly every scale has had a similar history—a global concept initially followed by evidence that the concept has multiple parts and that the scale may only measure some of them.

With this caution in mind, it pays to realize that any instrument will only partially measure the concept originally held. This in itself is an important lesson. All the scales are only partially complete tools that can at best begin to approach what was originally hoped for.

In the end, the researcher will have to be satisfied with what can be measured by the current off-the-shelf instruments, none of which may measure exactly what was originally intended. The other alternative is to develop a new instrument—a costly and time-consuming venture.

Defining Populations—Who Will Be Measured?

After selecting an instrument that compromises least what one first intended, the next question is *who* will be measured. Defining the target population is almost as difficult as defining the concept to be measured, and defining the target population may force a change of measuring instruments.

For example, assuming we want to measure the dependency (on the environment) of elderly people, we select a printed test on learned helplessness, only to realize that many elderly will not be able to read this test because of poor eyesight. Either we change the form of administration (that is, use larger type) or we pick a test that already has large type. In addition, if the test picked specifies a time limit, new norms will have to be developed for an elderly population.

In much of environmental design research the relevant population will be the potential users of the new design. Sometimes it is possible to find a design similar to the one contemplated, so that by measuring people living in that design, one has a *comparison* group to use. But this comparison cannot ignore the problem of *history*. Very often a client organization that wants a new building has a population of employees that has a unique history. For example, IBM employees have a history of job security that makes them a different population to measure than the employees of some other company making similar products. Thus, picking a population that lives in a similar design must be tempered with some knowledge of the history of the population.

Children and the elderly are the most difficult populations to administer printed tests to (Kane and Kane 1981; Johnson 1976). Both are easily distracted and both may have reading problems. Other groups, such as Hispanics and Blacks, may show cultural differences that invalidate tests. Sometimes, however, one is lucky and discovers tests that were developed specifically for these groups. In any case, it must be determined whether the test selected is applicable to the population selected. This can only be determined by finding examples in the literature reporting data from these populations. Assume that if such data are not reported, the test has not been validated for the population in question.

Any population should be randomly sampled for valid results or, at least, scientifically matched. (Random sampling is discussed in chapter 2.)

Searching the Literature

The Ninth Mental Measurements Yearbook (Mitchell 1985) is a publication devoted exclusively to reporting the uses and results of psychological instruments. Many of the instruments used in design research, however, are so new that they will not be included in this publication. Usually a search of the literature is required. Often a way to shorten this search is to call or write the author of the instrument and ask for a list of publications reporting results of its use.

In any case, before selecting an instrument for use, a search of the literature should be made to decide whether it has been used previously and what the results were. Some questions need to be answered from this search:

1. Do the results support the intended use of the instrument? Often, this means did it measure what it was supposed to?
2. Was it used with success among various populations? Or, are there indications that its use is limited, not applicable for the elderly, for example?
3. Can you find data showing reliability and validity? These concepts will be discussed more fully below, but every instrument should have evidence of both.
4. An instrument that does not report data on the above questions is one that has not passed the ''hurdles of acceptability.'' A complete definition of these ''hurdles'' is contained in the publication *Standards for Educational and Psychological Tests* published by the American Psychological Association (APA 1974). Note especially the chapter on reliability and validity, pages 25–55. It would pay to study this booklet thoroughly before using any psychological instrument.

Problems of Overuse

Some psychological tests have been given to differing populations indiscriminately and in circumstances never intended. The tendency of the novice researcher is to assume that the other researchers ''knew what they were doing,'' when this may not have been the case. For example, if the researcher who used the instrument makes no attempt to apply external checks for validity and reliability, but assumes that they are self-evident, the instrument should be viewed with skepticism. In some cases instruments that were once widely used are now restricted to a purely local application, indicating that local reliability and validity do not necessarily provide a sound basis for wider use.

Planning Problems

One of the commonest errors of the novice researcher is to fail to plan for the amount of time the administration of tests will take and, especially, how the data will be analyzed. Certain rules of thumb have been adopted, more or less by custom, in the administration of tests. One is to provide a minimum of ten subjects for every variable. Thus, if there are ten questions on a test and each question will be analyzed separately, then one hundred subjects are required. Of course, if all ten items will be added and only a total score issued, then one hundred subjects are not necessary; but the minimum—ten—are usually not enough for statistical comparison. Generally, about thirty-two subjects are needed to obtain a statistically "robust"[1] distribution of scores.

All of the items should take no more than half an hour, or ideally, twenty minutes of the subject's time. Many research instruments, however, tend to "load up" and take more than an hour. Increasingly, people are concerned with their time and one of the commonest questions asked is, "How much time will it take?" Researchers who can answer honestly that it will take less than half an hour get more cooperation.

Analysis of data is done by parametric or nonparametric statistics. If measures are taken independently, the data are in scale form that is linear, subjects are randomly assigned and scores are not correlated, then parametric statistics can be used. These are the t-tests, ANOVA, discriminant function, factor analysis, and other measures of any standard statistics textbook. If data are only counts of numbers of people, however, or yes-no answers only, or not randomly assigned subjects, then nonparametric tests are used, which are Chi square, Phi correlations, and so on. Siegel (1956) is still a standard text for nonparametric statistics. Planning the analysis makes one think about the kind of data that will be obtained by a particular test before selecting it. In many cases, certain tests will be eliminated because they do not result in the proper kind of data. For example, ranking is a task that many subjects have trouble with, and the ranked data often have to be collapsed and often cannot be analyzed by parametric measures.

The Reliability-Validity Vise

In this case, we mean a vise that tends to bind rather than one that dissipates (vice). Being caught within the reliability-validity vise is the dilemma of all tests. They *must* have both. Validity is a measure of whether the test measures what it was intended to measure. Reliability is a measure of consistency. You can be consistent but still not be valid, but you can never have validity without first having consistency.

Validity is really an independent measure that shows the same result. A high correlation between intelligence tests and school grades is a measure of validity. The school grades tend to validate the test results. More than one method is almost always used in a research project. When two or more methods agree, this is called *convergent* validity.

Another form of validity that is often neglected is the ability of tests to show that environments or methods are different. Called *discriminant* validity, this feature is especially important when using self-report instruments, those where the subject reports his or her own feelings and beliefs.

Reliability is measured by giving the same test more than once to the same population under the same conditions. Frequently, redundant questions are included within a test so that one can divide the test in half and get split-half reliability measures.

Often, however, a researcher wants to get a reliability measure of some stimuli, such as slides, to determine whether they produce a consistent response. In this case, the stimulus is given to different populations to see if the responses are reliable over those populations. This is called the *reliability of environmental response* to a specific stimulus.

The importance of reliability and validity cannot be overemphasized. In a very real sense, every administration of a test should be treated as a unique situation in which reliability and validity must be demonstrated anew. The burden is on the researcher to show both.

Tying Results to Design

At the end of all this is the original purpose of environment and behavior research. Somehow results must be tied in to design or environmental aspects, but researchers are not used to making such leaps of logic and faith. Design often contains many variables not measured. The commonest way for the connection to be made is for researcher and designer to collaborate at the beginning of the research to make sure the research results give meaningful answers to design questions.

An example of standardized instrument use occurred when a post hoc analysis was made of the population that rioted in Kansas City in April of 1968 (Bechtel 1970). This was done by reanalyzing the data from a preriot survey done on the population. In the presurvey subjects were administered Cantril's self-anchoring scale, an instrument that measures future aspirations. It is a simple device that asks the respondent to imagine that ten rungs on a ladder represent steps toward the best possible life at the top and the worst possible life at the bottom. When asked where they are on the ladder at present, most people locate themselves at about the fifth rung. When asked where they expect to be five years from now, most will indicate two rungs or so higher. The difference between the present and future rung chosen constitutes a quantitative measure of aspiration.

In the post hoc analysis, census tracts that rioted were matched on demographic variables with those that did not. The hypothesis was that those with higher aspiration levels are more likely to riot than those with lower aspiration levels. This is consistent with the old Kropotkin hypothesis that the downtrodden (that is, those without aspirations) do not rebel. It takes a higher aspiration level to motivate rebellion.

The finding was that those in the riot zones did, in fact, have higher future aspiration levels as measured by rungs on the ladder. Cantril's (1965) self-anchoring scale has been thoroughly standardized on United States and foreign populations.

An example of an experimental pencil and paper instrument that was used was the comparison of ratings of the environment by populations living in Fort McMurray, Canada, and Dhahran, Saudi Arabia. Matthiasson administered the list of adjectives to residents of Fort McMurray, a tar sands mining community in Northern Canada (Matthiasson 1970). The same list was presented to expatriates living in the oil community of Dhahran by Bechtel (1975), and these results were compared with those from the survey of the residents of Fort McMurray. Since the list had not been standardized either for items or populations, the results are correspondingly limited. For example, the rankings of both administrations of the list correlated very highly, 0.825. But is this because the list is incapable of discriminating among the environments, or because it measures a true agreement (convergence)? There is discrimination, however, on one item, the ranking of heat and cold. Cold showed less prominently in Canada than heat in Saudi Arabia. It gets very cold in Fort McMurray and very hot in Saudi Arabia. Then why the difference in ranking? The researcher speculates that it is because the residents of the Canadian community have accepted cold as a part of their environment, since many of them had lived in Canada all of their lives, while the expatriates had had less time to get used to the heat of Saudi Arabia. However, there is no independent confirmation of this interpretation (validity), nor is there any data on the stability of the responses (reliability). Such are the limitations of use of many experimental paper and pencil instruments.

The Unanswered Questions— The Research Dilemma

Every research project ends with some questions unanswered. Sometimes more questions are raised by the research than are answered. Such an outcome is not necessarily disturbing to researchers, who may, in fact, be delighted to add to the string of questions that were originally presented. Designers, and to an even greater degree, policy makers are likely to find such an attitude frustrating, however. Such clients engage in research for the purpose of finding answers to problems. One common difficulty is that research may make the problem appear worse merely because the problem was not stated properly in the first place. Design clients, policy makers, and lay people in general are not aware of the heuristic nature of research. (''Heuristic'' is a ten-dollar word meaning ''tending to provoke discovery.'') Most nonresearchers ask questions from a naive perspective, and the researcher may innocently accept their view only to discover that the basis on which the original question was asked is riddled with false assumptions. More experienced researchers will renegotiate the original question into a more researchable framework.

A degree of diplomacy is required in preparing the designer for the kinds of outcomes that research produces. It must always be remembered that even the best research may lead to more searching questions rather than answers.

THE SEMANTIC GAME AND CONFLICT

Since the original chapter on this subject frightened untold numbers of students and researchers away from the semantic differential, other researchers (Danford and Willems 1975; Daniel and Ittelson 1981) have entered the fray and the controversy has reached a stand-off, with the semantic differential users determinedly ignoring the critics and the critics just as determinedly battling them. In fact, as Boring (1950) so aptly put it, nothing creates progress in research as quickly as a good controversy.

The semantic differential is a device first invented by Osgood (Osgood, Suci, and Tannenbaum 1957) and intended to measure connotative (not dictionary) meanings. Its simple format consists of bipolar adjectives with seven spaces between each pole. For example, the most frequently used pair is good/bad. The subject checks off one of the seven spaces to indicate how close the object being rated is to either adjective. These spaces are then given numbers and a ''profile'' is obtained by the number assigned to each pair. Pairs are averaged so that a mean score can be given for how good (or bad) an environment (or word) is. These scores are also factor-analyzed, a method for summarizing the adjectives into higher dimensions. A typical semantic differential is shown in figure 3-1.

The main points of the criticism of the semantic differential still stand. It was intended to measure the connotative meanings of words and its overuse in design research has led to nine ways to confuse results. Rather than repeat this lengthy series here, these will be given in an appendix to this chapter so that the reader can consult them whenever the urge is felt to use a semantic differential.

Meanwhile the level of controversy has raised itself to a new pitch that applies not only to the semantic differential but to *any measure of environmental responses*. The outlines of the controversy are as follows:

1. Scott Danford and Ed Willems (1975) established that use of the semantic differential among groups exposed to: (a) a particular environment, (b) slides of that environment, and (c) neither slides nor environment, can produce no differences on the semantic differential. Prior to this, many studies had used similarities of responses between slides

RUSSIA

Rating

	1		2		3		4		5		6		7	
good	______	:	______	:	______	:	______	:	______	:	______	:	______	bad
timely	______	:	______	:	______	:	______	:	______	:	______	:	______	untimely
kind	______	:	______	:	______	:	______	:	______	:	______	:	______	cruel
beautiful	______	:	______	:	______	:	______	:	______	:	______	:	______	ugly
successful	______	:	______	:	______	:	______	:	______	:	______	:	______	unsuccessful
important	______	:	______	:	______	:	______	:	______	:	______	:	______	unimportant
true	______	:	______	:	______	:	______	:	______	:	______	:	______	false
wise	______	:	______	:	______	:	______	:	______	:	______	:	______	foolish
hard	______	:	______	:	______	:	______	:	______	:	______	:	______	soft
rich	______	:	______	:	______	:	______	:	______	:	______	:	______	poor
liberal	______	:	______	:	______	:	______	:	______	:	______	:	______	conservative
strong	______	:	______	:	______	:	______	:	______	:	______	:	______	weak

3–1. Typical semantic differential.

and environmental exposures to validate the use of slides as substitutes for "real" environments. Danford and Willems' conclusion (512) was that "the responses were determined or constrained by the technique of presentation and measurement and, therefore, are useless for practical purposes."

2. Starr and Danford (1979) went further in a later experiment, essentially instructing subjects to respond to *any* environment. They found no differences in responses of subjects exposed to slides and "real" environments. These results brought forth a stream of protests and frustrations. Danford's results were also often misunderstood. He did not claim that one would *always* get no differences in the use of the semantic differential and other self-report measures; he merely maintained that the nature of such instruments could lead to erroneous results. As a consequence of such misunderstanding, careful users of the semantic differential tended to ignore Danford's caution if they were able to show differences with a control group that did not see the environment either on slides or in "reality." Most just ignored the caution altogether.

3. Daniel and Ittelson (1981) raised a more critical issue concerning the type of research Ward and Russell (1981) were doing with a combination of verbal scaling techniques that included the semantic differential. The problem was that although the verbal methods discriminated among environmental stimuli, one could not be sure whether it was the environments or the verbal stimuli that were producing the results—in fact, there is every reason to believe that the latter were responsible. The practical consequence of this is that if it is really the verbal concepts that are producing the results, why bother to show people environments at all? And, of course, the answer to this is that getting people to respond to environments is one of the primary purposes of environment and behavior research!

The dilemma is pictured in figure 3-2.

Dilemma: Does response come from environment or verbal concept? Ward and Russell (1981) say: Environment. Daniel and Ittelson (1981) say: Word or Concept. Solution: Somehow to separate concept from environment.

To put it another way: the use of verbal methods such as the semantic differential often does not get beyond the stereotypes for any environment that are contained in the words denoting such environments. For example, Starr and Danford (1979), using a law school, offered slides of a law school, a tour of the law school, and verbal instructions to rate what a law school should be like, and got no differences across groups. In short, the use of the semantic differential obscures differences in environments because it summons verbal responses at the expense of environmental. The semantic differential was found to give three basic factors: evaluation, power, and activity (EPA). Even though verbal scales may yield seemingly different factors, they are still verbal components rather than environmental responses—that is, *abstractions* of environmental features rather than direct and specific responses to the particular environment. Daniel and Ittelson (1981, 156) conclude, "to put it quite bluntly, the most-used verbal methods for studying environmental perception have nothing (or virtually nothing) to do with the environment." This dilemma is taken up again in the final chapter.

How does one solve the problems presented? The answer is simple: through ecological validity. Simulated environments, slides, or verbal representations of environments cannot be compared to real environments using verbal instruments alone. More behavioral measures must be used. Each attempt to simulate or use slides for a particular en-

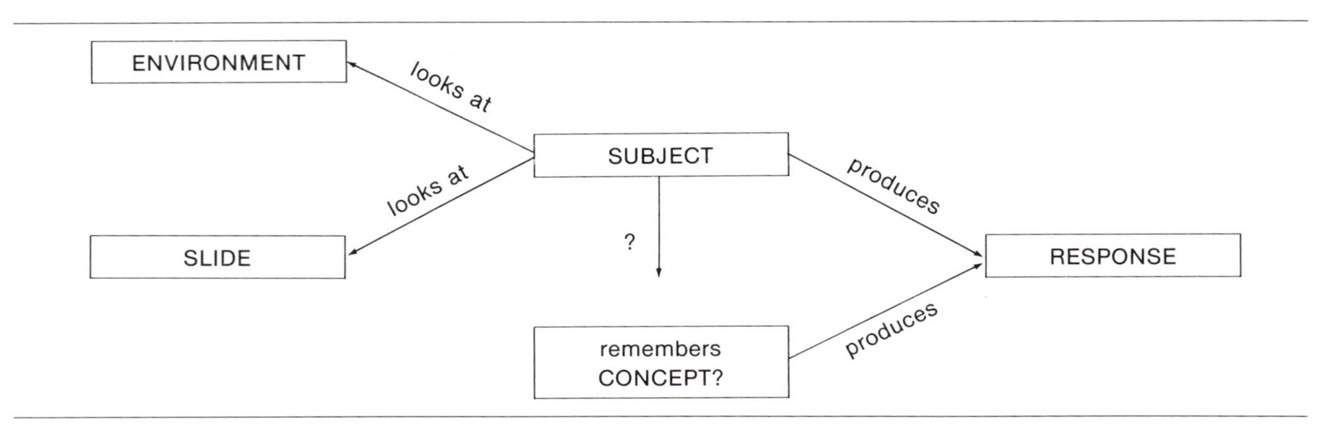

3-2. Dilemmas produced when discriminant validity fails and environmental response is confused with verbal concepts.

vironment must be validated by a wider range of instruments than the verbal ones used heretofore. Scales like the Scenic Beauty Estimate (SBE) (Daniel 1976; Daniel and Boster 1976) are only a partial answer because these deal with only one dimension. Moos' social climate scales (Moos 1974) are closer to the answer, but even these leave out many dimensions of the physical environment that are of central interest in design research. The simple truth is that no adequate scales have yet been developed, and much work remains to be done.

ENVIRONMENTAL INSTRUMENTS

Design research often requires a standard format for measuring how people respond to environments that goes beyond the usual verbal format of questions and answers. A number of instruments of the paper and pencil kind have been developed. These include adjective checklists, the Scenic Beauty Estimate, and cognitive mapping.

Adjective Checklists and Scaling

Along with the semantic differential, the use of adjective checklists has been a favorite of design research. Kasmar (1970) presented one of the first systematically tested checklists. Unfortunately, the adjective checklist suffers from the same problems of over-abstractness and verbal stereotyping that the semantic differential has. Kasmar's words (see fig. 3-3), although tested on various environments, do not produce the kind of discriminant validity Danford and Willems (1975) speak about nor the ecological validity that Daniel and Ittelson (1981) require.

Active/Passive	2a[3]
ADEQUATE SIZE/INADEQUATE SIZE	
Affected/Unaffected	2a
Alive/Dead	2a,b
APPEALING/UNAPPEALING	
Ascending Color/Receding Color	2a
ATTRACTIVE/UNATTRACTIVE	
BEAUTIFUL/UGLY	
BRIGHT/DULL	
BRIGHT COLORS/MUTED COLORS	
Busy/Calm	3e
Calming/Upsetting	3a,e
Changeable/Unchangeable	3e
CHEERFUL/GLOOMY	2a
CLEAN/DIRTY	
Coarse/Smooth	
COLORFUL/DRAB	
COMFORTABLE/UNCOMFORTABLE	
COMFORTABLE TEMPERATURE/ UNCOMFORTABLE TEMPERATURE	
Complete/Incomplete	3e
COMPLEX/SIMPLE	2a
Confused/Clear	
Consonant/Dissonant	2a,c
CONTEMPORARY/TRADITIONAL	
Content/Discontent	2a
CONVENIENT/INCONVENIENT	2b
Coordinated/Uncoordinated	
Cozy/Monumental	3c,e
Cultured/Uncultured	3a,b,e
Dated/Timeless	2a,b
Decorated/Stark	3c

(*continued*)

3-3. Kasmar's list of environmental adjectives. J. Kasmar, "The Development of a Usable Lexicon of Environmental Descriptors," **Environment and Behavior,** *Vol. 2, No. 2 (September 1970), pp. 153-64. Copyright © 1970 by Sage Publications, Inc. Reprinted by permission of Sage Publications, Inc.*

Deep/Shallow	2a	GOOD TEMPERATURE/BAD TEMPERATURE	
Defined Space/Undefined Space	2a	GOOD VENTILATION/POOR VENTILATION	
Definite Volume/Indefinite Volume	2a	Graceful/Clumsy	2b
Depressing/Exhilarating	3e	Happy/Sad	3a,b,e
DIFFUSE LIGHTING/DIRECT LIGHTING	3a,e	Hard/Soft	2a,b
Dignified/Undignified		Hard Texture/Soft Texture	2a
Directed/Undirected	2a,c	Harmonious/Discordant	2c
DISTINCTIVE/ORDINARY	2a,c	Healthy/Unhealthy	2a
Downward Scale/Upward Scale		Heavy/Light	2a
DRAFTY/STUFFY	3e	Heterogeneous/Homogeneous	2a,b,c
Dry/Humid		High/Low	2a,b
Dynamic Space/Static Space	2a,c	Honest/Dishonest	2a
EFFICIENT/INEFFICIENT		Horizontal Volume/Vertical Volume	2a,c
ELEGANT/UNADORNED		Hospitable/Inhospitable	3a,e
EMPTY/FULL		Hot/Cold	3b,e
Encouraging/Discouraging	2a	HUGE/TINY	
Euphonious/Diseuphonious	2c	Human Scale/Inhuman Scale	2a,c
Even Texture/Uneven Texture	2a	Imaginative/Unimaginative	3b,e
Exciting/Unexciting	3a,e	Impersonal/Personal	3e
EXPENSIVE/CHEAP		IMPRESSIVE/UNIMPRESSIVE	
Expressive/Unexpressive	3e	Inner-directed/Outer-directed	2a,c
Familiar/Unfamiliar	2d	Inspiring/Discouraging	3a,e
FASHIONABLE/UNFASHIONABLE		Interesting/Uninteresting	3e
Fatiguing/Invigorating	2d	INVITING/REPELLING	
Feminine/Masculine	3a,b,e	LARGE/SMALL	
Finished/Unfinished	3e	Lazy/Energetic	2a,b
FLASHY COLORS/SUBDUED COLORS		LIGHT/DARK	
Flexible/Rigid	2a	Livable/Unlivable	3a,b,e
Formal/Informal	3e	Lively/Dull	3e
Formed/Formless	2a	Long/Short	3e
Fragile/Sturdy	2d	Meaningful/Meaningless	2a
FREE SPACE/RESTRICTED SPACE		Mechanical Space/Nonmechanical Space	2a,c
FRESH ODOR/STALE ODOR		MODERN/OLD FASHIONED	
Friendly/Unfriendly	3a,e	MULTIPLE PURPOSE/SINGLE PURPOSE	
Frilly/Tailored	3a,b,c,e	Mystic/Nonmystic	2a
FUNCTIONAL/NONFUNCTIONAL		Natural/Artificial	3a,b,e
GAY/DREARY		NEAT/MESSY	
Gentle/Brutal	2a	NEW/OLD	
Glaring/Unglaring	2a	Nice/Awful	3e
Good/Bad	2a	No Odor/Strong Odor	2b
GOOD ACOUSTICS/POOR ACOUSTICS		Open/Closed	3e
GOOD COLORS/BAD COLORS		ORDERLY/CHAOTIC	
GOOD LIGHTING/POOR LIGHTING		ORGANIZED/DISORGANIZED	
GOOD LINES/BAD LINES		ORNATE/PLAIN	
Good Odor/Bad Odor	2d	Orthodox/Unorthodox	2b

Figure 3–3 continued

PLEASANT/UNPLEASANT	
PLEASANT ODOR/UNPLEASANT ODOR	
Pleasing/Annoying	3e
Plush/Austere	2c
Polished/Unpolished	2a
Popular/Unpopular	2a
Positive/Negative	2a
Pretentious/Unpretentious	2a,b,c
PRIVATE/PUBLIC	
Progressive/Conservative	3a,b,e
Proportional/Unproportional	3e
QUIET/NOISY	
Real/Phony	2a
Rectilinear/Curvilinear	2a,b,c
Refined/Unrefined	3a,e
Refreshing/Wearying	3e
Regular/Irregular	2a
Related/Unrelated	2a
Relaxed/Tense	2a,b
Reputable/Disreputable	2a
Reserved/Uninhibited	2d
Resonant/Flat	2a,c
Restful/Disturbing	3e
Restrained/Unrestrained	2a
Restricted/Unrestricted	2a
Reverent/Irreverent	2a
Rhythmic/Unrhythmic	2a
Rich/Poor	2b
Rickety/Stable	2a,b
Romantic/Unromantic	3a,b,e
ROOMY/CRAMPED	
Scenic/Unscenic	2a,c
Sectionalized Space/Undifferentiated Space	2a,c
Secure/Insecure	2a
Sedate/Flamboyant	2c
Sensitive/Insensitive	2a
Sensual/Prim	2a,c
Serene/Disturbed	3e
Serious/Humorous	2a
Shaped/Shapeless	2a
Sharp/Blunt	2a
Sincere/Insincere	2a
Sociable/Unsociable	3a,b,e
SOFT LIGHTING/HARSH LIGHTING	
Soothing/Distracting	3e
Sophisticated/Unsophisticated	3a,b,e
SPARKLING/DINGY	
Spiritual/Nonspiritual	2a
Stereotyped/Unstereotyped	3c,e
Sterile/Filthy	2b
Stimulating/Unstimulating	3e
Strong/Weak	2a
Structured/Unstructured	2a
STYLISH/UNSTYLISH	
Symmetrical/Asymmetrical	3c,e
TASTEFUL/TASTELESS	
Temporary/Permanent	2a
Textured/Untextured	2a
Threatening/Unthreatening	2a
TIDY/UNTIDY	
True/False	2a
UNCLUTTERED/CLUTTERED	
UNCROWDED/CROWDED	
UNUSUAL/USUAL	
Urban/Rustic	3a,b,c,e
USEFUL/USELESS	
Valuable/Worthless	2a
Varied/Repetitive	2a
Versatile/Nonversatile	3e
WARM/COOL	
WELL BALANCED/POORLY BALANCED	
WELL KEPT/RUNDOWN	
WELL ORGANIZED/POORLY ORGANIZED	
WELL PLANNED/POORLY PLANNED	
WELL SCALED/POORLY SCALED	
WIDE/NARROW	

1. Descriptors retained are shown in upper-case lettering
2. The stage in which descriptor was eliminated is indicated: Stage 2 or 3
3. Reason for elimination of descriptor: (a) low median, (b) wide interquartile range, (c) excessive question mark ratings, (d) median sex differences—Stage 2, (e) low Q^1—Stage 3.

Figure 3–3 continued

A fruitful approach has been exemplified in the Scenic Beauty Estimate (SBE) (Daniel 1976; Daniel and Boster 1976). This instrument deals with only one visual dimension of the environment as opposed to the much wider ambitions of the adjective checklist and the semantic differential. As with most paper and pencil instruments, the more precise and limited the concept, the better it is measured. SBEs are used to measure which parts of a forest or park are considered more scenically beautiful than others. It was validated by comparing measures of the actual environments with slides taken of identical scenes. Such scales avoid the dilemmas of the semantic measures because they use a Likert Scale system to measure relative degrees of a simple concept (see SBE Scale with instructions in fig. 3-4).

Sample Rating Scale Instructions

I am going to read some standardized instructions.

Today, more than ever, prudent management of wildlands such as our National Forests is very important. Many wildland researchers are conducting investigations on the effects of alternative vegetative management on water, forage, and timber yields; others are investigating influences on recreational use. In our own research, we are attempting to determine the public's esthetic or scenic perception of such management alternatives, and we greatly appreciate your time in this effort.

We are going to show you, one at a time, some color slides of several wildland areas. Each scene represents a larger area. We ask you to think about the *area* in which the slide was taken rather than about the individual slide itself.

The first slides will be shown very quickly, just to give you an idea of the range of areas you will be judging. Try to imagine how you would rate these slides, using the "rating response scale" on the top of your scoring sheet. Note that the scale ranges from zero, meaning you judge the area to be very low in scenic quality, to nine, indicating very high scenic quality.

Then, after the initial slides, I will announce that you are to begin rating the next set of slides. You should assign one rating number from zero to nine to each slide. Your rating should indicate your judgment of the scenic beauty represented by the slide. Please use the full range of numbers if you possibly can and please respond to each slide.

Are there any questions before we start?

3-4. Scenic beauty estimate instructions.

Scaling itself is an old problem of psychology (Torgerson 1958). The problem of scaling is how to calibrate the scale to demonstrate that any two points represent half the value of any four points. This is easy for a thermometer but not for an IQ test. Since there has been a general failure to demonstrate the unitary value of scales, scaling theory has fallen back on a ranking of values and a demonstration of the utility of this procedure (Binder 1964), or on multidimensional scaling (Kruskal and Wish 1978), the latter involving the notion that scaling can occur simultaneously in several dimensions.

If one wishes to use an adjective checklist to measure an environment, the same dilemma rears its ugly head as with the semantic differential: how does one interpret results? Are the results due to a response to concepts inherent in the adjectives themselves, or to something in the environment? The evidence would seem to point to the former.

Cognitive Maps

The central concept of cognitive mapping is to portray graphically the way people organize environmental spaces in their heads. (See Downs and Stea 1977, 6-7, for a more detailed definition.)

The idea for cognitive maps came from Tolman (1948). Running rats through mazes, he came up with the concept of a cognitive map to explain why rats remembered *places* where things were located rather than directions of travel. He devised clever mazes to demonstrate that rats could find food by orienting toward an external cue such as a light rather than remembering a series of right and left turns.

Downs and Stea (1973, 1977) cover cognitive mapping research in two volumes, and the method has remained an important part of design research since Lynch (1960) popularized its use. The most common form of cognitive mapping is to have a subject draw a map of the area in question, a neighborhood, city, a park, or even a room, and conclude from the map what features of the environment are important in orienting the subject. A variant of cognitive mapping is called *wayfinding,* a field of research concerned with testing out the use of signs and directions in helping people find their way about an environment (Levine 1982).

Figure 3-5 shows an example of a map drawn by a subject for Florence Ladd (1970). She wanted to know how knowledge about the environment (in this case, a neighborhood) was related to age. The assumption was that knowledge of the neighborhood would increase with age, and the method was to compare cognitive maps of younger and older subjects.

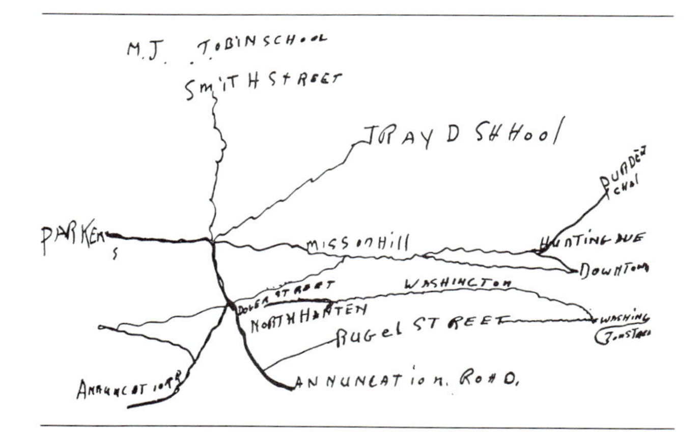

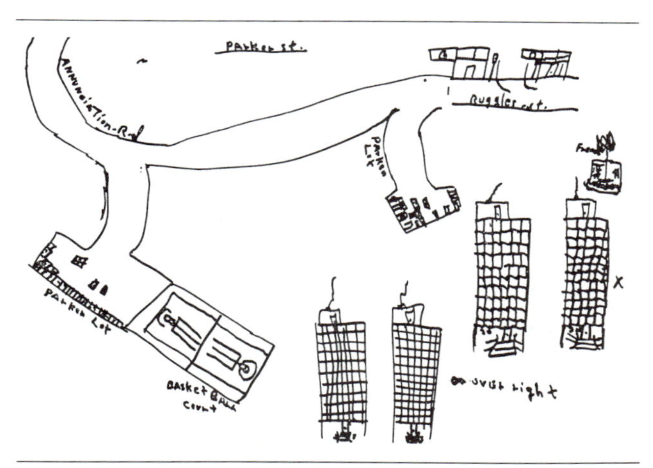

3-5. Ladd's cognitive maps obtained from young blacks. F. Ladd, "Black Youths View Their Environment,"* Environment and Behavior, *Vol. 9, No. 7, pp. 74-99. Copyright © 1970 by Sage Publications, Inc. Reprinted by permission of Sage Publications, Inc.

A problem that is generic to cognitive maps is how to score their details. Lynch's (1960) original categories for a cognitive city map were landmarks, nodes, pathways, barriers, and districts. Objects in categories of this kind can easily be confused, however. Pathways such as interstate highways can also serve as barriers, and district boundaries may be so ill-defined that there is little agreement on where the district begins and ends. These confusions often make for low reliability in scoring cognitive maps. Still another confusion is that many people do not draw their maps well enough to interpret what is meant. Does an "X" indicate a crossroad or a building? Much of the data on cognitive maps are lost.

The only way to resolve this problem is to train the researchers who collect the data to be very clear and consistent on what is to be included, to go over the map with the subject after it is drawn to make certain what each feature represents, and to conduct thorough tests of reliability among the researchers who score the maps.

STANDARDIZED INSTRUMENTS

As discussed above, a standardized instrument is one that has been pre-tested and applied to various populations and found to have a reasonable reliability and validity. College entrance examinations and Graduate Record Examinations are examples of instruments that must be standardized annually. Several instruments that have been more or less standardized for use in environmental design research are discussed below.

MEAP and the Classroom Environment Scale (CES)

Moos (1974) and his colleagues at the social ecology laboratory at Stanford University have developed a series of questionnaires, first called social atmosphere scales, lately more oriented toward both the social and physical environments. The Multiphasic Environmental Assessment Procedures (MEAP) was developed to measure sheltered environments such as nursing homes, residential care facilities, and federally assisted apartment houses. These questionnaires, which have been carefully pre-tested and have validity and reliability data reported, are available in a standardized format with a handbook for users (Lemke et al. 1979). There are five separate scales: a Physical and Architectural Features checklist (PAF), a Policy and Program Information Form (POLIF), a Resident and Staff Information Form (RESIF), a Rating Scale (RS), and a Sheltered Care Environment Scale (SCES). Specific details on each scale can be found in the user's handbook. The Physical and Architectural Features scale is of interest especially to design researchers, however, because it involves a rating of neighborhoods, buildings, community accessibility, and many other details. Figure 3-6 illustrates the Physical and Architectural Features scale (Moos and Lemke 1980, p. 573). The Classroom Environment Scale (CES) is a much shorter instrument directed at school environments of various kinds. A user's handbook (Moos and Trickett 1974) describes the reliability and validity data with normative populations and supplies details on how to administer and score. Figure 3-7 lists some items from this scale.

The importance of these scales from the Social Ecology Laboratory is that they represent a new generation of instruments, not first developed in psychology and then later applied to design research, but designed with full consciousness of environmental influences and with a serious attempt to meet all the standard hurdles of instrument development. Their best use is for global assessments of environments to determine the relative influence of management practices and architectural features.

The Environmental Response Inventory (ERI)

McKechnie (1977) describes the current use of the ERI, an instrument that comprises eight substantive scales and one validity scale. The manual (McKechnie 1974) reports data on validity. Subjects read an item and score it 1 through 5 (1 = strongly agree, 5 = strongly disagree). There are a total of 184 items (fig. 3-8 shows sample items). The ERI has been used in migration studies, family planning, environmental decision making, recreation, and cognition and perception studies (see McKechnie 1977).

The Internal versus External (IE) Scale

The IE scale is also referred to as the locus of control (LOC). Its principal concept is that human beings differ in the belief about whether they con-

	Subscale Descriptions and Item Examples
1. Physical Amenities	Measures the presence of physical features that add convenience, attractiveness, and special comfort. (Is the main entrance sheltered from sun or rain? Are the halls decorated?)
2. Social-Recreational Aids	Assesses the presence of features that foster social behavior and recreational activities. (Is the lounge by the entry furnished for resting and casual conversation? Is there a pool or billiard table?)
3. Prosthetic Aids	Assesses the extent to which the facility provides a barrier-free environment as well as aids to physical independence and mobility. (Can one enter the building without having to use stairs? Are there handrails in the halls?)
4. Orientational Aids	Measures the extent to which the setting provides visual cues to orient the resident. (Is each floor color coded or numbered? Is a map with local resources marked on it available in a convenient public location?)
5. Safety Features	Assesses the extent to which the facility provides features for monitoring communal areas and for preventing accidents. (Is the outside walk and entrance visible from the office or station of an employee? Are there call buttons in the bathrooms?)
6. Architectural Choice	Reflects the flexibility of the physical environment and the extent to which it allows residents options in performing necessary functions. (Does each resident have access to both a bathtub and a shower? Are there individual heating controls?)
7. Space Availability	Measures the number and size of communal areas in relation to the number of residents, as well as size allowances for personal space. (How many special activity areas are there? How large are these areas altogether? What size is the smallest per-person closet area?)
8. Staff Facilities	Assesses the presence of facilities that aid the staff and make it pleasant to maintain and manage the setting. (Are the offices free of distractions from adjacent activities? Is there a staff lounge?)
9. Community Accessibility	Measures the extent to which the community and its services are convenient and accessible to the facility. (Is there a grocery store within easy walking distance? Is there a public transportation stop within walking distance?)

3–6. Moos and Lemke's Physical and Architectural Features (PAF) scale. Copyright © 1984, Rudolf H. Moos, Department of Psychiatry, Stanford University and VA Medical Center, Palo Alto, CA.

trol their environment (internal) or are controlled by it (external). Figure 3–9 shows sample, but not actual, items. This test was developed by Rotter (1966), with much of the population data reported in Lefcourt (1980). The most dramatic use of the IE in design research was by Sims and Bauman (1972), where it was shown that southerners had a more external (fatalistic) orientation toward tornadoes, therefore took fewer precautions, and thus tended to suffer a higher mortality rate from this cause. Schiff (1977) did not replicate the finding but tended to use a different method of assessing IE. The internal orientation seems especially relevant to organization and managerial research. Spector (1982) feels that most research in organizational behavior is relevant only to the internal orientation, while those who are externally oriented react in a different mode than most research

1. Students will put a lot of energy into what they do here.
2. Students in this class will get to know each other really well.
3. This teacher will spend very little time just talking with students.
4. Almost all class time will be spent on the lesson for the day.
5. Students will not feel pressured to compete here.
6. This will be a well-organized class.
7. There will be a clear set of rules for students to follow.
8. There will be very few rules to follow.
9. New ideas will always be tried out here.
10. Students will daydream a lot in this class.

3–7. Classroom Environment Scale items. Reprinted by permission of Consulting Psychologists Press from **Classroom Environment Scale** *by Rudolf H. Moos and Edson J. Trickett, 1974.*

findings to date. The IE has had a long history of useful research and continues to be current.

The Self-anchoring Scale (SAS)

A useful instrument in measuring expectations and reflections about self or external entities such as nations or colleges, the SAS has had wide use in the United States and abroad (Cantril 1965). Figure 3–10 shows the simple visual device by which the subject "anchors" his responses. The instructions below are a model of clarity and have been translated across cultures many times. This, more than any other scale, comes closest to being a true cross-cultural instrument.

The A's and B's of Survival

Friedman and Rosenman (1974) drove a bolt of fear through the heart of many an American male when they linked a personality trait (Type A) to heart disease. They characterized Type A as "an action-emotion complex that can be observed in any person who is aggressively involved in a chronic, incessant struggle to achieve more and more in less and less time . . . " Among the traits associated with Type A are impatience with slowness, trying to do more than one thing at a time, dissatisfaction with life, and competing even in noncompetitive situations. If you feel you must take reading matter to the toilet in order not to waste time you fit into the Type A pattern. Type B, by contrast, is the opposite, not responding to time pressures—in short, just the kind of person most likely to irritate the Type A. There are three in-

Scale Designation and Major Themes	***Sample Items***
PA (Pastoralism). Opposition to land development; concern about population growth, preservation of natural resources, including open space; acceptance of natural forces as shapers of human life; sensitivity to pure environmental experiences; self-sufficiency in the natural environment	Our national forests should be preserved in their natural state, with roads and buildings prohibited. Birth control practices should be accepted by everyone. Natural resources must be preserved, even if people must do without. It is good for man to submit to the forces of nature. The idea of walking into the forest and "living off the land" for a week appeals to me.

3–8. McKechnie's items from the ERI. G. McKechnie, "The Environmental Response Inventory in Application," **Environment and Behavior,** *Vol. 9, No. 2, pp. 255–76. Copyright © 1977 by Sage Publications, Inc. Reprinted by permission of Sage Publications, Inc.*

Scale Designation and Major Themes	***Sample Items***
UR (Urbanism). Enjoyment of high-density living; appreciation of unusual and varied stimulus patterns of the city; interest in cultural life; enjoyment of interpersonal richness and diversity	I would enjoy riding in a crowded subway. I like the variety of stimulation one finds in the city. The cultural life of a big city is very important to me. Cities bring together interesting people.
EA (Environmental adaptation). Modification of the environment to satisfy needs and desires and to provide comfort and leisure; opposition to governmental control over private land use; preference for highly designed or adapted environments; use of technology to solve environmental problems; preference for stylized environmental details	A person has a right to modify the environment to suit his needs. There should [not] be a law against anyone owning more than a thousand acres of land. I like to go to shopping centers where everything is in one place. Making rain by artificially "seeding" clouds is a great technological advance. I like crystal chandeliers.
SS (Stimulus seeking). Interest in travel and exploration of unusual places; enjoyment of complex and intense physical sensations; breadth of interests	I would enjoy traveling around the world on a sailing ship. I like to ride on roller coasters. I like experimental art. I would enjoy driving a racing car. Alleys are interesting places to explore.
ET (Environmental trust). General environmental openness, responsiveness, and trust; competence in finding one's way about the environment vs. fear of potentially dangerous environments; security of home; fear of being alone and unprotected	Sometimes I am afraid of too much stimulation—from sounds, colors, odors, etc. [rejected]. I shudder at the thought of finding a spider in my bed [rejected]. I feel most secure when I am working around the house [rejected]. I would be afraid to live in a place where there were no people nearby [rejected]. I often have trouble finding my way around a new area [rejected].
AN (Antiquarianism). Enjoyment of antiques and historical places; preference for traditional vs. modern design; aesthetic sensitivity to man-made environments and to landscape; appreciation of cultural artifacts of earlier eras; tendency to collect objects for their emotional significance	Modern buildings are seldom as attractive as older ones. I enjoy browsing in antique shops. I am quite sensitive to the "character" of a building. It would be fun to own some old-fashioned costumes. I enjoy collecting things that most people would consider junk.
NP (Need for privacy). Need for physical isolation from stimuli; enjoyment of solitude; dislike of neighboring; need for freedom from distraction	There are often times when I need complete silence. I am happiest when I am alone. I get annoyed when people drop by without warning. I am easily distracted by people moving about.
MO (Mechanical orientation). Interest in mechanics in its various forms; enjoyment in working with one's hands; interest in technological processes and basic principles of science; appreciation of the functional properties of objects.	I enjoy tinkering with mechanical things. I would enjoy the work of an architect. I usually save spare nuts and bolts. I would like to work with computers. I like things that have precision parts.
CO (Communality). A validity scale, tapping honest, attentive, and careful test-taking attitude; response to items in statistically modal manner.	I like to visit historic places. As a child, I was taught respect for all living things. I have vivid memories of where I lived as a child. Traveling is not really worth the effort [rejected]. I seldom pay attention to what I eat [rejected].

Figure 3–8 continued

I more strongly believe that:	*OR*
Promotions are earned through hard work and persistence.	Getting promoted is really a matter of being a little luckier than the next guy.
In my experience I have noticed that there is usually a direct connection between how hard I study and the grades I get.	Many times the reactions of teachers seem haphazard to me.
The number of divorces indicates that more and more people are not trying to make their marriages work.	Marriage is largely a gamble.
When I am right I can convince others.	It is silly to think that one can really change another person's basic attitudes.
In our society a man's future earning power is dependent upon his ability.	Making a lot of money is largely a matter of getting the right breaks.
If one knows how to deal with people, they are really quite easily led.	I have little influence over the way other people behave.
In my case the grades I make are the results of my own efforts; luck has little or nothing to do with it.	Sometimes I feel that I have little to do with the grades I get.
People like me can change the course of world affairs if we make ourselves heard.	It is only wishful thinking to believe that one can really influence what happens in society at large.
I am the master of my fate.	A great deal that happens to me is probably a matter of chance.
Getting along with people is a skill that must be practiced.	It is almost impossible to figure out how to please some people.

3–9. I-E example items. Reprinted with permission from **Psychology Today** *Magazine. Copyright © 1971, American Psychological Association.*

struments that measure Type A: the Structured Interview of Rosenman (1978); the Jenkins Activity Survey (Jenkins et al. 1971); and the Framingham Type A Scale (Haynes et al. 1980). The Framingham Scale is the shortest, having only ten items, and is not equivalent to the other scales. Despite all the studies of Type A behavior (Haynes et al. 1980), it is still not clear exactly how to define and measure it. Even so, this type of behavior shows great potential for being exacerbated by environmental influences. For example, future angina patients indicate on the Jenkins Activity Survey that they are reactive to environmental stimulation and frustration. In the Medalie and Goldbourt (1976) study of thirteen thousand Israeli males, angina patients showed greater reactivity to environmental stress.

As is typical of most psychological concepts, it is now being recognized that "Type A" is multidimensional and not yet adequately measured by current methods (Haynes et al. 1980). In any case, this concept is one of the many new measures linking personal behavioral attributes to environmental variables. Eventually it should be possible to prescribe less Type-A-exacerbating environments and/or environments that will encourage more Type B behavior. Obviously, these environments will deemphasize time constraints and production orientations.

Another example of person–environment mea-

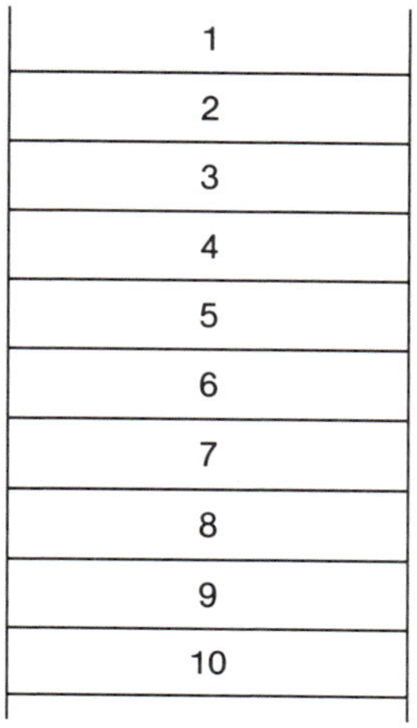

1
2
3
4
5
6
7
8
9
10

Instructions
Here is a picture of a ladder. Suppose we say that the top of the ladder (*pointing*) represents the best possible life for you and the bottom (*pointing*) represents the worst possible life for you.

A. Where on the ladder (*moving finger rapidly up and down the ladder*) do you feel you personally stand at the present time? Step number ________

B. Where on the ladder would you say you stood five years ago? Step number ________

C. And where do you think you will be on the ladder five years from now? Step number ________

3–10. Cantril's self-anchoring ladder.

sures is Petrie's discovery (1967) of *augmenters* and *reducers*. An augmenter is a person who consistently enhances, or increases, incoming stimulation, whereas a reducer diminishes or decreases stimulation. The implications of responses to environments are obvious. Augmenters can take less noise, crowding, and so forth. The usual problems of definition exist (Herzog and Weintraub 1982). For example, augmenters are usually defined by their tendency to overestimate the thickness of a board. This may not always occur, however; their estimates may be accurate.

Twenty Questions

The Who-Am-I test remains a stable item in the repertoire of paper and pencil instruments. Developed by Kuhn and McPartland (1954), this instrument was used by Garretson (1962) to match the way students relate with types of college environments. The Who-Am-I uses four basic types: A is the individual who defines the self by physical attributes, B is the person who relates mostly with social structures, C is the type who relates through desires, and D is not clear how he relates to anything. Figure 3–11 shows the scale with instructions, and figure 3–12 defines the types more comprehensively.

Satisfaction Scales

The most comprehensive scales in terms of measuring how biological drives relate to satisfaction with environmental locations were developed by Maynard Shelly (1969). Figure 3–13 shows Shelly's questionnaires for pleasant and unpleasant experiences. Basically, Shelly discovered that people tend to use the environment in two fundamental ways—as places of increasing arousal versus places of decreasing arousal, a sort of resting versus excitation polarity, with all environments on a continuum from one extreme to the other.

NONSTANDARDIZED TECHNIQUES

Many nonstandardized instruments exist. Sommer's Evaluator Cookbook (1971), Spindler and Spindler's Instrumental Activities Inventory (1965), and Kaplan's Environmental Preference Questionnaire (EPQ) (1977) are just a few of the many in the literature, and more are being created in what seems to be a daily progression.

There are twenty numbered spaces on this sheet. Just write twenty different things about yourself in the spaces. Do not worry about how important they are or the order you put them in. Just write the first twenty answers you think of to the question "Who am I?"

1.	______	11.	______
2.	______	12.	______
3.	______	13.	______
4.	______	14.	______
5.	______	15.	______
6.	______	16.	______
7.	______	17.	______
8.	______	18.	______
9.	______	19.	______
10.	______	20.	______

3–11. The Who-Am-I test.

FOUR WAYS IN WHICH PEOPLE DEFINE AND ANCHOR THEMSELVES TO THEIR ENVIRONMENTS

Category A

Some responses of many respondents (and many responses of some respondents) identify the self in terms of physical attributes and other information of the kind commonly found on identity cards, drivers' licenses, and the like. This kind of statement is illustrated by such examples as "I am blond," "I am five feet, seven inches tall," "I live at 1709 Elm Street," or "I live in Xville." Statements of this kind provide identification without suggesting anything about social behavior, since they refer to a more concrete level than that on which social interaction ordinarily is based. They constitute the *A* category of response. They contain information about the self that can be validated with a mirror, a yardstick, or a scale, that is, without social interaction. One can determine telephone number or home address from a directory without involving another person in the validation procedure. This is not to say, of course, that identifications in these terms do not refer to socially useful categories, but only that they do not imply any particular interactive context or any particular behavior in such contexts.

Category B

The *B* category used in the analysis of responses to the twenty-statements problem differentiates statements that imply involvement in more or less explicitly structured social situations. This category contains references to sta-

3–12. Instructions for scoring the Who-Am-I test.

tuses that are socially defined and can be socially validated. The identifications of self placed in this positional category are illustrated by such statements as "I am a father," "I am a bricklayer," "I am a college graduate," "I am a home owner," and the like. Statements placed in this category imply an interactive context and refer to positions that depend on performance in defined social contexts for their establishment and maintenance. It also can be said of statements in this category that they imply norms for the behavior of the person who identifies himself in this way and that they permit rather specific predictions about social behavior.

Category C

The *C* category of self-identifying statements includes those that are abstract enough to transcend specific social situations. They describe styles of behavior that the respondent attributes to himself. This category of *situation-free* styles of behavior is exemplified by such statements as "I am a happy person," I am economical," "I like good music," "I like to drink socially," "I dislike hypocrites," and so on. Statements in this category of action responses can also be characterized by the fact that they do not pin the respondent down to specific behaviors but leave him free to behave in various ways in various situations while maintaining his style. Viewed as a basis for prediction, action statements support predictions about the manner in which a person will behave but not about the contexts in which he will behave.

Category D

The *D* category of identifications of the self consists of statements that are so comprehensive in their references that they do not lead to socially meaningful differentiation of the person who makes the statement. Said another way, these kinds of statements are so vague that they lead to no reliable expectations about behavior, for example, "I'm a thinking individual," "I am a person who wishes the best for everyone." This category also includes statements that are offered as replies to the twenty-statements problem but which, in fact, deny the question. This kind of reply is exemplified by such statements as "People are not trustworthy." The internalized *others* implicit in *D* statements about the self are transcendental ("the cosmos" or "mankind"), rather than "generalized" in the Meadian sense, and float beyond the possibility of consensual validation or even verifiable communication.

Although the *D* category is necessarily defined negatively, since it subsumes statements which by definition transcend consensual validation, it is worth noting that it is *not* a residual category in the sense that statements that do not fall in categories *A, B,* or *C* are collected in *D.*

Viewed together, the four categories of self-identifying statements represent a spectrum that runs from conceptions of the self as a physical structure in time and space (category *A*), through conceptions of the self as existing in social structures (category *B*) and as a social interactor somewhat abstracted from social structures (category *C*), to conceptions of the self abstracted from physical being, from social structure, and from social interaction (category *D*). The letters used to designate the categories reflect the logical order of successive abstractions that is implicit in this conceptualization, and at the same time avoid any inferences about "goodness" or "badness," which more descriptive designations might invite.

Figure 3–12 continued

CONCLUSION

How can the reader reach a resolution of this bewildering and complex array of choices, especially when each choice is fraught with so many cautions? The most usual approach is to attempt a convergence of results by using several methods. But the Danford and Willems and the Daniel and Ittelson controversies cannot be overlooked, and the researchers must continually strive for discriminant as well as convergent validity. It is no longer possible to be content just because several methods agree. The question now is: have you measured a true response to an environment, or only responses to verbal concepts?

PLEASANT AND UNPLEASANT EXPERIENCE

For Pleasant Experience

Everyone has some experiences that are much more pleasant than others. We want you to think of one place where you recently had a pleasant experience. This experience may have been at a party, at a club, in your own house, a friend's house, at a lake, etc. It is not important where it occurred. This experience may have taken place when you were alone, with one other person, or with many others. It is not important how many others were present. The only important thing is that you think of one experience that was pleasant for you. We are not interested in what the experience was. We just wish you to answer questions about it. Remember to think of only *one* pleasant time that occurred in *one* place.

1. How many people, not including yourself, were present at the place where you had this experience?
   1. None
   2. One
   3. Two
   4. 3 to 5
   5. 6 to 10
   6. 11 to 20
   7. 21 to 50
   8. More than 50

2. How many people did you meet for the first time at the place where you had this experience?
   1. None
   2. One
   3. 2 or 3
   4. 4 to 6
   5. 7 to 10
   6. 11 to 15
   7. More than 15

3. Was this experience a new experience for you?
   1. No.
   2. Somewhat new
   3. Yes

4. Did you move around a lot (such as frequently walking from one place to another) at the place you had this experience?
   1. No
   2. Somewhat
   3. Yes

5. Did this experience involve your work (occupation)?
   1. No
   2. Somewhat
   3. Yes

6. Did this experience involve your family?
   1. No
   2. Somewhat
   3. Yes

3–13. Shelly's satisfaction scale items.

7. Did this experience involve old friends?
1. No
2. Somewhat
3. Yes

8. How long did this experience last?
1. Less than one hour
2. Several hours
3. 2 or 3 days
4. About a week
5. Longer than a week

9. Did anything unusual happen at this place?
1. No
2. Somewhat
3. Yes

10. Was this place noisy?
1. No
2. Somewhat
3. Yes

11. Was there music?
1. No
2. A little
3. Yes

12. Was there dancing?
1. No
2. A little
3. Yes

13. Was food available?
1. No.
2. A little
3. Yes

14. Did you engage in (participate in) activities at the place you had the pleasant experience?
1. No
2. A little
3. Yes

15. Did you talk a great deal?
1. No
2. Somewhat
3. Yes

16. Did you have something to do with (converse with) people of the opposite sex?
1. No
2. Somewhat
3. Yes

17. Did the experience involve using something new?
1. No
2. Somewhat
3. Yes

(*continued*)

Figure 3–13 continued

18. Do you often go to the place where you had the experience?
1. No
2. Sometimes
3. Yes

19. Have you had pleasant experiences at this place before?
1. No
2. A few
3. Yes

20. Were many of your relatives present at the place you had the experience?
1. No
2. A few
3. Yes

21. Were most of the people present between 16 and 30 years old?
1. No
2. A few
3. Yes

22. Did the experience involve spending money?
1. No
2. A little
3. Yes

23. Was there anything to drink available?
1. No
2. A little
3. Yes

24. Have you had unpleasant experiences at this place before?
1. No
2. A few
3. Yes

25. Were the others present very active (moving around a lot or talking loudly)?
1. No
2. A few
3. Yes

For Unpleasant Experience

All of us also have had unpleasant experiences. We are interested in what is an unpleasant experience for you. Just as you were asked to think of a pleasant experience, I want you to think of one recent unpleasant experience. Again, we are not interested in *what* it was but in certain questions about it. Remember to keep thinking about only *one* unpleasant time that occurred in *one* place.

1. How many people, not including yourself, were present at the place where you had this experience?
1. None
2. One
3. Two
4. 3 to 5
5. 6 to 10
6. 11 to 20
7. 21 to 50
8. More than 50

Figure 3–13 continued

2. How many people did you meet for the first time at the place where you had this experience?
    1. None
    2. One
    3. 2 or 3
    4. 4 to 6
    5. 7 to 10
    6. 11 to 15
    7. More than 15
3. Was this experience a new experience for you?
    1. No.
    2. Somewhat new
    3. Yes
4. Did you move around a lot (such as frequently walking from one place to another) at the place you had this experience?
    1. No
    2. Somewhat
    3. Yes
5. Did this experience involve your work (occupation)?
    1. No
    2. Somewhat
    3. Yes
6. Did this experience involve your family?
    1. No
    2. Somewhat
    3. Yes
7. Did this experience involve old friends?
    1. No
    2. Somewhat
    3. Yes
8. How long did this experience last?
    1. Less than one hour
    2. Several hours
    3. 2 or 3 days
    4. About a week
    5. Longer than a week
9. Did anything unusual happen at this place?
    1. No
    2. Somewhat
    3. Yes
10. Was this place noisy?
    1. No
    2. Somewhat
    3. Yes
11. Was there music?
    1. No
    2. A little
    3. Yes

(continued)

Figure 3–13 continued

12. Was there dancing?
1. No
2. A little
3. Yes

13. Was food available?
1. No.
2. A little
3. Yes

14. Did you engage in (participate in) activities at the place you had the experience?
1. No
2. A little
3. Yes

15. Did you talk a great deal?
1. No
2. Somewhat
3. Yes

16. Did you have something to do with (converse with) people of the opposite sex?
1. No
2. Somewhat
3. Yes

17. Did the experience involve using something new?
1. No
2. Somewhat
3. Yes

18. Do you often go to the place where you had the experience?
1. No
2. Somewhat
3. Yes

19. Have you had pleasant experiences at this place before?
1. No
2. A few
3. Yes

20. Were many of your relatives present at the place you had the experience?
1. No
2. A few
3. Yes

21. Were most of the people present between 16 and 30 years old?
1. No
2. A few
3. Yes

22. Did the experience involve spending money?
1. No
2. A little
3. Yes

Figure 3–13 continued

23. Was there anything to drink available?
1. No
2. A little
3. Yes

24. Have you had unpleasant experiences at this place before?
1. No
2. A few
3. Yes

25. Were the others present very active (moving around a lot or talking loudly)?
1. No
2. Somewhat
3. Yes

SATISFACTION SITE RATING SCHEDULE

1. Part of day
1. Morning
2. Afternoon
3. Early evening (5:00 P.M. to 8:00 P.M.)
4. Late evening (after 8:00 P.M.)

2. Size of place occupied in square feet
1. 0–50
2. 51–100
3. 101–200
4. 201–400
5. 401–800
6. 801–1,600
7. 1,601–3200
8. Over 3200

3. Indoors or outdoors
1. Indoors
2. Partly indoors
3. Outdoors

4. Public or private
1. Public
2. Semipublic
3. Private

5. Complexity of visual environment
1. Simple
2. Moderate
3. Complex

6. Level of illumination
1. Very low
2. Moderate
3. Very bright

(continued)

Figure 3–13 continued

7. Relative number of men and women
1. More men than women
2. Equal number of men and women
3. More women than men

8. Median age
1. 0–10
2. 11–20
3. 21–30
4. 31–40
5. Over 40

9. Average duration of stay
1. Less than ¼ hour
2. ¼ to ¾ hour
3. ¾ to 1½ hours
4. 1½ to 2½ hours
5. Over 2½ hours

10. Cleanliness of site
1. Unclean
2. Moderately clean
3. Very clean

11. Music (percentage of time)
1. Less than 20%
2. 20–80%
3. More than 80%

12. Food present
1. Yes
2. No

13. Drink present (other than water)
1. Yes
2. No

14. Level of activity
1. Little activity
2. Moderate activity
3. A great deal of activity

15. Noise level
1. Almost quiet
2. Moderate
3. Very noisy

16. Percentage of people dancing
1. Less than 10%
2. 10–60%
3. More than 60%

17. Crowdedness
1. Most people far from each other
2. Most people neither separated nor close
3. Most people close to each other

Figure 3–13 continued

18. Average number of people present
1. 1–3
2. 4–9
3. 10–22
4. 23–46
5. 47–94
6. Over 94

19. Clustering of people
1. Evenly dispersed
2. Some in clusters
3. Clustered

20. Modal size of groups
1. Alone
2. Pairs
3. Triplets or more

21. Rate of movement around site
1. Few or none walking around site
2. Several walking around site
3. Many walking around site

22. Percentage of people talking
1. Less than 5%
2. 5–40%
3. More than 40%

23. Percentage of time those who talked engaged in conversation
1. Less than 20%
2. 20–80%
3. More than 80%

24. Physical contact (touching, holding, etc.)
1. Very little
2. Moderate
3. A great deal

25. Gesturing
1. Very little
2. Moderate
3. A great deal

26. Laughing
1. Very little
2. Moderate
3. A great deal

27. Number of people entering per half-hour
1. 1–3
2. 4–9
3. 10–22
4. 23–46
5. 47–94
6. Over 94

(*continued*)

Figure 3–13 continued

28. Number of people leaving per half-hour
1. 1–3
2. 4–9
3. 10–22
4. 23–46
5. 47–94
6. Over 94

29. Focus of attention
1. Most people focused on several things (no major focus)
2. About half focused on one thing or most focused on few things
3. Most people focused on one thing

Figure 3–13 continued

Finally, no researcher in the field of environmental research can achieve competency without a continually growing file of methods that work in specific environments. Such an archive is the most powerful tool at the professional's disposal. Without it, each project becomes a painful process of reinventing the wheel. With a carefully collected archive, however, any researcher can save time searching for instruments and improve measurably with each new project.

APPENDIX: THE SEMANTIC DIFFERENTIAL

The semantic differential is the most widely used instrument in the study of subject responses to architectural stimuli. Craik (1968), Hershberger (1972), Collins (1971), and Seaton and Collins (1972) are only a sampling of the more comprehensive studies using this instrument. Because of its popularity, the semantic differential has gained a certain acceptance that has resulted in uses for which it was never intended and in applications that are misleading.

Although many methodological cautions could be made about semantic differential use, it seems that in environmental studies, in which the stimulus is nonverbal and the responses are not often based on language sampling, there are nine problem areas:

1. A common failure to realize that the semantic differential measures connotative as opposed to denotative meaning, and the sometimes unfortunate confounding of the two
2. The problem of ambiguity of reference in the presentation of complex stimuli
3. A lack of representativeness of scales as they naturally appear in the language
4. Representativeness of the population to be studied
5. Representativeness of the architectural environments to be studied
6. Representativeness of media through which environments are shown to subjects
7. Confusion of response modes among new and habitual modes of behavior
8. Overemphasis on orthogonality in factors
9. Ambiguity of derived factors

Problem 1. Osgood, Suci, and Tannenbaum (1957, 290) state: "The semantic differential taps the connotative aspects of meaning more immediately than the highly diversified denotative aspects.'' But what do connotative and denotative aspects mean? Allport (1955) defines denotative meaning as being that with which we can come in contact. Nouns are denotative. They define objects we can touch, smell, taste, and see. Adjectives, on the other hand, are not denotative—they connote objects. Their meaning is secondary to the object, which is primary. But how does this relate to a study of the environment? Very simply, it means that the researcher must be sure of the kind of meaning he wants and the use of meaning he has in mind when presenting a stimulus. It is clear that the semantic differential is more likely to measure the emotive reaction to or the feeling about an architectural space than its usual meaning. Given the same architectural stimulus, a subject responding in denotative fashion would say, ''That's a house,'' while a subject responding in connotative fashion might say, ''It's warm, soft, small, and cozy.'' Given that people are usually aware of the differences between houses, churches, and factories, it might seem easy to pass off the importance of denotative meaning. But when the stimuli become highly ambiguous, the unfamiliarity, the inability to place the object into a familiar category, results in semantic chaos. This happened when nonartists judged abstract art, for example (Osgood, Suci, and Tannenbaum 1957).

Hence denotative meaning seems to delimit connotative meaning, and this has considerable importance if one wants to present, say, highly unconventional designs whose form and function are not clear to the average subject. The researcher can never relax in assuming what is clear for the subject. For example, on my own first extensive presentation of stimulus words to subjects for semantic differential measurement (Bechtel 1962), there was a denotative confusion that produced a semantic storm. When presented with the stimulus word ''China,'' just enough subjects felt it denoted crockery to conflict with those who felt it denoted a country in Asia, markedly influencing results.

And if denotative confusion can arise around a word like China, consider the possible confusions that may accompany the presentation of a total environment. Thus, although the intention of the semantic differential is to measure connotative aspects of a stimulus, unless the denotative aspect is consistently perceived as the same by the subjects, the results will be both unreliable and invalid.

Let us take a common example of semantic differential rating—the house. A simple design to one subject may denote a vacation house, to another a low-income subsidized house, and to still another a rural house. The semantic differential ratings of these three interpretations could be quite different—but because of denotative, not connotative, meanings. In short, the researcher must present a stimulus for which there is very high agreement on denotative meaning before he can measure with confidence the connotative meaning it evokes.

Problem 2. Related to, but not the same as, problem 1 is the reference point within the stimulus. When researchers present a stimulus in the design realm, they often assume that the subject responds to the whole stimulus rather than some part of it. This is an assumption that has not been tested, and it is again a likely source for semantic confusion. For example, to turn to our house stimulus, it may be quite likely that some subjects react to the amount of window space (or lack of it) while others are intrigued by the slope of the roof, and still others (followers of Wright, perhaps) by the way it fits into the contour of the landscape.

Obviously, as the chances for this kind of confusion are increased, the more complex the presentation stimulus becomes; yet it would also seem extremely important for the designer to know what aspects of the design the subjects are responding to most.

Problem 3. Semantic space, as it has been defined by well over 1,000 studies (Heise 1969), seems to have three basic dimensions: evaluation, power, and activity (EPA). These dimensions are actually a part of the structure of language itself, and they seem to exist in a fixed ratio to one another. Miron states:

> Put in terms of meaning, our language (and most interestingly, other languages as well) exhibits more Evaluative than Potency synonyms and, in turn, more Potency than Activity synonyms. Accordingly, the variation observed in natural language qualification predicts the Evaluation, Potency, Activity factor order [but see Osgood's (1971) rebuttal]. But this naturalistic condition may be grossly distorted if equal numbers of scales are used to represent the "normal" factor prominences, especially when the number of concepts being rated is small. [1972, 319]

What Miron is saying is that to be truly representative when concepts in language are being rated by semantic differentials, the scales should emulate the E–P–A ratio found in the language structure by having roughly twice as many evaluative synonyms as power and twice as many power as activity.

Of course, when substituting architectural stimuli for language concepts, as Collins (1969) and Hershberger (1972) have recognized, the semantic dimensions must be reestablished. Probably the process should be much like those begun by Tucker (1955) in attempting to establish the semantic dimensions for painting. Osgood, Suci, and Tannenbaum (1957, 290) expect that visual stimuli like painting and other forms of art will have far more complex semantic dimensions than language. And, indeed, Hershberger (1972) relates some sixteen dimensions derived by seven researchers using architectural stimuli. But we have no assurance that these researchers all tried to obtain *representative* scales as they occur naturally in the language. Furthermore, as in Tucker's (1955) study showing differences between artists and nonartists, where are the naturally occurring scales that separate the way designers react to architectural spaces as opposed to nondesigners? Designers have a highly specific language when referring to design elements, and it is altogether likely that they would be highly polarized and more heavily weighted in the evaluative dimension than nondesigners.

Although the work of Hershberger (1972), Craik (1968), Collins (1971), and Seaton and Collins (1972) provides the beginnings of building a semantic response space to architectural stimuli, their work suffers from a lack of the representativeness of scales. Thus the factors they derived may suffer from the criticism that Miron (1972) gives, that is, failure to use the scales in the same ratio as they occur in the language, as well as using too few concepts (objects) to be rated.

Problem 4. It has been pointed out (Higbee and Wells 1972) that the use of college sophomores as subjects in social psychological experiments has increased, despite the fact that many authorities (McGuire 1967; Sears and Abeles 1969) hoped for and predicted a trend toward more representative populations. In the architectural research world, the tendency to use the available university population is equally compulsive. However, except for university buildings, the students represent building users even less than they represent adequate and relevant populations for social psychological experiments. The elderly, who constitute a population of 28,000,000 in the United States, continue to be vastly underrepresented in these studies; along with other persons who may have handicaps or special requirements in environmental adaptation, they are estimated to total 40,000,000, or 20 percent of the total population (Vash 1972).

The relevant population for any architectural environment, however, continues to be the user population. Environments are designed with specific users in mind; these may be students, factory workers, or prisoners. Or, as with public buildings, there may be two populations, the transient public and the resident bureaucrats.

The problem is doubly compounded when the architect wants to be able to tell how people will react to his design without actually building it. The semantic differential seems to be an easy way to get a favorable or nonfavorable response. The design is presented sometimes even to random samples of the population as a whole. But the true user population can never be sampled because they have yet to occupy the building. The result is that user populations are almost never tested and semantic differentials have yet to demonstrate a validity for the prediction of user satisfaction.

Only when a body of information on user population is accumulated will the semantic differential have a chance to be tested for the validity of the purpose for which it is most used.

Problem 5. As Hershberger (1972) states, it would be extremely difficult to obtain a representative sample of architectural environments. Yet if a standardization of semantic space related to architectural environments is ever to be realized, this task must be undertaken someday. Perhaps it need not be so overwhelming if more general architectural principles and architectural styles can be standardized. Collins (1969, 1971) has made a start in attempting to standardize evaluations of architectural environments but has not dealt with the problem of representativeness. It would seem a fair appraisal of the field to say that most researchers have taken the case-study approach and are waiting for a sufficient accumulation of data before attempting any statements representative of all architectural environments.

Problem 6. Seaton and Collins (1972) compared the presentation of environments through various media, such as models, colored slides, black-and-white slides, and viewing the real building. Yet this study did not cover other media, such as television tape or movie film in color and black-and-white. Hershberger (1972) raises the question of whether any media are really adequate to represent the architectural environment. For although a comparison of the view of a real building with slides and models makes a measurement of the visual contact with the stimulus, actual contact with an architectural environment involves many sensory modalities, such as sound, smell, touch, temperature, and adaptation to all these over time (Helson 1964).

The question, then, is not which media of all that have been sampled adequately predict the response to the visual contact with the architectural environment, but the prediction of the ultimate response when the architectural environment is experienced in all its sensory modalities.

Problem 7. Barker (1953) pointed out that a new situation is one in which the subject is easily influenced and easily led. Thus in any new situation, such as being asked to rate a stimulus on a semantic differential, the subject is oversensitive to cues around him. For this reason Rosenthal (1966) and others have discovered that subjects are uncannily sensitive to being influenced by researchers. Likewise, when seeing a building for the first time, they are likely to notice aspects that would go unheeded if they went by it every day. The first time a subject enters a building he is experiencing an exploratory mode of behavior. Thereafter, when he regularly uses the building he is experiencing a habitual mode of behavior (Bechtel 1967). It is the latter mode that is of more importance in evaluating the architectural environment, for it is the habitual use of the building that determines its success or failure. A building cannot be evaluated before it has acquired its habitual patterns of behavior. No semantic differentials have as yet been linked to habit patterns. The closest link has been to semantic impressions of persons seeing a building for virtually the first time.

Problem 8. Miron (1972) criticizes semantic differential studies for their overemphasis on orthogonality of factors. It may be, of course, that many factors occur in oblique (that is, related or correlated) rather than orthogonal (unrelated) relationships. But this, and the next problem, may be an indication that factor analysis itself needs to be reexamined as the sole technique for analyzing semantic differential data.

Problem 9. When it comes to meaning, the meaning of a factor is as much a problem as the meaning of a stimulus or a response. For example, in his list of preferred factors, Hershberger (1972) places the scale *active* within the factor *aesthetic*. Of course, no one questions the high loading of the scale on the factor, but there is a question of why the factor should be called *aesthetic*. When one sees that *exciting* has an even higher loading than *active,* it begins to look as though we may have really uncovered the *activity* factor of Osgood, Suci, and Tannenbaum (1957). But no; *unique, simple,* and *specialized* are also loading fairly high on the same factor, and perhaps the factor could be called *aesthetic* to encompass these various meanings. But what is this? *Strong,* which clearly belongs in a *potency* factor, is also in *aesthetic* and loading about the same on both! How then can the factors be distinguished?

Of course, some of the reasons why these factors may not be clear is Miron's (1972) admonition to use representative scales. Such failures commonly result in confounding. We have no way of knowing how any of these researchers derive their scales, but few, if any, seem to have attended to the representativeness of language.

Possible Solutions to the Problems

The astute observer will notice that solving one or more of the problems may result in resolving one or more of the others. For example, choosing carefully representative scales may also result in orthogonal and/or more clearly labeled factors. An underlying principle beneath all the problems is Brunswik's (1955) probabilistic functionalism. For the semantic differential to tell us something about architectural space, it must approximate the probabilistic occurrences of nature in language, architectural environments, media, and behavior.

The denotative and ambiguous aspects of the stimulus (problems 1 and 2) could probably be ameliorated by Honikman's (1972) suggestion to ask the subject what particular part of the stimulus he is responding to most and then what part is next most salient and so on. In this way, it would become clear whether the denotative meanings were similar and whether subjects were responding to different aspects of the stimulus.

Problems 1 and 2 and others like them tend to cause individual differences to overwhelm the differences between concepts or objects rated. Heise (1969) suggests that the way to help overcome this difficulty is to use means of scales across subjects as data for the correlations rather than raw scores of subjects. Miron (1972) offers the proposition that when means are not used, the factors may be confounded, as in Reed's (1972) study. In any case, these are both important admonitions about the use of the semantic differential.

Problems 3, 4, 5, and 6 deal with representativeness. The failure to represent the natural distribution of language as it relates to architectural environments by choosing equal numbers of scales for each dimension can lead to confounded factors. Likewise, the selection of subjects, media, and environments needs to be as representative as possible. The measurement of the habitual mode of behavior is really an admonition to sample the most representative type of behavior in architectural environments.

The last two problems may be solved by trying new methods of cluster analysis. Tryon and Bailey's (1970) methods use pivotal variables to define clusters, rather than depending on the ingenuity of the researcher to guess underlying dimensions. Furthermore, overlapping variables can be eliminated by preset instructions, producing a much cleaner set of clusters than is obtainable by ordinary factoring. There is the further advantage of being able to classify subjects by their semantic differential scores to determine if any natural grouping scored significantly differently from any other group. Cluster analysis can be used as a test of control groups or a determination of significant individual variation.

Finally, what is the goal of the use of the semantic differential in architectural research? The ideal would be to produce a semantic index that would tell us the connotative meaning of every conceivable architectural configuration. But even if this were done, would we have anything really useful? The semantic differential is quite similar to many attitudinal measures, and one must bear in mind Wicker's reviews (1969, 1971), which show that there are possibly insurmountable obstacles in predicting human behavior from attitudinal measures. And is that not the true goal of semantic differential research, to predict human behavior for any architectural setting? It is well to bear in mind Altman's (1971) remarks at the 1971 American Psychological Association convention that self-report methods are probably not going to be the way to unlock the needed information about behavior in architectural environments, and that direct behavioral observation methods need to be developed for this purpose.

Given then that the researcher recognizes the semantic differential will not predict (nor should be confused with) behavior, what is its proper use in architectural research? Probably Tucker's (1955) study is the best example. Tucker demonstrated that artists and laymen have considerably different semantic dimensions in their responses to modern art. Therefore, the semantic differential could be extremely useful in comparing the architect's associations with, say, his clients or with the user population of a building he is designing. By the same token, it could provide a sensitive measure of architectural education, the goal of which must at least involve the increasing ability to discriminate subtle differences in architectural spaces. A carefully validated semantic differential would provide a good measure of both the quantitative and qualitative success of this goal—and compare teachers with pupils as well.

NOTES

1. *Robust* is a technical term referring to a distribution of scores following the shape of a normal curve.

REFERENCES

American Psychological Association (APA). 1974. *Standards for Educational and Psychological Tests.* Washington, D.C.: American Psychological Association.

Bechtel, R. 1970. The discovery of areas of potential social disturbance in the city. *Sociological Quarterly* 12:114–21.

———. 1975. *Profile of Housing Needs for ARAMCO Employees.* Washington, D.C.: Real Estate Research Corp.

Bechtel, R., C. B. Ledbetter, and N. Cummings. 1980. *Post-Occupancy Evaluation of a Remote Australian Community: Shay Gap, Australia.* Hanover, N.H.: Cold Regions Research and Engineering Laboratory.

Binder, A. 1964. Statistical theory. *Annual Review of Psychology* 15:277–310.

Boring, E. G. 1950. *A History of Experimental Psychology.* 2d ed. New York: Appleton-Century-Crofts.

Cantril, H. 1965. *The Pattern of Human Concerns.* New Brunswick, N.J.: Rutgers Univ. Press.

Danford, S., and E. Willems. 1975. Subjective responses to architecture displays: A question of validity. *Environment and Behavior* 7:486–516.

Daniel, T. 1976. *Prediction of Scenic Quality from Manageable Forest Landscape Features.* Tucson: Univ. of Arizona Press.

Daniel, T., and R. Boster. 1976. *Measuring Scenic Beauty: The SBE Method.* Rocky Mountain Forest and Experimental Station, Fort Collins, Colo.

Daniel, T., and W. Ittelson. 1981. Conditions for environmental research: Reactions to Ward and Russell. *Journal of Experimental Psychology: General* 110:153–57.

Downs, R., and D. Stea. 1973. *Image and Environment.* Chicago: Aldine.

———. 1977. *Maps in Minds.* New York: Harper & Row.

Eysenck, H., and L. Kamin. 1981. *The Intelligence Controversy.* New York: Wiley.

Friedman, M., and R. Rosenman. 1974. *Type A Behavior and Your Heart.* New York: Knopf.

Garretson, W. 1962. Consensual definition of social objects. *Sociological Quarterly* 3:107–13.

Haynes, S., M. Feinleib, and W. Kannel. 1980. The relationship of psychosocial factors to coronary heart disease in the Framingham study III: Eight year incidence of coronary heart disease. *American Journal of Epidemiology* 111:37–50.

Herzog, T., and D. Weintraub. 1982. Roundup time at personality ranch and branding: The elusive augmenters and reducers. *Journal of Personality and Social Psychology* 42:729–37.

Ittelson, W., H. Proshansky, and L. Rivlin. 1970. *Environmental Psychology: Man and His Physical Setting.* New York: Holt, Rinehart, & Winston.

Jenkins, C., S. Zyzanski, and R. Rosenman. 1971. Progress toward validation of a computer-scored test for the Type A coronary-prone behavior pattern. *Psychosomatic Medicine* 33:193–202.

Johnson, O. 1976. *Tests and Measurements in Child Development: Handbook II.* San Francisco: Jossey-Bass.

Kane, R., and R. Kane. 1981. *Assessing the Elderly: A Practical Guide to Measurement.* Lexington, Mass.: Lexington.

Kaplan, R. 1977. Patterns of environmental preference. *Environment and Behavior* 9:195–216.

Kasmar, J. 1970. The development of a usable lexicon of environmental descriptors. *Environment and Behavior,* 153–64.

Kruskal, J., and M. Wish. 1978. *Multidimensional Scaling.* Beverly Hills, Cal.: Sage.

Kuhn, M., and T. McPartland. 1954. An empirical investigation of self attitudes. *American Sociological Review* 19:68–76.

Ladd, F. 1970. Black youths view their environment. *Environment and Behavior* 9(7):74–99.

Lefcourt, H. 1966. Internal vs. external control of reinforcement: A review. *Psychological Bulletin* 65:206–20.

———. 1980. Research on the Focus of Control Concepts. Vols. 1–3. New York: Academic Press.

Lemke, S., R. Moos, B. Mehren, and M. Ganvain. 1979. *Multiphasic Environmental Assessment Procedure (MEAP): Handbook for Users.* Palo Alto, Cal.: Social Ecology Laboratory.

Levine, M. 1982. You-Are-Here maps: Psychological considerations. *Environment and Behavior* 14:221–37.

Lynch, K. 1960. *Image of the City.* Cambridge, Mass.: MIT Press.

McKechnie, G. 1974. *Manual for the Environmental Response Inventory.* Palo Alto, Cal.: Consulting Psychologists.

———. 1977. The Environmental Response Inventory in application. *Environment and Behavior* 9:255–76.

Matthews, K. 1982. Psychological perspectives on the Type A behavior pattern. *Psychological Bulletin* 91:293–323.

Matthiasson, J. 1970. *Resident Perceptions of the Quality of Life in Resource Frontier Communities.* Winnipeg: Center for Settlement Studies, Univ. of Manitoba.

Medalie, J., and U. Goldbourt. 1976. Angina pectoris among 10,000 men. *American Journal of Medicine* 60:910–21.

Mitchell, J., ed. 1983. *Tests in Print III.* Buros Institute of Mental Measurements. Lincoln: Univ. of Nebraska Press.

———. 1985. *The Ninth Mental Measurements Yearbook.*

Buros Institute of Mental Measurements. Lincoln: Univ. of Nebraska Press.

Moos, R. 1974. *The Social Climate Scales: An Overview.* Palo Alto, Cal.: Consulting Psychologists.

Moos, R., and E. Trickett. 1974. *Classroom Environment Scale Manual.* Palo Alto, Cal.: Consulting Psychologists.

Osgood, C., G. Suci, and P. Tannenbaum. 1957. *The Measurement of Meaning.* Urbana, Ill.: Univ. of Illinois Press.

Petrie, A. 1967. *Individuality in Pain and Suffering.* Chicago: Univ. of Chicago Press.

Rosenman, R. 1978. The interview method of assessment of the coronary prone behavior pattern. In *Coronary Prone Behavior,* ed. T. M. Dembroski, S. M. Weiss, J. L. Shields, S. G. Haynes, and M. Feinleib. New York: Springer-Verlag.

Rotter, J. 1966. Generalized expectancies for internal vs. external control of reinforcement. *Psychological Monographs* 80(11): whole no. 609.

Schiff, M. 1977. Hazard adjustment, locus of control, and sensation seeking: Some null findings. *Environment and Behavior* 9:233–54.

Shelly, M., ed. 1969. *Analyses of Satisfaction.* Vol. 1. New York: MSS Educational Publishing Company.

Siegel, S. 1956. *Non-parametric Statistics for the Behavioral Sciences.* New York: McGraw-Hill.

Sims, J., and D. Bauman. 1972. The tornado threat: Coping styles of the North and South. *Science* 176:1386–92.

Sommer, R. 1971. The new evaluator cookbook. *Design and Environment* 2:34–37.

Spector, P. 1982. Behavior in organizations as a function of employee locus of control. *Psychological Bulletin* 91:482–97.

Spindler, G., and L. Spindler. 1965. The instrumental activities inventory: A technique for the study of the psychology of acculturation. *Southwest Journal on Anthropology* 21:1–23.

Starr, N., and S. Danford. 1979. The invalidity of subjective ratings of the physical environment. In *New Directions in Environmental Design Research,* ed. W. Rogers and W. Ittelson.

Tolman, E. 1948. Cognitive maps in rats and men. *Psychological Review* 55:189–200.

Torgerson, Q. 1958. *Theory and Methods of Scaling.* New York: Wiley.

Ward, L., and J. Russell. 1981. The psychological representation of molar physical environments. *Journal of Experimental Psychology: General* 110:121–52.

CHAPTER 4

TRADE-OFF GAMES AS A RESEARCH TOOL FOR ENVIRONMENTAL DESIGN

Ira M. Robinson

Urban simulation games first began to appear in the United States in the early 1960s, and since then, interest in them and their application to a variety of urban problems has grown enormously. Numerous accounts of the design and use of such games have appeared in the popular press and on television, as well as in professional and academic journals. A large number of books, including directories of games that have been actually designed, have appeared, although only a handful have focused specifically on games for urban or environmental design purposes. Two periodicals expressly devoted to the subject of gaming and games have also emerged: *Simulation and Games,* an international journal of theory, design, and research that is published quarterly; and *Simulation/Games/News,* a bimonthly publication containing news about the latest developments in gaming.

Several professional associations—both national and international—that are concerned with games and gaming devote a large proportion of their activities to urban gaming. The National Gaming Council was formed in the mid 1960s, as an outgrowth of a group comprised mainly of military people, and in 1975 this organization was formally incorporated as the North American Simulation and Gaming Association. In 1970, the International Simulation and Gaming Association was formed in West Germany, and since then ISAGA has held its annual meetings all over the world. Establishment of the ISAGA reflected the widespread interest of foreign professionals and academics in gaming, including urban gaming, in various European countries, especially the German Federal Republic, where adaptations have been made of several well-known games developed in the United States, such as Metropolis, Metro, Clug, and Trade-off (Schran 1972).

Most of the early urban simulation games were developed by and for educators in urban studies, city planning, and the social sciences, who wanted a simpler way to convey to their students the complex ideas associated with urban systems—their characteristics and processes. They found that the traditional lecture and seminar mode was inadequate for exploring such complicated and interrelated concepts as land use, budgeting, regulatory systems, citizen participation, and political processes. These educators were also influenced by the then fairly prevalent viewpoint that challenged the traditional normative concept of education, with its emphasis on the transmission of information or "truths," and instead promoted the idea that instruction should be experience-based and involve problem solving, involvement, and "engagement" among learners and between learners and teachers. This interactive and participatory view of education contributed greatly to the acceptance of games in general, and urban games in particular, as a legitimate educational method. The structure of simulation games, with its use of "players" taking on different "roles," which have goals, sets of activities to perform, face constraints on what can be done, and confront different pay-offs (good and bad) as consequences of their actions—and in which there is some semblance of competition, conflict, or counter-interests among the participants—seemed particularly appropriate to an interactive and participatory approach to learning.

Urban simulation games also proved attractive to those who wanted a way to experiment with and adapt the emerging computer technologies and analytical methods, including formal mathematical models, for understanding and managing cities.

The sixties were also the period when citizen participation in decision making and in public planning in particular emerged as an important area of concern. "Games" were seen as a valuable technique for, first, educating citizens as to the complexity of our urban environment and the complexities of decision making in such an environment; and, second, getting citizens involved in the actual decision processes.

As a consequence, urban simulation games have become a widely accepted teaching and training technique complementing more traditional instructional modes and have been used in classrooms at all educational levels (ranging from elementary to post-secondary), and in training seminars, workshops, and conferences. Such games have also been employed by city officials, professional planners, community development experts, citizen groups, and a host of other persons interested in generating public participation in the planning, design, and political decision-making processes. They are used as means of helping to identify problems, formulate solutions, set priorities, implement programs, and react to feedback.

There are today literally hundreds of such games in existence, designed to meet a variety of purposes, and many of them available for purchase through commercial sources in the form of kits, including players' manuals, game materials, and so on—much like Monopoly and other popular parlor games.[1]

As implied in the above discussion, urban simulation games have been developed and used primarily for educational and training purposes, as well as for involving citizens in the planning and design decision-making processes. While the literature on the development and uses of urban games in general and of specific examples of such games often mentions "research and data collection" as another purpose (along with education, training, and public participation), rarely is there any description of either how they have been used, or how they potentially could be used for this purpose. In short, when this writer delved into the matter, carrying out a careful library search as well as corresponding with a number of well-known designers of urban simulation games, he discovered to his surprise that the utility of such games, for social and especially urban or environmental design *research,* has largely been ignored in the various texts and guides on gaming methods.

To be sure, there have been some isolated articles in the broad field of the social sciences containing arguments that games might be useful to the social researcher, but even here, a perusal of the literature reveals disparate ideas about work actually done and little in the way of organized thought outlining or describing modes of utilizing such games for research purposes. Indeed, while some games have been the object *of* research—that is, research aimed at evaluating the supposed advantages of games for education and training purposes (Monroe 1968, Greenblat 1981b), they have not been used *for* research.[2]

This finding is not completely new. A few writers, notably Raser (1969), McFarlane (1971), Schran and Kumpf (1972), and Greenblat (1981a) have reached a similar conclusion; and, as with this writer, deplore the fact that urban simulation games have had so little use as a research tool and that, moreover, little has even been written about their potential for this purpose. Raser (1969) discusses how simulation games might be used for theory building in research. Greenblat (1981a) describes the possible uses of gaming simulations under different "research modes." In particular, she discusses the possible use of certain "frame games," which were originally developed for teaching and training purposes (for example, Impasse?, At Issue!, and the Conceptual Mapping Game[3]) as "questionnaires" to gather system-specification data from experts and nonexperts regarding different urban issues or problems. McFarlane (1971) argues that simulation games possess many advantages over participant observation and traditional social-psychological laboratory methods for purposes of testing hypotheses and collecting social-psychological data, and discusses the nature of these advantages. Except for these few writers and references, however, this writer was unable to find any detailed discussion of the uses of urban simulation games in general for research and only a few actual examples where they have been used for this purpose.

A notable exception to this conclusion is a special type of urban simulation game known as a "trade-off game," whose primary purpose is to identify and quantify (where possible) the trade-off preferences of different groups in a population for various attributes or dimensions of the environment. Most of these games have been developed for research and data collection. Many of them have also been used to stimulate public participation and a few have been developed mainly for this purpose. As demonstrated later in this paper, the information and data derived from such games can be used for research purposes in a variety of planning, design, and decision-making situations.

For the above reasons, the remainder of this chapter deals only with trade-off games, and represents an updating and expansion of the material included in this original version of this paper (Robinson et al. 1975). First, it discusses the concept of trade-offs, and briefly describes the trade-off game method. Second, it describes four fairly recent games that were designed primarily as research tools for identifying the trade-off preferences of different population groups for a variety of environmental attributes or features.[4] Third, it assesses the value and utility of the trade-off game approach, especially as a research tool. Finally, it concludes with a brief discussion of important lessons in designing trade-off games.

THE CONCEPT OF TRADE-OFFS

The term "trade-offs" is being heard more and more often both in the literature and at meetings of the planning and environmental design professions. It is frequently brought up during discussions on identifying community goals, formulating criteria or standards for plans and designs, or evaluating proposed plans, policies, and programs. The increasing concern for environmental quality has underscored the issue of trade-offs in public decision making at all levels of government. Policies to encourage population and economic growth often appear to be in conflict with concurrent programs to improve the environment and both appear at odds with resource redistribution for the poor and disadvantaged. In these areas it is increasingly clear that compromises must be made, hopefully without causing undue harm to any of the parties involved. In general, the concept of trade-offs implies compromises, exchanges, or substitutability between and among multiple—often mutually exclusive—goals; it reflects the need to give up or sacrifice something in order to gain something.

Underlying the concept of trade-offs is the recognition that resources are limited and that, unfortunately, not all needs and desires can be met. Choices must be made and priorities have to be established. Realistically, we cannot always have our cake and eat it, too. Trade-offs are made by individuals and families to cope with the constraints of everyday life—finding a place to live, deciding what things to purchase, where to go on a vacation, and so on. For example, when choosing a place to live, a family is often faced with the decision as to whether to give up (that is, trade off) a desire for open space, privacy, and spacious housing in order to have ready access to public transportation and downtown amenities. Similarly, governments must do the same: when faced with sociopolitical and economic constraints, public decision makers are required to make trade-offs in deciding how to allocate resources. Today, choices before governments are difficult, full of unknowns, and lacking in some of the optimism and idealism of an earlier era. It is increasingly evident, for example, that economic prosperity, environmental improvement, speedy private transportation, energy conservation, and low-density suburban living are not completely compatible goals. In deciding on trade-offs, public decision makers must consider the costs and benefits of each alternative.

Many of the trade-offs faced by decision makers include either/or situations. In land use planning, for example, it is seldom possible to use the same piece of land for two or more different purposes, and the choice of one purpose means that the possible advantages of the other purpose or purposes have been traded off. Frequently, however, decisions involve working out what portion of each goal or preference can be satisfied. For example, planners, environmental designers, and decision makers are often faced with the decision as to how much environmental pollution might be permitted in order to achieve a certain number of new jobs; or how high residential densities should be permitted to rise in inner city neighborhoods (in order, for example, to minimize energy consumption) before the level of traffic congestion in these areas becomes intolerable.

In deciding the trade-offs of various alternatives, it is important for both individuals and governments to consider the real costs of each one. Choosing one alternative over another involves certain direct costs as well as indirect costs in the form of benefits foregone by not selecting some other alternative. These costs of a trade-off are also referred to as "opportunity costs." In short, every time individuals and governments face such a choice, they must make trade-offs and bear certain opportunity costs.

In Western democratic societies, especially at the local governmental level, public policy decision makers, whether they are aware of trade-offs or not, have traditionally allocated resources to meet community or local needs on the basis of priorities established through bureaucratic routine, conventional wisdom, "fair share" judgments, precedent, professional norms and standards, or bargaining (Robinson et al. 1975). Increasingly, though, it has come to be recognized that the planner's, designer's, and decision maker's perceptions of community preferences may be at variance with the public's, and that there is a need to obtain citizen "input" to assist in the development of policies and goals for the provision of public services, allocation of land, and a host of other public functions and programs.

In response to the widely accepted view that the public ought to participate in defining community preferences and in allocating public resources to meet community needs, planners and designers have been seeking ways and means of discovering the trade-off preferences of different groups in the population, when they are faced with limited resources and conflicting or incompatible—but equally desirable—goals. With such information available ahead of time, decision makers would be in a better position to avoid later costly mistakes. One of the innovative approaches developed for this purpose is the "trade-off game." In the following section, the underlying method used in trade-off games is briefly described.

TRADE-OFF GAME METHOD

Trade-off games should perhaps better be termed "semi-projective" gaming simulations; indeed, they are not "games" in the literal sense of this word as it is generally used in the literature on gaming. In these games there is essentially only one "player," the respondent being interviewed or playing the game. (There may, however, be several players who can form teams.) Moreover, the result of the player's decision does not cause a new situation to which he must respond and make another decision. Each is a game only in the sense that the respondent's decision depends on the interviewer's actions or questions. However, the interviewer's action is independent of the respondent's decision. The constraints on the player's decisions do not come from the actions of an opponent, but are built into the game. Although the choices are made individually by the player, it is possible to repeatedly alter these choices until some sort of "compromise" is reached. It is perhaps this feature that gives some justification for calling it a "game." In each game trade-offs occur in which the player incurs a loss to achieve a greater gain. The result is that the player, with conflicting goals, makes "moves" or decisions that ultimately help him to win.[5]

The basic method of most trade-off games is that players (respondents) are confronted with a number of environmental attributes (such as public services, housing attributes, environmental goods,[6] and public facilities), each with several possible quality levels. Typically, each attribute level has an associated cost, defined in terms of dollars, points, or some other value. Respondents are allocated a budget (or some other constraint mechanism) and are allowed to "purchase" the quality levels they desire. However, by making the total budget insufficient to permit purchase of the highest (or "best") levels of all attributes or by adding a set of constraints, the players are forced to make trade-offs. Players are permitted to iteratively reallocate their budgets among the alternative attribute levels until they achieve the most satisfactory combination, or "optimum mix."

The trade-off game method is related to the economist's theory of "utility," which tries to explain consumer choice. To the economist, trade-offs are defined as "marginal rates of substitution between commodities" (Houthakker 1961) and are conceptually related to the indifference-curve construct, which in turn is a surrogate for measuring "utility" (satisfaction) as a way of describing individual preferences. In brief, the economist's theory of utility states that a choice or trade-off between any two dimensions or attributes is dependent upon the cost and utility associated with various quantities of each dimension. The ratio of the costs of the dimensions, together with a given level of income, determines a budget function. The process of trading off to obtain an optimal mix of the dimensions is known as utility maximization. The question is: for a given budget, what combination of dimensions or attributes will yield the greatest level of satisfaction? Economists answer this by developing indifference curves; that is, each level of utility is viewed as a locus of points representing equal levels of satisfaction, with points of tangency between budget functions and the indifference curves yielding maximum levels of satisfaction for a given budget.

In theory, application of this concept is fairly straightforward. In practice, however, in matters of public policy, planning, and design, especially with respect to environmental attributes or environmental goods (such as aesthetics or lack of pollution), it is more difficult to apply this concept. Environmental goods are extremely difficult to cost out since so many of them are subjectively perceived and evaluated—it is not a matter of simply determining the "exchange rates" between, say, apples and oranges. Also, environmental dimensions such as privacy and lot size are neither truly independent nor dependent, but interactive, and thus combined pricing between these two dimensions is either impossible or extremely difficult, even in theory. Further, the planner's and designer's universe of concern does not comprise any single individual, nor only a few environmental attributes, but groups of individuals and many environmental dimensions, each group with (presumably) a different set of preferences. Ultimately the need is therefore to develop something like a "community" (or social welfare) trade-off preference function.

In the following section, four fairly recent trade-off games that were developed to operationalize the concept of trade-off preferences and to derive empirically useful data on users' trade-offs are reviewed. One of the games is concerned with the preferences of the respondents for different public services (in a rural area), another with housing attribute preferences (in a new town), while two deal with environmental elements (one on a university campus and one in a rapidly developing mountain area).[7]

SOME EXAMPLES

Community Preferences for Different Public Services

The first example of a trade-off game reviewed here, to illustrate its versatility in a variety of planning and environmental design situations, is one developed to identify community preferences in rural townships in southern Ontario for different municipal services, where limits on revenue force trade-offs to be made among the services. The game, and its several variations, was designed by researchers at the University of Guelph (Joseph et al. 1982; Smit and Joseph 1982, 1983; Joseph and Smit 1983). The game has been played (as of this writing) in three rural townships in southern Ontario, using the same approach in each township. The results for one of the townships (Erin) are described below, as illustrative of the basic approach and findings.

The trade-off game deals with services supplied to residents of the townships by the municipal and county levels of government and paid for wholly or in part by municipal property taxes. For the services studied (there were thirteen in all, ranging from libraries, recreation, garbage disposal, and fire protection, to roads and education), a survey of government and service agencies provided data on current levels of service, on feasible alternative service levels, and on the associated costs of current and alternative service levels.

A game board was developed, similar in many ways to the one developed early on by Wilson (1967), and to a few described below. For each service the current level is indicated, and the cost of that level, in terms of property tax dollars to the average taxpayer in the township, is represented by colored pegs. Also, for each service an improved level and the associated cost of such an improvement are indicated, and for most services a reduced level and its cost are also presented. (There were no reduced levels for fire and police protection and for county and township roads.) See figure 4-1.

The game was played by a randomly selected sample of the rural township residents. Each respondent examined the game board and identified those services that he or she wished to see improved and those that could be allowed to "deteriorate." The alternative levels on the board indicate the degree of change in a service that could be expected

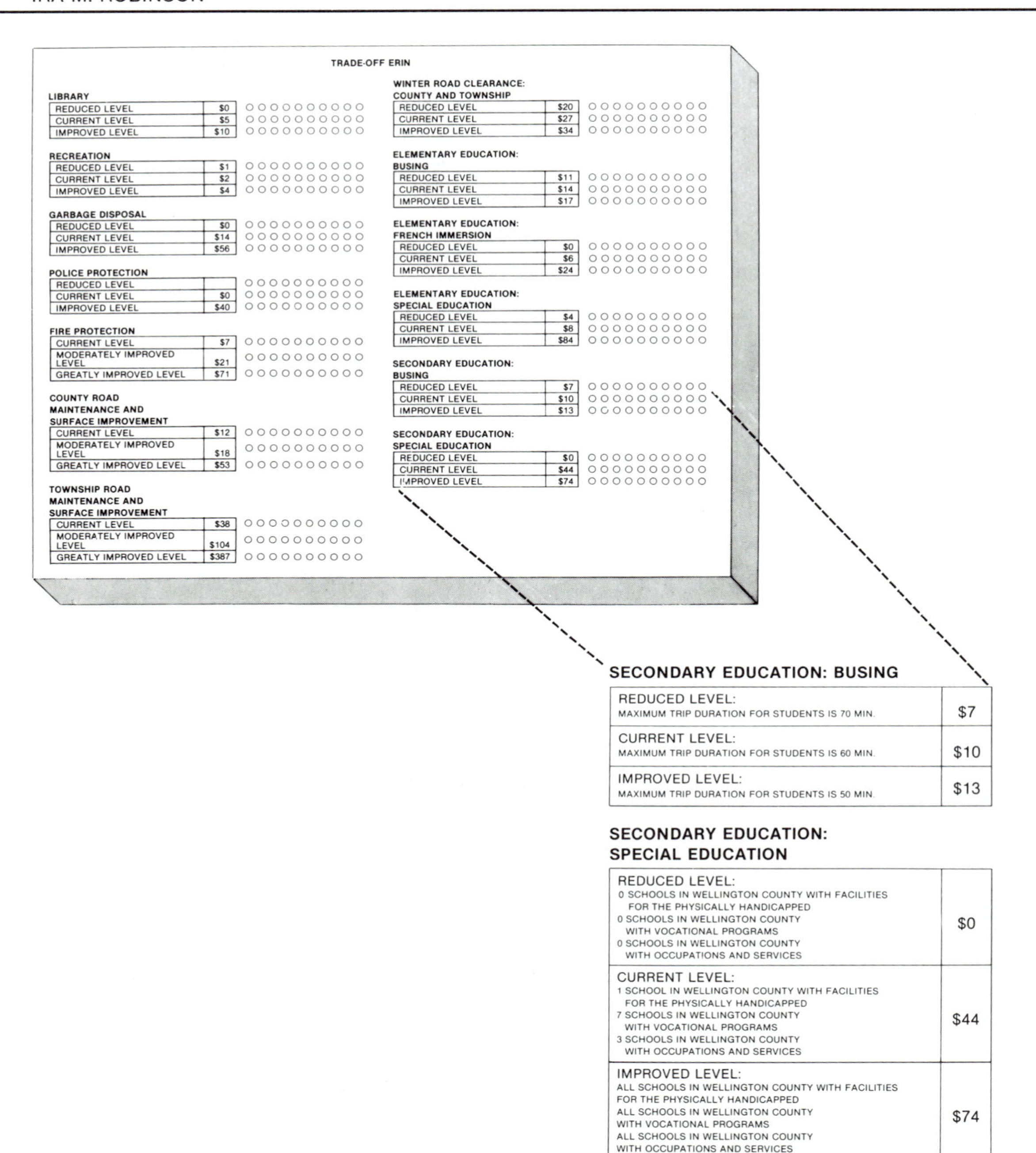

TRADE-OFF ERIN

LIBRARY

REDUCED LEVEL	$0
CURRENT LEVEL	$5
IMPROVED LEVEL	$10

RECREATION

REDUCED LEVEL	$1
CURRENT LEVEL	$2
IMPROVED LEVEL	$4

GARBAGE DISPOSAL

REDUCED LEVEL	$0
CURRENT LEVEL	$14
IMPROVED LEVEL	$56

POLICE PROTECTION

REDUCED LEVEL	
CURRENT LEVEL	$0
IMPROVED LEVEL	$40

FIRE PROTECTION

CURRENT LEVEL	$7
MODERATELY IMPROVED LEVEL	$21
GREATLY IMPROVED LEVEL	$71

COUNTY ROAD MAINTENANCE AND SURFACE IMPROVEMENT

CURRENT LEVEL	$12
MODERATELY IMPROVED LEVEL	$18
GREATLY IMPROVED LEVEL	$53

TOWNSHIP ROAD MAINTENANCE AND SURFACE IMPROVEMENT

CURRENT LEVEL	$38
MODERATELY IMPROVED LEVEL	$104
GREATLY IMPROVED LEVEL	$387

WINTER ROAD CLEARANCE: COUNTY AND TOWNSHIP

REDUCED LEVEL	$20
CURRENT LEVEL	$27
IMPROVED LEVEL	$34

ELEMENTARY EDUCATION: BUSING

REDUCED LEVEL	$11
CURRENT LEVEL	$14
IMPROVED LEVEL	$17

ELEMENTARY EDUCATION: FRENCH IMMERSION

REDUCED LEVEL	$0
CURRENT LEVEL	$6
IMPROVED LEVEL	$24

ELEMENTARY EDUCATION: SPECIAL EDUCATION

REDUCED LEVEL	$4
CURRENT LEVEL	$8
IMPROVED LEVEL	$84

SECONDARY EDUCATION: BUSING

REDUCED LEVEL	$7
CURRENT LEVEL	$10
IMPROVED LEVEL	$13

SECONDARY EDUCATION: SPECIAL EDUCATION

REDUCED LEVEL	$0
CURRENT LEVEL	$44
IMPROVED LEVEL	$74

SECONDARY EDUCATION: BUSING

REDUCED LEVEL: MAXIMUM TRIP DURATION FOR STUDENTS IS 70 MIN.	$7
CURRENT LEVEL: MAXIMUM TRIP DURATION FOR STUDENTS IS 60 MIN.	$10
IMPROVED LEVEL: MAXIMUM TRIP DURATION FOR STUDENTS IS 50 MIN.	$13

SECONDARY EDUCATION: SPECIAL EDUCATION

REDUCED LEVEL: 0 SCHOOLS IN WELLINGTON COUNTY WITH FACILITIES FOR THE PHYSICALLY HANDICAPPED; 0 SCHOOLS IN WELLINGTON COUNTY WITH VOCATIONAL PROGRAMS; 0 SCHOOLS IN WELLINGTON COUNTY WITH OCCUPATIONS AND SERVICES	$0
CURRENT LEVEL: 1 SCHOOL IN WELLINGTON COUNTY WITH FACILITIES FOR THE PHYSICALLY HANDICAPPED; 7 SCHOOLS IN WELLINGTON COUNTY WITH VOCATIONAL PROGRAMS; 3 SCHOOLS IN WELLINGTON COUNTY WITH OCCUPATIONS AND SERVICES	$44
IMPROVED LEVEL: ALL SCHOOLS IN WELLINGTON COUNTY WITH FACILITIES FOR THE PHYSICALLY HANDICAPPED; ALL SCHOOLS IN WELLINGTON COUNTY WITH VOCATIONAL PROGRAMS; ALL SCHOOLS IN WELLINGTON COUNTY WITH OCCUPATIONS AND SERVICES	$74

4–1. The Southern Ontario Public Services trade-off game. From Alun E. Joseph, Barry Smit, Ken Beesley, Public Input into Planning for Municipal Service Provision *(Guelph, Ontario: University School of Rural Planning and Development, 1982).*

with a specified change in tax dollars. These specified levels provide guidelines only; respondents could indicate the changes by smaller or larger amounts. Given these guidelines, each respondent rearranged the pegs to indicate preferred changes in expenditures on services and hence on the levels of service provision.

In this version of the game the total budget (the value of all of the pegs) is "fixed" at the total of the current value of services included in the game, and all the money must be allocated at the end of the game. (As described below, an alternative version of the game permits a variable budget, in which respondents can indicate preferences for decreases or increases in the total property tax and associated overall levels of service provision, as well as trade-offs amongst services.) With a fixed budget, no changes in the total tax bills are permitted, and improvements in services can be achieved only by allowing one or more services to deteriorate—that is, to move to a lower service level, by allocating fewer tax dollars to them. In this way the respondents were forced to consider desired improvements in certain services relative to the cost of such changes. Their preferences were constrained by the budget given to them, just as in the real world, the options available to municipal officials are limited by the municipal budget.

The results from the trade-off game were analyzed in a number of ways:

1. The propensities of respondents to trade-off expenditures on services—that is, the proportion of respondents willing to trade up or trade off—and the amount in dollars
2. The frequency and amount of trade-offs for different services—both improvements sought and reductions sought
3. Comparison of the current and preferred allocations for different services
4. Comparison of the preferred services allocations of users versus nonusers and of long-term versus short-term residents

Figure 4–2 shows the results of the analysis for "2" above. The results of the other analyses are not presented here; the interested reader is referred to the original works. Instead, a special feature of the game, undertaken after the initial game based on a fixed budget, will be described. Following completion of the above-listed types of analysis, the researchers decided that it would be useful to determine whether respondents would prefer to pay more taxes to improve services or would be willing to sacrifice levels of service provision for lower taxes, if given the option. Additionally, would the overall priorities revealed by the game be different if respondents were faced with an expanded or a reduced budget rather than a fixed one? Accordingly, the researchers examined the constrained preferences of the township residents for service provision elicited under two additional hypothetical budget "scenarios": in the first, respondents were asked to accommodate a reduction in the budget and in the second, they were required to respond to an increase.

In the first scenario, respondents were asked to reduce the total allocation by 10 percent below the original budget. The starting point for respondents was their set of preferred allocations at the end of the original game. In concert with the budget reduction, respondents were urged to reevaluate their overall allocation of resources. In the second hypothetical scenario, respondents were required to increase the total allocation by 10 percent above the original budget. The starting point for respondents was the same as in the second scenario—that is, the set of preferred allocations at the end of the original game. Respondents were again encouraged to reevaluate their overall allocation of resources in concert with the allocation of the budget increase.

Looking at the general preferences of the respondents in each of the three versions of the game, it appears there is a broad consistency in the overall pattern. In general, services such as garbage disposal and French immersion, for which the allo-

	Current Allocation	Reductions Sought		No Change		Improvements Sought		
			mean				mean	
Service	**($)**	**n(%)**	**($)**	**(s.d.)**	**n(%)**	**n(%)**	**($)**	**(s.d.)**
1. Library	5	18(14.8)	3.33	(0.69)	89(73.0)	15(12.3)	8.67	(3.13)
2. Recreation	2	4(3.3)	0.50	(0.58)	92(75.4)	26(21.3)	4.69	(2.48)
3. Garbage Disposal	14	16(13.1)	8.12	(3.32)	99(81.1)	7(5.7)	17.57	(3.21)
4. Police Protection	0	—	—	—	99(81.1)	23(18.9)	5.04	(3.10)
5. Fire Protection	21	1(6.8)	20.00	(0.00)	101(82.8)	20(16.4)	25.90	(6.80)
6. County Roads Maintenance and Improvement	12	5(4.1)	8.20	(2.17)	95(77.9)	22(18.0)	17.32	(4.41)
7. Township Roads Maintenance and Improvement	38	7(5.7)	31.28	(6.18)	88(72.1)	27(22.1)	43.11	(4.46)
8. Winter Roads Clearance	27	9(7.4)	21.56	(3.78)	99(81.1)	14(11.5)	29.71	(1.86)
9. Elementary Education: Busing	14	19(15.6)	10.37	(2.03)	99(81.1)	4(3.3)	18.75	(1.26)
10. Elementary Education: French Immersion	6	43(35.2)	2.30	(1.93)	76(62.3)	3(2.5)	9.67	(2.31)
11. Elementary Education: Special Education	8	4(3.3)	4.50	(3.11)	95(77.9)	23(18.9)	13.17	(4.39)
12. Secondary Education: Busing	10	17(13.9)	6.47	(2.29)	102(83.6)	3(2.5)	14.33	(2.08)
13. Secondary Education: Special Education	44	21(17.2)	31.52	(10.82)	95(77.9)	6(4.9)	47.33	(1.03)

4–2. Frequency and amount of service trade-offs—scenario 1, Ontario Public Services game. From Alun E. Joseph, Barry Smit, Ken Beesley, Public Input into Planning for Municipal Service Provision *(Guelph, Ontario: University School of Rural Planning and Development, 1982).*

cation of expenditure was reduced under a fixed budget, were further reduced when the overall budget was decreased. Similarly, services such as fire protection and special education at the elementary level, for which the allocation of expenditure was increased substantially under a fixed budget, were increased even more when the overall budget was increased. However, this broad consistency in overall preferences across the different budget scenarios is underlain by marked variability in priorities. Although the same services may be improved in each case, the degree of improvement varies relatively, as well as absolutely, from service to service.

After playing the trade-off game under the three scenarios, and thereby becoming aware of the relationship between alternative budgets and service provision opportunities, respondents were asked to indicate the scenario they preferred. Given the widespread and often vocal opposition in recent years to increases in property taxes, it might be expected that people would prefer the reduced budget. However, the results from this case study show that 40 percent preferred the status quo and 40 percent preferred an increased budget and the accompanying improvements of services, while only 19% preferred to save taxes by sacrificing service quality.

While this result may be surprising, given the widespread viewpoint that property taxes are too high, it probably demonstrates that once people realize that reductions in property taxes invariably represent reductions in service provision, as they are forced to do in the trade-off method, they may be less likely to opt for the tax reduction. Perhaps more and more people are willing to pay higher property taxes to maintain their public services. By conducting the trade-off game under alternative budgets, the implications of property tax changes for service provision became apparent to residents without the changes having to occur in reality. The results from this case study would seem to indicate that a large proportion of the population is prepared to forgo the opportunity to have reductions in property taxes because they would prefer to maintain or improve upon the levels of service they currently receive.

On the other hand, it is not clear, from this case study, whether there is any consistent relationship between scenario preference and respondent characteristics. The only statistically significant relationship revealed by a Chi-Square analysis is between scenario preference and age of respondent; proportionally more of the older respondents opted for the reduced budget and accompanying level of service provision. This suggests, according to the researchers,

> . . . a complex interplay of the forces underlying preferences for service provision rather than a simple relationship between scenario preference and individual respondent characteristics, and underlines once again the fragile basis for conventional wisdom as to the demands for public service in rural areas . . . [Joseph et al. 1982, 70]

Housing Preferences in Resource Towns

This writer conceived and helped develop, in conjunction with a western Canada social planning consulting firm, a housing trade-off game for use in planning resource towns (Praxis 1982). The trade-off game was part of a larger study undertaken for an Alberta oil development firm that had plans to construct an oil sands plant in northeastern Alberta. It was the intention of the company to participate in the building of a planned new town designed to house and service the workers (and their families) who would be employed by itself and several other companies also expected to operate in the area. The underlying purpose of the study was to assist the oil company develop its approach to the planning and building of the new town, especially in the area of housing and community development.[8]

Toward this end, the consultant (with this writer's assistance) selected five existing resource towns in western Canada to study in order to investigate, among other things, how the residents of these communities perceive the housing, services, and facilities in their community, and what their priorities would be if they should move to a new resource town. The housing trade-off game was played in conjunction with workshops held in each of the communities to discuss the preliminary study findings.[9] (A similar game, concerned with cultural and recreation facilities, was also developed and used.)

The underlying purpose of the housing trade-off game was to identify which housing attributes people really want, what they are willing to pay for, and, most importantly, what they are willing to give up in order to obtain the attributes or features they prefer.

The game focuses on sixteen attributes of housing, including among others, size of unit, size of property, level of dwelling completion, energy efficiency, privacy, access to work, access to the town center, view, and extent of landscaping. Each attribute is divided into a number of levels. For example, size of unit ranges from 600 square feet to 2,000 square feet. An interesting innovation used in the game is that a number of attributes have special constraints, penalties, or bonuses attached. The constraints either eliminate certain choices that could be made regarding other attributes or assign a series of penalties or bonuses when specific choices are made. As an example, if the respondent shows "country acreage" as the preferred size of property, he or she cannot live within walking distance of the town center. Likewise, if the respondent prefers a "super" energy-efficient house, he or she must pay a higher initial cost as a penalty but would also receive a credit or bonus because of anticipated savings in future energy costs.

Costs or prices are assigned to each attribute level. Because the cost of housing varies so widely across all the communities, it was decided to use "artificial" dollar values. However, the costs assigned are generally proportional to real housing costs so that realistic trade-offs can be achieved.

The game was designed to be played by individuals or in groups of twenty to thirty individuals. (In actuality some 175 participants in the five communities played the game.) A printed questionnaire form (see fig. 4-3) was given to each respondent. To launch the respondents into the game, they were initially asked a series of simple questions, including their demographic characteristics, current housing type, and extent of satisfaction with their existing housing based on a seven-point scale.

Individuals were first asked to identify (that is, check off) the level of each of the attributes in their existing home (identified as Step One in fig. 4-3). At this point participants were not required to calculate the costs associated with their existing housing situation. These were calculated as part of the analysis at a later stage.

The players then had to decide what features they would like in their next home, without any financial constraints (other than those noted above), were they to move within the town or region. These values were transcribed to a summary table, the costs totalled, and any debits or credits were calculated to produce a net total cost (Step Two—Round One). Participants rated their satisfaction with this unconstrained housing choice along the seven-point scale previously noted.

The next stage (Step Three—Round Two) forced the respondents to reduce their housing costs (in most cases) to a specified amount, $7,500, set by the study team. This stage was intended to identify which of the attributes of housing respondents would clearly not give up, as well as those they freely gave up, in the face of a constrained total housing cost. They were then asked to reassess their satisfaction with this final housing selection, using the seven-point scale.

Finally, the respondents were asked which of the

INTRODUCTION/INSTRUCTIONS

The household survey that was administered in the community two months ago helped to define people's preferences for housing and needs to be located close to certain services. Now we would like to determine what trade-offs you would be willing to make in terms of housing attributes and features.

There are several steps involved in this game. Please read the following carefully.

Before beginning the game, could you please identify the type of housing in which you presently live (check one) and indicate how satisfied you are with the house (check one level on the scale).

Step 1: Review the housing features (A through P) and choose the level that *best* represents your current situation. Circle the number, and then enter it on the summary form.

Step 2: Identify the level of each housing attribute you would *prefer* for your next home if you had the choice. Write the amounts for each category into the ROUND ONE column. Place the total $ into the summary table, and add up the column. Add or subtract any credits or debits and write in the final total. (Note: we have purposefully chosen a dollar value that does not reflect true construction costs.) Now, please rate your satisfaction with your choice of housing.

Step 3: Now we are going to give you a new set of rules. Go back to the list of attributes. We will set a *maximum* value that you cannot exceed. Record your new selections in the ROUND TWO column, and transfer the totals to the summary table. You must repeat and modify your selections until you are below the total cost we have given you. Total all costs in the summary table. Be sure to include all credits or penalties. Now, please rate your satisfaction with your choice of housing.

Step 4: Now we would like you to identify the three most important housing attributes (A through P) and rank them in order of importance (1, 2, 3), 1 being the most important. Now identify the three *least* important housing attributes (A through P) and rank them in order of importance (1, 2, 3), 1 being the least important.

Step 5: Now we would like you to suggest any attributes that you feel may be missing and are *important* to you. Please write in your responses. Now identify the most difficult trade-offs you had to make as well as the easiest. Please write in.

Now we will have a general discussion about your feelings and responses to the game so far.

Step 6: Following the discussion, we would like you to develop your own housing unit. Please use the same categories (A through P), but use your own words to describe what you would like based on the process we have gone through so far. Please write in the space provided. Following this, if you have any general comments, please write them in.

Your Current Housing Type (please indicate present type)

☐ Single-family housing
☐ Semi-detached housing
☐ Duplex
☐ Row or town house
☐ Low-rise, Medium-rise apartment
☐ High-rise apartment
☐ Mobile home
☐ Other (specify)

____

____

____

Background Information

Age: _____ yrs.

Sex: _____ M _____ F

Family size: _____ (inc. spouse)

Years in community _____ yrs.

Satisfaction with Present Housing

▼	▼	▼	▼	▼	▼	▼
extremely satisfied	very satisfied	satisfied	average	dissatisfied	very dissatisfied	extremely dissatisfied

(continued)

4–3. Resource community study: community housing game. From Praxis (A Social Planning Company), Resource Community Study, 1982. Reprinted with permission.

	Step 1		Step 2	Step 3
ATTRIBUTE	***LEVEL***	***COST***	***ROUND ONE***	***ROUND TWO***
A. Size of unit	1. 600 square feet 2. 800 square feet 3. 1,000 square feet 4. 1,200 square feet 5. 1,400 square feet 6. 1,600 square feet 7. 1,800 square feet 8. 2,000 square feet	$ 1,250 1,500 1,750 2,000 2,250 2,500 2,750 3,000		
B. Size of property	1. No land 2. Communal shared land 3. Zero lot line—small, private yard 4. Average size lot 5. Large size lot 6. Country acreage—1 acre** 7. Country acreage—5 acres** **If you choose this level of lot size, you *cannot* choose Level 1 or 2 of attribute K or L.	$ 100 800 1,300 1,600 2,000 2,100 2,600		
C. Level of lot servicing	1. Self-contained/no town services, gravel road 2. Water and power, paved road 3. Water, power, sewer, paved road 4. Water, power, sewer, paved roads, street lighting, sidewalk/curbs, underground wiring	100 600 800 1,100		
D. Level of dwelling completion	1. Empty lot (owner builds)* 2. Foundation, framing complete 3. Completed shell and partitions, not gyproc 4. Ready for painting 5. Complete—ready to occupy *Penalty: rent will have to be paid while building home ($400)	100 500 800 1,000 1,200		
E. Design quality	1. Manufactured/prefab—no choice in layout 2. Developer-built unit—little choice 3. Customized—some choice in layout 4. Architecturally designed, total choice in layout	100 200 400 600		
F. Dwelling features	1. Basic dwelling unit—no special features, inexpensive carpet, no appliances 2. Medium-quality carpet, stove, refrigerator 3. Medium-quality carpet, stove, refrigerator, dishwasher, washer, dryer, fireplace 4. High-quality carpeting/hardwood floors, all good-quality appliances	100 300 500 800		

Figure 4–3 continued

	Step 1		Step 2	Step 3
ATTRIBUTE	***LEVEL***	***COST***	***ROUND ONE***	***ROUND TWO***
G. Basement	1. No basement/storage space 2. Unfinished basement/storage space 3. Half-finished basement—family room/bedroom 4. Completely finished basement	0 200 400 600		
H. Garage	1. Street parking—no garage 2. Parking pad near unit 3. Carport at or near unit 4. Attached garage, 1 car 5. Attached garage, 2 car	0 100 200 300 400		
I. Energy efficiency	1. No special energy-conservation features 2. Added insulation/thermopane windows 3. Superinsulated/passive solar 4. Superinsulated/totally self-sufficient heating system* * Ascending credit for level of energy efficiency: 2. $ 50 3. $150 4. $400 Heating costs will be reduced over time due to improved energy efficiency.	0 100 300 800		
J. Privacy	1. Very limited privacy—shared accommodation 2. Limited privacy—sharing of common space and hearing/seeing neighbors 3. Private—views of neighbors' homes and neighbors 4. Very private—can't see or hear neighbors 5. Total privacy—no neighbors within 1 mile	10 100 300 600 1,000		
K. Accessibility to work	1. Within 5-minute walk 2. Within 15-minute walk 3. Within 15-minute drive 4. Within 30-minute drive 5. Within 45-minute drive 6. Within 15-minute bus ride 7. Within 30-minute bus ride 8. Within 45-minute bus ride	50 100 200 300 400 100 150 200		
L. Access to town center and major community facilities	1. Within 5-minute walk 2. Within 15-minute walk 3. Within 15-minute drive 4. Within 30-minute drive 5. Within 15-minute bus ride 6. Within 30-minute bus ride	50 100 200 300 100 150		

(*continued*)

Figure 4–3 continued

	Step 1		Step 2	Step 3
ATTRIBUTE	***LEVEL***	***COST***	***ROUND ONE***	***ROUND TWO***
M. Access to elementary school, local parks, and convenience store	1. Within 5-minute walk 2. Within 15-minute walk 3. Within 5-minute drive 4. Within 10-minute drive 5. Within 10-minute bus ride	100 150 150 200 50		
N. Proximity to emergency services	1. Not covered by local emergency services* 2. 5 minutes 3. 10 minutes 4. 20 minutes 5. 30 minutes * If you choose this option, you will pay a penalty of $300 for increased fire insurance.	0 300 200 100 50		
O. View	1. No view 2. Some view 3. Panoramic view	0 200 400		
P. Landscaping	1. Cleared site (owner does all landscaping) 2. Grass/lawn 3. Extensively landscaped 4. Natural treed site	0 100 300 300		

SATISFACTION WITH ROUND ONE HOUSING SELECTION

extremely satisfied	very satisfied	satisfied	average	dissatisfied	very dissatisfied	extremely dissatisfied

Summary

Step 4			Step 1	Step 2	Step 3
PRIORITY					
HIGH	***LOW***	***ATTRIBUTE***		***TOTAL COST ROUND ONE***	***TOTAL COST ROUND TWO***
		A. Size of unit			
		B. Size of property			
		C. Level of servicing			
		D. Level of dwelling completion			

Figure 4–3 continued

Summary

Step 4			*Step 1*	*Step 2*	*Step 3*
PRIORITY				***TOTAL COST ROUND ONE***	***TOTAL COST ROUND TWO***
HIGH	***LOW***	***ATTRIBUTE***			
		E. Design quality			
		F. Dwelling features			
		G. Basement			
		H. Garage			
		I. Energy efficiency			
		J. Privacy			
		K. Accessibility to work			
		L. Access to town center			
		M. Access to schools, parks			
		N. Proximity to emergency services			
		O. View			
		P. Landscaping			
			CREDITS (−)	$	$
			DEBITS (+)	$	$
			TOTAL	$	$

SATISFACTION WITH ROUND TWO HOUSING SELECTION

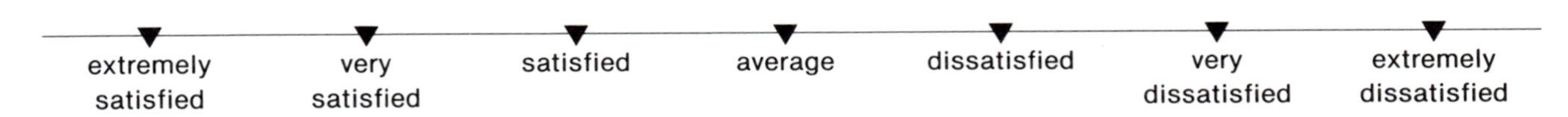

STEP 5

- Are there any other attributes you would like to add that are not included here? ____ yes ____ no
  If yes, what would you add?

(continued)

Figure 4–3 continued

■ Which of the housing attributes or features did you find the most difficult to trade off?

■ Which of the attributes did you find the least difficult to trade off?

STEP 6

■ Based on the housing attributes identified in the game, please take a few minutes to develop your own house. Use your own terms to describe it.

- In what *kind* of house do you want to live?
- *Where* do you want to live?
- What housing *features* do you really want?
- What special *qualities* do you want?

Figure 4–3 continued

housing attributes or features they found the most difficult, and which they found the least difficult, to trade off (Step Four).

There is no doubt about the success of this trade-off game in terms of "getting people involved," and, equally important, making them understand better the nature of the trade-offs they need to make when choosing housing. For example, following the unconstrained housing choice stage, each of the respondents was asked to call out his or her total housing costs to the discussion group, which generated a range of comments and controversy, especially between family members participating in the session who filled out their own separate questionnaires. Likewise, when the study team announced at the third stage that the respondents would have to reduce their housing costs to $7,500, this initially caused a great deal of consternation, but after the howls and protests died away they completed the game and recalculated their debits, credits, and total costs. While the game was being played, there was continuing discussion and verbal interchange among the various participants, many of whom would get up to discuss some aspect of the game with other participants.

With respect to the objective of obtaining relevant data for use in policy formulation, the findings are both interesting and useful. Figure 4–4 presents an overall summary of the findings. It should be noted that all figures represent median values for each attribute. Some highlights of the findings are as follows:

ATTRIBUTE	Existing House	Unconstrained Housing TOTAL COST ROUND ONE	Constrained Housing TOTAL COST ROUND TWO
Size of unit	$1946.69	$2241.20	$1988.25
Size of property	1609.77	2011.27	1609.52
Level of servicing	1029.41	1068.80	790.91
Level of dwelling completion	1196.43	1166.92	986.84
Design quality	206.38	436.11	233.95
Dwelling features	376.92	525.93	300.00
Basement	291.38	432.95	213.04
Garage	209.21	349.15	221.47
Energy Efficiency	61.05	345.45	141.98
Privacy	290.04	329.53	295.62
Accessibility to work	189.56	194.48	103.75
Access to town center	113.50	177.65	85.39
Access to schools, parks	122.99	133.00	96.92
Proximity to emergency services	278.42	215.07	180.60
View	211.82	288.17	190.76
Landscaping	98.97	286.75	23.10
Subtotal	$8251.25	$10046.25	$7504.60
Credits (−)*	30.46	173.66	70.94
Debits (+)	400.00	400.00	400.00
TOTAL	$8203.33	$ 9850.00	$7451.14

*These are median values for those who had debits or credits. Those who did not were eliminated. For this reason, the total will not add up to the value of the subtotal plus or minus the debits and credits.

4-4. Summary results of resource community housing game. From Praxis (A Social Planning Company), Resource Community Study, 1982. Reprinted with permission.

1. The median value of the *existing* homes was approximately $8,200 (''artificial'' housing costs). The *unconstrained* housing choice (Step Two) resulted in a median housing value of $9,850, an increase of about 20 percent over the existing dwelling. As there were no financial constraints on selection in this round, it can be seen that the respondents appeared quite conservative in their housing choice, establishing their own constraints in the selection process. Following this, as noted above, a cost limit of $7,500 was placed on all participants. In fact, once the respondents had reduced the costs, they actually ended up with a median of $7,450. This cutback actually ''forced'' them to accept accommodation that was below their existing standards of housing by almost 10 percent. Such a cutback ensured that the participants would be forced to make some substantial reductions from their unconstrained choice and even compared with their existing housing.

2. Keeping in mind that the objective of the game was to ''force'' the participants to identify the attributes (or levels of attributes) that they were not willing to trade off as well as those that they were willing to lose in order to retain these most desired attributes, the findings are perhaps surprising. Comparing their existing housing with the unconstrained choice round, as can be seen in figure 4–4, most attributes were increased in the unconstrained round with two exceptions. Proximity to emergency services was substantially lower in the unconstrained round. This seems to indicate that people felt the existing proximity was higher than absolutely necessary and reduced it *even though such a reduction was not required.* The level of dwelling completion was also lower in the unconstrained choice round because most residents chose houses that were completely finished when they moved in.

Also, design quality more than doubled when the existing and unconstrained choices are compared ($206 to $436). Several other attributes showed similar tendencies. Of particular importance was energy-efficiency. The low existing dollar value ($61) would seem to indicate that people thought their homes were generally energy-inefficient. When participants selected their unconstrained choice, there was almost a five-fold increase in their desire to pay for a more energy-efficient home. This was the greatest change in all the housing attributes. Landscaping was the only other attribute which rose substantially from the existing to the unconstrained choice round.

3. The most telling comparisons become apparent when existing housing is compared with the constrained housing choices (Step Three). It will be recalled that participants were being forced to reduce their constrained housing choice to a level below where they rated their own housing at present. The findings appear to indicate that participants were not willing to reduce the size of their house below the existing median of 1,200 square feet. Likewise, they were not willing to reduce the size of property below the existing median of $1,600, representing an average to large size lot in most of these communities. While they would not reduce these two attributes below the existing level, they were willing to pay more for better design quality, better energy efficiency, and privacy. Energy efficiency was far ahead of all attributes in terms of willingness to pay a higher price for it, even when they were being forced to take drastic cuts. The establishment of design quality as a high priority would seem to mean that people want greater choice in housing and more individuality in the unit. The willingness to pay more is quite understandable in view of the very limited number of basic plans that are used to develop most housing subdivisions in these and most other northern communities.

4. Of course, to obtain the above attributes, the participants had to reduce the attribute level in several categories. In order to achieve the things they desired, people appeared to be willing to accept lower levels of lot servicing, dwelling completion, and dwelling features. In addition, they were willing to reduce substantially their proximity to work, the town center, schools and parks, and emergency services. Landscaping experienced the most significant reduction.

In summary, participants in this trade-off game indicated they wanted a 1,200-square-foot home on a medium- to large-sized lot, more individually designed, with a much higher level of energy efficiency, and more privacy. To achieve this, they would be willing to see a reduced level of dwelling completion and landscaping (they were quite willing to do this themselves) and a reduction in their proximity to the town center, work, and most services. As the author of this report notes, these findings to a large extent go against many of the "norms" used in the planning of new resource towns. Most planners/engineers/architects advocate a high level of servicing as being essential in a new resource town. While the findings from this trade-off game seem to refute some long-held beliefs and assumptions, a note of caution is in order. Those responsible for designing and financing new resource towns should not act on the basis of one side of these results and reduce the levels of servicing and housing completion. If some attributes such as these are reduced, a balance must be achieved by increasing the attributes that people want, such as greater individuality of housing units, coupled with greater energy efficiency and privacy. In short, while people were willing to give up some things that are often seen as important, they did so with the knowledge that they would achieve something else that they wanted.

Moreover, it should also be remembered that these findings represent averages. There were many responses and desires for different choices outside the "medians." There were also some differences among the five communities studied. Generally speaking, however, the median data given across the board for all the communities were fairly representative of the attitudes of the residents of these towns and could be quite useful in developing future housing policy for resource towns built in the future.

5. The final step in the game (Step Four) involved the selection of the three most important attributes. This stage was included to give the participants, after they had gone through the trade-off process, a chance to determine and reflect on their priorities. The findings were very much in line with those from the trade-off game itself. The size of the unit and the size of the property were by far the highest priorities, while the least important attributes noted were view and landscaping, and proximity to all but the emergency services.

6. It will be recalled that after participants had selected the appropriate attributes for each step in the game—that is, existing, unconstrained, and constrained housing choices, they were asked to rate how satisfied or dissatisfied they were with each choice. The researchers analyzed the findings from a number of different standpoints. The highlights of this analysis are as follows.

Initially when asked how satisfied they were with their existing housing, a very large proportion indicated not only that they were satisfied, but that they were very satisfied (42.1 percent). Very few participants expressed dissatisfaction (7.4 percent). As would be expected, when participants completed the selection of their unconstrained home, nearly 80 percent expressed very high satisfaction with their choice. However, once the constrained choices had been completed, the level of satisfaction decreased substantially but not as significantly as anticipated, and only 3 percent noted high levels of dissatisfaction. This is perhaps surprising in light of the fact that the participants were being "forced" to accept a combination of attributes that would put them in housing slightly below their current housing standard.

In their effort to determine which attribute or combination of attributes increased participants' level of satisfaction, the researchers calculated a series of "satisfaction indicators," or "satisfaction ratios," designed to indicate the degree of change between the existing, unconstrained, and constrained housing choices. The satisfaction ratios compared the current with the unconstrained choice, the unconstrained with the constrained choice, and the current with the constrained choice. A ratio of less than 1.0 indicated that the participants were satisfied with their current or unconstrained situation. If the ratio was greater than 1.0, participants were generally dissatisfied with their current or unconstrained situation. In effect, the ratio indicates the extent of change from one situation to another; the greater the change, the greater the level of satisfaction or dissatisfaction with the particular attribute. The results, when comparing the existing with the unconstrained choices, show that the greatest levels of dissatisfaction focus on energy efficiency, design quality, and landscaping. Moreover, when the degree of change between the current and constrained choices is analyzed, energy efficiency and design quality still remain as the two attributes with which participants are least satisfied. At this point landscaping drops out almost entirely. This would seem to indicate that energy efficiency and design quality are the two areas where people would like to see improvements made to increase satisfaction with their homes. This was closely followed by unit size, size of property, garage, and privacy.

A regression analysis was also undertaken in an attempt to discover whether there were other attributes, or combinations of attributes, that caused the greatest increase in participant satisfaction with their housing. The findings indicated that *privacy* was the most significant variable affecting housing satisfaction, followed by unit size. Access to schools and parks is another factor that affects residents' levels of satisfaction. However, the results of the analysis indicate that the combination of the above attributes accounts for only 20 percent of the variation in housing satisfaction, while the remaining attributes account for even less. At best, if all the housing attributes are considered or met as conditions for developing housing policy, there would be only a 25 percent chance of satisfying potential residents. By implication there is another set of variables that accounts for the difference. These other variables, it would appear, include the actual cost of housing, interest rates, available down payment, and/or various subsidies available to the resident. However, these other attributes could not be treated as part of the housing trade-off game. If these other variables can be held constant, then it can be assumed that privacy, unit size, access to schools and parks, and a view are the most important variables in determining satisfaction with housing in a new resource town.

The above findings (and others from the overall study) were incorporated in the form of recommendations to the client (an oil company) to guide the development of its housing policy for the future new town in which it was expecting to participate. If and when the new town is built, the consultant's recommendations, flowing largely from the trade-off game, will no doubt be seriously considered by the client company. Moreover, the trade-off game findings, as well as the recommendations flowing therefrom should be valuable to those persons concerned with the planning and building of other new resource towns in Canada and elsewhere.

Application of the Priority Evaluator

The earlier version of this paper described the game known as Priority Evaluator, developed originally by Gerald Hoinville and his associates for the British Ministry of Transport (Hoinville and Berthoud 1970; Hoinville 1971; Robinson et al. 1975). Designed as an electrified game board, the Priority Evaluator (PE) is a simulation device that permits respondents to indicate their trade-off preferences between competing and costed environmental attributes so that the overall results of their choices are constantly visible to them.

Two Oregon State University researchers decided to test the application of the Priority Evaluator approach in the context of a planning/design problem on the Oregon State University campus. When a new administration building was completed, the Campus Plan Committee was faced with a difficult decision as to the future use of the site on which the old administration building had stood (Pendse and Wykoff 1974a, 1974b, 1978).

Two opposing groups, with different views as to the future use of this site, had already formed. One group wanted the space for a parking lot, arguing the value of improved staff and faculty parking in the central campus. The other group demanded that the site be used for a "people's park," claiming that this would increase the campus's natural beauty, provide a place for relaxation and recreation, and reduce vehicular traffic in the interior of the campus.

The researchers believed that a rational choice on the use of the site for a specific purpose could best be determined by identifying and evaluating the environmental preferences and quantifying the trade-off values of a representative group of students, staff, and faculty, by use of the Priority Evaluator approach.[10] While they did not build an electrified game board, in all other respects the researchers followed the PE approach. First, they selected six environmental variables to test (natural surroundings, various types of noises, recreation park facilities, vehicular traffic, travel time to work, and parking convenience), which were chosen on the basis of environmental conditions and the community interest at the university.

Second, they divided each of the six environmental variables into three levels or standards—low, medium, and high for noise level; 5, 10, and 15 minutes for travel time to work; and so on. Each standard was illustrated by black-and-white draw-

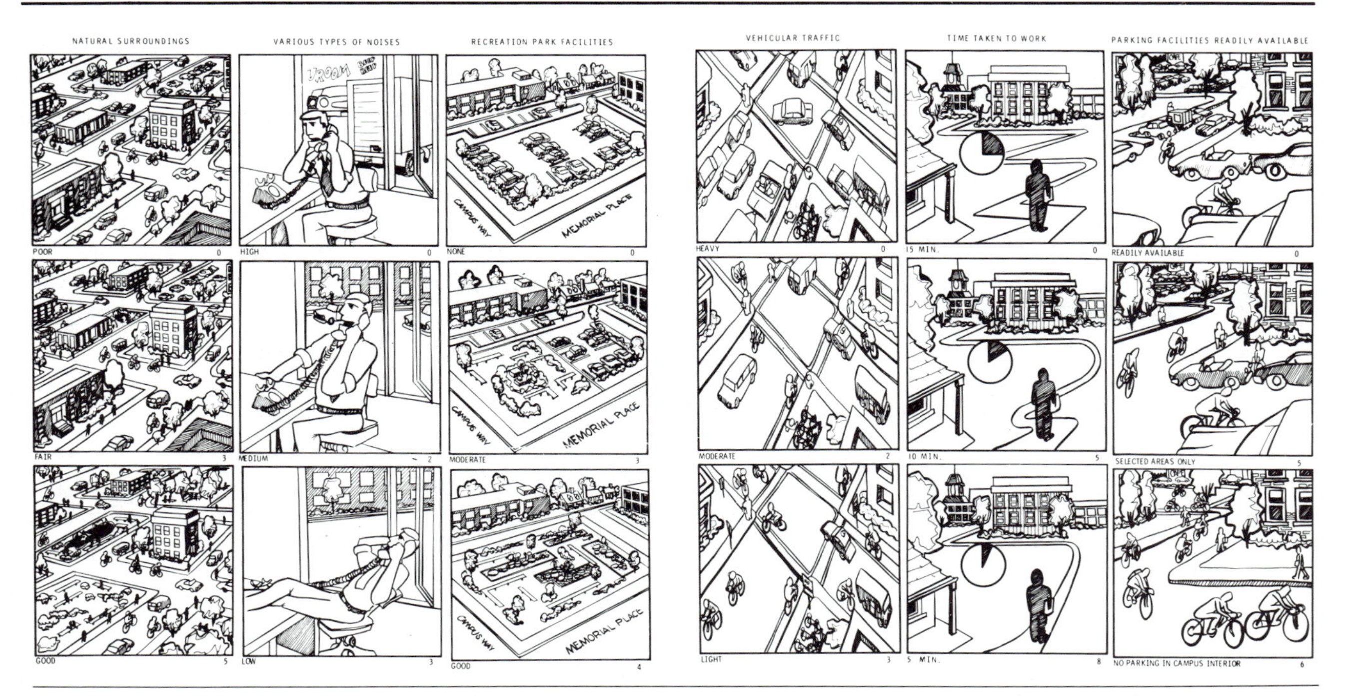

4–5. Oregon State PE game: six environmental variables divided into three levels. Reprinted with permission from D. Pendse and J. B. Wyckoff, ''Environmental Goods: Determination of Preferences and Trade-Off Values,'' Journal of Leisure Research 6(1) (Winter 1974): 70.

ings highlighting the main features rather than the specific views of the campus (see fig. 4–5).

Third, a sample of sixty respondents were subjects of a forty-minute interview during the summer of 1972 in Corvallis, Oregon. Precautions were taken to ensure that each respondent was given a similar explanation of the problem, objective, illustrations, and other related matters.

Fourth, prices representing the approximate annual per person cost were assigned to the standards, based on estimates of the yearly cost of maintaining shrubbery, green grass, parking lots, and roads at the university. The prices generally increased as environmental quality improved.

Fifth, a budget of $18, approximating the annual cost per person for maintaining the environment, was established; the budget was derived so that no one could simultaneously ''buy'' the highest standard of all six variables, thus requiring quality trade-offs.

The respondents were told that they should consider themselves in the position of the Campus Plan Committee, whose function was to plan the physical and visual environment of the university campus for the future and that their final preferences should provide themselves and the campus community at large the most satisfaction. The game procedure went as follows:

1. After the respondents had familiarized themselves with the eighteen environmental levels, they were asked to identify, from the illustrations, the levels that they felt most nearly represented their existing environmental situation. The responses were recorded by the interviewer. The average scores of the respondents' evaluations of their existing situation were calculated by assigning values of one for a poor situation, two for the average, and three for the best one chosen by the respondents (fig. 4-6). From the results of these scores, it can be inferred that the respondents faced relatively good conditions with respect to noise and travel time to work, and relatively poor conditions in regard to parking facilities and vehicular traffic.

2. The respondents were then presented with the given $18 budget to "buy" the desired standards or situations, each "priced" as previously indicated. The rules established that only one standard from each environmental variable could be selected in the allocation process; and further that the entire budget must be spent but the respondent could not overspend. These constraints forced the respondents to trade off different standards until they were indifferent to further trade-offs. The desired standards could differ from the identified existing situations, and the drawings constantly reminded the respondents of situations they had foregone or obtained in the process of allocating their budget.

3. The final responses (preferences) were recorded by the interviewer. This produced average scores for the so-called "optimum environmental conditions" for each of the attributes (fig. 4-7).

4. The procedure was repeated for different budget levels.

Underlying the Pendse/Wyckoff (and the PE) approach were two basic assumptions: first, allocation of the fixed budget among the alternative standards is optimum when the respondent cannot increase his or her satisfaction by further trade-offs; and, second, from the preferences revealed by the respondents, it is possible to establish the extent to which respondents are satisfied with the prevailing conditions, the magnitude and direction of changes sought, the quality trade-offs, and the respondents' value structure.

While the average scores provide some insight into the position of one variable relative to another, the degree of satisfaction respondents felt with the existing conditions, and their willingness to trade off certain standards (elements) at rates different from the rates of exchange used, were yet to be determined. The information was deduced from the optimum conditions desired by the residents. A satisfaction ratio (SR) was derived for each environmental situation. The satisfaction ratio was

Variable	*Average Score*
Parking facilities	1.80[a]
Vehicular traffic	1.90
Natural surroundings	1.98
Recreation park facilities	2.00
Travel time to work	2.14
Various noises	2.17[b]

Source: Pendse and Wyckoff, 1974, p. 71

a. Worst condition.
b. Best condition.

4-6. Oregon State PE game: existing environmental situation, average scores.

Variable	*Average Score*
Parking facilities	2.44
Vehicular traffic	2.61
Natural surroundings	2.36
Recreation park facilities	2.29
Travel time to work	1.14
Various noises	2.63

Source: Pendse and Wyckoff 1974a, p. 72

4-7. Oregon State PE game: optimum environmental situation, average scores.

computed by dividing the proportion of budget allocated for each of the environmental situations under optimum conditions by the proportion of total value of existing conditions assigned to each of the environmental situations. Thus, given the prices, and the alternatives, if the SR was greater than one, respondents were dissatisfied with existing conditions; if less than one, the respondents were satisfied; and if equal to one, respondents were indifferent to changing the existing conditions. The SR's were greater than one for all variables except travel time to work, thus indicating dissatisfaction with existing conditions, with that one exception. The greatest dissatisfaction existed in regard to vehicular traffic.

The data showed that respondents sought improvements in their environmental surroundings by: increasing the area of natural surroundings, reducing noise, reducing vehicular traffic, and imposing greater restrictions on parking facilities. As implied above, reducing vehicular traffic received top priority among the majority of residents. It was also clear that time was the least important factor relative to other variables because the respondents clearly indicated that they did not mind trading additional time (to reach the office) for more pleasant surroundings.

Next, the savings and investments resulting from the optimum distribution as compared to existing conditions were computed in dollars and cents, based on the average scores for the existing situation versus the optimum choices. With the given exchange rates, budget constraints, and limited alternatives, respondents chose to invest substantially in restricting parking spaces and vehicular traffic. They also chose to invest for the purposes of reducing noise level and beautifying natural surroundings. Overall, respondents reduced their budget allocated to "travel time to work" and distributed it among other alternatives. Reductions in vehicular traffic and parking spaces and an increase in areas of green grass, shrubs, and open spaces received top priority. Most importantly, respondents were clearly prepared to sacrifice extra time in exchange for pleasant surroundings.

The researchers show how the above information can be used for policy decisions, using the two variables "time" and "vehicular traffic" for illustrative purposes. First, based on estimates of the different levels of vehicular traffic on the campus and average times corresponding to each of the traffic flows, and using a budget of $18, they infer that the respondents sought to trade time and vehicular traffic as follows:

	Average Number of Vehicles/Hour	Average Time Taken to Work (Min.)
Existing situation	35	9
Optimum distribution	15	14

Second, using the data referred to earlier on average extra savings/instruments per respondent under different conditions, the researchers conclude that the respondents were indifferent to a reduction of 20 vehicles per hour (at a cost of $1.20 per head) and a sacrifice of 5 minutes of daily time (at a saving of $5.67 per head). From this, they deduce that 20-vehicle traffic flow per hour is roughly equivalent, as a trade-off, to 5 minutes of daily travel time. In other words, an exchange rate of four to one exists between vehicular flow per hour and minutes of travel time.

In short, the results obtained above provide quantitative information on the direction and the rate of exchange acceptable to respondents. These exchange rates are relative of course to various conditions imposed, such as budget, the given exchange rates and prices, and the alternatives available, and they could change if the conditions changed.

One of the innovative features of the methodology developed by the Oregon State researchers was their effort to value the unpriced environmental goods. The overall methodology in effect simulates the operation of a competitive market. According to theory, in a competitive market at equilibrium the marginal utility per dollar of any good (or unit of a good) is equal to the marginal utility per dollar of any other good (or unit of a good). The innovative aspect of the Pendse/Wyckoff method was to translate this condition by adjusting the experimental (given) prices to move toward the equilibrium prices. If the given prices perfectly reflected respondents' value structure, it would be expected that each combination of alternatives by chance would appear equally in the final selection. Comparison of the random or expected frequencies of choice (E) with the observed frequencies (O) will therefore show how well the given prices reflect marginal utilities—that is, the respondents' value structure. More specifically, an observed to expected (O/E) ratio greater/less than 1 implied that given prices underestimated/overestimated respondents' values and that prices needed to be increased/decreased to obtain the estimate of the equilibrium prices—an overall ''random'' balance of preferences. An O/E ratio of 1 indicated that the given prices perfectly estimated marginal utility and reflected the respondents' values and that no price changes were needed.

After obtaining the O/E ratios (fig. 4–8), a set of prices was deduced that reflected the relative values the respondents attached to the different variables. The budget and other factors were held constant and the prices of the overvalued and undervalued standards were modified until a balance was reached. Figure 4–9 represents the set of values that established overall balance among all variables at the $18 budget. The new prices, quite different from the given prices, reflect the values respondents would be willing to pay for an additional unit of each of the variables.

Space limitations do not permit an explanation of all the implications of figure 4–9. The primary findings were that respondents were willing to pay the same or more for an additional unit of the

	General Condition		
Variable	**Average**	**Good**	**Combined**
Vehicular traffic	1.04	1.84	1.45
Various noises	0.68	1.94	1.45
Parking facilities	0.99	1.59	1.27
Natural surroundings	2.05	0.89	1.26
Recreation park facilities	1.61	1.10	1.31
Travel time to work	0.34	0.04	0.13

Source: Pendse and Wyckoff 1974a, p. 91

4–8. Oregon State PE game: O/E ratios, $18 budget.

	General Condition	
Variable	**Average**	**Good**
Natural surroundings	$4.50	$4.50
Various noises	1.70	4.50
Recreation park facilities	3.90	3.95
Vehicular traffic	2.00	4.50
Travel time to work	0.90	0.55
Parking facilities	5.00	7.00

Source: Pendse and Wyckoff, 1974a, p.91

4–9. Oregon State PE game: equilibrium rates of exchange.

good situation than for "average" conditions in all classes but "travel time to work"; and that identical value was indicated for one unit of "average" and "good" natural surroundings. (See Pendse and Wyckoff 1974b for further discussion of the implications of the revised equilibrium prices.)

Given the small sample, specific environment, and prices and budget used, Pendse and Wyckoff do not claim that their results could be generalized for all situations or projected to the larger community. The equilibrium prices that were obtained, for example, are a function of the given prices, and thus small changes in the given prices could lead to a different set of equilibrium prices.[11] Despite these limitations, the authors believe, and this writer agrees, their study and the PE approach in particular demonstrates that it is possible to quantify visual, aesthetic, and other environmental goods and trade-off values. The results of their work would seem to justify testing the methodology on a large scale and under diverse conditions in order to obtain deeper insights into the effects of the form of presentation and the range of alternatives that can be handled. Such information, incorporated into benefit-cost analyses, could provide policy makers with a better vantage point for correctly assessing the value of environmental goods in public investment decisions. This, in turn, should lead to improved credibility with the public for a wider range of decisions related to the provision of environmental goods.

Jefferson County Game

Another novel application of the trade-off approach was developed by Jefferson County (state of Colorado) planners to assist in the preparation of a comprehensive land use plan for the mountainous part of the county (Dowall and Juhasz 1978). During the early 1970s this area was experiencing extreme development pressures due to its location on a most desirable fringe of the rapidly growing Denver metropolitan area. County planners, in responding to the citizens' concern over rapid land conversion and development, sought to discover the reasons why citizens prefer mountain living, and systematically to build this information into the planning process. After several attempts at traditional questionnaire designs, the decision to utilize trade-off techniques emerged. It was felt that by stressing the use of trade-off choices rather than by having people express agreements about desirable or undesirable courses of action, "citizens would be educated to the realities of resource allocation, and would yield unbiased and meaningful information."

Using a random example of 316 residences generated from property tax records, a trade-off questionnaire was designed to force residents to make realistic choices among desirable dimensions of living associated with land use. Ten dimensions were selected: travel to work, other travel, size of house, distance to nearest neighbor, number of visible man-made structures, recreation, personal expenditure, general public services, open space, and pollution. Each of the ten dimensions was paired with each of the other nine in turn, yielding forty-five unique trade-offs. The respondents were asked to indicate the position on a constrained choice line (displayed in diagrammatic form) that they would choose as the most acceptable or desirable with respect to the forty-five possible pairings of the ten dimensions.

Cluster analysis was then used to reduce the attitudinal items to significant dimensions. Cluster score patterns identified thirteen subgroups, which were then arranged on a continuum of convenience-versus-environment orientation. The subgroups were found to occupy distinctive subregions within the mountain area. The authors strongly believe that this environment-versus-convenience distinction is a powerful tool in developing regional land use plans (for example, with respect to population densities, road improvements, and water and sewer treatment requirements) and, specifically, that the alternative plans developed for the mountain area of Jefferson County should, to varying degrees, reflect both a high level of convenience and a high level of environmental quality.

ADVANTAGES AND BENEFITS OF TRADE-OFF GAMES

For planners and environmental designers, there would appear to be, in this writer's opinion, four distinct advantages and benefits to the use of trade-off games. First, trade-off games are an excellent learning mechanism, better perhaps than most urban simulation games. Second, they have immense advantages for getting people involved and participating in the planning and design processes. Third, they are a better way of identifying and measuring (where possible) preferences, especially the trade-off preferences of the users of the environment, compared with traditional research techniques. Fourth and most importantly, the trade-off game approach and, specifically, the data derived from such games are a valuable research tool in a variety of planning, design, and policy-making situations.

Learning Device

Trade-off games provide a learning experience for the respondents with respect to the exhaustibility of resources and goods. As evidenced by the USC trade-off game and others, it would appear that most people understand the concept of trade-offs and have a fairly good idea of their past and present trade-off preferences. However, when faced with specific trade-offs, they are often surprised to discover that what they believed to be their preferences do not match their past or present behavior or, for that matter, their own value system. Thus, the cognitive task of considering a series of trade-offs between various attributes affecting future options provides a unique opportunity that does not otherwise exist to sort things out in one's mind.

Most importantly, trade-off games allow the respondents to see the implications of their trade-off choices not only for their own purposes, but in relation to the community. In the southern Ontario public services game, for example, to gauge the effect that the information on services provided in the game had upon taxpayers' attributes, respondents were asked to indicate their degree of satisfaction with the current provision of services in the townships, both at the outset of the interview and at the end of the game. While a number of respondents indicated a degree of dissatisfaction with the current allocation of funds for services by trading off large amounts, almost 20 percent of the sample concluded, after considerable thought and playing the game, that they could not identify an expenditure pattern they would prefer over the current one, given a fixed budget. Moreover, many of the latter respondents at the beginning of the interview complained about the level of services available. In short, after examining the trade-off board and assessing the options, there was a common tendency among the respondents to indicate higher levels of satisfaction with existing municipal services. Indeed, for all services, both the average satisfaction and the proportion of satisfied respondents increased after the game.

The potential utility of such trade-off games as a learning device is thus apparent. When provided with the information about the effects of budget constraints on the possible service level options, respondents quickly became aware of the limits within which municipal officials, including planners, must work.

Participation

Trade-off games are a means of permitting citizens and residents (the actual users of the environment) to participate more fully in the planning and decision-making processes that affect their lives and sense of well-being. At an earlier time, planners and environmental designers assumed that they knew what was best for the public, what the public preferences were, what the real-world constraints were, and what the appropriate trade-offs were in the face of these constraints. Accordingly, the public was only minimally involved in the planning and decision processes. With the widespread recognition of the pluralistic nature of our society and with numerous demands for citizen input, the planner's and environmental designer's response in many cases was to conduct surveys of user's preferences (along the lines briefly described below) so as not to continue relying upon what may have been false impressions of the public's views. With this change, the expert at least knew what the preferences were, but, as noted later, they were unconstrained preferences. When faced with real-world constraints, the designers still had to modify the original preferences through a trade-off process to come up with a design solution. Thus, while the design process had been improved by citizen input from these questionnaires, there was still a large chance for error.

The merit of the trade-off game approach is that it carries citizen participation a step further along in the design process. It can get people involved in a serious way. Indeed, the experience of this writer with playing a number of such games with citizens' groups is that the players often had to be reminded, when feelings started to run high, that it was "only a game." During many gaming sessions in which the writer was involved, players remained half-standing through several hours of play, reflecting a level of attention and concern that would make any lecturer on the same subject envious. Equally important, this approach permits the different publics (user groups) to express their preferences, especially their trade-off preferences, and in a particularly salient fashion—that is, under a simulation of real-world constraints.

In particular, this approach permits population groups who are often excluded from the planning and decision-making processes (minorities and low-income and other disadvantaged groups) to indicate their preferences. Through this form of simulation, the participants are un-self-consciously able to express through actions (as well as words) their attitudes, preferences, and predilections, which they might find it difficult to verbalize in other circumstances (Taylor 1971, 107). Moreover, trade-off games appear to overcome most of the problems that have been experienced in using the typical simulation game with residents of "deprived" neighborhoods, among which the following might be mentioned (Law-Yone 1982):

1. Unlike students in a classroom, deprived residents find it difficult to assume theory-forming attitudes, venturing very little into generalizations (induction) or forecasts (deduction)—key elements in most simulation games; and this leads to a somewhat mechanistic form of play.
2. A predisposition to suspicion often gives rise to a tendency to see the simulation game as a form of propaganda or an attempt to sell something.
3. There is often a cultural bias against role playing among deprived residents, especially when in mixed (as to sex) and/or unfamiliar groups, with the result that many find it difficult to "act" in ways they consider frivolous, childish, or impractical in game play.

In spite of (or perhaps because of) the fact that the trade-off game approach is primarily an introspective and individualistic technique, Law-Yone (1982) found that in the playing of his trade-off game most of the residents felt more comfortable with it than with an interactive simulation game that he also used with the same people.[12]

Comparison with Traditional Techniques

Traditionally two basic research approaches and techniques have been used to elicit preferences.[13] The first approach is based on the economist's view that preferences and trade-offs can be inferred by studying market behavior. The basic assumption underlying the "preferences expressed as behavior" approach is that the choices users actually make in the real world are the best indicator of preferences and trade-offs; thus what is needed is information about what people actually do rather than what they say they will do, which is often quite a different thing. In line with this approach and viewpoint, planners and environmental designers have developed and used such techniques as mathematical simulation models, O-D (origin-destination) traffic surveys, market and consumer surveys, and time activity budgets, among others, to observe existing behavior and from this to predict future behavior.

The second approach to arriving at preferences and trade-offs is aimed at countering what is viewed as the disadvantages of the first approach. This viewpoint holds that there is an implicit assumption in the first approach that preferences cannot be changed. It argues that information on past or current behavior fails to take into account inadequacies in the existing environment and does not allow for unfulfilled preferences—preferences that might emerge in possible future environments with characteristics outside the range of current observations. This is important for planners and environmental designers who are interested in preferences—for example, for different types of housing, public services, or environmental goods—under alternative conditions, since their task is usually the rearrangement of the environment to suit better the needs and preferences of users. To satisfy this purpose, it has been argued that alternative environments (for example, a "new town") should be built on an experimental basis and then put to a "consumer test" (Webber 1973). However, unlike testing for new consumer products, experimental alternative environments would be impractical on the scale required, because of the cost.

For these reasons, planners and designers have turned to the use of questionnaires, or attitude and opinion surveys, to determine community preferences. The simplest instruments involve straightforward questions concerning preferences for, or satisfaction with, current housing, services, environmental goods, and so on. While such surveys do provide some valuable information about the attitudes of residents toward various elements in or attributes of the environment, they do suffer from certain basic weaknesses. First, while such surveys may indicate a preference ordering or ranking by respondents of different elements or attributes in the environment, they do not indicate trade-offs the respondents are prepared to make between these various elements or attributes. For example, a survey of community attitudes toward various environmental attributes in a community might show that air quality is considered the number one preference, schools number two, parks number three, and so forth. But is clean air, no matter how pure, always preferred to better schools? Is there a certain level of air quality beyond which better quality in schools would take precedence? These questions are not answered by the typical attitude survey.

Second, attitude questionnaires are weak because the questions about preferences are typically asked under *unconstrained* conditions. For example, a survey of community opinion on municipal services might ask residents to indicate their degree of satisfaction or dissatisfaction with existing services, or it might even have the residents specify those services in greatest need of improvement. Such surveys certainly provide valuable information on attitudes toward services, but are limited in that residents may or may not be aware of the feasibility of or the costs associated with alternative levels of service provision, or the fact that in order to achieve certain improvements, they may have to live with deterioration of other services. Thus, the respondents may indicate a desire for improvements that they might actually oppose if they were aware of their costs in increased taxes or reduced services in other areas. What is needed in this case is a method that allows residents to assess the implications of increasing or decreasing the provision and funding of various municipal services without actually doing it. Third, the typical attitude or opinion survey rarely attempts to determine the differences, let alone the differences in trade-off preferences, among various population groups. Yet we know that in the real world certain user groups might be willing to sacrifice, for example, better schools to achieve higher air quality, whereas under no circumstances would other groups forego their preference for good schools even to breathe the purest alpine atmosphere.

Thus, the first approach to identifying community preferences, described earlier, suffers from the basic weakness that it may endorse the status quo, so to speak, without any indication of preferences with respect to what might be; and the second approach may provide an unrealistic set of preferences and rankings. The former approach has a tendency to be entirely too present-day oriented while the latter may be too utopian. What is required is a technique which incorporates the advantages of both approaches and eliminates their weaknesses.

The trade-off game approach would appear to meet these objectives, combining attitudes and preferences with behavior information. As described earlier, in these games the respondents are typically asked to choose an ''optimum'' mix of variables (dimensions/attributes/elements) from a range of competing alternatives; and, in many of the games, prices or costs (often reflecting the real-world situation) are assigned to the alternatives and the respondents are given a ''fixed budget'' with which to make such choices or trade-offs. In this way, respondents are ''forced'' to indicate their preferences (that is, attitudes) under a constrained choice (that is, behavioral situation). In short, the trade-off game approach simulates behavior in the face of real-world constraints.

Research Tool for Planning, Design, and Policy Making

Perhaps the most valuable contribution of the trade-off game approach is its potential utility as a research tool to provide information in a variety of planning, design, and policy-making situations; to assist decision makers resolve current and emerging planning and design problems and issues involving complex trade-offs; and to help test and/or develop theories regarding the nature of urban development.

Including their uses previously discussed, games can provide research data potentially useful for:

- Planning and budgeting for different public services[14]
- Allocating resources to specific programs (Robinson et al. 1975)
- Developing quality-of-life indicators (Robinson et al. 1975)
- Assisting in cost-benefit analyses, where environmental goods are involved, for public investment decision making[15]
- Developing architectural programs (Berkeley 1968; Taylor 1971; Sanoff 1978)
- Determining housing policies for existing and new towns[16]
- Evaluating alternative plans and their effects on different population groups (Friend and Jessop 1969; Robinson 1972)

- Identifying citizen roles and attitudes and applying them to the development of alternative future urban scenarios (Robinson and Jamieson 1976)
- Assisting in the development of planning and environmental standards (Robinson et al. 1975)
- Reviewing environmental-impact statements (Robinson et al. 1975)

The previous sections, as well as the earlier version of this chapter (Robinson et al. 1975, 103–9), identified some of the ways data derived from trade-off games can be used in the above-mentioned situations. In this section, we shall attempt to summarize these conclusions, drawing, as well, upon the experience and research of this writer and other researchers and game designers.

At a minimum, the data from trade-off games can show the trade-off "propensities" of a community, with respect to different environmental attributes (such as housing, public services, and environmental goods). Trade-off propensities indicate the frequencies with which one or more attributes would be dispensed with or allowed to "deteriorate" in exchange for desired changes in other attributes. Such propensities were derived from the southern Ontario, Oregon State University, and USC games. For example, the USC game (Robinson et al. 1975, 106–7) found that respondents, generally speaking, were willing to trade off the "opportunity" attributes (such as access to work, friends, or shopping centers) for higher levels of the "ambience" attributes (air quality and personal and property safety). The Oregon State University game concluded that respondents did not mind trading off additional travel time to work for more pleasant surroundings (reduction in vehicular traffic and noise, restrictions on parking facilities, and an increase in the area of natural surroundings). This sort of information would be extremely useful in any planning, design, or policy-making situation in which resources were limited and trade-offs needed to be made among either the quantity or quality of environmental attributes.

As discussed by the USC researchers in the earlier version of this work (Robinson et al. 1975, 106–7), in addition to propensities it would be useful to state trade-offs in quantitative terms, in the form of exchange or trade-off "rates." While the data from the USC game did not permit the researchers to develop such rates, the Oregon State University game, described earlier, did. The USC researchers discussed the different ways that trade-off rates could be used in the development and evaluation of alternative plans and programs and in the development and administration of planning standards. In addition, they pointed out that an even better representation of trade-off relationships would be in the form of trade-off curves or functions for any pair of preferences or attributes (Robinson et al. 1975, 107). The idea of the trade-off curve or function is similar in concept to the economist's indifference curve, and the rates of exchange so represented are, as noted earlier, what the economist calls "marginal rates of substitution."

Data from the USC game did not permit the researchers to develop trade-off rates, curves, or functions. The closest they came to this idea was the development of trade-off domains or bands. The researchers note that, while admittedly a less precise form of aggregating trade-off relationships, the domains and bands are nevertheless useful for planning, design, and policy making.

If the above types of quantitative trade-off relationships were in fact available for a variety of goals, preferences, and attributes (and for different population groups, as discussed below)—in the form of rates, curves, functions, domains, or bands—they could be collected in a book or manual of planning trade-off "matrix" tables. Then, when faced with a planning, design, or policy-making situation involving trade-offs, the planner need only look up his or her particular situation in the appropriate tables to find the "solution" to his or her allocation problems. Indeed, the use of high-speed computers would make the various trade-off computations required fairly easy to calculate and interpret.

In planning, there is always a danger of focusing only on majority community preferences, at the expense of legitimate minority interests. Likewise, in using data from trade-off games, planners might focus only on the data on the statistical "means," and in this way ignore the preferences of those respondents who deviate one way or the other from the mean, and thus overlook the minority groups in the population. Needless to say, planners and other public officials should be aware of the special needs of minority groups within their community. Moreover, increasingly, planners and decision makers recognize that there is not one homogeneous public, but a number of publics, each with its own set of preferences. Analysis of community preferences (or demands) should identify these different sets of preferences and the nature and degree of similarities, differences, and incompatibilities among them.

Fortunately, the data yielded by most trade-off games permit examination of the nature and degree of group differences and similarities in preferences within a community. In the USC game, for example, the analysis produced trade-off propensities, domains, and bands for the different racial and income groups in the sampled population, showing that substantial differences in trade-off preferences existed among the different population groups. Likewise, in the southern Ontario game, the results for the population as a whole imply that the current budget apportioned for the library service, for example, is generally accepted as appropriate, but that there are minorities who would prefer increases or decreases in expenditures for this service. Further analysis of the data showed that these minority group differences reflected differences in preferences between users and nonusers of the library service and also between long-term and short-term residents of the township.

While the trade-off game method clearly does not provide a solution to the problem of accommodating minority concerns (this is ultimately a political decision), it does permit the accurate identification of minority trade-off preferences, and it facilitates comparison of minority preferences with those of the rest of the population. Such information would at least provide decision makers with a much wider understanding of the preferences of the different groups in their community, and thereby place them in a better position to make decisions with respect to the various decision-making situations noted earlier. For example, such information would be especially valuable for a community in which the composition of the population is changing rapidly. It would be possible, given known group preferences, to extrapolate the need for different services, housing, community facilities, or other environmental attributes in the light of specific trends in population composition.

The above discussion focused mainly on the value of data on community trade-off preferences for a variety of generic types of planning, design, and policy-making situations—on determining the preferences of different population groups for municipal services, housing types, community facilities, and so forth, and for developing or evaluating neighborhood or city-wide plans. In addition, as evidenced by several of the games described in the previous section and as implied in the earlier discussion of the rationale for such games, the information on community preferences can be used by planners, designers, and decision makers when faced with a pressing and immediate planning or design issue involving trade-offs.

For example, the Jefferson County game was used to aid planners and decision makers develop a comprehensive land use plan for the mountainous area within the county, which had been experiencing intense development pressures due to its proximity to the Denver metropolitan area. The plan was developed in response to citizens' concern over the rapid land conversion and development in the area. Likewise, Oregon State University researchers decided to test the application of the Priority Evaluator trade-off game to assist the university campus planners in deciding on the best way to develop a site on the campus.

The potential uses of a trade-off game in similar types of situations are innumerable. Currently, and for many years in the future, less favorable economic conditions in general and tightened municipal budgets in particular will confront local decision makers with a whole host of problems and issues involving complex trade-offs: job creation programs versus environmental quality regulations; economic stability versus social programs for the poor and disadvantaged groups; the traditional preference for single-family, low-density housing on undeveloped lands versus the need to limit the extension of physical infrastructure for cost reasons. Moreover, in all of these trade-off situations, decision makers will undoubtedly continue to want information on community preferences to assist them in making these complex and often delicate decisions.

A third use of data from trade-off games is to test various hypotheses or theories, or assist in the development of theories, regarding the nature of urban development. An example of such application is drawn from the work of the Ontario researchers in connection with their public service trade-off game. The major research question at issue here relates to the recent population trend, in Canada and the USA, toward diffusion of population outside major metropolitan areas. Called "exurban residential development," the term is used to describe development in the countryside that is urban-initiated (exurbanites reside in the country but maintain strong ties, chiefly through their jobs, with an urban center) but not contiguous with any urban area. This increasingly widespread form of residential development reflects changing locational opportunities and preferences on the part of a sizable proportion of the urban population.

Development in the countryside creates problems and issues that differ from those that have confronted most rural areas in the past. Among these problems are the implications of exurban residential development for the provision of public services in rural areas, especially at the municipal level. Increasing attention is being paid to the question of changing local demands for services, since the nature and level of services available to rural residents can vary considerably among localities even within the same region. This variability stems in part from localized differences in resident demands or preferences for municipal services. However, empirical evidence on service demands is lacking and, most importantly, we do not know the extent to which changed local demands for services result from the different demands of exurbanites, from changes in the demands of other rural residents, or simply from an increase in the local area's population.

If we are to develop or test any theory (or theories) on the demand for rural municipal services, we need answers to the following sorts of questions: Do the preferences of newcomers differ significantly from those of more established rural residents? Does the socioeconomic status of rural households influence service preferences? Do the preferences vary systematically and predictably according to the length of residence, household income, age, background, or other characteristics (or combination of characteristics) of rural residents? Or, in contrast to these questions, are community preferences for services merely a function of local conditions and pressures?

As described earlier, the trade-off game developed by the Ontario researchers does, indeed, provide some answers to these questions. Development and use of similar games in other rural areas should be encouraged so that we can build up a substantial body of empirical data to develop and/or test appropriate theories relative to the demand for municipal services in exurban areas.

CONCLUSIONS: DESIGNING A TRADE-OFF GAME

Based on this analysis of a number of trade-off games, including those described in the original version of this chapter, it can be concluded that the trade-off game approach does, indeed, provide useful research information for a variety of planning, design, and decision-making situations. Accordingly, it is expected to become a more popular research tool in the future. Some guidelines or criteria for designing a trade-off game, based on the experience of those trade-off games that have been developed to date, will therefore be offered below. Some of the points from the earlier paper (Robinson et al. 1975, 109–15) are highlighted, and lessons drawn from the review of the games described in this chapter are discussed, in terms of the following: (1) selection of the attributes for the games; (2) presentation media and response formats; and (3) good research design.

Selection of Attributes for the Game

In general, selection of the attributes or elements to include in a trade-off game relates, of course, to the basic problem under investigation. Determination of the specific attributes to be studied, including those that are important to the population groups under study, can be assisted by a review of the literature, open-ended pilot surveys of the population groups, and expert opinion, brainstorming, or even simplified versions of the Delphi technique.

In terms of the number of attributes, there should be a sufficient number to approach the complexity of real-world multiple choice situations. Of the various trade-off games reviewed by this author, the one designed by Redding and Peterson (1970) had the fewest number with only four; the game designed by Wilson (1967) had the greatest number—thirty-four. Unfortunately, the greater the number of attributes to be included in a game, the more difficult the game may be to explain and certainly the more difficult and time consuming to play (see ''Response Formats'' below for further discussion of this point). Given these constraints, however, an effort should be made to include the maximum number of relevant attributes in the game. The relationship between the number of different attributes and the number of different subject population groupings should be maximized. This criterion relates to the fact that not all attributes will be equally important to each population group under consideration. For example, the attribute, journey to work, may have little significance for the retired elderly; likewise, access to schools may have little relevance to single persons without children. The trade-off instrument should have enough attributes to ensure that important ones are represented for at least the major population groups to be investigated.

It is vital that the game designer guard against overselecting attributes that can be easily quantified. Both quantitative and qualitative attributes should be included. The easiest attributes to include in a trade-off instrument are those that reflect access to facilities, as these readily lend themselves to quantification in terms of either distance or time. The Wilson and Redding and Peterson games indeed were restricted to attributes concerned with access to facilities. On the other hand, in the Hoinville and USC games as well as those reviewed earlier, qualitative attributes were included. These attributes were quantified by using either a ratio or an ordinary scale. This point is discussed further below, under ''Response Formats.''

Presentation Media and Response Formats

A representation or simulation of the environment, more specifically of the environmental attributes or dimensions and their quality levels (or standards), must be developed for presentation to the subjects or respondents. This involves two aspects: the actual media of presentation, that is, the mode used to depict specific environmental attributes and quality levels; and the format or simulated device for obtaining the responses of the respondents.

Presentation Media. A variety of presentation media are possible:

1. Sketches, drawings, maps, models and replicas
2. Photography, cinema and television
3. Imagery presentation—that is, words and phrases

In the various games reviewed in this chapter and the earlier paper, the environment was simulated through a combination of two or more of these media, mainly the use of words and drawings.

It is important that the environmental dimensions or attributes and their quality levels be presented in as concrete and realistic a manner as possible to the respondents. Most of the games merely used word descriptors to describe the attributes and quality levels (for example, the Wilson, USC, University of Guelph, and Resource Community Housing games). However, several (such as the Hoinville and Oregon State University games) used symbolic drawings to depict each quality level for each attribute. According to the Oregon State University researchers, the respondents had little difficulty understanding the illustrations they showed and completing the simulation. Indeed many respondents showed great insight into the problem and were able to express themselves in detail (Pendse and Wyckoff 1974a; 1978). Nevertheless, while the purpose of these symbolic drawings is to make the different levels of quality more concrete and realistic, different respondents still might hold different interpretations of the drawings. For example, what one respondent judges as "heavy fumes from traffic" another respondent could conceivably judge as "medium fumes from traffic," even though both respondents came from the same environment. In part, the USC instrument attempted to eliminate misinterpretations by instructing respondents that they give a verbal description of the quality level that described their present environment, at least with respect to the four qualitative attributes. The descriptions, which were recorded in longhand by the interviewer, undoubtedly made the qualitative attributes more concrete. However, the descriptions also added time to the analytical phase of the study, as they had to be content-analyzed.

Response Formats. A number of different response formats can be employed to obtain subjects' responses. These include: (1) a game board (the Wilson, Redding and Peterson, and University of Guelph games); (2) an electrified game board (Hoinville game); (3) questionnaires (Resource Community Housing and Oregon State Games); (4) cards (USC game); and (5) chips (USC game).

Using these different formats, two basic techniques can be employed to obtain the respondent's responses. One involves the respondent actually recording the response. For example, in the Redding and Peterson game the respondents used arrows to mark on the game board their preferences for location of activities with respect to their own house. In the Resource Community Housing game, the respondents checked off their choices among housing attributes on the questionnaire form provided. In the initial and final chip allocation steps in the USC game, the respondents themselves allocated the number of chips in accordance with their priorities. In the Jefferson County trade-off game, respondents marked on a constrained choice line their most acceptable or desirable set of trade-off pairs. In the southern Ontario Public Service trade-off game the respondents allocated the funds for the different service levels by moving colored pegs on the game board in order to improve or reduce levels of service. With a fixed budget, all the money (pegs) had to be allocated at the end of the game. In Hoinville's trade-off game, the respondents also inserted their own pegs (representing money) into the holes of the electrified game board in accordance with the respondents' preferences, causing the corresponding attribute levels to light up.

By contrast, in a few of the games reviewed, the interviewers/researchers recorded the subject's response (the USC and Oregon State University games).

There are certain lessons regarding the handling of the information included in the response format (irrespective of the type used) that are worthy of the reader's attention.

Perhaps the key decision for the game designer is the degree of realism in the game setting to be used in the response format. There are two basic approaches to this issue. On the one hand, there is the view that the game setting must be absolutely realistic, for otherwise the respondents will not take the game seriously and not provide meaningful responses. For this reason, the games developed for Jefferson County, Oregon State University, and the rural townships in southern Ontario are all based on real-world planning situations, and use the actual attributes and costs applicable to each of the planning situations.

On the other hand, it is argued that when dealing with changes in the environment or in certain environmental attributes, respondents may become suspicious that in one way or another these changes will involve them in urban renewal, freeway routes or some other real-world physical or programmatic change in their environment as intended or planned by "City Hall" (Robinson et al. 1975, 113). This view contends that the game setting should avoid any association with potential negative images and instead should portray some believable but "let's pretend" situation, such as winning a house on a television quiz show (Wilson) or being shown a house by a real estate broker (Hoinville game), or deciding on the preferred type of housing if the residents were to move to a new resource town (the Resource Community Housing game). Clearly, a balance must be achieved between the real-world situation and a hypothetical setting.

Likewise, there is a difference of opinion as to the reality of the "costs" assigned to the attribute levels and of the "budgets" given to the respondents. One view (the USC and University of Guelph researchers) holds that the cost should be true and realistic, for the trade-offs derived are always a function of the prices stated. People have a different ranking of preferences depending upon the costs of achieving them. Such realistic costs were incorporated in the Oregon State University and Ontario public service games. Further, as demonstrated in the Oregon State University game, there is an issue of the appropriateness of the initial prices offered relative to the equilibrium prices, and to what extent the given prices will reflect marginal utilities—that is, the respondents' value structure. The adjustments made by the Oregon State University researchers were clearly subjective as O'Hanlon and Sinden (1978) note. Their approach—using re-surveys and tests to arrive at an equilibrium price matrix—has much to be said in its favor.

Existing as well as preferred levels of quality should be identified in order to determine the direction and magnitude of desired change. This criterion refers to the concept of preferences at the margin. The evidence appears to be that what people want improved is based on what they have now. Thus, to ask persons in the abstract what they most desire might provide quite a different ranking, and often a less realistic one, than to inquire about their preferences in terms of improving their existing situations. This points to the utility of starting with the attribute levels that are currently available, used, or experienced by individuals so that respondents can use their existing situation as a "bench mark." (Most of the games reviewed do this.) Respondents are then able to improve upon the quality level of one attribute only by sacrificing (or giving up) the quality of one or more of the other attributes. The benefits of relating desired improvements to the current bench mark situation is that individuals can indicate the direction and magnitude in which they would prefer changes to occur relative to their current situation, given, say, a finite budget and the cost of alternate quality levels. In short, the direction of change is reflected in the difference between the preferred and existing quality levels. Further, by identifying current quality levels, it is possible to examine the degree to which respondents might trade off attributes to gain some quality level of an attribute currently not available.

The listing in the response format of quality levels for each attribute should not appear to prejudice the desirability of the ordering. In designing the response format it is important to keep in mind that the order in which the levels are presented may inadvertently include the respondent's perception of what is desirable. This is particularly true if more than one dimension is involved in the descriptions of quality levels. For instance, in each of the six opportunity attributes used in the USC game, the quality levels were ordered into three categories according to transportation mode: pedestrian, automobile, or bus. The pedestrian mode appeared at the top of the list, followed by the automobile and bus modes. Within each category, the least amount of time appeared at the top of the list followed by successively increasing travel times. Hence, placing the 45-minute automobile drive higher than the 15-minute bus ride may have been perceived by respondents to be a clue that the automobile drive was "better" and the farther the respondent dropped down the list the greater the quality he was forfeiting. A similar "bias" may have been introduced into the Resource Community Housing game, where in the case of several "accessibility" attributes used in the game, the modes of transportation ranged from a 5-minute walk to a 15-minute drive to a 45-minute bus ride and were listed in that order.

Similarly, in determining a "price" for an attribute, the cost established should not prejudge the quality of the attribute in the eyes of the respondents. The price assigned to an attribute should not be interpreted as necessarily being a rigid indicator of quality. It is true that in general the higher the price the higher the quality of the attribute, but there may be exceptions to this rule. Different population groups may place a different valuation on an attribute regardless of the price. For any given attribute, the perceived quality level may or may not be directly proportional to the cost.

As suggested earlier, in selecting the attributes to be included in the game, there should be a sufficient number to approach the complexity of real-world, multiple-choice situations. Indeed, the whole point of the trade-off technique is to force respondents to operate in a multi-dimensional choice space—that is, to consider all quality levels of attributes and (where possible) their associated costs simultaneously, so that decisions are made within a realistic set of constraints. However, there is reason to believe that such tasks might be beyond the information-processing capabilities of most people. Clearly, one of the most difficult challenges in designing a trade-off game is, on the one hand, to maintain simplicity for the respondents, and, on the other hand, to approach the complex reality of multi-choice situations. This difficulty can be minimized, as is done in several of the games reviewed, by offering respondents the opportunity to reexamine their choices after the initial trade-offs are made. In this way, respondents approach their preferred combination of quality levels iteratively.

Good Research Design

The designer of a trade-off game, especially when the primary purpose of the game is research and data collection, must try to meet the criteria of good research design. Among these the following should be noted. First, is the set of hypotheses involving the relationships between the independent and dependent variables. Many of the games do not make this clear. The independent variables are generally specified: the quality levels (or standards) of different attributes or dimensions of the environment. What is not clear is the objective, the dependent variable of the trading-off process—that is, what the respondents are aiming to achieve and how this is measured. The exceptions are the USC, Resource Community, Oregon State University, and southern Ontario rural township games, in which the concept of "satisfaction" is explicitly or implicitly introduced as the dependent variable. In the first three cases, respondents were asked to rank their existing, preferred, and traded-off quality levels on a satisfaction scale (in the first two cases, a seven-point scale, and in the latter case, a five-point scale). In the Oregon State University game, "satisfaction ratios" were computed, based on a comparison of the respondent's evaluation of the existing conditions with the "optimum" conditions.

A second criterion of good research design, related to the first one, is the need for congruence between the conceptual and operational variables to be used in the trade-off game; the closer the congruence, the better the research design. Concepts such as "convenience," "safety," "crowdedness," "congestion," and so forth—environmental attributes often studied in trade-off games—must be translated into operational definitions. It is obviously easier to develop operational definitions for the so-called "accessibility" or "opportunity" concepts, where measures of time or distance can be used, as, for example, in the Redding and Peterson, USC, and Hoinville games.

Ambient, environmental, or qualitative variables such as natural surroundings, noise, and fumes from traffic, used in the USC, Hoinville, Jefferson County, and Oregon State University games, pose a greater challenge. These games used terms like "poor," "fair," and "good," or "heavy," "moderate," and "low" to describe the variables and employed symbolic drawings or photographs to help illustrate the meaning of these words. But, as noted earlier, these terms and the accompanying drawings or photographs can be interpreted differently by respondents. It is essential that the qualitative attributes or dimensions and their quality levels (or standards) be described concretely and, insofar as possible, in quantitative terms. The approaches of the Jefferson County planners (Dowall and Juhasz 1978, 729) and the Resource Community researchers (see fig. 4-3 above, especially questions E, F, J, and P) are worthy of attention.

A third criterion of good research design is the validity of the data, both internal and external. Internal validity is concerned with whether or not confirmation of a hypothesis can be explained away as an artifact of the way the measurement was taken. The standard remedy for this problem is to employ the triangulation of data technique—that is, to measure the same thing using several different methods.

There should be internal checks on the consistency of the subject's responses. While ultimately the "validity" of the responses can be checked only by observing the behavior of the respondents confronted with the actual situation depicted in the game, the consistency of response in the game provides some limited measure of validity. The less consistent, the less likely the validity. Among the various games reviewed, the techniques used in the USC game and in the Resource Community Housing game are worth noting. In the former, the criterion of validity was satisfied to the extent that three different means were used for eliciting preferences. Respondents were initially asked to allocate chips as a way of reflecting their priorities among the eleven attributes identified. The game itself, including the determination of the various trade-off propensities, provided the second method. At the end of the game, the respondents were once again asked to allocate their chips according to their priorities, to check on the effects of the trading-off process. The results of these methods showed fairly good consistency. In the Resource Community Housing game, following the completion of the game, the participants were asked to establish their priorities for the housing attributes. They were specifically asked to identify the three highest or most important attributes, along with the three lowest or least important attributes. As noted earlier, the results of this priority-setting exercise compared closely with the results of the trade-off game itself.

There should be compatibility of data across various subjects in the game. For the data from the trade-off games to be aggregated across subjects to derive meaningful results, each subject should receive the same instruction, media presentation, and set of environmental attributes to select from, and abide by the same game rules, so that it can be said that each subject has received the same stimulus. All the games reviewed satisfied this criterion.

External validity concerns the problem of generalizing from a sample to a larger population when interpreting the results. Here the standard remedy is to choose a random sample from the large population. As noted several times throughout this chapter, one of the primary objectives of trade-off games is to identify differences, where they exist, in the trade-off preferences of various population groups. Thus, in designing a game, the subjects selected should be from population groups that vary according to characteristics such as age, education, income, stage of the family or life cycle, and residential location. Determination of the appropriate population characteristics can be derived by reviewing previous research, and using pre-test pilot surveys, the Delphi technique, and similar measures. Once the characteristics have been identified, selection of the population to be included in the sample could be achieved by a random stratified sample.

Finally, an important criterion of good research design is reliability. Can the results be repeated over time? To demonstrate reliability, it should be sufficient to repeat the experiment several months later.

NOTES

1. For a comprehensive list and description of these various games, see Belch 1973; Horn and Cleaves 1980; Hasell 1980.
2. By research, I mean any efforts to examine systems and processes, experiment with actions or decisions, test hypotheses, discover or extract facts and relationships, predict possible future situations, or gain new perspectives on existing knowledge.
3. For a description of these games, see Duke and Greenblat 1979.
4. None of these games was discussed in the original version of this study, since they were all developed after it was completed. However, reference is made, where relevant and appropriate, to the games discussed in the original study in later sections of this chapter. Readers interested in some of the earlier trade-off games developed are referred to the original study.
5. Technically speaking, it is probably preferable to say that players in the trade-off game cannot lose, although they may not maximize their "win-

nings'' if they make incorrect choices (from their subjective point of view). In this respect trade-off games might be thought of as similar in concept to non-zero sum games.

6. Environmental goods include scenic beauty, human safety and health, tranquillity, sites of cultural and aesthetic importance, environmental quality, and related attributes.
7. The University of Southern California (USC) game is not one of the trade-off games reviewed in this chapter, as it was thoroughly described in the original version of this chapter (Robinson et al. 1975). Lessons from this game, however, are referred to in sections of this chapter.
8. In the spring of 1982, several of the major oil companies involved in the tar sands projects in northern Alberta decided to pull out of the venture, thus delaying, at least for several years, the building of the new resource town.
9. The writer participated in these workshops and in the playing of the Housing Trade-Off Game.
10. This game should not be confused with the game known as Trade-Off: The Land Use Planning Game, also developed at Oregon State University. Moreover, despite its name and current popularity (e.g., it was played at a planning commissioners' session of the Annual Conference of the American Planning Association held in Seattle), I do not consider ''Trade-Off'' to be a true trade-off game in the sense described in this chapter. It is basically an urban simulation game, its purpose being to provide a mechanism for the participants to understand the processes and pressures in deciding how lands will or should be used in a variety of community development situations. In this sense, it is in the tradition of the classic land use game, Clug. In the process of deciding how to use a piece of land, the participants do indeed learn about where and when trade-offs must be made. But in the game, the issue of trade-offs itself is not highlighted; nor is the nature of the trade-offs that must be made spelled out, nor are the procedures for determining the appropriate trade-offs specified. For these reasons, this game was not included among the examples of recent trade-off games reviewed in this chapter.
11. Two researchers from Australia (O'Hanlon and Sinden 1978), while acknowledging the innovative approach developed by Pendse and Wyckoff, have taken issue with the Oregon State University researchers' method for arriving at the equilibrium prices. The critics argue that, through the O/E ratios, the method does indicate the direction of the modification but it does not indicate the magnitude. The Australians argue that the process of ''balancing'' and ''deduction'' appeared to be entirely subjective. By contrast, O'Hanlon and Sinden, in their application of the Pendse/Wyckoff method, incorporated re-surveys and tests between sets of prices to select a price matrix in a rather more systematic manner. They feel that this procedure leads to more objectivity and permits a more reliable choice of final prices. In their rejoinder, Pendse and Wyckoff (1978) appeared to acknowledge the criticism and commended the Australians for the proposed modification to their approach.
12. Law-Yone (1982, 59) describes the use of a composite technique involving three types of games (word game, trade-off game, and simulation game) in the research he carried out in a neighborhood in Haifa selected for urban revitalization, and evaluates the relative merits of each type of game. However, as implied by the discussion, Law-Yone used his trade-off game, at least in the preliminary application, principally as an explanatory method for discussing problems and priorities with the respondents. He did not record systematically or undertake any rigorous analysis of the results from the game.
13. For a fuller discussion of these traditional approaches and techniques, see Robinson et al. 1975, 82–83, 101–2.
14. See discussion of the Ontario Public Services Game, *infra*.

15. See discussion of the Priority Evaluator, *infra.*
16. See Bell and Constantinescu 1974; and discussion of the Resource Community Housing Game, *infra.*

REFERENCES

Belch, J. 1973. *Contemporary Games.* 2 vols. Detroit: Gale Research.

Bell, L. I., and J. Constantinescu. 1974. *The Housing Game: A Survey of Consumer Preferences in Medium-Density Housing in the Greater Vancouver Region.* Vancouver: United Way of Vancouver, Sociology and Research Department.

Berkeley, E. P. 1968. The new gamesship. *Architectural Forum* 129(5):58–63.

County of Los Angeles, Department of Regional Planning. 1976. *General Plan Revision Program, Alternative Directions for Los Angeles County.*

Dowall, D. E., and J. B. Juhasz. 1978. Trade-off surveys in planning: Theory and application. *Environment and Planning,* series A, 10:125–36.

Duke, R. D., and C. S. Greenblat. 1979. *Game-Generating-Games: A Trilogy of Games for Community and Classroom.* Beverly Hills, Cal.: Sage.

Friend, J. K., and W. N. Jessop. 1969. *Local Government and Strategic Choice.* Beverly Hills, Cal.: Sage.

Greenblat, C. S. 1981a. Gaming-simulation as a tool for social research. In *Principles and Practices of Gaming Simulation,* ed. C. S. Greenblat and R. D. Duke, 189–201. Beverly Hills, Cal.: Sage.

———. 1981b. Teaching with simulation games: A review of claims and evidence. In *Principles and Practices of Gaming Simulation,* ed. C. S. Greenblat and R. D. Duke, 139–53. Beverly Hills, Cal.: Sage.

Hasell, M. J. 1980. Urban gaming simulations and evaluation. In *The Guide to Simulations/Games for Education and Training,* 4th ed., ed. R. Horn and A. Cleaves, 286–303. Beverly Hills, Cal.: Sage.

Hoinville, G. 1971. Evaluating community preferences. *Environment and Planning* 3:33–50.

Hoinville, G., and R. Berthoud. 1970. *Identifying and Evaluating Trade-off Preferences—An Analysis of Environmental/Accessibility Priorities.* London: Social and Community Planning Research.

Horn, R., and A. Cleaves, eds. 1980. *The Guide to Simulations/Games for Education and Training.* 4th ed. Beverly Hills, Cal.: Sage.

Houthakker, H. S. 1961. The present state of consumption theory: A survey article. *Econometrica* 29:704–40.

Joseph, A. E., and B. Smit. 1983. Preferences for public service provision in rural areas undergoing exurban residential development—A Canadian view. *Tijdschrift Vwor Economische En Sociale Geografie* 73(1).

Joseph, A. E., B. Smit, and K. Beesley. 1982. Public Input into Planning for Municipal Service Provision. University School of Rural Planning and Development, Report no. 14. Guelph, Ontario.

Law-Yone, H. 1982. Games for citizen participation. *Simulation and Games* 13(1):51–62.

McFarlane, P. A. 1971. Simulation games as social psychological research studies: Methodological advantages. *Simulation and Games* 2:149–61.

Monroe, M. W. 1968. Games as Teaching Tools: An Examination of the Community Land Use Game. Master's thesis, Center for Urban Development Research, Cornell University.

O'Hanlon, P. W., and J. A. Sinden. 1978. Scope for valuation of environmental goods: Comment. *Land Economics* 54(3):381–87.

Pendse, D., and J. B. Wyckoff. 1974a. Environmental goods: Determination of preferences and trade-off values. *Journal of Leisure Research* 6(1):64–76.

———. 1974b. Scope for valuation of environmental goods. *Land Economics* 50(1):89–92.

———. 1978. Scope for valuation of environmental goods: Reply. *Land Economics* 54(3):388–89.

Praxis [a social planning company]. 1982. *Resource Community Study.* Calgary, Alta.: Canstar Oil Sands Ltd.

Raser, J. R. 1969. *Simulation and Society: An Exploration of Scientific Gaming.* Boston: Allyn & Bacon.

Redding, M. J., and G. L. Peterson. 1970. The quality of the environment: Quantitative analysis of preferences for accessibility to selected neighborhood services. Northwestern University, Department of Civil Engineering. Evanston, Ill. Unpublished.

Robinson, I. M. 1972. A note on the determination of community "trade-off" preferences. *International Technical Cooperation Centre Review* 1(4):36–42.

Robinson, I. M., W. C. Baer, T. K. Banerjee, and P. G. Flacksbart. 1975. Trade-off games. In *Behavior Research Methods in Environmental Design,* ed. William Michaelson, 79–118. Stroudsburg, Pa.: Dowden, Hutchinson & Ross.

Robinson, I. M., and W. Jamieson. 1976. Values and alternative urban futures as the basis for policy making. In *Canadian Urban Agenda,* ed. H. P. Oberlander, 85–103. Ottawa: Community Planning Press.

Rockwell, M. L., et al. 1968. *Metropolitan Planning Guidelines—The Plan Study: Methodology, Phase Two: The Comprehensive Plan.* Chicago: Northeast Illinois Planning Commission.

Sanoff, H. 1978. *Designing with Community Participation.* Stroudsburg, Pa.: Dowden, Hutchinson & Ross.

Schran, H. 1972. Urban systems gaming: Developments in Germany. *Simulation and Games* 3(3):309–28.

Schran, H., and D. Kumpf. 1972. Environmental games in the United States: A review of a decade of confusion. *Simulation and Games* (3)4:465–76.

Smit, B., and A. E. Joseph. 1983. Taxpayers' views on the provision of municipal public services. *Plan Canada* 23(1):4–13.

———. 1982. Trade-off analysis of preferences for public services. *Environment and Behavior* 14(2):238–58.

Taylor, J. L. 1971. *Instructional Planning Systems: A Gaming Simulation Approach to Urban Problems.* Cambridge: Cambridge Univ. Press.

Webber, M. 1973. Alternative styles for citizen participation in transport planning. *DMG-DRS Journal: Design Research Methods* 7:60–64.

Wilson, R. L. 1967. Liveability of the city: Attitudes and urban development. In *Urban Growth Dynamics,* ed. F. S. Chapin and S. F. Weiss, 359–99. New York: Wiley.

CHAPTER 5

PERCEPTUAL SIMULATIONS OF ENVIRONMENTS

Peter Bosselmann and Kenneth H. Craik

The immediate on-site impressions of the environment that we experience in our everyday rounds constitute an important facet of our daily lives. But they are not the only environmental impressions we form. We also encounter environments through newspaper photos, movies, television shows, and perusal of our own tourist snapshots. Within the fields of environmental planning, design, management, and conservation, a substantial amount of professional communication about environments and their generation necessarily takes place through indirect presentations of sketches, floorplans and maps, and scale models (Appleyard 1977). Research on environmental perception and assessment, as well as other topics in environmental psychology, often uses indirect presentations of environments that are convenient and manipulatable (Craik 1971; Holahan 1982).

This chapter will describe the varieties of environmental simulation; attempt to determine some of the meanings in the question, "What is a good simulation?"; examine research issues in efforts to address some forms of that question; and describe research, design, and planning applications of a dynamic environmental simulation laboratory.

VARIETIES OF ENVIRONMENTAL SIMULATION

The notion of environmental simulation can be construed quite broadly to encompass a variety of simulation techniques. McKechnie (1977) has offered a useful typology based upon the dimensions of conceptual–perceptual and static–dynamic. *Conceptual simulation* seeks to convey abstract forms of environmental information. Static conceptual simulation includes maps and floor plans; dynamic conceptual simulation includes computer modeling of ecological processes (such as the Club of Rome's limits to growth simulations). *Perceptual simulation* aims at conveying specific physical environments or places. Static perceptual simulation includes photographs and sketches; dynamic perceptual simulation includes filmed modelscope tours of scale models of places.

Nested within McKechnie's typology, a further differentiation among dynamic perceptual simulations can be illustrated by three contexts of application: simulation in environmental planning and design; simulation in auto driving, flight, and navigational training; and simulation in entertainment feature films and television.

In environmental planning and design, visual simulation (such as film) is combined with contrivable environments (scale models or sketches, for example). The goal is to convey accurate impressions of a place—that is, what is seen to be present in it, what descriptions it evokes, and what evaluations it elicits. The purpose is to provide previews of proposed environments that do not yet exist so that response to them can be considered during the decision-making process (in planning and design development, or in public hearings, for example) prior to implementation and construction.

In auto driving, flight, and navigational training, visual simulation is combined with performance monitoring. Auto driver simulators, for example, typically consist of a cab in which the driver sits, a motion picture screen and projector, and scoring consoles. The cab approximates a mock-up of an actual vehicle, with steering wheel, brake, signal lights, and so on. During a simulated tour, the driver steers, brakes, and signals in reaction to various situations presented in the film, and this behavior is recorded and scored for appropriateness. By this kind of device, operators are trained and tested for real-world performance in automobiles, airplanes, space capsules, and ships. These applications entail the assumption that simulator performance predicts subsequent real-world performance. Unlike the context of environmental planning and design, contrivable environments are not essential for this application; motion pictures of real-world settings can be used. However, contrivable environments (such as scale models) are useful in presenting systematically varied situations for operator reaction.

Entertainment films and television are usually visual simulations of real-world settings, if not real-world events, although mock-ups in the form of stage settings are widely used. However, contrived environments achieved by cinematographic special effects and miniaturization have had an increasingly strong role in entertainment. As the recent accomplishments of space adventure films such as *Star Wars* and the genre of disaster films demonstrate, vivid and exciting experiences of imaginary worlds and extraordinary events can be evoked by outstanding expertise and elaborate technical facilities (Dykstra 1977; Kenworthy 1973). Unlike the context of environmental planning and design, visual simulation in entertainment is typically interwoven with action, plot, characters, and theme.

When employed in environmental planning and design, simulation has similar general aims. For example, in operator training it is used to predict responses in the real-world setting based on responses in the simulated setting. However, the appropriate response domains differ. Rather than *impressions of places,* auto driving, flight, and navigational simulations seek to predict real-world performances. In this sense, the criteria for appraising simulation effectiveness is more clear-cut in operator training simulation. In one empirical study, for example, two research staff members independently rated fourteen aspects of the real-world road performance of 304 taxi drivers, including turning without a signal, following too closely, and failure to stay in lane (Edwards et al. 1977). At the time, the drivers were not aware that they were being monitored in this way. Officially recorded accidents and violations over a five-year period were also obtained for all drivers. Then their performance was tested on two standard auto driver simulators. The key question was whether on-the-road performance can be predicted from simulator performance. This study failed to demonstrate the psychological effectiveness of the auto simulators; none of the simulator scores showed a significant relation to any of the on-the-road performance indices.

This study does underscore the goal of comparability between real-world and simulation responses that is shared by applications of simulation in operator training and in environmental planning and design, and illustrates the difference in appropriate response domains. In the former, the behavioral criterion has to do with skilled performance in operating a vehicle; in the latter, it bears upon more or less direct cognitive and evaluative responses to specific physical settings.

Simulation in entertainment films and video programs is also geared to cognitive and emotional responses, but comparability to real-world response is not an issue. Instead, the aim is a desired level of engagement, thrill, curiosity, excitement, and wonder on the part of the audience in the special social context of the theater. Unlike entertainment simulation, presentations of simulated physical settings in environmental planning and design are typically devoid of plot, characters, action, and theme. In this respect, these contexts (for example, environmental public hearings) also constitute special kinds of social situations. By calling for responses that are more or less directly and exclusively focused upon the physical environment, they differ from most, but not all, everyday life experiences.

At environmental public hearings, attention is directed to the proposed physical setting and structures. The project might be the renovation of an interior, the addition of an office building to the urban skyline, a planned residential community, or surface mining within an undeveloped valley. Responses to the simulated environment typically focus upon what is being proposed, how best to characterize it, and how to evaluate it. Another feature of this particular kind of presentation is that responses are usually first impressions. That is, the observers often are viewing the proposed project for the first time and only rarely are they afforded opportunities to examine it repeatedly and over a period of time.

EVALUATING THE PSYCHOLOGICAL EFFECTIVENESS OF PERCEPTUAL SIMULATIONS

During the past two decades, efforts have been made to appraise the psychological effectiveness of static and dynamic forms of perceptual simulation. The impetus for this research comes from two sources. First, within the process of planning and design, static and dynamic forms of perceptual simulation are ubiquitously employed. Photographs of the site are used within agencies and firms as surrogates for repeated site visits; sketches, renderings, plans, and scale models are an integral part of the process of formulating and communicating planning and design concepts and possibilities to colleagues, clients, and the public (Appleyard 1977; Cuff and Hooper 1979). Second, research on topics in environmental perception, cognition, and evaluation often uses photographic simulations of environmental settings. For example, Groat (1982) has studied the meaning of post-modern architecture among laypersons and experts. Prototypic examples of buildings for the design categories she examined are located in Chicago, Marseilles, Tokyo, Boston, Brasilia, Philadelphia, Newcastle-upon-Tyne, and elsewhere around the world. Rather than take research participants on a global tour, photographic presentations of the buildings were employed. Thus, appraisal of the psychological effectiveness of perceptual simulations has practical and scientific importance.

To convey the nature of this enterprise in environmental psychological research, three issues must be discussed. First, the question: "How good is a simulation?" must be unpacked of its various meanings. Second, the complexity of the research generated by the question must be appreciated and its several facets described. Third, the alternative ways of analyzing findings and converting them into evidence relevant to the question must be reviewed and illustrated.

UNPACKING THE QUESTION: HOW GOOD IS THE SIMULATION?

By limiting ourselves to the use of static and dynamic perceptual simulations in (1) environmental planning and design and (2) environmental psychological research, the question, How good is the simulation? can be reformulated as: How well do responses to the simulation predict first impressions of the real-world setting?

This phrasing places a noteworthy yet reasonable limitation upon what simulation is expected to accomplish. Responses to a single presentation of a simulated novel physical setting should predict first impressions of the actual, real-world place, but need not forecast long-term reactions to it and behavior within it. Presently, little is known about the process of acquaintance with places and the extent to which first impressions of real-world settings relate to later conceptions and evaluations of them or conduct in them. Of course, future research may show some orderly relations between first impressions and later adaptations. Only to the degree that these links exist, however, should impressions formed on the basis of simulations be expected to forecast long-term reactions and behavior. Thus, the critical issue for the psychological appraisal of environmental simulations appears to be the comparability of first impressions to simulated and real-world places.

This line of thought leads us in a straightforward fashion to the nature of environmental impression formation. When visiting a new place or being presented with a tour of it, how do people experience environments and form impressions of them? Actually, our knowledge of how people comprehend and evaluate everyday physical settings is not well developed. The topic of environmental perception has only recently received concerted scientific attention, as part of the agenda for the field of environmental psychology (Craik 1970, 1973, 1977; Stokols 1978; Russell and Ward 1982; Holahan 1982; Daniel and Vining 1983; Saarinen and Sell 1981).

The study of environmental perception seeks to understand the impressions we form of settings and places, which constitute an aspect of everyday experience, and focuses upon the processes and factors influencing the varied impressions that observers form of environments. In this context, the term "perception" has been used broadly, to encompass not only immediate visual and auditory perception but other forms of environmental awareness and pertains to both descriptive and evaluative responses. The topic of environmental perception has generated one of the most active lines of research in environmental psychology and has engaged the efforts of geographers, architects, and planners as well as psychologists (Craik 1973; Holahan 1982; Ittelson 1978; Porteous 1977; Rapoport 1977; Saarinen and Sell 1981; Daniel and Vining 1983; Zube et al. 1982; Feimer 1983).

The research to date on environmental perception reveals that the levels of responding to places are multi-faceted, subtle, and complex. Of course, an individual's experience of a place is not directly accessible to others, but must be expressed and communicated if it is to be studied. One of the major tasks facing environmental psychology is the development of standard devices for assisting the individual in recording descriptions, inferences, knowledge, evaluations, and other reactions to places and judgments of them. Thus, in order to compare the degree of match or equivalence between impressions of a place formed on the basis of direct site visit versus simulated presentation, adequate means of recording this domain of responses must be at hand.

In light of our purposes, another complicating recognition has emerged from research on environmental perception. That is, many factors other than medium of presentation of a place influence the impression individuals form of it. Four sets of variables have been identified as integral to investigations of environmental perception: (1) characteristics of the observers (for example, environmental attitudes and dispositions; and professional training); (2) medium selected for presenting the settings (that is, how the place is encountered—via direct site visit, photoslides, scale models, sketches, and so on); (3) the response formats used and the range of reactions they encompass; and (4) the environmental attributes of the settings (Craik 1968, 1971, 1981; Goodey 1971; Pervin 1978; Saarinen 1969; Zube 1974). A fifth set of variables that has also received attention deals with the nature of the transaction with the specific setting, such as cognitive and instructional sets and prior familiarity (Craik 1983a; Leff et al. 1974).

Our general question, How good is the simulation? perhaps inevitably requires a narrower specification before it can be properly addressed. How good is what kind of simulation, for what kind of environment, with regard to whose impressions of the place, formed under what conditions of encounter with it, and as recorded on which response formats? As we shall see, decisions must be made about each facet of this specification statement in any psychological appraisal of environmental simulation. Before discussing these matters in more detail, however, a preliminary strategic option must be dealt with.

We have established the need to compare impressions of a place based upon a simulated presentation with those based upon a direct site visit. One option is to select an existing place, develop a simulation of it, and compare impressions formed in direct and simulated presentations of it. An alternative that appears to fit more closely with the application of simulation in environmental planning and design is to select a proposed project, develop a simulation of it, obtain impressions based upon the simulated presentation, and at a later time, when the project has been implemented, obtain impressions of the actual place.

Despite its appeal on many counts, the second option introduces a formidable array of confounding factors into an effort to appraise the psychological effectiveness of the simulation itself. Planning and design development are incremental processes that occur in an on-going social context. Because they are incremental, the level of detailing of the plan or design varies from point to point in the process and probably is never as comprehensive, thorough, explicit, and inclusive as the details of an existing place. This observation implies, of course, that any implemented plan or design inevitably yields a host of unanticipated outcomes that have not been clearly conceived or considered in advance of implementation or construction. Because the process occurs in an evolving or at least ever-changing social context, detailing becomes more precise but also increasingly subject to modification as financial and institutional commitment to implementation of the project advances (Sheppard 1982a, 1982b).

The practical consequence for appraisal of environmental simulation is that if this strategy is adopted, any failure to achieve comparability between impressions formed on the basis of pre-construction simulations and post-construction places may be due either to incompleteness or errors in the detailed project information used in the simulation or to inherent limitations of the simulation medium. In contrast, the first option—that is, taking an existing place, simulating it, and comparing impressions based upon the place and its simulation—offers a more straightforward and interpretable appraisal of the capabilities of the simulation medium.

By adopting this option, however, one cannot thereby escape the problems that the second option carries for the application of simulation in environmental planning and design. That is, incompleteness and error in the information available about the proposed place, upon which simulations must be formed, may significantly reduce the accuracy of predictions of post-construction response to the place. This issue warrants empirical study in its own right, but it can be put aside here, since it does not bear directly upon the psychological appraisal of simulation effectiveness.

FACETS OF THE RESEARCH DESIGN

Any appraisal of the psychological effectiveness of perceptual simulations inescapably entails decisions regarding (1) which modes of presentation of the environment to compare, (2) what domains of response will be compared, and (3) who will serve as participants in the research. Drawing upon simulation appraisal studies that have been reported, each of these facets of the research design can be reviewed and illustrated.

Modes of Presentation

The modes of presenting research environments to observers fall into three major categories: (1) *direct presentations,* including auto tours, walking tours, use of the facilities, and viewing from specified vantage points; (2) *postconstruction simulations,* including film, photography, and television for indirect presentations of already existing environments; and (3) *preconstruction simulations,* usually combining the techniques of model-making or sketching with film, photography, or television for presentations of proposed or experimental environments prior to their construction or development. Some modes of simulation, such as computer graphics, have been notably neglected in empirical appraisals, while holography has been the focus of only one study. With the exception of film and video presentations (Acking and Küller 1973; Appleyard and Craik 1974, 1978), the visual simulations are static rather than dynamic in character, although the use of photoslide sequences may achieve a dynamic quality.

Most empirical appraisals include at least one direct presentation that serves as a criterion standard for appraising visual simulations (see, for example, Appleyard and Craik 1978; Craik 1983b), but some simply compare preconstruction with postconstruction simulations (Cunningham et al. 1973), or even two preconstruction simulations (Canter et al. 1973). Color slides used singly or in sequences for postconstruction simulations appear to be the most frequently studied mode of presentation (as in Daniel and Boster 1976) (see fig. 5-1).

The selection of modes of presentation in these studies appraising simulation may not adequately represent the frequency with which various forms of perceptual simulation are employed in practice and research. Little is known in particular about the base rate of usage for forms of perceptual simulation in everyday planning and design contexts. Sheppard (1982a, 1982b) conducted a survey of working simulations for projects involving large-scale landscape impacts. Out of a sample of 130 project presentations using a form of perceptual

I. Direct Presentations
  A. Auto tours
  B. Walking tours; use of facilities
  C. Viewing stations
II. Postconstruction Simulations
  A. Color films
  B. Black-white films
  C. Black-white video or videotape
  D. Color photoslides
  E. Color photoslide sequences
  F. Black-white photoslides
  G. Color photographs
  H. Black-white photographs
  I. Aerial photographs
  J. Black-white sketches
III. Preconstruction Simulations
  A. Illustrated plans
  B. Renderings, sketches, perspective drawings
  C. White scale models
  D. Color models
  E. Color model film
  F. Black-white model film
  G. Black-white model video or videotape
  H. Color model photoslides
  I. Black-white model photoslides
  J. Black-white model photographs
  K. Model hologram
  L. Black-white and color photomontages
  M. Verbal description-label only

5–1. Media of presentation.

simulation, tonal and line drawings accounted for 39 percent of all portrayals, followed by black-and-white photomontage (18 percent), full-color renderings (14 percent), scale models (9 percent), computer graphics (9 percent), color photomontage (8 percent), and others (3 percent). Thus, this set of findings raises the possibility that film and photographic simulations are overrepresented and sketches are underrepresented in appraisal studies, perhaps reflecting researchers' concern with scientific rather than practical applications of perceptual simulation.

Response Formats

Research appraising perceptual simulations requires the specification of appropriate criterion measures. Progress in environmental psychology has not yielded a comprehensive array of standard response measures. Furthermore, different applications of perceptual simulation may entail varying forms of appraisal. While an adequate delineation of criterion measures remains a complex and open-ended matter, empirical appraisals of perceptual simulation have commonly opted for a small number of descriptive and evaluative dimensions for recording responses to actual and simulated environments.

As figure 5–2 indicates, the use of bipolar descriptive–evaluative dimensions, often presented as a version of semantic differential ratings, has predominated. Indeed, this technique has served as the sole response format in many investigations despite its limitations (Ward and Russell 1981; Craik 1981).

Although research in environmental perception and assessment has sought to identify a basic set of descriptive and evaluative measures (Craik 1971;

I. Descriptive-evaluative Dimensions
II. Free Descriptions or Descriptive Checklists
III. Evaluative Judgments
IV. Behavioral Intentions or Self-predictions
V. Interest Registrations
VI. Judgments of Objective Properties
VII. Cognitive Measures
VIII. Route Trackings
IX. Direct Media Evaluations

5–2. Response formats.

Craik and Feimer, in press; Feimer 1984; Craik 1971; Daniel and Vining 1983), it has not yet produced a standard set of response formats commonly accepted in evaluation research in visual simulation. Consequently, empirical appraisals of perceptual simulation tend to employ lists of descriptive-evaluative adjectives that vary in content and length.

Supplements to descriptive-evaluative dimensions that have been employed from time to time are noteworthy. Closely related are free descriptions and descriptive checklists, on the one hand, and more explicit forms of evaluative judgments, on the other. Judgments of objective properties include estimates of size, distance, and height. A toggle switch apparatus has been employed to register interest patterns during dynamic presentations (Cunningham et al. 1973). Behavioral intentions and self-predictions include judgments of how much one would enjoy residing in a setting (Rabinowitz and Coughlin 1971) and how far one would be willing to walk to use a facility (Wood 1971). The most overt behavioral criterion remains the monitoring of routes through a museum, in the research of Bonsteel, Sasanoff, and Winkel (Bonsteel and Sasanoff 1967; Winkel and Sasanoff 1976). Cognitive indices have been relatively neglected (but can be illustrated by the use of map sketches and inferences regarding the function of buildings (Wood 1972; Appleyard and Craik 1978; Craik 1983b; Bryant 1984). Surprisingly, in this research tradition, direct judgments of the subjective adequacy of simulation media (in contrast to responses to the environments simulated) have rarely been reported (Anderson 1970; Wood 1972).

Research Participants

The external validity, or potential generalizability, possessed by empirical appraisals of perceptual simulation is partially determined by the representativeness of research participants. As figure 5-3 shows, most investigations have studied university students. However, about half of these studies have employed architecture and design students, representing a pertinent domain of simulation users. Studies enlisting the participation of practicing environmental professionals also focus upon important populations of simulation users. Some investigators have sought out members of the general public, typically having recourse to ready-at-hand groups (such as office workers), while systematic sampling from specified populations is rare.

I. University Samples
   A. Architecture, planning and design students and faculty
   B. Other university students
II. Environmental Professionals
III. Community Samples

5-3. Research participants.

The museum visitors in Seattle (Bonsteel and Sasanoff 1967; Winkel and Sasanoff 1976), the campus visitors at the University of British Columbia (Seaton and Collins 1972), and the residents of a county in California (Appleyard and Craik 1978; Craik 1983b) constitute the most broadly representative samples thus far recruited to appraise perceptual simulation.

ANALYZING THE FINDINGS OF PERCEPTUAL SIMULATION APPRAISALS

The question, How good is the simulation? takes on further and more specific meanings when an appraisal study has been conducted and the findings are available for analysis. The form of the analysis inevitably generates a more detailed specification of our question.

In order to illustrate these analytic options, a simulation appraisal project will be described, and the analytic alternatives and their implications will be discussed.

The simulation appraisal project was linked to an effort to create an innovative laboratory at the University of California at Berkeley. Its goals were to develop new techniques in dynamic environmental simulation, to appraise the psychological effectiveness of the techniques, and to explore the range of new applications of dynamic perceptual simulations in environmental decision making, public communication, and psychological research. The laboratory was initiated by the late Donald Appleyard (Anthony 1983; Craik 1982; Cuff 1983). The present facility was constructed in 1971 through a National Science Foundation grant to Appleyard and Craik (1974, 1978).

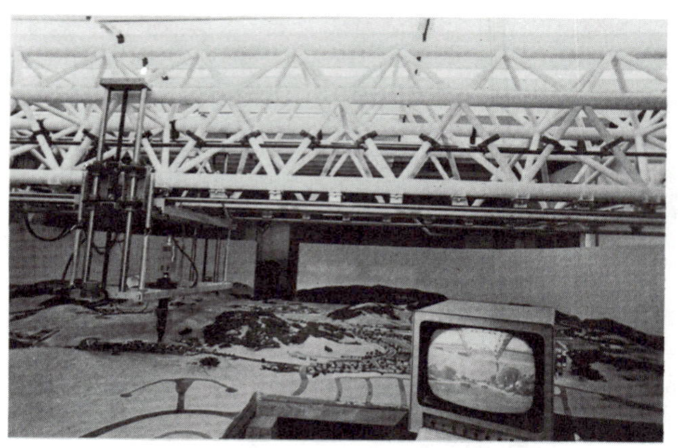

5–4. The Berkeley Environmental Simulation Laboratory, showing the modelscope, camera, carriage, and gantry. The probe is moving through the Marin County research site model. The eye-level image is being projected on an in-house video monitor.

The Berkeley Environmental Simulation Laboratory

The primary component of the laboratory is a dynamic environmental simulator that enables one to "walk" or "drive" through small three-dimensional scale models of urban, suburban, and natural environments. A remotely guided television camera equipped with tiny viewing attachments moves through scale models of the environment and projects continuous eye-level views on closed-circuit television screens. Trips through miniature environments can be displayed "live" to large television audiences. Color films and videotapes can also be made, by using either a manual or computer-controlled guidance system, for comparative feedback, permanent records, and later presentation. The laboratory has model-making and film-making facilities (fig. 5–4).

The use of the laboratory in facilitating decision making, citizen participation, and psychological research is a topic to which we will return. Now let us examine the issues presented by attempting to gauge the psychological effectiveness of this form of dynamic perceptual simulation of environments.

Research Choices

The first decision was to select an existing place, develop simulations of it, and compare descriptive and evaluative impressions formed in direct and simulated presentations of it. The second decision was to recruit samples of the general public and of environmental professionals to participate in the appraisal project. Their experience of the study depended upon further decisions regarding the setting, the media of presentation, and the response formats.

The Setting and the Scale Model. After considering several possibilities, a research site was selected in Marin County, which is located north of San Francisco, just across the Golden Gate Bridge. While Marin County is internationally known for the extraordinary scenic beauty of its coastal zone, including Point Reyes National Seashore, the research site lies within the inland, eastern, more developed Route 101 corridor and is more representative of the low rolling hills and valleys common to northern California. The setting for our study, approximately two by four miles in extent, embodies a broad array of land uses, including several types of residential areas, a regional shopping center, an older commercial highway strip, a light industrial park, an office complex, and some grazing land. The topography features hillsides with extensive grasses and occasional oak and bay trees. The small hills throughout the site create a system of differentiated places. The residential areas, mostly along the valley floors, are cultivated with vegetation that is not native to the area, including eucalyptus trees, liquidambars, and oleanders.

Settings vary in the adequacy of the challenge they offer to the effectiveness of environmental simulation. Little is learned about the capability of a simulation technique if the difficulty level of the research site is not set sufficiently high. Initially, we had considered Nicasio Valley, which runs east–west across the northern part of the county, as a research site. Extensive ecological information had been gathered on it by colleagues in the College of Environmental Design, which would have been available in constructing a scale model. However, an auto tour of the valley offers a predominantly linear route moving through dairy farms and open hillsides. Thus, even a quite primitive simulation might succeed in conveying the uncomplicated and redundant character of this setting. In contrast, the research site we eventually selected consists of a number of distinct places characterized by varied land uses and a more complex system of roadways, including a major highway, a parkway, connector roads, residential roads, and even a stretch of unpaved road. In addition, because of the small hills throughout the central portion of the site, observers never see the setting in a single glance but must instead organize its spatial layout cognitively.

A scale model of the research site, at one inch to thirty feet, was then constructed. This scale appeared to be compatible with the current state of the art of model building while permitting the construction of models within our laboratory to depict regions several square miles in area and thus large enough for the study of new communities, transit system projects, high-rise buildings, and the like. Aerial photographs of the site provided contour information for cutting and shaping the basic polyurethane terrain model. The detailed "dressing" of the model with roadbeds, vegetation, signs, equipment, vehicles, and structures was guided by photographic field studies of the setting and a color film of the auto tour through it. Photo-reduction techniques were used for some signs and building façades; other features and the cycloramic background were hand painted.

The Media of Presentation, Standard Tour Route, and General Instructions. In everyday life, we encounter places in varied ways: we stride, stroll, jog, rollerskate, bicycle, skateboard, and drive through places, and some of us fly, glide, and parachute over them. The closest analog to our dynamic environmental simulator, with its moving point of vision and variable acceleration and viewing direction, seems to be the auto tour. Because it is also a ubiquitous way of becoming acquainted with a place for the first time, the direct auto tour (AT) of the research site was selected as the basis for comparing and appraising three forms of simulated tours of the setting: a color film of the scale model tour (MF), a color film of the auto tour (AF), and a videotape of the scale model tour (MV). The primary focus of appraisal was upon the principal product of the dynamic simulator: a 16mm eye-level color film of the scale model tour (fig. 5-5). A 16mm color film of the real-world auto tour, made with a camera mounted in the front passen-

5–5. Eye-level views from the tour through the scale model of the Marin County research site.

ger side of an auto after its windshield had been removed, afforded an opportunity to differentiate between possible effects due to use of color film, with its fixed orientation and restricted angle of view, and effects due to the use of a scale model, with its inevitable detail distortions of the real-world setting. Finally, a black and white videotape of the scale model tour was included in the study to appraise the form of simulation employed in the laboratory for live, direct feedback uses. (We now use color video.)

In seeking to appraise the effectiveness of environmental simulation in conveying impressions of a place, we must operate at the boundaries of our knowledge of environmental perception and cognition. Thus, we are unable to appeal to prior scientific findings to judge the consequences of our focus upon the auto tour, in contrast to the stroll or helicopter flight. That these differing ways of encountering a place affect the impressions visitors form of it is a reasonable hypothesis but one not yet examined by environmental psychologists. All we can assert at this time is that by having to choose one of them, we have added another specification to our inquiry, How good is the simulation?

Nevertheless, the auto tour is an attractive option because in our society it represents an important form of everyday environmental experience. After much exploration along the roadways of the research site, we devised a standard tour of about twenty-five minutes covering nine miles. We had considered the alternative of developing much briefer and shorter tours through more restrictive models of several research sites. These presentations, however, would not be typical of an auto drive, and the scale models would not be useful for other research applications. The present standard tour is more representative of the social context of "going for a drive" and also affords a sufficiently challenging level of complexity for appraising the simulations. The findings from this study can also provide base-line findings for subsequent research examining the effects of briefer tours and tours combining several travel modes (such as ground level auto tours plus helicopter overflights).

As a full-fledged social event, an auto tour requires a purpose. Of course, our research volunteers would already be endowed with purpose: to enact the role of research participant ably and to advance the overall goals of our project through their cooperation. We considered the possibility of adding a hypothetical social purpose to the research design, for example, by instructing our participants to assume that during the tour, (1) they were searching for a particular restaurant where they were to meet a friend for dinner; or (2) as newcomers to the region, they were evaluating this area as a possible place of residence. However, the hypothetical nature of these purposes and their openness to individual variation in interpretation lent an unwanted complexity to the research design. Yet some orientation for the participants would be expected. We finally settled upon pretour instructions that combine the scenic tour or "Sunday drive" with the context of an environmental public hearing at which a new proposed project is being previewed.

Thus, prior to their tour, participants were informed that they would be touring an area of Marin County and that they were to take a good look at it, to note what impressions it made upon them, what caught their attention, what they liked and disliked about it, and in general, to size up the place. They were informed that following the tour, they would complete procedures that would assist them in recording their impressions of the tour area. They were requested not to smoke during the tour nor to take notes. Individuals in the auto tour condition were asked to aim for a minimal yet comfortable level of social conversation, rather than complete, awkward silence, but not to talk about the area being toured. Individuals in the other conditions were told they would be viewing a film of the tour, film of the scale model tour, or video tape of the scale model tour, as appropriate.

Response Formats. The appraisal project required a full-day commitment. In the morning session, participants were presented with the tour either directly or via simulation and then completed an extensive battery of procedures. In this systematic debriefing of their descriptions, cognitions, and evaluations of the research site, participants completed mood checklists, map sketches, environmental adjective checklists, and regional Q-sorts; inference, information, and recognition tests; and environmental evaluation forms (Appleyard and Craik 1978; Craik 1983b; Bryant 1984; Feimer 1984). Following lunch, they completed additional procedures dealing with personal background, environmental attitudes and dispositions, leisure activity styles, and related observer characteristics.

Analytic Strategies. The question, How good is the simulation? is constrained at yet another level by the options selected in analyzing the findings of a simulation appraisal. Three examples can be illustrated from results of the simulation of the Marin County research site.

First, the overall *congruence* in the descriptive impressions and evaluations of a place yielded by direct and simulated encounters with it can be gauged. For example, all participants rated how satisfactory they found the research site on twenty-eight dimensions of residential quality. For each sample, these twenty-eight dimensions can be ordered, according to mean ratings, from the attributes found to be most satisfactory to those found to be least satisfactory. In summary, the auto tour sample rated these features as most satisfactory about the research site:

- nearness to professional offices (doctor, dentist, and so on)
- nearness to shopping
- good climate
- nearness to freeway
- maintenance of public areas (such as streets and sidewalks)
- resale value of homes
- nearness to schools

and found these features the least satisfactory:

- amount of community spirit
- good places for children's play
- amount of visiting among neighbors
- availability of public transportation within region
- diversity of residents' age

- diversity of social status and life styles
- adequacy of separation from neighbors' houses (to insure privacy)

The similarity with which two samples, say, the auto tour (AT) and the model film (MF), evaluate a place can be estimated by the correlation between their mean ratings, across the twenty-eight attributes. For the Marin County research site, that correlation was above +.90, indicating substantial congruence in the overall evaluation of features of the site, regardless of the mode in which it was presented. Indeed, strong congruence in both descriptive impressions (as recorded on environmental adjective checklists and Q-sort decks) and evaluations prevailed in the findings from this study (Craik 1983b).

Second, the question of whether the mode of presentation has any significant impact upon the mean levels of the many dependent descriptive, cognitive, and evaluative variables can also be addressed. This form of the basic question: "How good is the simulation?" quickly moves us into the realm of advanced multivariate statistical analysis. Several issues, however, can be noted briefly: factor analysis, analysis of variance, and discriminant analysis.

Factor analysis can be employed to simplify the analytic and interpretive task by providing a smaller set of orthogonal summary variables. Thus, the 300 items of the environmental adjective checklist yield five factor scales (satisfying-delightful; monotonous-ordinary; beautiful-scenic; neat-maintained; active-busy). Similarly, the 67 items of the regional Q-sort deck provide five factor scores and the 28 items of the environmental evaluation form generate five factor scores (Craik et al. 1978). These new factor scores still represent descriptive, cognitive, or evaluative variables whose influence by the mode of presentation must still be examined. A similarity in factor structure across media conditions itself grants no assurance that specific research sites will be described or evaluated comparably (Craik and Feimer, in press; Wiggins 1973).

Even with a reduced set of factor scores and other summary variables, an ambitious appraisal of perceptual simulation still retains a large number of dependent variables, calling for the use of multivariate *analysis of variance.* This analytic approach allows us to pinpoint any specific dependent variables that show a significant influence due to the mode of simulation employed. For example, the auto film (AF) condition resulted in significantly lower mean scores on the EACL scale *beautiful-scenic,* and on a set of four landscape descriptors (Craik 1983b). Closer examination of the media suggests that an atmospheric haze and glare were picked up in the auto film presentation that were less noticeable in the direct auto tour setting and absent from the brightly lighted laboratory conditions of the model film (MF) and model video (MV) settings. As a second example of this kind of finding it can be noted that the research site was seen as lower on the EACL scale *neat-maintained* under the model film (MF) condition. One of the challenges of the model-making task was miniaturization of residential lawns and shrubbery. In the model film (MF) presentation, the residential landscaping did appear somewhat overgrown and unkempt, which probably led to this effect in the simulated presentation.

The detailed search for specific effects of simulation provides precise feedback and guidance for improvements in simulation techniques and for better understanding of the processes involved. Another form of multivariate statistics, known as *discriminant analysis,* provides a means for judging how functionally important the detailed media effects may be. Discriminant analysis weights and combines the entire array of dependent variables linearly to achieve maximum possible separation between media conditions. It tests the utility of the overall diagnostic value of the full set of descriptive, cognitive, and evaluative variables in predicting which media conditions the participants had been assigned to. That is, if we had available to us only all thirty-four dependent measures and knew nothing else about the individuals, how successfully could we use this information to decide which of the participants had taken the direct auto tour and which had seen, say, the model film simulation?

The diagnostic separation turned out to be the most successful for the auto tour (AT) versus auto film (AF) contrast, followed by the auto tour (AT) versus model video (MV) contrast, and finally the auto tour (AT) versus model film (MF) contrast. Obviously, the worse the diagnostic ability of the full set of dependent variables, the more psychologically effective the simulation. In fully effective simulation, the responses of observers should offer no basis for estimating which medium of presentation observers used in encountering the setting.

Third, the question, How good is the simulation? must be placed in a comparative context. The magnitude of the effects of simulation on descriptive, cognitive, and evaluative variables is difficult to appraise in an absolute fashion. Craik (1983b) has reported that the proportion of variance accounted for by the media of presentation is modest (less than 10 percent for most dependent variables). As a comparison variable, the amount of prior familiarity with the site accounted consistently for more of the variance. In a somewhat different but complementary analysis of these data, Feimer (1979, 1984) estimates that the media of presentation accounted for about 3 percent of the variance, while a combination of personality and other observer characteristics accounted for five to ten times as much of the variance in the descriptive–evaluative variables. The effects of the media of presentation upon spatial-cognitive variables is somewhat higher (Craik 1983b), and in a thorough analysis by Bryant (1984) it is estimated to approximate the magnitude of the effects of personality factors.

TRENDS IN RESEARCH FINDINGS ON THE PSYCHOLOGICAL EFFECTIVENESS OF PERCEPTUAL SIMULATION TECHNIQUES

We have identified three ways of reformulating the question, How good is the simulation? from a statistical viewpoint. Most research findings thus far have focused upon the first formulation: How good is the overall congruence of descriptive and evaluative impressions between direct and simulation presentations? Most studies have reported substantial congruence, with correlations in the +.70 to +.95 range (Craik and Feimer, in press).

Simulation appraisal studies have devoted less attention, and less adequate statistical analysis, to the second formulation: How extensive and of what kind are the detailed differences in descriptive, cognitive, and evaluative responses due to the use of various forms of perceptual simulation? As figures 5-1 through 5-3 indicate and as our analysis of our basic question has suggested, this formulation highlights the potential complexity of our research task. The number of forms of simulation and their combinations with the facets of observer characteristics, transactional contexts, and response formats pose a formidable but worthwhile research program. The studies to date amount to a sampling from this larger range of experimental conditions and do not provide the basis for generalizations. This research can be reviewed (Craik and Feimer, in press) but its primary message at present is that detailed, fine-grain understanding of alternate forms of perceptual simulation techniques and their contexts of application will require an imposing and long-term program of inquiry.

The third formulation of our question, How consequential is the mode of presentation of places in comparison with other factors influencing impressions of them? recasts our inquiry in the form of basic research on the understanding of environmental perception. It suggests that appraisal of the psychological effectiveness of perceptual simulation techniques may be best conducted within a larger scientific framework. The few analyses to date that have framed the question in this way derive from our study of the Marin County simulation project. In those findings, the media of presentation studied have consequences that tend to trail in magnitude to those due to prior familiarity with the site, personality characteristics of the observers, and sociodemographic backgrounds of the observers. However, once again, the detailed implications warrant more attention (Craik 1983b; Feimer 1980, 1984; Bryant 1984) than any generalizations that can be supported by them.

Overall, a review of studies on this topic suggests a falling off in the amount of research directed at the question, How good is the simulation? (Craik and Feimer, in press). Clearly, this decline makes no sense in light of our very modest and fragmented knowledge and the generally thin amount of empirical evidence that has been gathered to date.

APPLYING ENVIRONMENTAL SIMULATION IN PLANNING AND PUBLIC COMMUNICATION

Capturing the vision of the city as a communicable form began with the work of Kevin Lynch (1960). To convey the motion, light, wind, color, and tempo of the city as perceived by all of us became a special kind of design problem (Appleyard et al. 1964) (fig. 5-6). Although many planning professionals consider the visual aspects of the environment to be trivial in comparison with economic, fiscal, and social issues, the fact is that the public is extremely sensitive to the visual environment, for its symbolic quality as well as the immediate experiences it affords. Matters of scale, color, shape,

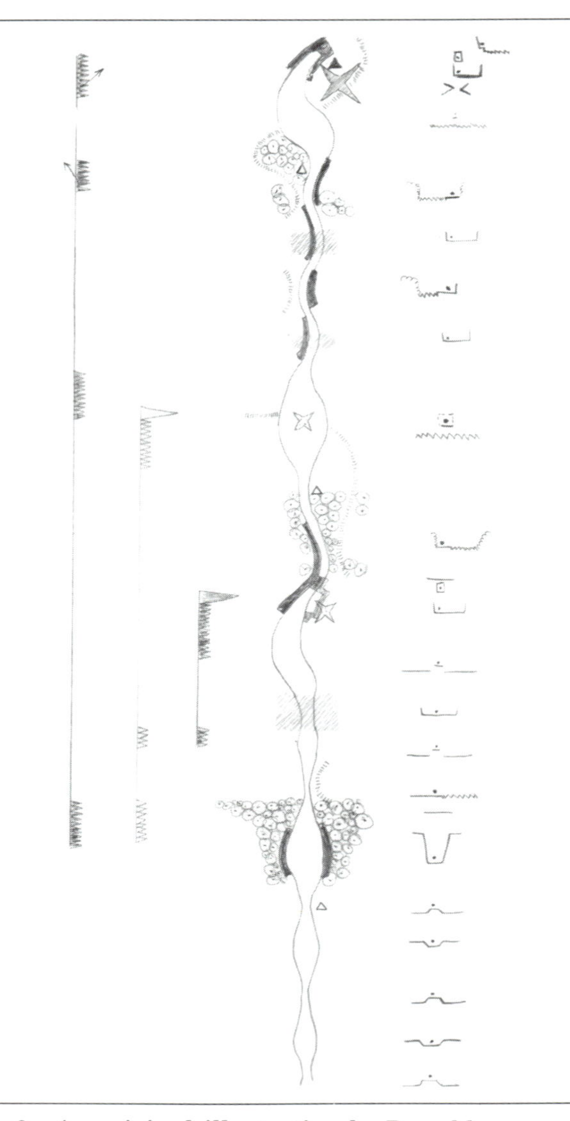

5-6. An original illustration by Donald Appleyard for **The View from the Road** *(Appleyard, Lynch, and Myer 1964). The notational system was an offspring of Lynch's earlier* **The Image of the City** *(Lynch 1960), aimed at communicating the experience of driving along a roadway.*

street character, and view affect a population's image of its city and of itself. The visual qualities convey powerful emotive messages that imply who runs the city, who dominates its environments, and the character of those in power (Appleyard 1984).

Much needs to be improved in the way that planners and design professionals communicate projects and future plans. If the aim is to let the public become more involved in the planning process, better methods of communication have to be developed. This advance would be to the benefit of all parties involved. Planners and designers are bound to learn as much about their own plans as the public. The ability to describe in experiential terms effects of designs and plans is a skill rarely found among professionals. The terms professionals use to describe such qualities as "urbanity" are vague and fall short of the qualities ordinary citizens directly experience in existing places. A lack of professional knowledge currently exists in this regard. Professionals have taken more and more to conceptual methods of explaining their ideas. This step has appeared to be a safer route, in that it leaves many visual impacts unrevealed and unexamined.

Even if planners wanted to explain the experience of a new development or plan more effectively, few techniques are available to serve these purposes. The experiential media of twentieth-century film and video are currently granted little importance in the planning and design professions. The development of the Berkeley Environmental Simulation Laboratory and the challenges of each new project undertaken by it have focused our thinking on all aspects of simulation and have prompted continuous appraisal of the validity of its products and their relation to practices within planning and design. Staff at the laboratory have become more and more aware of the politics of simulation, the relative utility of different media, and the hidden power that media have over our designs, decisions, and environment. If done well, simulation can be a tool for realizing a more democratic urban form. It can reach out and involve larger segments of the public whose opinions have traditionally not been sought or heard.

At the Berkeley Environmental Simulation Laboratory progress has been made with five major applications of perceptual simulation.

Illustrating Basic Planning Issues

First, simulation has been used to illustrate basic planning issues. A scale model of San Francisco housed in the laboratory has been used to examine proposed changes in the downtown zoning ordinance (Bosselmann and Gerdes 1980; Bosselmann 1983b). Simulations were made to illustrate (1) the effects of transfer development rights, (2) the consequences of new building bulk and height regulations, and (3) the impact of new high-rise development on the skyline and neighborhoods of the city (fig. 5-7). Film simulations illustrated the consequences of alternative planning controls on street scale, mix of uses, and openness of the street to sunlight and air (Bosselmann 1983a) (figs. 5-8 and 5-9). The film clips produced at the laboratory were shown to planners and planning commission members. The public saw the film with the alternatives as part of a community affairs program on television. The process educated policy makers and the public about the choices implied by alternative zoning controls. These analyses have led to pioneering development guidelines based on sun-access criteria (Bosselmann et al. 1983; Bosselmann et al. 1984).

Using Visual Previews to Develop and Review Proposed Projects

A second level of application uses perceptual simulation to offer previews of specific major new proj-

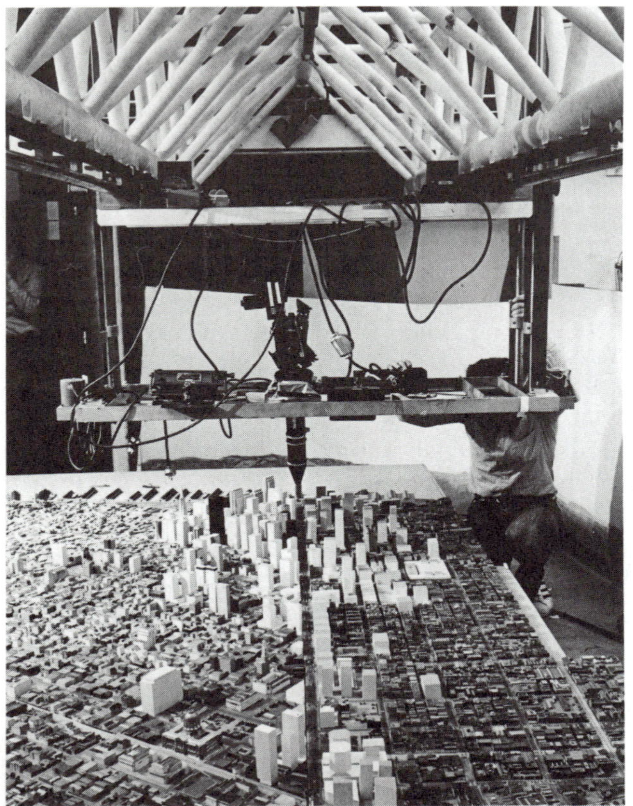

5–7. A 1935 scale model of San Francisco, continuously updated, is used at the Berkeley Environmental Simulation Laboratory to produce perceptual simulations of future zoning and urban design controls. The scene includes buildings projected as a consequence of a specific zoning alternative.

ects to the public. Simulation is also used as a testing tool in the planning and development process. In an analysis of the visual impact of alternative highway route alignments across a recreational lake, the modelscope technique provided film presentations of the before-and-after views generated by each alternative (fig. 5–10). Residents of the region were systematically sampled and invited to special viewing sessions, where they recorded their judgments of visual impacts (Atkins and Blair 1983). Other projects have dealt with the visual impacts of a redesign of the Great Highway along the ocean coast of San Francisco, a marina development in Richmond, California on San Francisco Bay, and development alternatives for the Berkeley bay waterfront area (Appleyard et al. 1979).

Increasing Public Participation

A third mode of application has explored ways of increasing public participation in the planning and design process. The systematic sampling of participants who viewed alternative highway alignments in a visual impact assessment procedure has already been noted above. In another project, the design of a mini-park involved neighbors through the use of a model-kit to shape initial ideas, followed by eye-level model tours at the environmental simulation laboratory, which led to additional modifications of the project by the neighborhood participants (Appleyard et al. 1979).

For another application, a citizens advisory committee charged with assigning preservation priorities in a county open-space program was presented with an array of prototypical development possibilities for the areas under consideration. The various possibilities were simulated for each type of land parcel. Through the use of an electronic switchboard system, their immediately recorded preference votes were tallied and fed back to them for further discussion and consideration.

Advancing Environmental Education

A fourth form of application of perceptual simulation of environments furthers educational aims.

5–8. A scale model of a typical downtown street permits the perceptual simulation of alternative development controls and their impacts on street scale, mix of uses, and openness of street to sky and sun.

Using our San Francisco scale model, a film was developed showing the changes in that city's skyline between the 1930s and the 1970s. An early film from the laboratory showed the uses of a proposed automated guideway system for highways. Finally, a recent simulation film conveys the findings and planning implications from Appleyard's (1981) examination of the use of diverters and controllers in managing traffic in residential neighborhoods (Appleyard and Bosselmann 1982; Bosselmann and O'Hare 1983) (see also fig. 5–11).

Facilitating Research in Environmental Psychology

A final level of application can be found in the use of perceptual simulation in basic research on land-use compatibility. The degree of fittingness of new uses to present contexts is a pervasive issue in urban design and landscape management (Groat 1983; Wohlwill 1977). With the modelscope technique, land use can be systematically introduced in combination with various current uses and topo-

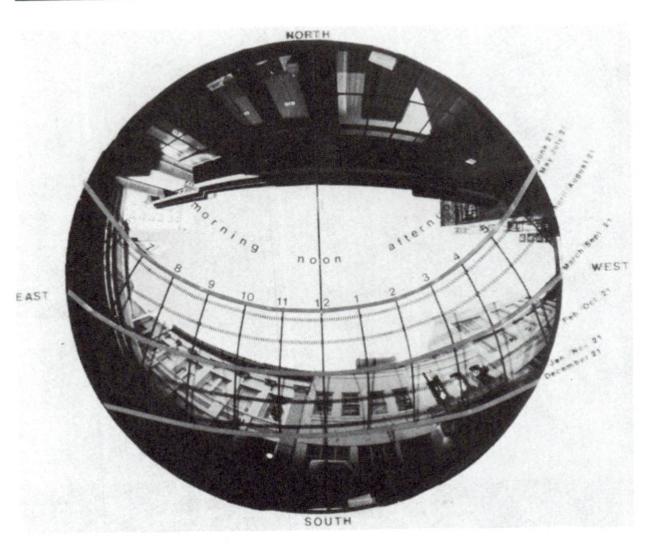

5–9. Photographic sunlight simulations. The superimposed lines represent the path of the sun in June, March, September, and December for this site. The photographic analysis is used to measure the duration of sunlight and shade upon streets and open spaces, given varying high-rise development in the vicinity.

graphic settings. Judgment techniques can be employed to analyze the compatibility of the land-use combinations and to provide guidelines for predicting the impact of specific kinds of projects upon perceived environmental quality. For example, Wohlwill (1977) used the facilities of the Berkeley Environmental Simulation Laboratory to investigate the effects upon observer response of different levels of incongruity in three kinds of structures, each of which was systematically varied in color, texture, and size, as located in two different coastal settings (fig. 5–12). This application of the modelscope technique makes full use of its capability of affording systematic manipulations of the environment for scientific and planning purposes. A more recent research project using perceptual simulations generated by our modelscope technique has

5–10. Simulation of a proposed freeway across a recreational lake in Louisiana. The photo at top shows the scale model (at 30 feet to 1 inch); on the bottom is an eye-level view through the modelscope.

5–11. Berkeley street diverter plan. Detailed scale models are used to explain the impact and options of neighborhood traffic management devices. The two photos* at left *show the scale models and the photo* at right *shows eye-level views through the modelscope.

investigated the effects of pathway configurations and the presence of landmarks upon environmental cognition (Evans et al. 1984).

These five applications of environmental simulation represent a sampling of the broad range of purposes to which environmental simulations can be put. The illustrations are drawn from the work and experience of a single environmental simulation laboratory. The examples are restricted to those generated by the specific technical apparatus of that laboratory. The range of simulation techniques is wider in scope and encompasses considerable diversity, including the recent emphasis upon full scale mock-up versions of proposed environments in pre-construction evaluation (King et al. 1982) and in user participation (Lawrence 1982).

Many researchers and planners have no access to modern simulation facilities. As Sheppard has found, the static sketch and photomontage have predominated in the simulation of projects entailing potential large-scale impacts (Sheppard 1982a, 1982b).

5–12. Views of a scale model of a coastal site showing three land uses: top, *a small resort hotel;* center, *a larger resort hotel;* bottom, *a lumber mill. Developed by J. F. Wohlwill.*

Often design proposals are approved based upon static two-dimensional drawings (fig. 5–13). The selection of viewpoint, perspective, and focus of view is highly controlled by the producer of such simulations and is usually restricted in diversity and coverage. If a colored rendering is produced, the light, shadow, texture, color, and usage of environmental features is easy to distort or overemphasize. Sequences of drawings or photomontages, however, can provide understandable visual presentations of motion through space. In a recent study in the Environmental Simulation Laboratory, five important views of an undeveloped waterfront were selected. Through photomontage, alternative development proposals were superimposed onto the existing ones. The development proposal had been generated by community representatives. The simulated views in turn were presented to the original group. The alternative views described a continuum of change from low to high intensity development (fig. 5–14). Upon seeing the images, the community groups engaged in an active discussion about the appropriate level of development. The "trade-offs" were negotiated be-

5–13. A line drawing of a potential high-rise development near San Francisco's Chinatown. Courtesy William Gray.

5–14. A sequence of photomontages onto one base view of the Berkeley hills, taken from the bay waterfront. The sequence shows alternative development options of increasing intensity.

tween the citizen group and the developers in order to move toward a range of suitable development.

Advances in computer technology have been explosive in the last ten years and are likely to continue. Virtually all conventional training simulators for pilots, drivers, and train engineers use electronically generated imagery. The imagery is still very abstract and has a cartoon-like quality. Images for a recently developed driver-simulator for Daimler-Benz are of very high quality—multicolored and rich in detail (fig. 5–15). Such effects as shadows moving with the vehicle, fog, and dusk views can be realistically simulated. The driver, however, is taken through a quite abstract landscape with few visual clues or details. The trees and building façades represented are poor reflections of their real-world counterparts. Due to the high cost factor, computer simulations are available only to large firms and research centers. Nevertheless, significant amounts of research and development funds are being devoted to advances in computer graphics and substantial improvements and reduced costs can be anticipated over the next decade. Also, the entertainment industry has devel-

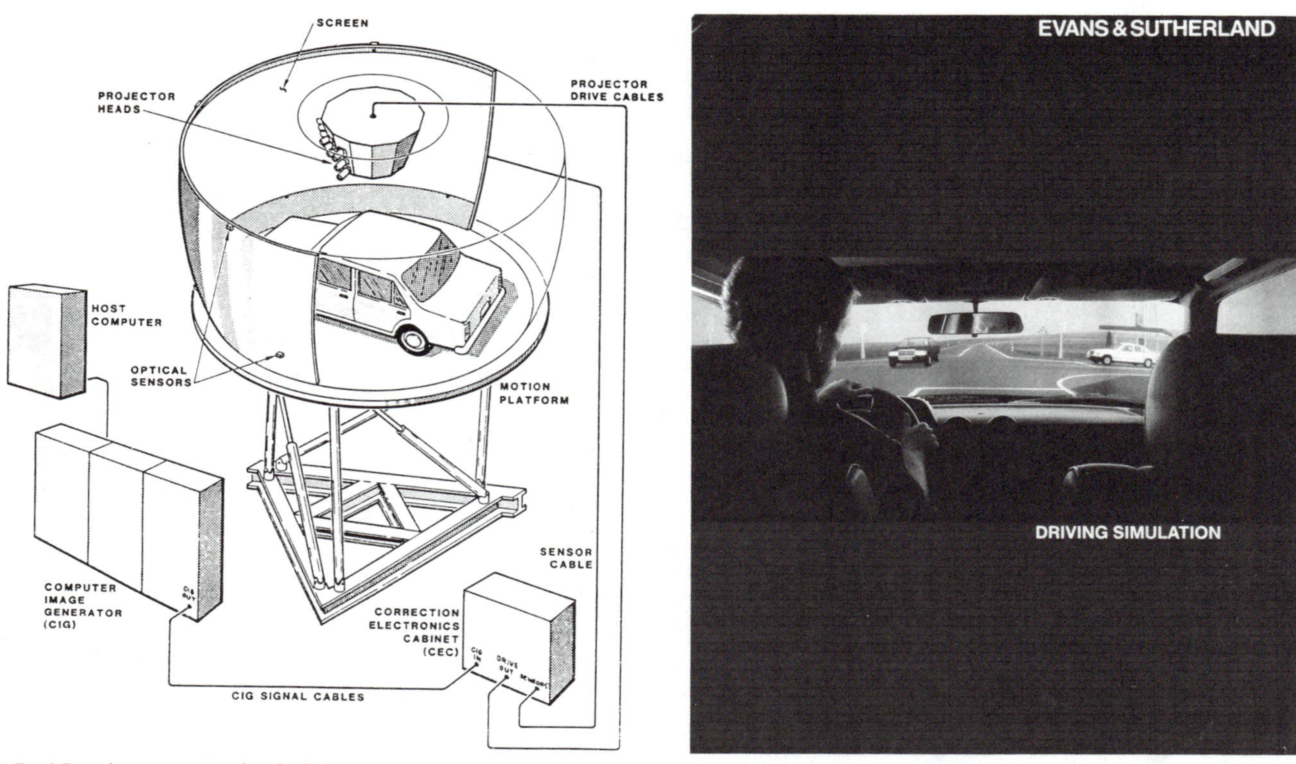

5–15. A computerized driver simulator for an automobile manufacturer. The drawing is a diagram of the apparatus; the photo shows the computer-generated views from the test automobile. Courtesy of Evans and Sutherland, Salt Lake City, developed for the Daimler-Benz Driving Simulator.

oped its own computer generated images. As noted earlier, the aim here is to create illusions and fantasies. The technical capacities for doing so are impressive, as demonstrated by the road scene with a rainbow (fig. 5–16).

Now, fifteen years after the Berkeley Environmental Simulation Laboratory was established, techniques have been developed for producing model simulation with relative ease and at low cost. Frequently architectural firms bring models to the laboratory for eye-level simulation tours through them. The videotape production of simulations in conjunction with modelscopes has reduced costs, at some sacrifice to depth of field and crispness of image (see, for example, Carpman et al. in press). The turnaround times for film, videotape, and photoslide recordings of modelscope views are normally a few hours and work can be done on a day's notice.

Our perceptual simulations are often presented at public hearings. For example, a new ordinance in San Francisco requires all developers of downtown office buildings to construct a scale model of the proposed design. The building is placed into the laboratory's scale model of downtown San Francisco and photographed from various angles. Any reasonable number of views can be readily recorded. The simulations are part of the Planning

5–16. A computer simulation produced by Lucasfilm, Ltd., entitled "Road to Point Reyes." This landscape was defined using patches, polygons, fractals, particle systems, and a variety of procedural models. The various elements were rendered separately and later composited. Rob Cook designed the picture and did the texturing and shading, including the road, hills, fence, rainbow, shadows, and reflections. Loren Carpenter used fractals for the mountains, rock, and lake, and a special atmosphere program for the sky and haze. Tom Porter provided the procedurally drawn texture for the hills and wrote the compositing software. Bill Reeves used his particle systems for the grass and wrote the modeling software. David Salesin put the ripples in the puddles. Alvy Ray Smith rendered the forsythia plants using a procedural model. The visible surface software was written by Loren Carpenter, and the antialiasing software by Rob Cook. The picture was rendered using an Ikonas graphics processor and frame buffers, and was scanned on FIRE 240, courtesy of MacDonald Dettwiler & Associates Ltd. The resolution is 4K × 4K, 24 bits/pixel. Credit: "Road to Point Reyes," directed by Robert L. Cook, Computer Division of Lucasfilm, Ltd.

Commission's design review process. In this work the laboratory serves as an extension of the San Francisco Planning Staff.

The simulations have to be accurate and open to accuracy control. In our procedure, developers as well as opponents of the development have access to the model and can take measurements of the dimensions of the proposed and existing development to check for accuracy. The perceptual simulations have to be realistic in color, texture, and façade treatments. The simulated sun and shadow patterns have to be consistent, and the choice of sun angles has to be realistic and representative. The simulations has to be objective. Not only the most attractive or devastating views are taken; instead, views are recorded from an array of representative viewing stations from which the development would be seen. In some instances the corresponding real-world locations are visited and on-site photographs are taken to verify the model simulation (Appleyard et al. 1979).

San Francisco's new ordinance is useful and innovative. It is the result of continuous concern by citizens and environmental groups for development compatible with the character of the city. As in other cities, planners often find themselves in an adversary situation. For example, a proposal to expand a hospital has caused neighborhood groups to unite and fight to block the project. The group presented a simulation that strongly exaggerated the negative impacts of the proposal. If the planners respond by showing only diagrams that remain abstract, the public feels misled and has little trust in the professionals. Perceptual simulation should provide a balanced, objective viewpoint that allows the identification of conflict areas, and a procedural mechanism for critiques, modifications, and the generation of supplemental views. A two-way design process can then be established that permits various compromises to be discussed, simulated, and reexamined.

The gradual withdrawal from the use of modern simulations that appears now to be a trend among planning and design professionals would widen the gap between the professionals and the general public. With the loss of credibility in the predictions advanced by planners, the public is demanding, and will continue to demand, complete information and full disclosure regarding the impacts of proposed projects.

CONCLUSION

This chapter has had three main purposes. First, the varieties of environmental simulation have been reviewed and the use of perceptual simulation in environmental decision making and in environmental psychological research has been distinguished from other forms of application. Second, the conceptual and strategic research design issues presented by the task of evaluating the psychological effectiveness of perceptual simulations have been delineated. Third, the wide range of useful applications of perceptual simulation in environmental planning and design has been illustrated.

Two major conclusions can be reached regarding psychological appraisals of perceptual environmental simulations. First, these investigations must be placed within the context of basic research on environmental perception and cognition. Second, an extensive agenda of appraisal research remains before us.

Three major conclusions emerge from an examination of specific forms of application of perceptual environmental simulations. First, the diversity of current and possible uses of perceptual simulations calls for more detailed evaluations of their effectiveness within these specific contexts of use. Second, perceptual simulation techniques used in environmental planning and design and in environmental psychological research must keep pace with the rapid technological advances now found in the field of simulation. Third, perceptual environmental simulations are currently underused in environmental decision making, and their forms of useful applications are limited only by the ingenuity and insightfulness of environmental professionals and researchers.

ACKNOWLEDGMENTS

This chapter derives from a program of innovation and research on perceptual environmental simulation initiated at the University of California, Berkeley by the late Donald Appleyard. His contribution to this chapter cannot be overestimated. We also wish to thank the extensive number of technical staff, research staff, graduate students, visiting scholars, project participants, and institutional supporters who have made the work of the Berkeley Environmental Simulation Laboratory possible over the decade and a half of its operation.

REFERENCES

Acking, C. A., and R. Küller. 1973. Presentation and judgment of planned environments and the hypothesis of arousal. In *Environmental Design Research,* ed. W. F. E. Preiser, vol. 1, 72–83. Stroudsburg, Pa.: Dowden, Hutchinson, & Ross.

Anderson, J. M. 1970. A television aid to design presentation. *Architectural Research and Teaching* 1:20–24.

Anthony, K. 1983. Major themes in the work of Donald Appleyard. *Environment and Behavior* 15:411–18.

Appleyard, D. 1977. Understanding professional media: Issues, theory and a research agenda. In *Human Behavior and Environment,* ed. I. Altman and J. F. Wohlwill, vol. 2. New York: Plenum.

Appleyard, D., with M. S. Gerson and M. Lintell. 1981. *Livable Streets.* Berkeley, Cal.: Univ. of California Press.

———. 1984. Identity, Power and Place. Institute of Urban and Regional Development, University of California. Typescript.

Appleyard, D., and P. Bosselmann. 1982. *Urban Design Guidelines for Street Management.* University of California, Institute of Urban and Regional Development, Working paper no. 385. Berkeley.

Appleyard, D., P. Bosselmann, R. Klock, and A. Schmidt. 1979. Periscoping future scenes: How to use an environmental simulation lab. *Landscape Architecture* 69:487–88, 508–10.

Appleyard, D., and K. H. Craik. 1974. The Berkeley Environmental Simulation Project: Its use in environmental impact assessment. In *Environmental Impact Assessment: Guidelines and Commentary,* ed. T. G. Dickert and K. R. Domeny, 121–25. Berkeley, Cal.: Univ. of California Extension.

———. 1978. The Berkeley Environmental Simulation Laboratory and its research programme. *International Review of Applied Psychology* 27:53–55.

Appleyard, D., K. Lynch, and J. R. Myer. 1964. *The View from the Road.* Cambridge, Mass.: MIT Press.

Atkins, J. T., and W. G. E. Blair. 1983. Visual impacts of highway alternatives. *Garten und Landschaft* 8:632–35.

Bonsteel, D. L., and R. Sasanoff. 1967. *An investigation of a televised image in simulation of architectural space.* University of Washington, Architecture/Development Series no. 6. Seattle.

Bosselmann, P. 1983a. Shadowboxing: Keeping sunlight on Chinatown's kids. *Landscape Architecture* 73:74–76.

———. 1983b. Visual impact assessment at Berkeley. *Urban Design International* 7:34–37.

Bosselmann, P., J. Flores, and T. O'Hare. 1983. *Sun and Light for Downtown San Francisco.* Berkeley, Cal.: Institute of Urban and Regional Development, Univ. of California.

Bosselmann, P., J. Flores, T. Priestley, and H. Gerdes. 1984. *Sun, Wind and Comfort.* Berkeley,

Cal.: Institute of Urban and Regional Development, Univ. of California.

Bosselmann, P., and H. Gerdes. 1980. Film and video in the planning process. *American Planning Journal* 46:12–14.

Bosselmann, P., and T. O'Hare. 1983. Traffic in urban American neighbourhoods: The influence of Buchanan. *Built Environment* 9:127–39.

Bryant, K. J. 1984. Geographical spatial orientation ability and the representation of real-world and simulated environments. Ph.D. diss., University of California, Berkeley.

Canter, D., M. Benyon, and S. West. 1973. Comparisons of a hologram and a slide of a room interior. *Perceptual and Motor Skills* 37:635–38.

Carpman, J. R., M. A. Grant, and D. A. Simmons. (in press). Hospital design and wayfinding: A video simulation study. *Environment and Behavior.*

Craik, K. H. 1968. The comprehension of the everyday physical environment. *Journal of the American Institute of Planners* 34:29–37.

———. 1970. Environmental psychology. In *New Directions in Psychology,* ed. K. H. Craik, B. Kleinmuntz, R. L. Rosnow, B. Rosenthal, J. A. Cheyne, and R. H. Walters, vol. 4, 1–122. New York: Holt, Rinehart & Winston.

———. 1971. The assessment of places. In *Advances in Psychological Assessment,* ed. P. McReynolds, vol. 2, 40–62. Palo Alto, Cal.: Science & Behavior.

———. 1973. Environmental psychology. *Annual Review of Psychology* 24:402–22.

———. 1977. Multiple scientific paradigms in environmental psychology. *International Journal of Psychology* 12:147–57.

———. 1981. Environmental assessment and situational analysis. In *Toward a Psychology of Situations,* ed. D. Magnusson, 37–48. Hillsdale, N.J.: Erlbaum.

———. 1982. Obituary: Donald Appleyard, 1928–1982. *Journal of Environmental Psychology* 2:169–70.

———. 1983a. A role theoretic analysis of scenic quality judgments. In *Managing Air Quality and Scenic Resources at National Parks and Wilderness Areas,* ed. R. D. Rowe and L. G. Chestnut, 117–26. Boulder, Col.: Westview.

———. 1983b. The psychology of the large-scale environment. In *Environmental Psychology: Directions and Perspectives,* ed. N. R. Feimer and E. S. Geller, 67–105. New York: Praeger.

Craik, K. H., D. Appleyard, and G. E. McKechnie. 1978. Impressions of a Place: Effects of Media and Familiarity among Environmental Professionals. Institute of Personality Assessment and Research, Berkeley, Cal.: Univ. of California. Unpublished report.

Craik, K. H., and N. R. Feimer. In press. Environmental assessment. In *Handbook of Environmental Psychology,* ed. D. Stokols and I. Altman. New York: Wiley.

Cuff, D. 1983. A tribute to Donald Appleyard. *Places* 1(1):3–17.

Cuff, D., and K. Hooper. 1979. Graphic and mental representation of environments. In *Environmental Design: Research, Theory and Applications,* ed. A. Seidel and S. Danford. Washington, D.C.: Environmental Design Research Association.

Cunningham, M. C., J. A. Carter, C. P. Reese, and B. C. Webb. 1973. Toward a perceptual tool in urban design: A street simulation pilot study. In *Environmental Design Research,* ed. W. F. E. Preiser, vol. 1, 62–71. Stroudsburg, Pa.: Dowden, Hutchinson, & Ross.

Daniel, T. C., and R. S. Boster. 1976. *Measuring landscape aesthetics: The scenic beauty estimation method.* USDA Forest Service Research Paper RM-167. Fort Collins, Colo.: Rocky Mountain Forest & Range Station.

Daniel, T. C., and J. Vining. 1983. Methodological issues in the assessment of landscape quality. In *Behavior and the Natural Environment,* ed. I. Altman and J. F. Wohlwill, 39–84. New York: Plenum.

Dykstra, J. 1977. Miniature and mechanical special effects for "Star Wars." *American Cinematographer* 58:702–5, 732, 742, 750–57.

Edwards, D. S., C. P. Hahn, and E. A. Fleishman. 1977. Evaluation of laboratory methods for the study of driver behavior: Relationship between simulator and street performance. *Journal of Applied Psychology* 62:559–66.

Evans, G. W., M. A. Skorpanich, T. Garling, K. J. Bryant, and B. Bresolin. 1984. The effects of pathway configuration, landmarks and stress on environmental cognition. *Journal of Environmental Psychology* 4:323–36.

Feimer, N. R. 1979. Personality and Environmental Perception: Alternative Predictive Systems and Implications for Evaluative Judgments. Ph.D. diss., University of California, Berkeley.

———. 1983. Environmental perception and cognition in rural contexts. In *Rural Psychology,* ed. A. W. Childs and G. B. Melton, 113–50. New York: Plenum.

———. 1984. Environmental perception: The effects of media, evaluative context and observer sample. *Journal of Environmental Psychology* 4:61–80.

Goodey, B. 1971. *Perception of the Environment.* Occasional Paper no. 17. Birmingham: Centre for Urban and Regional Studies, Univ. of Birmingham.

Groat, L. 1982. Meaning in post-modern architecture: An examination using the multiple sorting task. *Journal of Environmental Psychology* 2:3–22.

———. 1983. Measuring the fit of new to old: A checklist resulting from a study of contextualism. *Architecture* 72:58–61.

Hershberger, R. G., and R. C. Cass. 1974. Toward a set of semantic scales to measure the meaning of architectural environments. In *Environmental Design: Research and Practice,* ed. W. J. Mitchell, 6-4-1 to 6-4-10. Los Angeles: Univ. of California at Los Angeles.

Holahan, C. A. 1982. *Environmental Psychology.* New York: Random House.

Ittelson, W. H. 1978. Environmental perception and contemporary perceptual theory. In *Environment and Cognition,* ed. W. H. Ittelson. New York: Seminar.

Kenworthy, N. P., Jr. 1973. A remote camera system for motion-picture and television production. *Journal of the SMPTE* 82:159–65.

King, J., R. W. Marans, and L. A. Solomon. 1982. *Pre-construction Evaluation: A Report on the Full Scale Mock-up and Evaluation of Hospital Rooms.* Ann Arbor, Mich.: Architectural Research Laboratory, Univ. of Michigan.

Lawrence, R. J. 1982. A psychological-spatial approach for architectural design and research. *Journal of Environmental Psychology* 2:37–52.

Leff, H. L., L. R. Gordon, and J. G. Ferguson. 1974. Cognitive set and environmental awareness. *Environment and Behavior* 6:395–447.

Lynch, K. 1960. *The Image of the City.* Cambridge, Mass.: MIT Press.

McKechnie, G. E. 1977. Simulation techniques in environmental psychology. In *Perspectives on Environment and Behavior: Theory, Research and Applications,* ed. D. Stokols, 169–90. New York: Plenum.

Pervin, L. A. 1978. Definitions, measurements, and classifications of stimuli, situations and environments. *Human Ecology* 6:71–105.

Porteous, J. D. 1977. *Environment and behavior: Planning and everyday urban life.* Reading, Mass.: Addison-Wesley.

Rabinowitz, C. B., and R. E. Coughlin. 1971. *Some Experiments in Quantitative Measurement of Landscape Quality.* Discussion paper no. 43. Philadelphia, Pa.: Regional Science Research Institute.

Rapoport, A. 1977. *Human Aspects of Urban Form.* New York: Pergamon.

Russell, J. A., and L. M. Ward. 1982. Environmental psychology. *Annual Review of Psychology* 33:651–88.

Saarinen, T. F. 1969. *Perception of Environment.* Resource Paper no. 5. Washington, D.C.: Commission on College Geography, Association of American Geographers.

Saarinen, T. F., and J. L. Sell. 1981. Environmental perception. *Progress in Human Geography* 5:525–47.

Seaton, R. W., and J. B. Collins. 1972. Validity and reliability of ratings of simulated buildings. In *Environmental Design: Research and Practice,* ed. W. J. Mitchell, 6-10-1 to 6-10-12. Los Angeles: Univ. of California at Los Angeles.

Sheppard, S. R. J. 1982a. Landscape Portrayals: Their Use, Accuracy, and Validity in Simulating Proposed Landscape Changes. Ph.D. diss., University of California, Berkeley.

———. 1982b. Predictive landscape portrayals: A selective research review. *Landscape Journal* 1:9–14.

Stokols, D. 1978. Environmental psychology. *Annual Review of Psychology* 29:253–95.

Ward, L. M., and J. A. Russell. 1981. The psychological representation of the molar physical environment. *Journal of Experimental Psychology: General,* 110:121–52.

Wiggins, J. S. 1973. *Personality and prediction: Principles of Personality Assessment.* Reading, Mass.: Addison-Wesley.

Winkel, G. H., and R. Sasanoff. 1976. An approach to an objective analysis of behavior in architectural space. In *Environmental Psychology: People and Their Physical Settings,* 2d ed., ed. H. M. Proshansky, W. H. Ittelson, and R. G. Rivlin, 351–62. New York: Holt, Rinehart & Winston.

Wohlwill, J. F. 1977. What belongs where: Research on fittingness of man-made structures in natural settings. In *Assessing Amenity Research Values,* ed. T. C. Daniel, E. H. Zube, and B. L. Driver, 48–57. Fort Collins, Colo.: U.S. Forest Service.

Wood, W. 1971. Simulation: A Comparison of Color Film, Black and White Film and Video Tape to Reality in the Simulation of Architectural Environments. University of British Columbia, School of Architecture, unpublished report. Vancouver, B.C.

———. 1972. An Analysis of Simulation Media. University of British Columbia, School of Architecture, unpublished report. Vancouver, B.C.

Zube, E. H. 1974. Cross-disciplinary and intermode agreement on the description and evaluation of landscape. *Environment and Behavior* 6:69–90.

Zube, E. H., D. G. Pitt, and T. W. Anderson. 1975. Perception and prediction of scenic resource values of the Northwest. In *Landscape Assessment: Values, Perceptions and Resources,* ed. E. H. Zube, R. O. Brush, and J. G. Fabos, 151–67. Stroudsburg, Pa.: Dowden, Hutchinson & Ross.

Zube, E. H., J. L. Sell, and J. G. Taylor. 1982. Landscape perception: Research, application and theory. *Landscape Planning* 9:1–33.

CHAPTER 6

ECOLOGICAL PSYCHOLOGY

Robert B. Bechtel

One of the most pervasive and least dealt with problems of planning and design research is how to gather data on the great number of questions that need to be answered in programming and design. The designer and/or programmer wants to know the answers to a variety of questions. What are the functions and activities of the building? How do these functions and activities relate to one another? Which ones should overlap, and which ones need to be separated? How much space is required for each activity? How many people take part in each activity and at what times? Can some activities be scheduled in the same space because they operate at nonoverlapping times?

These and many other questions must be asked and answered in order to program and/or design any room, building, development, or community. Yet answering these kinds of questions in one study is largely beyond the scope of most of the social sciences. The social sciences, psychology and sociology in particular, focus all their research and training on testing hypotheses—precise questions phrased to establish an unambiguous relationship between a single cause and a single effect. Furthermore, a good researcher in these fields will spend a great amount of time and energy attempting to answer just one hypothesis. The testing of one hypothesis may continue for years.

Thus, when confronted with the myriad questions the designer wants answered, the average social scientist throws up his or her hands in horror, contemplating several lifespans of work just to begin such a task. And, confronted with this kind of response, the average designer despairs of getting answers that are needed within months or even weeks. How do we solve this dilemma?

One of the ways is to collect data in a non-hypothesis-testing mode, to look at the whole cloth of human behavior and present this information to the designer. Such a method was developed in the 1940s and 1950s by psychologist Roger Barker and his colleagues, working in small Midwestern towns.

Rather than take all of human behavior in one gigantic swallow, Barker discovered that behavior can be studied in ''bite-size'' bits called *behavior settings.* A behavior setting is a standing pattern of behavior that is tied to a particular place and occurs at regular intervals. They are easily seen and recognized as the ordinary events of daily life. Barker saw that people in a town (or building, for that matter) sort themselves out into these behavior settings in order to get the daily business of life accomplished. All one needs to do to design is to snip off the settings and enclose them into a building envelope. Admittedly, this is oversimplified, but let us examine how it can be done.

In the case of a mental hospital, the question that arises is how to design a building that will satisfy the needs of patients and staff. An examination of hospital behavior settings (Srivastava 1978) shows that there are too many activities for the spaces provided. A better design provides a space for each behavior setting, alleviates the crowding, and stops forcing patients into spaces not designed for them.

In remote communities of the Arctic, many design questions become more critical than in other geographical areas because the climate forces more behavior indoors for the long winters. An examination of community behavior settings (Bechtel and Ledbetter 1976) shows how to plan better large communities by separating single and married quarters and how to plan better small remote installations by building composite buildings that house most of the activities. An examination of behavior settings in a harsh desert community (Bechtel et al. 1980) shows that an encirclement of hills provides an ideal site location and a community building appears to tie the community together socially. Other behavior setting studies show how to staff a national park (Wicker 1979b) and improve the design of a rehabilitation hospital (LeCompte and Willems 1960). These are a few of the examples of how behavior settings have been used to program better design. Before understanding how these examples worked it is necessary to examine the methods used.

BACKGROUND AND LITERATURE

Ecological psychology had its beginning in 1947, when Roger Barker and Herbert Wright opened the Midwest Psychological Field Station at the down home farming community of Midwest (code name), Kansas. The original modest purpose was to study the development of children in a town small enough to observe and measure. Some time in the early 1950s it became apparent that the community influence on behavior was not easily captured by conventional psychological methods; and new techniques, first called psychological ecology, were developed to deal with the problem. Along with new methods, a new view of human behavior evolved that saw behavior and environment as occurring in inseparable units called behavior settings. This linking of behavior with environment has led to the claim that the psychological field station gave birth to environmental psychology itself (Holahan 1982).

The methods were so new and different from conventional psychology that they remain obscure and unknown to many psychologists even today. It would be fair to say that despite Barker's tremendous influence on the field of environmental psychology, the techniques of ecological psychology are not widespread, partly due to the belief that ecological techniques are long and cumbersome (Smith 1974). This objection is no longer valid, because shorter and more varied techniques have been derived from the original methods (Bechtel 1977). The techniques evolved as studies in ecological psychology moved from an attempt to characterize behavior in one community to comparisons of behavior across communities.

The first report in the field of ecological studies was *One Boy's Day,* published in 1951, a study describing in full detail the activities of one person during the course of a typical day. The second text, *Midwest and Its Children,* was published in 1955 and became the standard text until Barker's *Ecological Psychology* appeared in 1968. By 1960, however, Barker began comparing communities and organizations and first proposed his undermanning theory (Barker 1960). Barker and Gump's *Big School, Small School* (1964) applied this theory to schools, and the *Qualities of Community Life* (1973) by Barker and Schoggin described the stability of the comparative data over a ten-year period. Other books such as *Stream of Behavior* (1963) and *Habitats, Environments and Human Behavior* (1978) describe studies and methods of various projects in ecological psychology. Theoretical work is reported in Wicker (1973, 1979a) and applied work in Bechtel (1977).

The standard introductory text and the main recommendation for further reading is Wicker's *Introduction to Ecological Psychology* (1979b).

THE BEHAVIOR SETTING AND THE K-21 SCALE

Central to the understanding of all ecological psychology and its methods is the behavior setting. Barker discovered the behavior setting by listening to and observing the people in his small town. When they talked about the behavior of their lives they described activities and events. These same events were reported in newspapers and recorded in various kinds of archives. When Barker looked at these events and activities, he discovered they had rather permanent and enduring qualities in terms of repeated behavior, time, place, and physical attributes. He began experimenting with ways to measure these attributes and came up with a series of scales, which became the heart of ecological psychology measurement. The primary scale was called the K-21 (see fig. 6–1).

The K-21 scale was developed to answer the problem of how to tell whether two putative behavior settings are actually separate or constitute a single setting. While common sense can easily discern most behavior settings, in some cases it is difficult to tell them apart. The K-21 consists of seven subscales that are added together. If the sum is 21 or more, the behaviors are considered separate behavior settings. If below 21, they are deemed too interdependent to be separate; and scores between 18 and 23 seem to indicate boundary problems (Bechtel 1977). By this use, the scale becomes a diagnostic tool as well as a descriptive definition of behavior settings.

By doing a few K-21 scales on behaviors in any environment, it will become clear that overlaps seem to have a cut-off point of roughly 50 percent. If each subscale shows less than 50 percent overlap, the behaviors being measured are separate, but if overlaps are more than 50 percent the total will add up to less than 21. It is thus convenient, in estimating interdependence, to judge whether overlaps in time, population, and so forth, seem to overlap more or less than 50 percent. When it becomes too difficult to tell, or if the overlaps seem marginal, it is better to do a K-21 on the site, using actual observations to arrive at scores. Traditionally, Barker and his associates would do K-21 scales on *all* behavior settings.

The K-21 is actually the defining instrument for a behavior setting. Barker (1968) defined a behavior setting as "a standing pattern of behavior synomorphic and circumjacent to the milieu." This means that a behavior setting can be discerned as a separate entity even though it is surrounded by and is a part of surrounding behavior, much in the way that a waterfall is part of a stream.

Only by doing a number of K-21 scales can the novice gain a "feeling" for behavior settings. While most behavior settings such as grocery stores, boy scout meetings, and school classes are easily identified, it is often difficult to intuit whether, for example, the lunch counter at a drug store is a separate behavior setting from the pharmacy counter.

In this regard, there is no substitute for field experience. An excellent exercise is to gain experience in obtaining reliability with the K-21 scale. When architect Burgess Ledbetter and I were learning to work together, it was an important part of our training to learn to do K-21 scales with a high degree of reliability. We picked two rather complex activities to start with—a sergeant's desk in one corner of a room, and a secretary's desk in the opposite diagonal corner (see fig. 6–2). These two people carried out their duties despite being able to hear and see each other constantly and despite the many interruptions and intrusions of people walking through the space between them.

THE IDENTIFICATION OF K21 BEHAVIOR SETTINGS

The K-Test of interdependency of two behavior settings is based upon ratings of the degree to which:

1. The same people enter both settings
2. The same power figure or leaders are active in both settings
3. Both settings use the same or similar spaces
4. Both settings use the same or similar behavior objects
5. The same molar action units span the two settings
6. Both settings occur at the same time or at times that are near together
7. The same kinds of behavior mechanisms occur in the settings

Rating of Population Interdependence

This is a rating of the degree to which people who enter setting A (P_B) are the same as those who enter setting B (P_B). The percent overlap is judged by the following formula:

$$\text{Percent Overlap} = \frac{2\,P_{AB}}{P_A + P_B}$$

Where P_A is number of people who enter setting A; P_B is number of people who enter setting B; P_{AB} is number of people who enter both setting A and setting B.

This percent overlap is converted to an interdependency rating by the following scale:

Rating	*Percent Overlap*
1	95–100
2	67–94
3	33–66
4	6–32
5	2–5
6	trace–1
7	none

Rating of Leadership Interdependence

This is a rating of the degree to which the leaders of setting A are also the leaders of setting B. It is determined in the same way as population interdependence for persons who penetrate to Zones 4, 5, or 6 in both settings A and B.

Rating of Spatial Interdependence

This rating indicates the degree to which settings A and B use the same or proximate spatial areas. Rate on the following scale. In the case of scale points with two definitions, the most appropriate one applies; if more than one applies, give the lowest scale rating.

Rating	*Percent of Space Common to A and B*	
1	95–100	
2	50–94	
3	10–49	or A and B use different parts of same room or small area
4	5–9	or A and B use different parts of same building or lot
5	2–4	or A and B use areas in same part of town*
6	trace–1	or A and B use areas in same town but different parts of the town*
7	none	or A in town, B out of town

*Deciding how to separate a town or area into parts should not be completely arbitrary. Sometimes census tracts can be used. If a building is being studied, floors can be the "parts." Sometimes a town can also be divided into fourths.

Rating of Interdependence Based on Behavior Objects

This rating measures the extent to which behavior setting A and behavior setting B use identical or similar behavior objects. Rate on the following scale. In the case of scale points with two definitions, the most appropriate one applies; if more than one applies, give the lowest rating.

6–1. K-21 scale.

Rating		
1	Identical objects used in setting A and setting B; i.e., all behavior objects shared	
2	More than half of the objects shared by A and B	or virtually all objects in A and B of the same kind
3	Half of the objects shared by A and B	or more than half of the objects in A and B of the same kind**
4	Less than half the objects shared by A and B	or half the objects in A and B of the same kind**
5	Few behavior objects in A and B identical	or less than half the objects of A and B of the same kind**
6	Almost no objects shared by A and B	or few behavior objects of same kind** in A and B
7	No objects shared	or almost no similarity between objects in A and B

**Objects of the same kind are different instances of objects that have the same dictionary definition; for example, spoons are used in the behavior setting School Lunch Room and the setting Clifford's Drug Store Fountain, but they are different spoons.

Rating of Interdependence Based on Molar Action Units

This is the degree to which molar behavior units are continuous between setting A and setting B. The molar behavior settings A and B may be integrated in two ways. The inhabitants of setting A may interact across the boundary with the inhabitants of B; for example, the person in the cytosetting Preacher interacts directly with the members of the cytosetting Congregation in the Church Service. On the other hand, behavior begun in one behavior setting may be completed in the other, for example, delivering lumber for a construction project starts at the setting Lumberyard and is completed at the setting House Construction. Scales for the former situation are found in column I, for the latter in column II. For each kind of behavior integration, use the highest percent that applies. The average of the two ratings is the final rating.

Rating	*I*	*II*
1	95–100	95–100
2	67–94	67–94
3	34–66	34–66
4	5–33	5–33
5	2–4	2–4
6	trace–1	trace–1
7	none	none

Rating of Interdependence Based on Temporal Contiguity

This is the degree to which settings A and B occur at the same time or at proximate times. Most behavior settings recur at intervals. Any pair of settings, therefore, may occur together on some occasions and be temporally separated at other times. For example, the American Legion meets monthly, while the Boy Scout Troop meets weekly; once a month their meetings occur during the same week. The closest temporal proximity of setting A and setting B determines the column to enter the table below. The percent of contact at the point of closest proximity determines the interdependence rating in the column at the right. The percent of contact is computed as the ratio between the number of occurrences of both settings at this closest point of contact divided by the total number of occurrences of both behavior settings.

Interdependence Rating	Simultaneous	Same Part of Day	Same Day	Same Week	Same Month	Same Year
1	.75–1.00					
2	.50–0.74	.75–1.00				
3	.25–0.49	.50–0.74	.75–1.00			
4	.05–0.24	.25–0.49	.50–0.74	.75–1.00		
5	0–0.04	.05–0.24	.25–0.49	.50–0.74	.75–1.00	
6		0–0.04	.05–0.24	.25–0.49	.50–0.74	.50–1.00
7			0–0.04	.05–0.24	.25–0.49	0–0.49

(continued)

Figure 6–1 continued

Interdependence Based on Similarity of Behavior Mechanisms

This scale rates the degree to which behavior mechanisms are similar in setting A and setting B. Ratings are based on the following twelve behavior mechanisms:

Gross Motor	Writing	Eating
Manipulation	Observing	Reading
Verbalization	Listening	Emoting
Singing	Thinking	Tactual feeling

The interdependence score is determined by the number of behavior mechanisms present in one setting and absent in the other as indicated in the following table.

Interdependence Rating	*Number of Mechanisms Present In One Setting and Absent in the Other*
1	0–1
2	2–3
3	4–6
4	7–8
5	9–10
6	11
7	12

Figure 6–1 continued

6–2. Overlapping behavior settings of the secretary and the sergeant.

Population

Because of the fact that most of the people counted in the room walked through both spaces, including the occupants of the desks themselves, it was obvious that the population overlap was 95 to 100 percent, or a rating of 1 on the scale.

Leadership

Observing how both people performed their duties revealed that the sergeant had to leave the room frequently and that this meant the secretary answered his phone more often than he answered hers. Moreover, she would never go near his vehicle assignment charts, nor would he use her typewriter, or the telecopier. It seemed that leadership overlap was very little—only a trace to one percent of the time both occupied the space.

Spatial Interdependence

Barker's phrase, "different parts of the same room" (see K-21 Scale, fig. 6–1) is applicable here and gets a rating of 3. When actual overlap in terms of square feet was calculated, the space commonly used by both is less than 49 percent.

Behavior Objects

Few objects are shared between the two. They have their own phones, pens, desks, writing pads, and so forth. The secretary has her typewriter, telecopier, and locked filing cabinets, while the sergeant has his scheduling and assignment charts. This was the only rating, however, in which the architect and I disagreed. I gave it a 5 and the architect gave it a 6.

Molar Actions

Observing the behavior of both, it is noted that the phoning, typing, writing, and conversing overlap very little. Only answering the telephone calls occurs across both boundaries; it accounts for less than 33 percent of the time both spent in the space. The rating was 4.

Temporal Contiguity

The time both spent in the space overlaps nearly 100 percent and is rated 1. They both work the same hours on the same days and only during vacation times is there no overlap.

Behavior Mechanisms

Observation of both people reveals that they perform largely the same kinds of bodily tasks: talking, phoning, and writing. The tasks that are different do not account for much time. Both observers rated 1.

The K-21 rating showed these two behavior patterns to be just at the point of independence, 21. The two raters differed on only one scale, showing an agreement of over 90 percent. Obviously, not all ratings will show such close agreement among observers. Much is to be learned from areas of disagreement, however. For example, some of the disagreement on behavior objects could be resolved by actually making an inventory of every object in each location, finding which ones are shared, and calculating the percentage. Nearly all disagreements in K-21 ratings can be resolved by more careful counting of the overlapping and nonoverlapping elements.

In addition to using this exercise as a reliability test, it can also serve as a design guide. Reexamining the seven dimensions shows boundary problems between the settings. The sergeant must leave his desk to counsel his soldiers because they can be overheard if he were to stay there. The secretary feels uncomfortable when she has a confidential phone call. Both the sergeant and the secretary must exert energy *not* to learn each other's job. These kinds of boundary problems are very common in open office situations. One can calculate how the problem would be alleviated by erecting physical, soundproof barriers between the two settings. Population overlap would be cut down considerably. Observation would be needed to confirm the new scores, but it is also likely that with effective barriers, the two offices would then be treated as two rooms and spatial dependence and molar action overlaps would also be decreased, making a new possible score of 27, well beyond the boundary conflict range.

In fact Ledbetter did K-21 scales for the entire office complex and was able to derive a remodeling design that resulted in higher K-21 scores (Bechtel 1977, ch. 3). Thus, the K-21 score itself can be used as a design tool for discovering and measuring solutions to behavior setting boundary problems.

THE BEHAVIOR SETTING SURVEY

A community is "measured" by doing a behavior setting survey. This is really a census or count of all the behavior settings in a community. It differs from a survey of people because behavior settings rather than people are counted, and in this process, the same people may actually be counted several times. The final arbiter of whether a behavior setting is included in the survey is the K-21 scale.

A behavior setting survey usually has four stages: (1) preliminary list, (2) research on the list and potential behavior settings, (3) final list, and (4) analysis of data.

The preliminary list of behavior settings is obtained from a wide variety of sources. Going into a new community afresh, how can a researcher come up with a preliminary behavior setting list? The telephone book is a primary source, particularly the yellow pages, which usually will list every business. The white pages typically will list every residence. Newspapers, covering an entire year, will probably report the greatest number of public meetings, events and happenings for the community. School year books, neighborhood newspapers, bulletin boards, church bulletins, and organizational newsletters are also important sources. Once these sources have been combed, the researcher has acquired a fairly comprehensive grasp of the range of activities in the community. These become a basis for asking about behavior settings not included in the initial sources.

The second and most time-consuming task in the behavior setting survey is the second phase, which has the dual purpose of discovering any settings missed in the preliminary list and filling in the technical data on all the behavior settings.

Behavior settings missed in the previous list are often discovered by using informants. A standard procedure, for example in filling out behavior settings in a school, is to go over the preliminary list with the school principal and a group of teachers, followed by a group of students. They often will report on unexpected behavior settings such as smoking in the furnace room (the furnace room itself becomes a behavior setting by the K-21 scale, while smoking is one of several behaviors there). And from the students you learn that they sneak smokes there, as do the teachers. The principal, of course, knows nothing of this, but a new behavior setting has been catalogued.

At the same time that one is adding behavior settings to the preliminary list, informants can add to and confirm data on attendance, leadership, and other aspects of behavior that need to be collected for each behavior setting.

The behavior setting survey virtually exhausts every method of collecting data on behavior settings. For this reason, it then becomes impossible to verify the data by some independent method, and since validity is always established by independent methods, how can behavior settings be shown to be valid? The question really addresses ecological psychology from the point of view of hypothesis-testing standard psychology, which uses only one or a few methods in testing a hypothesis. The question is better understood when it is realized that the behavior setting survey exhausts *all* independent sources of measurement, making it the most valid method available in social science. Furthermore, since this process is a part of the ordinary data collection, and not just a means of establishing validity, it is the most continuously valid source of data!

A behavior setting code sheet, shown in figure 6-3, demonstrates a method of recording data on each behavior setting for a computer analysis. A newer method uses the data sheet as the basis for constructing a questionnaire administered to randomly selected respondents in order to get the behavior setting information (Bechtel 1977, 177-79).

It is important first to have a general knowledge of the lifestyles in a community. For example, in a

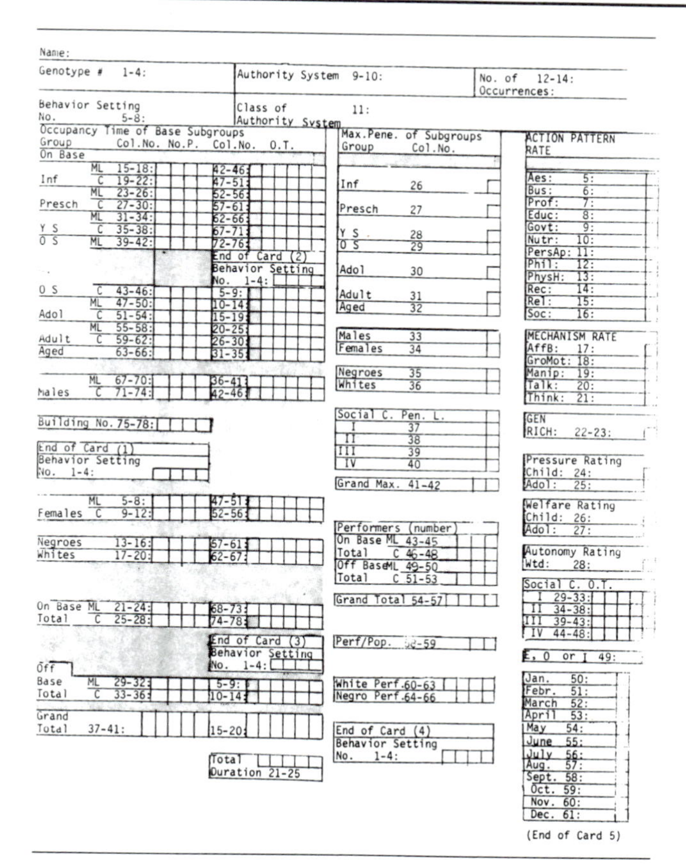

Name:
Genotype # 1-4: | Authority System 9-10: | No. of Occurrences: 12-14:
Behavior Setting No. 5-8: | Class of Authority System 11:

Occupancy Time of Base Subgroups
Group Col.No. No.P. Col.No. O.T.
On Base
Inf ML 15-18: 42-46:
Inf C 19-22: 47-51:
Presch ML 23-26: 52-56:
Presch C 27-30: 57-61:
Y S ML 31-34: 62-66:
Y S C 35-38: 67-71:
O S ML 39-42: 72-76:
End of Card (2) Behavior Setting No. 1-4:
O S C 43-46: 5-9:
Adol ML 47-50: 10-14:
Adol C 51-54: 15-19:
Adult ML 55-58: 20-25:
Adult C 59-62: 26-30:
Aged 63-66: 31-35:
Males ML 67-70: 36-41:
Males C 71-74: 42-46:
Building No. 75-78:
End of Card (1) Behavior Setting No. 1-4:
Females ML 5-8: 47-51:
Females C 9-12: 52-56:
Negroes 13-16: 57-61:
Whites 17-20: 62-67:
On Base ML 21-24: 68-73:
Total C 25-28: 74-78:
End of Card (3) Behavior Setting No. 1-4:
Off Base ML 29-32: 5-9:
Total C 33-36: 10-14:
Grand Total 37-41: 15-20:
Total Duration 21-25

Max. Pene. of Subgroups
Group Col.No.
Inf 26
Presch 27
Y S 28
O S 29
Adol 30
Adult 31
Aged 32
Males 33
Females 34
Negroes 35
Whites 36
Social C. Pen. L.
I 37
II 38
III 39
IV 40
Grand Max. 41-42
Performers (number)
On Base ML 43-45
Total C 46-48
Off Base ML 49-50
Total C 51-53
Grand Total 54-57
Perf/Pop. 58-59
White Perf. 60-63
Negro Perf. 64-66
End of Card (4) Behavior Setting No. 1-4:

ACTION PATTERN RATE
Aes: 5:
Bus: 6:
Prof: 7:
Educ: 8:
Govt: 9:
Nutr: 10:
PersAp: 11:
Phil: 12:
PhysH: 13:
Rec: 14:
Rel: 15:
Soc: 16:
MECHANISM RATE
AffB: 17:
GroMot: 18:
Manip: 19:
Talk: 20:
Think: 21:
GEN RICH: 22-23:
Pressure Rating
Child: 24:
Adol: 25:
Welfare Rating
Child: 26:
Adol: 27:
Autonomy Rating
Wtd: 28:
Social C. O.T.
I 29-33:
II 34-38:
III 39-43:
IV 44-48:
E, O or I 49:
Jan. 50:
Febr. 51:
March 52:
April 53:
May 54:
June 55:
July 56:
Aug. 57:
Sept. 58:
Oct. 59:
Nov. 60:
Dec. 61:
(End of Card 5)

6–3. Behavior setting code sheet.

military community, the work patterns are a fairly routine matter that can be easily discovered. Civilian communities are much more varied. Factory workers may have different shifts round-the-clock, and working mothers present extremely full schedules.

Some knowledge of the work schedule is necessary so that it can first be blocked out of the 8,760 hours of the year for each person. The average work year is about 2,080 hours if vacation is not taken into account (52 × 40). Individual vacations will reduce this amount by from 80 to 160 hours (two to four weeks), and holidays, sick days, and other days absent will reduce it even more.

The researcher begins with large blocks of time, whittles them away with detailed questions, and finally arrives at figures denoting specified time of activities within the various behavior settings. Figure 6–4, an exercise sheet, shows how to determine time spent in one type of setting—a house. An additional exercise would be to attempt to design a house that would enclose the above behaviors. What specialized spaces within the rooms will be necessary?

Behavior setting data is collected on the basis of a one-year period. Before a behavior setting survey is begun, the year period is arbitrarily agreed upon. This, of course, usually applies to a complete community study or a building. Shorter time periods should be weighed carefully. Use of time periods shorter than a year sacrifices data on seasonal variations in behavior, certain holidays, and many other aspects that may be critically important.

Assuming a year is the base, each behavior setting has data collected on:

Frequency is the number of times it meets in one year. Since some settings may meet more than once per day, there is a high theoretical limit on this number. More often, a setting will not meet more than once a day, so the upper limit is usually 365.

Duration is the total amount of time (in hours) a setting meets in one year. The maximum possible is 8,760 in one year (365 days × 24 hours).

Population is the total number of *different* persons who have entered the setting during the year. Population is often divided into age subgroups, in town/out of town, or by race or other variables (see Barker 1968, 48, or Bechtel 1977, 97).

Occupancy time is the number of person hours in each setting. This is usually reported as total occupancy time (number of persons multiplied by the number of hours each person has spent in the setting). Often this is calculated by the average attendance times the average length of each occupancy. Even sleeping is accounted for in the behavior setting of a home.

A. Hours of waking time

1. Total hours for the average year, *8760*
2. Person A (male) sleeps 8 hours every weekday night, an extra hour on Sunday.
3. Person B (female) sleeps 7½ hours every weekday night, an extra hour on Saturday, and 2 extra hours on Sunday.
4. Person A works 8 hours per day during the week. His travel time to and from work is 30 minutes each way.
5. Person B works part-time 6 hours on Saturday and 2 hours each weekday afternoon. Travel time is 15 minutes each way.
6. Both A and B spent a two-week vacation away from home.
7. A goes bowling every Wednesday night for two hours. Travel time is 20 minutes each way.
8. B goes to the hairdresser every Tuesday morning for two hours. Total travel time is 20 minutes.
9. A had a business trip for 10 days in September.
10. A and B went to the movies 12 times in the year. Travel time to and from is 10 minutes each way. They usually stop for a cup of coffee afterward for 30 minutes.

B. Questions you should have asked

1. What does *usually* stopping for a cup of coffee mean? More than half? 75%? 90%? (Answer: 60%)
2. Does A go bowling all year-round? (Answer: Only September 1 through December 20)
3. Were there any times during the year when either A or B was home sick from work (Answer: A two days, B one day)
4. Can A and B think of any other times they were away from the house? (Answer: Shopping on Saturday mornings for both—three hours)
5. Any visits to neighbors, relatives? (Answer: No)

C. Calculations of waking time

1. A's sleeping time: 8 hours per day during week plus weekends.
2. A's working time: 8 hours per day less vacation time and sick time.
3. Other times away from the house for A: bowling, business trip.
4. Total for A.
5. B's sleeping time.
6. B's working time.
7. Other times away from house for B: hairdresser.
8. Total for B.
9. Times away for A and B together: vacation, movies and coffee, shopping.
10. Sum of A's time away plus B's time away plus time A and B spent away together, plus A's sleeping time and B's sleeping time.
11. No. 10 subtracted from 2 × 8760 is the sum of the total waking hours in the house.

D. Action pattern calculations

1. *Aesthetics*
   a. Time spent cleaning the house each day by A or B or both. Check for differences on weekends. (Answer: B clean 1½ hours on weekdays, none on weekends)
   b. Time spent by A and B in hobbies like painting, sculpting, dancing, etc., or in correspondence courses on such subjects in the home. (Answer: B paints on Sunday afternoons, average 3 hours)
   c. Time spent reading about such subjects (receives a trace, if any). (Answer: A reads 3 hours per week; B reads 4 hours per week)
   d. Time spent preparing or practicing for these activities outside the home. (Answer: None)
   e. Total time in these activities. (Note: A or B may actually *teach* such activities in the home, may have a studio, or may use a certain space for teaching.)
2. *Business*
   a. Is anything bought or sold in the home? This includes time spent in ordering through catalogs, buying from door-to-door salesmen, over the phone, or from newspaper ads. It does not include going through the

6–4. Worksheet for calculating time spent in house.

catalogs for fun (recreation), or giving to charities. (Answer: Order from Sears twice a year. Have Fuller Brush man twice a year, 30 minutes each time)
   b. Is there any time spent in the home preparing for business activities outside the home? (Answer: No)
   c. Total of time in business activities.

3. *Professionalism*
   a. Is any time spent earning a living in the home? (Answer: No)
   b. Have any visitors earned a living while there (e.g., doctors, salesmen, repairmen)? (Answer: TV repairman, 4 hours; plumber, 2 hours)
   c. Was any time used in preparation for earning a living outside the home? (Answer: A writes reports at home, 2 hours every week)
4. *Education*
   a. Is any time spent being taught or doing lessons in the home? (Answer: No)
   b. Does any teaching take place in the home? (Answer: B teaches one pupil painting, 1 hour every 2 weeks)
   c. Is there any preparation for education that takes place in the home? (Answer: None)
   d. Do any activities that stimulate education take place in the home (e.g., teacher's meetings)? (Answer: Two PTA meetings held at home—20 people, 2 hours each time)
5. *Government*
   a. Is any time spent making or carrying out laws? (Answer: Yes, filing income tax, paying taxes)
   b. Is there any government activity? (Answer: No)
6. *Nutrition*
   a. How much time is spent preparing and eating meals each day? Test for weekend differences. (Answer: 2 hours prep, 1½ hours eating on weekdays, only 2 meals on Sunday)
   b. Special events preparation and grooming (dances, dates, social events). (Answer: Parties, 2 hours per month for both)
   c. Is there any time spent learning about food preparation? (Answer: None)
7. *Personal appearance*
   a. How much time is spent getting dressed and groomed each day? (Answer: 15 minutes a day for both)
   b. Special events preparation and grooming (dances, dates, social events). (Answer: Parties, 2 hours per month for both)
   c. Time spent washing clothes and drying or ironing them. (Answer: 3 hours on Saturdays)
   d. Are any clothes washed for outside the home (time spent)? (Answer: None)
8. *Physical health*
   a. Any time spent at home sick—not just from work but additional time sick, less sleeping, plus doctor's visits, etc. (Answer: Yes, A had a cold for 10 days)
   b. Any time spent in preventive health measures, brushing teeth, taking vitamins? (Answer: 2 minutes a day for each)
   c. Any time spent learning or teaching about improving health? (Answer: None)
9. *Recreation*
   a. Time spent in recreational activities such as watching television, playing (games or children's play), visiting, talking on the phone, reading. (Answer: A watches TV 3 hours every weekday, B watches TV 4 hours every weekday, both watch 6 hours over weekend; have visitors every Thursday evening, 3 people, 3 hours, and every other Sunday evening, 2 people, 3 hours)
10. *Religion*
   a. Are there any religious meetings in the house? (Answer: None)
   b. Do people in the house say prayers at mealtime or bedtime? (Answer: None)
   c. Are there any religious counseling visits (e.g., pastor, deacon)? (Answer: None)

(*continued*)

Figure 6–4 continued

11. *Social contact*
    a. What are the times spent in visits from neighbors, friends? (Answer: Every Thursday, 3 people, 3 hours; every other Sunday evening, 2 people, 3 hours; neighbors Saturday evening 2–3 hours)
    b. What amount of time is spent with child visitors (friends of children of the household)? (Answer: None)
    c. What is the amount of time residents of the house spend talking (observational sample)? (Answer: Rather quiet couple)

E. Each action pattern as a percentage of waking time—the family profile (Fill in data gathered above)

Aesthetics:
Business:
Professionalism:
Education:
Government:
Nutrition:
Personal appearance:
Physical health:
Recreation:
Religion:
Social contact:

Figure 6–4 continued

These four measures provide the basic working data for behavior settings. One might suppose that it would be easy to check on the accuracy of a behavior setting survey by multiplying the population times 8,760, the number of hours in a year. This figure then should equal the total occupancy time of all behavior settings. In actual fact, since some behavior settings overlap, some people are counted more than once in a behavior setting survey, the total occupancy time arrived at by adding total occupancy time for all behavior settings should be a higher figure.

Behavior Measures

The basic demographic measures above do not get at any of the flavors of different behaviors that occur across the range of behavior settings. Barker (1968) developed three global scales to try to make this type of analysis more specific: action patterns, behavior mechanisms, and the general richness index. Barker began with thirteen action patterns, but only ten are used currently: aesthetics, business, education, government, personal appearance, physical health, professionalism, recreation, religion, and social contact.

Aesthetics is any behavior that improves the appearance of the physical environment, like adding a statue, painting a house, or raking the lawn.

Business is any behavior involving an exchange of goods or services where payment is obligatory.

Education is any behavior that requires the formal role of teacher. Incidental learning is not counted.

Government is any behavior that has to do with the making or enforcing of laws—local, county, state or federal. Sheriff's offices, lawyer's offices, and legislative committee meetings are examples.

Personal appearance has to do with trying to look one's best as opposed to merely getting dressed. Local differences vary widely as to what is "dressed up." Barker (1968) has developed a clothing scale to measure this objectively.

Physical health refers to any behavior that contributes directly to physical well-being, such as taking medicine, exercise, and the like.

Professionalism has to do with the payment of wages for anything from babysitting to consulting on a research project.

Recreation is any behavior that gives immediate

pleasure and ranges from watching television to climbing mountains.

Religion is usually tied to a worship service but may include a prayer said at a banquet or other celebration.

Social contact is personal relations of any kind.

Action patterns are scored according to what percentage of the occupancy time they take up. A score of zero is given if the action pattern does not take place during any part of the total occupancy time, and the following are coded percentage scores, (% of total occupancy time).

1–10%: 1	31–40%: 4	61–70%: 7
11–20%: 2	41–50%: 5	71–80%: 8
21–30%: 3	51–60%: 6	81–100%: 9

The reader needs to be aware that this scoring system is a simplification of Barker's original scales (1968), which included three subscales for each action pattern for a possible total of 14 points. The system presented here is intended to preserve the original intent of the measures and yet render the administration of the scale easier and make it fit more easily on a computer card.

An even more simplified version would be to count only three values, absent, present, or prominent. Absent would be counted as zero, present at 2.5 or 3, and prominent as 7.5 or 8. In the last analysis Barker himself emphasized these three summary measures because of low reliability for his more complex scales (1968).

The action pattern scores are useful for design purposes when one wants to know the quality of the behavior enclosed by a building. For example, in the Bechtel and Ledbetter study (1976), it was discovered that *recreation* was the only prominent action pattern in the family housing of a military base, yet that housing, like most housing everywhere, was designed only for the bare necessities. Since the location was a far northerly climate, it was more imperative that recreation be provided in the home. The long dark winter nights made it a necessity. The design solution was to finish the basements as recreation rooms and provide day beds for the children's bedrooms so they could use the bedrooms for play when not sleeping. Without the action pattern scale it would have been difficult to prioritize which kind of behavior was most important and merited design changes.

Behavior mechanisms are a second global behavioral scale but they have been found not to discriminate well across environments (Bechtel 1977, last chapter). They may be used, however, in special cases and *must* be used if one wants to calculate the general richness index later. There are five behavior mechanisms:

Affective behavior is any behavior expressing emotions such as laughing, crying, yelling, and more sedate activities such as singing.

Gross motor activity is any behavior that involves the large muscles of the body, such as walking, running, or swimming.

Manipulation is any use of the hands such as typing, working with tools, or turning pages.

Talking is any form of verbal expression, even use of sign language.

Thinking is scored whenever a person has to make a decision or solve a problem.

Behavior mechanisms are scored the same as action patterns on a 1 to 9 scale according to the percentages of total occupancy time.

Responsibility Measures

The autonomy scale aims to measure whether the people in any environment (or behavior setting or community) have control over deciding four basic matters: (1) appointment of leaders, (2) admittance of members, (3) determination of fees and prices, and (4) establishment of programs and schedules.

These four areas are scored according to the level at which the decision is made. If it is made at the federal level the score is 1; state level 3; county level, 5; school district, 7; and local level, 9. Sometimes another value, 12, is added to indicate a level within the behavior setting itself. These scores are calculated for each of the decision levels and then averaged. Maximum autonomy for a behavior setting would be 12, for a community, 9; the minimum (entirely controlled by the federal government) would be 1.

The autonomy scale is called a responsibility measure because it approximates how responsible people are for decisions that control their own behavior settings. It has been useful in describing low responsibility levels in public housing environments (Bechtel 1977). These circumstances can lead to dependency and a psychological condition called learned helplessness (Seligman 1975).

The penetration level scale is a second type of responsibility measure that rates the level of leadership in behavior settings. If there is a single leader of a behavior setting whose position is such that without that person the setting could not function, the penetration level is 6. Most leaders share their power so that if they did not appear at a behavior setting, another could take their place. These are rated a 5. Officials, or people with a formal functional role such as secretaries or treasurers, are rated 4. Legitimate members of a setting or organization are rated a 3. Visitors are rated a 2, and onlookers who are contributing nothing to the setting are rated a 1. Levels 6 to 4 are called performers or leaders, levels 1 to 3 are called nonperformers.

This arbitrary assignment of numbers to leadership functions measures responsibility levels available to persons in any environment. Coupled with the autonomy scale, they are useful instruments to determine whether any population segment is subordinate to outsiders or in control of its own environment.

These scales are especially useful as measures in testing responsibility theory (see below); and the penetration level can also be a subtle measure of segregation, testing whether a minority group has access to levels of leadership (Bechtel and Ledbetter 1976).

A good example of testing access of minorities to leadership positions was found in the Arrowhead study (Dumouchel 1972). The settlement house that supplied social services to residents was found to make only very minimal levels of leadership roles available to residents. Consequently, activities were initiated, such as African drums classes and preschool classes, in which residents could take leading roles; and new spaces were provided for them.

Autonomy measures showed that residents had 68 percent of the decisions made for them by off-the-site agents such as the housing authority or the federal government. This finding led to giving the on-site manager more authority and providing residents with more authority through the resident council.

General Richness Index

The General Richness Index (GRI) is calculated on the basis of scores for action patterns, behavior mechanisms, and penetration levels. The formula is

$$\text{GRI} = ([\Sigma\text{PenR} + \Sigma\text{ApR} + \Sigma\text{BmR}]\ \text{cOT})/(100)$$

where:

- ΣPenR is the sum of the penetration level ratings for each age group
- ΣApR is the sum of the eleven action patterns
- ΣBmR is the sum of the five behavior mechanisms
- OT is a code number assigned to the total occupancy time for the behavior setting

(See Barker 1968, app. 1, 209–10.)

The General Richness Index can be calculated for an individual behavior setting, averaged over any number of behavior settings, or calculated for an entire community. It is a handy way of quantifying the richness of behavior available to the occupants of any behavior setting. Since its score is derived by adding sums of the various behaviors, it becomes obvious which behavior settings are rich and which ones are less rich. A city market, with its wide variety of populations and behaviors, is very rich compared to the same functions separated into individual scores.

The GRI indices for the Arrowhead Housing Project show that the local behavior settings were very low in richness (Dumouchel et al. 1972). Conversely, the GRI's of two composite buildings at two remote radar stations were found to be very high (Bechtel 1977), justifying that type of design for remote stations.

The above scales account for most of the data collected in a behavior setting survey. The reader may wish to use other scales such as welfare and raison d'être (Barker 1968), but the ones discussed above are used more frequently.

DATA ANALYSIS

The data can be analyzed in many ways. A discriminant function analysis can be used to test for differences among communities or among groups of behavior settings within a community, or nonparametric statistics such as chi square can be used to test for differences within settings or between two or more settings.

BEHAVIORAL FOCAL POINTS

A frequently asked question is, How does one design a community? The question is not answerable unless some basic sociological concept by which communities form can be identified and used to design a physical environment to enhance that growth. Fortunately, a number of observations have led to a simple principle from which a design schema can be derived. This concept, which at the same time leads to new ecological psychology methods for evaluating and studying communities and other organizations, is known as the behavioral focal point.

The behavioral focal point is the behavior setting that is most accessible to the largest numbers of the various kinds of people in any geographical area. A behavioral focal point helps any geographical entity become a community by providing an essential condition: to become a community, people must have a place where they can meet each other regularly on a face-to-face basis. A behavioral focal point best serves this purpose by helping to attract the greatest numbers of different kinds of people. It can do so by incorporating several complementary functions such as eating, drinking, socializing, and the selling of goods and services of various kinds.

"Good" focal points combine several complementary functions, which attract more people together than they would separately. A theory of behavioral focal points would assert that, left on their own, the members of any community would naturally organize into their own behavioral focal points in the course of their daily lives. Thus, able to meet each other on a regular basis, the members of the community would develop the ability to recognize each other on sight and evolve a sense of who belongs. Of course, if the community is not designed to include a place that allows this to happen, it may be difficult or impossible for this sense to develop.

Focal points tend to be centrally located at a crossroads of traffic, have a maximum degree of richness without requiring a social commitment, have high visual access so everyone can see everybody else, and involve central areas where a fair proportion of the community can be seated. Usually the seating area involves the serving or at least the eating of food.

Where does one find behavioral focal points? In small towns they are places like the downtown drugstore where everybody goes to see what is happening and has a cup of coffee or a soda. One can sit there, sipping, and pick up on all the latest gossip while being able to meet with virtually every member of the community. Larger communities tend to form several behavioral focal points that follow community functions. For example, corporations have "break" rooms or cafeterias. This fragmentation prevents larger entities from forming focal points for the community as a whole. Redfield (1960) called this difference between face-to-face interactions in small communities and the role behaviors of cities the folk-urban continuum.

Analysis of behavioral focal points can provide a sophisticated diagnosis of the social workings of a community. By coding the GRI for each behavior setting according to the size of the circle (the more richness, the larger the circle), behavior settings of a community can be arranged on polar coordinates by their interrelatedness on a diagram. A fragmented community will not have a rich behavioral focal point but will have richer unrelated settings, arranged at some distance from it. An integrated community, however, will have a rich behavioral focal point with many behavior settings around it.

Illustrations of focal point analysis diagrams are given in figures 6–5 and 6–6. Figure 6–5 shows the

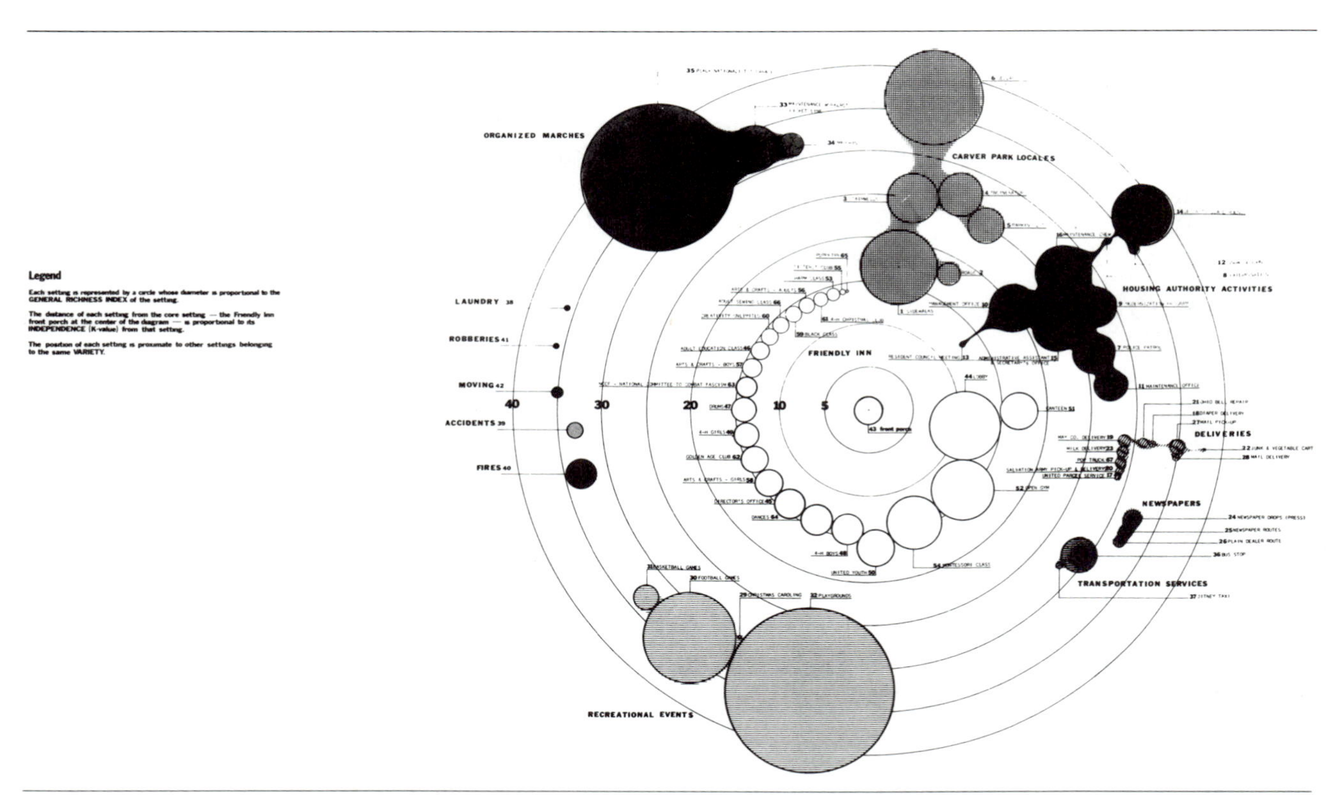

6–5. Arrowhead behavioral focal point diagram.

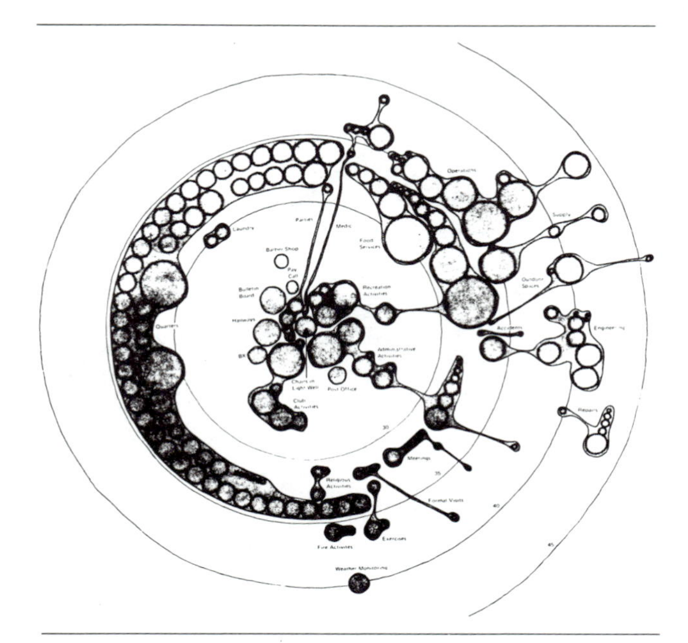

6–6. Base map of behavior settings of Cape Lisburne.

relatively fragmented community of Arrowhead, where the very weak behavioral focal point of the settlement house steps does not have a seating or even a very large standing capacity. Consequently, richer behavior settings tend to draw people away in fragmented subpopulations that do not regularly meet together. Figure 6–6 shows a central cluster of fairly rich behavior settings around a rich focal point at Cape Lisburne, a U.S. radar station in northern Alaska.

ECOLOGICAL PSYCHOLOGY AND DESIGN

For many design research and evaluation purposes, the methods of ecological psychology would not be used as extensively as Barker uses them. For example, it would be much more common to evaluate a building rather than a whole community. The essential purpose would be to describe and measure the behavior settings that would need to be considered for the design. The behavior settings and their scales then make up the necessary behavioral information for programming.

By using the framework of ecological psychology as a starting point, the designer and/or researcher can ask some critical design questions. For example, should the building try to act as a community with a behavioral focal point? It might be that the building will be composed of a number of tenants who have no reason to form a community. But it may also be that the client or tenants want to establish a strong community sense, in which case they will need to have a focal point designed.

Ecological psychology comes close to supplying the totality of behavioral information that the designer wants. It *can* be used for hypothesis testing but it doesn't need to be. By collecting information on all the behavior that takes place in an architectural space, it can be used to answer many questions that the hypotheses did not include.

It is often assumed, by those who have not used ecological methods, that because these methods are taken with a present time reference, they do not show the need for change. Certainly, no method at present can give a complete diagnosis of needed changes, yet ecological methods are extremely useful in uncovering problems that call for change.

For example, the penetration level scores and the autonomy scale scores of Arrowhead showed that the citizens had very little control over their own behavior settings (Bechtel 1977, 102, 106–8). Through analysis of the behavior settings of one building (the settlement house), it became obvious that the services for the residents did not permit participation in leadership roles.

In the cold regions studies (Bechtel and Ledbetter 1976), the penetration level data showed a subtle discrimination between large and small military bases. Black men had a much better opportunity for leadership in the smaller bases. While the behavior setting data itself does not prescribe solutions, it often reveals where solutions or changes are needed. It can pinpoint the specific behavior settings that need change or, as in Srivastava's (1978) studies, it can show where more behavior settings are needed. By no means, then, are behavior setting data limited to a static picture of the present.

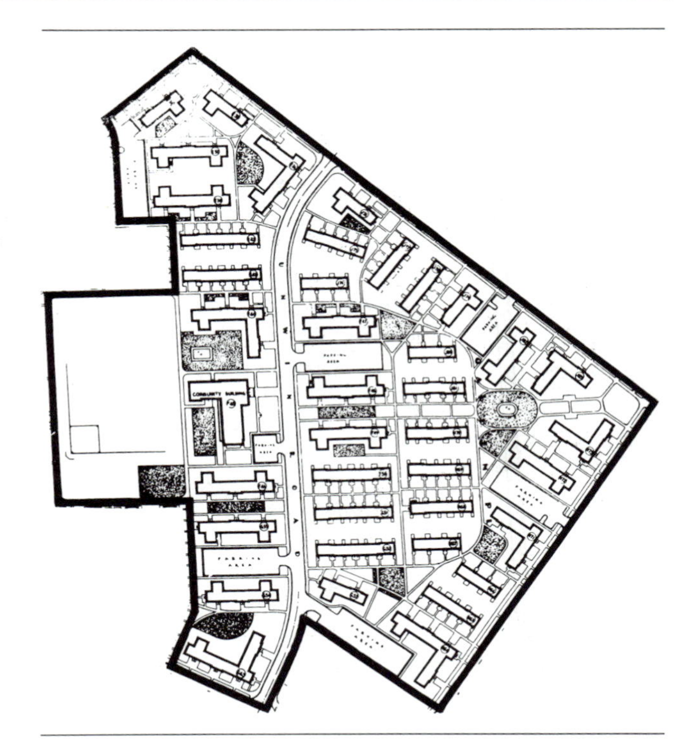

6-7. Map of arrowhead.

ECOLOGICAL PSYCHOLOGY AS A POE METHOD

Post-occupancy evaluations are an especially fruitful use of ecological methods (see chapter 9). However, it should be noted that the common practice is to use behavior setting surveys along with normal questionnaire items. For example, when residents are asked what they like and do not like about the environment, these questions become more meaningful against the background of the behavior settings and, conversely, the behavior settings are better understood when it is clear which aspects are liked and which disliked. Two examples will be considered.

The first, Arrowhead, was an evaluation done of a large public housing project (see fig. 6-7). Its purpose was to define problems and make recommendations for design modifications to the *exterior* only. A group of researchers moved to the site, recruited observers from among the residents, and collected data over a period of several months (Dumouchel et al. 1972). The behavior setting data, as mentioned above, provided evidence that too many decisions were being made for the residents and too many things being done *to* them instead of by or with them. Additional ecological data linked vandalism to the children of the project rather than outsiders and indicated that children had too few designated play areas. Observations also showed that many residents and nonresidents had difficulty finding their way around the project. These data led directly to design recommendations. Long discussions took place between the architects and the researchers until there was clear understanding of the nature of the problem.

One critical aspect of this project was the realization that architectural solutions were not enough. The central change that needed to take place was one that focused on management. Design, then, was a secondary level of change that would reinforce the changes in management.

Because management practices had inadvertently fostered dependence, management changes were aimed at encouraging participation and lowering the level at which decisions were made. Architectural changes were needed that would help to further these aims. The principle was translated into a density reduction, better definition of locations and pathways, more space for new activities and fewer "protective" barriers for management, making them more accessible.

A few years later the appearance of the project was noticeably improved, vandalism decreased, and a whole new pattern of healthier play was shown in the children. In addition, residents had more decision-making opportunities and were leading new activities.

Shay Gap (see fig. 6–8) was an Australian mining community designed as a temporary town that could be moved when the iron ore was exhausted. Lawrence Howroyd selected the site and designed the entire community. Ecological methods were used to evaluate the design of the completed community (Bechtel et al. 1980). Howroyd provided the researchers with no less than fifty-five design hypotheses used in making decisions about the town's design. He began by studying middle eastern communities and tried to learn how they used design to adapt to the harsh desert climate. He observed that a wall around the community had the dual purpose of providing shade from the sun and also of psychologically separating the residents from the harsher world of the desert. The wall principle was incorporated by selecting a site that was surrounded on three sides by hills.

Another central concept was the clustering of houses close together to take advantage of the shade offered and to provide a psychological closeness in pathways among the houses. This made passageways among the houses too narrow for cars and the automobile was relegated to a perimeter road around the outside of the community. Consequently, the entire residential area was made safer for children.

These and many other design hypotheses were tested by a behavior setting survey of Shay Gap conducted in about two weeks (see fig. 6–9, Shay Gap questionnaire). Howroyd's basic hypotheses were confirmed. The hills did provide a protective surrounding to the residents; children not only felt safer, but had higher penetration levels (were members of a wider variety of settings) than children of other communities, and the clustering of housing did not create a feeling of crowdedness.

In addition to providing data on the hypotheses, the ecological data also demonstrated that the community building served as an effective behavioral focal point, a result not anticipated by the architect. He felt he had "tried to put too much" in the building but it turned out that it worked very well as a behavioral focal point (a diagram of the shopping center as a behavioral focal point is shown in fig. 6–10). This was one POE that showed design results that were more successful than the designer anticipated.

ISSUES TO CONSIDER IN THE USE OF ECOLOGICAL METHODS

Ecological methods are appropriate in situations where a large amount of global behavioral data is needed. They should not be used in situations where the meaning of behavior, attitudes, or feelings needs to be measured in depth, but no data is needed on activities or the time they take.

While doing a behavior setting survey, all of the available sources for behavior setting data are used. This effectively exhausts all the independent sources for validity measurement. Usually when one method is used, independent sources are tapped to get a validity measure. Thus, newspaper reporting of an event would be a validity confirmation of a behavior setting observed by a researcher. However, in doing an ordinary behavior setting survey, newspapers, telephone books, observations, informants—*all* sources are utilized so that there are no independent data sources left to

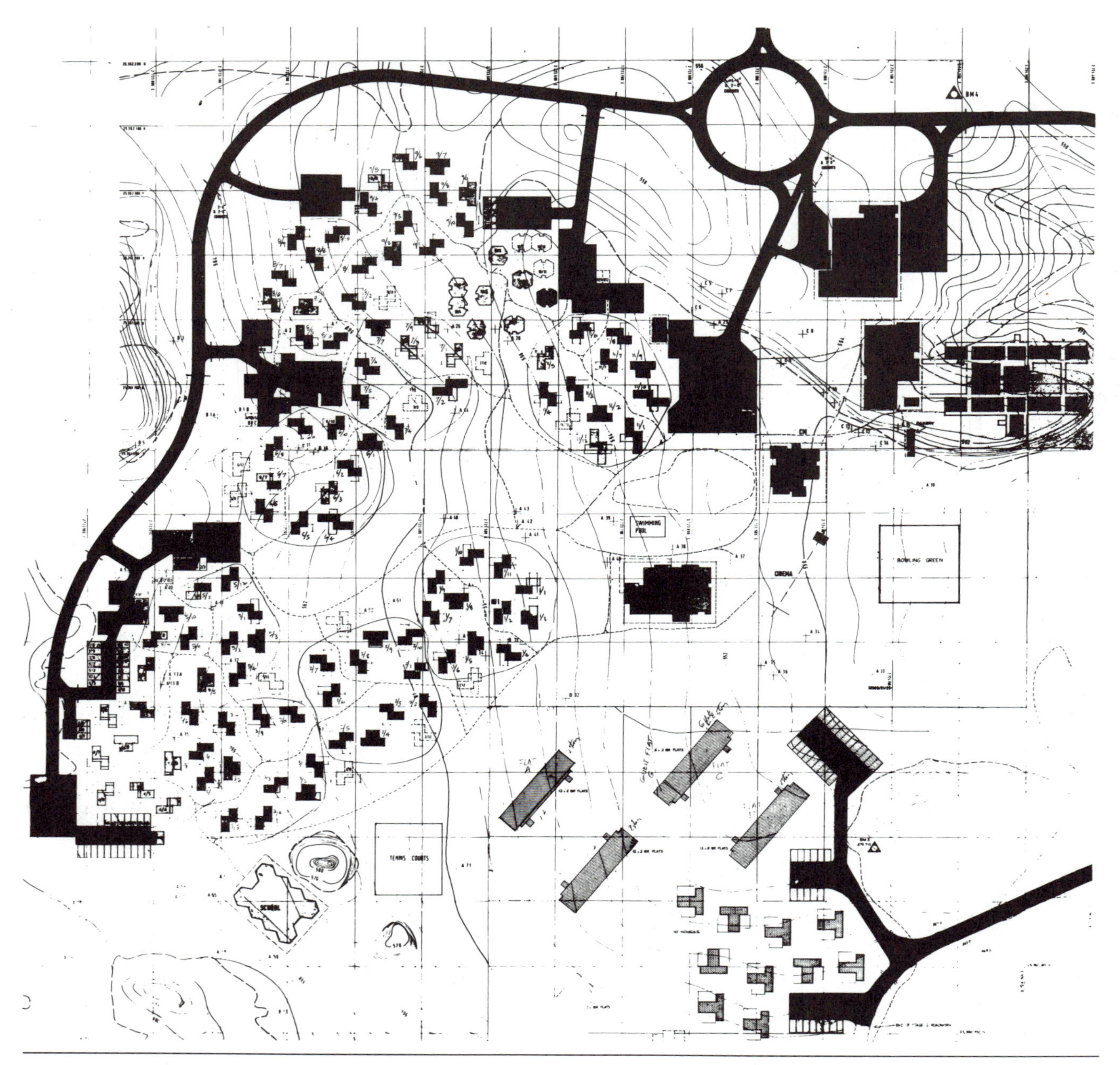

6–8. Map of Shay Gap.

Have you lived in other company towns? ☐ cities? ☐ rural? ☐

Probe: Where have you lived most of your adult life?

Names of towns:

Names of cities:

What is your precinct color and number? Correct ☐ Wrong ☐

How would you rate SHAY GAP compared to those other places in which you recently lived?

A. Site

1. Compared to the average of other places you recently lived in, are the surrounding hills:

comforting and protective	5
pleasant	4
no different from towns without hills	3
slightly uncomfortable (confining)	2
confining and limiting	1

other ____________________

Do you prefer hills or an open view? ____________

2. Compared to the average in other places you have recently lived, the wind in SHAY GAP is:

least in volume and annoyance	5
less than most	4
same	3
more than most	2
the most in volume and annoyance	1

3. Compared to the average in other places you have recently lived, the dust at SHAY GAP is:

least in volume and annoyance	5
less than most	4
same	3
more than most	2
most in volume and annoyance	1

4. Compared to the average in other places you have lived in recently, the whole town of SHAY GAP has:

most space of any	5
more space than most	4
same	3
less space than most	2
least space of any	1

5. Compared to the average in other places you have lived in recently, the amount of shade in SHAY GAP is:

best of any	5
better than most	4
same	3
worse than most	2
worst of many	1

A. due to hills
B. due to roof
C. due to vegetation

6. Compared to the average in the places you have lived in recently, SHAY GAP is:

most isolated	1
more isolated than most	2
average in level of isolation	3
less isolated than most	4
least isolated	5

7. Compared to the average in the places you have lived in recently, SHAY GAP is:

most permanent	5
more permanent than most	4
average in permanence	3
less permanent than most	2
least permanent	1

B. Community

8. Compared to the average in places you have lived in recently, are the groceries and other store goods available in SHAY GAP:

best	5
better than most	4
average	3
worse than most	2
worst	1

9. Compared to the average in places you have lived in recently, the houses in SHAY GAP are:

closest together	1
closer together than most	2
average	3
not as close as most	4
farthest apart	5

(*continued*)

6–9. Shay Gap questionnaire.

10. Do you find you go outside of SHAY GAP to buy things?

more than in any other place	1
more than in most places	2
average	3
less than in most places	4
least of any place	5

11. Compared to the average in places you have lived in recently, the shopping center at SHAY GAP is:

best	5
better than most	4
average	3
worse than most	2
worst	1

12. Compared to the average in places you have lived in recently, the space for raising and exercising pets in SHAY GAP is:

best	5
better than most	4
average	3
worse than most	2
worst	1

13. Compared to other areas you have lived in recently, the storage areas in SHAY GAP are:

Outdoor

best	5
better than most	4
average	3
worse than most	2
worst	1

Indoor

best	5
better than most	4
average	3
worse than most	2
worst	1

14. Compared to other areas you have lived in recently, the space for gardens in SHAY GAP is:

best	5
better than most	4
average	3
worse than most	2
worst	1

Where do you garden? ______________________

15. Compared to other areas you have lived in recently, the number of clean areas in SHAY GAP is:

best	5
better than most	4
average	3
worse than most	2
worst	1

16. What building is the place most used by everybody?

Probe: More people go there than any other

17. What is the most popular recreational activity in SHAY GAP?

C. Social and Daily Living

18. Compared to other areas you have lived in recently, at SHAY GAP the relations between family and single personnel are:

best	5
better than most	4
average	3
worse than most	2
worst	1

19. Compared to other areas you have lived in recently, do you or your spouse spend:

most time in the house	1
more time	2
same	3
less time	4
least time in the house	5

20. Compared to other areas you have lived in recently, do you notice noise from your neighbors:

most	1
more	2
average	3
less	4
least	5

21. Compared to other areas you have lived in recently, do you feel that at SHAY GAP you interact with people:

most	5
more than most	4
average	3
less than most	2
least	1

Figure 6–9 continued

22. Compared to other areas you have lived in recently, do you experience a loss of energy (get tired) at SHAY GAP:
Probe: Over the whole year

most	1
more than most	2
average	3
less than most	4
least	5

23. Compared to other areas you have lived in recently, do you feel you got to know:

most people in Shay Gap	5
more than most	4
average	3
less than most	2
least	1

24. Compared to other areas you have lived in recently, do you feel you walk

most	5
more than most	4
average	3
less than most	2
least	1

25. Compared to other areas you have lived in recently, do you think that living in SHAY GAP is:

best	5
better than most	4
average	3
worse than most	2
worst	1

D. Children

26. Compared to other areas you have lived in recently, are children in the streets and pathways of SHAY GAP:

safest	5
safer than most	4
average	3
less safe than most	2
least safe	1

27. Compared to other areas you have lived in recently, are children endangered by the climate at SHAY GAP:

worst	1
worse than most	2
average	3
less than most	4
least	5

28. Compared to other areas you have lived in recently, do children at SHAY GAP have:

most playmates	5
more than most	4
average	3
fewer playmates	2
fewest	1

29. Compared to other places you have lived in recently, do children in SHAY GAP have (outside):

most places to play	5
more than most	4
average	3
worse than most	2
worst	1

E. The House

30. Compared to other areas you have lived in recently, are the houses at SHAY GAP:

best looking	5
better than most	4
average	3
worse than most	2
worst	1

31. Compared to other areas you have lived in recently, are the courtyards at SHAY GAP:

most private	5
more private than most	4
average	3
less private than most	2
least private	1

32. Compared to other areas you have lived in recently, do you use the courtyards at SHAY GAP:

most often	5
more than most	4
average	3
less than most	2
least often	1

(*continued*)

Figure 6–9 continued

33. Compared to other areas you have lived in recently, do the houses at SHAY GAP seem like a suburban single-family house:

most	5
more than most	4
average	3
less than most	2
least	1

34. Compared to other areas you have lived in recently, do the interiors of the houses at SHAY GAP seem:

most bland (uninteresting)	1
more bland than most	2
average	3
less bland than most	4
least bland	5

35. Compared to other areas you have lived in recently, are the interiors of the houses:

most easily decorated	5
more easily decorated	4
average	3
less easily decorated	2
least easily decorated	1

36. Compared to other areas you have lived in recently, the windows in the houses (rooms) at SHAY GAP provide:

most privacy	5
more privacy than most	4
average	3
less privacy than most	2
least privacy	1

37. Compared to other areas you have lived in recently, the plumbing in the houses (rooms) at SHAY GAP is:

noisiest	1
noisier than most	2
average	3
less noisy than most	4
least noisy	5

38. Consider the areas you move around and live in at SHAY GAP and please rank them in terms of the most private to the least private:

inside the house
living court (barbeque, etc.)
service court (laundry)
paths and streets
play areas, common areas
public buildings (shopping center, club, etc.)

Figure 6–9 continued

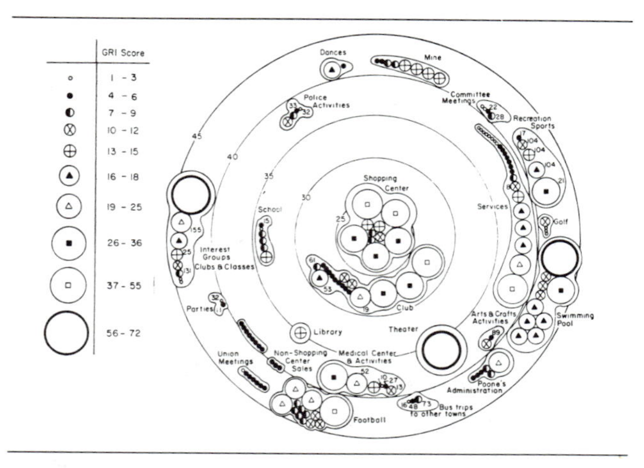

6–10. Shay Gap shopping center as a behavioral focal point.

establish validity. It is assumed that, since all these independent sources converge, the data are valid and the behavior setting data can be used to validate other methods.

Behavior setting surveys, like all other methods, are almost never used alone. When Shay Gap was surveyed, residents were also questioned directly about how they responded to the surrounding hills and other aspects of the community.

Reliability data in ecological methods is sometimes a problem. Scoring action patterns and behavior mechanisms and the use of the K-21 scale should not be done until reliability is established among different observers or scorers.

Attempting to arrange behavior settings into a meaningful whole presents a number of problems in time sequence and behavioral relationships. Here, a combination of methods like time geography and the skillful use of informants can be of help. Similarly, the K-21 scale can produce a hierarchy of dependencies among all settings if it is done on every setting versus every other.

REFERENCES

Barker, R. 1960. Ecology and motivation. In *Nebraska symposium on motivation,* ed. M. Jones. Lincoln, Neb.: Univ. of Nebraska Press.

———. 1963. *Stream of Behavior.* New York: Appleton-Century-Crofts.

———. 1968. *Ecological Psychology.* Stanford, Cal.: Stanford Univ. Press.

Barker, R., & Associates. 1978. *Habitats, Environments and Human Behavior.* San Francisco, Cal.: Jossey-Bass.

Barker, R., and R. Gump. 1964. *Big School, Small School.* Stanford, Cal.: Stanford Univ. Press.

Barker, R., and R. Schoggin. 1973. *Qualities of Community Life.* San Francisco, Cal.: Jossey-Bass.

Barker, R., and H. Wright. 1951. *One Boy's Day.* Evanston, Ill.: Row, Peterson.

———. 1955. *Midwest and Its Children.* Evanston, Ill.: Row, Peterson.

Bechtel, R. 1977. *Enclosing Behavior.* Stroudsburg, Pa.: Dowden, Hutchinson & Ross.

Bechtel, R., and C. B. Ledbetter. 1976. *The Temporary Environment.* Hanover, N.H.: Cold Regions Research and Engineering Laboratory.

Bechtel, R., C. B. Ledbetter, and N. Cummings, 1980. *Post-Occupancy Evaluation of a Remote Australian Community: Shay Gap, Australia.* Hanover, N.H.: Cold Regions Research and Engineering Laboratory.

Dumouchel, J. R., E. Ash, M. Stevens, U. Owens, and R. Bechtel. 1972. *Arrowhead Final Recommendations.* Environmental Research and Development Foundation, Kansas City, Mo.

Holahan, J. 1982. *Environmental Psychology.* New York: Random House.

LeCompte, W., and E. Willems. 1960. Ecological analysis of a hospital. In *EDRA 2: Proceedings of the Second Annual Environmental Design Research Association Conference,* ed. J. Archea and C. Eastman, 236–45. Pittsburgh: Environmental Research and Development Foundation.

Redfield, R. 1960. *The Little Community and Peasant Society.* Chicago: Univ. of Chicago Press.

Seligman, M. 1975. *Helplessness.* New York: W. H. Freeman.

Smith, M. B. 1974. Psychology in two small towns. *Science* 184:671–73.

Srivastava, R. 1978. Ecological approach to mental health facility design. In *New Directions in Environmental Design Research,* ed. W. Rogers and W. Ittelson. Tucson, Ariz.: Environmental Design Research Association.

Wicker, A. 1973. Undermanning theory and research: Implications for the study of psychological and behavioral effects of excess populations. *Research in Social Psychology* 4:185–206.

———. 1979a. Ecological psychology: Some recent and prospective developments. *American Psychologist* 34:755–65.

———. 1979b. *Introduction to Ecological Psychology.* Monterey, Cal.: Brooks/Cole.

CHAPTER 7
MEASURING MACROENVIRONMENT AND BEHAVIOR
THE TIME BUDGET AND TIME GEOGRAPHY

William Michelson

When viewing the progress of mankind, we typically fail to acknowledge a major achievement—that most people manage to get through the complexities of the average day. The lives of most people in a modern, urban setting are highly complex and varied. Included in the everyday round are varieties of goals, activities, people, places, and means of movement to join them—clearly a logistical problem-set exemplifying the most basic perspectives of person–environment relations.

Nonetheless, the complex of activities, specific settings, and participants making up everyday life is at a higher, more inclusive level of generality than what environmental researchers study in specific settings like rooms, buildings, playgrounds, or plazas. Therefore, a methodology must be geared to the special requirements involved in measurement concerning macroenvironments and their interface with people. This chapter examines two major converging approaches to the understanding of human activity in its larger physical context: the time budget and time geography.

Given the divergence of perspective from the more conventional microenvironments, it is necessary to commence with a discussion of basic considerations facing the measurement of behavior in macroenvironments. Then specific methodological aspects will be explored. Some examples of applications pertaining to the built environment will conclude the chapter.

BEYOND IMMEDIATE ENVIRONMENTS

Of what do our lives consist? At the least, we perform activities in specific settings in relation to other people. We are typically not stationary. And we put values on how well things work out.

Many settings are primarily geared for specific activities: kitchens, laundries, examining rooms, restaurants, and so on, but even small settings like these typically allow for and are designed for more than just a single activity. While the interface of human activity requirements with the physical design that should support them is not always readily apparent, it is nevertheless tangible enough for comprehension and planning. Researchers can assess through observation and questioning which activities are desired for a particular place. Designs can be programmed to accommodate a reasonable combination of these. Various techniques may be employed to see whether a given setting is successful in accommodating such activities and in satisfying users on a more subjective plane (see chapter 9, on post-occupancy evaluation).

Few people, however, spend all their time in a single behavior setting. Human activities and the behavior settings in which they take place relate to one another in time and in space. Behaviors not only follow each other in sequence, for example, but must be made to fit vis à vis each other into the time frames that conventionally face us—days, weeks, years, or lifetimes. Insofar as human beings do not have the power to be everywhere at once, they have to be able to move among physical settings for activities that are bound to specific places within the dictates of appropriate time frames. A pilgrimage across the world need only be fit into a lifetime, but a daycare center and a workplace have to be physically situated to fit into every workday.

Hence, people's daily lives reflect not just the adequacy of individual behavior settings, but the aggregation of relevant activities and the logistics of their relationships in time and space. As Mårtensson puts it, "Each person's biography is constructed out of events and experiences in continual interaction with components in the environment" (Mårtensson 1979, 12).

City and community planning deal with activities in time and space, sometimes explicitly but mostly implicitly. Land-use planning, for example, fixes people and activities within certain limits of proximity or separation (Michelson 1970), usually on grounds that have to do with health, functionality, or aesthetics as they pertain to particular sites and areas. The overall texture that emerges in a behavior setting constitutes a set of opportunities for and limits to everyday behavior (Gutenschwager 1973). A challenge to adequate planning is to come up with a design that reflects the behavioral propensities of residents and other users (Chapin 1965; 1974). While not done as a matter of course, it is increasingly necessary to conceptualize cities, as does Tuan, as "time made visible" (quoted in Parkes and Thrift 1980, 28). Transportation planning does this most clearly, working with resources and propensities, on the one hand, and with travel-associated timing, on the other (Matzner and Rüsch 1976; Pant and Bullen 1980; Chumak and Braaksma 1981).

Any consideration of the linkage of at least two spatially separate activities, at the simplest level, all the way up to the aggregate of daily activities for an individual or the agglomeration of activities in a place, requires focusing on human use of time and on the physical context in which it occurs. As Ås put it,

> [A]ctivity must be seen as an interaction of humans and their immediate environment. . . . Information on at least three "stage-coordinates" must be provided before we are able to understand what goes on, namely: a) actor type or who is acting, b) spatial location or where it takes place, and c) time frame . . . [1982, 49]

Burke went even further: "[A]ny complete statement . . . will offer *some kind of* answers to these five questions: what was done (act), when or where was it done (scene), who did it (agent), how he did it (agency), and why (purpose)" (cited by Asplund 1979, 12).

One may wish to add as well the *consequences* of any such activity.

Such a focus on human activity in time and space becomes useful when analytic interests turn from settings in which activities can be monitored accurately in situ by observers to those where an observer cannot follow the movement of one or more persons to other locations or activities within the system of interest. This focus is justified when the functioning of even a simple, finite setting should be understood within the context of a user's broader scheme of movement, activity, or daily routine (for example, the apartment laundromat with respect to time of use, simultaneous demands on users, and so on). You cannot observe the broader considerations at the site of primary interest.

The analysis of temporal and spatial dimensions of activity is thus relevant to various levels of design decision. In a micro setting such as the home or office, a detailed record of who does what for how long, in what sequence, and with whom is helpful in arranging internal space for optimal flow and function.

At a somewhat more macro level, such time analysis is useful in the design of land-use mixtures and facilities within neighborhoods. It can be used to provide information about the actual use of facilities compared to one another, to document the time that people spend in and out of their homes, to illustrate what recreational activities are participated in by what combinations of persons, and a whole host of other questions. At this level the time-budget perspective enables some merger of the considerations of both physical and social planners.

It is as important to know when and under what conditions an activity or a use of space does *not* occur. To what extent, for example, is there a regular withdrawal from the streets that leads to increased crime, and vice versa?

At a still more macro level, time-use studies may be used as an input to planning that is concerned with the overall form of cities and metropolitan areas. The stochastic linkage of land-use-specific activities is quite relevant here, since people are not inclined to make all their stops in a rational, logical order. The distance to and from home has been shown to be a major part of most trips, an indication of the relevance of facility location to residential location and the importance of what consumers view as convenience, as compared to, for example, the views of downtown businessmen.

At the same level, one can use the time-budget approach to compare the uses of different social milieux within a metropolitan area, since different sections of town may have different physical requirements, designs, and land-use mixtures. Not all cities have the same form or the same combinations of interior neighborhood forms, and hence the documentation of the variations in residents' behavior between one metropolitan area and another is an important input to overall conceptual planning.

Physical planning, of course, is not just a matter of levels and designs. Among the many other relevant components is time management, which is concerned with such issues as the opening and closing hours of public facilities. The logic of the optimal time of day for various establishments to be open and available certainly lies somewhere between the extremes of complete simultaneity and complete randomness. Time and space-use information is one way of documenting the logic that underlies sensible management practice.

The study of activity in time and space becomes necessary when simple settings must be related to a larger context, extending into the kinds of complex systems customarily dealt with in multi-use structures, communities, urban areas, and regions. When push comes to shove, all of these are planned with at least minimal acknowledgment that they should fit harmoniously into people's lives, whether the relevant time frame be a day, a week, or longer. Even when this is acknowledged, the less tangible nature of the phenomena involved, compared to activities conducted within the bounds of simple settings, has confounded practitioners who want to come to grips with how environments fit into people's lives.

The complex cannot, however, be wished away. Complexity must be dealt with on its own terms.

Therefore, when we extend into the analysis of more complex environments, we need methods that deal with human use of time and space and with the potential inherent in environments for human activity (measured most simply in terms of time and space). Fortunately, two complementary approaches have emerged that provide conceptual and operational tools to deal with larger-scale considerations of the built environment. They are the time budget, used to measure many aspects of human time and space use, and time geography, used to consider behavioral potential in environments.

THE TIME BUDGET

The time budget is very simply a record of what a person has done during a specified period of time—usually a twenty-four-hour day or a given number of days. A detailed record, it lists in chronological order a person's activities during the period and usually states when each activity began and terminated. Time budgets usually assess, for each activity in order, what other persons were involved, where the activity took place, and whether other simultaneous activities transpired. Time budgets allow as well for other time- and activity-specific data, and more attention has recently been given to subjective aspects of the daily round.

Perspectives

The general pattern of data from time budgets has been treated in very different ways. One view takes time as a *resource* to be consumed (Reed 1976; Chapin 1974). Time consumption is seen as an expression of values and preferences, reflecting the priorities of the individuals and groups involved. Others see time use as an *outcome* of contextual logistics and constraints. This approach involves comparisons of what people do in different circumstances or settings, or how their behavior changes in a changed environment (Cullen 1978). Either or both of these approaches may be appropriate, depending on the specific uses to which time-budget data are applied. Let us now look more deeply into various perspectives on time use.

The earliest uses of time budgets, from the 1920s, were more value-neutral, placing description before interpretation. Strumulin conducted a comprehensive survey of factory workers in Moscow in 1923 (Ottensman 1972), while Lundberg and his colleagues focussed on five thousand diary records of daily activity in Westchester County, New York, nine years later (Lundberg et al. 1934). A few years later, Sorokin and Berger (1939) conducted a well-known study in Boston. At the time these comprehensive studies were taking place, more limited studies by researchers in American land grant institutions assessed by the same technique the situation of farm families (particularly housewives) (Vanek 1974). Swedish researchers developed domestic analyses as well (Boalt and Carlsson 1949). In these applications, the main interest was to ascertain what people *do* during the course of the day.

Time budgets were found desirable for this basically descriptive information, because a chronological log of a particular time period enables the tabulation of information that people do not typically picture with much accuracy in their own minds. Few people, for example, can state accurately how much time in a day or week they devote to specific aspects of housekeeping such as cooking, child care, leisure, or travel, all of which are broken up into many short episodes. Yet, tracing through actual activity in the context of a tangible time period enables the reasonably accurate representation of such information, as well as its aggregation over the time period involved by the analyst. Social analysts and policy makers find such purely descriptive data useful to assess the need and direction for change in areas like transportation, working hours, plant locations, recreation planning, and public institutions.

In recent years, Japan has conducted huge, repeated national surveys (Nakanishi 1966, 1968; Matsushima 1982). Such diverse nations as the German Democratic Republic and the United States have also made important discoveries about changes in daily life over recent years through the comparison of representative data on average, daily time use taken at intervals of five or ten years (Manz 1978; Robinson 1977).

Clearly the most massive undertaking in this tradition was a multinational comparison of time use among twelve nations, the United States and eleven countries in Eastern and Western Europe (Szalai et al. 1972). A common approach to sampling and field methodology enabled the amassing of nearly identical data and hence the fascinating assessment of similarities and differences among nations regarding such features of daily life as employment, commuting, housework, child care, and social life. More detailed analyses on specific topics have also been pursued (see, for example, Stone 1978).

Nonetheless, while such descriptive information about how populations (and categories within them) spend their time, with whom, and where is helpful to planners as base-line data, planning researchers increasingly adopt one or more of the more interpretative perspectives. These turn away from societal averages, focussing instead on subpopulations to whom specific planning processes may be directed.

One approach, as mentioned above, is to assess special time-use propensities of certain subgroups in comparison to others, inferring that greater amounts of time devoted to certain kinds of activity reflect higher priorities. How subgroups consume time and space is taken as a basis for more sensitive land-use, transportation, and/or recreation planning. The kind of inference involved is parallel to that used by economists regarding expenditures of money (Becker 1965), and the potential fallacies are also similar. Expenditures of time or money that reflect necessity and constraint do not reflect values or free choice. Nonetheless, studies assessing regularities in commercial, recreational, and domestic time usage among subgroups have been felt to contribute to planning in their own right. F. Stuart Chapin, Jr. and a number of colleagues have advanced what they term a *transductive* approach (Parkes and Thrift 1980), in which the particular behavior patterns of subgroups differing on such bases as class, race, and ecological situation have been isolated for planning purposes (Chapin 1974).

A roughly similar approach is taken by researchers at Cambridge University (Shapcott and Steadman 1978). These observers see everyday behavior within subgroups not only as regularized but as culturally determined. Planning, according to this view, requires the understanding of cultural influences, not the unguided search for behavior patterns.

A third use of time-budget data as reflecting behavioral propensities is relatively recent. A number of researchers feel the necessity to supplement the market economic activity reported in the Gross National Product with nonmarket activities that potentially substitute for market transactions. According to this view, one needs time expenditures to complement expenditures of money in order fully to report economically meaningful activities. In a parallel vein, economic indicators are seen as inadequate indices of welfare, and time-use statistics are highly desirable social indicators (Felson 1981; Harvey 1978; Juster et al. 1979). Analyses of the economic value of housework are roughly parallel (see, for example, Walker and Woods 1976).

Time-budget data may also be used as a reflection of constraining phenomena—activities that represent selections within given limits rather than completely free choices. While a culture or subculture may itself be viewed as such a limit, it is not generally felt as such by those who are well integrated into it. In any case, researchers' focus for constraints on time use centers on more tangible factors in the everyday environment, such as housing (Michelson 1977) and employment (Michelson 1980, 1985). Within limits set by such factors, people are said to arrange routines, which become habitual and hence not problematic from one day to the next, though often they are far from ideal (Cullen 1978). This approach studies how aspects of planned environment—interior design, land use, transportation, employment, social planning, and so on—constrain, channel, or otherwise limit time use, as a basis for replanning such environments. It involves such methods as studying the time use of persons subjected to certain environments in comparison to that of persons in other environments—all else being equal—or in comparison to their own previous time use after changes occur.

Format

Time budgets are typically generated in one of two ways: by means of a self-administered diary or through an interview schedule. The content recorded could be identical; the difference lies in when and where each instrument is completed. Both have distinct advantages and disadvantages.

With the diary method, each respondent is given a form as physically compact and portable as possible on which to record the day's activities and the time when each was begun and ended. The respondent may be instructed to record this information either with every change in activity or at natural break-points in the day, such as coffee and meal breaks and immediately before retiring.

The claimed advantages of this mode of data acquisition are that (1) the short time span between activities and recording them results in higher accuracy and reliability, and (2) it is the only way to acquire accurate time-use data for periods of time longer than one full day. The disadvantage of this method is that keeping a diary while engaging in activities can affect what and how activities are carried out. Respondents are also less likely to complete the task than when in an interview context.

With the interview schedule, the respondent is asked to provide details about activities, with times, places, and coparticipants, for the *preceding* day. Engagement with the interview process is considered an asset of this approach.

The method selected is largely a function of the time period that you wish to cover, as well as the return that you expect to get. At least one study has shown that when you are concerned about only the activities of the immediately preceding day, it does not matter whether one uses interview or diary approaches. However, if you wish to gather information on more than a single day, the diary is far superior. The usual practice is to leave a diary with a respondent, outline the period for which the diary should be completed by the respondent, and then arrange a time for study personnel to pick up the completed time diary. On the last occasion, research personnel look through the time diary and try to obtain any information that seems to be missing.

The use of an interviewer to pick up a self-administered questionnaire doubtless adds to what would otherwise be a relatively low cost compared with the use of a questionnaire alone. However, the time budget questionnaire is a sufficiently detailed instrument that a personal visit is often required to explain how it should be filled out, as well as to provide some incentive for the person actually to do it. It is very common for a respondent to throw out a questionnaire that looks the least bit complicated or threatening. Similarly, the call-back after completion prompts the respondent to realize that someone does have expectations of his or her performance, and it similarly allows the interviewer to have the opportunity of checking the completeness and quality of the finished record before it is too late to do anything about it. Although this does take the time of interviewers, which could have been utilized equally well to take a record of the previous day's time budget by interview techniques, it is reasonable to utilize this procedure when the period to be covered is more than just a previous day. Accounts of activities for periods of a week are not uncommon.

The trouble with the time diary, however, is that, in spite of their best intentions and promises, many people do not follow through and complete it. There is also little chance to question or to discuss their categorization of activities; whoever picks up the diaries may spot questionable responses, but it is normally only blanks that draw strong attention at that time.

An interview relies on a respondent's memory of the period involved; therefore, a valid reconstruction is generally possible only for the previous day. Nonetheless, the level of cooperation by respondents is considerably higher for this mode of data acquisition. The oral time budget, however, takes a large amount of interviewer time, and frequently interviewers discover that they have at least as much difficulty as their respondent, since quite some strain is involved in ensuring that all levels of detail are completed for as complex a matter as a person's day.

Interviewers normally ask less complex questions than those of the time-budget series, such as people's preferred brand of orange juice or their opinions about political leaders. Hence interviewers feel that they may be straining the attention of their respondents when going through the necessary details of the time budget, and this frequently interferes with their perseverance. This problem is avoided by sufficient interviewer orientation before the actual interviews. Payment of respondents appears to relieve interviewer anxieties of exploitation and enables the latter to work more effectively. In fact, as long as the interviewer is not on edge, people seem to enjoy reconstructing their daily lives.

It could be extremely time-consuming to conduct time-budget interviews with all family members, when complete family coverage is desired. My colleagues and I have experimented with group sessions in which all persons simultaneously fill out a time-use questionnaire about yesterday under the continuous direction and guidance of an interviewer, who circulates and double-checks results as they work (Michelson 1985). This method provides multiples of results for little more than the time a single interview would take. (Children under ten, however, are less able to do this themselves and hence require the extra time and attention of an adult for their time-budget data.)

Researchers are now turning as well to the telephone, establishing contact and confidence through initial personal interviews and then arranging for time-budget coverage of subsequent days by telephone contacts the day following each day to be covered.

Whether for use in diaries or in an interview schedule, there are two general types of time-budget questions—precoded and open-ended. The precoded structure has a set of alternative answers from which the respondent must choose his or her replies. This format limits the range or variety of answers and makes the task somewhat easier for the respondent; however, the alternative answers must be simple, relevant, inclusive of nearly all possibilities, and clearly different from one another. This may result in both the oversimplification and prejudgment of the results. An open-ended format allows full freedom for response and is almost always used in interviews, as the interviewer can in any case monitor the answers to ensure that they are on target.

Figure 7-1 shows a partially precoded time diary (self-administered). Figure 7-2 shows the first of the many pages needed in a thorough time-budget interview schedule that is open-ended.

The format in figure 7-2 is sometimes used without specifying exact time points, allowing (theoretically, at least) the respondent to fill in his own recollection of the exact time of the beginning and

Please complete this activity record for your activities during waking hours on:

______ (day of week) ______ (month) ______ (day) ______ (year)

NOTE: Any time spent working at your job (or jobs) should simply be recorded as "At work."
However, please remember to include any lunch or coffee breaks.

Others participating: 1 Alone, 2 Family, 3 Friends, 4 Work associates, 5 Other

Location: 1 At home, 2 At work, 3 Travelling, 4 Other

	ACTIVITY	Office Use only	STARTING TIME	FINISHING TIME	OTHERS PARTICIPATING	LOCATION	
01							(if other, specify)
02							(if other, specify)
03							(if other, specify)
04							(if other, specify)
05							(if other, specify)
06							(if other, specify)
07							(if other, specify)
08							(if other, specify)
09							(if other, specify)
10							(if other, specify)
11							(if other, specify)
12							(if other, specify)
13							(if other, specify)
14							(if other, specify)
15							(if other, specify)
16							(if other, specify)
17							(if other, specify)

7–1. Time diary. Courtesy of the Department of Secretary of State, Ottawa.

Now I'd like to get some idea of what an average day for you might include. Let's take yesterday. (Last weekday) *Use respondent's own words as much as possible.*

At what time did you get up? (*circle time*)
Then what did you do? How long did it take you?
Was anyone else with you?
Where did you do it?
Were you doing anything else at the same time?

Begin by asking the respondent the time he (she) got up that morning and what he did first. Ask how long this activity took and then record it on the sheet at the appropriate times. Ask whether or not anyone was with the person when he did it; determine whether the presence of the other individual(s) was incidental or whether he was asked to accompany the respondent such that it was really an interaction process. Ask where the activity took place and whether or not the respondent was doing anything else at the time. If a person goes to a store or somewhere, be sure to check the time to store, shopping, and home again. Finally, ask the respondent what he did next, and then repeat the above line of questioning. *Do not attempt to record what was being done at each time given on the sheet;* rather, use the sheet simply as a method of calendaring the day's activities.

The minimum time span to be considered for an activity is fifteen minutes. Record start and stop time to the nearest quarter-hour. Do not record for any activity that is less than a quarter-hour.

Time spent traveling to *or* from an activity *is a separate activity and should not be included with that activity.*

Time	***What did you do? How long did it take you?***	***Was anyone else with you?***	***Where did you do it?***	***Were you doing anything else at the same time?***	***Typical activity***
6:00 A.M.					
6:15 A.M.					
6:30 A.M.					
6:45 A.M.					
7:00 A.M.					
7:15 A.M.					
7:30 A.M.					
7:45 A.M.					
8:00 A.M.					
8:15 A.M.					
8:30 A.M.					
8:45 A.M.					

7–2. Time-budget interview.

ending of each activity, as in figure 7-1. This usually fosters a false sense of precision. By displaying specific time points ten to fifteen minutes apart, recall of activities is assisted; that is, respondents may be able to recall activities better when they think first about the time at which they took place. Additionally, the format in figure 7-2 avoids the redundancy of asking both when each activity was begun and when completed, since the time when any activity begins almost always implies termination of the previous activity.

Since no evaluative research has been done on the various formats, choosing between them now depends more on the ultimate purpose to which the data will be put.

A different format for taking down family time-use data in a relatively general way was suggested by Swedish researchers (Carlstein et al. 1968). Only information on respondents' behavior settings is gathered, with a unit of one hour as the minimum. Our own adoption of this is shown in figure 7-3 (Michelson 1984). It covers the hours of the previous weekend, remembered by respondents approximately but not in the same detail as the preceding weekday. Each family member is assigned a separate colored or textured (horizontal) line on a time-use chart. Behavior settings are the rows, and hours are the columns. When such a chart is completed, one can immediately see various patterns of togetherness, travel, home-use, external recreation, use of outside space, and so on. The chart can also become the basis for complex data analyses.

Subjective Aspects

We think time budgets are useful because they tell us something important about respondents' behavior. The meaning and intent of activity, however, are never self-evident; they must be inferred. The duration and frequency of activities are not certain indicators of importance to the respondent. For example, twenty minutes spent reading the newspaper may be more important (or "less replaceable") than three hours spent watching television. In addition, activities may have both manifest and latent functions; eating or walking may be done for their own sake or as a means of achieving a particular objective. Hence inferences of some kinds can be made only with extensive analysis of data and additional qualifying information from respondents.

Some degree of evaluation of the component parts of the time-budget data is made possible by the addition of supplementary questions on each activity. As part of the regular time-budget exercise, a person is sometimes asked to evaluate whether or not he is satisfied with the amount of time he devotes to an activity or whether a given location is adequate for the performance of that activity. Although it adds to the time, expense, and trouble of the time-budget interview, this further step adds an entirely new, useful dimension of practical importance. A diary that adds this dimension is illustrated in figure 7-4. Another researcher, Patrushev, applies a five-point scale of satisfaction to leisure time in particular (1982).

Cullen and Phelps (1978) emphasize that respondents are better able to identify negative aspects of time use than positive. In their work, they found that stress and annoyance in an activity are associated most with unpleasant or difficult conditions (46 percent), followed by disruptions (19 percent), greater than expected difficulty (17 percent), interference with subsequently planned activity (10 percent), and difficulty in fitting it in (8 percent). They also measured the degree that individual activities were routinized, running from specifically arranged or planned, on the one hand, to time-filling, on the other.

In our own work (Michelson 1985), dimensions of choice/no choice and tense/relaxed were measured on seven-point scales. These proved useful to help interpret activities vis à vis each other in

Family Code no. ____________

Now I would like to ask you about last weekend. I would like to chart how you spent Saturday and Sunday. Let's look at this form, which allows us to go through the whole day. Each person will get his or her own color line. The day starts on thé left. What time would the first of you get up? How long would you (he, she) remain at home? (Start line accordingly, keeping lines apart, with the person number at the left.) What time would each person go to sleep? When would they wake up again? (Put dots on the line to signify going to sleep and waking up.)

SATURDAY	AM	4	5	6	7	8	9	10	11	12	NOON	1	2	3	4	5	6	7	8	9	10	11	12	MIDNIGHT
Work place																								
Shopping or commercial place, including restaurants																								
Public office clinic, etc.																								
Outside, near home																								
At home																								
Place of worship																								
Recreation, etc.																								
Someone else's home																								
School, day care																								

SUNDAY	AM	1	2	3	4	5	6	7	8	9	10	11	12	NOON	1	2	3	4	5	6	7	8	9	10	11	12	MIDNIGHT AM	1	2	3	4	5	6	7	8	9
Work place																																				
Shopping or commercial place, including restaurants																																				
Public office, clinic, etc.																																				
Outside, near home																																				
At home																																				
Place of worship																																				
Recreation, etc.																																				
Someone else's home																																				
School, day care																																				

7–3. Time chart for all family members.

TIME BEGAN	TIME ENDED	WHAT DID YOU DO?	WERE YOU DOING ANYTHING ELSE AT THE SAME TIME? (Specify Activity)	CHECK ONE: WHEN YOU WERE DOING THIS HOW DID YOU FEEL?					WERE YOU WITH YOUR CHILDREN?
				1 pleased or delighted	2 mostly satisfied	3 mixed or neutral	4 mostly dissatisfied	5 unhappy or terrible	
									☐ YES ☐ NO
									☐ YES ☐ NO
									☐ YES ☐ NO
									☐ YES ☐ NO
									☐ YES ☐ NO
									☐ YES ☐ NO
									☐ YES ☐ NO
									☐ YES ☐ NO
									☐ YES ☐ NO
									☐ YES ☐ NO
									☐ YES ☐ NO
									☐ YES ☐ NO

7–4. Diary with a subjective scale. Courtesy of Survey Research Center, University of Michigan.

subjective terms and to place similar perspectives on the (weighted) aggregation of activities over the whole day.

Such subjective scales, when attached at the level of the individual activity, help resolve the dilemma as to whether a given use of time is a freely chosen expenditure of a valuable resource or the result of a constraining factor.

Coding

Time budgets are normally coded and placed on data cards and/or tape for analysis. Coding a time budget following open-ended responses is generally extremely time consuming and hence expensive. Individual researchers have worked up computer programs to facilitate time-budget analyses, which are available to others by arrangement. There is as yet no standardization of programs, however, nor any regular arrangement for program distribution. Needless to say, with great amounts of information on large numbers of persons, the costs of storage and analysis can be sizable.

There is no single agreed-upon set of activity categories or codes (see, for example, Swedner and Yague 1970). One set of ninety-nine categories was devised and utilized in the Multinational Comparative Time-Budget Research Project (Szalai 1966, 1972), and it has been utilized by others subsequently. This set of codes is reproduced in figure 7-5 in the form adapted for a study on housing (Michelson 1977).

Other researchers find, however, that even such an international set of codes does not provide a level of subtle detail sufficient to distinguish among certain kinds of activities in which they have a special interest—that is, a measure intended to cover the entire spectrum of activities in a variety of cultures, but yet remain relatively uncomplicated, may not be sufficient to differentiate among forms of behavior relevant to a particular problem. In work on parent-child contact, for example, we found it easy to expand the standard ten categories on "care of children" to thirty-five (Ziegler and Michelson 1981).

In addition, there is a tension between the creation of a large number of codes to describe behavior, so as to be complete and accurate, and the desire to have as few codes as possible, so that analysis can be efficient and relatively uniform. If there is a large number of codes, many of them will not apply to most people, and the results of an analysis may be extremely uneven and difficult to comprehend. The use of only small numbers of categories, however, may mean that they are too general to differentiate sensitively enough among the groups being compared.

Ås, for example, has argued for the use of relatively few, hopefully even precoded categories in studies that focus on specific enough topics or subgroups to make this substantively adequate. It would surely save much coding. He has, for example, suggested the reduction of all activity categories, in an extreme case, to a division between what he calls necessary, contracted, committed, and free time. Large, broad-based surveys nonetheless demand the full range of potential activities assessed and coded, according to Ås (1982).

In the process of coding, intercoder reliability is extremely important, and the validity of what is later reported depends on the accurate understanding by coders of how the categories of the code differ from one another, so that they may accurately assign them. Considerable training and practice are necessary before a coder is either accurate or fast.

A very specific problem in coding has to do with the recording of points of time. For accuracy and simplicity, the twenty-four-hour clock is optimum. However, many coders are not accustomed to it, and errors may creep into the data set, without extensive checking as to the accuracy of the figures.

More difficult to solve are the problems of accurately recording time spent sleeping and the length of a day. Some time budgets begin with midnight and continue through the following midnight. Others start at the time the person gets up at the beginning of the day and continue until he goes to bed. Absolutely accurate construction of a person's day, including his or her sleep time, requires either the assumption that a person has the same rising habits on two consecutive days or that the time budget be continued from the time a person gets up until the time that his sleep ends the

WORKING TIME AND TIME CONNECTED TO IT (00–09)

- **00** Normal professional work (outside home)
- **01** Normal professional work at home or brought home
- **02** Overtime if it can be specifically isolated from 00
- **03** Displacements during work if they can be specifically isolated from 00
- **04** Any waiting or interruption during working time if it can be specifically isolated from work (e.g., due to supply shortage, breakdown of machines, etc.)
- **05** Undeclared, auxiliary, etc., work, spouses-children, unpaid members to assist family
- **06** Meal at the workplace
- **07** Time spent at the workplace before starting or after ending work
- **08** Regular breaks and prescribed nonworking periods, etc., during work time
- **09** Travel to (return from) workplace, including waiting for means of transport

DOMESTIC WORK (10–19)

- **10** Preparation and cooking of food, putting away groceries
- **11** Washing up and putting away the dishes
- **12** Indoor cleaning (sweeping, washing, bed-making), general nonspecific housework
- **13** Outdoor cleaning (sidewalk, disposal of garbage)
- **14** Laundry, ironing
- **15** Repair or upkeep of clothes, shoes, underwear, etc.
- **16** Other repairs and home operations, packing and unpacking, washing or repairing car
- **17** Gardening, animal care, walking dog[a]
- **18** Heat and water supplies—upkeep
- **19** Others (e.g., dealing with bills and various other papers, usual care to household members, etc.)

CARE OF CHILDREN (20–29)

- **20** Care of babies, feeding baby
- **21** Care of older children
- **22** Supervision of schoolwork (exercises and lessons)
- **23** Reading of tales or other nonschool books to children, conversations with children
- **24** Indoor games and manual instruction
- **25** Outdoor games and walks
- **26** Medical care (visiting the children's doctor or dentist or other activities related to the health of children)
- **27** Others
- **28** Not to be used
- **29** Travel to accompany children, including waiting for means of transport

PURCHASING OF GOODS AND SERVICES (30–39)

- **30** Purchasing of everyday consumer goods and products, shopping
- **31** Purchasing of durable consumer goods
- **32** Personal care outside home (e.g., hairdresser)
- **33** Medical care outside home
- **34** Administrative services, offices, bank, employment agency, customs, etc.
- **35** Repair and other services (e.g., laundry, electricity, mechanics, car wash)
- **36** Waiting, queuing for the purchase of goods and services, house or apartment hunting
- **37** Others, signing lease or contract to buy
- **38** Selling house or house contents; showing own house
- **39** Traveling connected to the above mentioned activities, including waiting for means of transport

[a]Gardening and animal care are to be recorded as Domestic Work only if not part of professional work or gainfui employment.
[b]A number of special types of meals outside home and the canteen have special codes, different from 44 (see Spectacles, Entertainment, Social Life, 70–79).

(*continued*)

7–5. Activity codes.

PRIVATE AND NONDESCRIBED ACTIVITIES (40–49)

- **40** Personal hygiene, dressing (getting up, going to bed, etc.)
- **41** Personal medical care at home
- **42** Care given to adults, if not included in household work
- **43** Meals and snacks at home
- **44** Meals outside home or the canteen, essential other than 70–79[b]
- **45** Night sleep (essential)
- **46** Daytime sleep (incidental), long time, e.g., 1 hour or more
- **47** Nap or rest, 1 hour or less
- **48** Private activities, nondescribed, others (using sauna alone)
- **49** Traveling connected to the above mentioned activities, including waiting for means of transport

ADULT EDUCATION AND PROFESSIONAL TRAINING (50–59)

- **50** Full-time attendance in classes (undergraduate or postgraduate student), studies being the principal activity
- **51** Reduced programs of professional or special training courses, driving lessons (including after-work classes organized by the plant or enterprise in question)
- **52** Attendance at lectures (occasionally)
- **53** Programs of political or union training courses
- **54** Homework prepared for different courses and lectures (including related research work and self-instruction)
- **55** Reading of scientific reviews of books for personal instruction, specific to own profession
- **56** Others
- **57** No response, no further activity
- **58** No secondary activity
- **59** Traveling connected to the above mentioned activities, including waiting for means of transport

CIVIC AND COLLECTIVE PARTICIPATION ACTIVITIES (60–69)

- **60** Participation as a member of a party, union, etc.
- **61** Voluntary activity as an elected official of a social or political organization
- **62** Participation in meetings other than those covered by 60 and 61
- **63** Nonpaid collective civic activity (e.g., volunteers)
- **64** Participation in religious organizations
- **65** Religious practice and attending religious ceremonies
- **66** Participation in various factory councils (committees, commissions)
- **67** Participation in other associations (family, parent, military, etc.)
- **68** Others
- **69** Traveling connected to the above mentioned activities, including waiting for means of transport

SPECTACLES, ENTERTAINMENT, SOCIAL LIFE (70–79)

- **70** Attending a sports event
- **71** Circus, music hall, dancing, show, nightclub (including a meal in entertainment local), parade
- **72** Movies
- **73** Theater, concert, opera
- **74** Museum, exhibition, library (educational purposes)
- **75** Receiving visit of friends or visiting friends, relatives at airport
- **76** Party or reception with meal or snack offered to or offered by friends, relatives
- **77** Café, bar, tearoom
- **78** Attending receptions (other than those mentioned above)
- **79** Traveling connected to the above mentioned activities, including waiting for means of transport

Figure 7–5 continued

SPORTS AND ACTIVE LEISURE (80–89)

80 Practice a sport and physical exercise
81 Excursions or drive, hunting, fishing
82 Walks, browsing, window shopping
83 Technical hobbies, photography and developing, collections
84 Crafts (confection, needlework, dressmaking, knitting, etc.)
85 Artistic creations (sculpture, painting, pottery, literature, writing poetry, etc.)
86 Playing a musical instrument, singing
87 Society games (cards, etc.), crosswords, board games, chess
88 Others
89 Traveling connected to the above mentioned activities, including waiting for means of transport

PASSIVE LEISURE (90–99)

90 Listening to the radio, piped music
91 Watching television
92 Listening to records, tape recording
93 Reading books
94 Reading reviews, periodicals, magazines, pamphlets, etc., including proofreading done at home
95 Reading newspapers
96 Conversations, including telephone conversations
97 Writing private correspondence, reading mail, writing in diary
98 Relaxing, reflecting, thinking, planning, doing nothing, no visible activity (arrive home, use on Sunday if long interval between activities)
99 Travel connected to the above mentioned activities, including waiting for means of transport

Figure 7–5 continued

following day. There are, almost inevitably, logical difficulties in analysis, however accurate the information given the investigator.

Information is usually placed on tape or disk in the form of a large number of identical "fields," each one of which deals with one episode during the day—that is, an activity, the times involved, the people involved, the location, and all other activity-level information. Standard social science analysis programs may be used with time-budget data to a greater extent if one episode is placed on one card (or card image). One major difficulty in conducting analyses is that the number of episodes a day will vary greatly by respondent. Standard programs can be applied more readily to summary tabulations on each individual over the day regarding the activity, contact, and other codes.

Analysis

Results may be produced in a variety of forms. Each of these is available not just for a whole aggregate of people who were subjected to time-budget procedures but also for different subgroups being compared (from place to place, time to time, or both, as discussed earlier). One may, for example, report the average time devoted to each of the activities coded by members of the whole aggregate or by persons in each of the relevant subgroups.

One can report not just averages, but also extremes in time usage that might apply to one subcategory as opposed to another; this is indicated by standard deviations, deciles or quartiles, interquartile ranges, or other such measures of dispersion.

One can measure not only how much time was devoted to what activity, but also how much time was devoted to certain activities by particular kinds of people, or to what activities in what places, or what activities with which other people, in what places with which other people, and so on. Two-way and three-way analyses involving the type of activity, the location, and the persons present—all with respect to the amount of time spent—are both possible and fruitful with this technique. It is these analyses that are normally most useful for design purposes.

The scope can be widened even more by inclusion of subjective information. The degrees of pleasure, stress, choice associated with particular activities, places, people, and combinations thereof can be computed without unusual difficulty.

As continuous data, time-budget values can be examined not only with the widest variety of descriptive statistics but with respect to tests of association and significance.

One can also use time-budget data as input to more complex analytic techniques. If one wants to look for certain regularities or alternatives in behavior within a given population, the quantitative statistical properties of time-budget data make them ideal for use with such techniques as factor analysis.

Of certain relevance in this context is the fact that one can portray the spatial components of activity graphically. Plotters facilitate portrayal of the spatial distribution of particular activities or indeed of the whole spectrum of life activity. One can also ascertain the relationship of residential locations to other locations frequented. This of course requires that locations be reported exactly in the time budgets and then geo-coded; considerable attention to detail is necessary, but the task clearly can be done. Figures 7-6 and 7-7, for example, compare the daily round of husbands and wives living in suburban homes, from a study in Metropolitan Toronto (Michelson 1977). The maps show not only greater travel by the husbands but more of a centralized direction to their travel.

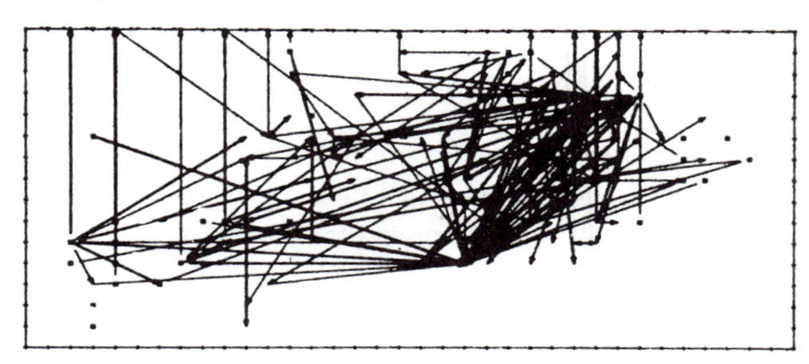

7-6. The relationship of home to daily trip destinations among a sample of men living in suburban houses in metropolitan Toronto.

Pitfalls

We have so far discussed largely the merits and applications of time budgets. Their weaknesses require mention, however, since some are not readily apparent. When we ask people for information, we usually try to select people so that they reflect or represent a much larger group; we then assume that their responses are typical or representative of both the individuals who give them and the larger group. This is the sampling of persons. In time-budget studies, it also matters how you sample for *time*.

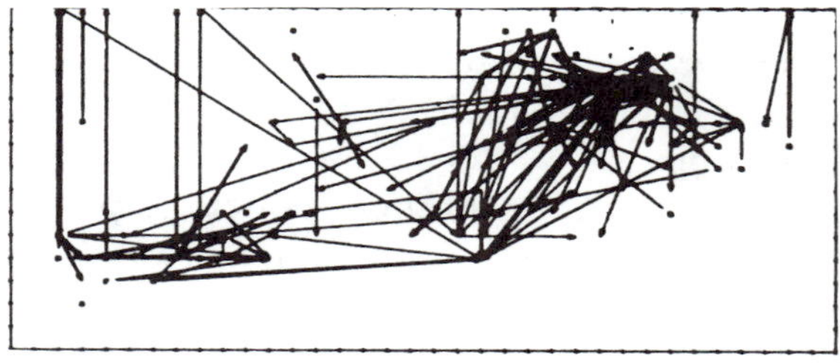

7-7. The relationship of home to daily trip destinations among a sample of women living in suburban houses in metropolitan Toronto.

There is some question as to whether a time budget for one or two days in an individual's life provides accurate, representative evidence of typical activity patterns, since these shift with the day of the week, season, physical and social locale, and so on. It is commonplace to request from respondents time-use profiles of at least one weekday (that is, a workday) and possibly also a weekend day. To ask for more results in the necessity for a self-administered format, with its trade-offs between coverage and response.

Researchers seeking to use time budgets in the construction of a social accounting scheme attempt to sample so as to cover the equivalent of a whole year in their data. They sample a small number of random days each from a large number of individuals so as to create what they call a *synthetic year.*

Others have argued for the interpretation of time use within a *lifetime* of behavior (Szalai 1975; Hägerstrand 1963). In any case, the point is that the sampling of time should be appropriate for the questions under investigation. (See a more complete discussion in Altergott 1982.)

If one is interested in activities that do not occur every day or that are very brief, one should base the time budget on more than a single day in a person's life. Otherwise, it is a matter of chance as to whether this use of time will emerge. This is particularly relevant in comparisons of different time periods. If the period of time sampled is insufficient for very many people to have exhibited an activity of interest to the researcher, then whether a person has increased or decreased the amount of time devoted to the activity is not easily determined. An analysis would show, for example, that on an average day most people did not engage in the activity and only small numbers showed an increase or decrease in their patterns. If one sampled a larger period of time, the analysis would easily be more accurate. However, another way of finding out such information on activities are rare occurrence is to ask directly about them and not utilize the time budget as a vehicle. This is advisable if data on more regular activities are of no special interest. The time budget is advantageous, however, with a suitable sampling of time because it does capture—no matter how indistinct at times the focus—a wide range of activities with one battery of questions.

I noted earlier that the retrospective interview has been shown to produce results as valid as a self-administered diary for the immediately preceding day. A deeper question of validity must be faced: Do respondents report what actually transpired during the time period in question?

One aspect of the issue of representativeness is underenumeration of certain kinds of activity. It is a documented fact that all questionnaires and interviews evoke responses significantly affected by the respondent's acquiescence to and perceptions of social desirability; hence, time-use protocols are very unlikely to contain explicit records of body function activity, sexual activity, or any other behavior regarded as very private, generally disapproved of (whether mildly or totally), or deviant, no matter how "normal" or commonplace any of these activities may be. Furthermore, simultaneously executed activities (such as watching television while eating, talking, or working) usually result in only one being recorded. Mental activity or purposeful nonactivity (such as relaxing or contemplating) are unlikely to be reported very frequently. And many activities of less than ten or fifteen minutes' duration are likely to be forgotten and unrecorded, particularly if a questionnaire is preblocked in such time segments.

My colleagues and I at one point had contacts with families on three days, the latter two consecutive. On Day 2, the interviewer acted as a participant observer, taking a careful record of what family members did for a two- to three-hour period, from late afternoon to early evening, when most family members return home and are together. The next day, she took retrospective time budgets from family members. The time-budget data could be compared with observation of what went on in a micro setting.

The results (Ziegler and Michelson 1981) indicated that activities reported in the time budgets accounted for a large proportion of the time observed but that respondents were not accurate in pinpointing the exact times their activities occurred. They were also more likely to remember to mention active, positive, and sustained behaviors, and less likely to cite passive, negative, or fleeting behaviors. The latter could be retrieved to some extent by a follow-up checklist, but interview time limits the number of subjects on which a follow-up is possible. The degree of validity of the time budget is ultimately a function of the specificity of the subject under study. In a specific comparison between observation and the time budget on the topic of type of parent–child contact, we found extremely high correlations (+0.75 to +0.80) for the time devoted to each type of contact during the period of observation between the two methods.

Another problem is that the tabular presentation of results is almost always detailed and difficult for the inexperienced reader to decipher. Although these results can be parceled out into a great number of simple tables, summary measures of general time-budget results are not well developed. Clark, Elliott, and Harvey (1982) suggest the use of what they call *hypercodes,* a method of grouping activity, place, and person codes for an episode together as a three-digit number. After running distributions, they find it possible to remove a number of possibilities and to focus on modal patterns.

A final pitfall worth mentioning is related to the interpretation of time-budget data. These data are inherently a measure of what exists under current conditions, and not necessarily what might emerge under other conditions. They are thus ideal for use in evaluation. Under other circumstances, however, the researcher must always be aware of the range of constraints above and beyond those that he wishes to measure, which may be accounting for the behavior observed. In other words, what you see people doing is not always a measure of what people might want to do in the best of all possible worlds. How they might change under realistic alternative conditions is something not intrinsic to time-budget data, but a consideration that must be used in their interpretation.

TIME GEOGRAPHY

Time geography, which has seen less general use than time-budget data, is credited almost entirely to the Swedish geographer Torsten Hägerstrand, in conjunction with students and colleagues. In recent years, however, their ideas have gained wide acceptance, particularly within the British Commonwealth, and a field sometimes called chronogeography (Schurer 1978; Parkes and Thrift 1980) has recently emerged.

Just as sociologists looked primarily at the behavioral side of time use, Hägerstrand, as a geographer, explored the other side of the coin in this connection: the environment. His basic ideas were most clearly introduced to international scientists in 1969, when he presented a seminal paper to the Regional Science Association titled, "What About People in Regional Science?" (Hägerstrand 1970a). His aim was to provide a tangible linkage between what people do and the physical conditions under which they do them. In the years since, Hägerstrand's scheme has been explicated in English (see, for example, Lenntorp 1976; Carlstein 1978a, 1978b; Schurer 1978; Mårtensson 1979; Parkes and Thrift 1980; Pred 1977, 1981), and many applications have been made.

What Hägerstrand advances is a way of looking at environment in terms of its potential for behavior, with time and space as central variables. He conceptualizes each individual as on a path through space within a time frame. One's ultimate time frame is a lifetime, and typical movements in space at that scale can be shown (Hägerstrand 1963). For environment and its behavioral potential in daily life, the weekday is a preferred time frame. As figure 7-8 indicates, Hägerstrand charts paths with time (that is, twenty-four hours) as the vertical axis and space as the horizontal axis; all paths go from the bottom of the chart to the top.

Movement in space and time is inherently constrained, according to Hägerstrand. Several premises underlie this outlook. (1) People cannot be in two places at once. (2) It is difficult to do more than one major activity at a time. (3) Each task takes time that cannot be devoted to another and that therefore delays subsequent activities. (4) The number of activities possible in one place is limited, requiring movement. (5) Movement between points in space takes time. (6) One can only go so far in a day, and hence activities are limited also by space.

Different places in space are called stations—geographic equivalents to what psychologists call behavior settings (Barker 1968). Hence, a daily path proceeds upward in time and laterally among stations, as shown in figure 7-9.

The potential path through the typical day takes the shape of a prism, under the constraints in force (fig. 7-10). Because you start from one place and because it takes time to get elsewhere, the distance in (horizontal) space away from the starting point is limited during the initial part of a (vertical) time frame but gradually increases with the passage of time. The top end of the potential prism is similarly tapered, insofar as most people return to the point of their daily origin by the end of the day and hence lose travel options as the day comes to a close. How wide or narrow a prism will be depends, at the most simple level, on what a person needs or wants to do during the day, where in space the stations for these activities are located, and what type and speed of travel are available to get to and from these sta-

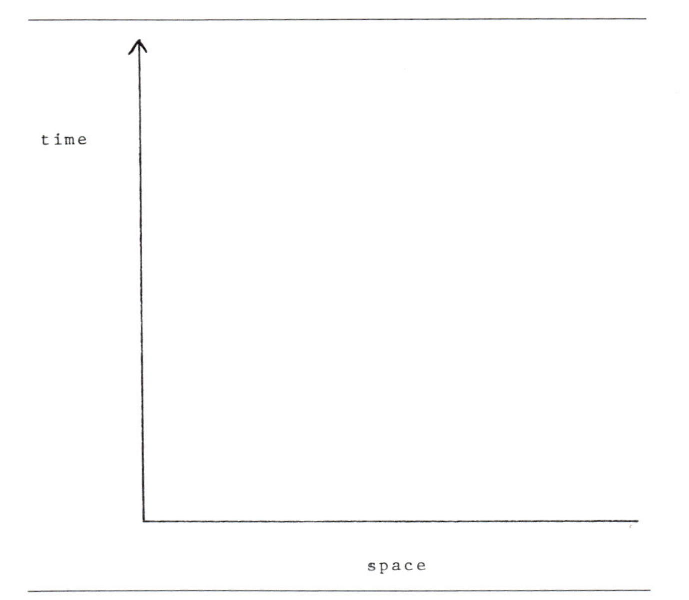

7-8. The axes of Hägerstrand's path charts.

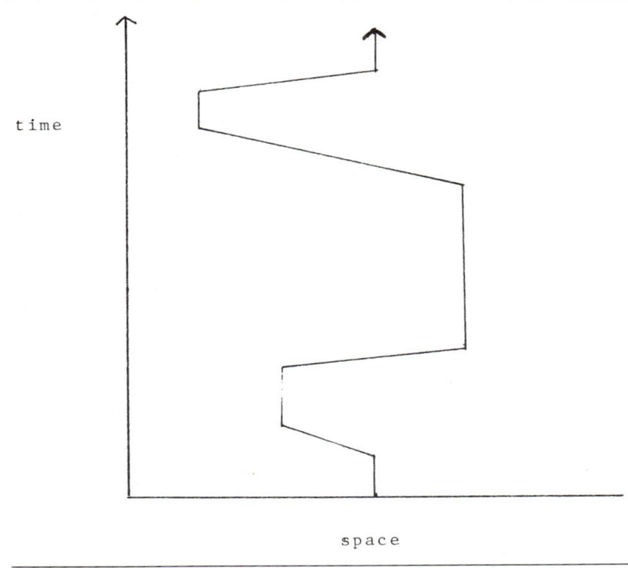

7-9. An individual path among stations.

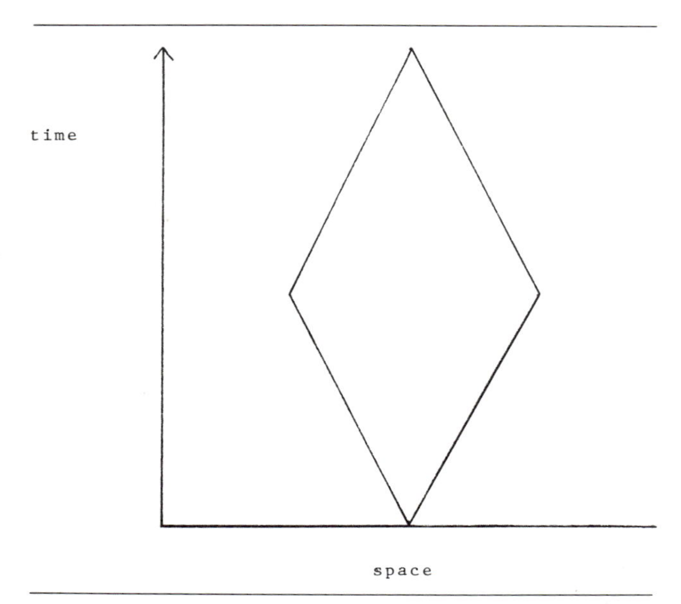

7–10. *Potential for an individual's daily activity.*

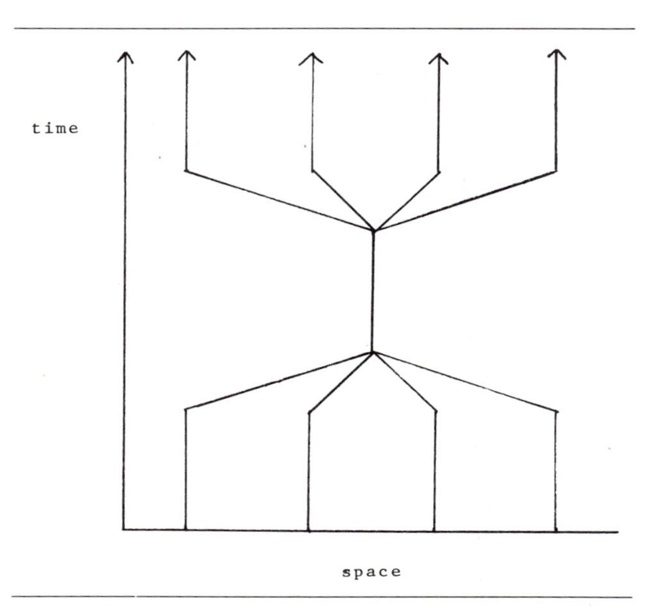

7–11. *People converging during day.*

tions. Prisms take on greatly different shapes depending on differences in obligations, environments, and resources—and in three or four dimensions.

Paths are charted not just for individuals but, as bundles, for aggregates. A number of people who come from their homes and join together in an activity are illustrated in figure 7–11, while family members who disperse to different activities during the day are shown in figure 7–12.

The potential for individuals and groups to follow particular paths and form particular bundles is conditioned not only by absolute limitations of time and space but by certain macro constraints.

Capability constraints represent limits to the "reach" a person has during the day under the conditions in which he lives and works. Can you, for example, physically get to the beach in the time available between work and dinner?

Coupling constraints are those that determine whether or not sufficient numbers and appropriate

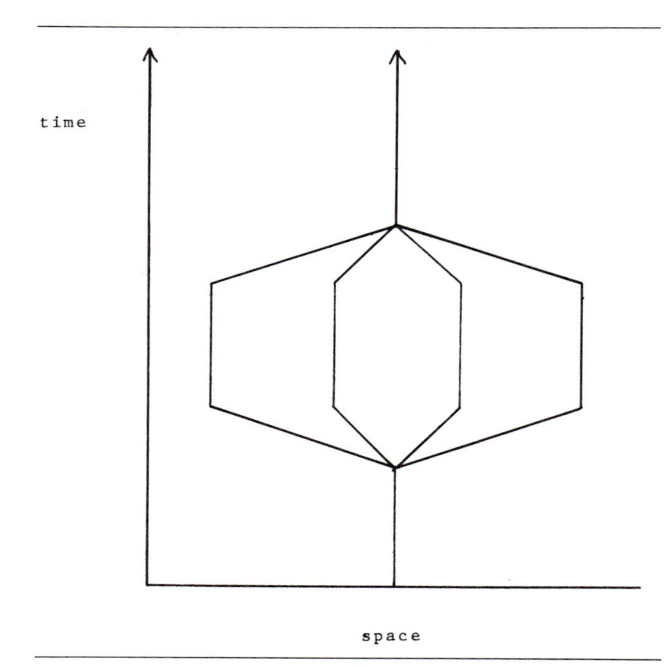

7–12. *People dispersing during day.*

types of people can get together within existing temporal and spatial conditions to make an activity possible. How realistic, for example, are specialty leisure or educational activities requiring large numbers of adult participants in the suburbs during weekdays?

Authority constraints are aspects of the organization of activities that potentially narrow what a person can do. Are the hours of certain stores or services such that, with necessary travel, it is difficult or impossible to visit them before, during, or after working hours (with a given work location)?

Hägerstrand is not a spatial determinist. He does not see the environment as dictating any particular activity. Nonetheless, what he makes explicit are some "real, physical limits and the real impossibilities which are created by time and place in connection with physiological and technological abilities, social ties and institutional domains" (van Paasen 1981, 27). Within these limits lies freedom of choice, yet the nature of encroachment upon freedom may be significant and have significant effects. Since many of the constraints arise from aspects of community environment that are potentially open to change or redesign, the understanding of environmental factors in everyday behavior is a positive step in the process of amelioration through planning and design.

In practice, time geographers look at both time budgets and environmental contexts. The former are taken according to both of the interpretations discussed earlier. Time geographers clearly assume that the time use observed in any group of people is at least in part a function of surroundings. Hence they utilize time budgets experimentally, for example, before and after an intervention designed to enhance the range of possibilities in daily activity, ascribing differences to the intervention in the absence of other compelling sources of change in the behavior monitored. On the other hand, ideal daily time budgets, capturing aspects of life considered desirable but not always attainable under current conditions, are modeled, to test whether they might be achieved with specific alterations in community environment/infrastructure. Mårtensson (1978, 1979), for example, compared two cities in Sweden, to determine the extent to which the infrastructure in each made feasible such activities as medical care or evening cultural or political participation, in combination with a typical day's employment. To do this, she had to assess the temporal and spatial requirements of employment and minimum domestic commitments and then spell out what would be entailed by the addition of the activities under examination. Could the latter fit into the remainder of the day, without sacrifice of the givens, under prevailing scheduling, organization, transportation arrangements, distances, and the like? Different community environments and infrastructures are in fact shown to allow different degrees of opportunity for daily behavior.

When time geographers measure an environment's behavioral potential, they turn to referents of time and space in the community: opening and closing hours of places of employment, stores, institutions, and bureaucracies; locations and relationships of these land uses and activities, not least in connection with where residents live; and modes, routes, and characteristics of the various relevant forms of travel. Insofar as the incorporation of all aspects of environment in even a small city is incredibly complex, the selection of relevant aspects is a function of the focus of any given study.

One operational, general model of urban movement was generated by Lenntorp (1976). Called PESASP (Program for Evaluating the Set of Alternative Sample Paths), this model is set up to accommodate data from a specific municipality on all relevant stations (including their type, location, and hours), transport systems (including routes of public transportation, constraints to movement in time and space for various forms of travel, together with their speeds), and activity programs (how much time typical activities demand, where they take place, and when). With PESASP, one can determine whether the resident of a particular area who works for a given employer and who does or does not drive a car to work is capable of participating in a specific additional daily activity, or set of them (for example, getting shoes repaired or going to the bank), as the local environment is currently arranged and organized. PESASP can also test to see what changes would have to be made to allow a given combination of desired daily activities or to make a current set easier to complete.

The logic and operationalization of time geography, however, can be implemented by degrees without PESASP per se, and even researchers in Lund, where Hägerstrand, Lenntorp, Mårtensson, Carlstein, and others are based, work with parallel approaches to measurement, despite the systematic process offered by the formal model.

INTEGRATIVE APPLICATIONS

Our examination of the time-budget and time-geography approaches indicates that while social scientists have found merit in the use of time budgets without the obligatory incorporation of contextual constraints, time geographers find it a necessity to utilize either real or ideal behavior as one of the two sectors of their analyses of environment and behavior. When planners and other designers are arranging or making interventions in an environment on the basis of direct or indirect behavioral considerations, the more explicit both dimensions can be made, the more realistically research can serve to orient functional change.

Hägerstrand, who developed his approach in conjunction with a national task force on regional development in Sweden, rethought earlier geographic theories on hierarchies of settlements, which primarily reflected agricultural market relationships. He focussed instead on the temporal and spatial aspects of relationships of citizens to public institutions and services (like hospitals, government offices, and universities), which help support quality of life and health while providing jobs and helping to support the economy of a region. His formulations about individual access to such institutions (Hägerstrand 1970b) became the basis for regional planning based on the real power governments have to distribute their offices and institutions in a pattern promoting relatively equitable, and, in an everyday perspective, functional access for the population. An outcome of this research-based exercise of legislative power is the reduced likelihood that economically disadvantaged areas will become increasingly isolated from the mainstream.

A smaller-scale Swedish study by Mårtensson (1982) illustrates the application of both time-budget and time-geography approaches. An experiment with the dial-a-bus system in and around the town of Nynäshamn required an evaluation. Did the transportation innovations measurably change people's activities and modes of travel? While it was a relatively straightforward procedure to conduct a panel study involving the comparison of time budgets for the same people before and after the inception of the changes, determining what could be attributed to these particular changes required a more detailed examination of the possibilities facing particular sectors of the population before and after dial-a-bus. Hence, the population was disaggregated according to geographic area and age (children, adults, and mobile pensioners). Before the commencement of dial-a-bus, opportunities for travel by public transport to specific activities were calculated for commuting, school, shopping, and recreation. It was then possible to see where constraints were originally present and to analyze the extent to which the new system might help mitigate these constraints. The comparison of time-budget results from one period to another then documented increased activities in those realms and on the part of those groups for whom greater opportunities were provided (such as recreation for rural children, shopping for the elderly). The time-geographic analysis was necessary to assess how in fact the planners were intervening on behalf of people's potential opportunities, while the time-budget results documented whether this potential was meaningfully actualized.

A second application of the convergence of these methods deals with exposure to risk. If you can document people's routine behavior, on the one hand, and the degree of danger associated with the environments involved in their routines, on the other, then people's exposure to risk can be calculated. Armstrong (1973), a geographer working in the field of public health, applied time budgets and time geography to travel safety. He independently measured the weekly time-use routines of a sample in a rural area in Hawaii and the degree of danger inherent in the roads they would take to implement their rounds. Drawing out typical needs for movement and weighting the degree of danger by this empirical measure of exposure gives a new view of the perils accompanying a given road system. Planning for the future can be based on how the present system penetrates the daily lives of local residents and what potential it presents for them. Armstrong's method can be applied to a variety of other concerns in the environment and behavior area—for example, to dwelling unit safety features, defensible space in buildings and grounds, and children's pedestrian safety in neighborhoods. One can measure exposure without waiting for the results of a sudden rash of "accidents," and one can set priorities for ameliorative actions.

A third application reflects the growing trend among the mothers of young children to hold outside employment. Joining the responsibilities of employment to domestic commitments that have declined only in part creates a daily routine that many mothers find challenging. I recently completed research seeking to document how the lives of women and children in Metropolitan Toronto are affected by maternal employment, not least with respect to how community structure facilitates or hinders people—men, women, and children alike—in the pursuit of everyday activities (Michelson 1985). One aspect of the community that is explicitly organized to support employed mothers is child care. Besides daycare centers, there is individual provision of child care by others in their homes. Relatives provide care, as do preschools and before-school, lunchtime, and after-school programs. While the availability, quality, and cost of such services are at times in question, they are recognized as providing an essential service. Using time budgets and simple contextual information, we were able to examine child care supports in terms of one aspect of their logistical adequacy—their location.

As part of a lengthy interview procedure, time budgets were elicited, as mentioned earlier, from all family members, and considerable information about her daily routine and her feelings about it was given by each mother. Data about child care options utilized, including type and location, were gathered. All data about places in and out of the time budgets were geo-coded according to a standard kilometer grid of Metropolitan Toronto, and thus distances could be calculated on a straight-line basis, the hypotenuse of the triangle formed by the distance between the places on each of the two axes. (This distance is of course conservatively understated, because few people can travel from one place to another in a straight line.) We could also calculate the degree of tension associated with travel, having utilized the seven-point scale of tension–relaxation discussed earlier with respect to each activity.

Mothers are involved in most trips for child care.

They are the lone adult family chaperone in 55.6 percent of such trips, and they and their husbands go together another 14.8 percent of the time, accounting for over 70 percent of child care trips. It is therefore advisable to look at distances and travel times connected with women's child care and work trips. If child care were immediately adjacent to home or workplace, then it still might take longer to get from door to desk or bench, but the child care drop-off would not represent extra travel time or distance. In our sample, the mean distance from home to child care is 1.71 kilometers. In terms of net travel, about half a kilometer is added (in each direction) by child care to the home-to-work distance. No less than 28 percent of child care travel is out of the way.

The daycare centers used by families in the Toronto sample are, on average, 3.58 kilometers from home—more than twice the general average; in contrast, home daycare averages within a kilometer of home (0.9 kilometers), while the distance to grandparents is in between.

The value of paying attention to the location of child care services is seen by analyzing tension associated with mothers' daily travel. Tension does not vary significantly according to either the distance from home to work ($r = +.10$, NS) or the total distance of home to child care to work ($r = -.04$, NS). Rather, it is the amount of *extra* distance added by the child care drop-off that is significantly (though still mildly) related to travel tension over the day ($r = +.16$, $p = .004$). Fathers do not show the same pattern of tension, reinforcing our interpretation that the daycare drop-off makes a significant incursion primarily in the mother's day.

These data suggest the personal value to women (not to speak of differences in commuting by very young children) of locating daycare centers more sensitively in the future with respect to places of residence and employment, and possibly also to transportation nodes, so as to minimize debilitating marginal increases in daily commuting associated with a presumed support.

CONCLUSION

The varieties of application and operationalization of time budgets and time geography with respect to planning and design are virtually endless. Work to date is but suggestive. Conceptual developments linking behavior to environment through the media of time and space are relatively recent, as is the recognition of the need to establish such conceptual clarity as part of dealing with design settings that are larger and more complex than those traditionally studied. The time-budget and time-geography studies make available quantitative empirical data that can include vital subjective dimensions and that can be manipulated with the aid of modern computers to shed light on this next level of environment and behavior without undue difficulty. These approaches are not optimal for all types of problems, but offer encouraging prospects for enhancing the quality and behavioral potential of community infrastructures and other human spaces.

ACKNOWLEDGMENTS

This chapter represents a major revision of one coauthored by Paul B. Reed in the original volume (Michelson 1975). Reed's influence on the current effort through his original contribution is hereby gratefully acknowledged. I wrote this while on sabbatical leave as a visiting researcher at the Institute of Cultural and Economic Geography and the Institute for Building Functions Analysis, University of Lund, Sweden. I am grateful in this regard to Carin Boalt, Tommy

Carlstein, Torsten Hägerstrand, Birgit Krantz, Bo Lenntorp, Solveig Mårtensson, and Olof Wärneryd for helpful suggestions and more general kindness. The personal data mentioned in the manuscript were collected and analyzed with grants from the Welfare Grants Division, Health and Welfare, Canada, the U.S. Urban Mass Transportation Administration (through Grant CA-11-0024-1), and the Institute of Transportation Studies and Program in Social Ecology, University of California, Irvine. The Child in the City Programme, University of Toronto, and its major sponsor, The Hospital for Sick Children Foundation, generated the project and managed its progress. I want to express my thanks to everyone associated with these supporting organizations in relation to this research project. Howard Andrews provided useful feedback on a previous draft.

REFERENCES

Altergott, K. 1982. Role relationships across the life span. In *It's about Time,* ed. Z. Staikov, 123–26. Sofia: Jusautor.

Armstrong, R. W. 1973. Tracing exposure to specific environments in medical geography. *Geographical Analyses* 2:122–32.

Ås, D. 1982. Designs for large scale time use studies of the 24-hour day. In *It's about Time,* ed. Z. Staikov, 17–53. Sofia: Jusautor.

Asplund, J. 1979. *Teorier om framtiden* (Theories about the Future). Stockholm: Liber.

Barker, R. 1968. *Ecological Psychology.* Stanford: Stanford Univ. Press.

Becker, G. S. 1965. A theory of the allocation of time. *Economics Journal* 75:493–517.

Boalt, C., and G. Carlsson. 1949. *Mor och barn från morgon till kväll* (Mother and Child from Morning to Night). Hemmets Forskningsinstitut Report no. 2. Stockholm.

Carlstein, T. 1978a. Innovation, time allocation and time-space packing. In *Human Activity and Time Geography,* ed. T. Carlstein et al., ch. 8. New York: Halsted.

———. 1978b. A time-geographic approach to time allocation and socio-ecological systems. In *Public Policy in Temporal Perspective,* ed. W. Michelson, 69–82. The Hague: Mouton.

Carlstein, T., et al. 1968. *Individars dygnsbanor i några hushållstyper* (Individual Routines within Several Household Types). Lund: Institute for Cultural Geography, Univ. of Lund.

Chapin, F. S., Jr. 1965. *Urban Land Use Planning.* Urbana: Univ. of Illinois Press.

———. 1974. *Human Activity Patterns in the City.* New York: Wiley.

Chumak, A., and J. P. Braaksma. 1981. Implications of the travel-time budget for urban transportation modeling in Canada. *Transportation Research Record* 794:19–27.

Clark, S., D. Elliott, and A. S. Harvey 1982. Hypercodes and composite variables: Simple techniques for the reduction and analysis of time-budget data. In *It's about Time,* ed. Z. Staikov, 66–92. Sofia: Jusautor.

Cullen, I. 1978. The treatment of time in the explanation of spatial behavior. In *Human Activity and Time Geography,* ed. T. Carlstein et al., 27–38. New York: Halsted.

Cullen, I., and E. Phelps. 1978. Patterns of behavior and responses to the urban environment. In *Public Policy in Temporal Perspective,* ed. W. Michelson, 165–81. The Hague: Mouton.

Felson, M. 1981. Social accounts based on map, clock, and calendar. In *Social Accounting Systems,* ed. F. T. Juster and K. C. Land, 219–39. New York: Academic Press.

Gutenschwager, G. A. 1973. The time budget-activity systems perspective in urban research and planning. *Journal of the American Institute of Planners* 39:378–87.

Hägerstrand, T. 1963. Geographic measurements of migration: Swedish data. In *Human Displacements: Measurements and Methodological Aspects,* ed. J. Sutter, 61–83. Monaco: Entretiens de Monaco en Sciences Humaines.

Harvey, A. S. 1978. The role of time-budgets in national and regional economic accounting. In *Public Policy in Temporal Perspective,* ed. W. Michelson, 11-22. The Hague: Mouton.

———. 1970a. What about people in regional science? *Papers of the Regional Science Association* 24:7-21.

———. 1970b. Tidsanvändning och omgivningsstruktur (Time-use and Environmental Structure). *Statens Offentliga Utredningar* 14, no. 4:1-146.

Juster, T. F., P. N. Courant, and G. K. Dow. 1979. *Social Indicators: A Framework for the Analysis of Well-being.* Institute for Social Research, University of Michigan, 1979.

Lenntorp, B. 1976. *Paths in Space-Time Environments: A Time-Geographic Study of Movement Possibilities of Individuals.* Lund Studies in Geography, no. 44. Lund: C. W. K. Gleerup.

Lundberg, G., M. Komarovsky, and M. A. McInerny. 1934. *Leisure: A Suburban Study.* New York: Columbia University Press.

Manz, G. 1978. The time budget in national economic planning. In *Public Policy in Temporal Perspective,* ed. W. Michelson, 23-27. The Hague: Mouton.

Mårtensson, S. 1978. Time allocation and daily living conditions: comparing regions. In *Human Activity and Time Geography,* ed. T. Carlstein et al. 181-97. New York: Halsted.

———. 1979. *On the Formation of Biographies.* Lund Studies in Geography, no. 47. Lund: C. W. K. Gleerup.

———. 1982. *Tidsbudjetstudier in anslutning till försök med anropstyrd busstrafik* (Time-budget Studies in Connection with an Experiment with Dial-a-bus). Lund: Department of Geography, University of Lund.

Matsushima, C. 1982. Time-input and household work-output studies in Japan. In *It's about Time,* ed. Z. Staikov, 188-208. Sofia: Jusautor.

Matzner, E., and G. Rüsch, eds. 1976. *Transport as an Instrument for Allocating Space and Time—A Social Science Approach.* Vienna: Technical Univ. in Vienna, Institute of Public Finance, no. 11. Vienna.

Michelson, W. 1976. *Man and His Urban Environment: A Sociological Approach.* Rev. ed. Reading, Mass.: Addison-Wesley.

———. 1977. *Environmental Choice, Human Behavior, and Residential Satisfaction.* New York: Oxford Univ. Press.

———. 1980. Spatial and temporal dimensions of child care. *Signs: Journal of Women in Culture and Society* 5(3):S242-47.

———. 1985. *From Sun to Sun: Daily Obligations and Community Structure in the Lives of Employed Women and Their Families.* Totowa, N.J.: Rowman & Allanheld.

Michelson, W., ed. 1975. *Behavioral Research Methods in Environmental Design.* Stroudsburg, Pa.: Dowden, Hutchinson & Ross.

Nakanishi, N. 1966. *A Report on the How-do-people-spend-their-time Survey.* NHK Public Opinion Research Institute. Tokyo.

———. 1968. *A Study of International Comparisons of Time Budget.* NHK Public Opinion Research Institute. Tokyo.

Ottensman, J. 1972. *Systems of Urban Activities and Time: An Interpretative Review of the Literature.* Center for Urban and Regional Studies, University of North Carolina. Chapel Hill.

Pant, P. D., and A. G. R. Bullen. 1980. Urban activities, travel and time: Relationships from national time-use survey. *Transportation Research Record* 750:1-6.

Parkes, D. N., and N. Thrift. 1980. *Times, Spaces, and Places.* New York: Wiley.

Patrushev, V. D. 1982. Satisfaction with free time as a social category and indicator of way of life. In *It's about Time,* ed. Z. Staikov, 259-67. Sofia: Jusautor.

Pred, A. 1977. The choreography of existence: Comments on Hägerstrand's time-geography and its usefulness. *Economic Geography* 53:207-21.

———. 1981. Of paths and projects: Individual behavior and its societal context. In *Behavioral Problems in Geography Revisited,* ed. R. Golledge and K.

Cox, 231–55. New York: Methuen.

Reed, P. 1976. Lifestyle as an Element of Social Logic: Patterns of Activity, Social Characteristics, and Residential Choice. Ph.D. diss., University of Toronto.

Robinson, J. P. 1977. *Changes in Americans' Use of Time: 1965–1975.* Cleveland State University, Communication Research Center. Cleveland.

Schurer, G. A. K. 1978. *Chrono-geography: An Interpretative Review of Related Literature.* University of Adelaide, Urban and Regional Planning Working Paper no. 6. Adelaide.

Shapcott, M., and P. Steadman. 1978. Rhythms of urban activity. In *Human Activity and Time Geography,* ed. T. Carlstein et al. 49–74. New York: Halsted Press.

Sorokin, P. A., and C. Q. Berger. 1939. *Time Budgets of Human Behavior.* Cambridge, Mass.: Harvard Univ. Press.

Stone, P. 1978. Women's time patterns in eleven countries. In *Public Policy in Temporal Perspective,* ed. W. Michelson, 113–50. The Hague: Mouton.

Swedner, H., and D. Yague. 1970. Proposals for a nomenclature for human activities with particular reference to cultural activities. *Society and Leisure* 2.

Szalai, A. 1966. The multinational comparative time budget research project: A venture in international research cooperation. *American Behavioral Scientist* 10, no. 12.

———. 1975. Informal paper presented to workshop on the application of time-budget research to policy questions in urban and regional settings, Laxenburg, Austria, 7–9 October.

Szalai, A. et al. 1972. *The Use of Time.* The Hague: Mouton.

van Paasen, C. 1981. The philosophy of geography: from Vidal to Hägerstrand. In *Space and Time Geography: Essays Dedicated to Torsten Hägerstrand,* ed. A. Pred, 17–29. Lund: C. W. K. Gleerup.

Vanek, J. 1974. Time spent in housework. *Scientific American* 231, no. 5:116–20.

Walker, K., and M. E. Woods. 1976. Time Use: A Measure of Household Production of Family Goods and Services. Washington, D.C.: Center for the Family of the American Home Economics Association.

Ziegler, S., and W. Michelson. 1981. Complementary methods of data gathering in literate, urban populations. *Human Organization* 40:323–29.

PART II

APPLICATIONS

CHAPTER 8

ENVIRONMENTAL PROGRAMMING

Kent Spreckelmeyer

Programming is the process of defining environmental problems and suggesting to the designer strategies for solving those problems. Programmers translate owner, user, and community needs into concepts that can be implemented by the architect or planner. The interaction among competing client, occupant, and community groups is a necessary and crucial component of this process. This chapter outlines ways in which such an interaction can be facilitated and enhanced with the use of behavioral research techniques. Specifically, it focuses on the use of methods that have been applied in architectural programming.[1]

The chapter is divided into three sections. The first part is an overview of programming theory and a definition of the programming process as it relates to environmental design. This section ends with a discussion of the various roles that programmers play in the design process. A number of analytic techniques are presented in the second part of the chapter to acquaint the reader with the range of research methods that are available to the programmer. Most of the techniques are described in depth in the preceding chapters of this book. The purpose of this section is to show how the different roles of the programmer defined in the initial part of the chapter are related to specific types or classes of research techniques. Finally, one example of the use of decision analysis research techniques in programming is given to illustrate the application of these methods in the design process.

DEFINITION OF PROGRAMMING

Programming is an activity that precedes environmental design and provides the designer with the functional, technical, and behavioral requirements of design. Technically, it is defined by architects as an additional service to be rendered over and above the standard design activities. It is listed among such technical services as site investigations, feasibility studies, and engineering analyses and is intended to provide definitions of the owner's needs and to determine the requirements of a design project (AIA 1977). Beyond this contractual distinction, the design professions in the United States have tended to leave the analysis of environmental needs and functions to the discretion of individual practitioners.[2]

The Canadian Department of Public Works has attempted in recent years to standardize the content of pre-design services and combine it formally with the building process. An initial survey of architectural programmers confirmed the personalized and informal nature of the process. The department concluded that this lack of common understanding in analyzing environmental problems was a major detriment to the delivery of well-designed buildings and prevented the orderly transfer of information, not only from one problem to another but also between the various members within the single architectural project (Public Works Canada 1979).

If there is a unifying thought that runs throughout the design professions concerning the nature of programming it is the view that programming and design are distinct and separate activities. Peña argues forcefully for such a separation because of the dual purposes of the analyst and synthesizer in design.

> Designers are subjective, intuitive, and facile with physical concepts. Programmers must be objective (to a degree) and analytical, at ease with abstract ideas and able to evaluate information and identify factors while postponing irrelevant materials . . . if a person can manage both analysis and synthesis, they must have two minds and use them alternately. [Pena 1977]

Wade, although taking a more lenient view of the separation of analysis and synthesis in design, gives a detailed explanation of how information entering environmental problems must be transformed from behaviorally based concepts to functional and object-related data in the programming and planning processes (Wade 1977). Preiser's (1978) compilation of approaches to pre-design services highlights a wide range of approaches to programming and the use of behavioral research methods.

Implicit in the definition of programming as the analytic antecedent of design is the idea that it must also be a communicative link that translates abstract ideas and data into physical concepts and strategies. Diagrammatically, this link has been described as the process of determining an owner's statement of need and environmental goals and producing a set of instructions that the designer can then use to fashion a physical solution. That process is characterized as a linear progression from abstract ideas and concepts concerning an environmental problem, to the development of design solutions, the construction of a building, its use as a response to that initial problem statement, and, finally, an assessment of the facility with respect to the original goals and needs.

Figure 8–1 illustrates the relationship between programming and the architectural design process. Programming has traditionally been viewed as the initiation of the design process and the point at which the data collection procedures of that process are begun. Recently, however, it has become more apparent to designers that the connection between the evaluation of existing environments and the programming of new environments is a critical point of departure in the traditional view of design. The importance of the completed loop created between the evaluation and programming steps of this process has been documented by Zeisel (1981) and implemented in a number of design projects (Farbstein 1984; Friedman et al. 1978; Marans and Spreckelmeyer 1981). The purpose of environmental evaluation is especially important in designs that will serve users who may not be fully represented within the design process. By looking critically at the effects of built environments on the occupants of office buildings, congregate housing, hospitals, and other large institutional settings, the programmer can more accurately determine the behavioral requirements of a proposed design solution.

The continuity of the design process and the creation of new knowledge implied within this diagram is also an important concept in terms of environmental programming. Although programming is viewed as the initial step of design, it is in fact the culmination of information that has been generated and accumulated over a number of past design efforts and within environments similar to the one presently being programmed. The connec-

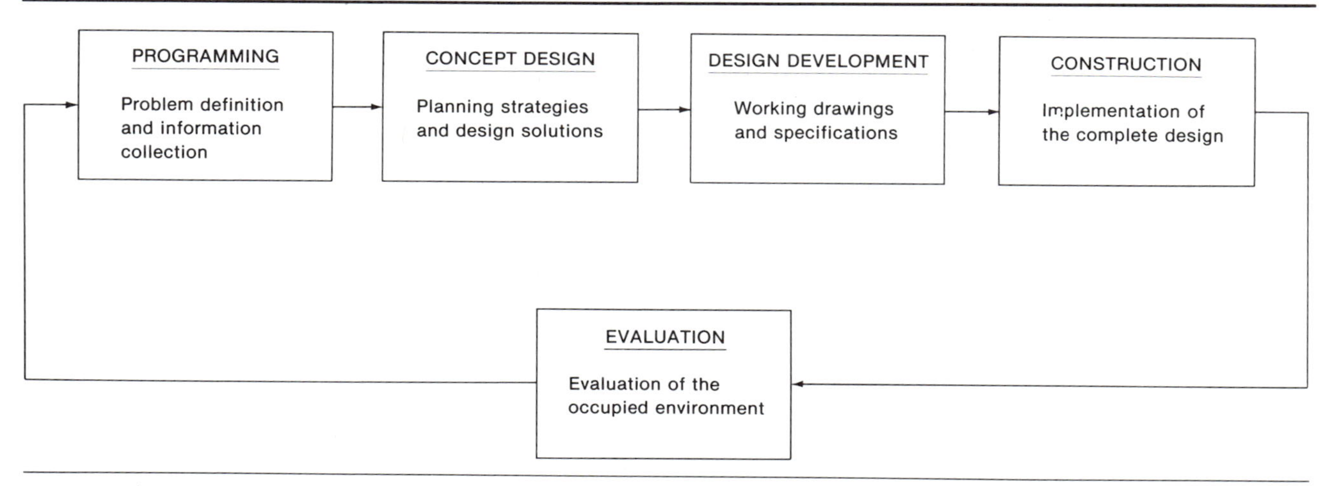

8–1. Relationship between programming and the architectural design process.

tion of programming to evaluation should be recognized in any process that attempts to clarify the behavioral aspects of design, and many of the analytic tools used in each share common theoretical and application principles.

The primary distinction between programming and the later phases of the design process is the fact that programming is primarily an exercise in making decisions. Although many techniques of data collection are common to both programming and evaluation, the latter is an investigation of environments that are complete and operational. Programming, on the other hand, is concerned with the creation of something new. The techniques of behavioral analysis that are most applicable to programming are those that help the designer understand the relationships between conflicting user needs and weigh the consequences of distinct planning strategies.

APPROACHES TO PROGRAMMING

Programming can be viewed from a number of perspectives, each of which describes the ways the programmer deals with environmental information. The four approaches outlined here define a range of possible roles the programmer may be required to assume given the kinds of information relevant to a particular environmental problem. It is not suggested that these approaches are definitive programming models or that they are mutually exclusive. On the contrary, most programming efforts will probably contain elements of all four approaches, and the programmer will no doubt switch roles throughout each project. Programs evolve from general statements and information concerned with owner and user needs to concrete analyses and presentations of design strategies. In other words, programming begins with the search for human needs and desires, proceeds to the collection of environmental data that describes those needs, continues with the analysis or interpretation of those data, and concludes in a decision as to the physical solutions that will satisfy those needs.[3]

The Facilitator

This approach to programming assumes a close relationship between the programmer and the users of a proposed environment. The facilitator helps the client define a course of design action and allows the user to become involved in the design process. Facilitator roles are characterized by participatory design sessions and community inputs. Sanoff (1977, 1978) has highlighted a number of these programming philosophies, which are characterized by the emphasis they place on the people affected by the design. The programmer in this instance is concerned with action and serves as an advocate of human needs.

The facilitator employs methods that bring the user into direct contact with an environmental problem. In certain respects, the facilitator is responsible for changing the definition of environmental problems to conform to the needs of a client group. In general, the behavioral methods can be defined as ''hands-on'' techniques that act as communication devices between the immediate users of environments and the designer. The facilitator is involved in the early steps of programming in order to assure that the most relevant questions can be asked in later phases and that those most directly affected by design decisions have the opportunity to express their needs and aspirations.

The Collector of Information

Simply stated, this is the role that requires the programmer to take in as much information as possible without being extremely concerned about its immediate usefulness or meaning. This is not to imply that the information is to be arbitrarily or poorly collected, but rather that the process of actually taking in the data outweighs, for the moment, its content. The collector is interested in technique and instrumentation and will place a great deal of importance on the precision with which information is gathered.

The programmer in the role of the collector is concerned with such issues as sampling procedures, instrument testing, statistics, and field procedures. The range of methods can be quite broad, from the casual observation and recording of human behavior to the detailed description of a population's subjective feelings about a particular environmental feature. The collector is the person who provides the designer, users, and owners with the basic information that can be interpreted or manipulated within the other roles of the programmer.

The Interpreter of Information

This approach can be defined as the ''processing of raw data into useful information'' (Peña 1977). The interpreter is the analyzer of information and the person who objectively translates large amounts of complex data. This point of view depends upon the assumption that programming is essentially a problem-defining activity, while design is a problem-solving exercise. The interpreter, because of this detachment, can assign meaning to information that would be impossible when the problem is given form and substance.

The Manager of Information

This approach to programming is defined as a decision-making process. It assumes that the primary task of the programmer is the resolution of conflicting points of view and the arrangement of owner and user information in well-defined categories. The programmer as the manager of information is a role characterized by the notion that environmental decisions must be hierarchical and areas of responsibility must be assigned to each step within the programming process. Since environmental decisions are ultimately concerned with the allocation of limited resources, the programmer cannot escape this need for control in the design process (Davis and Szigeti 1979).

The manager depends upon behavioral techniques that aid in prioritizing, managing, and sorting programmatic data. The nature of the information itself becomes important to the manager, since he or she must eventually decide on its usefulness in the assignment of program resources.

Figure 8-2 gives a brief summary of these four approaches to programming. Although this diagram should not be interpreted as a linear progression from facilitator to manager, it should be noted that each of these approaches is useful for dealing with a certain type of programming information, ranging from general statements of user and client needs to concrete decisions about resource allocation.

PROGRAMMING TECHNIQUES

It is useful to examine some of the tools that apply to each of the four approaches the programmer might take to analyze an environmental problem. Figure 8-3 outlines six types of research methods and indicates which may be of some use to the various roles the programmer might assume. Again, this diagram should not be thought of as complete or definitive. Rather, it should be viewed as a way of cataloging methods in relation to the various points of view that a programmer may wish to focus on at any given time in the programming proc-

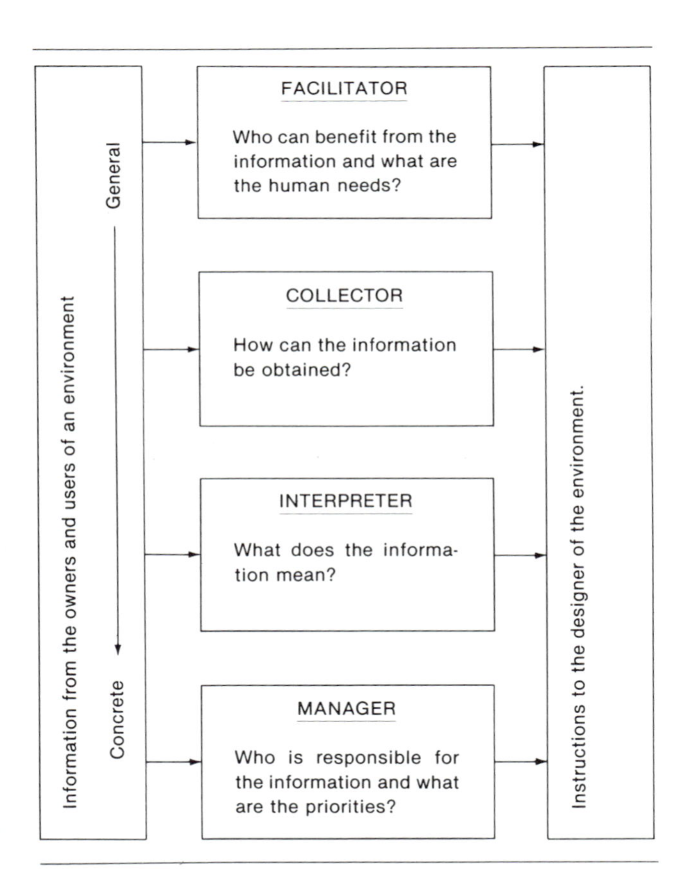

8–2. Approaches to programming.

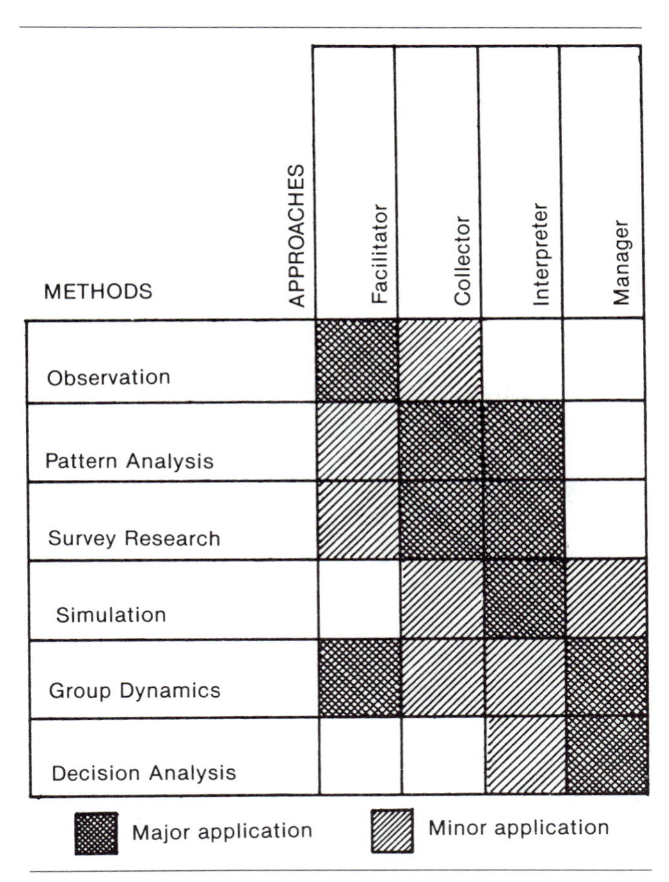

8–3. Methods and approaches in programming.

ess. The collector of program information may be more concerned with techniques that are useful for assembling as much information as possible rather than with how this information relates to the broader issues of the problem as, for example, would the manager or facilitator of that information. The first five methods are covered in depth in other sections of this book. The sixth—decision analysis—will be illustrated in the case study at the conclusion of this chapter.

Observation

Observation methods are concerned with the collection of information through watching the ways that environments are used. While some research techniques stress the scientific testing of a limited number of variables, observation methods are useful when many variables interact in such a way as to make the isolation of the components of the environmental setting infeasible or undesirable. Such techniques are often described as the "unobtrusive" measurement of an environment (Webb et al. 1981).

The recording of observed events in environmental settings can be accomplished through written checklists or photographic equipment. The latter form of data collection is recommended when the setting being observed includes a large number of activities or if the people using the environment change their behavior in the setting over time. Davis and Ayers (1975) provide an example of the use of time-lapse photography in the design of an airport terminal to determine the requirements of circulation space and the location of critical signage.

Existing environments are used by the programmer to observe situations similar to the ones proposed in a program statement. In some instances, however, full-scale mock-ups of the proposed environments are constructed and occupied by the intended users so that more accurate observations of human response can be achieved. Robert Bechtel and John Zeisel outline a number of specific observation methods in chapter 1 and show how these methods are used in various stages of the design process.

Pattern Analysis

Pattern analysis techniques typically depend upon observation techniques as a means of collecting behavioral data, but differ from the latter in that they use anthropological and psychological theories to interpret the behavior observed in specific settings. Programmers can use pattern analysis methods to focus information within a unique cultural or social setting and provide a basis for comparing design strategies from a number of user perspectives. The term "pattern" refers to environmental settings or situations that are associated with particular cultural norms or ethnological standards of behavior (Alexander et al. 1977).

The concept of cross-cultural comparisons is an important aspect of pattern analysis methods (Rapoport 1982). This type of study can aid the programmer in understanding how certain physical forms are associated with culturally specific human needs. Petronis et al. (1978) illustrate the use of behavioral research techniques in a culturally unique setting during the programming of a Cochiti Indian community food preparation facility. Specific research tools associated with pattern analysis are behavior mapping, activity logs, archival searches, and historical analyses. Chapters 6 and 7 contain material that is relevant to the programmer in this area of behavioral research.

Survey Research

Survey techniques are used to determine the needs and opinions of a user group by asking large numbers of people to respond to standardized questions concerning an environment. They are useful techniques in that they do not necessarily require the population's direct participation in the programming process nor does the group need to be aware of the extent of the design problem. Needs and opinions are determined by identifying trends in the combined responses of the user group. Uses of these techniques in programming are typically directed to the establishment of project goals and the determination of program priorities. Sanoff has used surveys in programming to define project goals and resolve conflicts within facilities with multiple uses (Palmer 1981, 234–40). A unique feature of survey research methods is that the exact user group of a proposed design need not be questioned in the survey as long as a comparable user group can be identified and systematically queried (Johnson 1980).

Questionnaires and interviews are used in survey research as data collection instruments. These techniques require a careful selection of the population to be surveyed and a clearly defined collection instrument. An important requirement in the analysis of information generated from these techniques is the establishment of hypotheses that determine how the various questions relate to the problem as a whole (Marans and Spreckelmeyer 1981). Robert Marans gives a detailed explanation of the construction of survey instruments and their use in environmental problems in chapter 2 of this book.

Simulation

Whereas the previous methods have depended on the observation of real environments or the polling of building users as the source of behavioral data, simulation methods rely on laboratory settings or symbolic models to predict how people respond to environments. Simulation techniques are capable of rapidly analyzing a limited number of well-defined variables within a large set of alternative conditions. Although some theorists such as Friedman (1975) have speculated that computer-aided techniques might be used for huge networks of user inputs and interactions, the more successful uses of these methods have been found in intricate but limited programming problems such as material and pedestrian flow (Zilm 1980).

Environments such as critical-care areas in hospitals require detailed programming studies in order to determine the human and technical requirements to be incorporated in these facilities. A number of programming studies have been conducted at the University of Michigan, where full-scale patient-care rooms were constructed during programming and tested by the hospital staff (Clipson and Wehrer 1973; King et al. 1982). Computers have also been programmed to simulate the behavior of complex urban systems, thereby reducing the time required for the programmer to study the effects of alternative strategies to design problems (Negroponte 1975; Cross 1977). The main advantage of simulation techniques is the ability to predict the environmental consequences of programmatic decisions without interacting directly with an affected population. The simulation techniques outlined in chapter 5 will give the programmer a more detailed understanding of their use in behavioral research.

Group Dynamics

The active participation by the users of an environment in the programming process is the purpose of these techniques. While the previous methodologies have focused on the organization and analysis of information, group dynamic techniques emphasize the creative aspects of programming. The underlying theory behind these techniques is that the collective knowledge of the users of the environments is the best source of programming and design data. Sanoff (1977 and 1978) presents this approach to participatory design as a way for programmers to bring the opinions and expectations of the users to bear directly on the design process. Peña (1977) uses the term "Squatter Session" to describe the process of allowing user groups to interact directly during programming to help the programmer determine the goals and generate programmatic concepts.

Group dynamic techniques are employed with small user groups to act out environmental scenarios that relate to an environmental problem. Gaming is a group dynamic method that condenses the facets of a design problem into a simple and clearly delineated set of events (Duke 1974; Sanoff 1979). Games have been used both to generate ideas in a user group and to sensitize users and programmers to the special problems of populations that are often overlooked in designs, such as the handicapped, the elderly, or children (Hasell and Taylor 1981). Trade-off games are sometimes used to help user groups prioritize the components of environmental problems and to predict the consequences of programming decisions. Chapter 4 contains information about the use of gaming techniques in urban-scale problems.

Group dynamic techniques are characterized by intensive workshop sessions composed of users directly affected by a proposed design. An important aspect of these techniques is the free and spontaneous exchange of ideas and opinions among the group members and the recording of these ideas either through game boards or concept cards. Craig Zimring gives an example of how workshop sessions are useful in generating information in evaluation studies in chapter 9.

Decision Analysis

Decision analysis tools are useful management techniques in dealing with a large amount of programmatic information when the connections between the data are unclear or confused. They allow the programmer to elicit value judgments from a small set of client and user representatives and prioritize the goals and objectives of the program statement. The remainder of this chapter will be used to describe the use of decision techniques and to present a model of decision making in programming.[4] It should be noted that the preceding discussions of research techniques are used primarily to formulate hypotheses of human behavior, collect data to test these hypotheses, and facilitate the communication of user needs and owner goals. Decision analysis techniques are used in the latter stages of programming in order to select from the data collected and ideas generated the programming strategy that best satisfies these needs and goals.

Originally associated with the field of operations research, decision analysis techniques have been used in a number of environmental design problems (Keeney and Raiffa 1976). Designers and programmers have used these techniques to evaluate programmatic alternatives as well as to organize the step-by-step process of design (Clipson and Wehrer 1977). Decision analysis techniques are used to weigh the consequences of different approaches to an environmental problem and help the client and programmer prioritize the goals and objectives of a design project. These methods have been used in areas of environmental design that are concerned with cost and material selection (Dell'Isola and Kirk 1981; Mattar et al. 1978) as well as those concerned with human values and judgment (Spreckelmeyer 1981).

The Delphi technique of group decision making is a method that allows a diverse owner and user group systematically to generate and analyze programming data. Delphi sessions are actually brainstorming exercises in which a wide range of ideas and design concepts are collected from building users and design consultants in order to creatively analyze a variety of programming strategies (Delbecq et al. 1975; Linstone and Turoff 1975). These techniques are similar to social surveys in that they attempt to collect opinions from people directly affected by programming decisions, but are distinct from surveys in that they are primarily concerned with developing a consensus within a group with conflicting values and perceptions. The Delphi technique was developed at the Rand Corporation during the 1960s as a way of simplifying and focusing the process of collective decision making, although the essential ingredients of this method have been used informally since the inception of the "decision-by-committee" (Thomas 1979).

The model of decision making that is presented here is a structure that orders programmatic information. In using observation or survey research methods in the earlier stages of programming, for example, data will have been collected by the researcher that describe the basic environmental attitudes and desires of a user group. Gaming techniques or simulation methods may have been used to generate alternative programming strategies that the users would like to see incorporated into an environmental design. The decision model organizes this data in two separate categories: (1) the client and user groups' design objectives and (2) a set of environmental alternatives that can be used to satisfy these objectives. Design objectives are the goals and aspirations of the people who will construct and occupy an environment and the relative degrees of importance of these goals. The various programming alternatives feasible for accomplishing these objectives are typified by space and functions diagrams, patterns of people and material flow, and activity analyses that have been made during programming. The balance of the objectives and alternatives constitutes the definition of the problem and the selection of a specific programming strategy to solve that problem. The decision model outlined in figure 8-4 acts as an evaluation tool to achieve such a balance.

The basic requirements or assumptions in using this model are:

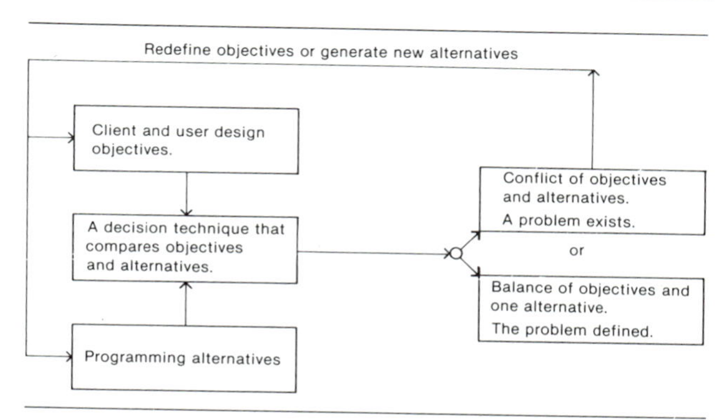

8-4. A decision technique in architectural programming.

1. One decision maker or a unified group presents design objectives and evaluates programming alternatives
2. The objectives are assumed to be independent of one another and in some way measurable
3. Judgments of relative importance can be made by the decision makers among the various client objectives
4. Probabilities can be assigned to the alternatives that describe the likelihood of each alternative achieving specific levels of the objectives

It can be seen from the definition of the above requirements that the technique is a normative model of decision making and is limited to a select set of user values. It is a tool that is used after a large amount of behavioral data has been collected and when the programmer and client are ready to search out and select environmental solutions.

A PROGRAMMING CASE STUDY

An important component of environmental programming is the establishment of a consensus within a diverse programming team. That team—

composed of representatives of the owner and user, the programmer, cost analysts, and design consultants—must make sense of the information that has been collected during programming and provide direction to the designer. One architectural consulting firm has used the decision model described above to achieve such a synthesis of information during programming and has found that the use of the model can have a positive effect on the ways that program decisions are made. The following case study illustrates the use of the model during the formulation of a program for a large corporate headquarters facility.[5]

At a point in the programming process when a number of program alternatives have been generated and the goals of the owner and users have been defined, all members of the programming team are assembled for an intensive review and evaluation of this information. This assembly, or workshop, is a creative activity in which the various opinions and experiences of the team are pooled to arrive at a collective understanding of the problem. At the completion of the workshop, an agreement should be reached among the team members that defines the nature of the problem and suggests a range of possible design implications for its solution.

In this case study the team consisted of three client/user representatives, two programmers and technical consultants, the designers, and three members of the consulting firm acting as the managers of the workshop and providing cost, mechanical, and site expertise. The workshop was conducted over a two-day period in the office of the programmers.

A critical step in any decision-making process is the selection of the workshop team. It is necessary to limit the number of workshop participants, both in order to simplify the mechanics of information transfer and to create a feeling of cohesiveness within the working group. At the same time it should also be the objective of the programmer to include within the decision-making process as many points of view and conflicting opinions as possible. This is especially true for designs that will contain a large number of competing factions that will each demand that the programmer listen to a specific set of concerns and design issues. One user group, for example, may be particularly concerned about the quality of the environment—aesthetics, noise control, natural lighting—while yet another may be very sensitive to the degree of functional efficiency within a plan layout. Management, on the other hand, will probably be most concerned with operating costs and worker productivity, while the design professionals themselves will no doubt have a responsibility to incorporate a high degree of safety and economy into the proposed design.

Each of these concerns and perspectives represents a specific and narrow view of the program. Many of these concerns are probably in conflict with every other concern and therefore must be brought into balance. It is the programmer's responsibility to ensure that this balance is achieved by including within the programming team a representative of each interest group that will be affected by the facility design. Each workshop participant should represent a specific point of view and should be conversant with all the behavioral and functional details that embody that point of view. In this particular project the list of participants consisted of both management and staff personnel from the user organization, engineering consultants, the designer, and the programmer. The perceptions of each of these individuals were unique with respect to the problem and each brought a separate set of priorities to the programming process.

It is common at the initiation of a decision-making or Delphi workshop to reverse the roles of the team members in order to create a feeling of mutual respect and to sharpen the differences that exist within the group. Gaming or simulation techniques are used to sensitize the team to the complexity of the problem and to begin the process of consensus building, which will be critical to prioritizing the program objectives. A gaming exercise held at the beginning of the workshop, for example, might be useful in ranking a set of goals and in initiating detailed discussions between the team members. If, at this point, the clerical staff representative and the owner of the project were to find themselves in each other's position, it might be easier in later phases of the decision-making process to arrive at a collective understanding of the importance of each team member's perspective on the problem.

The proposed facility was the headquarters of a large manufacturing company and was to contain twelve separate but functionally interrelated departments. The primary goals of the user group were the creation of an efficient, functional, and attractive environment for the occupants of the facility. At the same time the construction was to be of such a quality that the building would project an impressive exterior image and optimize life-cycle costs. In the initial construction phase, the facility was expected to be comprised of approximately 210,000 square feet of administrative and technical work space. Five hundred employees were expected to occupy the facility initially, with an ultimate workforce of two thousand projected.

CLIENT AND USER OBJECTIVES

The first task of the workshop team was to define in precise terms the objectives of the client and user groups. These objectives were formulated in general terms earlier in the programming process as a result of group discussions among the team members and company employees. The objectives were listed at the beginning of the workshop and, from a larger list of general goal statements, five independent statements of owner and user needs were defined. Figure 8-5 shows this list of objectives.

Objective	***Description***	***Rank***
Circulation	Movement of workers and materials in a well-defined and efficient manner.	4
Function	Organization and arrangement of activities to allow for maximum work productivity.	1
Expandability	The ability to grow and change within the building and on the site.	5
Sensory Environment	Comfort of the user in physical and psychological terms. Positive corporate image.	2
Life-Cycle Costs	Minimization of capital, operating, maintenance, salvage, and tax costs.	3

8-5. Initial client and user objectives.

The rank order in the right-hand column indicates the first estimate by the team of the relative importance of the various goal statements.

The use of survey research techniques to gather and analyze user goals is often employed by the programmer to expand the programming team's understanding of the opinions of a larger client group. One of the drawbacks of programming facilities that will be occupied by a large number of people is the lack of contact between the professionals planning the facility and those who will eventually occupy it. Obviously, in this particular example, the entire affected building population could not participate in the definition and ranking of the project objectives nor could they all be given the opportunity to act as user representatives within the programming team. By soliciting the opinions of the users of the organization through random-sample questionnaires and selective interviews, however, the programming team can incorporate the collective knowledge and desires of the larger group into the decision-making process. The listing of objectives found in figure 8–5, therefore, is drawn from not only the views of those representatives present at the workshop sessions but also the ideas generated from focused discussions of the entire staff of the company.

One problem that is frequently encountered in programming is the creation of a consensus within the programming team in terms of the various design objectives. It should be noted that most of the five objectives listed in figure 8–5 are subjective concepts and, except for *Life-Cycle Costs,* not susceptible to exact measurement. It would be very difficult, for example, to conceive of a scale that could effectively measure—from good to bad—the concepts embodied in an objective such as *Circulation,* especially in this case, given the fact that there were ten team members, each with a somewhat different set of values and prejudices. If *Circulation* is a major program objective, how can this concept be described in such a way that both (1) defines in general terms the basic meaning and intent of the attribute and (2) measures a specific range of value limits? Figure 8–6 is an example of how the case-study group attempted to solve this problem.

When the client and user group's objective of *Circulation* was presented at the workshop, the participants were asked to think of the extreme levels of acceptable and desirable pedestrian flow characteristics that should be present in the new facility. In other words, "What is the lowest level of expectation you would accept for the circulation patterns in this facility?" was posed as a question to prompt the group to consider carefully the *Circulation* scale. The team was asked to consider a num-

Project—Corporate Headquarters Date 3/23/81

Objective Number 1 Objective Name Circulation

LOW VALUE

1. Extended amount of employee walking for communication purposes.

   Circulation system that satisfies simple, clear, and direct movement with life safety.
   Mixed circulation for people, vehicles, and service.
   Controlled access to buildings.

2. Tolerable amount of employee walking for communication purposes.

   Circulation system that satisfies simple, clear, and direct movement with life safety.
   Separate circulation for people, vehicles, and service.
   Controlled access to buildings.

3. Moderate amount of employee walking for communication purposes.

   Circulation system that satisfies job function and personal needs and life safety. Separate circulation for people, vehicles, and service. Controlled access to buildings.

4. Minor amount of employee walking for communication and life safety purposes.

   Circulation system that improves job function and personal needs. Separate circulation for people, vehicles, and service. Restricted access to buildings and parking with separated visitor entry point.

5. Minimal amount of employee walking for communcation and life safety purposes.

   Circulation system that greatly improves job function and personal needs. Separate circulation for people, vehicles, and service. Restricted access to buildings and parking with controlled entry points for employees and visitors. Link between HII and HWH/HVS with limited access.

HIGH VALUE

8–6. Value descriptions of circulation objective.

ber of selected intervals within this scale to check for accuracy and consistency within the group, as in the comparison between the first and third and the third and fifth scale pairs. If the perceived intervals between these three points are judged to be equal, then at least the overall structure of this particular scale can be considered valid.[6]

After each scale had been constructed the team turned its attention to the relative degrees of importance—or value priorities—between the five separate objective definitions. In order to verify the relative degrees of importance between the objectives, a trade-off exercise was performed. Starting with the assumption that functional efficiency represented to the programming team the most important client and user goal, every other objective was compared to this critical attribute. In comparison to circulation patterns, for example, a trade-off diagram was presented for consideration by the programming team. A question was posed to the team: "If *Function* and *Circulation* could be compared one to the other, and if the latter were to be increased to its highest scalar value (i.e., 5), how much of the more preferred *Function* objective could be traded-off in order to achieve this level of *Circulation?*" In essence, the group was asked to consider the relative degree of one objective definition that could be sacrificed in order to get value from a less important objective. As can be seen in figure 8-7, the distinction of importance between *Function* and *Circulation* was fairly great, primarily because the members of the programming team considered efficiency within the proposed building to be more important than the ease of communicating between the activities within that building.[7]

The mechanics for establishing the relative orderings of the objectives are shown in figure 8-8. It should be noted that the completion of this exercise produced a rank ordering different from the one shown originally in figure 8-5. This is a common and useful outcome of decisions made during programming, since it indicates that a simple discussion and analysis of the goals of the program have led to a deeper and possibly more complete definition of the problem.

a. The client and user objective of FUNCTION has been judged by the programming team to be more important as a program goal than CIRCULATION.

b. The question is posed to the team: "How much of the FUNCTION objective would the team be willing to trade-off to insure that the CIRCULATION objective could attain its highest level of value (i.e., 5)?"

c. In terms of the following diagram, what is the point of equality between the CIRCULATION objective at a level of 5 and the FUNCTION objective of a lower value or trade-off point *x*?

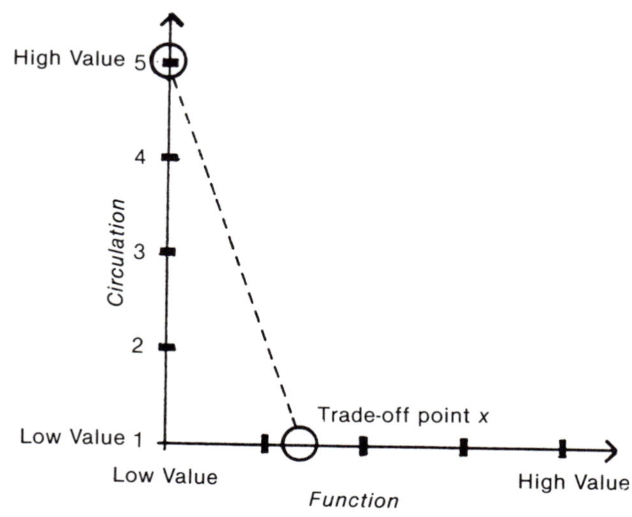

d. The team felt that the FUNCTION objective was considerably more important to CIRCULATION and therefore assigned a relatively low trade-off value (i.e., 2.3 on the FUNCTION scale).

8-7. Trade-off exercise to determine relative weights of importance of function and circulation objectives.

Programming Alternatives

When the workshop began, the programmer had already completed a preliminary investigation of

Function
This goal was judged to be the most important. Set the weight at 1.00.

Circulation
A trade-off value at the 2.3 point on the Function scale was established (see figure 8-7). Since this point is approximately a third of the distance up the scale, use a weight of importance of .33.

Life-cycle Cost
A trade-off value of 3.75 on the Function scale was chosen by the team. Since this value is somewhat less than three-quarters of the distance up this scale, use a weight of importance of .69.

Expandability
A trade-off value at the 3.50 point on the Function scale was chosen. This value is just slightly less than assigned to the Life-cycle Cost goal. Assign a weight of importance of .65.

Sensory Environment
A trade-off value of 2.3 was chosen. Assign the same weight as Circulation at .33.

The new normalized weights of importance of the value statements (in descending order) are:

Function = 1.00/3.00 = .33
Life-cycle Cost = .69/3.00 = .23
Expandability = .65/3.00 = .22
Circulation = .33/3.00 = .11
Sensory Environment = .33/3.00 = .11

8–8. Weights of importance and rank orderings of objectives.

the proposed building site and had compiled a detailed list of spatial needs for the activities that were to be housed in the facility. Blocks of space had been defined in earlier programming phases and specific functional requirements of the individual building activities had been defined. At this point in the programming process the use of observation and simulation techniques is essential in order to arrive at specific functional and behavioral solutions. The existing organizational setting of the company was recorded and detailed measurements were made to determine the exact size requirements necessary to satisfy the needs of each workstation setting. From these detailed descriptions of the individual's work area, larger groupings of departmental layouts were combined into overall building blocks. The programming team then began to organize these large building blocks around a number of conceptual ordering devices. Six schemes, or programming alternatives, were developed and presented to the entire workshop team (fig. 8–9).

Initially, the team, when presented with the al-

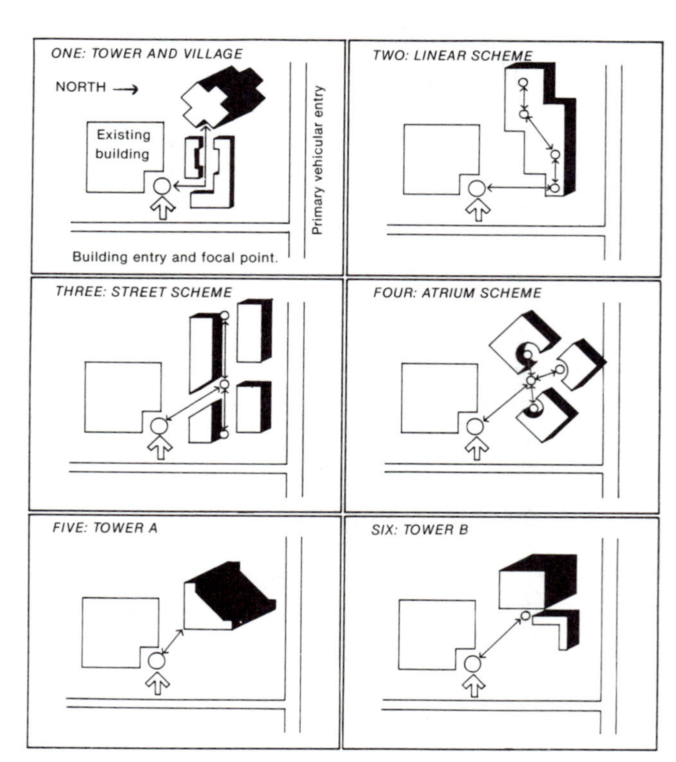

8–9. Programming alternatives.

ternatives, brainstormed informally about the strengths and weaknesses of each scheme, using a Delphi questionnaire.[8] Because the team was composed of people with a wide range of client, user, and technical viewpoints, the discussion produced a large number of ideas and suggestions concerning the six alternatives. Each member was given a form for each of the six schemes and asked to list the factors that might be considered strengths or weaknesses of each. Figure 8-10 is a compilation of ideas for the fifth alternative. The free association of ideas was encouraged and no proposition or suggestion was considered too unusual for inclusion in the discussion. When approximately thirty ideas had been recorded, the team was asked to respond to each one in relation to the five objectives that

IDEA GENERATION
THE DELPHI METHOD

ALTERNATIVE FOUR: ATRIUM

PROJECT CORPORATE HEADQUARTERS
DATE 3/23/81 CYCLE 1
TEAM PROGRAMMING

Idea	***Advantage***	***Disadvantage***	***Rank****
More department entries to west edge	Improved parking efficiency	Increased walking distance	Yes
Orient building true north	Increased site utilization	Less visual interest	Maybe
Consider parking entry parallel to diagonal buildings	Increased parking efficiency	—	Maybe
Rotate orientation to east/west axis	More compact site configuration	Increased solar loads	Maybe
Improve access from main vehicular route	Direct entry from main street	Increased street congestion	Maybe
Eliminate secondary atrium spaces	Larger central space; increased visual contact	Decrease in unit isolation potential	Maybe
Design segments of atrium for smaller unit of growth	Increased efficiency	—	Yes
Investigate parking south of main site	Expandability potential	Cost of land acquisition	Yes
Develop entry access from both east & north	—	Isolation of central access point	No

*Yes—incorporate in next cycle for evaluation.
Maybe—consider at a more detailed design phase.
No—no merit to consider.

8-10. Delphi evaluation worksheet for "Atrium" alternative scheme.

had previously been constructed. Each of the thirty ideas were rated as an advantage or disadvantage with respect to each objective. Not surprisingly, these advantages and disadvantages were found to bring into conflict a wide range of client and user values and began to highlight to the team the need to clarify and reinforce the rankings they had originally established in those value definitions. It should be noted that at this point in the programming process, the alternatives considered by the team were of a relatively large scale and the decisions made concerning these schemes were strategic in nature. The advantages of high-rise versus low-rise construction, for example, were an important factor in this programming exercise. In planning the more detailed aspects of a design, however, the same questionnaire techniques of group consensus can be used with a much wider audience. The decision as to the appropriateness of either open-office or bullpen workstation layout might be considered by a large representative group within the organization, and, using a system of computerized scoring, an interactive form of collective decision making can be achieved (Linstone and Turoff 1975, 489–549).

When widely divergent opinions are investigated in Delphi exercises, new approaches to a problem are often uncovered. In order to capitalize on this process, the case-study team used the first Delphi exercise to evaluate informally the six programming alternatives. It was found that by openly discussing the ideas generated in the Delphi session, the programming group was able to view the alternatives in a creative, as well as critical, manner. In the first scheme, for example, the group began to discuss the merits and problems of mixed construction techniques in light of the client and user objectives as well as the comments of the team members. These discussions were systematically recorded, and a number of modifications to the schemes were suggested to the programmer.

Alternative Evaluations

At the end of the first day of the workshop the team had used a number of decision analysis techniques. Trade-off exercises were used, for example, to establish the relative degrees of importance among the design objectives, and Delphi methods were introduced to begin an initial discussion of the six alternative schemes. The second day was devoted to the systematic evaluation of the alternatives with respect to the five design objectives. At completion of the Delphi exercises the workshop team had established some crude estimates of how well the various alternatives met or failed to meet the goals of the program. These initial judgments were formalized and verified during the second day of the workshop.

In order to begin the evaluation process, each member was again familiarized with the objectives and the five-point measurement scales of each. This was an important aspect of the decision-making process, because the team members were to be asked to make very specific value judgments using these scales. In terms of the "Village and Tower" scheme, for example, each team member was asked whether the *Circulation* objective was met by the first, second, third, fourth, or fifth level of the scale defined in figure 8–6. This process was repeated for all six schemes. The collective assessments of the ten team members are shown in figure 8–11 for the "Village and Tower" scheme.

After the schemes were assessed, the workshop group met again for a second Delphi session to discuss the ranges of value assessments that had been assigned to the various schemes by the team members. On the first scheme, for example, the group considered the reasons why the first member rated this alternative poorly with respect to *Expandability* while the fifth person gave a positive assessment of this same objective. It was found that the Delphi method helped to bring the collective expertise of

		Objectives				
		CIRCULATION	FUNCTION	EXPANDABILITY	SENSORY ENVIRONMENT	LIFE-CYCLE COSTS
Programming Team Members	1	2	2	2	4	2
	2	2	3	4	3	1
	3	2	3	2	3	1
	4	2	3	2	3.5	2
	5	2	2	5	4	3
	6	3	3.5	4	2.5	2
	7	1.5	4.5	4.5	3	2
	8	2	3	3	4	2
	9	2	3	4	4	2
	10	2	3	4	3	1
AVERAGE SCORES		2.05	3.00	3.45	3.40	1.80

8–11. Assessments for the "Village and Tower."

the group to bear on the problem and highlighted those areas of the program that might be too loosely defined or in need of special attention by the designer later in the project. At the completion of this discussion, several group members had changed their assessments in light of the opinions of their colleagues, and an arithmetic average score for each column of the matrix was calculated.

It should be noted that the arithmetic average score for each value statement is only a crude approximation of how the collective body of the team has analyzed the effectiveness of a particular alternative in satisfying that objective. In order very quickly to analyze the overall rankings of the six schemes using these average value scores, a series of simple summation equations were used.[9] These calculations used the weights of importance found in figure 8–8 to determine how well each scheme satisfies—on the average—the full range of the five design objectives. The "weighted average" value for the first scheme, with respect to the *Circulation* objective, was determined by the equation:

$$\begin{gathered}\text{(Weight of Importance for Circulation)}\\ \times\ \text{(Average Circulation Score)}\\ (.11) \times (2.05) = .23,\end{gathered}$$

while the *total* weighted average value for this scheme with respect to *all* objectives was:

$$\begin{gathered}(.11 \times 2.05) + (.33 \times 3.00) + (.22 \times 3.45)\\ + (.11 \times 3.40) + (.23 \times 1.80)\\ = (.23 + .99 + .76 + .37 + .41)\\ = 2.76.\end{gathered}$$

A calculation of all six schemes indicated that three alternatives were clearly favored by the team members (fig. 8–12). After discussing these ratings and considering the relative merits of each scheme, the workshop team performed a series of sensitivity analyses to confirm the above evaluation. These analyses consisted of the adjusting and reevaluating of the weights of the objectives as well as a reconsideration of the scores outlined in figure 8–11. Even though these adjustments caused the overall rankings of the schemes to vary, it was found that the "Street," "Atrium," and "Tower B" schemes were consistently the most highly rated alternatives. It was also considered important to allow the client and user representatives to express their views in isolation from the technical staff of the workshop group. A separate evaluation, therefore, was undertaken in which only the client and user members of the team were asked to evaluate each

		Objectives					
		CIRCULATION	FUNCTION	EXPANDABILITY	SENSORY ENVIRONMENT	LIFE-CYCLE COSTS	ALTERNATE SCORES (Sum of Weighted Average Values)
Weights of Importance (See figure 8-8)		.11	.33	.22	.11	.23	
Programming Alternatives	ONE: VILLAGE TOWER	.23 / 2.05	.99 / 3.00	.76 / 3.45	.37 / 3.40	.41 / 1.80	2.76
	TWO: LINEAR	.26 / 2.35	1.01 / 3.05	.59 / 2.70	.30 / 2.75	.56 / 2.45	2.72
	THREE: STREET	.40 / 3.65	1.22 / 3.70	.74 / 3.35	.45 / 4.10	.98 / 4.25	3.79
	FOUR: ATRIUM	.41 / 3.70	1.16 / 3.50	.89 / 4.05	.50 / 4.50	.79 / 3.45	3.75
	FIVE: TOWER A	.32 / 2.95	.83 / 2.50	.51 / 2.30	.31 / 2.80	.30 / 1.30	2.27
	SIX: TOWER B	.32 / 2.93	.97 / 2.95	.67 / 3.03	.34 / 3.10	.78 / 3.40	3.08

Key:

8-12. Calculation of programming alternative scores.

scheme. This evaluation indicated that although the relative scores of the six schemes changed, the same three alternatives that were strongest in the first assessments remained those that were preferred by the client and users.

In order to validate the rankings of the six schemes precisely, a more sophisticated method of value assessment was undertaken at the completion of the workshop session.[10] Using this technique, the team members were able not only to assign a single objective value for each alternative scheme, but also to assess the schemes with a range of feasible values. Instead of using the simple average scores shown in figure 8–11, the group established a probability frequency for the values that were thought to be likely in each scheme. Although the basic theory of this decision technique is similar to the weighted average method, the use of a computer program was required to input and calculate the assessments of the workshop group because of the larger number of probability calculations.[11] In this manner the team was able to take into account the full range of opinions and assessments that had surfaced in the earlier Delphi session. When all probability assessments were completed, the computer program was used to calculate the rankings of the six schemes. It was found that, with minor exceptions, the same three alternative schemes (numbers 3, 4, and 6) were still most favored by the workshop members.

At the completion of the workshop sessions the program team documented a number of findings that emerged from the decision analysis exercise. First, it was obvious that the ideas contained in the "Street" and "Atrium" schemes should be further developed in the schematic design phase. Second, upon reflection by the team, it was determined that the sixth alternative contained many ideas found in both the "Village and Tower" and "Linear" schemes. It was recommended that this scheme be investigated carefully by the designer and the "Tower A" scheme be eliminated from further consideration. Finally, the team members considered once more the five design objectives and their associated definitions. It was found, based upon the various group discussions and decision analysis assessments, that the five value statements were descriptive of the desires and needs of the client and user representatives. With minor adjustments the initial definitions were incorporated into the program document.

CONCLUSION

This case study has illustrated an approach to decision making in the programming process. Group dynamic and decision analysis techniques were used to develop a consensus opinion within a programming team and to explore a number of programmatic alternatives to an environmental problem. The approach is presented as a general model of programming and should be viewed in light of the matrix shown in figure 8–3. Although only a limited number of user representatives participated in the actual decision analysis exercise, attempts were made to incorporate information from a large number of the users of the proposed facility. Survey research and observation methods are directly applicable to this model and were used to augment and enrich the decisions made.

This model of decision making can also be used during the succeeding phases of the design process. Although this particular case study focused on the use of the method in programming, the model itself is applicable to decisions that occur in concept and schematic design, design development, the construction process, and even as the environment is being occupied by the building users. In this respect, the methods and approaches to programming should be viewed by the designer as tools that apply to problems throughout the life of a design project. It should also be noted that the levels of detail that will form the basis of the alternatives and objective definitions depend upon the degree to which environmental information is understood by the design team at any given point in a project. The information that is considered by the design team early in a project is necessarily general in nature and as the process proceeds over time the specificity of the data will become more concrete.

The ultimate purpose of the programming techniques used in this case study is to evaluate the information entering a project in order to guide and enlighten subsequent design decisions. In the traditional design process programmatic decisions are evaluated only after an environment has been occupied. This is evident in the process outlined in figure 8-1. A more cyclical and repetitive approach, however, is implied in the model outlined in the above case study and illustrated in figure 8-13.

The differences between this definition of programming and the one presented in figure 8-1 are the combination of programming and evaluation into a single activity and the inclusion of this activity as an important function in all subsequent phases of design. Using this approach, the programmer analyzes and evaluates information not only in the early pre-design phases or after an environment is occupied, but at each critical decision point in the design process. The approaches to programming and the techniques that were discussed in this chapter are applicable to the entire range of decisions that must be considered during environmental planning or design. The programmer and evaluator, in this proposal, become key members of the design team and assume the various roles of facilitator, collector, interpreter, and manager of information throughout the life of a design project.

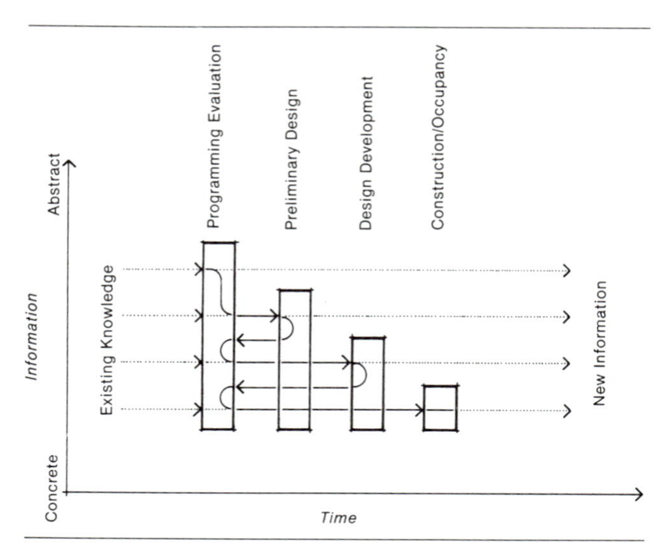

8-13. A proposal for a decision process in architecture.

The case study presented in this chapter was an example of how this process of decision making might be conducted in the early phases of design. In this phase the programmer is dealing with imprecise and abstract information. The use of a limited number of user and client representatives is often necessary in this phase of the design process in order to set the stage for more detailed and concrete investigations of the behavioral aspects of the problem. The generation of functional concepts and the definition of a small number of design objectives early in the process will be used in later stages as working hypotheses that can be tested and refined in community surveys and simulation techniques. The Delphi exercises, for example, can be expanded from brainstorming sessions composed of a compact and select programming team to evaluation networks of large numbers of the eventual users of the proposed facility. The process of programming, therefore, is one that extends throughout the life of the design and acts as an evaluation device within the design team.

A number of practitioners have begun to incorporate behavioral research methods into the design process and use the techniques outlined in this chapter to augment the traditional skills and tools of the designer. The work of Jay Farbstein (1984) is cited as an example of how the programming process has been extended throughout the life of design projects and expanded to include a wide range of behavioral research techniques. The model of programming and the relation of evaluation methodologies to the entire design process he presents is supportive of the view of programming outlined in figure 8–13. Again, the key to the successful use of the program as a continually growing and changing decision-making instrument is the inclusion of mechanisms that allow the design team constantly to measure and evaluate the products of design against well-defined objectives and performance criteria. The program, in this respect, becomes a measurement tool that helps the owners, users, and designers of environments monitor their progress through the various stages of design. Instead of becoming an exercise in data collection and problem definition that results in a static set of instructions to the designer, programming should be viewed as a flexible and interactive procedure for matching human needs with design solutions.

NOTES

1. A large part of this chapter is abstracted from research by Spreckelmeyer (1981) funded by the Seabury Foundation.
2. Some programming firms have begun to render specific services to client groups that are consciously devoid of traditional design elements (Davis and Szigeti 1979), while most architectural and planning firms have diversified their pre-design services into the more technical fields of value management and human factors.
3. See Palmer (1981) and Preiser (1978) for discussions of programming approaches in architectural design.
4. See Spreckelmeyer (1982) for a detailed description of this programming model and its use in six case studies.
5. This example is provided by Stephen J. Kirk of Smith, Hinchman and Grylls Associates (Washington, D.C.). Special attention is drawn to other projects for which Mr. Kirk has been responsible that use similar decision and group dynamic techniques (Kirk 1981).
6. For a complete discussion of this scaling technique see Coombs (1976).
7. It should be noted that for the purposes of simplifying this discussion of decision methods, all five measurement scales are assumed to be linear. In the case study, a risk assessment technique was used to determine the exact shape of these scales. At the completion of this process an exact utility function was produced for each value definition. In only one design objective (*Function*) did a nonlinear utility function appear. See Keeney (1977) for the procedures of this assessment process.
8. A modified form of the traditional Delphi method was used in this project and is outlined in Kirk (1980).
9. See Dell'Isola and Kirk (1981) for a detailed description of this form of decision analysis.
10. This form of decision analysis, commonly referred to as Expected Utility Theory, is outlined in Keeney and Raiffa (1976). A number of programming uses of this method are detailed in this reference.
11. See Spetzler and Holstein (1975) for a discussion of this probability assessment technique.

REFERENCES

Alexander, C., et al. 1977. *A Pattern Language.* New York: Oxford Univ. Press.
American Institute of Architects (AIA). 1977. *Owner-*

architect agreement, AIA Documents B141 and B161. Washington, D.C.: American Institute of Architects.

Clipson, C. W., and J. J. Wehrer. 1973. *Planning for Cardiac Care.* Ann Arbor: Health Administration Press, Univ. of Michigan.

———. 1977. *Design Process and Methods.* Ann Arbor: College of Architecture and Urban Planning, Univ. of Michigan.

Coombs, C. H. 1976. *A Theory of Data.* Ann Arbor: Mathesis.

Cross, N. 1977. *The Automated Architect.* London: Pion.

Davis, G., and V. Ayers. 1975. Photographic recording of environmental behavior. In *Behavioral Research Methods in Environmental Design,* ed. W. Michelson, 235–79. Stroudsburg, Pa.: Dowden, Hutchinson & Ross.

Davis, G., and F. Szigeti. 1979. Functional and technical programming. *Proceedings of the Fourth International Architectural Psychology Conference,* Louvain-La Neuve, Belgium.

———. 1980. Proposal for a Conceptual Framework for the Knowledge Base Relevant to Environmental Design Research. The Environmental Analysis Group. Unpublished paper. Ottawa.

Delbecq, A. L., A. E. Van de Ven, and D. H. Gustafson. 1975. *Group Techniques for Program Planning.* Dallas: Scott, Foresman.

Dell'Isola, A., and S. J. Kirk. 1981. *Life Cycle Costing for Design Professionals.* New York: McGraw-Hill.

Duke, R. D. 1974. *Gaming: The Future's Language.* New York: Sage/Halsted.

Farbstein, J. 1984. Using the program: Applications to design, occupancy and evaluation. *Proceedings of the 15th Annual Conference of the Environmental Design Research Association,* San Luis Obispo, Cal., 240–51.

Friedman, A., C. Zimring, and E. Zube. 1978. *Environmental Design Evaluation.* New York: Plenum.

Friedman, Y. 1975. *Toward a Scientific Architecture.* Cambridge, Mass.: MIT Press.

Hasell, J., and J. Taylor. 1981. Gaming/simulation: An approach to the study of environmental change and development. *Proceedings of the 12th Annual Conference of the Environmental Design Research Association,* Ames, Iowa, 119–32.

Johnson, R. E. 1980. *Assessing House Preference for Low-Cost Single Family Home Buyers.* Ann Arbor: Architectural Research Laboratory.

Jones, J. C. 1981. *Design Methods: Seeds of Human Futures.* New York: Wiley.

Keeney, R. L. 1977. The art of assessing multiattribute utility functions. *Organizational Behavior and Human Performance* 19:267–310.

Keeney, R. L., and H. Raiffa. 1976. *Decisions with Multiple Objectives.* New York: Wiley.

King, J., R. W. Marans, and L. Solomon. 1982. *Pre-Construction Evaluation.* Ann Arbor: Architectural Research Laboratory.

Kirk, S. J. 1980. Delphi: An aid in project cost control. *Architectural Record,* Dec., 51–55.

———. 1981. Value assessments in facility designs. *Proceedings of the International Conference of the Society of Value Engineers.* St. Louis.

Linstone, H. A., and M. Turoff, eds. 1975. *The Delphi Method: Techniques and Applications.* Reading, Mass.: Addison-Wesley.

Marans, R. W., and K. F. Spreckelmeyer. 1981. *Evaluating Built Environments: A Behavioral Approach.* Ann Arbor: Institute for Social Research.

Mattar, S., et al. 1978. A decision model for the design of building enclosures. *Building and Environment* 13:201–32.

Negroponte, N. 1975. *Soft Architecture Machines.* Cambridge, Mass.: MIT Press.

Palmer, M. 1981. *The Architect's Guide to Facility Programming.* Washington, D.C.: American Institute of Architects.

Peña, W. M. 1977. *Problem Seeking.* Boston: Cahners Books International.

Petronis, J. P., L. S. Kline, and R. Pugh. 1978. Programming across cultures: A cultural food preparation center for Cochiti Indian Pueblo. In *Facility Programming,* ed. W. F. E. Preiser, 54–66. Stroudsburg, Pa.: Dowden, Hutchinson & Ross.

Preiser, W. F. E., ed. 1978. *Facility Programming.* Stroudsburg, Pa.: Dowden, Hutchinson & Ross.

Public Works Canada (Quebec). 1979. *Mandat du programmateur.* Montreal.

Rapoport, A. 1982. *The Meaning of the Built Environment.* Beverly Hills, Cal.: Sage.

Sanoff, H. 1977. *Methods of Architectural Programming.* Stroudsburg, Pa.: Dowden, Hutchinson & Ross.

———. 1978. *Designing with Community Participation.* Stroudsburg, Pa.: Dowden, Hutchinson & Ross.

———. 1979. *Design Games.* Los Altos, Ca.: Kaufmann.

Seaton, R. 1978. Modeling architectural problems. *Design Methods and Theories* 12(1):46–52.

Spetzler, C. S., and A. S. S. von Holstein. 1975. Probability encoding in decision analysis. *Management Science* 22:340–58.

Spreckelmeyer, K. F. 1981. Application of a Computer-Aided Decision Technique in Architectural Programming. D.Arch. diss., University of Michigan.

———. 1982. Architectural programming as an evaluation tool in design. *Proceedings of the 13th Annual Conference of the Environmental Design Research Association,* College Park, Md., 289–96.

Thomas, L. 1979. On committees. In *The Medusa and the Snail,* 115–20. New York: Viking.

Wade, J. W. 1977. *Architecture, Problems and Purposes.* New York: Wiley.

Webb, B., et al. 1981. *Nonreactive Measures in the Social Sciences.* Boston: Houghton Mifflin.

White, T. 1972. *Introduction to Architectural Programming.* Tucson: Architectural Media.

Zeisel, J. 1981. *Inquiry by design.* Monterey, Cal.: Brooks/Cole.

Zilm, F. S. 1980. *Computer Modeling in Hospital Planning: Three Case Studies.* Ann Arbor: Architectural Research Laboratory.

CHAPTER 9

EVALUATION OF DESIGNED ENVIRONMENTS

METHODS FOR POST-OCCUPANCY EVALUATION

Craig M. Zimring

Evaluation of designed environments, post-occupancy evaluation (POE), has arrived. POE is routinely performed by organizations as large as AT&T and the U.S. General Services Administration and as small as one- or two-person consulting firms. A 1978 survey found over one thousand persons actively evaluating housing alone (Bechtel and Srivastava 1978). Yet, for all its apparent success, much POE remains methodologically weak, limited in its contribution to the development of theory and of uneven usefulness to those faced with decisions about designed environments. This chapter will attempt to address these problems by proposing a process for conducting successful POEs and describing several methods that have been used effectively in POE. Finally, several issues involved with the implementation of POE will be discussed.

DEFINITIONS

Post-occupancy evaluation has been defined as "the examination of the effectiveness of designed environments for human users" (Zimring and Reizenstein 1980). Some observers of POE interpret this definition fairly narrowly, suggesting that the term *post-occupancy evaluation* be reserved for applied, problem-focused studies intended to be used in a given setting, and that *research* or other labels be used for broader or more theoretical studies of designed settings (Connell 1986). This chapter takes a more inclusive view: post-occupancy evaluation is what post-occupancy evaluators do (Sommer 1984). This definition incorporates controlled field experiments as well as field studies, theoretical as well as applied research. However, several qualities tend to characterize POE (Zimring and Reizenstein 1980): (1) post-occupancy evaluation tends to focus on a single type of building or other designed setting such as housing, offices, schools, or public plazas; (2) evaluators tend to describe rather than manipulate a setting; (3) the work is almost always conducted in actual settings rather than in the laboratory.

There is considerable diversity in what post-occupancy evaluators are hoping to achieve, in how studies are carried out, and in what the resulting information is to be used for. POE represents the confluence of several research traditions, each of which brings their goals and methods to the process. Although categorization is always dangerous, one can discern at least three research streams in POE:

1. A desire to gather and represent the views of the nonpaying user, such as rental tenants or office workers. This work, which can be traced to the tenement reform movements of the late 1800s, typically uses interviews and questionnaires to survey building users' attitudes and satisfaction levels (see, for example, Weidemann et al. 1982).
2. An interest in exploring conceptual issues such as way-finding or environmental stress. These POEs often reflect a desire to make tight, unequivocal, scientific arguments and as a result may use field experiments in which the evaluator has as much control as possible (see, for example, Weisman 1981).
3. A concern with influencing the decisions an organization makes about settings or people. These decisions may include programming or designing a new building, settling into a new building when it is completed, fine-tuning an existing building after organizational needs have changed, and planning and managing space. These evaluators are often strongly influenced by practices of organizational development. Rather than focusing on making scientific arguments, they attempt to create a process whereby the setting users and environmental decision makers feel they are participating and their needs are represented. As a result, instead of using standardized, controlled methods, evaluators with this orientation principally employ interactive methods such as group and individual interviews and walk-throughs.

Hundreds of books have been written on research methods; much of this discussion, however, is often more obfuscating than illuminating, partly because of disagreement on terms and definitions. This chapter discusses three levels of methodological decisions: choice of the *research strategies*, which are the basic approaches to research, such as use of laboratory experiments, field experiments, field studies, and the like; development of *research design*, including the overall plan of how the strategy study is to be carried out—sampling of participants and sites, timing, and such; and development of *research methods,* including the specific form of data-collection instruments and analysis procedures, such as questionnaires or interviews (McGrath 1982).

Although decisions in these three areas may be interrelated, separating them into levels helps to clarify some of the confusion that plagues the methodological literature. It is not appropriate, for example, to discuss the relative merits of laboratory experiments versus qualitative research methods. These are at different levels: laboratory experiments are strategies; qualitative data-gathering techniques are methods and can be used either in the laboratory or field.

McGrath's 1982 categorization of general goals of research helps focus the discussion of the objectives of various kinds of POEs. POEs have three basic goals. The first is to learn as much as possible about a specific setting, including its specific users, history, structure, and so on. This can be called *setting sensitivity*. The second goal is to be able to generalize as accurately as possible about some larger category of settings, users, or times. This can be called *generalizability.* The final goal is to be able to make statements of research outcomes that are as unambiguous as possible—that discount all plausible alternative explanations. This goal may be termed *precision.*

Furthermore, McGrath argues that methodological decisions relate directly to goals. Choice of strategies inevitably maximizes one goal while minimizing others. Laboratory experiments, for example, offer researchers considerable control and therefore allow them to discount alternative explanations. However, because the laboratory does not include the characteristics of any given setting, it necessarily sacrifices setting sensitivity.

To summarize briefly, POE can be characterized by a least three research traditions: giving a voice to the nonpaying user; researching theoretical questions; and affecting decision making. These traditions bring their own complex approaches to problems but can be generally characterized in terms of the three kinds of research goals. For example, evaluators concerned with fine-tuning or space planning in a given setting focus principally on setting sensitivity; evaluators testing a theoretically derived hypothesis may be more concerned with precision.

The purpose of this chapter is not to suggest that one set of goals should take precedence. Rather, methodological decisions need to follow a clear definition of goals. The following section suggests a multistep process for conducting POEs. The final section includes more detail on seven methods commonly or potentially used in POE.

THE POE PROCESS

Although POEs range dramatically in scale, resources, goals, and methods, and in the expertise and interests of the evaluators, most evaluations have several principal phases in common. Although they are presented below as linear, they seldom are, and a large number of formal and informal feedback loops usually occur. Each of the five steps, which are illustrated in figure 9-1, will be briefly discussed. In the next section several specific POE methods will be presented in more detail.

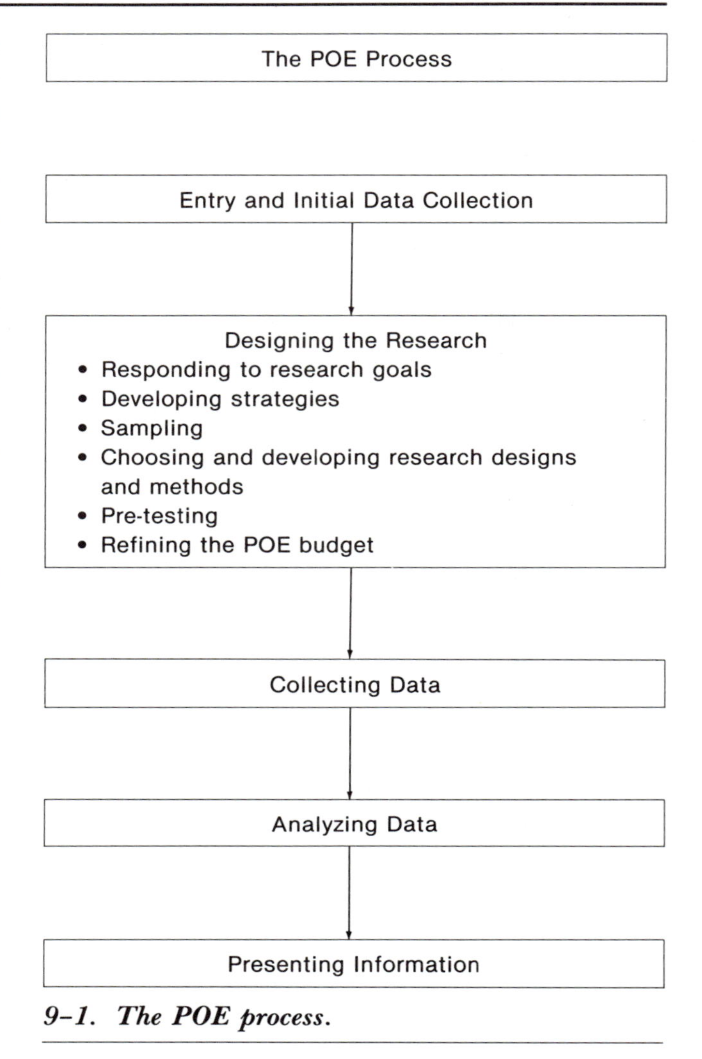

9-1. The POE process.

Phase I: Entry and Initial Data Collection

In every POE there is a critical set of initial contacts between the evaluator and the organization and setting being evaluated (and with the client if different from the organization being evaluated). Moreover, the evaluator identifies available resources, establishes a general time frame for the POE, and studies the context and history of the setting being evaluated.

Sometimes the evaluator is approached by an informed and eager client. At other times the evaluator is faced with selling the evaluation to a suspicious and dubious organization. In either case, the initial contacts can dramatically affect the subsequent ease of doing the evaluation, the validity of the results, and the likelihood of recommendations being implemented.

Keys and Wener (1980) pointed out two key issues during the entry phase: (1) the need for support from multiple levels within the client organization; (2) the prehistory of the project. Any organization has a range of levels of authority that can support—or sabotage—a project. If the goal of the POE is to provide information that is to be used by these decision makers, the evaluator has a special responsibility to understand their needs and perspectives. Even for a POE where the results are to be used in other ways—to be published in a scholarly journal, for example—the support of people in the setting being evaluated is often critical. Often, whereas initial permission is needed from upper management—who may also pay for the POE and implement findings—much of the data collection typically occurs among lower level personnel, whose attitude may affect response to questionnaires or influence the candidness of responses.

A range of strategies is often appropriate to enlist support by people at multiple levels of authority. Personal contact usually must be made with individuals at all levels to explain the project and to understand their needs and perspectives. The evaluator needs to understand what the individual stands to gain or lose by participating in the POE and by using the results.

Evaluation can be defined as understanding and exploiting self-interest: that of the evaluators and that of the participants. Although many people are motivated by altruism and do things for the good of society and of the organization, they are less likely to participate in a POE if they feel that they are in jeopardy because their performance is being evaluated or if participation represents an additional task that robs time from other, more demanding or rewarding activities. A common cry is "we don't have time for more paperwork." In contrast, someone will probably participate if it is felt that the POE will result in better conditions or is interesting or will help in getting work done. Shibley (1984) has suggested that several questions can be posed to decision makers to help learn what is important and useful to them: How do you know you are doing a good job? What are you rewarded for? What did you spend your time doing today? Last week? What would you see as the best possible outcome of the POE? The worst possible outcome?

Often these questions may reveal a discrepancy between avowed goals and practical self-interest. A school administrator may espouse—and genuinely believe in—the importance of trusting students and in enhancing student independence. He or she may also be primarily rewarded by the school board for keeping the maintenance budget low. As a result, great value may be placed on a POE that provides information on reducing vandalism even if it does not necessarily address larger ideological goals. There is nothing wrong with self-interest. It is entirely appropriate for people to be concerned with doing their job so that they will be rewarded and with making their job as easy as possible. It is the evaluator's job to discover how the POE can make those things possible—or, at least not make things worse.

It is also often useful to get some sort of endorsement of the project. In a highly hierarchical organization, it may be enough to have someone in authority write memos or make phone calls. (In any large organization, it is usually necessary to have an authorizing letter for the evaluators to carry when they are not being accompanied by someone in authority.) However, such an endorsement may sometimes backfire: a letter from the boss may confirm employees' suspicions that the evaluators are really performing clandestine job performance evaluations. To help counter this possibility, it is usually valuable to enlist other trusted people to support the POE.

In a POE my colleagues and I conducted of an institution for the mentally retarded (the project was called the "ELEMR" project, short for "Effects of the Living Environment on the Mentally Retarded"), we needed to observe attendants in their everyday activities (Zimring et al. 1982). However, the attendants were concerned that the data would be used against them in job evaluations. We gradually developed their trust by having the union president accompany us during many of our initial visits. (We also developed a simple system that ensured their anonymity by using arbitrary numbers rather than names when collecting data.) The endorser need not be a person of high authority but should be someone who is recognized and trusted.

In addition, an informal authority structure may dramatically help—or hinder—the evaluation. Everyone has had experience with a secretary or shop steward or bookkeeper who knows what is going on, and who can, if motivated, rapidly make a key appointment, process an order, or cut a check. Evaluators spend much time learning the formal authority structure; it is often useful to understand the informal one as well.

Keys and Wener's (1981) concern with project prehistory—learning what went on before the evaluators entered—is part of a larger activity of understanding the project's general context. (Marans and Spreckelmeyer [1981] call this *reconnaissance.*) The evaluator tries to develop a general picture of how the setting operates, what it is like, and how it came about. Part of this activity involves understanding the previous experiences that people in the setting have had with evaluation. In the ELEMR Project, for example, some television reporters had previously passed themselves off as researchers and had run a major expose, a fact that only emerged after extended discussion. This experience had made many at the state school quite research-shy and limited the possibility of using filming as a data-collection method.

Generally the context is understood through group and individual interviews and by assembling and briefly summarizing key documents such as facilities programs, memos, and correspondence. (These techniques are discussed below in more depth.) Also, the growth of POE and the increasing availability of published studies in journals such as *Environment and Behavior* and in the proceedings of the Environmental Design Research Association give evaluators the opportunity and responsibility to build on past studies.

It is useful to have a general framework to guide this phase of the investigation, although it needs to be quite open and flexible. Friedmann et al. (1978) proposed that five components are involved in most POEs and should be understood as part of the entry and initial data-collection phase: setting, users, neighborhood or physical context, design and space management activity, and social-historical context.

The *setting* is the project being evaluated, and setting characteristics are physical and social aspects such as the qualities of the overall design; relevant materials; ambient qualities such as heat, light, and noise; elements with symbolic value for users and others; condition of temporary and permanent elements including maintenance; and organizational goals, needs, and communication patterns.

The *users* are the people who directly or indirectly use the setting being evaluated (including, for example, both the people who actually set foot in a park and others living in the city who might use it but thus far have not). Frequently the users are quite diverse and may have little leverage because of a lack of access to the people actually contracting for the POE. It is usually important in a POE to describe the users and their needs, perceptions, and activities.

All projects exist within a *neighborhood and physical context* such as hilly terrain that might limit activity by older people or climates that might cause special problems for user comfort. This category also includes surrounding land users and architectural styles.

The *design and space management activity* is perhaps the single most ignored aspect of environmental design evaluation to date. The designer is only one of the actors in a complex process that can involve the client, users, financiers, boards and committees, public officials and agency representatives, space managers, and others. Several steps can be identified in this process—programming, design, construction, and occupancy—and each step represents decisions that can be evaluated through a POE. During the initial data-gathering phase the evaluator may want to develop a rough chronology of the project and gather whatever drawings, documents, and correspondence are available. Also, it is easy to overlook the changes made by users after the completion of the project, which may indicate changed needs or post hoc efforts to compensate for cases where perceptions and values of designers or other decision makers were incongruent with those of users.

In addition to the above four components, it is often important to document the social and physical changes affecting the project: the *social-historical context*. For example, how well does a facility for mentally retarded people fit the accepted treatment model? How has this treatment model changed since the inception of the project?

Some evaluators have also proposed more specific models that aid in their initial and subsequent data-gathering. For example Archea (1984b) has proposed that people choose how to behave and where to locate themselves in public places at least in part based on the proportion of the setting they can see and the proportion from which they can be seen. (For example, single people tend to sit in corners or around the periphery of a setting where they can see most of the setting but are relatively less likely to be observed.) Archea's model helps guide his initial data-gathering: he looks for areas where visual access and visual exposure vary. (Archea's method is discussed further below in "Methods of Assessing the Physical Setting.")

During this phase the evaluator should also explore the appropriate role of the client or people in the setting. Questions to be considered include: What role does the client want? What resources—such as time, money, space, expertise, and materials—is the client willing to commit?

In sum, the purpose of this phase is to explore the setting initially and develop a working relationship with the client. Some important questions during this phase include:

1. Have people at all levels of authority who might affect the project been contacted?
2. Have the benefits of the project been explained to them? (These may include specific help in doing their jobs or personal satisfaction in helping the organization.)
3. Have appropriate endorsements been secured?
4. Has a framework or heuristic been developed to help guide data-gathering?
5. Has a general picture of the designed setting been established?

Phase II: Designing the Research

In the first phase, the goals, issues, and context of the POE were established. In this phase the specifics of the POE should be developed.

Responding to Research Goals. There are no "best" methods, only methods that best fit given goals. Before the evaluator makes key methodological decisions, he or she must review the goals for the POE: How will the information be used? In fine-tuning a specific project? If so, who will make the key decisions? Is the intention to provide input into programming of new projects? If so, what are the major questions the programmers will be facing? Is the POE aimed at contributing to knowledge in environmental psychology or sociology or corrections or housing? Where might it be published?

What methods and analysis schemes do other researchers in those areas use?

Developing Strategies. The first, and most global, decision to be made concerns research *strategy.* McGrath (1981) has suggested that social psychologists have seven basic strategies available to them: field experiments, field studies, computer simulations, formal theory sample surveys, judgment tasks, laboratory experiments and experimental simulations. Because of the nature of the problems to be solved, most evaluators must use field studies: research that takes place in actual settings, where the evaluator cannot control the conditions. (Many methodologists reserve the term *experiment* for cases in which the researcher can randomly assign people to situations.) Of the three general kinds of goals described above—learning about a specific setting (setting sensitivity), generality, and precision in making arguments—field studies are most conducive to setting sensitivity. The lack of control inherent in them makes being very precise difficult. For example, people may say they like their housing. But it may be difficult or impossible to decide whether they like it because the housing genuinely suits their needs or because they chose it. Randomly assigning people to housing, if it is possible, may resolve this problem, but it also creates a very artificial situation.

Field studies also make generality difficult to achieve. The need to conduct site visits in field studies makes getting a broad cross section of people, sites, and times expensive and difficult. (In a telephone survey, such a cross section may be relatively easy.) For studies concerned with precision or generality, it is worthwhile to consider more controlled strategies such as lab or field experiments. Because studies using these strategies are not normally considered POE, they are not discussed in this chapter.

Sampling. Sampling is a sophisticated practice, and a detailed discussion is beyond the scope of this chapter (see chapter 2 for further information). However, sampling of participants, sites, and times seriously affects the kinds of arguments that can be made in a POE. In addition to affecting the generalizability that can be expected from an evaluation, sampling helps reject (or create) alternative explanations of the results. For example, questionnaires may be filled out only by people designated by departmental managers, who may choose people known to have a positive attitude. If the setting is positively evaluated, do most users view it that way, or does it reflect the view of specially chosen people? To combat these problems of biased selection, evaluators use random selection wherever possible. In the instance above, if respondents were randomly chosen, one could assume, on average, that selection factors equalize over time. Random sampling is also often combined with stratified sampling where a given number of individuals from designated groups are chosen. For example, in the study of an architecture building at Florida A&M University, we are randomly choosing a given number of students within each class level to respond to a questionnaire, in order to assure equivalent representation of each group.

Random sampling in POE is the exception rather than the rule, however, because the evaluator typically has relatively little power over the setting being evaluated. In fact, whereas some types of random assignment, such as randomly choosing people to respond to a questionnaire or interview, are rare, others are almost nonexistent. For example, if an evaluator were performing jail evaluations in the hope of obtaining findings that generalize to all U.S. jails, ideally a sizable random sample of all U.S. jails should be chosen for evaluation. Realistically, an "opportunity sample" of jails that are convenient, represent a range of characteristics, and have a cooperative staff is usually established. If sampling is nonrandom or if assignment is made to control groups on a nonrandom basis, a range of problems may occur including both initial differences between groups and different change rates over time. (For example, if a comparison is made between an open plan and a traditional office without randomly assigning workers to each setting, there may be differences in job satisfaction initially based on the criteria used to assign people to settings: more valued people are generally provided traditional offices.)

Although random assignment is usually not possible in a POE and may in fact be disruptive to the setting, the consequences of sampling are seldom discussed in final reports, and methods for addressing sampling problems are seldom employed. Examples of such methods are quasi-experimental design (see Cook and Campbell 1979) and the use of comparison groups (see Carson et al. 1980). This represents a serious weakness in many POEs.

Choosing and Developing Research Designs and Methods. In their review of housing evaluations, Bechtel and Srivastava (1978) identified fourteen data-gathering methods commonly used in POEs (listed in fig. 9-2). In addition, Bechtel and Srivastava and others (see, for example, Friedmann et al. 1978, Zimring and Reizenstein 1980) have noted several methodological trends: most POEs employ a combination of data-gathering techniques, with several methods used more commonly than others. The most frequently used methods include questionnaires, interviews, and photography or some other type of physical survey. These more common methods as well as several others will be described in this chapter. (Most of the less common methods are discussed elsewhere in this volume.)

How does one choose appropriate data-gathering methods? First, the evaluator must examine his or her POE plan and goals; the methods must incorporate the evaluation criteria and address the goals for use of the information. For instance, if influencing the client's decision making is an important goal, then in addition to addressing the specific issues in the POE plan, methods should be chosen that involve and engage the client, such as the client walk-through, workshops, and interviews. (Some methods tend to separate the evaluator from the client, such as direct observation, and these are sometimes less useful in helping the client become committed to the POE process. Other methods, such as questionnaires, are particularly efficient ways to gather large amounts of information.)

In addition, methods should be chosen so that the strength of one type compensates for weaknesses in another. For example, "self-report measures" such as interviews and questionnaires are valuable because respondents can be asked about the motives and rationales for their actions, but are limited by the respondents' skills or interest in discussing their feelings, by lapses in memory, and by the desire to appear intelligent, rational, or "with it." By contrast, methods such as direct observation or measurement of traces the users have left in the setting (such as signs of wear and tear) may be less affected by the respondents' perceptions, memories, or worries. However, using observation to evaluate "internal" states may present difficulties in interpretation, because subjective feelings

1. Interviews, open ended
2. Interviews, structured
3. Cognitive maps
4. Behavioral maps
5. Diaries
6. Direct observation
7. Participant observation
8. Time-lapse photography
9. Motion-picture photography
10. Questionnaires
11. Psychological tests
12. Adjective checklists
13. Archival data
14. Demographic data

9-2. Fourteen methods commonly used in POE. From Bechtel and Srivastava, 1978.

such as satisfaction or dissatisfaction are difficult to observe. As a consequence, self-report measures are frequently combined with direct observation or other techniques.

Pre-testing Methods and Procedures. Pre-testing is a critical step that is often bypassed due to time pressures—usually to the peril of the evaluators. At least two steps are called for. The evaluator should personally complete all questionnaires and other instruments to help identify any ambiguities or potential problems. Next, all methods and procedures need to be tested in the actual setting and *completely analyzed.* In addition to serving as a test of the methods and procedures, this will test the analysis scheme. Most people who skip pre-testing find that they are forced to make adjustments during actual data collection or during analysis. It is less expensive and more satisfactory to do so earlier.

Refining the POE Budget. Typically, a POE is budgeted early in the process, and the budget is refined as the goals, issues, and methods become clearer. POEs have ranged in cost from a few hundred dollars to over one million dollars and have ranged in scope from one-day walk-throughs of a single department to multi-year, multi-site efforts. Because of the diversity of POEs, it is hard to provide clear guidance in costing.

Some evaluators, such as White (n.d.), have proposed that evaluations can be figured as costing about the same as programming and that the same rough rules of thumb apply. For example, White suggests that an evaluation may cost ¼ percent to 1¼ percent the cost of construction, 5 to 8 percent of the design fee or $.12 to $1.00 per gross square foot of construction. This would mean, for example, that a POE of a $2 million, 33,000-square foot building would cost between about $5,000 and $35,000.

However, a better system (as White also states) is to budget each step independently. Figure 9-3 represents a sample budget spreadsheet. Because of overlap, some phases have been combined; some evaluators may want to separate them. Spreadsheets work well on microcomputers using programs such as Lotus 1-2-3.

In sum, during the fourth phase, designing the research involves refining research goals, and especially defining the uses of the information, choosing an appropriate sample, choosing and developing methods and procedures, pre-testing, and refining the POE budget. Some key questions about this phase include:

1. Have goals for the use of the results been clarified, including necessary generalizability?
2. Does the sampling reflect the project goals?
3. Have possible biases due to sampling been considered?
4. Have methods been chosen that address the criteria in the POE plan?
5. Have multiple methods been employed so that the weaknesses of some are at least partially compensated for by strengths in others?
6. Have all methods been pre-tested?
7. Has the project budget been refined?

Phase III: Collecting Data

The specifics of data collection depend considerably on the given research method used; these are further discussed below and elsewhere in this volume. It is important to consider a general problem with data collection: ethics. Whereas much POE is benign, some post-occupancy evaluations gather sensitive or potentially harmful information such as data from medical or employment records or observation of job performance. In almost all cases the evaluator is using the participants' time and good will. This situation initially requires an overall assessment of the ethical acceptability and overall benefits of the study: Do the potential benefits outweigh possibilities for disruption, embarrassment, and harm to participants?

Even if benefits are greater than potential risks,

	Entry & Initial Data-gathering	***Developing POE Plan***	***Designing the Research***	***Pretesting***	***Collecting Data***	***Analyzing Data***	***Present***
Staff Time							
Wages							
Consultants							
Computer Time							
Travel							
Reproduction							
Materials							
Printing							
Presentations							
Multiplier							
Total							

9–3. Sample spreadsheet for budgeting a POE.

if the participants are involved in such a way that they are identified individually and that their daily life is affected, written "informed consent" must be received from them. The nature of the study must be explained and participants told that they can discontinue participation at any time. If they are being compensated for their participation, they must be told that they will receive compensation no matter whether they complete the study or not. For minors or institutionalized people, informed consent is usually required from guardians and, if possible, from participants themselves. In general it is normally assumed that direct observation where individuals are simply counted without recording their identity does not require informed consent, and that if people consent to be interviewed or fill out a questionnaire they have provided "implied consent." However, special care is needed where participants are in some way dependent on the evaluator (as in the case of employees or students) to ensure that participation is genuinely voluntary. In almost all situations feedback about the nature of the study is desirable, and a summary of results should be made available to participants at the completion of the POE. Although I am unaware of any ethical principles developed explicitly for POE, the ethical principles for psychologists listed in figure 9–4 are highly relevant.

The following are basic questions to be asked regarding the data collection phase:

1. Have data-collection procedures been established in writing in advance, pre-tested, completely explained to all members of the evaluation team, and practiced by them?

a. In planning a study, the investigator has the responsibility to make a careful evaluation of its ethical acceptability. To the extent that the weighing of scientific and human values suggests a compromise of any principle, the investigator incurs a correspondingly serious obligation to seek ethical advice and to observe stringent safeguards to protect the rights of human participants.

b. Considering whether a participant in a planned study will be a "subject at risk" or a "subject at minimal risk," according to recognized standards, is of primary ethical concern to the investigator.

c. The investigator always retains the responsibility for ensuring ethical practice in research. The investigation is also responsible for the ethical treatment of research participants by collaborators, assistants, students, and employees, all of whom, however, incur similar obligations.

d. Except in minimal risk research, the investigator establishes a clear and fair agreement with research participants, prior to their participation, that clarifies the obligations and responsibilities of each. The investigation has the obligation to honor all promises and commitments included in that agreement. The investigator informs the participants of all aspects of the research that might reasonably be expected to influence willingness to participate and explains all other aspects of the research about which the participants inquire. Failure to make full disclosure prior to obtaining informed consent requires additional safeguards to protect the welfare and dignity of the research participants. Research with children or with participants who have impairments that would limit understanding and/or communication requires special safeguarding procedures.

e. Methodological requirements of a study may make the use of concealment or deception necessary. Before conducting such a study, the investigator has a special responsibility to (i) determine whether the use of such techniques is justified by the study's prospective scientific, educational, or applied value; (ii) determine whether alternative procedures are available that do not use concealment or deception; and (iii) ensure that the participants are provided with sufficient explanation as soon as possible.

f. The investigator respects the individual's freedom to decline to participate in or to withdraw from the research at any time. The obligation to protect this freedom requires careful thought and consideration when the investigator is in a position of authority or influence over the participant. Such positions of authority include, but are not limited to, situations in which research participation is required as part of employment or in which the participant is a student, client, or employee of the investigator.

g. The investigator protects the participant from physical and mental discomfort, harm, and danger that may arise from research procedures. If risks of such consequences exist, the investigator informs the participant of that fact. Research procedures likely to cause serious or lasting harm to a participant are not used unless the failure to use these procedures might expose the participant to risk of greater harm, or unless the research has great potential benefit and fully informed and voluntary consent is obtained from each participant. The participant should be informed of procedures for contacting the investigator within a reasonable time period following participation should stress, potential harm, or related questions or concerns arise.

h. After the data are collected, the investigator provides the participant with information about the nature of the study and attempts to remove any misconceptions that may have arisen. Where scientific or humane value justify delaying or withholding this information, the investigator incurs a special responsibility to monitor the research and to ensure that there are no damaging consequences for the participant.

i. Where research procedures result in undesirable consequences for the individual participant, the investigation has the responsibility to detect and remove or correct these consequences, including long-term effects.

j. Information obtained about a research participant during the course of an investigation is confidential unless otherwise agreed upon in advance. When the possibility exists that others may obtain access to such information, this possibility, together with the plans for protecting confidentiality, is explained to the participant as part of the procedure for obtaining informed consent.

9–4. Ethical principles in research with human participants.

2. Is the adequacy of the data-collection procedure monitored, such as by spot checks by the principal evaluator?
3. Have the ethical implications of the POE been fully considered and has informed consent been received where necessary?

Phase IV: Analyzing the Data

Analysis of data represents one of the weakest aspects of many POEs (Bechtel and Srivastava 1978). Not only are many evaluators naive about appropriate statistical analysis techniques, analyses often do not address the central questions in the evaluation. The most serious problems in POEs are not the traditional statistical problems of falsely accepting or rejecting the null hypothesis but rather what can be called "Type III error": the evaluator consults a statistician who does not really understand the problem and suggests an analytic technique that is not quite appropriate, whereupon the evaluator uses the technique and misreports the results, not really understanding what the technique provides. This problem is exacerbated by the realities of doing research in real settings, which often involves small sample sizes, nonrandom selection, and other potential threats to validity.

It is beyond the scope of this chapter to discuss data analysis in any depth, especially given the diversity of methods available and the range of POEs. However, a few simple principles may be appropriate. First, analyses should proceed from the simple to the complex. If several quantitative variables are involved, the analysis should consider single variables before moving on to multiple variables. The analyses should help the evaluator understand the structure of the data. A number of methodologists have recently developed particularly clear ways of visually presenting preliminary results (see Carmines and Zeller 1979 for a discussion of preliminary quantitative data analysis and for a discussion of qualitative analysis).

Perhaps the most important overall conclusion is that *understanding is critical.* The evaluator should clearly understand the purpose of the analytic techniques, what the analysis yields, and the implications of any methodological problems for interpretation of the results. This may mean that the analysis will remain extremely simple; in all cases clarity is preferable to quasi-scientific mystification.

An additional problem with the data analysis step is that it often occurs out of sight of the client or setting (Keys and Wener 1980). The evaluators may disappear for weeks or months, and the client may feel conspired against or at least let down after the intense interaction of the data-gathering phase. An obvious conclusion is that key people in the setting being evaluated need to receive periodic reports and need to participate during analysis as well as data collection.

To summarize, many problems in POE have resulted from evaluators' lack of understanding of appropriate quantitative and qualitative analysis methods, and more care is needed. Some central questions about the analysis step include:

1. Do the analysis methods directly address the issues and criteria?
2. Are the assumptions behind the methods understood? (For example, for statistical methods, what are the requirements for equal sample sizes? minimum sample sizes?)
3. Are the implications for the results of the methods and procedures understood and acknowledged?

Phase V: Presenting Information

Increasingly, evaluators are realizing that the way information is presented has an important impact on whether it is used. Reizenstein (1980) suggested that evaluators should generally present information in several ways. Different disciplines and individuals are accustomed to different ways of presenting materials. For example, social scientists are used to reading written reports, and designers respond better to visual presentations. The various information users should have the information of significance to them presented in a way they find clear and meaningful. A visual presentation such as slides or video tape may supplement written final reports, and the reports themselves may be in different formats. For example in their study of psychiatric group homes, ARC produced a large format (11 × 14 inch) magazine-style final report broken up into booklets (Bakos et al. 1979, 1981). Heavily illustrated, the booklet organizes individual topics into columns after the fashion of *Newsweek* and similar magazines. In a recent POE of a juvenile detention center my colleagues and I prepared a 22- by 28-inch poster that shows the purpose of the study, major issues, results, and some sample graphics. This poster, which helped provide feedback to resident and staff participants, is a concise representation of a complex project.

Despite growing sophistication in the formats of final reports, few evaluators take the next step and publish results. Whereas some POEs are proprietary, most can be published if only to show that the client is progressive and cares about employees. Journals such as *Environment and Behavior, Journal of Architecture and Planning Research,* and *AIA Journal* have begun to publish POEs, and Sommer (1984) has suggested that it may be even more meaningful to publish POEs in trade periodicals such as *The Office, Contract Magazine, Plant Engineering, Building Science,* and *Skyscraper Management.* (Decision makers are more likely to read these specialized trade periodicals than the first set of journals.)

The following are key questions about the presentation of information:

1. Was the "targeted" information presented to the key information users? (For example, was information intended for research peers published in an appropriate outlet? Was information relevant to codes presented to code officials in sources they are likely to read and in a form they can understand?)
2. Was the information presented in a clear, jargon-free manner?
3. Were multiple modes of presentation considered?
4. Were findings presented in key trade journals?

POE METHODS

There are a large number of data-collection methods available for performing POEs, many of which are described elsewhere in this volume. In this chapter I will briefly discuss seven methods as a way of illustrating the POE process. The discussion will emphasize particular methods or applications of methods that are unique to POE: walk-throughs, workshop sessions, interviewing, questionnaires, recording participants' use of time, observation, and methods of assessing the physical setting.

Walk-through Interviews

This technique is an unstructured interview procedure that has been proposed by Bechtel and Srivastava (1978), Zeisel (1981), and others and serves as the basis of a major POE program conducted by the Ministry of Works and Development in New Zealand (Daish et al. 1982). It uses the physical environment as a prompt to help respondents articulate their reactions to the setting. Daish and his colleagues have developed an extremely useful booklet entitled *Process Guidelines,* which explains the procedure in considerable detail (Daish et al. 1982). In a typical evaluation they conduct a two-and-a-half- to four-day walk-through program in which seven to ten "participant groups" are interviewed while walking through the building.

The walk-through procedure reflects the New Zealand group's view that the opinions of building users are more important than expert judgments: participants are asked open, unstructured questions to determine what is important to *them* about the buildings.

Daish and his colleagues propose a seven-step procedure for accomplishing a walk-through evaluation. These steps are illustrated in figure 9-5. First, a task group is established that will plan, carry out, and write up the evaluation. In the New Zealand POEs this is usually composed of four people, two from the Ministry of Works and Development and two from the client organization, with the expectation that at least one of the client representatives will be familiar with the building to be evaluated and will have contacts there.

Second, the task group plans the walk-through, choosing the participant groups to be interviewed and preparing a work plan for the task group. The participant groups are chosen from people who have an interest in the building: occupants, managers, designers, builders, financiers, owners, visitors, maintenance staff, and so on. The participant groups are interviewed in groups of three to seven people of similar interests. (In a study my colleagues and I are currently undertaking of the Florida A&M University School of Architecture building, we will do walk-through interviews with groups of students, with faculty, with the architects, and so on.) Some roles that include relatively few people, such as designers, may be represented by one participant group. Other roles, such as students, may require several participant groups to gain an adequate view of the group as a whole. It is helpful if, as in New Zealand, all task groups have some funds for fine-tuning the building being evaluated. Having "money in their back pocket" to correct small problems ensures that the evaluation receives cooperation by people in the evaluation setting and provides some immediate reinforcement concerning the value of POE. During this step a work plan is developed in which dates and work assignments are established. (In our own work we have found it useful to make this up as a poster and put it outside our offices.)

The third step is to choose and organize the individual participants. In the New Zealand system the participants are not chosen completely randomly. Instead, people are picked to represent a range of experience, ages, and ethnicity, as well as the "interest group" from which they are drawn. Prior to inviting anyone to participate, a list of all potential participants is drawn up, and the entire task group agrees on the list. In cases where too few good candidates are known to the task group, aid is enlisted from someone in the setting. A union steward or shift supervisor, for example, may be enlisted to fill out the list of potential participants in the maintenance worker group. After participants are chosen they are invited individually by mail or phone, and acknowledgments are obtained at least four to five working days before the walk-through. It is important during the preparation stage that the building management be kept informed of the scheduling and of any possible disruptions in the building operation. The building management is asked to explain the purpose of the walk-through to nonparticipants who work in the setting so that disruption is kept to a minimum.

The fourth step is to search documents to help clarify the background of the project, as in the initial data gathering step described above. In the document review step, the task group collects documents concerning the history of the project such as the program, plans and drawings, and correspondence. Choosing the documents that have had the greatest impact on design decision making, the task group makes a one- or two-page annotated list itemizing key events and briefly explaining why things happened as they did. Key questions are addressed. For example: How and why was there a

STEP 1: FORM TASK GROUP

- Task group plans, conducts and reports POE.
- Task group should include about four people, including, where possible, a member of the client organization who is familiar with the building.

STEP 2: PLAN WALKTHROUGH

- Task group chooses "participant groups" to be interviewed (occupants, managers, designers, etc.).
- Task group develops work plan and, where possible, acquires fine-tuning money for buildings to be evaluated.
- Areas to be visited on walkthrough are selected.

STEP 3: CHOOSE AND ENLIST PARTICIPANTS

- Task group makes list of potential participants for each participant group, choosing people with a wide range of experience and without idiosyncratic views.
- Participants are individually invited to join the walkthrough.

STEP 4: SEARCH DOCUMENTS

- Task group skims selected documents such as the program, plans, and memos to determine key events and decisions during design, construction, and occupancy.

STEP 5: PREPARE WALKTHROUGH

- Task group prepares data-recording sheets.
- Task group acquires necessary equipment.
- Task group confirms arrangements with POE site and participants.

STEP 6: FACILITATE WALKTHROUGHS

- Task group conducts: introductory meeting (about ½ hour); touring interview (1½ hours); and review meeting (about 1½ hours).
- In introductory meeting the task group explains purpose and structure of the walkthrough.
- During the touring interview, a facilitator asks participants unstructured questions such as "What do you think is important about this space? What do you think works well? What do you think doesn't work well?"
- A recorder marks down responses, using the participants' own words wherever possible.
- Either during the walkthrough or afterward, the features and problems noted are photographed and otherwise explored (using thermometers, light meters, sound level meters, etc.).
- During the review meeting, recommendations are solicited regarding problems and strengths noted. Recommendations are noted on flip charts, or by other "visual" devices.

STEP 7: CODE AND PRESENT DATA

- Recommendations are coded by key words such as building type (e.g., dormitories), behavioral processes (e.g., use of recreation space) or building elements (e.g., carpeting).
- Recommendations are further categorized into "action categories," such as fine-tuning, programming, or building management. (If action is required, the person to conduct the action is identified.)
- Report is submitted in three forms: a POE file containing all recommendations, a condensed report, and a one-page poster.

9–5. The Victoria University of Wellington/Ministry of Works and Development (New Zealand) walkthrough procedure. After Dalish, Gray, and Kernohan, 1982.

decision to build? Who decided what was required? Were there any unusual functional requirements? Is the present use of the building in line with the original plan? Is there anything unusual about design, construction, or environment?

Fifth, the walk-throughs are prepared. Data-recording sheets are set up, and equipment is secured. Final arrangements are made with the POE site, including reserving rooms for an introductory meeting before the "touring interview" and a review meeting afterward. Because the walk-through also involves documenting physical problems, a range of recording equipment—such as light and sound meters—is made available.

Sixth, the walk-through is conducted. The New Zealand walk-through has three parts: an introductory meeting of about half an hour; a "touring interview" lasting a half hour to an hour; and a one-hour review meeting. All take place in the building being evaluated. During the introductory meeting the participants are introduced, the purpose and procedure of the walk-through are explained, and the participants are asked to describe their roles and activities with respect to the building. The walk-through includes unstructured interviews taken while visiting a representative set of spaces inside and outside the building. Whereas some spaces may be included in all walk-throughs, other spaces, such as the maintenance shop, may only be part of selected walk-throughs. In buildings with duplicated spaces such as hospital rooms, a sample of such spaces may be chosen.

To conduct a walk-through, at least two roles are required: a facilitator and a recorder (and perhaps a photographer). As used by the New Zealanders, the walk-through is intended to discover what is important to the *users* rather than to follow any prearranged agenda. As a result, the facilitator asks open-ended questions such as: What do you think is important about this space? Do you know what happens here? What do you think works well? What do you think doesn't work well? (Although it changes the nature of the walk-through, I have also successfully used this technique with more directed questions such as: Do you ever feel threatened here? or, How good would you say the lighting is?) The recorder indicates comments on the data sheets, writing down comments in the participant's own words if possible. Areas referred to in comments should be photographed and tested for light levels, noise, and so forth during or after the walk-through.

During the review meeting, comments and recommendations are solicited about the building and the spaces visited, and any other responses the participants might have about issues such as the building, maintenance, and design process are collected. The participants are reminded of their comments and asked for both positive and negative recommendations. These may be recorded on a flip chart during the meeting and transcribed later.

In the seventh step the data are coded and presented. Daish and his colleagues suggest that recommendations be coded by key areas such as policy or management matters, behavioral issues (for example, use of recreation space or privacy at telephones), room types, or building elements such as carpeting or walls. It is further suggested that the recommendations be coded into categories such as fine-tuning, programming, or building management. The reports are presented in three forms: a POE file containing all comments, a condensed twenty- to fifty-page report, and a one-page poster describing the process and the findings. (Issues involved with presenting POE information are discussed in a separate section below.)

In the New Zealand work, the presentation of the final report is followed by meetings in which the various participant groups and other interest groups negotiate strategies for action and attempt to reconcile divergent viewpoints. It is felt that this consensus-building process is critical in making the transition between research and implementation.

Some advocates of the walk-through, such as

Bechtel and Srivastava (1978), propose that it be used early in a POE to help define the major issues in the evaluation, and that it can be a central part of initial data-gathering, followed by more directed methods such as questionnaires or observation. Other walk-through practitioners, such as the New Zealand group, use the walk-through as the main data-gathering instrument in the POE (although they sometimes also do more in-depth "focus" studies as well).

The strengths of the walk-through are that it is relatively inexpensive, it discovers what is important for users, and helps the client become committed to the POE process. A potential weakness is that comparability between sites and over time is difficult. For example, a multi-site evaluation of different office systems may be hard to interpret because the different organizational cultures and personalities of the walk-through participants may have colored the responses. However, establishing a data base of case studies as part of an ongoing project may build comparability over time.

Workshop Sessions

An increasing number of POEs are using participant workshops as a method to combine information gathering with the providing of feedback to the client. For example, in the Florida A&M University project, an "Advisory Task Force" is being assembled that will include representatives of the various relevant user groups: faculty, students, Board of Regents, and state legislature. Although participants will be involved throughout the process, the task force will meet only four times during the thirty-month project: initially to help establish the central issues of the POE, during development of methods, during data collection, and finally near the end of the project.

In addition to providing specific information about the users' reactions to the School of Architecture building, the workshop sessions present a forum where intergroup differences, such as those between students and faculty, may be aired and considered. These sessions help to clarify important evaluation criteria as judged by the various groups. However, workshop sessions share the potential pitfalls of other self-report measures in that social pressures may cause respondents to misrepresent personally or professionally sensitive questions. It is also true that one or two dominant personalities may strongly influence the course of a workshop session unless the moderator is careful to draw out other participants.

Nonetheless, the workshop format may be a fairly rapid way of learning about participants' perceptions and of working toward the implementation of POE findings. For example, if the evaluator wishes to develop an action plan to implement these findings, participants might be asked: What problems do you face presently? What recommendations do you have for solving these problems? What are the barriers for implementing these problems? How may these barriers be overcome? The answers to these questions may be recorded on flip charts or by some other method so that all participants can see what is recorded.

A caution is in order. Evaluators like to consider themselves "facilitators" who mediate between various groups in workshops. Realistically, extreme power differences, such as between a corporate board of directors and secretaries may make such mediation impossible. Knight and Campbell (1980) somewhat facetiously suggested that trying to mediate between such disparate job classifications is a bit like trying to negotiate between slaves and slave owners on a 1790 North Carolina plantation.

Participant workshops are useful ways to involve the client in the POE. Because the time commitment to participate in the workshops is clear and bounded, clients often find this approach more attractive than being involved in a more time-consuming task group. Workshop sessions tend to be active and stimulating and as a result help build commitment to the POE process.

Interviewing

Almost all POEs include some sort of interviewing of users, designers, passersby, financiers, space managers, or others. Because this technique is described clearly and in detail elsewhere in the present volume and in other sources (such as Zeisel 1981), I will discuss it only briefly here.

Interviews vary greatly in the amount of control exercised by the interviewer in choosing the topic for discussion and in structuring the response. National political polls are at one extreme in the dimension of control: the question is read verbatim (If the presidential election were held today, whom would you vote for?) and the possible responses are constrained (for example, candidate *X* or candidate *Y*). This degree of control aids in comparability; the researchers can compare responses regionally and over time. By contrast, many researchers use unstructured interviews guided simply by a list of topics such as ''safety'' or ''crowding'' and conducted like a social conversation, in which participants are free to dwell on issues they consider important. The value of unstructured techniques is that they reveal what is of significance for the respondent, who may choose whatever he or she wishes to discuss. However, because there is no assurance that the same issues were raised at each interview, it is difficult to make comparisons among sites or over time.

Zeisel (1981) and others have suggested that an intermediate level of control over topic and responses is often appropriate for POE. This level of control is obtained through a method they call the *structured interview.* The interviewer has an *interview schedule,* a detailed list of questions or issues that serves as a general map of the discussion. However, the respondent answers in his or her own words and need not respond to questions in the order listed.

Reizenstein and Grant (1983) have recently developed a useful set of interviewing techniques for their ongoing project. Reizenstein (now Carpman) and Grant are gathering patient and visitor input into the design and planning of the University of Michigan Replacement Hospital. Borrowing techniques from design, marketing, and other disciplines, they use many graphic aids. For example, when considering several design alternatives for a given space, they build a model that can be easily altered to show each alternative and photograph each solution. Respondents are asked to rate each photograph comparatively.

The use of models, computer graphics, or other simulations in POE allows some efficiencies in procedure. For example, users can be interviewed about visual attributes of settings without being brought to the site, and large groups can be tested at one time by using slides. Users can also compare unbuilt design alternatives with the setting being evaluated. Simulation, of course, has the disadvantage that it taps only visual aspects of settings and that the generalizability of ratings of simulations to the actual setting is uncertain. Kaplan (1978), however, has found that ratings of photographs of even quite simple, undetailed models are good predictors of reactions to the actual environments.

In another example, Reizenstein and Grant (1983) were trying to determine what labels to use in signage for hospital departments. They made cards with technical names in bold type such as ''Radiology'' and asked what the words meant, as well as providing more generic definitions, and asked patients and visitors for their best ideas of what the technical titles for those departments might be. These bold, clear, and engaging stimuli helped make the interviewing quite rapid as well as interesting for participants.

Although the Reizenstein and Grant work is properly labeled "facilities programming" rather than POE, the techniques they have developed are clearly applicable to evaluation research. The use of graphic aids makes the interview more interesting for participants and helps reduce variation in response due to ambiguities in language. Also, the use of fixed responses, requiring respondents to choose a "best" alternative among several presented, allows rapid analysis of results.

The cost-effectiveness of interviews needs to be considered by the evaluator when designing POE methods. Individual interviews are useful because people being questioned may be more honest than if friends or colleagues are present. However, individual interviews are expensive. Including scheduling, waiting time, running the interview, and coding, a brief individual interview may require a minimum of several hours. Many interviewers use small group interviews of from two to ten people to reduce costs. Group interviews are often quite successful because participants stimulate each other and may forge a consensus, as in the workshops described above.

In summary, interviews are valuable because people can tell you their feelings, motives, and actions directly. Faulty memory, however, and the desire to make socially acceptable responses may limit their usefulness, although these problems are unlikely to be serious unless the questions are very sensitive. Interviews vary in the amount of control the evaluator exercises in structuring the issues and responses. Zeisel (1981) and others have suggested that a structured interview may offer an appropriate level of control in many situations, although Reizenstein and Grant have used very controlled interviews with considerable success.

Questionnaires

Questionnaires have been called "written interviews" and as such share many of the qualities described above. Since questionnaire development is discussed in Marans' chapter in this volume, it will be only briefly described here. The evaluator typically has a high level of control over the topic, because the questions are written down, and often has control over the response as well. Questionnaire construction has been raised to a fine art. Considerable attention has been paid to the impact of the ordering and wording of questions and responses and to format. There are many useful volumes available explaining this technique in depth (for example, Galtung 1967).

Zeisel (1981) has suggested that there are three critical issues in questionnaire construction: rapport, conditioning, and fatigue. He suggests that the initial explanation of the purpose of the questionnaire and the tone of the initial questions (Zeisel suggests starting by asking what is good about a building) help to engage or turn off the respondent.

Many of the principles described in the "entry" step are applicable here. The overall appearance and design of the questionnaire is important: Does it look interesting? Is there a picture on the cover? Does it look professional? Does it have sufficient white space, or does it look heavy and gray? Are the response formats clear? Having a letter of endorsement by a recognized authority such as the president of the tenants' organization is also helpful.

Noting that one can influence responses to the questionnaire by the order of questions, Zeisel proposes starting with general questions and moving to more specific ones. Fatigue can be reduced by grouping questions focused on similar topics and with similar response formats.

Many of these qualities are reflected in a series of studies of resident satisfaction with housing performed by Francescato, Weidemann, Anderson, and their colleagues at the University of Illinois (see, for example, Francescato et al. 1979; Weidemann et al. 1982). Using both written and verbal questionnaires, they have attempted to discover the principal components of satisfaction with the residential environment. They have found that the percentage of questionnaires completed is affected by appearance, personal appeal, and follow-up. (The "response rate" is an important criteria of success both because higher rates result in obtaining more data for the same effort and because low response rates often mean that specific types of respondents have not returned the questionnaire.) Butterfield and Anderson (1980) expanded on some early work on this issue by Dillman (1972; Dillman and Frey 1974), who found that by carefully developing a questionnaire package, the typical 20–40 percent response rate could be raised to 80 percent or higher.

Butterfield and Anderson conducted two studies in which they examined the impact of three factors: individually addressing questionnaires as opposed to sending letters addressed "Dear Resident"; providing well laid-out questionnaires versus poorly assembled ones; and using zero, one, or two follow-ups. They found that personalization and professional appearance (which were presented together and hence not separable in the analysis) had no apparent impact on the response rate. However, the respondents were students in developments near campus who may have been sufficiently swayed by the university letterhead to be unaffected by lack of personalization; their response rate was relatively high in any case (41–55 percent). Follow-ups did have a significant impact on response rates. A postcard sent seven to fourteen days after the questionnaire resulted in an additional 10–22 percent of questionnaires being returned, and a follow-up letter with a replacement questionnaire after three weeks resulted in an additional 11–14 percent. The questionnaires in the follow-up group had individual code numbers on them to allow tracking of responses. The purpose of the code was explained in the cover letter, and absolute anonymity was promised.

As the field of POE matures, standardized questionnaires are taking on increased importance. For example, Moos and his colleagues at Stanford University have developed questionnaires that have been applied to large national samples of settings of various types such as correctional facilities (Moos 1975) and health care settings (Moos 1974). Anderson, Francescato, Weidemann, and their colleagues have used similar questionnaires focusing on housing satisfaction in the United States, Australia, and England (Weidemann et al. 1982); while Farbstein and Wener have developed standardized questionnaires for the evaluation of jails (Farbstein and Wener 1982).

Standardized questionnaires have the obvious advantage that they do not require preparation; they are already developed. Perhaps more important, however, is that they allow norms to be established. The evaluator can tell how his or her setting compares with similar settings nationally or internationally.

In summary, questionnaires share the characteristics of other self-report measures—respondents can describe their own activities and opinions but may also intentionally or unintentionally distort the results. Questionnaires, however, are usually the most cost-effective way of gathering data from a large number of respondents. Because the evaluator has comparatively high control over the topic and the response, comparability is also greater than with more "open" methods such as the walk-through, and quantitative analysis may be easier as well.

Recording Participants' Use of Time

A POE is often concerned with how users of the setting spend their time over the course of an hour, day, month, or year. For example, a POE of housing for the elderly may be concerned with how much time the tenants spend in shared spaces

(Howell et al. 1980), while an office evaluation may assess the amount of time workers spend at their desks (Wineman 1982).

Information about use of time is derived from three sources: interviews; time budgets (usually logs or diaries); and observation. Through interviewing—asking people how they spend their time—a profile of activity can be developed, although large errors in estimation are quite common. Alternatively, building users may be asked to keep a log or diary of their own activities. These logs may be selective by activities ("record each time a visitor asks you directions") or selective by time of day ("record activities for one hour preceding each dinner"), or may attempt to be exhaustive ("record your activity every fifteen minutes"). Logs are discussed more fully in the Michelson chapter in this volume.

The ELEMR project (Zimring et al. 1982) used the "critical incidents technique" (Flannagan 1953) to gather specific incidents of resident behavior from staff members. Index cards (see fig. 9-6) were preprinted with key questions on an incident (Where did the incident occur? Who was involved? How did it start? What happened? How did it end? and so on) and staff members were asked to record at the end of each shift specific kinds of resident incidents, such as conflicts over territory. Staff were paid a modest additional amount of money ($5 per hour in 1974) to spend their break

INCIDENT RECORDING CARD

For Office Use:
Incident Code ______________________

Where did the incident occur?

Who was involved?

How did it start?

What happened? (Use other side if necessary)

How did it end?

9-6. Sample card for recording a critical incident. From Knight, Weitzer, and Zimring, 1978.

times filling out the cards. The evaluators collected the cards after the first few days to ensure that the staff understood the task and then about once per week afterward. When necessary, the evaluator would question the staff member to fill out sketchy details.

The critical incident technique seems to work well because the participants are asked for very concrete information shortly after it occurs. A second, related method was used in a small evaluation of group homes (Wineman and Zimring 1982) for the mentally retarded. This log pressed the live-in house parents into service as observers and asked them to record the residents' location and activities during meal times (fig. 9–7). The log worked well for similar reasons: the form asked for clear, simple responses. In addition to time budgets and critical incidents, use of time may be recorded by observing people in a setting. For example, observation may reveal where children play in playgrounds or where institutional residents spend their time in a dayhall. The procedures for observation are discussed in the following section.

In summary, time budgets provide a profile of how people spend their time in a setting. The profile may be established through self-report measures such as interviews, questionnaires, or logs or by direct observation of user activities.

mealtime

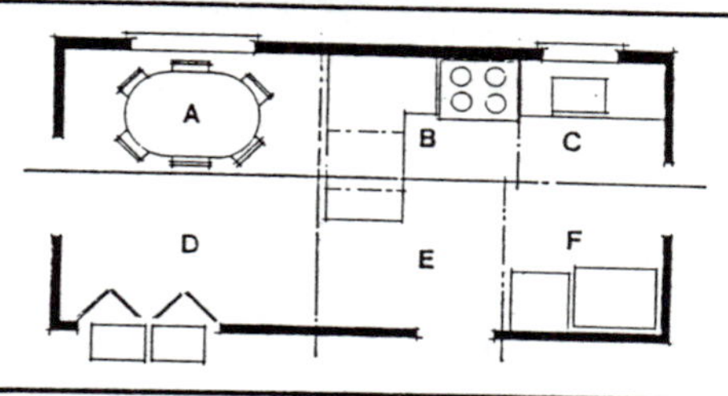

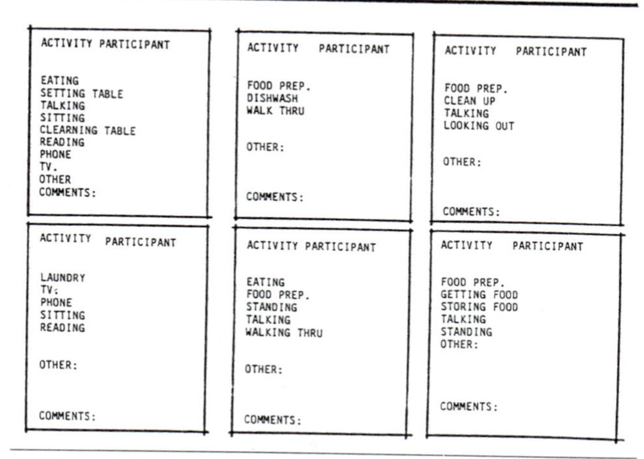

ACTIVITY PARTICIPANT
EATING
SETTING TABLE
TALKING
SITTING
CLEARNING TABLE
READING
PHONE
TV.
OTHER
COMMENTS:

ACTIVITY PARTICIPANT
FOOD PREP.
DISHWASH
WALK THRU
OTHER:
COMMENTS:

ACTIVITY PARTICIPANT
FOOD PREP.
CLEAN UP
TALKING
LOOKING OUT
OTHER:
COMMENTS:

ACTIVITY PARTICIPANT
LAUNDRY
TV:
PHONE
SITTING
READING
OTHER:
COMMENTS:

ACTIVITY PARTICIPANT
EATING
FOOD PREP.
STANDING
TALKING
WALKING THRU
OTHER:
COMMENTS:

ACTIVITY PARTICIPANT
FOOD PREP.
GETTING FOOD
STORING FOOD
TALKING
STANDING
OTHER:
COMMENTS:

9–7. A log filled out by houseparents in a study of group homes for mentally retarded people.

Observing Environmental Activity

In an effort to overcome the problems inherent in self-report data collection techniques, many post-occupancy evaluators use some sort of direct observation of behavior. Observation is particularly useful in building a rapid, empathetic understanding of the setting, because the evaluator stays in the setting and is exposed to its full range of verbal and nonverbal behaviors, sights, sounds, and activity (Zeisel 1981) and may provide a stable data base that can be quantitatively analyzed (Landesman-Dwyer et al. 1978).

Zeisel (1981) suggests that, depending on the situation, observers can vary their role in the setting from "secret outsider" to "recognized outsider" to "marginal participant" to "full participant." For example, Whyte (1980) was a "secret observer" in his study of urban public spaces; he placed movie cameras with telephoto lenses on adjacent rooftops and recorded activities in plazas without users' knowledge. At the opposite extreme, as part of the ELEMR project, Hollis Wheeler, a sociology graduate student, worked full time as a staff member for several weeks in the institution being evaluated. Although her affiliation with the research team was known by the staff at the institution, she performed the most menial tasks alongside other employees and was quickly accepted by them (Wheeler 1978).

There are a number of devices for recording observations commonly used in POE, including various narrative notation systems, "behavior maps" noting behaviors directly on floorplans, precoded checklists, and other methods. For example, a recent study of fifteen psychiatric group homes used observation effectively (Bakos et al. 1979). The research group Architecture/Research/Construction (ARC) was funded to examine the relationship of privacy and other day-to-day behaviors to the design of group homes and specifically to see whether homes that were more "normalized" had different characteristic patterns of activities. Like many POEs, this study used a multi-methodological approach employing interviews with residents and staff, written and orally read questionnaires including standard measures of social climate, behavior mapping, and other techniques.

The ARC group used the behavior mapping technique first developed by Ittleson, Proshansky, and Rivlin (1970), which uses a checklist to record categories of behaviors and where the behaviors occur. In the group home study, behavior was recorded during the "free times" that were of principal interest to the researchers: from one-half hour before meal times to one-half hour after meals, including the meal itself. Every five minutes a new checklist (illustrated in fig. 9–8) was filled out showing the location and behavior of each staff member and resident. Analysis of the data revealed that there were some differences in behaviors in the homes with different levels of normalization and that the amount of talking with others was particularly higher in normalized settings.

Observation has the advantage that it is direct and dynamic and, if some quantifiable checklist is used, can produce numerical quantities for statistical analysis. Observation extensive enough for quantitative analysis is quite expensive and time consuming, however. It may also create a distance between the researcher and the setting, an observer-observed gap that may limit the commitment-building potential of the POE. However, the replicability and apparent objectivity of quantitative observation can make it very persuasive—statistical analyses sometimes provide very powerful support for an argument.

Briefly, observation has the advantage that it is vivid and engaging; it forces the evaluator to spend time in the setting itself. Because it does not rely on the users' own comments it avoids some of the problems of self-report techniques, and it can be coded for statistical analysis. However, observation can be costly, and interpretation of some subjective qualities may be difficult.

Methods of Assessing the Physical Setting

In addition to exploring the perceptions, attitudes, and behaviors of users, POEs typically assess the setting itself. Although the techniques for this vary greatly according to the needs of the evaluation, several examples deserve mention here.

Energy Assessment. As energy-conscious design becomes increasingly important, the links between physical building performance and user performance are seen as critical. In housing, for example, it has been found that about 50 percent of the variability in energy use is attributable to life-style variables, such as where occupants set their thermostat, when they open and close windows, and so on, rather than to the design of the structure (Benton 1984). In addition, it is unclear whether some of the decisions that may come with energy-conscious design are well accepted by users. For instance, large amounts of south-facing glass or open-plan interiors often result in significant reductions in visual or auditory privacy.

The U.S. Department of Energy Passive Solar Commercial Buildings Program is currently instru-

Mapping Form
Time: Date: Mapper: ARCPR·1978

				Time				Who			Location								General				Specific Activity										Inter.				Speech				With			
individual	house number	meal	non-meal	11-1	1-3	3-5	5-7	resident	staff	other	living room	music room	sun room	hallway·stairs	dining room	kitchen	pantry	game room	cooperative	solitary	passive	null	moving·walking	talking	eating	meal related	phone	television	games	house cleaning	sleeping	other	cooperative -3'	cooperative +3'	parallel -3'	solitary +3'	cooperative	solitary	hostile	none	resident	staff	other	no one
1																																												
2																																												
3																																												
4																																												
5																																												
6																																												
7																																												
8																																												
9																																												
10																																												
11																																												
12																																												
13																																												
14																																												
15																																												
16																																												
17																																												
18																																												
19																																												
20																																												
21																																												

BEHAVIORAL MAPPING: STATISTICAL SUMMARY

		Breakdown of the Four Continuum Groups				
Variable	Total Survey Mean %	Institutional Group	Low Medium Group	High Medium Group	Normally Supportive Group	p**
PERSON						
1. Resident	76	78	79	71	76	*
2. Staff	17	12	16	22	21	*
LOCATION						
1. Large living room	30	39	28	25	26	*
2. Small living room	7	2	14	6	3	*
3. Dining room	25	12	23	30	43	p < .04
4. Kitchen	22	18	22	22	25	*
5. Hall	9	13	11	8	2	*
6. Recreation room	3	8	0	3	0	*
7. Other room	5	8	3	6	2	*

(continued)

9–8. Mapping form used to record behavior. From ARC, Community Group Homes *(New York: Van Nostrand Reinhold, 1985).*

BEHAVIORAL MAPPING: STATISTICAL SUMMARY

Variable	Total Survey Mean %	Breakdown of the Four Continuum Groups				p**
		Institutional Group	Low Medium Group	High Medium Group	Normally Supportive Group	
ACTIVITY						
1. Cooperative activity	25	17	25	27	37	$p < .05$
2. Solitary activity	9	3	15	10	9	*
3. Moving, walking, in transit	9	16	6	8	2	*
4. Meal-related activity	14	13	10	18	13	*
5. Eating	17	14	15	20	18	*
6. Watching TV	18	40	24	20	16	$p < .04$
7. Talking on the telephone	2	1	2	3	2	*
8. Passively watching others	7	10	12	2	4	*
LEVEL OF INTERACTION						
1. Cooperative activity, within 3 feet of other person(s)	27	18	17	42	36	$p < .03$
2. Cooperative activity, more than 3 feet from other person(s)	15	6	22	16	16	$p < .05$
3. Parallel, within 3 feet of other(s), but not engaged in cooperative activity	35	56	36	16	28	$p < .01$
4. Solitary, more than 3 feet from other(s), not engaged in cooperative activity	23	20	25	26	20	*
LEVEL OF INTERACTIVE SPEECH						
1. Talking with other(s)	41	25	36	53	56	$p < .03$
2. Talking alone, using telephone	3	1	6	3	1	*
3. Hostile, yelling, arguing	1	0	2	1	0	*
4. No speech	55	74	57	42	43	$p < .02$
FOCUS OF INTERACTION						
1. Interaction with another resident	32	16	45	33	37	$p < .03$
2. Interaction with staff	11	7	8	15	16	*
3. Interaction with other, visitor	6	4	5	11	7	*
4. No interaction	51	74	42	42	40	$p < .02$

* Nonsignificant difference between groups; *p* is significant only when less than .05.
** Significance levels were determined from chi square analysis of the four continuum groups. Value *p* denotes the odds of a particular result being found by chance.

Figure 9–8 continued

menting some twenty-three buildings in the United States, including such diverse structures as office buildings, libraries, and schools (Gordon et al. 1984). In each building sophisticated monitoring systems have been installed, which record internal and external temperatures and energy usage in various parts of the building. In addition, light, heat, and noise levels are periodically recorded. Overlaying user-behavior and building-behavior data allows questions such as the following to be answered: Are energy-conscious features well accepted? Are innovative aspects, such as display spaces lit mostly by daylight, in fact used by building occupants? Does usage vary by light levels?

Researchers exploring the relationships of energy and behavior increasingly are exploring ways to record user behavior mechanically as well as instrumenting the building. Whereas user behavior has typically been documented by self-report measures such as interviews and questionnaires, evaluators are exploring ways to record automatically whether windows are open or closed, where thermostats are set, and other energy-relevant activities (Kantrowitz 1984).

Privacy. Although privacy has traditionally been considered a perceived quality, evaluators are beginning to look at its physical aspects. As stated above, Archea (1977) has hypothesized that people in public settings regulate their behavior according to both their "visual access" and their "visual exposure." People in high visual exposure areas (places where many people can see them) perceive themselves as being more accountable for their actions than people in lower exposure areas. This may help explain why solitary diners in a restaurant tend to sit around the periphery of the room, choosing high visual access, low visual exposure locations. Archea (1977) argues that access and exposure can fairly precisely predict where people will congregate in a space and thus whether a space will be acceptable for various kinds of behaviors.

Archea and his students assess visual access and exposure by dividing a plan of the space to be investigated into the equivalent of 3-foot by 3-foot grid squares (Archea 1984). For each square, "visual access" is the number of squares a person in that square can view, and visual exposure is the number of squares from which it can be viewed. Procedurally, Archea lays a template with a 30-degree angle on the midpoint of each square and counts the number of midpoints of other squares that are included in that 30-degree arc. (This procedure simulates a 30-degree arc of central vision.) He then rotates this arc twelve times (to include all 360 degrees). The total number of midpoints of squares included in all twelve arcs radiating from the midpoint of each square becomes the visual access figure for that square. Each time a square is counted as being visually accessible from another square, a notation is made, and the total for each square is its visual exposure figure.

Whereas Archea's method seems quite powerful in predicting people's location and behavior in space, it is computationally cumbersome. Several microcomputer programs are being developed to compute these figures (Archea 1984).

Accessibility and Normalization. Several checklists have recently been developed for evaluating these key physical aspects of settings that affect society's growing consciousness about the importance of "normalizing" buildings and making them accessible to the handicapped. Figure 9–9 was developed by Zube, Palmer, and Crystal (1976) to examine the accessibility to disabled people of National Park Service visitor interpretive centers.

As the role of the physical environment becomes better understood, increased attention is being paid to measures of the setting itself. The three issues mentioned above are examples of the use of physical measures in POEs. Levels and color of light (Wineman 1982), noise levels and reverberation (Zimring et al. 1982), internal air pollution (Wineman 1982), and other physical measures are often included in evaluations.

SUMMARY

A five-step process can be used in making POEs. *Phase I—entry and initial data collection*—is devoted to developing support by key individuals at all levels of the formal and informal organizational hierarchy, and to learning about the prehistory of the project. Its purpose is also to find out what is important to key decision makers and to learn in gen-

CIRCULATION

Parking spaces
- Width: 12 feet wide to permit room at side of car for wheelchair access to or from spaces
- Path of movement: should avoid need to pass behind parked cars

Walks
- Width: minimum 48 inches
- Grade: maximum 5 percent

Ramps
- Width: minimum 48 inches
- Grade: maximum slope of 1 in 12 or 8.3 percent
- Length: maximum of 30 feet of continuous slope between level platforms
- Surface: nonslip
- Handrails: minimum 1 side, preferably on both sides, height of 32 inches, provide additional rails at lower heights where children will use the facility, extend rails 1 foot beyond top and bottom of ramp on the side of the continuing wall or guardrail

Entrances
- Service either on grade or by ramp (see above)

Doors
- Width: minimum of 32 inches when door is open
- Operation: single action

Stairs
- Risers: maximum height of 7 inches
- Nosing: avoid projecting nosings
- Handrails: minimum one side, height of 32 inches, extend rail 18 inches beyond top and bottom risers

OTHER FACILITIES

Toilet stall
- Width: 3 feet
- Depth: minimum 56 inches, preferably 60 inches
- Door: 32 inches wide when door is open
- Handrails: on each side, 33 inches high, parallel with floor, strong and well supported

Water closet
- Seat height: 20 inches
- Type: wall hung most desirable; if floor supported, understructure should not interfere with close approach of wheelchair

Urinal
- Wall hung, opening 19 inches above floor; floor mounted at same level as floor

Mirrors
- Height: not greater than 40 inches above the floor

Towel racks, dispensers, or shelves
- Height: not greater than 40 inches above the floor

Water fountains
- Height and type: hand operated or hand-and-foot operated; floor-mounted side fountain, 30 inches, wall-hung basin, 36 inches; recessed mounting not recommended; alcoves should be wider than wheelchair

9–9. Accessibility checklist for National Park Service visitors centers. From Zube, Palmer, and Crystall, 1976.

Lavatory (sink)
Clearance: 27 inches beneath the sink
Public phones
Dial and handset should be within reach of person in wheelchair, coin slot should be at a height of 51 to 56 inches
Identification for the blind
Raised letters or numbers for room identification, placed 54 to 66 inches high to the side of the door

Figure 9–9 continued

eral about the project. *Phase II—designing the research*—includes responding to the research goals; developing strategies; sampling, choosing, and developing methods and procedures; pre-testing them; and refining the POE budget. The purpose of *phase III—data collection*—is to gather information, while not neglecting the significant ethical problems that may arise. *Phase IV—analyzing the data*—represents a serious weakness in many POEs: greater sophistication is needed as well as a willingness to eschew quasi-scientific methods and adopt simple approaches when appropriate. *Phase V—presenting the data*—usually requires multiple presentation techniques as well as particular care to ensure that each information user receives information in a way he or she finds meaningful.

Seven POE methods were discussed. *Walk-through interviews* are used both for initial data-gathering and as the major data-collection strategy in a POE. As used by the New Zealand group, the walk-through includes a two-and-a-half- to four-day program in which seven to ten participant groups are interviewed during a touring interview and immediately afterward in a review meeting. Walk-throughs are rich in information and relatively quick to carry out but may suffer from a lack of comparability. *Workshop sessions* serve the dual purpose of learning about the setting and reporting progress. They are useful in helping the client feel a part of the POE but also may be distorted by group dynamics and politics. *Interviewing* is perhaps the most common POE method. It is useful in that it helps clarify the motivations and rationales of users; it is less useful in cases where respondents have difficulty remembering or are worried about sensitive questions. *Questionnaires* are very efficient ways of collecting large amounts of information but share the potential problems of interviews: people may forget or misrepresent their answers. *Recording participants' use of time* may be done through interviews, time budgets, and observations. The critical incidents technique can be used to gather specific incidents of user behavior; the specificity of this technique can be used to combat vagaries of memory. *Observing environmental activity* is useful because it is not susceptible to the problems of self-report measures and can be quantitatively analyzed, but it does not reveal reasons or motivations for activity. *Methods of recording the physical setting,* including checklists and other techniques, can be used to measure and observe the setting directly. Like other observation techniques they bypass problems with self-reporting but do not reveal motivation or intention.

ACKNOWLEDGMENTS

For their thoughtful comments on previous drafts I would like to thank Richard Barnes, Robert Bechtel, Jan Reizenstein Carpman, John Gray, Robert Marans, Stephen Margulis, William Michelson, and Richard Wener.

REFERENCES

Archea, J. C. 1977. The place of architectural factors in behavioral theories of privacy. *Journal of Social Issues* 33:116–38.

———. 1984a. Personal communication.

———. 1984b. *Visual Access and Exposure: An Architectural Basis for Interpersonal Behavior.* Ph.D. diss. Pennsylvania State University.

Bakos, M., R. Bozic, D. Chapin, J. Gandrus, S. Kahn, W. Mateer, and S. Neuman. 1979. *Group Homes: A Study of Community Residential Environments.* Cleveland: Architecture/Research/Construction.

Bakos, M., R. Bozic, D. Chapin, J. Gandrus, S. Kahn, and S. Neuman. 1981. *Group Home Booklet.* Cleveland: Architecture/Research/Construction.

Bechtel, R. B., and R. K. Srivastava. 1978. Post-occupancy evaluation of housing. Report submitted to the U.S. Department of Housing and Urban Development.

Benton, C. C. 1984. Personal communication.

Butterfield, D. I., and J. R. Anderson. 1980. An examination of return rates for mail questionnaires. Paper presented at the Council of Educators in Landscape Architecture Conference, Madison, Wisconsin.

Carmines, E. G., and R. A. Zeller. 1979. *Reliability and Validity Assessment.* Beverly Hills, Cal.: Sage Publications, Inc.

Carson, D. H., S. T. Margulis, R. Carson, and R. Wehrili. 1980. Post-occupancy evaluation: A practical strategy for obtaining control groups. *Environment and Behavior* 12:541–51.

Connell, A. 1986. Personal communication.

Cook, T., and D. Campbell. 1979. *Quasi-experimentation: Design and Analysis for Field Settings.* Skokie, Ill.: Rand McNally.

Cooper, C. C. 1975. *Easter Hill Village.* New York: Free Press.

Daish, J., J. Gray, and D. Kernohan. 1982. *Post-occupancy Evaluation Process Guidelines.* Wellington, New Zealand: Victoria University School of Architecture.

Dillman, D. A. 1972. Increasing mail questionnaires response in large samples of the general public. *Public Opinion Quarterly* 36:254–57.

Dillman, D. A., and J. A. Frey. 1974. Contribution of personalization to mail questionnaire response as an element of a previously tested method. *Journal of Applied Psychology* 59:297–301.

Farbstein, J., and R. E. Wener. 1982. Evaluation of correctional environments. *Environment and Behavior* 4:671–95.

Flannagan, J. C. 1953. The critical incident: Techniques in the study of individuals. In *Modern Educational Problems:* Report of the 17th Educational Conference, New York, October 30-31, 1952, ed. A. E. Traxler. Washington, DC: American Council on Education.

Francescato, G. S., S. Weidemann, J. R. Anderson, and R. Chenoweth. 1979. *Residents' Satisfaction in HUD-assisted Housing: Design and Management Factors.* Washington, D.C.: U.S. Department of Housing and Urban Development.

Friedmann, A., C. M. Zimring, and E. Zube. 1978. *Environmental Design Evaluation.* New York: Plenum.

Galtung, J. 1967. *Theory and Methods of Social Research.* New York: Columbia Univ. Press.

Gordon, H., J. Estogue, M. Kantrowitz, and K. Hart. 1984. Nonresidential buildings: Program description and performance overview. *Proceedings of the Ninth Annual Passive Solar Conference,* September.

Howell, S. C. 1980. *Designing for Aging: Patterns of Use.* Cambridge, Mass.: MIT Press.

Ittleson, W. H., L. G. Rivlin, and H. M. Proshansky. 1970. The use of behavioral maps in environmental psychology. In *Environmental Psychology: People and Their Physical Settings,* ed. H. M. Proshansky, W. H. Ittleson and L. G. Rivlin. New York: Holt, Rinehart & Winston.

Kantrowitz, M. 1984. Report on occupancy evaluation from the passive solar commercial buildings program. In the *Proceedings of the Passive and Hybrid Solar Energy Update.* Washington, D.C.: U.S. Department of Energy.

Kaplan, R. 1978. Participation in environmental design: Some considerations and a case study. In *Hu-*

manscape: Environments for People, ed. S. Kaplan and R. Kaplan. North Scituate, Mass.: Duxbury Press.

Keys, C. R., and R. E. Wener. 1980. Organizational intervention issues: A four-phase approach to post-occupancy evaluation. *Environment and Behavior* 12:533–41.

Knight, R. C., and D. E. Campbell. 1980. Environmental evaluation research: Evaluator roles and inherent social commitments. *Environment and Behavior* 12:520–33.

Landesman-Dwyer, S., J. G. Stein, and G. P. Sackett. 1978. A behavioral and ecological study of group homes. In *Observing behavior* Vol. 1: of *Theory and Applications in Mental Retardation,* ed. G. P. Sackett. Baltimore: University Park Press.

Linton, M., and P. S. Gallo. 1975. *The practical statistician: Simplified handbook of statistics.* Belmont, Cal.: Wadsworth.

McGrath, J. E. 1982. Dilemmetics: The study of research traces and dilemmas. In *Judgment Calls in Research,* ed. J. E. McGrath, J. Martin, and R. A. Kulka. Beverly Hills, Cal.: Sage.

Marans, R. W., and K. F. Spreckelmeyer. 1981. *Evaluating Built Environments: A Behavioral Approach.* Survey Research Center. Ann Arbor.

Moos, R. 1974. *Evaluating Treatment Environments: A Social Ecological Approach.* New York: Wiley.

Moos, R. H. 1975. *Evaluating Correctional and Community Settings.* New York: Wiley.

Picasso, J. 1984. Post-occupancy evaluation at AT&T. Paper presented at the annual meeting of the Environmental Design Research Association, San Luis Obispo, California.

Preiser, W. F. E. 1981. *Navajo Mission Academy New Student Housing.* Albuquerque, N.M.: Univ. of New Mexico School of Architecture and Planning.

Reizenstein, J. E. 1980. The importance of presentation format. *Environment and Behavior* 12:551–59.

Reizenstein, J. E., and M. A. Grant. 1983. *Report No. 16: Design Guidelines for Hospital Signage and Wayfinding Aids.* Ann Arbor: Office of Hospital Planning, Research and Development, Univ. of Michigan.

Shibley, R. 1984. Personal communication.

Sommer, R. 1984. *Social Design.* Englewood Cliffs, N.J.: Prentice-Hall.

Weidemann, S., J. R. Anderson, D. I. Butterfield, and P. M. O'Donnell. 1982. Residents' perceptions of satisfaction and safety. *Environment and Behavior* 14:695–725.

Weisman, G D. 1981. Evaluating architectural legibility: Wayfinding in the built environment. *Environment and Behavior 13,* 189–204.

Wener, R., and R. Olsen. 1980. Innovative correctional environments: A user assessment. *Environment and Behavior* 4:478–94.

Wheeler, H. 1978. These kids aren't babies—they're grownups: The socializations and work world of attendants in a changing institution. In *Opportunity for Control and the Built Environment: The ELEMR Project,* ed. R. C. Knight, C. M. Zimring and W. H. Weitzer. Amherst, Mass.: The University of Massachusetts Environmental Institute.

White, E. T. (n.d.) *Building evaluation in professional practice.* Tallahassee, Fla.: School of Architecture, Florida A&M University.

Whyte, W. H. 1980. *The social life of small urban spaces.* New York: Municipal Art Society of New York. Film.

Wineman, J. D. 1982. Office design and evaluation: An overview. *Environment and Behavior* 14:271–99.

Wineman, J. D., and C. M. Zimring. 1982. A study of group homes for developmentally disabled people. Report to the National Endowment for the Arts.

Zeisel, J. 1981. *Inquiry by Design: Tools for Environment-Behavior Research.* Monterey, Cal.: Brooks/Cole.

Zeisel, J., and M. Griffin. 1975. *Charlesview Housing: A Diagnostic Evaluation.* Cambridge, Mass.: Architecture Research Office, Harvard Graduate School of Design.

Zimring, C. M., and J. E. Reizenstein. 1980. Post-occupancy evaluation: An overview. *Environment and Behavior* 12:429–51.

———. 1981. A primer on post-occupancy evaluation. *AIA Journal* (November), 52–57.

Zimring, C. M., W. H. Weitzer, and R. C. Knight. 1982. Opportunity for control and the designed environment: The case of an institution for the developmentally disabled. In *Advances in Environmental Psychology, volume IV: Environment and Health,* ed. A. Baum and J. Singer. Hillsdale, N.J.: Erlbaum.

Zube, E. H., J. H. Crystal, and J. F. Palmer. 1976. *Visitor Center Design Evaluation.* Amherst, Mass.: Institute for Man and Environment, Univ. of Massachusetts.

CHAPTER 10

CHILDREN AND BUILT ENVIRONMENTS

A REVIEW OF METHODS FOR ENVIRONMENTAL RESEARCH AND DESIGN

Suzanne Ziegler and Howard F. Andrews

A variety of reasons may be suggested for the consideration of children and built environments as a discrete topic in a volume about research methods in environmental design. All of these reasons derive ultimately from the truism that children and adults differ as individual actors and population groups along dimensions that are critical for environmental design, including, for example, physical size, cognitive development, social competency, personal mobility, autonomy, and control. Thus, children *act* differently from adults within and upon the built environment; secondly, children *react* differently from adults to the built environment; thirdly, certain environments are designed explicitly for children's activities or for children as users. Finally, given the basic differences between adult and child subjects outlined above, different methods of data collection and measurement are necessary to capture the quality of children's interactions with the (built) world around them.

As actors, children generally have less input into the design of the built spaces they inhabit than do adults. Adults exercise choice over their house or apartment layout, so long as personal financial constraints or an extremely high occupancy rate do not disallow choice. Children are not usually important as decision makers in family housing choices; although their needs (for a private room, or proximity to an acceptable school, for example), may be important considerations for their parents (see, for example, Michelson 1977). As active participants in choice of house or neighborhood, however, the child's role is generally small, although it may increase with age.

As inhabitants of a home and a neighborhood, children may be very active users of facilities, and often the facilities they use the most are little used or unused by adults. Sometimes children's usages are in conflict with those of adults; more often they are simply separate.

It is not unreasonable to suggest that, to a considerable extent, children who cohabit with adults are occupying a different, albeit contiguous, space. The playgrounds, corridors, and other indoor and outdoor built public spaces that they use are either unused, little used, or very differently used by adults. Within the residential unit, rooms that are much used by adults—like bathrooms and living rooms—may be less used by children, who may spend much of their time—depending on their age—in their own sleeping or play area.

In part because children are physically and cognitively different from adults and in part because they do, to some extent, use different physical spaces and facilities, we can expect their perceptions and evaluations of their built environment to be different from those of their parents and of other adult users of the same spaces.

Finally, and most pertinent to the present discussion, we can expect that, in order to find out how children interact with the built environment, how they use it, perceive it, and evaluate it, we will need different tools from those used to study the behavioral interactions of adults with their environments. Some research methods that are frequently used with adults may be less useful with children; others, of quite limited utility in studies of adults and the built environment, may be eminently practical with children. And still others may be invented solely for work with children.

Differences between studying adults and children in interaction with their physical environment stem not only from differences between those two subject groups but also from the difference in the relationship between subjects and investigator. Since investigators are virtually always adults, their basic understanding of objects and events is likely to be qualitatively similar to that of adult subjects, but qualitatively different from that of child subjects. In this sense, an adult investigator of children's environmental interactions is akin to an ethnologist working in a culture foreign to his or her own, and therefore faced with having to build in safeguards against culturally biased interpretation of the data (see for example, Little 1980).

Given the distinctive characteristics of undertaking research with children as a population of subjects, many of the substantive questions of research in person-environment relations involving children remain similar to those addressed in research involving adults. These may be broadly grouped into three categories: questions concerning children as users of the built environment—*behavior,* patterns of activities, and utilization of environmental settings and facilities; questions concerning children's perception of the built environment—relating in particular to the development and formulation of the child's *cognitive representations* of environmental settings of different scales; and questions concerning children's perception of environmental settings that focus on the child's evaluation and appraisal of environments—that is, on the nature and quality of children's *attitudes* towards given environmental settings. The ultimate goals of research practice involving children and built environments are entirely compatible with the broad objectives of environmental research in general: to identify, utilize, and evaluate alternative appropriate *methods* and alternative appropriate *research designs,* for given *populations* with respect to given *environmental settings,* and given *research questions.* In terms of day-to-day research practice, the questions concerning the selection of particular methods for collecting and analyzing information are addressed once the research problem, environmental setting, and subject population have been adequately specified. Far less attention to date has been given to research strategies designed to evaluate alternative research methods per se in systematic fashion, and particularly in the case of research on children and the built environment.

A NOTE ON METHODS OF DATA COLLECTION

A number of points raised in the preceding paragraphs may be illustrated by noting briefly some of the considerations involved in obtaining data about children and built environments. Given the difficulties and differences involved in gathering data from children, it is perhaps not surprising that they have been so much ignored by environmental designers and evaluators. A common alternative to dealing directly with children is instead to ask adults—parents, teachers, or neighbors—to report on children's usages and preferences. Sometimes this is done in addition to, rather than in place of, querying or observing the children themselves. For example, Medrich et al. (see Berg and Medrich 1980; Medrich et al. 1982) in their study of the out-of-school activities of sixth-grade school children in Oakland, California, had parents fill out a questionnaire about the children's activities at the same time as an interviewer spent an hour with each child, asking questions about his or her activities. Children of this age (eleven to thirteen years) are able to respond to an interviewer's reasonably straightforward questions without great difficulty, and various pencil-and-paper instruments may be used to collect data. Some investigators have used maps, drawings, and diaries to collect what is essentially self-report data from children on their perceptions, use, and evaluation of their environments.

Much younger children have far greater difficulty in responding to directed inquiry. Because their language and literacy skills are less developed than those of adults, direct observation of physical behavior is more common than interviewing. Researchers often use both strategies, with observation usually preceding interview and generating the relevant questions. As with interviewing, observation may be more or less structured and it may build in reliability and validity checks. Although it is usually performed by human observers with cameras, sometimes either hand-held still or movie cameras are used or even a time-lapse method. Observers may be intrusive and interact verbally with the children as participant-observers; or, more usually, may seek to be unobtrusive and noninteractive.

Mark (1972) lists a number of techniques that have been used for eliciting children's topographical representations of the physical environment (see fig. 10–1). These include four direct techniques: pictorial sketches and drawings, maps constructed by the subject, modeling environments using toys, and verbal descriptions and reports. All four methods have been used experimentally by Piaget and his associates, as well as by other researchers. Only the last requires a primarily linguistic mode, which is the weakest mode with young children. Drawing pictures and maps requires graphic competence, which is unreliable in children before the concrete operational stage (elementary school age, or about age seven to twelve).

Two indirect techniques used to elicit children's spatial knowledge are direct observation of children's actions and verbal behavior, followed by derived inferences as to the processes underlying the observed behavior; and way-finding tasks in which the subject's movements in response to a direction are observed, or the subject is asked directions to or locations of places. Again, both involve children's ability to produce and receive sometimes complex verbal messages. The avoidance of linguistic and graphic tasks as the sole or primary tool for eliciting children's spatial perceptions is a hallmark of the studies of pre-adolescent children.

THE MEASUREMENT OF ENVIRONMENT-RELATED BEHAVIORS

As with adults, children's perceptions and usages of the built environment are of interest to designers who wish to understand such interactions as a guide to effective user-tested design. Children's behavior, as it may be influenced by their built environment, is also of interest to social and health sci-

A. EXTERNAL REPRESENTATIONS

Technique	Outline of Procedure	Competence Variable	Illustrations of the Technique
Pictorial sketches and drawings	Subject is asked to "draw a picture" of an environment as seen from a horizontal or oblique perspective.	graphic motoric	Anderson and Tindal (1972); Arnheim (1967); Hart (1971); Ladd (1970); Lee (1964); Piaget & Inhelder (1967).
Maps constructed by the subject	Subject is asked to show the location of objects in the environment (a) at a reduced scale, (b) from a vertical point of view, (c) using designated symbols to represent landscape elements.	graphic motoric	Appleyard (1970); Gittens (1969); Hart (1971); Laurendeau & Pinard (1970); Lynch (1960) ; Piaget & Inhelder (1967); Piaget et al. (1960); Rand (1969); Shemyakin (1962); Wood (1971).
Modeling environments using toys	Subject is asked to place toy block replicas of elements in the environment in positions corresponding to their placement in the environment.	motoric	Laurendeau & Pinard (1970); Piaget & Inhelder (1967); Piaget et al. (1960); Stea and Blaut (1972).
Verbal description and reports	Subject's verbal comments and descriptions of an environment are analyzed. Analysis of literature and other popular culture for the images conveyed. Use of scaling devices and environmental inventories.	linguistic	Anderson & Tindal (1972); Gittens (1969); Lynch (1960); Piaget & Inhelder (1967); Piaget et al. (1960); Von Senden (1960); Boulding (1968); Strauss (1970).

B. INFERENCES FROM BEHAVIOR

Technique	Outline of Procedure	Competence Variable	Illustrations of the Technique
Experimentation with animals	Animals (rats) are studied as they move through mazes. Their choice of pathways to the goal are noted for the effects of learning or "past experience" from previous trials.		Tolman (1948).

10–1. Techniques for eliciting topographical representations. Adapted from L. Mark, "Modeling through Toy Play: A Methodology for Eliciting Topographical Representations in Children," in **Environmental Design: Research and Practice,** *vol. 1, Proceedings EDRA 3, ed. W. Mitchell. Los Angeles, 1972.*

Technique	Outline of Procedure	Competence Variable	Illustrations of the Technique
Inferences from animal behavior in their natural habitat	Animal behavior is observed in a natural setting (e.g., in a jungle). Inferences are drawn about the internal processes responsible for particular behaviors.		Altman & Altman (1971).
Observations and inferences from the behavior of the subject	Experimenter observes the behavior of people in the environment. He then draws inferences about the processes underlying that behavior. These inferences are sometimes tested with a more controlled experimental design. This technique is often used in observations of children's play behavior in a naturalistic setting. Inferences are drawn about the underlying processes through analysis of the child's actions and verbal outputs.	motoric linguistic	Freeman (1916); Werner (1948); Brown (1932); Mandler (1962); Von Senden (1960); Shemyakin (1962); Piaget (1954); Piaget & Inhelder (1967); Piaget et al. (1960).
Way-finding tasks	The subject's movements in response to specific directions are observed. Subject is asked directions of locations of landscape elements.	linguistic	Follini (1966); Lynch (1960); Ryan & Ryan (1940).

Figure 10–1 continued

entists who look at possible influences of built environments on children's behavior both within and beyond the immediate settings in question. The tools used to measure children's environmental perceptions and usages differ from those used to measure adult–environment interactions in these respects: they are less often based exclusively on self-report; they less often depend mainly on verbal feedback; they more often depend on direct observation, especially of children's manipulation of concrete objects, such as models.

A theoretical model for the understanding and prediction of children's spatial perceptions and behavior that has had profound influence on how researchers investigate children's environmental interactions is that developed by Piaget. Piaget's investigations of children's spatial understanding (Piaget and Inhelder 1967; Piaget et al. 1960; Hart and Moore 1973) have strongly influenced both what is believed about children's environmental awareness and also how such perceptions are measured, in any specific environmental context. Piaget's theory of children's development of spatial cognition follows his general theory of cognitive development, which asserts that children become increasingly capable of encompassing formal, abstract dimensions with age, and that young children lack understanding of abstractions and can learn only if they can manipulate concrete objects. He describes four major periods of spatial cognitive development: the sensorimotor period (infancy); the preoperational period (preschool years); the concrete operational period (middle childhood); and the formal operational period (adolescence and adulthood). These stages are associated with specific capabilities for understanding symbols, having a concept of object permanence, combining points on a route, reversing a route, and so on.

Piaget devised various experiments to test the appearance and degree of development of spatial abilities in children. These tests, given to preschool and school age children, all involved the manipulation of placed objects in space. For example, children were asked to build in a sand-box a model of their built and material environment—the school buildings, roads, rivers, and so on; to trace in the sand their route from home to school; to draw the model; and to reorient the model after the school building was rotated 180 degrees. While these tests avoid the gross underestimate of accuracy of young children's environmental perceptions introduced by verbal or graphic self-report techniques, there may be problems for children in translating from larger to smaller scale that mask real environmental knowledge (see Siegel et al. 1978, 228–29). Nonetheless, these tasks, which Piaget devised to test children's understanding of spatial relations in the physical environment, have been adapted by geographers, planners, and others to be used as tests of children's perceptions and representations of specific environment and behavior settings; and these concrete measures can be a valuable supplement to interviews, drawings, and especially observation as indicators of which aspects of his physical environment a child is aware of, afraid of, satisfied with, and so on.

Given the enduring significance of Piaget's work for our understanding of child-environment relations and of the developmental path for cognitive representation in particular, the following discussion of methods for investigating children's environmental interactions is organized according to Piaget's four age-stage periods of cognitive development. An alternative organizing schema might follow increasing spatial scales of environmental settings for children's activities and experiences (see, for example, Saarinen 1977). Such scales are themselves not independent of age (Andrews 1973), however, and with children as subjects, research methods are more directly determined by age-related factors of competency and are, by and large, less influenced by the nature of the environmental setting under investigation.

Infancy (Sensorimotor Period)

From birth to age two, children's interactions with the environment are very confined in range, compared to older children, and their movements and place-uses tend to be heavily determined by others. During this period, infants develop the concept of object permanence—that an object still exists when it is temporarily hidden from sight—and become able to move in a coordinated way through limited terrains. Children this young cannot be interviewed, so any direct contact between researcher and subject must be essentially observational, not interactive.

Interest in infant-environment interactions centers on two kinds of health concerns: first, a concern for the infant's safety and physical well-being; and second, a concern for his developmental stimulation (Bronfenbrenner 1979).

The relationship between infant morbidity and mortality and conditions of housing is usually established through some kind of epidemiological survey that depends wholly on aggregate data. The investigator looks at data on hospital admissions for infants, for example, and relates them to neighborhood of residence. A major problem in such studies, as is well known, is in assigning significance to one aspect of the environment rather than another (Andrews 1982). For example, slum residence may be found to be related to much higher frequency of hospital admission for infants with upper respiratory and gastrointestinal disorders (Christensen 1956). Are the age, condition, and amenities of the infants' housing responsible, or are the major causes poor nutrition, poor hygiene, or other aspects of the social/human environment that may not be directly related to housing? Some dangers to infants are clearly aspects of the man-made environment whose alteration would eliminate significant hazards even in the absence of any social change (lead-free paint is one example; windows above a certain minimal height from the floor are another). More often, however, the effects of the physical environment may be expressed only indirectly, or in combination with nonphysical environmental qualities. This is true in all man–environment studies; but it is particularly true for the very young, whose "access . . . to the physical environment and . . . [its] features . . . that are salient are to a very large degree under social control" (Parke 1978, 35; see also Michelson and Roberts 1979).

Thus, scrutinizing hospital admissions or accident records and relating pathology to housing or neighborhood may be useful and valid, but only if nonphysical, social environmental characteristics are known to be of little direct relevance or, alternatively, are subject to control. An example of the latter is the work of Essen and his associates in England (1978a, 1978b), who looked at relationships between health and achievement indices and housing history, including indices of crowding, amenities, and tenancy type. Their methodology consisted of health-oriented interviews with parents, followed by correlational analyses of health and educational achievement of the children. Data on crowding and access to basic amenities (sole use of a bathroom, hot water supply, indoor lavatory) were gathered during the parent interviews. Unlike many earlier and more naive investigations, these studies controlled for social class, and looked for possible health and achievement correlates of crowding and other conditions within social class. Like some other studies that attempt to relate physical environment during infancy and early childhood, the methodology was retrospective and consisted of interviewing the parents some years after the events in question. Their results showed a significant relationship between crowding and lowered academic achievement but not poorer health. (For similar findings on crowding, see Parke 1978, 70–72. Gad [1973] contains a thorough review of a variety of conceptual difficulties involved in research on the effects of crowding.)

The advantage of the epidemiological method that surveys institutional records for incidence of infant morbidity and mortality, and relates incidence to area and type of residential environment, is that it is noninvasive: it does not require home visits. To make home visits to observe characteristics of infants and their environments requires considerable cooperation and trust from parents and caretakers, is subject to refusals and thus to sampling bias, and, not least of all, is costly. Since built environments in which infants spend almost all of their time are private homes, we have relatively few infant–environment studies. Perhaps, as increasing numbers of mothers go to work and put their infants in daycare centers, more studies will be done on infant–environment interaction, because access and economies of scale will make such work easier to execute. Such studies will not address the lack of information we have on the home environment, however, nor will they aid in the development of research methods ideally suited to the home setting. As Parke notes,

> It is one of the issues of the history of psychology that so little attention has been paid to one of the most important settings for the developing child—the home. In fact, until recently more was known about orphanages, institutions, hospital wards, preschools, and playgrounds than home environments . . . in spite of the recent increase in child-care environments outside the home for infants and young children, the home environment remains a principal setting in which the child's early social and cognitive development takes place. The early social and physical environment that the home provides for the child has a marked impact on his later social and cognitive development. [1978, 34–35]

In the existing home-based infant–environment studies that focus on environmental stimulation, the principal research methodologies used are, first, direct observation of infants in interaction with the physical environment; and second, inventories of amenities and facilities available to the infant. Some instruments, such as the Caldwell Inventory of Home Stimulation (Caldwell 1968) include both methods. The Caldwell inventory has almost twice as many items based on parent interview as on direct observation by the researcher, and such a ratio is clearly more economical of time than would be the reverse.

Much of the interest focuses on the extent to which the environment stimulates or retards the child's cognitive and social development. Since, following Piaget, child development specialists attach considerable importance to the infant's opportunity physically to manipulate concrete objects in his environment (that is, the contingency-responsiveness of the environment), much of the observation (laboratory as well as home-based) focuses on the child's interaction with toys and other small, mobile objects, rather than on the influence of room or house layout, major furnishings, and so on. Nonetheless, one can derive room and furniture layouts from Piagetian principles (for an example, see Burnette 1972). Also, since barriers to the infant's motoric, visual, and tactile exploration have been found to be negatively related to cognitive development, it becomes important to designers to consider the minimization of such barriers in planning safe and stimulating interiors.

Just as the safety of the domestic environment depends in great part—though not entirely—on how adults control children's use and access, so does the potential stimulation level of that same setting. The extent to which infants are allowed to explore their environments and thus to be stimulated depends not only on how the builder has designed the space, but as much or more on how the adult residents arrange objects within it. Chase et al. (1974) used questionnaires, videotapes, and still photography to document the use by infants and their caretakers of various three-dimensional play materials designed to enhance development. Findings from these documented records were used as a basis for improving the developmental potential of the toys. Toys made of more flexible materials, for example, were found to be more responsive to infants' manipulations. Color and movements (for example, using encapsulated water, or plastic objects in a tub) permit caretakers to observe infants' visual tracking.

The issue of privacy and the physical environment is a clear example of behavior whose dimensions are social, but are affected by space. While it is an important issue in the research literature, it is rarely focused on infants or very young children. An exception is a study that looked at possible effects of the presence in the house of a "stimulus shelter"—a room in which a one- to two-year-old child could escape intense stimulation—as it might relate to later cognitive development (Wachs 1971). High intensity stimulation in the home from which a child cannot escape is negatively correlated with several aspects of psychological development in infants of seven to eighteen months. A stimulus shelter, a quiet place out of the flow of home traffic and high visual and aural input, may serve a protective function for infants.

Negative effects of noise as an over-stimulator of infants has also been studied (see Parke 1978, 60–65). The methodology is most often one of direct observation: measurement and recording of interior or exterior noise levels. Some measures of noise can be inferred from information obtainable in the absence of direct observation; for example, whether or not a television set was turned on at a particular time, or how many people were present in the home. Such information can be gathered through parental self-report measures, such as the time budget, with or without an interviewer present. Heft (1976), for example, determined the level of interior and exterior background noise as well as the activity level of the home, entirely from interview-based data. From this self-report data, he developed indices of distinctive versus overlapping sounds and of the frequency of sudden, unexpected sounds. Although his subject population consisted of five-year olds, the same or a similar parental interview could be used in studying background noise exposure for infants.

Exterior noise can be measured much more directly, without intruding into homes. The noise from an expressway or airport can be measured at a residential site without going inside. Estimates can be made of differences between first floor and progressively higher floors in the same apartment building. Thus, Cohen et al. (1973) found a significant association of noise level, by floor, with auditory discrimination loss in young children. This loss was shown, increasingly over time, to be a significant predictor of lowered reading achievement in school-age children. The significance of this study, in the words of its authors, is that "it demonstrates that despite seeming adaptation . . . prolonged exposure to high intensity noise is related to deleterious after effects." It is also worth noting, from the point of view of research design and data collection, that *parents'* subjective rating of the noisiness of their apartments was not related to measured noise level by floor, suggesting that direct observation of noise level (that is, independent measurement) is superior to interview- or questionnaire-obtained self-reports for detecting outcome effects in the situation.

Outcome measures of infant–environment interactions—effects of the built environment in combination with social factors—are most often health measures or measures of cognitive development or intelligence. These may be aggregates or individually collected; and they may be coincidental with or very much later than the presumed stimuli. Essen et al. (1978a, 1978b) related health measures obtained on sixteen-year olds to housing histories from birth. Wachs et al. (1971) related interior residential noise level to the cognitive development of infants in the seven- to twenty-four-month age range. Both the retrospective and simultaneous relating of infants' environment to behavior are common research strategies. The issue of whether or not to use mechanical instrumentation in addition to observation is addressed by Bechtel (1974), who suggests that mechanical aids such as cameras or tape-recorders are most useful when the behaviors of interest can be precisely defined and/or are ephemeral (for example, particular facial gestures). He notes that, even when such instrumentation is suitable, cost factors may make it impractical.

Perhaps the best combination of methods to use is one that includes structured parent or caretaker interviews with brief, direct observation. Items of both kinds, from the Caldwell inventory referred to earlier, were used in the study by Wachs et al. (1971) to examine the relationship between infants' social and physical home environment and their cognitive development. The latter was measured with the Infant Psychological Development Scale (which is based on Piaget's model of intellectual development), and includes assessments of the infant's abilities to track visually, to attain goals through manipulating tools, and to relate to objects. Physical environmental attributes related to such abilities include noisiness of neighborhood and home (negatively) and variety in interior decor and colors (positively).

In summary, infant–environment interactions are most often studied either indirectly, through examination of aggregated records, or interviews with parents; or directly, through observation. The fact that infants are typically home-based and indoors makes observation costly, and relatively rare.

Preschool Children (Preoperational Period)

Preschool children (ages two to six or seven), unlike infants, are capable of some mental manipulation even in the absence of concrete phenomena, and they are able to represent the external world symbolically. They have the necessary motoric competence and, at the upper end of this age range, some of the graphic and linguistic abilities to describe topographies that Mark identifies (fig. 10–1). But these abilities are much less developed than they are in older children, and consequently researchers frequently depend heavily on direct observation and the manipulation of concrete objects in studying environmental interactions of preschool children.

Preschool children do show a fully developed ability to recognize and use landmarks by the age of four or five years. Children of this age are able to operate in an objective (nonegocentric) frame of reference, although this ability may not extend from small to large spaces. Studies testing these abilities generally bear out Piaget's conclusions about the timing and sequence of the development of landmark recognition and frames of reference. Some work suggests that children of this age can also follow simple plans of rooms, with some assistance in initial orientation and alignment (see, for example, Spencer and Darvizeh 1981). They have difficulty, however, coordinating landscapes in space to construct routes. Thus the "cognitive maps" (or pre-maps) of preschool children are normally uncoordinated networks of landmarks (Siegel et al. 1978). Some researchers have found, however, that kindergarten children are capable of fairly sophisticated symbolic place recognition, involving the reading of aerial photos of familiar and unfamiliar communities (see, for example, Stea and Blaut 1973; Stea and Taphanel 1974).

Unlike infants, preschool and young school-age children spend considerable amounts of time playing outdoors, where they can be observed publicly. In fact, the study of child–environment interaction for preschool and young school-age children is overwhelmingly the study of children outdoors: in parks, playgrounds, streets, lanes, empty lots, backyards, and other public, private, and semipublic spaces. Correspondingly, the most common source of *interview*-elicited data about these children, unlike infants, is the children themselves rather than their adult caretakers.

In the majority of studies of children and the outdoor environment, the subject population is children, either of unspecified ages (all of the children playing in a particular setting or area), or ranging from four to twelve years in most cases. Studies whose subjects are all in the preschool age range are, not surprisingly, carried out in nursery schools, daycare centers, and kindergartens, where the age range is from two to six years. One such study in a daycare center (Rohe and Patterson 1974) employed stop-frame movie camera techniques to observe the behavior of twelve children, aged two to five, under varying levels of density and resources. Filming was done from opposite corners of the room for two minutes per take. Raters (whose inter-reliability was established) then recorded every instance of four categories of behavior (social interaction, participation, constructiveness, use of area) for each ten-second (twenty-frame) sequence.

The behaviors observed in the last of each of these sequences (the twentieth frame) were then recorded on behavior checklists. Thus the behaviors observed in the single frames recorded were understood in their situational contexts. While density was found to be associated with aggressive behavior, the quality of resources available was shown to alter and sometimes to reverse this relationship.

Kinsman and Berk (1979) used direct observation without a camera in two play areas of a nursery-kindergarten room. The observers focused on each of the two areas in turn for five minutes per observation, and dictated every twenty seconds into a hand-held recorder the identity of each child in the setting, the size and composition of the group, the type of play, and the affective expression of each child. These observations were used to document changes in group size, sex ratio, and type of play activity (relevant/irrelevant; integrative/uninvolved), the spatial arrangement of activities, and affect. Changes were found to be significantly related to deliberate changes made by the experimenters in the arrangement of the spaces. For example, girls made much more use of existing blocks and building toys when a partial wall separating these items from a playhouse area was removed.

Several studies have been made in nursery and in laboratory settings of the effects of spatial density (room size and design) on children's behavior. Loo (1978) observed a group of preschool children who had been ranked on several characteristics (hyperactivity, behavior disturbance, and motor inhibition) in a larger and a smaller room, and counted their avoidance, distractibility, and affective behaviors in the two settings. The author found that hyperactive boys were more affected than others by higher density. They sat less and paced more; their "predisposition toward restlessness and a short attention span tended to be elicited in the high density condition through motoric channels" (ibid., 502–3). Another study showed that while increasing (spatial) density tended to increase aggressive behavior, sheltering activity areas by inserting partitions increased cooperative behavior. Both density and partitioning affected children's activity choices (Rohe and Nuffer 1977; reviewed in Gump 1978, 141). Ellis (1972) briefly describes several studies of children at play in a laboratory setting, where he was able to use cameras to produce a film strip, which was projected onto a grid, so that coordinates of position in space of an observed child-actor were easily calculated and made machine scorable. From such raw data are derived measures of frequency of use of items in the room, time on the apparatus, and so on (see also Herron and Frobish 1969; Wuellner et al. 1970).

All these studies used direct observation to examine the use of space by young children in play groups. In focus and in method, they typify the relatively scant literature that is exclusively concerned with children in the preschool age group. Several such studies of two- to five-year olds are reviewed by Smith and Connolly (1972), who liken their common methodology to animal ethology: the unobtrusive observation of animal behavior in naturally occurring behavior settings. The literature on tools for observing human behavior and social interactions derives principally from this ethological tradition (see Jones 1972), and notably from the research of Barker and Wright (Wright 1960). For a collection of observational tools and schema, see Sackett (1978, vol. 2) and Simm and Boyer (1970). Figure 10–2 provides an example of an observation checklist, recording "social behavior on the playground," developed by Hambleton and Ziegler (1974) for use in a study of the integration of trainable mentally retarded (TMR) children into a regular elementary school building. Observers spent fifteen minutes on the playground at recess times, each noting the behavior of a single child from the experimental group. The behaviors noted in the columns from left to right in figure 10–2 represent least to most friendly interactions between the target child and other children in the playground. For

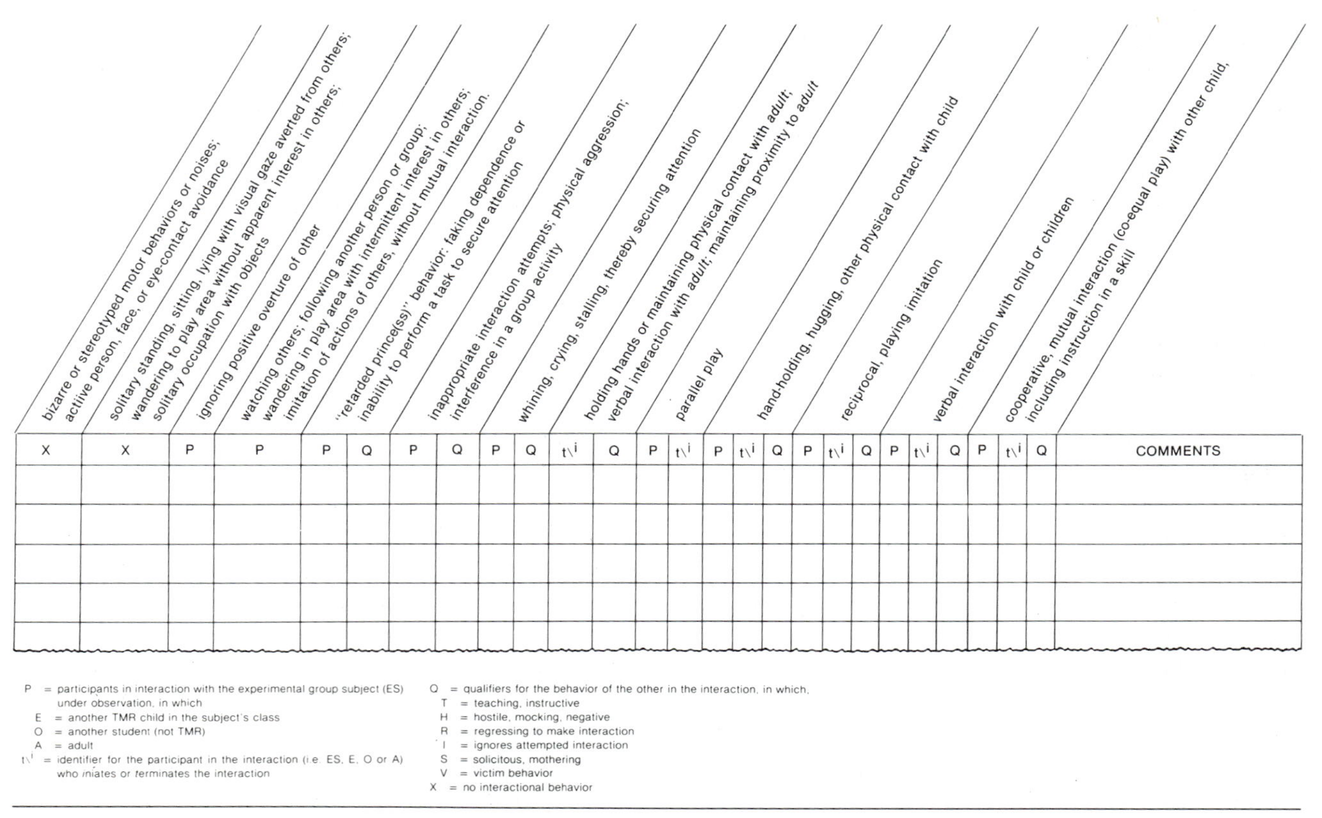

bizarre or stereotyped motor behaviors or noises; active person, face, or eye-contact avoidance
solitary standing, sitting, lying with visual gaze averted from others; wandering to play area without apparent interest in others; solitary occupation with objects
ignoring positive overture of other
watching others; following another person or group; wandering in play area with intermittent interest in others; imitation of actions of others, without mutual interaction.
"retarded prince(ss)" behavior: faking dependence or inability to perform a task to secure attention
inappropriate interaction attempts; physical aggression; interference in a group activity
whining, crying, stalling, thereby securing attention
holding hands or maintaining physical contact with adult; verbal interaction with adult; maintaining proximity to adult
parallel play
hand-holding, hugging, other physical contact with child
reciprocal, playing imitation
verbal interaction with child or children
cooperative, mutual interaction (co-equal play) with other child, including instruction in a skill

X	X	P	P	P	Q	P	Q	P	Q	t\i	Q	P	t\i	P	t\i	Q	P	t\i	Q	P	t\i	Q	P	t\i	Q	COMMENTS

P = participants in interaction with the experimental group subject (ES) under observation, in which
E = another TMR child in the subject's class
O = another student (not TMR)
A = adult
t\i = identifier for the participant in the interaction (i.e. ES, E, O or A) who iniates or terminates the interaction

Q = qualifiers for the behavior of the other in the interaction, in which,
T = teaching, instructive
H = hostile, mocking, negative
R = regressing to make interaction
I = ignores attempted interaction
S = solicitous, mothering
V = victim behavior
X = no interactional behavior

10–2. Checklist for recording social behavior on the playground. From Hambleton and Ziegler 1974.

the interactive behaviors, the observer records not simply presence/absence, but also whether the target child initiated and/or terminated the interaction, as well as other qualitative characteristics of the interaction.

Smith and Connolly (1972) point out that these types of study have produced extensive "behavior dictionaries" or taxonomies, which are valuable because they make reliable classification and comparison possible. The fact that such studies have not greatly expanded in number in the last ten years, as these authors anticipated, may be accounted for by their cost in man-hours. Another reason may be that the independent variable being manipulated in many of these studies was density/crowding, and this area may have become research-saturated by the mid-1970s. The importance of this work, however, is that it recognizes the value of structured and reliable observation for producing data that is comparable across time and place. It is disappointing that there has not been more cumulative use and development of specific behavioral observation guides. Observation, despite its cost, remains the best tool for evaluating place- and space-related variables for young children, and the nursery and play-group-based studies have the additional advantage that children can be observed doing what is both natural and constructive for them: manipulating concrete, play objects (note also, Schwartzman 1978, 308–15).

Observation of children outdoors, around houses, and in parks, streets, and lanes has produced an extensive literature (Cooper-Marcus and Moore 1976). The quality of the data collection ranges from slapdash to exceedingly exacting. The studies most often cited include Hole (1966) and Cooper-Marcus (1974, 1975). Hole reports on extensive studies of children's play behavior in high- and lower-density housing estates in Britain. The studies combined methods, including a detailed analysis of site utilization from layout plans and site inspections; interviews with residents, caretakers, and housing managers; and systematic observation of children's play use of all types of spaces, with more intensive studies of playgrounds. It was this last technique—systematic observation of children at play—that became the hallmark of the British housing estate studies in the 1960s and inspired a host of careful, ethologically based descriptions of children's play use of space. Characteristic of the methodology in this group of studies is a preplanned route, walked through (as in the Hole studies) or driven through at pre-scheduled intervals (that is, using time-sampling) to guarantee thorough and equally distributed observations. Hole, for example, observed at each of fifteen housing estates for up to four days, walking through the same route at several pre-appointed times each day, for a total of about ten thousand observations. These were supplemented by time-lapse photography. Rhodeside et al. (1970), finding that most children at the housing estate they studied did not confine their play to the planned play areas, concluded that "it would be better to see the entire estate as a potential play area. Emphasis would then fall on making this [entire] environment a safe . . . place which could withstand the rigors of such activity and [where] there is a minimal amount of annoyance to residents from this general activity spread." Rhodeside's recommendation was a practical, observation-based alternative to another suggestion that had been made for "bigger and better" planned play areas.

Following in the same tradition, Cooper-Marcus (1974, 1975) trained observers, checked on and obtained high inter-rater reliability, and distributed walk-through observations over weekdays and weekend days, to obtain and analyze detailed descriptions of children's use of outdoor space in a newly developed urban housing project in California. The site plan was divided into sub-areas, each with a specific observation site. Observations were made every twelve minutes, for twelve hours a day for five days, for a total of three hundred observations. Each sub-area was observed once during each hour of the day. Moore (1974a, 1974b) looked specifically at a neighborhood playground in a high-density public housing project, and at two school playgrounds in Berkeley, to compare childrens' differing usage of layouts and sets of play equipment. Moore et al. (1979) developed verbal and graphic reporting forms for observations of children's activities. Cohen et al. (1978) described fifty facilities and settings for play and child care at U.S. military establishments. One goal was to identify key design features that facilitate child development. They used a combination of architectural inventories of physical context, site, built facility, and furnishings; observations of the spatial behavior of children and staff; and focused interviews with facility planners, directors, staff, and sometimes with children and parents. Observations were recorded with behavioral maps, sketches, and photographs.

The technique of describing the users, by age, gender, and sometimes ethnicity, and the uses of specific built sites is often called behavior mapping (Ittelson et al. 1970). It can be used (as, for example, by Coates and Sanoff 1972) to describe behavioral density and diversity, and to yield profiles of activity types and group types (see fig. 10–3). Activity maps can be constructed to compare the

BEHAVIORAL PROPERTIES OF PHYSICAL ELEMENTS

	A. Behavioral Density (Number of Observations)		*B. Number of Activity Types*	*C. Behavioral Diversity Index A/B*	*D. Number of Children Observed*
	No.	*%*			
Front stoop and private side walk	17	11.3	4	4.25	21
Backyard	12	8.0	5	2.40	20
Public sidewalk	17	11.3	4	4.25	52
Street	9	6.0	3	3.00	18
Parking lots	22	14.7	7	3.14	48
Woods	14	9.4	4	3.50	59
Public open space	25	16.6	5	5.00	128
Community open space	34	22.7	8	4.25	173

PHYSICAL ELEMENTS AND AGE GROUPS

	Front Stoop and Private Sidewalk		*Backyard and Backyard Patio*		*Public Sidewalk*		*Street*		*Parking Lots*		*Woods*		*Public Open Space*		*Community Open Space*		*Chi-square*
	No.	*%*	*No.*	*%*	*No.*	*%*	*No.*	*%*	*No.*	*%*	*No.*	*%*	*No.*	*%*	*No.*	*%*	
Infant (under 2)	2	9.5	1	5.0	2	3.9	0	0.0	3	6.2	9	15.2	2	1.6	6	3.5	0.01
Preschool (3-5)	5	23.8	0	0.0	9	17.3	4	22.2	6	12.5	11	18.7	24	18.7	9	5.2	0.01
Young child (6-9)	3	14.3	8	40.0	18	34.6	3	16.7	13	27.1	27	45.8	60	46.9	36	20.8	0.01
Adolescent (10-13)	5	23.8	7	35.0	1	1.9	10	55.6	6	12.5	9	15.2	33	35.8	62	35.8	0.01
Teenager (14-18)	6	28.6	4	20.0	22	42.3	1	5.5	20	41.7	3	5.1	9	7.0	60	34.7	0.01
Totals	21	100.0	20	100.0	52	100.0	18	100.0	48	100.0	59	100.0	128	100.0	173	100.0	0.01
Chi-square	ns		0.05		0.01		0.01		0.01		0.01		0.01		0.01		

10–3. Reporting results of observations of children's activities. From G. Coates and H. Sanoff, "Behavior Mapping: The Ecology of Child Behavior in a Planned Residential Setting," in **Environmental Design: Research and Practice,** *vol. 2, Proceedings EDRA 3, ed. W. Mitchell. Los Angeles, 1978.*

distribution of activities over environmental settings; and individuals can be tracked and their behavior recorded at intervals, to compare level of social behavior (verbal, nonverbal, isolated) over settings (see Holahan 1978, 33–35).

Rothenberg et al. (1974) combined activity sampling, behavioral mapping, individual tracking (in behavioral settings) and interviews with children to describe the site use at three different kinds of playgrounds. While the authors do not comment on the relative weight given to each method and instead report all their data in the aggregate, one must assume that interview data, with children of preschool and early school age, must be primarily a supplement to, and not a substitute for, data obtained from observation.

With preschool children, as with infants, direct observation of behavior in the environment of interest is the preferred method of study. However, advances in cognitive and linguistic abilities in the two- to six-year-old period makes structured interviewing a useful supplement to observation. This is especially so when interviewing takes the form of probing around concrete stimuli, such as the environmental features themselves (ideally), or three-dimensional models or photographs.

Somewhat neglected but potentially useful are unobtrusive mechanical methods of observation or measurement of children's activities. One example that might be replicated for a child population is described by Bechtel (1970), where a hodometer was used to measure the volume of pedestrian traffic at particular points in a defined area. Pressure plates sensitive to a child's weight might be located at strategic points in a particular setting to record automatically the movement of children passing by.

School-age Children (Concrete Operational Period)

School-age children, especially the pre-adolescent group, are the age group most studied by scholars interested in the relationship between the physical environment and children's behavior. There are several reasons for this, both pragmatic and programmatic. Children between the ages of six and thirteen years of age are outside a great deal. They are principal users of playgrounds; they exercise increasing freedom to play unsupervised, so that they are more clearly demonstrating their own choices and expressing their own preferences in where they go and what they do there. And they are generally somewhat more accessible to an adult than are adolescents, whose relationships with the adult world are more guarded.

The ethological or naturalistic observation procedure associated with Hole, Cooper-Marcus, Moore, and others has been discussed above in the section on preschool children. When older children are the subjects of investigation, other techniques may be used to supplement or substitute for direct observation.[1]

While most researchers continue to prefer to include observation as a basic tool when investigating the interaction of school-age children with their physical environment, they also use questionnaires, interviews, cognitive maps, and various other self-report techniques that depend on verbal and/or graphic skills. Aiello et al. (1974) used a walk-through strategy to document children's outdoor activities in a suburban residential area, making thirty trips, two hours each, over three months, and sampling to cover all times of the week. They supplemented their observations with interviews with some of the children in the area. The same strategy was used by Thomsen and Borowiecka (1980) to arrive at design guidelines for outdoor winter play environments (see also Rothenberg et al. 1974).

While they depend on children's capacity for concrete operational thought, interviews do not require literacy skills, fine motor development, or good eye-hand coordination. Techniques that do, including map drawing, should probably be reserved for use with children twelve years and older, unless they are being supplemented with other, more age-appropriate techniques (but note the findings reported by Maurer and Baxter [1972]). While younger children can and do draw pictures of their physical worlds, it is questionable whether such pictures and diagrams can be relied on to reflect accurately children's environmental perceptions and knowledge. Individual differences in drawing skills may interfere, to make drawings noncomparable. One study asked young children (five- to eight-year olds) to draw "what you like best in the playground" in order that their preferences could be elicited for traditional or modern play structures. While some apparently real preferences emerged, with significant differences between boys and girls, the authors note that some facilities with relatively low visibility (such as hopscotch squares) were underrepresented compared with the use of the facilities as directly observed by the researchers. They note that the pictures, while useful, cannot replace observation and/or structured interviews (Moore and Wochiler 1974). One of these authors, in another paper, describes the use of children's drawings, in combination with informal and systematic observation, interviews, and on-the-spot user feedback, to evaluate two school playgrounds (Moore 1974a). A pictorial technique that does not depend on children's memories supplies them with photographs of locations or objects in a particular environmental setting (such as a playground, schoolroom, or library) and asks them to sort the pictures into two or more piles according to given criteria ("the ones you like and those you do not like," for example). This fairly simple version of the Q-sort technique has the potential for revealing pertinent characteristics of objects or settings to which children respond, but about which they may be unable to verbalize.

Weinstein (1982) found that ten-year old children's self-reported desire for privacy was uncorrelated with their observed use of privacy booths placed in a classroom. Even though there are problems with operationalizing a multi-meaning phenomena such as privacy for empirical research (see Wolfe 1978, for example), Weinstein's report suggests that observation, rather than self-report/interviews, may be a more reliable method for evaluating likely facility usage with children of this age.

The principal methods for studying school-age children in environmental settings are thus observation and personal interview. Two major studies of child–environment interactions have focused on the middle childhood period. These include Roger Hart's study of the children of a small New England town, where all but four of the eighty-six children were in grades one to six (Hart 1979); and the Oakland study (Medrich et al. 1982), which sampled from all sixth graders in the city. The first uses a wide range of methods, including observation and interview; the second depends entirely on personal interviews. Given the relatively comprehensive nature of these two studies, it is well worth describing the methods utilized in each in greater detail.

Hart's study *Children's Experience of Place* (1979) is comprehensive in several respects. First, he followed *all* the six- to eleven-year-old children of a small, suburban New England village (n = 86); secondly, he studied them intensively over a considerable period of time (about a year and a half); and finally, he used a considerable number of different methods to obtain the desired information (fig. 10–4) relating to children's spatial activities, place knowledge, place values and feelings, and place use. His theoretical framework is Piagetian, and research tasks were structured with a clear sense of children's age-related cognitive abilities.

The basic methodological approach is descriptive, rather than experimental. While some controlled experimentation was included, it is clear that naturalistic observation, of an ethnographic or ethological sort, was the preferred technique. Hart's goals were both substantive and methodological: to describe the landscape as it exists for children, and, in the process, to develop and test methodologies for investigating children's environments and behavior. His intention was to observe them closely and intensively in the ethnographic tradition, and to come to know their environmental behaviors as fully as possible. Such an investment of an investigator's time in face-to-face relationships with his subjects is unusual, and while it can rarely be replicated, it has the potential to elicit data about children's private uses of and feelings towards their physical environment on a scale that is both more extensive and intensive than most studies can encompass.

Hart was not able to use standardized observation as a primary data-gathering technique because of the large scale of the environment he studied (children's whole territorial range). He did use it, however, as the "ultimate check on questions aris-

Date	Procedure	Population
October 1971	Census of village population by age, sex, and occupation	Town children
November–December 1971	Meeting children, making preliminary observations, pre-testing the child activity survey	Town children
February 1972	Child activity survey—winter (2 weeks)	Town children
March–April 1972	Landscape modeling exercise (8 weeks)	Town children
March 1972	Winter play place drawings (3 days)	Town children
April–May 1972	Child activity survey—spring (1 week)	Town children
May 1972	Place familiarity exercise—color transparencies (4 weeks)	Town children
June 1972	Child activity survey—summer (1 week)	Town children
June–July 1972	Range restrictions: structured interview (2 weeks)	Subsample
July 1972	Geographic diaries (2 weeks)	Subsample
August–September 1972	Place feeling expeditions: photography (6 weeks)	Subsample
September 1972	Summer play place drawings (3 days)	Township children
September 1972	Weekend geographic diaries (2 days)	Town children
September 1972	Place familiarity exercise—aerial slides (1 week)	Subsample
October 1972	Range restrictions interviews (1 month)	Town children
November 1972	Parents' questionnaire (1 week)	Parents of sample population
November 1972	Child activity survey—fall (1 week)	Town children
Spring 1973	Landscape modeling—follow-up exercise	3 children
Spring and summer 1973	Pursuit of unanswered and new questions through individual interviews of children and parents	Town children and parents

10–4. Field procedures in a comprehensive study of children's experience of place. From Hart 1979.

ing out of other procedures'' (33). This was done through very frequent drive-around tours of the town, often supplemented with photographs. The observations made during these tours and recorded, and the photographs, were kept as a log. Together they provided a check on locations, activities, and materials used during play, as well as the routes of ''secret paths,'' and so on. The usual length of a tour was forty-five minutes to an hour and a half, and the route taken and sequence and direction of visual scans were previously mapped, to avoid flaws in sampling. One drawback of such activity surveys by automobile is the difficulty of identifying individuals and their activities at a distance, particularly in loosely textured environments with numerous opportunities for activities away from roads and streets. However, Hart did manage to gather a good deal of information in this way.

Two types of self-report techniques were employed: the geographic diary and a variety of interview formats. For the first, to investigate their spatial activity and place use, children were given seven identical aerial photographs of the town. Each day they were to record on an accompanying sheet their locations, companions, and activities, and to draw with different colored pens the foot or bike and vehicular routes followed that day. With such material, Hart obtained a pattern of the child's spatial activities for one week in summer, and was able to derive a variety of measures including maximum daily distance traveled, number of daily journeys from home, means of transport, and proportions of accompanied versus unaccompanied, and adult- versus child-directed journeys.

Each child was visited between 5 and 7 P.M. daily by the investigator, who gave any assistance in the task that was needed. Depending on the child's age, the assistance varied from considerable to minimal. Because of the amount of time required from the researcher, the diaries could be used with a subsample of the children only, and for relatively brief periods of time (one week). This technique is really a variant of the time budget, collected for out-of-school hours and supplemented by the graphic device of route-tracing. Some of Hart's findings demonstrate clear sex and age differences for various activities recorded in this fashion.

Hart used interviews at several points in his study. Children and parents were interviewed separately, and information was obtained on where children were permitted to go, where they could go without parental permission, and where they could go alone and with peers. Children were asked a series of four questions about such locations and they watched while the investigator colored in each location on an aerial photograph. Such photographs, used in both the diary and direct interview instruments, served to keep the children's interest at the same time as increasing the accuracy of their reporting. For both these reasons, the use of aerial photographs for collecting data on macroenvironments and children's activities can be strongly recommended. A subsample of parents was asked a series of questions on the restrictions they place on their children's wanderings. Hart notes, in his review of the relevant literature, that parents are not reliable reporters of their children's spatial activities, and thus cannot be depended on as the primary source of information. In addition, he observed a considerable discrepancy between the rules as stated by parents and as followed by children. Both children's actual place use and their permitted place use can be of interest to planners, but it is important to note that parents' input may be more valid for ''permitted'' and far less for ''actual'' place uses by children.

Another interview technique used color photographs and still a third used aerial photographs for eliciting place knowledge of the town and asked children to tell anything about these places, if they recognized them, including name and location. Their responses were tape recorded. The amount of data gathered in this way made this method practical only for individual, not aggregate, analyses. No single scoring/coding system could be found to summarize it. A further interview was used to elicit data on children's preferences for places. This was structured by asking the child to name his or her ten favorite places; the places disliked; the places considered by the child to be dangerous; and those considered frightening (always in the home town). The investigator then colored in all places named on aerial photographs, obtaining verbal descriptions where necessary. A drawback of the method was a tendency to deemphasize private or unique places, which were harder to describe or locate verbally. A combined interview-observation format was used in the place-expedition strategy, in which the child is asked to take the investigator along to all the places that are important to the child. This strategy does not depend solely on the child's verbal responsiveness or facility, since subjects were asked to demonstrate their uses of and feelings towards a place. They were also given a polaroid camera and asked to think of ten best places, to go to each, and to photograph it. At each site, children were asked to say and show what they liked about it in a series of five open-ended questions. Finally, children ordered the photographs from most to least favorite. Each expedition occupied between one and three days during the summer.

Besides these observational and self-report techniques, themselves demonstrating considerable ingenuity and creativity on the researcher's part, Hart also incorporated a number of experimental techniques into his study. Landscape modeling, a variant of one of Piaget's tests, was used, in which children were asked to place tokens representing home, school, and "all the places you know" on an 8- by 8-foot piece of white paper. Their goal was to build a giant model of their town. Besides the wooden models and toys, they could also use crayons and modeling clay. When the child was satisfied with his product, he and the investigator pretended to "drive through" the scheme. The child was to name each place represented, while the investigator traced around the objects and labeled the outline. Children's verbal and nonverbal activity during the experimental situation was recorded, to aid in analyzing the maps, and as a record of the order in which the elements were placed on the paper. Several different kinds of analysis were performed on the maps, to yield information on children's spatial knowledge and cognitive spatial development.

The difficulties involved in this method are several. For the older children, the amount of time and detail they wanted to use made the task impracticable. But smaller maps (2 feet × 2 feet) proved to be unmotivating. Younger children often used crayon in lieu of models and were reluctant to make changes in the finished products even when they discovered errors. In this respect, three dimensional objects are superior.

Hart's methodology is impressive in its extensiveness and variety. Unlike most studies, his was of sufficient duration and intensity to include a great deal of individual data, gathered over a long period of time. Most investigators will be unable to duplicate many of his strategies, except with very small samples. But if one were focusing on a much smaller scale than the children's whole local range and emphasizing built rather than natural environments, some of the techniques he describes might be practical. The geographic diary, for example, could be adapted for particular behavior settings, like rooms in a house, or a school, or particular parks or streets, to learn how children use particular structures or constructed spaces. Place expeditions could be limited to home–school routes and associated paths and hangouts, where children spend much of their time. Similarly, favorite place photographs could be limited to built spaces. All such limitations should make the task easier to do and the results more useful for specific design or planning purposes.

The recently published "Oakland" study by Medrich et al., *The Serious Business of Growing Up,* (1982) uses a very different methodology to explore child–environment–activity relationships. Hart had a strong interest in children's development of spatial cognition and was interested in testing developmental theory in his sample of six- to eleven-year olds. Medrich et al. do not explore developmental sequences or stages. Their sample was chosen so as to minimize age as a factor, by using children drawn from a single grade in school (grade six). Hart's study was place, not activity, centered. While it examined place usage in relation to activities, it was children's experience of place that was his primary focus. Medrich et al. focus primarily on children's out-of-school activities and consider places as activity settings. To use a photographic metaphor, Hart's pictures emphasize the frame and setting, while Medrich et al. emphasize the activity observed within the frame. Differences in methodology were to some extent determined by these different foci but were also related to a differential emphasis on methodology itself. Hart had a strong interest in exploring a variety of research strategies—in part because of his developmental focus, which suggests the need for different tools for different ages. Medrich et al. are content, not methodology, focused. They use a single format—the participant-interview—supplementing their subjects' responses with a questionnaire used with the parents. The interview questions were mostly directed (for example, About how often do you play in the school yard after school or on weekends?); and a number of Likert-scale type items were also included (such as: How safe do you think it is going around the neighborhood by yourself—very safe, fairly safe, or not very safe?). In addition, the interviewer handed the child a questionnaire to complete by himself, requiring the child to circle precoded responses (such as: My classroom is too noisy—yes/no).

Care was taken to ensure a random and representative sample. The 764 children who completed the interview were 87.2 percent of the "eligible cases," defined by a randomly selected 20 percent of the grade six population of twenty-two elementary schools, stratified to reflect the socioeconomic variation of the city. Sampling bias, while small, was introduced by (1) the refusal of one of twenty-two randomly chosen school principals to involve his grade six children; (2) the inability to reach 5 percent of the total sixth-grade enrollment because of lack of current addresses or telephone numbers; (3) a parental refusal rate of 10.6 percent; and (4) inability to complete the interview in 2.2 percent of cases. Similar sources of bias have been noted in other large-scale studies (for example, Hill 1980).

The authors assert that the high completion rate of 87.2 percent, well-distributed across gender, ethnic, and socioeconomic groups, in combination with the carefully randomized and stratified sampling procedure, must result in a highly representative sample. While this is a reasonable assertion, the limitations to its validity listed above are worth noting because, in a one-time, single-method approach, any sampling bias assumes significance, since it usually cannot be corrected for by a comparison of results over time, or a comparison of results from different methods. Careful pre-testing of instruments for reliability and validity is usual. In the present case, the researchers pre-tested and compared various formats, and on this basis chose the personal interview over self-administered time-use diaries, questionnaires administered in class or sent home through the mail, and telephone interviews. They found personal interviews to be superior because (1) they minimize the need for reading skills; (2) they can cover more ground in a fixed time; (3) they are not perceived by the subjects as test-like; (4) it was easier to get permission to interview children at home than at school or elsewhere; and (5) they also allowed for interviewing the parents.

No pre-test for reliability or validity of the items was reported. A post-test for reliability (stability of responses over time) was made by recontacting the subjects three months later, by telephone, and asking them a subset of the original questions. The authors report "remarkably stable" results from this post-test across all socioeconomic and ethnic groups. They also point to evidence, from another study, that children's responses to questions are most stable over time when (1) the subject matter is personal, and (2) the questions do not ask about attitudes or opinions (Medrich et al. 1982, 29; Vaillancourt 1977). While the Oakland questionnaire definitely stresses factual reporting of one's activities, there are, however, a significant number of items that ask for evaluations and opinions as responses (for example, Is your classroom too noisy? or, What things don't you like about this neighborhood?).

The composition of the interview derived from three time-research tools: time budgets, single activity analyses, and activity enumerations. Time budgets link activities to both time and place. Single activity analyses may or may not document time used. Sometimes they focus on children's activity preferences, or on their use of facilities such as parks or recreation centers. Activity enumerations are usually checklists of activities, and children are asked about their participation in each. Like single activity analyses and time budgets, they may include (but very often do not) reference to the locations of activities.

While the emphasis in this study was on activities, not places, the built environment was examined as a barrier and a facilitator to movement, as well as the focus of specific activities. Reference to location and activity setting was included in many of the questions. For example, in the series of items about the child's reading activities, one question was: When you're here at home, do you spend any time reading—not for school, but just reading for fun? Response to this item could, potentially, be analyzed in combination with the information collected by the interviewer on number of persons residing in the household, kind of residence and neighborhood, noisiness of the household, and so on, to yield some suggestive data on the relationship between the physical environment, the social environment (socioeconomic status, ethnicity, language spoken in the home, parents' facility in English, and so on) and children's tendency to spend time at home in leisure-reading. But an emphasis on the built environment does not characterize the study, although some activity/place correlations (by gender or ethnicity) are reported.

Locations of activities were usually ascertained. In the list of questions asked about the lessons taken by children and the sports and groups in which they participated, the "where" question was always asked. For public and semipublic facilities such as school, library, and YMCA or YWCA, usage could be examined by children's place of residence, to determine the association between distance, quality of amenity or facility, and frequency of use. As there is also information on the frequency and duration of activities at these various locations, this data base is useful as a source of information on how much structured, out-of-school time children in this age group spend in various facilities.

There is also a list of places that children may visit in any capacity—as an individual or part of an organized or loose social group—with the question as to how often they have done so in the current school year. The settings listed are public and private places of education and/or recreation—museums, zoos, parks with pools, skating rinks, and the like. Again, simply knowing how frequently pre-teens use such facilities is of interest to planners. By using a personal, home-based interview on a large and representative sample of an appropriate age-set in an urban setting, and by depending mainly on the self-report method for objective data on activities, the Oakland study presents a useful model for collecting activity and place-related data, although it is clearly unlikely to tap more private place use and less organized activities, as Hart was able to do. A particular interest in the built environment would dictate more emphasis on the quality of settings and their facilities, but should maintain an objective tone for the majority of items: using a question such as, What activities have worked well at ______ place? as opposed to, How well do you like ______ place for studying? The latter question, while it may usefully be asked, should not stand alone as an indicator of the quality of the setting, because its subjective nature weakens the reliability of the response, especially from a child.

The advantage of highly structured interviews and questionnaires is that of facilitating the comparison, aggregation, and quantification of individual data. A disadvantage of the procedure is the potential loss of information through closed-ended questions, which make it less likely that unanticipated and possibly interesting data will be obtained.

Another large-scale study of school-age and adolescent children that relied wholly on interview data but that does focus on developmental aspects of spatial perceptions is reported by Wolfe (Wolfe and Laufer 1974; Wolfe 1978). The subject was children's concepts of privacy, and the nine hundred respondents were between five and seventeen years old. Children were asked open-ended questions, and responses were content-analyzed to yield user-generated response categories. Thus, for example, thirty-nine coding categories were derived from responses to a question about the meaning of privacy. The relationships of age to response categories were examined. Other studies of privacy and territoriality in the use of home by pre-adolescent and adolescent children (see Parke 1978, 66–70) should indicate to designers the importance of private spaces for older children and their belongings. (Even such small and overlooked spaces as clothes closets are significant.)

Studies of School Buildings. In the 1960s and early 1970s, many elementary schools were redesigned or constructed in North America on what was called the open plan—which indicated many fewer interior walls and a differing and more fluid use of space than in the traditional "egg-crate" design of fixed, rectangular rooms of equal size. How children, teachers, and curricula fitted into and functioned in such an open environment became the subject of several investigations. Durlak et al. (1972), Durlak and Lehman (1974), Brunetti (1972), and Rivlin et al. (1974) investigated aspects of open school–person interactions. For example, Durlak et al. used trained observers to record numbers of people occupying spaces at varying times; group composition; activities; the amount of movement; and the number of tools being used. They used this data to describe the general structure of activity settings, teaching style, and student activities. They then compared traditional with two models of open-plan schools on these dimensions, finding "higher" general activity patterns (flexible use of space, arrangement of furniture, and grouping of students) in the most physically open schools.

In another paper (Durlak and Lehman 1974), the authors describe a questionnaire methodology used to collect further information on which to compare the different kinds of school buildings. While the observationally gathered data (on furniture layout, the proximity of teacher to students, numbers and sizes of student clusters, and so on) in each setting were used to provide a basis on which to compare environmental usages, the questionnaires provided information on teachers', principals', and students' perceptions of the environment. This is a typical use of a direct (observation) and an indirect (questionnaire) technique to elicit objective and subjective data to describe and compare environments. The same combination characterizes Brunetti's 1972 study, "Noise, distraction and privacy in conventional and open school environments." He measured noise level in two open-space schools and one traditional school, and related his observations to data gathered from questionnaires asking students about perceived noisiness and distraction in the school settings.

Rivlin et al. (1974) had children in open classrooms in grades two, three, and four furnish scale models of their room in two ways: as it currently existed and as they would like to see it. The children "were able to translate their images of the room to the model . . . and to use the model to answer detailed questions about the room" (151). There are several good points to note in the design of this study: The use of concrete stimuli was appropriate for the age group from a developmental theory perspective; the initial task of translating to the scale model an observable environment provided a means of validating the methodology before applying it to elicit children's preferences; and utilizing a concrete stimulus such as the child-designed model made direct questioning of young children more reliable than attempting to elicit information about a subject that lacks such a concrete referent.

Peterson, Bishop et al. studied eight-year-old children's perceptions of school playground equipment by showing them photographs of existing pieces of play equipment during personal interviews and asking them to state their preferences in two different formats: paired comparison and rank order. The use of photos makes verbal response brief and simple, which is clearly advantageous with young children. The two formats produced identical results, and reliable and valid scales of preference. The authors then used these preference scales to predict probability of use of each piece of equipment, which they measured with a hidden time-lapse camera on the playground. They point out that while they found very high correlations between the interview and observational data, the direct observation is more sensitive to differences in rates of use/preference among alternatives than are the scales. In a second study, the authors used the same photographs and asked adult designers to predict children's preferences: They did so with remarkably low accuracy (see Bishop et al. 1972; and Peterson et al. 1973).

Another use of photography in school settings is to record the location of teacher–pupil interactions. Several investigators have established that where a child sits influences how much on-task interaction he has with the teacher (see Gump 1978, 155).

Generally, researchers who deal with pre-adolescent populations avoid methodologies that are very indirect, and/or that depend on verbal/literacy skills. Observation and personal interview on topics that are either highly factual (such as, How many times this school year have you gone to the YMCA?) or straightforward and personal (for example, Which play structure do you like better?) are the most direct approaches to studies of children's environmental usages and perceptions, and require no reading or writing; and they are, as we have noted, the preferred techniques. Such methods are, necessarily, more time-consuming and more expensive than group-administered questionnaires, whose use with pre-teen populations is generally avoided. Bunting and Semple (1979), however, report very high levels of internal consistency of items and reliability of scales for an instrument they call ERIC—the Environmental Research Inventory for Children. Based on a previously developed measure for adults (McKechnie 1972, 1977) ERIC attempts to measure children's environmental dispositions as they are reflected in beliefs, attitudes, and values. The measure has eight content scales, including such dimensions as *urbanism, environmental adaptation,* and *need for privacy.* Each scale is derived from the configuration of several items: for example, I would enjoy riding in a crowded subway (urbanism scale); I like to go to shopping centers where everything is in one place (environmental adaptation scale); I am happiest when I am alone (need for privacy scale). The measure was used with 105 children, from grades four to ten. It was administered during class time, in the classroom. Children read the test items silently and asked for help when needed. Help was solicited by a high percentage of the youngest group, but by none in the oldest group, indicating the difficulty of the use of the questionnaire format with young children.

No data on validity is reported. Test-retest reliability was quite high overall, but lower for some scales. The authors indicate that further item revisions will precede validity testing. They foresee the utility of their measure for investigating many aspects of childhood environments. If further tests do prove the validity of this measure, it has the potential to yield interesting information on environmental stimuli and settings, but the application of a version of McKechnie's ERI protocol to such a wide age range of children may be fraught with problems in attempting to establish concept validation across obviously differing stages in cognitive development. A detailed study using the original ERI protocol with older teenage children (graduating high school students) is reported in Roberts (1976; note also, Burchett 1971; Horvat 1974).

There is a general consensus that, with school-age children as with younger age groups, the most reliable methods of investigating environmental behaviors involve direct observation, either through photography, or more commonly, by personal observation. However, self-report data can be used with some apparent success, as Medrich and his associates show in their study of Oakland children. (Medrich et al. do not report on the validity of subjects' responses, which would, of course, be extremely difficult to establish.) Such self-report data depends, however, on considerable interviewer presence and input and the tailoring of items to the concrete and personal. Whether the responses of young adolescent children to a formal, large-group-administered protocol such as ERIC are indeed valid, and if so for which lowest age group, remains to be demonstrated.

In dealing with children's uses of and preferences within the built environment, the opportunity for combining experimentation and observation is often overlooked. Such two-pronged research strategies have potential advantages over observation alone: They are likely to be more economical because they focus the subjects' attention/behavior on the central interests of the research and may indeed reduce the total amount of "pure" observation time that might otherwise be required. This is most readily illustrated where the researcher is interested in responses to particular objects or concrete environmental elements and attributes, such as a piece of playground equipment or a movable barrier in a classroom. Base-line observations can be made before the item is introduced, and at some time afterwards, with comparisons of the children's use of the item or other behavior being recorded. While daycare centers and schools remain the likeliest and most accessible settings for such studies, they can also be carried out in homes, where variations in parental response that influence children's access and behavior can also be observed.

Adolescents (Formal Operational Period)

By the beginning of adolescence (after age twelve), children are becoming adultlike in their capacity for formal, abstract, relational thinking; by its end, they are adults and have realized their cognitive potential. Thus it is not surprising that the research methods considered appropriate for use with adolescents are substantially the same as those used with adults. Graphic and literacy production skills, whose reliability is uncertain before this age, can now be called upon. Pencil-and-paper questionnaires can be group-administered; maps and diagrams can be not only read, but produced. In some cases, a particular technique that was first developed as a method for collecting information from adults on their place or space knowledge, usage, or perception is adapted with few or no changes to an adolescent population.

Cognitive Maps. Map drawing is a graphic skill that has been much used in combination with observation and/or other techniques, and by itself, as a tool for examining adolescents' environmental knowledge and perceptions (Kosslyn et al. 1974). Lynch, who used the technique in work with adults, later made it a central methodology of his study of children, aged twelve to fourteen years, growing up in cities in four nations (1977). The field researchers were also instructed to use systematic observation to record children's behavior in public spaces; but the individual map-centered interviews were to precede the observations, both in time and in emphasis. In the interview, children were first asked to draw a map of their area of the city and then asked a series of questions about places and activities, with reference to the maps. Scanlan

(1980) used the same combination of observation and ''mental map'' with working-class children in apartment house neighborhoods in five cities around the world. He analyzed the maps for the presence/absence of particular features, such as cars, houses, and stores; and he used the observational data to describe behavior settings (public spaces and playgrounds), play group composition, activities, and the ratios of adults to children in outdoor settings.

Generally, cognitive or mental maps are used as reflections of the cartographer's perceived space. They may be construed as indicating what is important to him, what features he recalls, uses, or is concerned about. As reflections of fact—of knowledge of an environment—they are suspect, because they are subject to systematic errors, especially of distortion reflecting a divergence between actual and perceived size and/or position of given features of the built or natural environment (see Golledge et al. 1977; Holahan 1978, ch. 9; Saarinen 1973, 1977). As projective tools, however, as Lynch and many others have used them, cognitive maps are useful and revealing of older children's (and adults') observed and perceived environments. With younger children a map-drawing task may be too difficult, physically and conceptually, to produce useful results across any number of respondents; but simplifications that require less production and a more receptive mode may be possible (note Siegel and White 1975). There is evidence, cited earlier, that young children can ''read'' aerial photographs with considerable accuracy. Coates and Bussard (1974) found that school-age children (over age ten) were able to draw on a local outline map covered by a transparent overlay, the places to which they went, the places they could not go to, and the paths they used. A summary of their findings for this age group, compared to those for younger age groups, is included in figure 10-5. An earlier example of this particular use of base-maps for children's self-reported spatial behavior is to be found in the work of Martha Muchow (Muchow and Muchow 1935).

The ability of adolescents to understand and express themselves in writing means that the full spectrum of direct and indirect, pencil-and-paper self-report techniques available for use with adults can be used with adolescents, sometimes with some modification of vocabulary and/or referents. These methods, which lend themselves to group administration in secondary and post-secondary classroom situations, are very much cheaper in time and money than direct observation. Observation, in addition to its high cost, is more difficult to employ with adolescents, because they are more exclusionary. Wolfe (1978) has shown that adolescents define privacy as ''aloneness'' and autonomy significantly more often than do younger children.

Self-reports. Self-report questions may be direct in approach: What places do you go to? What do you do there? How much do you like it? and so on. Or they may be indirect: the researchers may intend to analyze the responses in a way not obvious to the respondent. Semantic differential scales, for example, which ask respondents to choose one each in a series of paired adjectives to describe a place, may be scored to derive a single, unitary measure of attitude toward that place. Another example is the essay, on a given topic, which may be read for a purpose other than that implied in the title. For example, university students are asked to describe the place where they lived longest during their first ten years. Such essays could be read simply as straightforward descriptions and analyzed for their inclusion or omission of specific features (such as the number of rooms in a house or the size of a dwelling). In fact, these essays have frequently been used as a basis for analyzing sex differences in degree of personalization and social emphasis found in these descriptions of childhood physical environments (see Holahan 1978, ch. 8).

Hart's 1979 study of younger children's place behavior was of particular interest to us because it

Parameters	***4–5 Years***	***6–9 Years***	***10–12 Years***
HOME BASE	Compact bubbles out front doors to boundaries (usually about 50′); lateral expansion to boundary (90′–140′) and within a 120° cone of vision. Bubble out back doors (only for town houses, family private zones to a maximum 30′).	Expands by a factor of 10 in area and a factor of 5 to 8 in path length. Often includes friends' home base. Almost all girls' friends live within immediate vicinity. Boys' friends spread throughout own subdivision of site. Boys use unowned areas more than girls. Boys home base larger.	Similar to 6–9 years for both sexes. Exceptions: two boys and one girl with 4-5-year-old bubbles around house and long walking/biking paths to off-site nodes. Boys' pattern result of choice. Girls' result of parental restriction.
Activities	Triking, biking, play with dolls, toys, in dirt, jacks, jump rope, hide and seek, ball games. No sex differences.	Girls: quiet, e.g., jacks, dolls, role play. Boys: ball games, tag.	Girls define "play" as playground activity; actually they dominate playground. Boys define "play" as activities (see 6–9 years) that occur in wild areas with friends.
Zones	Family public, family private, group and section public if within sight lines. May include playgrounds (if safe path) and nearby friend's house.	Girls: mostly family public and private of own and friends' houses. Also, used playgrounds more.	Girls regularly use section public now. Boys regularly use unowned areas on-site.
TERRITORIAL RANGE	Existed for only half of all children. Usually short paths to playgrounds.	Girls: half had none or only one node within site; half went to nearby store or, rarely, to nearby scrubby area. Boys: all boys had off-site range that included stores and wild areas equally.	All children had off-site ranges. All girls went to stores, while only half went to wild areas; only one went to water area. Boys went more often to wild areas than stores and to more distant wild areas and water play areas.
Activities		Boys: fishing, catching frogs and tadpoles, shooting BB gun.	See 6–9 years.

10–5. Spatial ranges of children. From Coates and Bussard, 1974.

Parameters	***4-5 Years***	***6-9 Years***	***10-12 Years***
CHAPERONED TRAVEL	For only half of children: two went to playgrounds not used independently, two to town, one to nearby wild areas.	Half boys and three-quarter girls had chaperoned walks. Girls chaperoned to more places, half of which were stores.	More frequent for girls than boys. Girls averaged two chaperoned destinations, half of which were stores. Boys mentioned one place each, none of them stores.
Contributing Factors			
PARENTAL ATTITUDES	All wanted children within view and easy access of house. Children allowed out of sight only to go to playgrounds within boundaries or to known friend's home (never more than 2 bldg. away). Firm boundaries existed.	Much stricter with girls than boys. Girls often still kept within view of home but never boys. No girls allowed off-site. Girls were required to ask permission to leave area of house; boys were required to ask permission only when leaving the site. Firm boundaries set for girls.	For boys no distinctions made between going with friends or alone. Boys had no boundaries except truck route on South. Required to tell parents when leaving site. Girls still directly supervised. Were allowed to go shorter distances with friends. Had to tell parents when leaving vicinity of house.
SITE INFLUENCES	Boundaries set for children were small-scale differences in placement of buildings, roads, parking areas, playgrounds, etc. Sometimes even a crack in the sidewalk would be used. Large-scale site divisions not used at all.	Large-scale structure of development split site into three unequal sections to which children confined Home Bases. Availability, location and size of group private, section public, and unowned areas accounted for most differences in shape and structure of home bases and territorial ranges. Clear on-site/off-site boundaries reinforce boundaries set by parents (especially for girls).	The dynamics of site influence are the same as described for 6-9 years.

Figure 10-5 continued

employed a number of research methods in an experimental fashion. A recent Toronto-based study of adolescents similarly employed several tools appropriate to this older age group. Like Medrich et al.'s study of sixth-grade children (1982), the Toronto study used a grade-sampling method, which resulted in a sample of more than seven thousand grade nine pupils and three thousand grade twelve pupils from across the Metropolitan area. Direct observation was not used; instead group-administered questionnaires (grade nine) and student-produced area maps (grade twelve) were the key tools.

The Toronto Study. One intention of the Toronto study was to document "the distribution of all the facilities, land uses, spaces, places, activities and programs relevant to children and teenagers through Metropolitan Toronto" (Hill and Michelson 1981, 207). To aid in this ambitious effort, pairs of grade twelve students in urban geography classes were to compile a map and inventory of all these resources for an assigned area (a basic planning unit) near their school. They were given an outline map and a lengthy inventory-checklist, while their teacher, who had previously been briefed and provided with detailed instructions, was to be certain they read and understood the instruction sheets provided to them. The mapping and inventory exercise was to be done by walking through the area and noting, on a map and on the inventory checklist provided, the location of various built facilities (different types of stores, pinball machines, arenas, outdoor ice rinks, parks, and so on) as well as less building-defined places such as "places to take lessons," "where kids play," and "hazards." The intention was to compare the distribution of resources and density of children of various ages by area in order to measure neighborhood differences in children's accessibility to resources, including public, semipublic, semiprivate, and private facilities.

The second major goal of the Toronto study was "to examine the extent to which . . . teenagers' activity patterns vary from one neighborhood to another in Metropolitan Toronto . . . " (Hill and Michelson, 212). For this purpose, a questionnaire was presented to grade nine students (ages thirteen to fourteen) across Toronto. Like the Medrich et al. study of somewhat younger children in Oakland, the Toronto study gathered fairly comprehensive information on how, where, and with whom these young people spent their out-of-school time. It also included attitudinal data on what they liked and disliked about their neighborhood, and what they thought was lacking. All of this information was collected by group-administered questionnaire; no personal interviews occurred. As all questionnaires were geo-coded by location of the respondent's home (using nearest major intersection), and as certain other facts are known about the residences (for example, if they were private or public housing) it is possible to compare both within and across neighborhoods, and to pose and answer such questions as the extent to which neighborhood perceptions, activities, and perceived opportunities differ between adolescents living in state-subsidized (public) and private housing in the same neighborhood, as well as across the city (Phillips and Andrews 1982). The attitudinal questions have similar potential. Do children from Italian-speaking homes in neighborhood *X* or across Metro, differ substantially from children from English-speaking homes in neighborhood *X* or across Metro, in their satisfaction with their neighborhood or their attitudes toward ethnically or racially different neighbors? Aggregate data of this sort, gathered from an approximately one-in-four census of same-age persons in an urban area, has real utility for physical and social planning (Hill 1980; Andrews 1981). It would be virtually impossible to collect the same kind and extent of information from anything like a universe of much younger children, because of the difficulty of using a group-administered form. With adultlike linguistic, conceptual, and graphic abilities, adolescents can be studied as environment actors and perceivers with considerably more economy than younger children. The full range of oral and written self-report techniques available for use with adults can be used with adolescents, provided their language competencies (especially written) are average. Caveats pertaining to particular techniques of adult self-report (see, for example, Bechtel's comments on the semantic differential [1973]) would apply equally to adolescent populations.

SUMMARY

The purpose of this chapter has been to review methods of investigating children's relationship to the environment, stressing the built environment, and emphasizing age-appropriate methodologies. The literature on methodology, in this subject area, tends to be dispersed in articles on specific methods or contexts ("the semantic differential" or "school environments"). It is unusual to find syntheses of information on methods appropriate to child-environment investigations, and there are no comprehensive guides for this topic, as may be found in other areas of child research (for example, Boyer et al. 1973; Johnson 1976; Goodwin and Driscoll 1980). Further, some sources suggest that certain types of methodology are appropriate for "children" without distinction by age group. As we have emphasized, interviews, drawings, questionnaires, and behavior mapping are not equally valid and useful for subjects from infancy through adolescence; and techniques for eliciting information on child-environment relations depend far more on the age group of the subjects than they do on either the general research questions being addressed or the particular scale and nature of the environmental setting being examined. Similarly, one cannot expect to adapt all the methods available for use with adults to children.

Lozar (1974) offers an excellent discussion of behavioral measurement techniques for use in environmental design research. By way of a summary to this selected review of methods for studying the child-built environment interface, figure 10-6 expands on Lozar's taxonomy of various measurement techniques by suggesting, for each of the methods identified by Lozar, its appropriateness for the specific age groups from infancy to adolescence that we have utilized to organize our own discussion.

Just as children of different ages see the world through different eyes, so must we, in seeking to explore their worlds, approach them in a variety of ways. Children's cognitive development and their awareness and use of the world around them are achieved essentially through processes of creative learning: furthering our understanding of these processes similarly requires creativity in research design, ingenuity in the development of age-appropriate methodologies, and sensitivity in their application. As the child's cognitive and physical world expands, so do our paths to and within it.

NOTES

1. In cases where the children are intellectually or emotionally handicapped in their ability to respond to an interview situation, however, observation becomes the sole tool of value. See, for example, Wolfe and Rivlin's excellent study of space utilization and activities in a children's psychiatric hospital, which uses careful behavior mapping to provide a mini-longitudinal study (Wolfe and Rivlin 1972; Rivlin and Wolfe 1972; Rivlin et al. 1973).

Measurement Technique	***Appropriate Age Categories***			
	Infants	***Pre-schoolers***	***School Children***	***Adoles-cents***
Self-report methods				
1. Survey attitude instruments				
• open-ended questions				x
• directed questions				x
• Likert scales				x
• semantic differential				x
• cognitive mapping			x	x
• diaries—activity log			x	x
• photographic simulation		x	x	x
• games		x	x	x
• scale models		x	x	x
2. Interview techniques				
• unstructured		x	x	x
• structured		x	x	x
• participant interview		x	x	x
• content analysis		x	x	x
• Q-sort		x	x	x
Non-self-report methods				
3. Instrumental observation				
• time-lapse photography	x	x	x	x
• still photography	x	x	x	x
• video taping	x	x	x	x
4. Direct observation				
• behavior setting	x	x	x	x
• personal space			x	x
• time sampling		x	x	x
• mapping	x	x	x	x
• structured observation	x	x	x	x
• specimen record (from parent)	x	x	x	x
5. Sensory stimuli observation				
• lighting	x	x	x	x
• noise	x	x	x	x
• thermal comfort	x	x	x	x
6. Indirect methods				
• tracks		x	x	x
• records	x	x	x	x

10–6. A summary of age-appropriate measurement techniques. Adapted from Lozar 1974.

REFERENCES

Aiello, I., B. Gordon, and T. Farrell. 1974. Description of children's outdoor activities in a suburban residential area: Preliminary findings. In *Man-Environment Interactions: Evaluations and Applications,* ed. D. Carson, vol. 3, 187–96. Stroudsburg, Pa.: Dowden, Hutchinson & Ross.

Altman, I., and J. Wohlwill. 1978. *Children and the Environment.* New York: Plenum.

Altman, S., and J. Altman. 1971. *Baboon Ecology: African Field Research.* Chicago: Univ. of Chicago Press.

Anderson, J., and M. Tindall. 1972. The concept of home range: New data for the study of territorial behavior. In *Environmental Design: Research and Practice,* vol. 1 of *Proceedings, EDRA-3,* ed. W. Mitchell, 1-1-1 – 7. Los Angeles.

Andrews, H. 1973. Home range and urban knowledge of school age children. *Environment and Behavior* 5(1):73–86.

———. 1981. *Managing Urban Space for Children.* Centre for Urban and Community Studies, Child in the City Report 13. Toronto.

———. 1982. *Preventive Intervention for the Health and Well-being of Urban Children.* Centre for Urban and Community Studies, Child in the City Report 17. Toronto.

Appleyard, D. 1970. Styles and Methods of Structuring a City. *Environment and Behavior* 2(2):100–18.

Arnheim, R. 1967. *Art and Visual Perception: A Psychology of the Creative Eye.* Berkeley: Univ. of California Press.

Bechtel, R. 1970. Human movement and architecture. In *Environmental Psychology,* ed. H. Proshansky, W. Ittleson, and L. Rivlin. New York: Holt, Rinehart & Winston.

———. 1973. Architectural space and semantic space. In *Environmental Research and Design,* ed. W. Preiser, vol. 2, 274–79. Stroudsburg, Pa.: Dowden, Hutchinson & Ross.

———. 1974. Direct and instrumented observational techniques: A comparison. In *Man-Environment Interactions: Evaluations and Applications,* ed. D. Carson, vol. 3, 231–42. Stroudsburg, Pa.: Dowden, Hutchinson & Ross.

Berg, M., and A. Medrich. 1980. Children in four neighborhoods: The physical environment and its effect on play and play patterns. *Environment and Behavior* 12(3):320–48.

Bishop, R., J. Peterson, and R. Michaels. 1972. Measurement of children's perceptions for the play environment. In *Environmental Design: Research and Practice,* vol. 1 of *Proceedings, EDRA-3,* ed. W. Mitchell, 6-2-1 – 6-2-9. Los Angeles.

Boulding, K. 1968. *The Image: Knowledge in Life and Society.* Ann Arbor: Univ. of Michigan Press.

Boyer, E., A. Simon, and G. Karafin, eds. 1973. *Measures of Maturation: An Anthology of Early Childhood Observation Instruments.* Philadelphia: Research for Better Schools.

Bronfenbrenner, U. 1979. *The Ecology of Human Development: Experiments by Nature and Design.* Cambridge, Mass.: Harvard Univ. Press.

Brown, W. 1932. Spatial integration in a human maze. *University of California Publications in Psychology* 5(6):123–34.

Brunetti, F. A. 1972. Noise, distraction and privacy in conventional and open school environments. In *Environmental Design: Research and Practice,* vol. 1 of *Proceedings, EDRA-3,* ed. W. Mitchell, 12-2-1 – 6. Los Angeles.

Bunting, T., and T. Semple. 1979. The development of an environmental response inventory for children. In *Environmental Design: Research, Theory and Application, Proceedings EDRA-10,* ed. A. Seidel and S. Danford, 273–83. Washington, D.C.: Environmental Design Research Association.

Burchett, B. 1971. A Descriptive Study of Fourth, Fifth and Sixth Grade Students' Attitudes to Environmental Problems. Ph.D. diss., Indiana University.

Burnette, C. 1972. Designing to reinforce the mental image: An infant learning environment. In *Environmental Design: Research and Practice,* vol. 2 of *Proceedings, EDRA-3,* ed. W. Mitchell, 29-1-1 – 7. Los Angeles.

Caldwell, B. 1968. *Inventory of Home Stimulation.* Little Rock, Ark.: Center for Early Development and Education.

Chase, R., D. Williams, D. Welcher, J. Fisher III, and S. Gfeller. 1974. Design of learning environments for infants. In *Man–Environment Interactions: Evaluations and Applications,* ed. D. Carson, vol. 2, 127–52. Stroudsburg, Pa.: Dowden, Hutchinson & Ross.

Christensen, V. 1956. Child morbidity in a good and bad residential area. *Danish Medical Bulletin* 3(2):93–98.

Coates, G., and H. Sanoff. 1972. Behavior mapping: The ecology of child behavior in a planned residential setting. In *Environmental Design and Practice,* vol. 2 of *Proceedings, EDRA-3,* ed. W. Mitchell, 13-2-1 - 11. Los Angeles.

Coates, G., and E. Bussard. 1974. Patterns of children's behavior in a moderate-density housing environment. In *Man–Environment Interactions: Evaluations and Applications,* ed. D. Carson, vol. 3, 131–42. Stroudsburg, Pa.: Dowden, Hutchinson & Ross.

Cohen, S., D. Glass, and J. Singer. 1973. Apartment noise, auditory discrimination and reading ability in children. *Journal of Experimental Social Psychology* 9(4):407–22.

Cohen, V., T. McGinty, and G. Moore. 1978. *Case Studies of Child Play Areas and Support Facilities.* Milwaukee: School of Architecture and Urban Planning.

Cooper-Marcus, C. 1974. Children's play behavior in a low-rise inner-city housing development. In *Man–Environment Interactions: Evaluations and Applications,* ed. D. Carson, vol. 3, 197–211. Stroudsburg, Pa.: Dowden, Hutchinson & Ross.

———. 1975. *Easter Hill Village: Some Social Implications of Design.* New York: Fall Press.

Cooper-Marcus, C., and R. Moore. 1976. Children and Their Environment: A Review of Research 1955–1975. *Journal of Architectural Education* 29(4):22–25.

Durlak, J., B. Beardsley, and J. Murray. 1972. Observations of user activity patterns in open and traditional plan school environments. In *Environmental Design: Research and Practice,* vol. 1 of *Proceedings, EDRA-3,* ed. W. Mitchell, 12-4-1 - 8. Los Angeles.

Durlak, J., and J. Lehman. 1974. User awareness and sensitivity to open space: a study of traditional and open plan schools. In *Psychology and the Built-Environment,* ed. D. Carter and T. Lee, 164–69. London: Architectural Press.

Elardo, R., R. Bradley, and B. Caldwell. 1975. The relation of infants' home environments to mental test performance from six to thirty-six months: A longitudinal analysis. *Child Development* 46(1):71–76.

Ellis, M. 1972. Play: Theory and research. In *Environmental Design: Research and Practice,* vol. 1 of *Proceedings, EDRA-3,* ed. W. Mitchell, 5-4-1 - 5. Los Angeles.

Essen, J., F. Fogelman, and J. Head. 1978a. Childhood housing experiences and school attainment. *Child: Care, Health and Development* 4(1):41–58.

———. 1978b. Children's housing and their health and physical development. *Child: Care, Health and Development* 4(6):357–69.

Follini, M. 1966. The construction of behavioral space: A microgenetic investigation of orientation in an unfamiliar locality. M.A. thesis, Clark University.

Freeman, F. 1916. Geography: Extension of experience through imagination. In *The Psychology of Common Branches,* 161–78. Boston: Houghton-Mifflin.

Gad, G. H. K. 1973. "Crowding" and "pathologies": Some critical remarks. *Canadian Geographer* 17(4):373–90.

Gittens, J. 1969. Forming impressions of an unfamiliar city: A comparative study of aesthetic and scientific knowing. M.A. thesis, Clark University.

Golledge, R., V. Rivizzigno, and A. Spector. 1977. Learning about a city: Analysis by multidimensional scaling. In *Spatial Choice and Spatial Behavior,* ed. R. Golledge and G. Rushton, 95–118. Columbus: Ohio Univ. Press.

Goodwin, W., and L. Driscoll. 1980. *Handbook for Measurement and Evaluation in Early Childhood Education.* San Francisco: Jossey-Bass.

Gump, P. 1978. School environments. In *Children and the Environment,* ed. L. Altman and J. Wohlwill, 131–74. New York: Plenum.

Hambleton, D., and S. Ziegler. 1974. *A Study of Integration of Trainable Mentally Retarded Students into a Regular Elementary School Setting.* Toronto: Metropolitan Toronto School Board.

Hart, R. 1971. *Aerial Geography: An Experiment in Elementary Education.* Worcester, Mass.: Clark University, Graduate School of Geography, Place Perception Report 6.

———. 1979. *Children's Experience of Place.* New York: Irvington.

Hart, R., and G. Moore. 1973. The development of spatial cognition: A review. In *Image and Environment: Cognitive Mapping and Spatial Behavior,* ed. R. Downs, and D. Stea, 246–88. Chicago: Aldine.

Heft, H. 1976. An Examination of the Relationship between Environmental Stimulation in the Home and Selective Attention in Young Children. Ph.D. diss., Pennsylvania State University.

Herron, R., and M. Frobish. 1969. Computer analysis and display of movement patterns. *Journal of Experimental Child Psychology* 8, no. 1:40–44.

Hill, F. 1980. *The Lives and Times of Urban Adolescents: Activity Patterns and Neighborhood Perceptions.* Toronto: Centre for Urban and Community Studies, Child in the City Report 8.

Hill, F., and W. Michelson. 1981. Towards a geography of urban children and youth. In *Geography and the Urban Environment: Progress in Research and Applications,* ed. D. Herbert, and R. Johnston, vol. 4, 193–228. New York and London: Wiley.

Holahan, C. 1978. *Environment and Behavior: A Dynamic Perspective.* New York: Plenum.

Hole, V. 1966. *Children's Play on Housing Estates.* Ministry of Technology, National Building Studies, Research Paper 39. London.

Horvat, R. 1974. Fifth and Eighth Grade Students' Orientation Toward the Environment and Environmental Problems. Ph.D. diss., University of Wisconsin.

Ittleson, W., L. Rivlin, and H. Proshansky. 1970. The use of behavioral maps in environmental psychology. In *Environmental Psychology: Man and His Physical Setting,* ed. H. Proshansky, W. Ittleson, and L. Rivlin, 658–68. New York: Holt, Rinehart & Winston.

Johnson, O. 1976. *Tests and Measurements in Child Development: Handbook II,* vols. 1 and 2. San Francisco: Jossey-Bass.

Jones, N. B. 1970. *Ethological Studies of Child Behavior.* Cambridge, Mass.: Cambridge Univ. Press.

Kinsman, C., and L. Berk. 1979. Joining the block and housekeeping areas: Changes in play and social behavior. *Young Children* 35(1):66–75.

Kosslyn, S., H. Pick, and G. Fariello. 1974. Cognitive maps in children and men. *Child Development* 45(8):707–16.

Ladd, F. 1970. Black youths view their environment: Neighborhood maps. *Environment and Behavior* 2(1):74–79.

Laurendeau, M., and A. Pinard. 1970. *The Development of the Concept of Space in the Child.* New York: International Universities Press.

Lee, T. 1964. Psychology and living space. *Transactions of the Bartlett Society* 2:9–36.

Little, B. 1980. The social ecology of children's nothings. In *Managing Urban Space in the Interests of Children,* Canada/MAB Report 14, ed. W. Michelson and E. Michelson, 12–19.

Loo, G. 1978. Behavior problem indices: The differential effects of spatial density on low and high scores. *Environment and Behavior* 10(4):489–510.

Lozar, C. 1974. Measurement techniques towards a measurement technology. In *Man-Environment Interactions: Evaluations and Applications,* ed. D. Carson, 171–92. Stroudsburg, Pa.: Dowden, Hutchinson & Ross.

Lynch, K. 1960. *The Image of the City.* Cambridge, Mass.: MIT Press.

———. 1977. *Growing Up in Cities: Studies of the Spatial Environment of Adolescence in Cracow, Melbourne, Mex-*

ico City, Salta, Toluca and Warszawa. Paris/Cambridge, Mass.: UNESCO/MIT Press.

Mandler, G. 1962. From association to structure. *Psychological Review* 69(5):415–27.

Mark, L. 1972. Modeling through toy play: A methodology for eliciting topographical representations in children. In *Environmental Design: Research and Practice,* vol. 1 of *Proceedings, EDRA-3,* ed. W. Mitchell, 1-3-1 – 9. Los Angeles.

Maurer, R., and J. Baxter. 1972. Images of the neighborhood and city among Black-, Anglo-, and Mexican-American children. *Environment and Behavior* 4(4):351–88.

McKechnie, G. 1972. A Study of Environmental Life Styles. Ph.D. thesis, University of California, Berkeley.

———. 1977. The Environmental Response Inventory in action. *Environment and Behavior* 9(2):255–76.

Medrich, E., J. Roizen, V. Rubin, and S. Buckley. 1982. *The Serious Business of Growing Up: A Study of Children's Lives outside School.* Berkeley: Univ. of California Press.

Michelson, W. 1977. *Environmental Choice, Human Behavior and Residential Satisfaction.* New York: Oxford.

Michelson, W., and E. Roberts. 1979. Children and the urban physical environment. In *The Child in the City: Changes and Challenges,* W. Michelson, S. Levine, A-R. Spina et al., 410–77. Toronto: Univ. of Toronto Press.

Moore, R. 1974a. Patterns of activity in time and space: The ecology of a neighborhood playground. In *Psychology and the Built-Environment,* ed. D. Canter and T. Lee, 118–31. London: Architectural Press.

———. 1974b. Anarchy zone: Encounters in a schoolyard. *Landscape Architecture* 64(5):364–71.

Moore, G., V. Cohen, J. Oertel, and L. van Ryzin. 1979. *Designing Environments for Handicapped Children.* New York: Educational Facilities Laboratories.

Moore, R., and A. Wochiler. 1974. An assessment of a "redeveloped" school yard based on drawings made by child users. In *Man–Environment Interactions: Evaluations and Applications,* ed. D. Carson, vol. 3, 107–20. Stroudsburg, Pa.: Dowden, Hutchinson & Ross.

Muchow, M., and H. Muchow. 1935. *Der Lebensraum des Grosstadtkindes.* Hamburg: Martin Riegel.

Parke, E. 1978. Children's home environments: Social and cognitive effects. In *Children and the Environment,* ed. I. Altman and J. Wohlwill. New York: Plenum.

Peterson, S., R. Bishop, R. Michaels, and G. Rath. 1973. Children's choice of playground equipment: Development of methodology for integrating user preferences into environmental engineering. *Journal of Applied Psychology* 58(2):233–38.

Phillips, E., and H. Andrews. 1982. *Residential Satisfaction and the Neighborhood Perception of Young Adolescents in Public Housing.* Centre for Urban and Community Studies, Child in the City Report 15. Toronto.

Piaget, J. 1954. *The Child's Construction of Reality.* New York: Basic Books.

Piaget, J., and B. Inhelder. 1967. *The Child's Conception of Space.* New York: Norton.

Piaget, J., B. Inhelder, and A. Szeminska. 1960. *The Child's Conception of Geometry.* New York: Harper.

Rand, G. 1969. Some Copernican views of the city. *Architectural Forum* 132(9):77–81.

Rhodeside, D., F. Peters, and G. Watkins. 1970. *Play Observation on Six Council Estates.* London: Ministry of the Environment.

Rivlin, L., and M. Wolfe. 1972. The early history of a psychiatric hospital for children. *Environment and Behavior* 4(1):33–72.

Rivlin, L., M. Wolfe, and M. Beyda. 1973. Age-related differences in the use of space. In *Environmental Design Research,* vol. 1 of *Proceedings, EDRA-4,* ed. W. Preiser, 191–203. Blacksburg, Va.

Rivlin, L., M. Rothenberg, F. Justa, and A. Wallis. 1974. Children's conceptions of open classrooms through use of scaled models. In *Man–Environment Interactions: Evaluations and Applications,* ed. D. Carson, vol. 3, 151–60. Stroudsburg, Pa.: Dowden, Hutchinson & Ross.

Roberts, E. 1976. Environment, Community and

Life Style: Components of Residential Preference for Cities. Ph.D. diss., University of Toronto.

Rohe, W., and E. Nuffer. 1977. The Effects of Density and Partitioning on Children's Behavior. Paper presented at the annual meeting, American Psychological Association, San Francisco. Mimeo.

Rohe, W., and A. Patterson. 1974. The effects of varied levels of resources and density on behavior in a day care center. In *Man-Environment Interactions: Evaluations and Applications,* ed. D. Carson, vol. 3, 161–71. Stroudsburg, Pa.: Dowden, Hutchinson & Ross.

Rothenberg, M., D. Haywood, and R. Beasley. 1974. Playgrounds: For whom? In *Man-Environment Interactions: Evaluations and Applications,* ed. D. Carson, vol. 3, 121–30. Stroudsburg, Pa.: Dowden, Hutchinson & Ross.

Ryan, T., and M. Ryan. 1940. Geographical orientation. *American Journal of Psychology* 53(2):204–15.

Saarinen, T. 1973. Students' views of the world. In *Image and Environment: Cognitive Mapping and Spatial Behavior,* ed. R. Downs and D. Stea, 148–61. Chicago: Aldine.

———. 1977. *Environmental Planning: Perceptions and Behavior.* Boston: Houghton Mifflin.

Sackett, G. 1978. *Observing Behavior.* Baltimore: University Park.

Scanlan, T. 1980. *Cities: A Human Perspective,* Toronto: Is Five Foundation.

Schwartzman, H. 1978. *Transformations: The Anthropology of Children's Play.* New York: Plenum.

Shemyakin, F. 1962. Orientation in space. In *Psychological Science in the USSR,* ed. B. Anan'yev et al., vol. 1, OTS Report 62-11083, 86–225. Washington, D.C.

Siegel, A., K. Kirasic, and R. Kail. 1978. Stalking the elusive cognitive map: The development of children's representations of geographic space. In *Children and the Environment,* ed. I. Altman and J. Wohlwill, 223–58. New York: Plenum.

Siegel, A., and S. White. 1975. The development of spatial representations of large-scale environments. In *Advances in Child Development and Behavior,* ed. H. Reese, vol. 10, 75–93. New York: Academic Press.

Simm, A., and E. Boyer. 1970. *Mirrors for Behavior.* Philadelphia: Classroom Interaction Newsletter.

Smith, P., and K. Connolly. 1972. Patterns of play and social interaction in pre-school children. In *Ethological Studies of Child Behavior,* ed. N. Blurton-Jones, 65–95. Cambridge: Cambridge University Press.

Spencer, C., and Z. Darvizeh. 1981. The case for developing a cognitive psychology that does not underestimate the abilities of young children. *Journal of Environmental Psychology* 1(2):21–31.

Stea, D., and J. Blaut. 1972. *Exploration in the Use of Toy Play for Landscape Modeling.* Worcester, Mass.: Clark University, Graduate School of Geography, Place Perception Report 9.

———. 1973. Some preliminary observations on spatial learning in school children. In *Image and Environment: Cognitive Mapping and Spatial Behavior,* ed. R. Downs and D. Stea, 226–34. Chicago: Aldine.

Stea, D., and S. Taphanel. 1974. Theory and experiment on the relation between environmental modeling ("toy play") and environmental cognition. In *Psychology and the Built-Environment,* ed. D. Canter and T. Lee, 170–78. London: Architectural Press.

Strauss, A. 1970. *Images of the American City.* New York: Free Press.

Thomsen, C., and A. Borowiecka. 1980. *Winter and Play: Design Guidelines for Winter Play Environments on the Canadian Prairie.* CMHC, Children's Environmental Advisory Service, Research and Development Programme, Project 10. Ottawa.

Tolman, E. 1948. Cognitive maps in rats and men. *Psychological Review* 55(3):189–208.

Vaillancourt, P. 1977. Stability of children's survey responses. *Public Opinion Quarterly* 40(4):373–87.

Von Senden, M. 1960. *Space and Sight.* London: Methuen.

Wachs, T. 1973. The measurement of early intellectual functioning. In *Socio-Behavioral Studies in Mental Retardation,* ed. G. Tarjan et al., 47–65. Washington, D.C.: American Association on Mental Deficiency.

Wachs, T., I. Uzgiris, and J. Hunt. 1971. Cognitive

development in infants of different age levels and from different environmental backgrounds: An exploratory investigation. *Merrill-Palmer Quarterly* 17(2):283–317.

Weinstein, C. 1982. Privacy-seeking behavior in an elementary classroom. *Journal of Environmental Psychology* 2(1):23–35.

Werner, H. 1948. *Comparative Psychology of Mental Development.* New York: International Universities Press.

Wolfe, M. 1978. Childhood and privacy. In *Children and the Environment,* ed. I. Altman and J. Wohlwill, 175–222. New York: Plenum.

Wolfe, M., and R. Laufer. 1974. The concept of privacy in childhood and adolescence. In *Man–Environment Interactions: Evaluations and Applications,* ed. D. Carson, vol. 2, 29–54. Stroudsburg, Pa.: Dowden, Hutchinson & Ross.

Wolfe, M., and L. Rivlin. 1972. Evolution of space utilization patterns in a children's psychiatric hospital. In *Environmental Design: Research and Practice,* vol. 1, *Proceedings, EDRA-3,* ed. W. Mitchell, 5-2-1 - 10. Los Angeles.

Wood, D. 1971. Fleeting Glimpses. M.A. thesis, Clark University.

Wright, H. F. 1960. Observational child study. In *Handbook of Research Methods in Child Development,* ed. P. Mussen. New York: Wiley.

Wuellner, L., P. Witt, and R. Herron. 1970. A method to investigate the movement patterns of children. In *Contemporary Psychology of Sport,* ed. G. Kenyon, 799–808. Chicago: Athletic Institute.

Zeisel, J. 1970. *Sociology and Architectural Design.* New York: Russell Sage Foundation.

CHAPTER 11
METHODS IN ENVIRONMENTAL RESEARCH WITH OLDER PEOPLE

M. Powell Lawton

Not all gerontologists would agree that a special chapter on research methods is necessary for this age group. Particularly from the psychological literature one would have to conclude that similarities across different adult ages are far more remarkable than age differences. The assertion that chronological age is irrelevant is partly ideological, however, perhaps as a reaction against the glib invocation of age as an explanation for many observed cross-sectional group differences whose causes have later been found not to be causally related to age per se (see Schaie 1974, for a discussion of age-irrelevant factors in cognitive performance, for example). There certainly are age differences in biological functioning and in social experience. If one interprets research knowledge in a discriminating fashion one can also find some psychological functions (for example, psychomotor speed) for which age is a relevant variable.

The approach taken in this chapter will be to review briefly some basic conclusions about age differences that may be relevant to gathering data about the environment from older people. The remainder of the chapter will discuss traditional environmental research methods from the vantage point of these differences. In unusual instances hard data are available to demonstrate the differential effectiveness of different methods with older subjects or age differentials within a single method. Much more often, however, discussions will be based upon simple experience in the use of particular methods with older people, with qualitative observations on how age-related characteristics may influence response. Since most methods are discussed generically in other chapters, this chapter will deal in a cursory fashion with method issues that are general to all ages.

RESPONSE-RELEVANT AGE DIFFERENCES

One consequence of added years is a decrease in general physical energy, as in decreased vital capacity (Klocke 1977), cardiovascular stress recovery rate (Kohn 1977), or motor performance (Botwinick 1978). Unless the demands of a research task involve physical energy expenditure, however, these age changes should affect most behavioral test responses minimally. For example, one would think that energy might be depleted more rapidly over the course of a day among older people. However, time of day proved to have no effect on older people's performance on a cognitive test battery (Kaplan et al. 1964).

Sensory deficits perhaps constitute the major limitation on older people's ability to respond to the usual visual or auditory mode of inquiry (Pastalan 1979). Losses in these areas are far more prevalent than are most other clinical or physical limitations. Multi-modal presentations during an interview (such as showing questions or response devices on display cards to a respondent while an interviewer asks the questions) are thus often effective. Large dark print on questionnaires and slow, distinct speech at slightly above-average volume will elicit responses from a small group of marginally receptive people who might otherwise be lost.

The more complex and novel the task demand, the more difficulty will older people have, especially as time pressure is added. Psychomotor speed and decision processes are slowed by aging (Botwinick 1978), which makes novel or complex tasks selectively more difficult for older people. The most familiar types of task, such as the interview, may elicit the fewest such response problems. In environmental research, however, one frequently wishes to approach the subject in a way that goes beyond the direct question. Therefore tasks such as the trade-off game (see chapter 4 above), semantic differential (Hershberger 1972), distance and location estimates (Golledge and Zannaras 1973), or the repertory grid (Kelly 1955) have been used to probe environmental responses that resist eliciting through conscious inquiry. Such novel approaches may be more difficult for respondents of all ages than a straight question-and-answer approach. To the extent, however, that more detailed explanation is required, more choices are presented, and ambiguity is introduced into the stimuli or into connection between the task and the purpose of the encounter as construed by the person, the ease of response of younger and older adults will proportionately differ. Such techniques are within the power of most older people to use. A great deal more care is necessary to introduce, explain, and provide practice in such tasks than might be true for the college student subject. The practice session, with feedback, is essential, as is repeated emphasis that the time taken to complete the task is inconsequential.

A social factor, the acceptability of the total research context, adds to the central processing problem. The present cohort of older people, with a mean educational experience in 1980 of less than ten years (White House Conference on Aging 1981), is not as likely as young adult cohorts to accept social research as a natural feature of their world. Extended explanation and conversation designed to legitimize the researcher's goals and personal acceptability, while worthwhile for all subjects, are particularly helpful in raising the level of motivation in the older subject. No data are at hand to suggest that inquiries in the environmental domain may be selectively responded to by older people differently in any way than by younger people. The researcher should be aware, however, that open-ended questions and ambiguous stimuli (for example, pictures used to elicit stories, such as the Thematic Apperception Test, Murray, 1938) are likely to evoke shorter and less rich responses from older people (see Lawton et al. 1980 for a review of the evidence). This type of verbal constriction may be wholly cohort-related or a more age-related phenomenon emanating from the demonstrably greater cautiousness of the older person (Botwinick 1966).

To the extent that the older subject is reasonably well educated and unimpaired physically or mentally, the considerations mentioned above will be minimally relevant. However, some subgroups of less-advantaged older people are often the subjects of research and deserve special attention. For example, minority aged and rural aged are likely to have been disadvantaged in education and therefore may require more explanation and less complex modes of inquiry than the more advantaged. In particular, older people with major health impairments or those in service-receiving situations are likely to be the focus of research. The need to tailor the type of research instrument to particular perceptual, motor, or cognitive capabilities is obvious, an extreme case being the person so cognitively impaired (suffering, for example, from a disease of the central nervous system) that no verbal inquiry at all is possible.

Verbal and nonverbal modes of response will be used to distinguish the methods to be discussed, though some methods may use either verbal or nonverbal stimuli and response modes. The major methods include the interview, direct observation, the time budget, cognitive mapping, and models and simulation. It is very likely that the most complete and reliable information will be obtained from a manifold methodological approach, in which, for example, the older person's verbal responses, natural behavior, and experimentally elicited behavior are studied simultaneously. Such an approach is sometimes taken by ethnographers. However, use of this method involves an accompanying loss; problems can be created by the multiplicity of the data and the researcher's uncertainty regarding the relative weight to be assigned to the results obtained from each method. Choices will usually have to be made to emphasize one approach and give others more limited treatment.

VERBAL STIMULI AND RESPONSE MODES

The Interview and Questionnaire

The interview is unquestionably the most ubiquitous research method in environmental studies of older people. While there are many differences between the interview and the questionnaire, they share a number of general qualities. This discussion will deal with age-related aspects, while Marans (in chapter 2) treats the topic more generally.

Both the interview and the questionnaire assume the availability of environment-relevant knowledge, attitudes, or affect in the respondent and the latter's ability to share these with the researcher—assumptions that are by no means always tenable. It may be more difficult for older people to introspect regarding their environmental experiences than it is for younger people. First, since the social space (Sivadon 1970), or motility in space, of older people is less and their residential mobility less, they may have a lesser breadth of environmental experience. Second, since the overall size of their social networks is smaller (Fischer 1982), less personally transmitted knowledge regarding the external environment is likely to flow in both directions. Finally, younger cohorts are now being sensitized to environmental concerns in a way that was missing during the early socialization stages experienced by today's elderly. (Later cohorts will no doubt approach environment in a different manner.) It may be possible in asking questions about the environment to equalize to some extent the experience of people with an environmental attribute. Information designed to orient the respondent may be included in the inquiry. For example, the term ''senior-citizen housing'' may communicate unequally to people. If further definition is needed, all subjects could be shown a few photographs of such housing, or be read a short verbal definition.

The hazards of the hypothetical question are well known. It is exceedingly difficult for a person to answer a question about an environment that he or she has never experienced. The set toward cautiousness may make older people, more than others, answer in noninformative ways. Similar effects may be elicited by negative age-stereotyped attitudes that make the older respondent hesitant to express an opinion or risk a guess. For example, many older people are overly concerned about the acceptability of their opinions to the researcher. Others are convinced that any response will betray their ignorance.

A small amount of empirical data is at hand to inform us of the magnitude of such limitations on reliability and validity of data from direct questions. Although this knowledge is not specific to environmental research, the frequent use of interview methods justifies its inclusion here.

It has often been asserted, with occasional data-based verification (for example, Botwinick and Thompson 1968), that older people are more diverse than people of younger ages in virtually every attribute. One recent attempt to verify this hypothesis through a meta-analysis of variances by age did not uphold it (Bornstein and Smircina 1982). On the other hand, examination of large pools of survey interview data enabled Rodgers and Herzog (1982) to conclude that item variances were greater among the elderly. Should this occur generally in survey research data, it could reflect not only greater diversity among the people themselves, but also the possibility of greater response error, which in turn would affect the reliability and validity of the data. For the time being it would seem especially desirable for investigators to test and present new determinations of reliability and validity for previously standardized tests when used with the elderly. This suggestion is especially relevant when the respondents include older people whose impairments might be assumed to affect error rate.

Error variance was the focus of an analysis of six survey data sets (Andrews and Herzog 1983). As age increased, the proportions of random error and response error associated with item format increased, a relationship that remained even after controlling for education. The researchers also found that older respondents differentiated less among their responses to different concepts than did younger people, that is, there was a greater stereotypic tendency to rate many aspects of their lives similarly. Rodgers and Herzog (1982) also found that older people were more likely to use fewer response categories, to give the same rating to many questions, and to use extreme response categories more often than younger people did. However, controlling for education greatly reduced these tendencies, suggesting the possibility that over time, this covariation between age and interview response style may disappear. Working with semantic differential scales, Drevenstedt (1975) reported very similar findings, except that the less-educated older subjects showed overuse of the midpoint as well as the extremes on the response scales.

Memory, of course, is an increasing problem for the aging, although its significance has probably been overrated where "normal aging" is concerned (Fozard 1980). How substantial a problem memory is for the interview responses of older people is not at all clear. The literature contains cautionary studies showing recall problems for distant events (Powers et al. 1978). Among older subjects asked to provide retrospective information (whose accuracy could be checked), recall is better for "objective" than for evaluational responses given at an earlier time in life (Field 1981) and even over a short term (Ridley et al. 1979). Further, there seems to be a "sweetening of memory," whereby earlier events are evaluated more positively as time passes (Field 1981). However, there is no clear evidence of memory decay in many kinds of interview responses (Field 1981; Ridley et al. 1979). Neither is it well established that, for a type of memory that is problematic in general, decay is even age-related. Since evaluational questions in environmental research are likely to refer to contemporary events, and questions relating to the past are more likely to be objective, it does seem that the majority of older subjects would not suffer from memory-related interview distortions.

Response Formats. The presence of any of the deficits or other limitations on response capability mentioned above will guide the investigator in choosing questions. In most research endeavors one is likely to find some people of marginal competence in one's sample. It may thus be prudent to compromise to some extent the level of sophistication of questions and response formats in order to minimize the number who would be thus screened out as unreliable informants.

It is especially important in constructing questions for older subjects to keep them simple: Basic English, with careful deletion of words or terms that have attained a contemporary meaning different from their traditional meaning, is desirable. The fewer concepts contained in an instruction or a question the better. If conditional clauses, definitions, or other information must be conveyed, these should be given in separate sentences. If orally administered, much can be done with pauses between sentences, with voice emphasis, and eye contact to insure understanding. The pacing of orally presented material is extremely important. People with experience dealing with the elderly instinctively moderate the speed of their speech, but novices will need to be trained to speak considerably slower than usual unless they see that normal speed is unproblematic for a particular subject.

Rating scales are possible for most older subjects to use. For people who are extremely culturally deprived or who suffer from cognitive or perceptual deficits that limit their comprehension, a dichotomous response format (yes-no or agree-disagree) may elicit a response where a longer scale would not. Such a foreshortened scale also limits reliability, so the gains and losses of each approach must be carefully considered. Most older people do well with a rating scale of five points; marginally competent people may sometimes be added to the yield by a two-stage unfolding technique, that is, first an agree versus disagree option, followed by, Do you agree/disagree very much or a little? A visual display card where there are more than three response alternatives is helpful, as well as letters in boldface and large type.

The paired comparison is a response format that has particular advantages in insuring that every response is compared with every other response and in demanding only a dichotomous judgment for each presentation. However, the number of attributes that can be compared is limited; for example, ten pairs must be judged if there are five attributes. Older respondents appear to become impatient with the reappearance of the same item to a greater extent than the young. Thus in general five attributes may be the maximum to which paired-comparison judgments can be applied. Ranking also has problems, especially for those who find it hard to keep more than a few items in mind at once. Ranking is easier when approached by unfolding; for example, the three highest and three lowest may be chosen, followed by ranking within each set of three.

Research from large surveys does indicate that older people yield more missing data and more "don't know" responses than do other age groups (Sudman and Bradburn 1974), although education, rather than age, may be the critical determinant (Glenn 1969). It might seem logical, though not yet empirically demonstrated, that a "don't know" response should not be offered as an alternative to the older interviewee but instead accepted and freely used as a mean in missing-data substitution where that procedure can be justified. However, Herzog (personal communication) has indicated that the proportion of don't know responses produced by older subjects is high regardless of whether the alternative is offered. Carp (1974) found that there was a strong tendency for older people to rate more highly the first-presented items in an array, thus justifying the counterbalancing of response alternatives throughout the interview schedule. Factual items, however, did not show this primacy effect, nor was there any effect ascribable to a question's placement early or late in the interview. Long lists of items in a similar format may encourage response-set error. On the other hand, changing the format with every question could conceivably be too complex for some respondents. No data exist to define either the optimum balance between constancy and change in the format of consecutive questions, or the optimal length of an interview or testing session for the general population of the elderly. An informal rule of thumb tries to limit the time to sixty or ninety minutes. However, the literature is full of examples of successfully-completed three-hour interview sessions. In our own experience we have lost almost no elderly subjects by breaking at about ninety minutes and returning another day, although there are some older interviewees who themselves request that the data be completed at the first visit.

Questionnaires. A printed questionnaire probably puts more burden on the respondent than an interview. Visual problems are widespread, and it is not always possible to get really clear copy. Typewriters with large type frequently do not yield copy that reproduces very clearly. A substantial number of today's elderly feel insecure about their reading skills and even more insecure when asked to wield a pencil. However, there are many occasions when the saving in time makes a printed questionnaire almost mandatory. When administered in a group, the subjects may be chosen so as to maximize the probability that they will respond reliably. People who volunteer for a written test are likely to have screened themselves in terms of their capability for performing this task prior to volunteering. In any case, it is essential to have several monitors present on such occasions to answer subjects' questions and especially to see that responses are being indicated properly. No completed form should be turned in without such a check, followed by the request to correct responses or especially to complete omitted items (often whole pages).

Mailed questionnaires are potentially even less satisfactory because they do not allow face-to-face explanations or monitoring. However, when used with groups of known literate backgrounds (for example, Atchley [1969] used former employers' lists of retired teachers and telephone employees), acceptable response rates and quality of responses can be obtained from mailed questionnaires. Atchley obtained 90 percent from his group, while Lee and Finney (1977) obtained a 74 percent rate from a statewide sample of older people who had responded to an earlier screening inquiry.

Data are available that compare telephone and face-to-face interviewing of the elderly. Herzog et al. (1983), in an analysis of five large face-to-face and four telephone surveys, found that the primary hazards were an underrepresentation of older people and specifically of less well-educated elderly and the less healthy, as compared to face-to-face surveys. They failed to find telephone-survey-specific age differences in a number of indicators of response quality or response content, however. They did find some suggestion that older people may have less tolerance for long telephone interviews than do younger people.

Age and Satisfaction

Psychological processes in the respondent are the source of a number of possible distortions in the interview responses of older people. Whether any are really age-specific has not been demonstrated with certainty. These mechanisms have been identified to explain the recurrent finding that older people's degree of expressed satisfaction with a number of domains of everyday life is higher than that expressed by other age groups and also higher than might be expected on the basis of the "objective'' quality of the domain. This pattern, which might be called ''excess satisfaction,'' is expressed particularly well in older people's evaluations of their housing, neighborhood, and community (Campbell et al. 1976; Carp 1975; Lawton 1978). Herzog and Rodgers (1981), in fact, examined these age-satisfaction relationships after controlling for three objective factors where the elderly are most deprived (health, income, and education) and found that the tendency for the aged to exhibit excess satisfaction was enhanced.

Objective indicators from the U.S. Bureau of the Census' Annual Housing Survey (1974–1981) show the *quality of housing* occupied by older people to be measurably poorer than that occupied by younger people (Lawton 1980a). This fact alone argues against one hypothesis advanced by Campbell et al. to account for older people's higher satisfaction—that is, that they in fact may occupy better housing. However, another related hypothesis seems more tenable, that *progressive shopping* over a lifetime has enabled older people to approximate a match between their own needs, their assessment of what is possible, and their actual residential situation. The result is a state of perceived congruence, which is less parallel with objective quality than with quality as perceived from the individual's vantage point.

Another suggestion is that *familiarity* itself leads to liking, for reasons including emotional attachment, symbolic meaning, or the security associated with intimate knowledge of an environment (Lawton, in press[a]). Some support for the power of familiarity alone to elicit liking may be found in experimental work with younger adults (Zajonc 1968). Herzog and Rodgers (1981), however, were unable to confirm length of residence as a strong determinant of the relationship between age and residential satisfaction.

The personality trait *acquiescence* has been suggested as more prevalent among present-day older people, leading to excess satisfaction (Kogan 1961). In addition, some older subjects when interviewed about their environmental situations, such as institutions and planned housing, may feel that expressions of dissatisfaction will evoke negative reactions from management or staff. It has been frequently noted anecdotally that such respondents will answer positively to a structured question asked by an interviewer but very differently in informal conversation with someone else who is known and trusted. However, this explanation has not been tested empirically and is explicitly rejected by Campbell et al. (1976).

A related explanation has been sought in the suggestion that the older cohort is more subject to the response set toward *social desirability.* Campbell et al. (1976) found a correlation of 0.26 between age and a social desirability scale, for example. Using these same data, Herzog and Rodgers (1981) found that controlling for social desirability reduced the excess satisfaction of the elderly to a barely perceptible degree. Bradburn and Sudman (1979) hypothesized that what appears to be a social desirability set may be a cohort-related tendency to think in terms of extremes or ''either-or'' categories. This suggestion is consistent with the findings of Drevenstedt (1975) and Rodgers and Herzog (1982) regarding stereotypic response distributions.

Carp (1975) identified the phenomenon of *cognitive balance* in determining the interview responses of the aged. In her evaluation of a housing project for the elderly, her subjects' expressed satisfaction with their current housing in the community was relatively high, notwithstanding its objectively poor quality and the fact that all had applied for the new housing. Decisions regarding acceptance were then announced and another interview was done before any had moved. In this second interview the unsuccessful applicants' satisfaction did not change, but there was a marked drop in satisfaction among successful applicants. Thus it required the existence of a realistic alternative for these people to be able to tolerate the imbalance between an objective evaluation of their present housing and their personal evaluation of it.

Understanding of this phenomenon was aided by further findings from the Campbell et al. (1976) study, which showed that excess satisfaction was increased by *lower aspirations* and by an *ignorance of alternatives,* which are clearly facets of the cognitive balance effect. Older adults show at one and the same time little discrepancy between aspiration and actuality and narrower experience in recent years with other types of living situations. Their acceptance of the residential status quo is thus understandable. Carp et al. (1982), on the other hand, found that when social *comparison* factors (that is, perceived equity or reference-group comparative evaluations) were considered, these factors explained considerably more variation in residential satisfaction than did aspiration-discrepancy. However, it should be emphasized that the *lack* of discrepancy between the actual and the ideal is what is so notable about older people's judgments. With so little variance in this measure of disjunction, it is no wonder that the discrepancy measure added more predictability of environmental satisfaction in younger but not older people.

A final response style is *ego-defensiveness,* identified by Carp and Carp (1981a) as a very strong influence on older people's judgments of environmental satisfaction. When older people evaluated an environmental object in terms of its being a "problem" for them, they seemed to view the question as one that called into question their competence. The rate of "problem" endorsement was quite low. When the object was judged in terms of "satisfaction," evaluations were less positive than evaluations made in terms of "how well they managed things" in the domain.

Herzog and Rodgers (1981) examined the effect of life events in accounting for excess satisfaction. The sum total of life events as a covariate predictor decreased slightly the set of age–satisfaction correlations. Since age and life events showed a correlation of −.40, it may be that the relative absence of these disturbances allows the older person to be more satisfied with all domains of everyday life.

The evidence reviewed in this section argues that evaluative interview responses by older adults of environmental objects probably contain a significant portion of true excess expressed satisfaction. A major question yet to be answered is how much of this tendency is age-related and how much is cohort-related. Age, income, and education are confounded in most of the research demonstrating excess satisfaction, thus cautioning us against glib explanations in terms of chronological age. However, neither can we accept at face value the highly sanguine judgments of older people about their environmental situation (for example, the Harris Survey finding that 95 percent of all older adults expressed no problem with their housing, National Council on the Aging 1981). Neugarten (1982) has wondered whether drawing this conclusion means that we think older people are "lying" when they express satisfaction. The psychological processes detailed above are clearly something different from lying. They represent mechanisms used by all people, perhaps a little more by today's elderly, to moderate the gap between the objective and the perceived environment. These mechanisms represent for most people, most of the time, a positive means of coping with the external world.

It is possible to use evaluative or preferential judgments other than as absolute indicators of satisfaction or demand. Relative satisfaction or preference constitutes a firmer basis for using such data. For example, if people are asked to make the same kind of judgment for a whole list of attributes, response sets should be equalized and the relative standing of each attribute thus reasonably well indicated. Similarly, the same attribute may be subjected to judgments by several contrasting subgroups of people. While one needs to be aware of the possibility of interactions between subgroups (such as age groups) and judgments, the order in which the subgroups' evaluations fall may be more meaningful than their absolute value. These uses have been discussed in greater detail elsewhere (Lawton 1977).

Because evaluative judgments of environmental attributes are the most frequent approach taken to research in this area, the foregoing discussion has paid less attention to other types of interview-based inquiry. However, there is high consensus that factual information or judgments of highly specific environmental attributes (for example, how well one's heating system works) are less subject to both memory decay and response-style distortion than are more global judgments (Campbell et al. 1976; Carp 1975; Carp and Carp 1981a; Field 1981).

Since more general evaluations of quality of life (''satisfaction with life as a whole,'' Campbell et al. 1976; life satisfaction, Neugarten et al. 1961; morale, Lawton 1975a; or happiness, Bradburn 1969) are frequently used as indicators of a favorable environmental outcome (dependent variables) in environmental research, a few points should be made about this practice. First, Lawton (1977) argued that such criteria may be very ''distant'' from the environmental transaction, in a psychological sense. Such indicators of generalized psychological well-being may not be the most appropriate domains for an environmental effect to be evidenced on well-being. In many instances it is more logical to look for an impact on behavior or mental states that have some logical connection with the environmental attribute being evaluated. An example may be cited where the physical characteristics of 150 housing projects and their dwelling units were correlated with the morale of their older occupants (Lawton and Nahemow 1979a). Although some significant and meaningful relationships were found, many more were found when housing satisfaction, rather than morale, was used as the dependent variable.

Second, the user should be aware that in general, the more the indicator refers to ''satisfaction,'' the higher older adults will score as compared to the young. The more the indicator refers to affect, the lower will older people score; for example, older people show fewer neurotic symptoms (Veroff et al. 1981), less negative affect, less positive affect, and less happiness than do younger people (Andrews and Withey 1976; Campbell et al. 1976). In contrast, age differences in traditional measures of life satisfaction or morale typically have not been found (Larson 1978).

In conclusion, it may be expecting too much of such ''soft'' global measures of well-being to find them sensitive to environmental features. It can thus be recommended that in addition to attempts to relate environmental factors to these generalized well-being measures, more environment-specific evaluative criteria or behavioral outcomes also be used.

DIRECT BEHAVIOR OBSERVATION

Since about 90 percent of older people live in ordinary homes in ordinary communities (Lawton, in press [b]), the behavior of this majority should be about as accessible to direct observation as that of people in general. Older people are less prevalent in schools and in the workplace; to the extent that decrements in the occupancy of these settings are converted into time within the dwelling unit, their behavior may be less accessible to observation for research purposes. However, about 5 percent of people sixty-five and over live in institutions (U.S. Bureau of the Census 1982) and another 5 percent in planned housing (Lawton, in press [b]). Because these settings are very important forms of service for older people (and also because they are unusually accessible to researchers!), they have received a disproportionate share of research attention. Further, in both settings an unusually high proportion of behavior occurs in public places. It is thus understandable that naturalistic observational studies should have been performed from time to time in both institutions and housing. This fact must alert us to the sampling issue—that is, that findings from these specialized settings cannot be used to generalize about older people's behavior. Even within the institution it is not always possible to sample the universe of all behaviors, and virtually everywhere else it is only public behaviors that are accessible.

Older people seem no more or less reactive to the presence of an observer than any other group. In planned housing, where concern for security runs high, it is necessary for the observer to establish legitimacy very clearly during the research endeavor. An introduction of the researcher to the tenants both in person and by posted notice should be solicited from the administration. Several observational occasions should be treated as pilot runs during the early stage until tenants have become familiar with the observer. Similar sensitivity among the people being observed has been found in both small towns and in urban neighborhoods. Naturalistic observation within a household introduces many problems, of course, and does not seem to have been applied to samples of older people except in case studies or qualitative approaches such as participant observation. Thus an intensive study of the "stream of behavior" of the older people in the fashion performed with a child by Barker and Wright (1967) remains to be done.

Behavior Setting Studies

Most of the other behavior-observational techniques described in the general literature have been used with the aged. Barker and Barker's (1961) full behavior setting study of the ecology of small towns in England and the United States included an analysis of their older subpopulations. Behavior-mapping studies where different environments and portions of environments are observed in replicative fashion in terms of the occupants, their location, and their behaviors have been reported in housing (Lawton 1970) and institutions (Lawton et al. 1984). In these studies clear preferences for various spaces were determined—for example, areas near the nurses' station and centrally rather than peripherally located lounges. Such findings have clear design implications. Data of this type are easy to obtain and are useful when the unit of comparison is the physical area and the aggregate of people within it. The usefulness of such ecological data is greatly increased when they can be combined for analysis with data on the individuals composing the environment. Thus Brent et al. (1984) were able to compose typologies of persons based on their patterns of space occupancy in institutions and in turn relate these types to characteristics of persons; for example, the cluster that denoted people who engaged in "backstage behavior" (such as sleeping) in public areas was less mobile and mentally alert than other clusters.

Behavior Mapping

The typical behavior map attempts to account for all behavior in its classification scheme (Ittelson et al. 1970). The resulting categories tend to be relatively general, with some loss in specificity. Thus when the individual is the focus of research interest, it is often desirable to focus on only a limited number of specific behaviors. For example, in a study of proxemic behavior (personal distance, touching) in public places by Berkowitz (1971), it was easy to classify each behavior at the same time that the sex and approximate age of the behavior were noted. A more extensive behavior-coding scheme might have been difficult for observers to apply in such well-populated settings. Another example of the direct behavior-observation method was a study by Barton (1980) of the environmental contingencies controlling the behavior of nursing home residents. They found that the dependent behavior of the older resident was reinforced by staff, while independent behavior was not.

The coding of some behaviors may be so demanding as to require visual recording, which also can under some conditions be less obtrusive, especially when the judgments of multiple coders are required. Azar and Lawton (1964), for example, studied pedestrian accidents by motion-picture recording of the foot and leg movements of older people as they negotiated ordinary pathways. In other research the proxemic behavior of nursing home patients with senile dementia was studied by a fixed-focus videotape recorder that picked up all behavior occurring in a hallway (DeLong 1974).

An age-specific advantage of direct behavior observation is its lack of dependence on verbal mediation. That is, the dementia patient (with Alzheimer's disease or a related condition) may not be amenable to the usual research methods; for this group, the focus of much present high-priority research, direct observation may be the main source of reliable data. Although it is difficult to arrange, videotape recording has recently been used in the home to study the interactions between dementia patients and their care-giving relatives (Niederehe 1982).

A last form of directly observed behavior may be called the *performance test,* where the examiner asks a person to perform a behavior that can occur in a natural setting under a condition that allows it to be observed at a given time, rather than requiring the observer to wait for it to occur. Kuriansky and Gurland (1976), for example, developed an activities of daily living performance test containing sixteen requests such as, Show me how you comb your hair, or, Put this jacket on for me and then take it off. It is very likely that performance tasks dealing with a variety of environmental manipulative skills could be constructed for particular research problems.

While there have been many general exhortations for the application of *human-factors research* methods to the aging (Fozard 1981; Parsons 1981, for example), only recently has empirical research in this tradition begun. Faletti (1984) has demonstrated the applicability of such methods in relation to the study of meal-preparation behavior in an ordinary kitchen. Norris-Baker and Willems (1979) formalized what they call an ''environmental negotiability survey,'' in which the examiner leads the subject through every structural feature of the relevant environment in order to judge its usability, through both demonstration and verbal report. Howell (1980) approached this task in a more limited form, focusing on particular environmental features through instructions like, Show me how you make coffee. Such a sequence moves through retrieval of utensils and supplies from storage, use of sink and stove, pouring, and clean-up. Quantitation is still primitive, but even the dichotomous ''yes-no'' judgments for negotiability used by Norris-Baker and Willems (1979) were able to distinguish in a gross way several levels of dwelling-unit accessibility.

Direct observational methods deserve greater use in gerontological research, especially in the transactional fashions described above. The advantages and disadvantages of this method with normal older populations conform well with those discussed elsewhere in this book and will not be repeated here.

TIME BUDGETS

The time budget is an alternative to the interview and direct behavior observation for finding out what people do. It is especially useful in highlighting differences among large subaggregates of people whose characteristics contrast in some basic manner—for example, groups exhibiting cross-national differences (Szalai 1972). The traditional interview requires people both to recall past behaviors and to rate them in terms of such attributes as frequency, intensity, or affective character. The time budget also requires the subject to make his or her own observations. It has an advantage over the interview because it avoids the need to sum activities mentally and minimizes the memory aspect. It is far superior to direct observation in obviating the time, expense, and intrusiveness of an observer.

Regrettably most of the important time budget studies of the past have either omitted the elderly (Robinson 1977; Szalai 1972) or reported inadequately on the aging segment (Chapin 1974). More limited samples of older adults have been studied in this way, however (Carp and Carp 1981b; Moss and Lawton 1982; Lawton and Moss in press).

One approach to the time budget is the time diary, in which the person keeps a record of his or her behavior as it occurs through the day. This method has proved difficult for older subjects. Moss and Lawton (1982), for example, found that only 49 percent of their subjects widely ranging in behavioral competence were able to produce usable one-day diaries, a much lower usable yield than reported among younger adults (Szalai 1972). On the other hand, with clearly more competent subjects, Carp and Carp (1981b) obtained completion rates of 58 percent, 61 percent, and 73 percent on seven-day diaries in three samples of older people.

The other major form of time budget is the "yesterday interview," which has been used in many such studies (for example, Chapin 1974). In this approach, the person accounts to the interviewer for the previous twenty-four hours; while recall is involved, this problem is minimized by the recency of the events. Apparently this is much easier than a diary for older adult samples that include many foreign-born and marginally competent people; 91 percent of those who completed a regular interview produced usable yesterday interviews in the Moss and Lawton (1982) study. This same study included a number of marginally competent subjects who could not be interviewed. It was possible, however, to solicit yesterday interviews from competent household members in a majority of the cases where the older subject could not respond. Not determined as yet is the reliability of informant-reported time budgets.

The yesterday interview, requiring the presence of an interviewer, is considerably more expensive than the time diary. For this reason, a single day has usually been the sample unit, imposing an obvious limitation on the reliability of the data. In particular the likelihood of obtaining stable estimates of infrequent events is considerably decreased (Robinson 1977).

Carp and Carp (1981b) found that seven-day diaries were reasonably valid. They found that the reliability of time distributions of a single subject across seven separate days was very poor in their seven-day diary approach to the time budget. In the aggregate, however, the group distributions of time over the separate twenty-four-hour periods were very similar. Their findings show clearly that cautious interpretations must be made when time budgets are estimated by one-day records.

On the other hand, Stephens and Willems (1979) found the reliability between reported and observed behavior to be acceptably high. Lawton and Moss (in press) also found that group prediction of time allocations based on one-day interviews by personal characteristics such as socioeconomic status and health was relatively good. Moss and Lawton (1982) compared a one-day diary and a one-day yesterday interview (two different days) for their sample of older people and found that the two methods yielded about the same number of entries (twenty-four and twenty-three, respectively). The median correlation between minutes spent in each of twenty-nine categories for the two days was 0.51, considerably higher than the median r of 0.08 reported by Carp and Carp (1981b) between a one-day yesterday interview and a seven-day diary, across eleven behavior categories. The poorer agreement between yesterday interview and time diary found by the Carps may possibly be explained by the fact that the error of reporting in the diary format may be greater; this explanation has not been verified empirically, however.

Several sources of bias were investigated by Carp and Carp (1981b). They compared time estimates using the seven-day diary data with time estimates derived from interview questions that asked people to estimate their "usual" time investments in activities. These latter aggregate responses overestimated the time spent in desired activities but were reasonably accurate in estimating time spent in activities that the subject felt occurred about as often as desired. Among those who were successfully interviewed, those who did not provide a usable diary had lower income, less education, belonged to an ethnic minority, and were in poorer health, but did not differ in age from those who completed the diary. The diary user must thus be prepared for the sample to overrepresent relatively competent subjects.

The specific environmental aspect of the time budget has typically consisted of a simple designation of the location of the activity, beginning with the category "at home." An example of the environmental use of the yesterday interview is seen in Stephens and Willems's (1979) study of older people in public housing, where their concern was the types of behaviors performed within the dwelling units. They were able to establish that behavior was not predominantly passive simply because it occurred within the apartment. A substantial amount of social behavior occurred there. Given the difficulty of installing an observer in the dwelling units, these findings could not have been elicited by direct behavior observation.

Moss and Lawton (1982) attempted in the piloting of their research to get people to report in which particular spaces within the dwelling unit behavior occurred. With the many other demands made of these particular subjects, this specification was difficult and was therefore dropped. However, for a project whose focus was spatial behavior, it would be very possible for good informants to differentiate more precisely the locus of their behavior. Where the research population is capable of keeping a time diary, this mode seems better suited to requesting more detailed environmental information than does the yesterday interview.

There is more that can be said about the environmental aspects of behavior than simply where it occurs. The meaning of activity is very inadequately carried by the category describing the behavior itself. Ideally a great deal more will be learned about the environment–behavior transaction when we also can understand how meaning varies as a function of both the behavior and where it occurs. Unfortunately it is very difficult to ask a subject to rate every activity in terms of its meaning. Moss and Lawton (1982) piloted a number of terms by which each time budget entry was to be rated. Perhaps because of limitations in the cognitive capabilities of some of their subjects, the simplest possible dimension, a three-point evaluative scale (liked, neither liked nor disliked, disliked) had to be used, after attempting unsuccessfully to use other more sophisticated concepts such as "meaningful" or "satisfying." As in the case of satisfaction ratings, a strong tendency toward liking most activities was found. If activities are to be rated in terms of a richer variety of dimensions, other approaches will be necessary. Although not yet used with older people, a pre-programmed beeper that signals at random times when a subject should note his current activity appears to have dealt well with some of the problems of response compliance, recall, and intrusiveness (Csikszentmihalyi and Graef 1980). With other response problems thus minimized, the subjects were able to perform ratings of the ongoing person–environment transaction that gave a better view of the meaning of the situation, such as perceived freedom, competence, attentiveness, involvement, and psychological state at the moment. As was recommended in the case of the environmental component, it seems desirable to explore further the dimensionality of the meaning of activities with time budget studies of subjects chosen expressly because they are good informants.

As in the case of direct behavior observation, the time budget approach may be used with more limited types of behavior, as in the ''trip diary,'' which logs all movements outside the home (Regnier 1981): all of his subjects were able to complete this instrument. On the other hand, an attempt to use a health-care diary in a less competent population failed and a yesterday interview format had to be substituted (Brody 1985).

To summarize the time budget approach, this method has thus far been used in environmental research primarily to determine the location of behavior along a very gross scale. Needed are attempts to explore other dimensions such as degree of environmental awareness, pleasantness or aesthetic quality, demand, problematic quality, or subjective meaning of the type investigated by Csikszentmihalyi and Graef (1980).

ENVIRONMENTAL COGNITION

Although this general topic, especially cognitive mapping and way-finding, has formed one of the major streams of research in general environmental psychology, a relatively small amount of this type of research has been done with older adults.

Dimensions of Environment

Few attempts have been made to determine whether the basic dimensions by which older people categorize their environments are any different from those used by younger people. This writer did attempt pilot work using the semantic differential in the way many environmental investigators have done (reviewed in Hershberger 1972). The semantic differential format, reduced to a 5-point rating scale, was usable; but the original adjectives (from Osgood et al. 1957), when not apparently relevant to the stimuli being used (that is, a series of building pictures that were to be rated on such Osgood scales as ''hard-soft'' or ''hot-cold'') gave major response problems to older subjects. Similar problems emanating from the complexity of the procedure arose when a repertory grid approach (Kelly 1955) was used to elicit unsophisticated subjects' constructs by which real and imagined residential environments were judged (Lawton, unpublished pilot data). Older people had problems first in complying with the long series of tasks demanded by this procedure. The demand to ''choose two that are the same and another that is different from the other two'' taxed the conceptual skills of some older subjects.

However, among a group of relatively well-educated adults, Jirovec (1977) was able to obtain age-comparative semantic differential ratings of home and neighborhood. He found many similarities among age groups in the dimensionality of these concepts. However, older people gave higher neighborhood preference ratings to ''brightness,'' ''age homogeneity,'' and ''familiarity.'' It is reasonable to think that all three of these attributes may have special meaning for the aged. In judging housing, older people generally chose more affective descriptors (''friendliness,'' ''quiet''), while younger people chose structural descriptors (space, shape), as if personal salience were a stronger basis for older people's perceiving housing.

Cognitive Maps

A series of studies of the cognitive maps of older adults has been reported by Regnier and his colleagues. While the author of this chapter was able to get only a small proportion of his poorly educated subjects even to try a freehand drawing of their neighborhood, Walsh et al. (1981) obtained such maps from all of their better-educated subjects. Although they characterized these maps as "limited in scope, disorganized, and minimally complex" (337), they did find suggestive relationships between map parameters and personal characteristics, spatial skills, and use of the environment.

Considerably easier to use is the cognitive map produced in response to the request to delineate the boundaries of one's neighborhood on an actual area map with some orienting features already identified. In a series of such studies (Regnier et al. 1973; Regnier 1976; Walsh et al. 1981), relationships were found between the degree of consensus among neighborhood residents and the location and frequency of service use. Many configurations were differentiated in terms of the salience of their resources to the respondent. For example, Regnier's (1981) mapping of the locations of goods and services used by older people showed that these tended strongly to lie within the "consensus neighborhood" defined by the composite neighborhood boundaries drawn by residents. Further, larger maps were produced by those who were healthier and more mobile.

Cognitive Imagery and Way-finding

There is a substantial body of literature dealing with space perception among the aged (primarily in laboratory settings), for example, Ohta et al. (1981). Walsh et al. (1981) related such laboratory performance in traditional spatial tasks to other more naturalistic spatial behavior. In one of their studies, a hybrid between laboratory and life, a room-sized model of a city, was utilized in tasks presented as both direct viewing (the subject stood overlooking the model) and a simulated "drive through the city" (that is, presented in videotape as if from a car traversing the city). Again, all of their subjects were able to comply with the tasks, which involved both judgments of relative location of elements and a more difficult vicarious perspective-taking task. Their findings suggested only small (though meaningful) degrees of generality across the entire range of space-related behavior, but they illustrate the great potential in experimental methods for expanding our knowledge of how older people deal with space.

The most ecologically valid test of cognitive orientation to space is how people perform in real environments (for example, Ohta and Kirasic 1982). There may be some age-related barriers to such research. Since our concern is often with the macroenvironment (whole buildings, city blocks, neighborhoods, communities), the time taken for such research is often increased by the researcher's need to travel with the subject. Such travel, in turn, may make strong physical demands on some older subjects, especially those with physical or mental impairments.

In a study of preparation for institutional relocation, in fact, Bourestom and Pastalan (n.d.) found some reason to be concerned about whether an actual visit to the prospective relocation site might even be harmful to some vulnerable nursing home residents. Hunt (1984) provided useful data on how knowledge might be obtained without actual travel. He demonstrated that knowledge of an unfamiliar building could be given as well (conceivably, in some instances better) through exposure to an architectural model and videotaped "walks" through a building as from a site visit. The usefulness of ordinary photographs in testing the environmental knowledge of even relatively low-competency older people was demonstrated in research done in nursing homes (Weber et al. 1978; Herman and Bruce 1981).

A very important principle for research of this kind was illustrated in studies done by Weisman (in press), who used approaches similar to those of

Hunt (1984) to examine way-finding in nursing home residents. In addition to the measures of accuracy of performance in the actual or simulated situations, Weisman obtained introspections from his subjects about the cues they had used in both successful and unsuccessful way-finding trials. These qualitative observations added considerably to his ability to translate the findings of his research into design-relevant guidelines.

OTHER METHODS

The remaining methods, to be mentioned only in passing, are primarily variants of other methods. *Projective tests,* such as the set of thematic pictures used by Tobin and Lieberman (1977) to elicit stories about institutional life, have been occasionally used with older people. Carp found them helpful in studying adjustment to new housing (1966). With these stimuli, as in the case of visual stimuli in general, visual capacity can become a limiting factor. In addition, other research on these methods (reviewed by Lawton et al. 1980) suggests that older people are less productive of such fantasies than are younger people.

Games have been used to study environmental preferences, the most effective being those that force the subject to engage in a trade-off—that is, an exchange of mutually exclusive environmental attributes with different advantages and disadvantages. Some of the most carefully designed (such as those described by Robinson, in chapter 4 of this volume) are unfortunately too complex and time-consuming for many older subjects.

Methods for the use of *archival* data hardly justify any age-specific focus. However, it is worth remembering that chronological age is one of the most ubiquitous of all data items. Many existing data sets have never been analyzed in terms of either age differences or within-age-group relationships. Thus one may find interesting and environmentally relevant material in such neglected archives as the Survey of the Low Income and Disabled (U.S. Department of Health and Human Services 1975) or the Survey of Institutionalized Persons (U.S. Department of Health and Human Services 1977), as well as better-known sets like the Annual Housing Survey (U.S. Department of Housing and Urban Development 1974–1981). Although frustrating for the researcher in their typical disarray, the archives of environment types like public housing or institutions for the aged are potential sources of usable information.

Also especially appropriate where knowledge is so thin are *qualitative methods* of inquiry. A foremost example of this approach is Rowles' series of studies of older people in urban (1978) and rural (1980) environments. This research yielded many innovative concepts, such as "environmental fantasy," a mechanism by which older people compensated for reduced geographic motility by nurturing vivid mental images both of places they had once been and of places they had not, and might never, visit. In this approach, people who are not articulate in the "elite" sense are made able to share their views of self and the world. Thus, the traditional large-scale methods given prominence in this chapter must be complemented by methods that, rather than "generating" data, allow the knowledge to emerge.

EXAMPLES OF RESEARCH WITH THE ELDERLY

Housing built especially for older people provides a particularly good opportunity to study person–environment transactions, since all tenants make a move from an ordinary dwelling to this unique type of environment.

The effects of environmental change per se, the effects of the specific environment, the congruence between expectations and reality, and the way needs and their satisfaction change over time are only a few of the research opportunities that have been used by gerontologists studying housing for the aged.

This section will illustrate the application of some of the principles discussed above in the conduct of research done by the author on older tenants in planned housing. The first study interviewed about 1,200 tenants in twelve such housing environments, 443 of them both immediately prior to entry and again twelve months after the housing was occupied (see Lawton 1975; 1980b for more complete accounts of this research). Among the many purposes of the research, one that assessed the social quality of the housing environment will be described here. Specifically, we were concerned about the acceptability of age segregation to older people and the functions of the common spaces in facilitating social behavior within the housing.

Age Segregation

The research design asked two questions: First, do people who live in age-segregated housing feel more positively about living only with others their own age than do older people who have not applied for such housing? Second, does experience with age-segregated housing alter people's preferences?

The structured interview was used for these questions. Community residents might or might not have had actual experience with "senior-citizen housing." Therefore we felt it necessary to preface the age-mix preference question with the statement, "Some buildings are being built for people who are over 62 years of age," followed by the question, "Would you prefer to live in a place with only people over 62 years old or a place with people of all ages?" Tenants who had been accepted for the housing but had not yet moved in would presumably know about age segregation, but the informative statement helped equate the amount of prior knowledge in the two groups. The percentage of community residents who would prefer a building with all ages was 42, as compared to 21 percent of prospective tenants. Because of the problems discussed above regarding the difficulty of anticipating how one might respond to a hypothetical environmental quality, we would not insist very strongly that the estimate of 42 percent already against age-segregated living represented a good estimate of actual future behavior. However, since neither group had yet lived in that kind of environment, the *difference* between the two was of great interest and of significant magnitude to interpret: Housing applicants had clearly sorted themselves out in terms of their prospective tolerance for age segregation.

Another finding of interest was that a full 40 percent of applicants were uncertain whether they would like the age density; only 39 percent were certain they would like it. By contrast, after becoming tenants, only 8 percent still would have preferred age mixing. This is another illustration of the effective use of relative evaluative judgments (in this case, before versus after occupancy), even though the absolute percentage estimates may be error-prone.

It is of interest to note that our successful interview rate was 89 percent, a very high rate for urban areas. Interviewers were trained for a full week, with considerable emphasis on how to explain the purpose of the study and the function of the subjects as "experts." In this case, since housing for the aged was still relatively new, it was very easy to convey to older people how useful their responses could be to future planners, architects, and administrators.

Social Behavior in Planned Housing

Some questions about the effectiveness of an environment in facilitating social behavior can be answered only by examining behavior in the aggregate, rather than by asking a sample of individuals interview questions about such behavior. This is where direct behavior observations, specifically, behavior mapping, was particularly useful. Our twelve housing sites varied considerably in the extent and layout of their common spaces. Our question asked, first, does the amount of social space affect the amount of social behavior, and, second, does the placement of these social spaces affect their use? (see Lawton 1980, ch. 6, for a complete report of this aspect of the research). Our method required observers to walk systematically through all common spaces in each building (space types consisted of halls, the lobby, other lounges, activity spaces, functional spaces, and outdoor spaces). Although we could theoretically have counted behaviors and classified them into many different categories, time limitations demanded that behavior be characterized only as social behavior, traffic, and other. A few of our findings were:

- The greater the use of common spaces, the more social interaction occurs.
- The greatest proportion of all people present in social spaces interact when they are concentrated in single areas such as a lobby, rather than dispersed over many areas.
- Centrally located social spaces received almost five times as much use as peripherally located lounges.
- Buildings with tenants who were less healthy had higher rates of use of social spaces, suggesting that environmental factors may be selectively critical for the less-competent elderly.

The advantage of such behavior mapping was that it could be done relatively unobtrusively, with high reliability and perfect compliance.

Other publications from our research program illustrate how satisfaction and preference questions may be used to best advantage (Lawton and Nahemow 1979a), how local-area census data and individual-level interview data may be combined (Lawton and Nahemow 1979b), and how useful data may be gained from very impaired people who cannot be interviewed (Lawton et al. 1984).

CONCLUSION

Despite the length of the discussions devoted to age differences, age similarities are considerably more striking, both in people's approaches to the testing situation and in the results of environmental research. One can confidently conclude that to the extent that one's subjects are physically and mentally healthy, perceptually competent, reasonably well educated, and native English speaking, they require few age-related accommodations in research procedures. A group that meets all these qualifications may, to be sure, constitute an elite among the aged. However, such high-functioning people are also apt to be particularly good informants about the environment, an area where useful introspections are still welcome. Thus, the researcher would do well to cultivate such expertise among his or her subjects.

The chapter will conclude with a summary of the recommendations for maximizing the quality of research data gathered on older people.

1. Selecting the basic mode of data collection
   - *The interview* is the best all-purpose method, but it is less effective with the deaf, the speech-impaired, the person not fluent in English, and especially the cognitively impaired.
   - *Direct behavior observation* is the method of choice for people with the above impairments, for situations where the behavior of interest can be easily observed, and for behaviors that are difficult for people to report.

- *The questionnaire* is relatively more demanding than an interview and should be reserved for relatively healthy and at least moderately well-educated people with no visual or language handicap.
- *The time budget* is less an alternative to the interview or direct behavior observation than a specific way to learn how behaviors are distributed in time and space. It is time-consuming but a more precise way to answer those specific questions.
- *Qualitative methods* such as ethnography or participant observation are extremely valuable and often may be used to precede a quantitative study, or by experts such as anthropologists, for a new view of phenomena studied by other methods.

2. Improving the quality of interviews
   - Explain at length the purpose of the interview
   - Define unfamiliar concepts
   - Emphasize objective facts in questions—responses will be more valid than for remembered subjective phenomena
   - Keep questions short and uncomplicated
   - Pace questions slowly, maintaining eye contact
   - Use short rating scales
   - Use multi-modal approaches (such as reading the questions aloud while the subject silently reads the question)
   - Keep lists short
   - Limit the interview to a maximum of sixty to ninety minutes, less for telephone interviewing
   - Frame questions in a way that makes it acceptable for people to disagree, give a negative response, or express dissatisfaction
3. Improving the quality of questionnaires
   - Use larger and bolder type than normal
   - Monitor subject's response during process and check when handed in
   - Reserve mail questionnaires for the especially well educated
   - Allow people to compare the present state with a past state, other people's state, or a desired state
4. Improving the quality of observational methods
   - Explain the observer's presence to all inhabitants of a setting
   - Spend time in a "dry run" so that inhabitants get used to the observer before "real data" are gathered
   - Use for research where behavior in public settings is of interest; private spaces are difficult to observe
   - Make use of experimental situations, where subject performs a standard task, for direct observation
   - Define carefully what behavior is to be observed and categorized and what is to be ignored
   - Use recording techniques for complex behaviors or those requiring detailed coding
5. Improving the time budget
   - Use direct self-generated time diaries only with exceptionally responsive and healthy subjects
   - Provide a sample of either a diary or yesterday interview during training
   - Use a seven-day, in preference to a one-day time budget; the number of subjects required to generate reliable estimates is much increased with the one-day budget
   - Attempt to keep the number of categories of behavior and the number of location categories to a minimum

In conclusion, this review has attempted to provide examples of the use of most environmental research methods as applied to older people. The number of such examples among which to choose was distressingly small as far as the more "interior" methods were concerned. For example, such areas as environmental meaning, symbolic aspects of the environment, personal taxonomies of the environment, and the affective connotations of environments have been rarely studied among older people. Many writers speak of "familiarity" as a basis for environmental choices by the elderly. "Attachment" has been invoked as an explanation of why older people move so infrequently. These constructs are highly subjective and have been explored inadequately. The great need at this point is a continued effort to merge the very productive qualitative approach and the more traditional quantitative methods so as to map the interior reaches of older people and environmental transactions.

ACKNOWLEDGMENTS

Many helpful comments and suggestions for additions to this chapter were made by A. Regula Herzog.

REFERENCES

Andrews, F. M., and A. R. Herzog. 1983. *The Quality of Survey Data as Related to Age of Respondent.* Univ. of Michigan, Institute for Social Research, Working Paper No. 8032. Ann Arbor.

Andrews, F. M., and S. B. Withey. 1976. *Social Indicators of Well-Being.* New York: Plenum.

Atchley, R. C. 1969. Respondents vs. refusers in an interview survey of retired women: An analysis of selected characteristics. *Journal of Gerontology* 24:42–47.

Azar, G. J., and A. H. Lawton. 1964. Gait and stepping as factors in the frequent falls of elderly women. *Gerontologist* 4:83–84.

Barker, R. G., and L. S. Barker. 1961. The psychological ecology of old people in Midwest, Kansas, and Yoredale, Yorkshire. *Journa! of Gerontology* 16:231–39.

Barker, R. G., and H. F. Wright. 1967. *Recording and Analyzing Child Behavior.* New York: Harper & Row.

Barton, E., M. Baltes, and M. Orzech. 1980. Etiology of dependence in older nursing home residents during morning care: The role of staff behavior. *Journal of Personality and Social Psychology* 38: 423–31.

Berkowitz, W. R. 1971. A cross-national comparison of some social patterns of urban pedestrians. *Journal of Cross-Cultural Psychology* 2:129–44.

Bornstein, R., and M. T. Smircina. 1982. The status of the empirical support for the hypothesis of increased variability in aging populations. *Gerontologist* 22:258–60.

Botwinick, J. 1966. Cautiousness in advanced age. *Journal of Gerontology* 21:347–53.

———. 1978. *Aging and Behavior.* 2d ed. New York: Springer.

Botwinick, J., and L. W. Thompson. 1968. A research note on individual differences in reaction time in relation to age. *Journal of Genetic Psychology* 112:73–75.

Bourestom, N. C., and L. Pastalan. n.d. *Death and Survival.* Univ. of Michigan, Institute of Gerontology, Relocation Report No. 2. Ann Arbor.

Bradburn, N. M. 1969. *The Structure of Psychological Wellbeing.* Chicago: Aldine.

Bradburn, N. M., and S. Sudman. 1979. *Improving Interview Method and Questionnaire Design.* San Francisco: Jossey-Bass.

Brent, R., E. E. Brent, and R. K. Mauksch. 1984. Common behavior patterns of residents in public areas of nursing homes. *Gerontologist* 24:186–92.

Brody, E. 1985. *Mental and Physical Health Practices of Older People: A Guide for Health Professionals.* New York: Springer.

Campbell, A., P. G. Converse, and W. Rodgers. 1976. *The Quality of American Life.* New York: Russell Sage Foundation.

Carp, F. M. 1966. *A Future for the Aged.* Austin: Univ. of Texas Press.

———. 1974. Position effects on interview responses. *Journal of Gerontology* 29:581–87.

———. 1975. Ego defense or cognitive consistency: Effects of environmental evaluation. *Journal of Gerontology* 30:707–16.

Carp, F. M., and A. Carp. 1981a. It may not be the answer, it may be the question. *Research on Aging* 3:85–100.

———. 1981b. The validity, reliability, and generalization of diary data. *Experimental Aging Research* 7:281–96.

Carp, F. M., A. Carp, and R. Millsap. 1982. Equity and satisfaction among the elderly. *International Journal of Aging and Human Development* 15:151–66.

Chapin, F. S., Jr. 1974. *Human Activity Patterns in the City.* New York: Wiley.

Csikszentmihalyi, M., and R. Graef. 1980. The experience of freedom in daily life. *American Journal of Community Psychology* 8:401–14.

DeLong, A. J. 1974. Environments for the elderly. *Journal of Communication* 24:101–12.

Drevenstedt, J. 1975. Scale-checking styles on the semantic differential among older people. *Journal of Gerontology* 30:170–73.

Faletti, M. V. 1984. Human factors research and functional environments for the aged. In *Elderly People and the Environment,* vol. 7 of *Human Behavior and Environment,* ed. I. Altman, M. P. Lawton, and J. F. Wohlwill, 191–237. New York: Plenum.

Field, D. 1981. Retrospective reports by healthy intelligent elderly people of personal events of their adult lives. *International Journal of Behavioral Development* 4:77–97.

Fischer, C. S. 1982. *To Dwell Among Friends: Personal Networks in Town and City.* Chicago: Univ. of Chicago Press.

Fozard, J. L. 1980. The time for remembering. In *Aging in the 1980s.* ed. L. W. Poon. Washington, D.C.: American Psychological Association.

———. 1981. Person-environment relationships in adults: Implications for human factors engineering. *Human Factors* 23:7–27.

Glenn, N. D. 1969. Aging, disengagement, and opinionation. *Public Opinion Quarterly* 33:17–33.

Golledge, R. G., and G. Zannaras. 1973. Cognitive approaches to the analysis of human spatial behavior. In *Environmental Cognition,* ed. W. H. Ittelson, 59–94. New York: Seminar.

Herman, J. F., and P. R. Bruce. 1981. Spatial knowledge of ambulatory and wheelchair-confined nursing home residents. *Experimental Aging Research* 7:491–96.

Hershberger, R. 1972. Toward a set of semantic scales to measure the meaning of architectural environments. In *Environmental Design: Research and Practice,* ed. W. W. Mitchell, vol. 1. Stroudsburg, Pa.: Dowden, Hutchinson & Ross.

Herzog, A. R., and W. L. Rodgers. 1981. Age and satisfaction: Data from several large surveys. *Research on Aging* 3:142–65.

Herzog, A. R., W. L. Rodgers, and R. A. Kulka. 1983. Interviewing older adults: A comparison of telephone and face-to-face modalities. *Public Opinion Quarterly* 47:405–18.

Howell, S. C. 1980. *Designing for Aging: Patterns of Use.* Cambridge, Mass.: MIT Press.

Hunt, M. E. 1984. Environmental learning without being there. *Environment and Behavior* 16:307–34.

Ittelson, W. H., L. G. Rivlin, and H. M. Proshansky. 1970. The use of behavioral maps in environmental psychology. In *Environmental Psychology: Man and His Physical Setting,* ed. H. M. Proshansky, W. H. Ittelson, and L. G. Rivlin, 658–68. New York: Holt, Rinehart, & Winston.

Jirovec, R. L. 1977. Optimal residential environments across the lifespan. Paper presented at the annual meeting of the Gerontological Society, San Francisco, Cal.

Kaplan, O. J., et al. 1964. Effects of level of surviving abilities, time of day, and test-retest upon psychological performance. *Journal of Gerontology* 18:55–59.

Kelly, G. A. 1955. *The Psychology of Personal Constructs.* New York: Norton.

Klocke, R. A. 1977. Influence of aging on the lung.

In *Handbook of the Biology of Aging,* ed. C. E. Finch and L. Hayflick, 432–44. New York: Van Nostrand Reinhold.

Kogan, N. L. 1961. Attitudes toward old people: The development of a scale and examination of correlates. *Journal of Abnormal and Social Psychology* 62:616–22.

Kohn, R. R. 1977. Heart and cardiovascular system. In *Handbook of the Biology of Aging,* ed. C. E. Finch and L. Hayflick, 281–317. New York: Van Nostrand Reinhold.

Kuriansky, J. B., and B. J. Gurland. 1976. The performance test of activities of daily living. *International Journal of Aging and Human Development* 7:343–52.

Larson, R. 1978. Thirty years of research on the subjective wellbeing of older Americans. *Journal of Gerontology* 33:109–25.

Lawton, M. P. 1970. Public behavior of older people in congregate housing. In *Environmental Design Research Association,* vol. 2, ed. J. Archea and C. Eastman, 372–80. Stroudsburg, Pa.: Dowden, Hutchinson & Ross.

———. 1975a. The Philadelphia Geriatric Center Morale Scale: A revision. *Journal of Gerontology* 30:85–89.

———. 1975b. *Planning and Managing Housing for the Elderly.* New York: Wiley-Interscience.

———. 1977. Methodologies for evaluation in environment and aging. In *The Behavioral Basis of Design,* ed. P. Suedfeld, J. A. Russell, L. M. Ward, F. Szigeti, and G. Davis, vol. 2. Stroudsburg, Pa.: Dowden, Hutchinson & Ross.

———. 1978. *Occasional Papers in Housing and Community Affairs,* no. 1, 39–74. Washington, D.C.: U.S. Government Printing Office.

———. 1980a. *Environment and Aging.* Monterey, Cal.: Brooks/Cole.

———. 1980b. *Social and Medical Services in Housing for the Aged.* Rockville, Md.: National Institute of Mental Health.

———. In press, a. Metaphors of environmental influences on aging. In *Aging as Metaphor,* ed. J. E. Thornton. Vancouver, B.C., Canada: Univ. of British Columbia Press.

———. In press, b. Housing and living environments of the elderly. In *Handbook of Social Gerontology,* 2d ed., ed. R. H. Binstock and E. Shanas. New York: Van Nostrand Reinhold.

Lawton, M. P., M. Fulcomer, and M. H. Kleban. 1984. Architecture for the mentally impaired elderly. *Environment and Behavior* 16:730–57.

Lawton, M. P., and M. Moss. In press. Objective and subjective uses of time by older people. *International Journal of Aging and Human Development.*

Lawton, M. P., and L. Nahemow. 1979a. Social science methods for evaluating the quality of housing for the elderly. *Journal of Architectural Research* 7:5–11.

———. 1979b. Social areas and the well-being of tenants in planned housing for the elderly. *Multivariate Behavioral Research* 14:463–84.

Lawton, M. P., W. M. Whelihan, and J. K. Belsky. 1980. Personality tests and their uses with older adults. In *Handbook of Aging and Mental Health,* ed. J. E. Birren and B. Sloane. New York: Prentice-Hall.

Lee, G. R., and J. M. Finney. 1977. Sampling in social gerontology: A method of locating specialized populations. *Journal of Gerontology* 32:689–93.

Moss, M., and M. P. Lawton. 1982. The time budgets of older people: A window on four life-styles. *Journal of Gerontology* 37:115–23.

Murray, H. 1938. *Explorations in Personality.* New York: Oxford.

National Council on the Aging. 1981. *Aging in the Eighties: America in Transition.* Washington, D.C.: National Council on the Aging.

Neugarten, B. L. 1982. Dilemma in Developmental Psychology. Paper presented at the annual meeting of the American Psychological Association, Washington, D.C.

Neugarten, B. L., R. J. Havighurst, and S. S. Tobin. 1961. The measurement of life satisfaction. *Journal of Gerontology* 16:134–43.

Niederehe, G. 1982. Measuring Family System Characteristics in Families Caring for Dementia Patients. Paper presented at the annual meeting of the Gerontological Society of America, Boston.

Norris-Baker, C., and E. P. Willems. 1979. Environmental negotiability as a direct measure of behavior–environment relationships. In *Environmental Design: Research, Theory, and Application,* ed. A. D. Seidel and S. Danford. Washington, D.C.: Environmental Design Research Association.

Ohta, R. J., and K. C. Kirasic. 1982. Environmental learning. In *Aging and Milieu,* ed. G. Rowles and R. J. Ohta. New York: Academic Press.

Ohta, R. J., D. A. Walsh, and I. K. Krauss. 1981. Spatial perspective-taking ability and young and elderly adults. *Experimental Aging Research* 7:45–63.

Osgood, C. E., G. J. Suci, and G. J. Tannenbaum. 1957. *The Measurement of Meaning.* Urbana, Ill.: Univ. of Illinois Press.

Parsons, H. M. 1981. Residential design for the aging (for example, the bedroom). *Human Factors* 23:39–58.

Pastalan, L. A. 1979. Sensory changes and environmental behavior. In *The Environmental Context of Aging,* ed. T. O. Byerts, S. C. Howell, and L. A. Pastalan, 118–26. New York: Garland.

Powers, E. A., W. J. Goudy, and P. M. Keith. 1978. Congruence between panel and recall data in longitudinal research. *Public Opinion Quarterly* 42:380–89.

Regnier, V. A. 1976. Neighborhoods as service systems. In *Community Planning for an Aging Society,* ed. M. P. Lawton, R. J. Newcomer, and T. O. Byerts, 240–59. Stroudsburg, Pa.: Dowden, Hutchinson & Ross.

———. 1981. Neighborhood images and use. In *Community Housing Choices for Older Americans,* ed. M. P. Lawton and S. L. Hoover. New York: Springer.

Regnier, V. A., R. A. Eribes, and W. Hansen. 1973. Cognitive Mapping as a Concept for Establishing Neighborhood Service Delivery Locations for Older People. Proceedings of the eighth annual Association for Computing Machinery Symposium, New York City.

Ridley, J. C., C. A. Bachrach, and D. A. Dawson. 1979. Recall and reliability of interview data from older women. *Journal of Gerontology* 34:99–105.

Robinson, J. P. 1977. *How Americans Use Time.* New York: Praeger.

Rodgers, W., and A. R. Herzog. 1982. *Response style characteristics and their relationships to age and to item covariances.* Ann Arbor: Institute for Social Research. Univ. of Michigan.

Rowles, G. D. 1978. *Prisoners of Space?* Boulder, Colo.: Westview Press.

———. 1980. Growing old "inside": Aging and attachment to place in an Appalachian community. In *Transitions of Aging,* ed. N. Datan and N. Lohmann, 153–70. New York: Academic Press.

Schaie, K. W. 1974. Translations in gerontology—from lab to life: Intellectual functioning. *American Psychologist* 29:802–7.

Sivadon, P. 1970. Space as experienced: Therapeutic implications. In *Environmental Psychology,* ed. H. M. Proshansky, W. H. Ittelson, and L. G. Rivlin, 409–19. New York: Holt, Rinehart & Winston.

Stephens, M. A. P., and E. P. Willems. 1979. Everyday behavior of older persons in institutional housing. In *Environmental Design: Research, Theory, and Application,* ed. A. D. Seidel and S. Danford. Washington, D.C.: Environmental Design Research Association.

Sudman, S., and N. M. Bradburn. 1974. *Response Effects in Surveys.* Chicago: Aldine.

Szalai, A. ed. 1972. *The Use of Time.* The Hague: Mouton.

Tobin, S., and M. A. Lieberman. 1977. *Last Home for the Aged.* San Francisco: Jossey-Bass.

U.S. Bureau of the Census. 1974–1981. Annual Housing Survey, 1973–1976. Washington, D.C.: U.S. Government Printing Office.

———. 1982. Households, families, marital status and living arrangements: March 1982. *Current Population Reports.* Series P-20, no. 376. Washington, D.C.

U.S. Department of Health and Human Services. 1975. Survey of the Low Income and Disabled.

Public-use data tape. Washington, D.C.: Social Security Administration.

———. 1977. Survey of Institutionalized Persons. Public-use data tape. Washington, D.C.: Assistant Secretary for Planning and Evaluation.

Veroff, J., R. A. Kulka, and E. Douvan. 1981. *Mental Health in America.* New York: Basic Books.

Walsh, D. A., I. K. Krauss, and V. A. Regnier. 1981. Spatial ability, environmental knowledge, and environmental use: The elderly. In *Spatial Representation and Behavior across the Life Span,* ed. L. S. Liben, A. H. Patterson, and N. Newcombe, 321–57. New York: Academic Press.

Weber, R., L. Brown, and J. Weldon. 1978. Cognitive maps of environmental knowledge and preference in nursing home patients. *Experimental Aging Research* 4:157–74.

Weisman, G. D. In press. Way-finding and architectural legibility: Design considerations in housing environments for the elderly. In *Housing for the Elderly: Satisfaction and Preferences,* ed. V. Regnier and J. Pynoos. New York: Garland.

White House Conference on Aging. 1981. Chartbook on Aging in America. Washington, D.C.: WHCOA.

Zajonc, R. B. 1968. Attitudinal effects of mere exposure. *Journal of Personality and Social Psychology,* Monograph Supplement 9:1–28 (2, part 2).

CHAPTER 12

LANDSCAPE ASSESSMENT AND PERCEPTION RESEARCH METHODS

Jonathan G. Taylor
Ervin H. Zube
and James L. Sell

The representation, design, and understanding of landscapes has been a topic of interest at least since the Renaissance. For a long time, the methods used by students of landscapes, notably landscape architects and geographers, were highly individual, consisting of procedures developed through personal experience and often molded by idiosyncratic interests and values. Usually there was no serious attempt to determine whether these personal assessments were similar to other people's perceptions of the landscape. Within the last two decades, however, there has been a broadening of interest, as well as a concern for a more general standardization of landscape values. This concern is an outgrowth of such laws as the U.S. National Environmental Policy Act of 1969, which called for the development of procedures " . . . which will insure that previously unquantified environmental amenities and values may be given appropriate consideration in decision making along with economic and technical considerations."

Implementation of such a mandate required environmental managers and policy makers to search for methods of landscape assessment that were explicit, able to stand up under public scrutiny, and provide some measure (often numeric) to compare against economic or technical measures. This need resulted in the broadening of the base of researchers in landscape assessment, to include such groups as psychologists, public land managers, lawyers, and ecologists. Many people in these areas, as well as those in the other landscape study disciplines, tended to ignore existing data and methods and to use their own disciplinary paradigms to develop tools to measure landscape aesthetics and other values. In short order a proliferation of landscape assessment techniques appeared based upon a number of different conceptual approaches. Although several conferences have demonstrated broad areas of common interest among a large number of researchers, they also indicate little agreement about how to assess landscape values (Zube et al. 1975; Craik and Zube 1975; Elsner and Smardon 1979). More recently, several attempts have been made to draw this diversity into some sort of order (Lowenthal 1978; Penning-Rowsell 1981; Porteous 1982; Zube et al. 1982; Daniel and Vining 1983). It has also been asserted that an important reason for this methodological Babel has been the lack of attention to theory, resulting in methods being developed without adequate consideration for the nature of humans, their activities, or their aesthetic response (Zube et al. 1982; Appleton 1975a; Appleton 1975b; Sell et al. 1984).

The primary purpose of this chapter is to present some of the methods used in landscape assessment. It is important as well to discuss some considerations in adopting and applying these methods, especially in terms of theoretical background, criteria for testing and measurement, the representation of real landscapes, and legal applicability.

The examination of the theoretical background of this body of literature requires some means of order. In a recent review the authors developed a classification scheme for landscape assessment research using a simple model (fig. 12-1) of the human-landscape interaction process (Zube et al. 1982). This model considers humans and their landscapes to exist in a situation of mutual influence, each affecting the character and quality of the other. The interaction between humans and landscapes leads to outcomes that feed back to the interacting elements. By examining various research techniques in terms of the model, it is possible to organize them into a number of research paradigms.

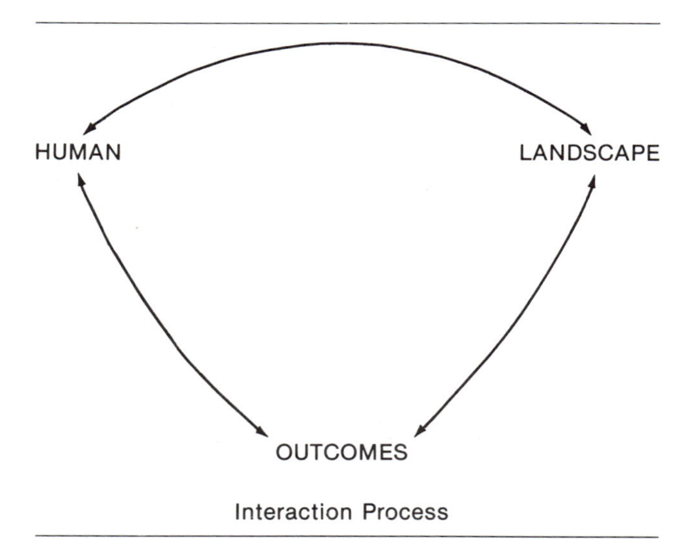

12-1. Model of landscape perception.

Four paradigms were identified on the basis of the model: expert, psychophysical, cognitive, and experiential. In the expert paradigm, the assessments are done by highly skilled observers such as landscape architects or ecologists. In the psychophysical paradigm, landscape values seem to derive from the actions of landscape stimulus features on passive human respondents. In the cognitive paradigm, people tend to be seen as "thinkers" whose aesthetic values come from the way information is given meaning in the mind or through social process. The experiential paradigm views people as active participants in the landscape, deriving their values from experience. Each of these paradigms has strengths and weaknesses, and each may be better suited for different kinds of problems. Choice of a technique must rest on realistic theoretical grounds, but there are also methodological criteria for evaluating approaches.

Daniel and Vining suggested four criteria for evaluating measurement techniques in the study of psychological testing (Daniel and Vining 1983). These criteria—validity, reliability, sensitivity, and utility—have been used in the assessment of various approaches to landscape assessment. *Validity* is the relationship between what is measured and what is purported to be measured. For example, there is assumed to be a valid relationship between IQ and intelligence, and in the context of landscape, between topographic relief and scenic quality. *Reliability* is the consistency of results from repeated measurements; if a test given under similar conditions does not yield similar results, it is not considered reliable. *Sensitivity* is the ability of the technique to measure actual differences; if the test is not able to measure a difference we know to exist, such as between a park and a garbage dump, we should doubt its sensitivity. *Utility* determines whether the test yields findings that can be used for what is intended; a measurement that does not show what landscape elements can be managed will not be useful for managers, no matter how valid.

A special problem of validity also pertains to the relationship between real and represented environments. In many cases it is difficult and expensive to obtain public assessments of real landscapes, especially when the effects of proposed changes are the subject of attention. This difficulty in dealing with the real landscape has led to extensive use of simulations and surrogates. It might be useful to distinguish between the two terms: a surrogate is a substitute for a real environment, such as a photograph; a simulation is an analogue, something that is similar to but not really representative of an actual landscape. A scale model is a simulation; so is a photograph retouched to show expected environmental changes (Daniel and Ittelson 1981). The major issue regarding simulations and surrogates is the degree to which they represent real landscapes, and whether or not people react to them in the same way. There is some evidence to suggest that photographs may be valid surrogates of real environments (Shuttleworth 1980) but that line drawings are not (Zube 1973). A second issue regarding simulations and surrogates is insuring that the representations provide an unbiased sample of scenes from the represented landscape. Strategies have included random sampling, cross-sectional sampling, and opportunity sampling.

Another criterion that is becoming increasingly important is usefulness in litigation. Judgments of landscape aesthetics have been argued in court, and specialists in landscape assessment have been called upon as expert witnesses. The role of various measurement approaches in an adversarial situation in a courtroom demands that legality be included, as well as theoretical and methodological considerations, in choosing a technique for landscape assessment.

RESEARCH PARADIGMS

In this section, we will discuss each of the four paradigms of landscape perception research from the perspectives of their theoretical origins and assumptions. The kinds of landscape evaluations that have been made within each paradigm will be discussed, and some illustrative examples will be given of methodologies within each paradigm.

The Expert Paradigm

Origins and Assumptions. Expert evaluation of landscape quality derives from two general intellectual traditions: (1) fine arts and design, and (2) ecology and resource management. Laurie suggested that artists, writers, and designers have become ''sensitized to beauty and ugliness'' through their profession and training and that this increased sensitivity qualifies them to be better judges of landscape aesthetic quality than ordinary people (1975). The landscape quality evaluation method that Litton and others have developed for the U.S. Forest Service depends heavily on formal landscape architecture criteria: scale, boundaries and edges, land form, plant cover, water elements, and focal attractions (1968). Arguments about the validity of the art expert approach rest on principles derived from the art and design disciplines, for this tradition draws upon the work of earlier professionals and the demonstrated successes or failures of designed landscapes and of specific landscape components.

The ecological tradition contains a strong implied assumption that natural, unmodified ecosystems have the greatest intrinsic aesthetic quality. This assumption is evident in Smardon's assessment work on inland wetlands of Massachusetts (1975). Leopold's model for evaluating river corridor aesthetics, developed for the U.S. Geological

Survey, assumes a strong positive correlation between "degree of naturalness" and "landscape interest" (1969). An assumption held by many resource managers is that proper natural resource management will automatically produce quality landscape aesthetics. Generally, this assumption is not explicitly stated, but can be seen as an implicit underlying assumption. Undoubtedly this opinion is true among resource professionals—a properly managed forest is a thing of beauty to the forester—but whether the same can be said for the perceptions of the general public remains unproven, at best.

Within the expert paradigm, evaluations of landscape quality are done by skilled experts, or others given specific training to enable them to conduct valid assessments. The assumption here is that landscape perception is an emotional, subjective reaction on the part of the general public, and therefore it is necessary to employ professionals in order to obtain more objective, reliable assessments. The "superior" ability of experts is sometimes tacitly assumed and sometimes expressly stated. For example, Carlson argued that "public opinion . . . [is] untenable . . . as an approach to aesthetics," and that the evaluation of a trained expert is far superior to surveys of the landscape preferences of the general public (1977). Wright noted that acceptable landscape assessments must either be "replicated throughout the community, or the status of the persons giving the opinion must be acceptable." To bring both of these criteria together, Wright stressed the importance of training, using "a team of inexperienced persons . . . trained to evaluate landscape in an internally consistent manner" (1974).

By looking at the expert paradigm in terms of our general model of the human–landscape interaction, we can make some broad statements about its underlying assumptions. The *human* side of the equation is defined in terms of an elite group of highly trained, skilled observers who are capable of making value judgments for the rest of society; although capable of being educated, the general public has no intrinsic capacity for judging landscape value. The *landscape* properties important to expert assessments are those the experts have been trained to see, either through principles of art and design (such as form, balance, contrast, or points of focus), or through principles of ecology and resource management (such as species, diversity, quality of timber, or lack of evidence of humans). The *outcomes* of the interaction tend to be some statements of landscape quality, which are expected to lead to the development of an enhanced sense of landscape beauty.

Applications and Examples. After the passage of the major environmental values legislation in the 1960s and 1970s, environmental managers in Great Britain and North America first turned to experts to develop approaches to landscape assessment. In fact, the expert approach generally has dominated the practical side of the field, especially in the early days. In the authors' literature survey, 40 percent of the landscape perception articles reviewed fell within the expert paradigm (Zube et al. 1982). The majority of these were concerned with forest land, river management, and rural planning. Rural planning was a special concern in Great Britain from the start, where it was necessary to control incursions of urban development in the rural countryside. Linton, for example, included urbanization as a negative factor in his rating of landscapes in Scotland (1968). Fines, working on the urban fringe of London, developed a classification of townscape types ranging from slums to "classic towns" (1968). Other rural landscape evaluations cover criteria for selecting "Areas of Outstanding Natural Beauty" in Great Britain or scenic rivers and scenic highways in the United States. The visual effects of a broad variety of man-made structures have been studied, including roads, park and recreation structures, dams, utility lines, and buildings. In addition, several expert paradigm articles deal with landscape quality in outdoor recreation areas, although most recreation aesthetics research involves user surveys and therefore falls within the psychophysical paradigm.

In the United States, the vast areas of government land and the competing interests in exploiting it have led the land management agencies to take special interest in expert ways of rating landscapes. Leopold's pioneering effort leaned toward ecological and human use factors in evaluating riverscape aesthetics (Leopold 1969). Leopold's work was sponsored by the U.S. Geological Survey in response to the Federal Power Commission's consideration of a dam in Hell's Canyon of the Snake River (Idaho); this technique was also used on rivers in several national parks (Leopold 1970; Wilson-Hodges 1978). The Bureau of Land Management (BLM) and U.S. Forest Service (USFS) have relied more heavily on design principles drawn from landscape architecture. Litton and Burke have worked on the development of techniques for use by the USFS. Litton stressed the appraisal of ''visual vulnerability'' using four major criteria: compositional types, feature landscape, enclosure, and focus (1972). Burke developed a set of ''characteristic landscapes'' for his evaluations, using features of contrast, sequence, axis, convergence, codominance, and enframement (1975). The Bureau of Land Management manual also stressed the importance of visual elements of design, especially in terms of the strength and variety of form, line, color, and texture (BLM 1980).

Linton's method used a ''Form and Mantle'' evaluation involving numerical ratings of land form and land use categories, which, when added (or subtracted), provided a general scenic rating (1968). Figure 12–2 illustrates the matrix provided by the two dimensions. The total numbers in the matrix cells are the scenic values; higher numbers are more scenic than lower ones. The classification system is designed for use by inexperienced people. All one needs to know is the category of land use or land form; once that is established, Linton's predetermined values can be added into the equation. Linton also added bonus points for the presence of water in the view, two points for water in the foreground or middle ground, and one for its presence anywhere in upland areas. Obviously, the numbers were determined by Linton's judgment of scenic quality and seem to reflect a preference for wild, mountain areas with a rejection of urbanized lowlands. This may perhaps be well suited to the aesthetic values of Scotland, where it was applied.

Fines developed a set of twenty ''exemplary photographs'' of representative landscape types in three general categories of highland, lowland, and townscape (1968). These photographs were given numerical ratings by a panel of experts (originally people without design training were also asked to rate these scenes, but Fines decided to use only the professionals' judgments for his final rating scheme). Comparison of the views in the field with the ''exemplary views'' was expected to provide a ''yardstick'' for a scenic classification of landscapes. Figure 12–3 shows how Fines scaled his values, and also provides a more detailed look at his landscape categories. By adding value ratings for all possible views of a tract of land, Fines could map scenic values in an area.

Leopold's procedure was designed to meet the practical consequences of river management, in the first instance to determine the aesthetic impacts of a dam in a scenic canyon (1969). Leopold's major goals were to develop a rating system for scenic beauty and to calculate the degree to which a site was unique. This system used a list of forty-six separate categories broadly grouped into the three areas of stream geomorphology, ecology, and human use and interest. For each category a number from one to five was assigned, one being the best rating. As can be seen in figure 12–4, these numbers tended to be quite specific for most physical and ecological criteria and more vague for human factors. This system is a fine example of the eco-

LANDFORM

Category and rating	***0 Lowland***	***2 Low Uplands***	***3 Plateau Uplands***	***5 Hill Country***	***6 Bold Hills***	***8 Mountains***
−5 Urbanized and industrialized	−5	−3	−2	0	+1	+3
−2 Continuous forest	−2	0	+1	+3	+4	+6
+1 Treeless farmland	+1	+3	+4	+6	+7	+9
+3 Moorland	+3	+5	+6	+8	+9	+11
+4 Varied forest and moorland	+4	+6	+7	+9	+10	+12
+5 Richly varied farmland	+5	+7	+8	+10	+11	+13
+6 Wild landscape	+6	+8	+9	+11	+12	+14

***12–2. Linton's Scenery Assessment Matrix. Adapted from Linton, 1968. Reprinted with permission of* Scottish Geographical Magazine.**

logical experts' partiality toward the natural ecosystem, in which any evidence of human use lowers the scenic rating.

The U.S. Forest Service developed a set of visual landscape manuals based on landscape architectural design principles (USFS 1973, 1974). The primary concern of the Forest Service scheme is to evaluate visual harmony using three fundamental concepts: the identifiable character of the landscape (''characteristic landscape''), the visual variety, and the deviations from the characteristic landscape (1973). These basic concepts are examined using three sets of criteria: ''dominance elements,'' ''dominance principles,'' and ''variable factors.'' Dominance elements (fig. 12–5) are the basic visual modes of form, line, color, and texture, which are assumed to be the basic ingredients of landscape perception. Dominance principles affect the perception of dominance elements. There are six of these principles (illustrated in fig. 12–6), consisting of contrast, sequence, axis, convergence, codominance, and enframement. Finally, the variable factors recognize that changes in visual condition can affect how the dominance elements are perceived. The manual identified eight variable factors (see fig. 12–7), including motion, light, at-

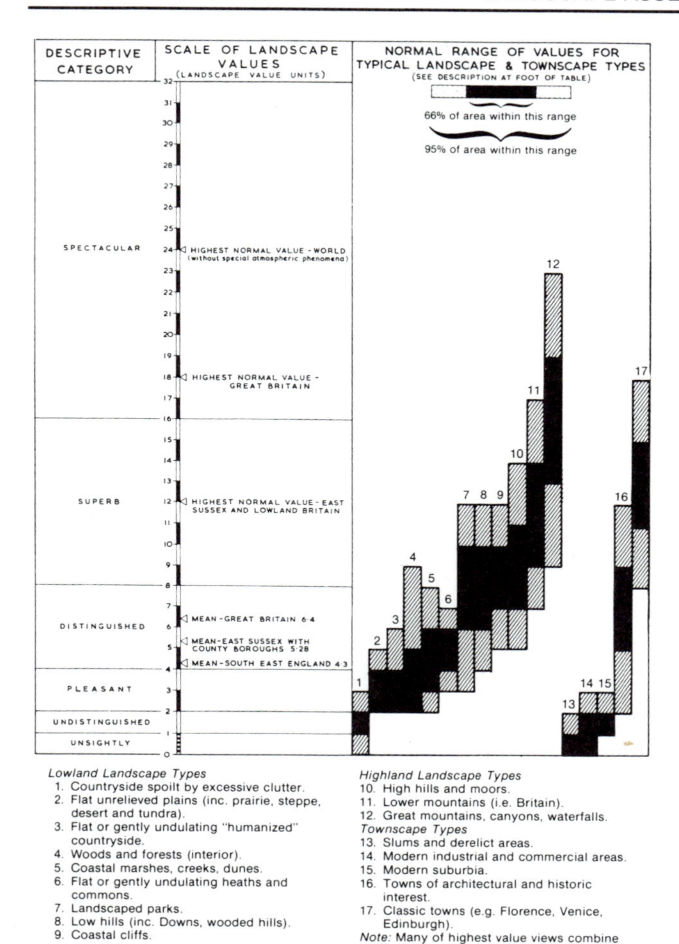

12–3. Scale of landscape values. Reprinted with permission from* Regional Studies, *2, K. D. Fines, "Landscape Evaluation: A Research Project in East Sussex," copyright 1968, Pergamon Press, Ltd.

mospheric conditions, season, distance, observer position, scale, and time (USFS 1973). Along with the fundamentals of landscape character, variety, and deviations, there was a consideration of the level of "sensitivity" in the USFS procedure (fig. 12–7). Actually, sensitivity (fig. 12–8) is not really a measure of public concern for environments. It is instead a measure of the degree to which places will be seen from travel routes, use areas, and water bodies. Areas of high sensitivity, then, need only be seen by many people; they are not necessarily the best scenery. The Forest Service manual does not specify any numerical ratings for this procedure, relying primarily upon subjective judgments of what are essentially unquantifiable qualities.

The Bureau of Land Management Visual Resources Management Program has many similarities to the USFS system; however, it adds a numerical rating (BLM 1980). The BLM process is based upon three stated premises that: (1) landscape character is primarily determined by the four basic visual elements of form, line, color, and texture; (2) the stronger the influence of these elements, the more interesting the landscape; and (3) the more visual variety, the more aesthetically pleasing the landscape—except that variety without harmony represents intrusion and detracts from aesthetic pleasure. There are seven "key factors" in the BLM landscape rating procedure: land form, vegetation, water, color, adjacent scenery, scarcity, and cultural modifications. The landscape factors are scored according to the chart in figure 12–9, and these scores are totaled to yield three Scenic Quality Classes:

- Class A (19–33 points): combines the most outstanding characteristics of each rating factor
- Class B (12–18 points): represents a mix of some outstanding and some common features
- Class C (1–11 points): represents features common to the area

As in the Forest Service procedure, the BLM combines these Scenic Quality classes with "sensitivity levels" to derive a set of Landscape Management Classes. Sensitivity levels are based upon a combination of user attitude and use volume, and of distance zones for the view—foreground, middleground, or seldom seen.

Factor Number	Descriptive Categories	Evaluation Numbers				
		1	2	3	4	5
	Physical Factors					
1	River width (ft.) (at	<3	3–10	10–30	30–100	>100
2	Depth (ft.) low	<.5	.5–1	1–2	2–5	>5
3	Velocity (ft. per sec.) flow)	<.5	.5–1	1–2	3–5	>5
4	Stream depth (ft.)	<1	1–2	2–4	4–8	>8
5	Flow variability	Little variation		Normal	Ephemeral or large variation	
6	River pattern	Torrent	Pool & riffle	w/o riffles	Meander	Braided
7	Valley height/width	≤1	2–5	5–10	11–14	>15
8	Steam bed material	Clay or silt	Sand	Sand & gravel	Gravel	Cobbles or larger
9	Bed slope (ft./ft.)	<.0005	.0005–.001	.001–.005	.005–.01	>.01
10	Drainage area (sq. mi.)	<1	1–10	10–100	100–1000	>1000
11	Stream order	≤2	3	4	5	≥6
12	Erosion of banks	Stable		Slumping		Eroding
13	Sediment deposition in bed	Stable				Large-scale deposition
14	Width of valley flat (ft.)	<100	100–300	300–500	500–1000	1000
	Biological Water Quality Factors					
15	Water color	Clear colorless		Green tints		Brown
16	Turbidity (ppm)	<25	25–150	150–1000	1000–5000	>5000
17	Floating material	None	Vegetation	Foamy	Oily	Variety
18	Water condition (general)	Poor		Good		Excellent
	Algae					
19	Amount	Absent				Infested
20	Type	Green	Blue-green	Diatom	Floating green	None
	Larger Plants					
21	Amount	Absent				Infested
22	Kind	None	Unknown rooted	Elodea duck weed	Water lily	Cattail
23	River fauna	None				Large variety
24	Pollution evidence	None				Evident
	Land flora					
25	Valley	Open	Open with grass, trees	Brushy	Wooded	Trees and brush
26	Hillside	Open	Open with grass, trees	Brushy	Wooded	Trees and brush
27	Diversity	Small				Great
28	Condition	Good				Overused
	Human Use & Interest Factors					
	Trash & litter					
29	Metal (no. per	<2	2–5	5–10	10–50	>50
30	Paper 100 ft. of	<2	2–5	5–10	10–50	>50
31	Other river)	<2	2–5	5–10	10–50	>50

12–4. Definition of class categories: Leopold model. Reprinted with permission from L. B. Leopold, "Landscape Esthetics," Ekistics *29: p. 272.*

Factor Number	Descriptive Categories	Evaluation Numbers				
		1	2	3	4	5
32	Material removable	Easily removed				Difficult removal
33	Artificial controls (dams, etc.)	Free and natural				Controlled
	Accessibility					
34	Individual	Wilderness				Urban or paved access
35	Mass use	Wilderness				Urban or paved access
36	Local scene	Diverse views and scenes				Closed or without diversity
37	Vistas	Vistas of far places				Closed or no vistas
38	View confinement	Open or no obstructions				Closed by hills, cliffs, or trees
39	Land use	Wilderness	Grazed	Lumbering	Forest, mixed recreation	Urbanized
40	Utilities	Scene unobstructed by power lines				Scene obstructed by utilities
41	Degree of change	Original				Materially altered
42	Recovery potential	Natural recovery				Natural recovery unlikely
43	Urbanization	No buildings				Many buildings
44	Special views	None				Unusual interest
45	Historic features	None				Many
46	Misfits	None				Many

KEY:
< less than
> greater than
≤ less than or equal to
≥ greater than or equal to
/ divided by

Figure 12–4 continued

As may be implied by the above examples, the expert approach tends to dominate in the visual management processes of at least two of the largest land management agencies in the United States. There are practical advantages to the expert approach, including the need for only a few trained personnel and the ease of application to field or air photo ratings. There is also, however, some awareness of the weaknesses of the expert paradigm, and the same agencies that have published the above manuals have also supported the development of alternative approaches (Elsner and Smardon 1979; Daniel and Boster 1976). The alternative that received the most interest from people in environmental management and policy making is the psychophysical.

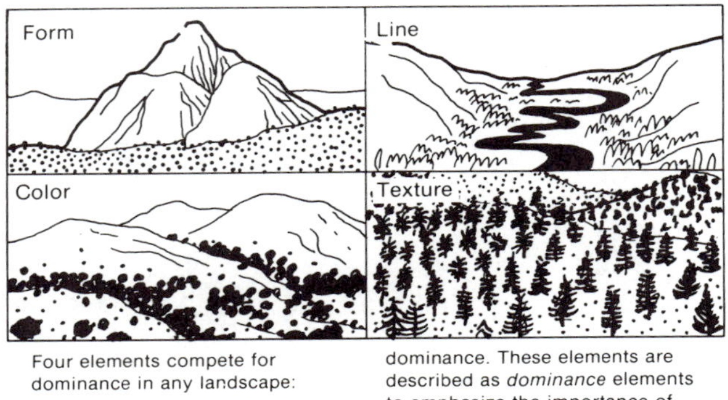

Four elements compete for dominance in any landscape:

- Form
- Line
- Color
- Texture

All four elements are usually present but exert differing degrees of visual influence, power or dominance. These elements are described as *dominance* elements to emphasize the importance of looking at both the landscape and the proposed management practice in two ways: (1) their basic visual ingredients and (2) the relative strengths of each.

12–5. Dominance elements.

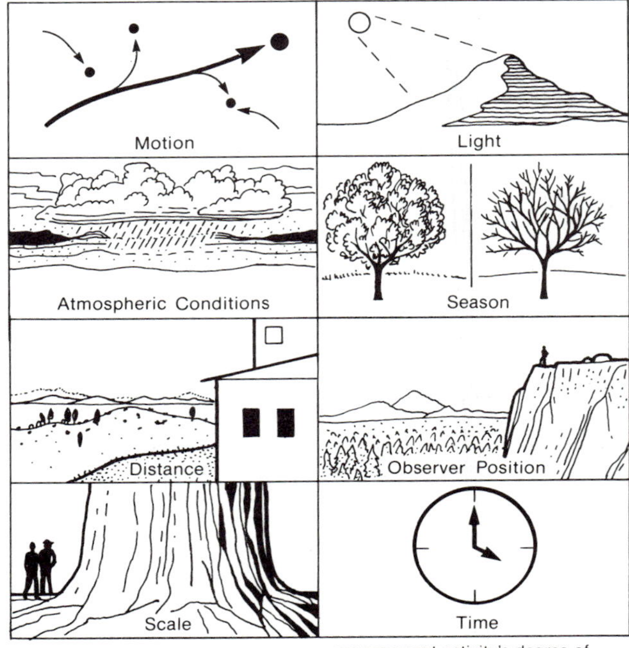

- Motion
- Light
- Atmospheric Conditions
- Season
- Distance
- Observer Position
- Scale
- Time

Eight factors affect how the dominance elements (form, line, color, or texture) are seen. These factors help to identify the most critical location or time to judge a management activity's degree of visual impact.

In analyzing the influence of variable factors on visual dominance, it is most important to choose the conditions which give the activity the greatest contrast with the characteristic landscape.

In other words, we want to judge the potential visual impacts under the most severe, most sensitive conditions possible.

12–7. Variable factors.

The Psychophysical Paradigm

Origins and Assumptions. The psychophysical paradigm is founded upon traditional experimental psychology, in which carefully controlled experimental manipulations are used to stimulate measurable reactions in subjects. In landscape perception research its special strength has been to widen the base of scenic assessments, by measuring the aesthetic values of the general public. Although some may consider this psychophysical approach to be atheoretical, closer consideration reveals several implicit assumptions about the nature of the human–landscape interaction. The most important assumption is that the landscape or elements of the landscape act as stimuli to which observers respond. The value of the landscape is assumed to be its stimulus property. This property is outside the observer, does not vary, and can be perceived without thinking. Thought processes are less likely to

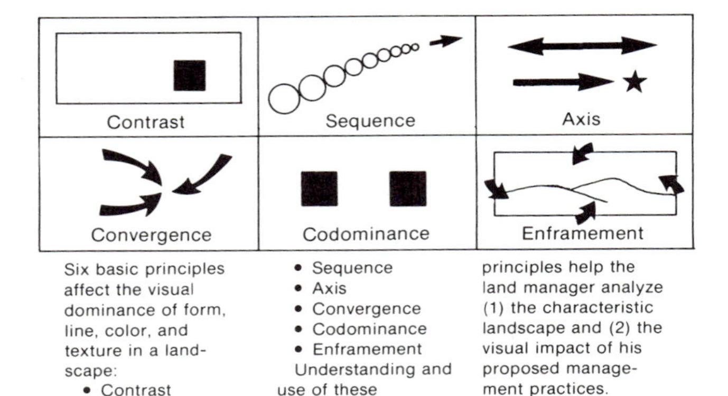

Six basic principles affect the visual dominance of form, line, color, and texture in a landscape:

- Contrast
- Sequence
- Axis
- Convergence
- Codominance
- Enframement

Understanding and use of these principles help the land manager analyze (1) the characteristic landscape and (2) the visual impact of his proposed management practices.

12–6. Dominance principles. From U.S. Forest Service, 1973.

	Primary importance	Secondary importance
Travel route	National importance High-use volume Long-use duration Forest land access roads	Local importance Low-use volume Short-use duration Project roads
Use areas	National importance High-use volume Long-use duration Large size	Local importance Low-use volume Short-use duration Small size
Water bodies	National importance High fishing use High boating use High swimming use	Local importance Low fishing use Low boating use Low swimming use

12–8. Sensitivity factors. From U.S. Forest Service, 1974.

be used in determining preferences than in justifying the decision afterward.

The psychophysical paradigm relies heavily on stimulus–response assumptions that originate in psychology, especially behaviorism. Gibson provided a considered modification of stimulus–response notions in his theory of "affordances" (Gibson 1977). In this theory, the observer perceives what is "offered" ("afforded") by the environment, in terms of possibilities for behavior. For example, a chair "affords" sitting down. Value is tied to the affordance of an object.

Evaluation of landscape quality, under the psychophysical paradigm, is done by the general public or by special-interest groups, rather than by experts. This approach assumes that if one wishes to identify or design landscapes of aesthetic appeal for the public, the most direct way is to test samples of the general public to learn what they find appealing. Special interest groups may be tested to determine the aesthetic or scenic preferences of the users of a particular landscape. Heberlein and Dunwiddie, for example, tested correlations between campground attractiveness and how much the campground areas were actually used (Heberlein and Dunwiddie 1979). In this instance, a special interest group was tested not only for perception, but to see if stated preference corresponded with actual behavior. Another use of special-interest group testing is to determine whether significant differences in landscape perception exist between different groups. Much of the psychophysical landscape perception research has been in response to agencies' needs to evaluate landscape quality, as was true for the expert paradigm research. Psychophysical researchers have tended, therefore, to concentrate on landscape properties that can be manipulated or changed by resource managers and designers.

In the model of human–landscape interaction, the *landscape* tends to assume the dominant role, with stimulus properties that are external to the observer, invariant, and perceivable without conscious thought. On the *human* side are passive observers, generalized into groups of "general public" or perhaps special interests, whose aesthetic response is conditioned by the stimulus properties of the landscape. The *outcomes* of such interactions are statistically verified measurements of public perceptions of landscape quality, with the identification of environmental elements that can be manipulated by resource managers.

Applications and Examples. As with the expert paradigm, much of the call for landscape perception research involving testing of general public samples comes from landscape and natural resource managers and designers. These professionals need to determine just what landscape visual quality is in order to be able to manage and protect it. In the authors' literature survey, 35 percent of the articles

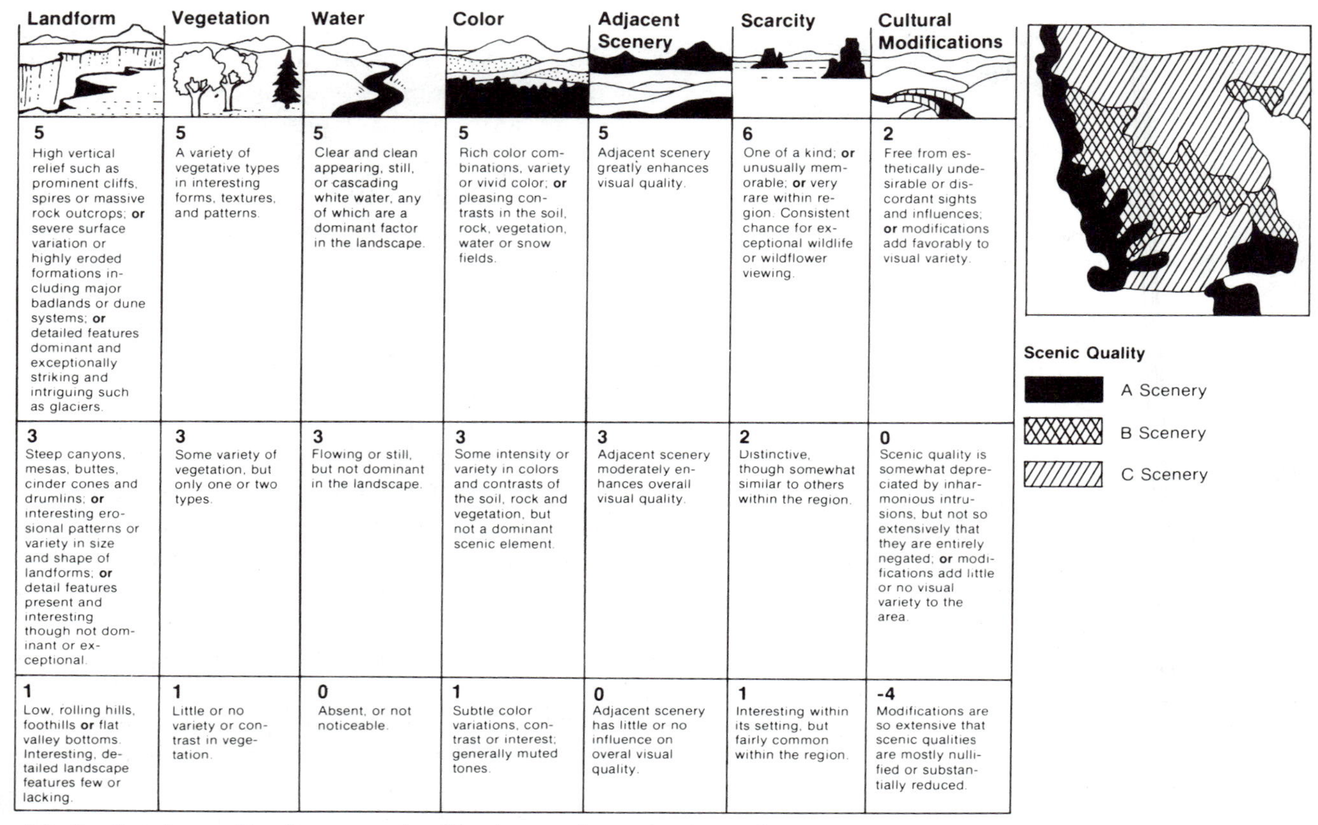

Landform	Vegetation	Water	Color	Adjacent Scenery	Scarcity	Cultural Modifications
5 High vertical relief such as prominent cliffs, spires or massive rock outcrops; **or** severe surface variation or highly eroded formations including major badlands or dune systems; **or** detailed features dominant and exceptionally striking and intriguing such as glaciers.	5 A variety of vegetative types in interesting forms, textures, and patterns.	5 Clear and clean appearing, still, or cascading white water, any of which are a dominant factor in the landscape.	5 Rich color combinations, variety or vivid color; **or** pleasing contrasts in the soil, rock, vegetation, water or snow fields.	5 Adjacent scenery greatly enhances visual quality.	6 One of a kind; **or** unusually memorable; **or** very rare within region. Consistent chance for exceptional wildlife or wildflower viewing.	2 Free from esthetically undesirable or discordant sights and influences; **or** modifications add favorably to visual variety.
3 Steep canyons, mesas, buttes, cinder cones and drumlins; **or** interesting erosional patterns or variety in size and shape of landforms; **or** detail features present and interesting though not dominant or exceptional.	3 Some variety of vegetation, but only one or two types.	3 Flowing or still, but not dominant in the landscape.	3 Some intensity or variety in colors and contrasts of the soil, rock and vegetation, but not a dominant scenic element.	3 Adjacent scenery moderately enhances overall visual quality.	2 Distinctive, though somewhat similar to others within the region.	0 Scenic quality is somewhat depreciated by inharmonious intrusions, but not so extensively that they are entirely negated; **or** modifications add little or no visual variety to the area.
1 Low, rolling hills, foothills **or** flat valley bottoms. Interesting, detailed landscape features few or lacking.	1 Little or no variety or contrast in vegetation.	0 Absent, or not noticeable.	1 Subtle color variations, contrast or interest; generally muted tones.	0 Adjacent scenery has little or no influence on overal visual quality.	1 Interesting within its setting, but fairly common within the region.	-4 Modifications are so extensive that scenic qualities are mostly nullified or substantially reduced.

12–9. Scenic quality inventory/evaluation rating criteria and score.

reviewed used psychophysical research methods (Zube et al. 1982). Research in the psychophysical paradigm has focused on forest landscape planning and management of rural landscapes, outdoor recreation settings, and comparisons of natural and man-made landscapes.

Of the forest landscape perception research, among the most widely known is the pioneering work done by Shafer and his colleagues (1969). Their work involves placing a grid over photographs that have been rated for scenic quality, and analyzing the elements hypothesized to contribute to high quality ratings. By counting the number of grid cells containing foreground vegetation, middle-ground and distant open space, water in the middle ground, and so on, Shafer claims to be able to account for over 60 percent of what contributes to visual quality. Daniel and his colleagues analyzed slides of forest scenes, which had been rated for scenic quality, for factors that are already in the forest manager's vocabulary—downed wood, tree diameter at breast height, low-level vegetation, and so forth (Daniel and Boster 1976). This method has been used for designing forest road corridors, for testing the visual effects of timber harvesting and management, and for creating scenic beauty maps of forest areas. Buhyoff and his colleagues have done extensive assessment of the effects of insect damage on forest scenic quality (1979), and Taylor and Daniel have studied the effects of fire on perceived forest landscape quality (1984).

Articles relating landscape quality to rural planning have covered a wide range of topics. Zube and others have done extensive landscape quality research in the northeastern United States, including evaluations of the Connecticut River Valley, comparisons of urban and rural landscapes, and tests of a number of elements as to their utility in predicting landscape scenic quality, including land form, land use, and the presence of water (Zube 1973). These researchers have experimented with a number of techniques, including Q-sort methods and rating scales, and have conducted comparative evaluations of groups from different disciplines and from different cultures. In England, Penning-Rowsell has done extensive rural landscape quality research, combining psychophysical with cognitive research methods to determine what is valued in landscapes, as well as the reasons for those evaluations (1975).

Much of the outdoor recreation landscape perception work has used psychophysical methods. Recreation planners and managers have an established tradition of testing user preferences, and therefore it is logical that they turn to psychophysical methods in evaluating landscape quality. Campground attractiveness has been tested by Heberlein and Dunwiddie (1979); by Shafer and Richards, who compared evaluations of U.S. and Scottish campers (1974); and by Foster and Jackson, who correlated camping satisfaction with structures in the area and with perceived vegetative screening (1979). Peterson compared perceptions of wilderness users with those of wilderness managers in the Boundary Waters Canoe Area (1974); and Cherem used a visitor-employed-photography technique to determine landscape scenic quality (1973). A number of articles have been written relating recreation perception with social context. Carls, for example, tested recreation preferences as they changed in response to crowding (1974).

A fair portion of psychophysical landscape perception research is methodological—suggesting, validating, or criticizing methods. A certain amount of controversy surrounds the use of photographs to depict landscapes, resulting in a number of comparative tests of evaluations of photos with evaluations done on the site where the photos were taken (Daniel and Boster 1976; Shafer and Richards 1974; Craik 1972b; Zube et al. 1974; Rabinowitz and Coughlin 1970). Several tests have shown differences between stated landscape preferences and behavior. Hancock, for example, showed that campers state preferences for vegetative screening, but actually tend to use areas with less vegetation (1973); while Lucas discovered that although wilderness users dislike crowding, they crowd nevertheless (1972). An especially interesting, cross-paradigm methodological study was made by Craik, who used psychophysical means to verify the validity of Litton's expert forest landscape model (1972a).

A good example of the application of psychophysical methods to landscape assessment is that of Daniel and Boster, which involves a standardized testing procedure, based on ratings of landscape photographs, which are then measured in terms of qualities foresters would use in forest management, such as tree diameter; number of stems per acre; cubic volume of downed wood; or volumes of grass, forbs, and shrubs per acre (Daniel and Boster 1976). This "Scenic Beauty Estimation [SBE] Method" asks respondents to rate landscape scenes, represented by thirty-five millimeter color slides, on a 1-to-10 (or 0-to-9) scale where 1 is low scenic beauty and 10 is high. The pictures are taken in random directions from points selected by pacing a predetermined distance on a course also determined at random (randomization avoids sampling bias). The slides themselves are placed in random order on slide trays and groups of observers are asked to rate each scene on the 10-point scenic beauty scale. The score sheets results are analyzed by a special SBE computer program, which permits both a "by-observer" and "by-slide" analysis. SBE scores for an area have been mapped and used for road siting (Daniel et al. 1977); and, in visual air quality studies, Scenic Beauty Estimates were compared to physical measurements of changes in the visible light spectrum (Latimer et al. 1980).

Brush and Shafer devised a regression equation describing the contribution of several landscape features to public preferences for forest vistas (1975). The base data were derived from rank-order preferences given for one hundred black and white photographs by 250 randomly selected campers. Rank-order preferences were determined simply by having respondents place the photographs in order from the most to the least preferred scenes. The 8- by 10-inch photographs were then overlain with a transparent ¼-inch grid, and the number of cells counted that contained: part of a perimeter of close-up vegetation; perimeter of intermediate vegetation; perimeter of distant vegetation; area of intermediate vegetation; area of water surface; and distant area without vegetation. Judicious weighting of the above variables have yielded an equation that, Shafer and his colleagues report, accounts for 66 percent of the variance in respondent scenic preference rankings.

A variation on rating or ranking landscape scene photographs is a forced distribution technique borrowed from psychology called the "Q-sort method" (Pitt and Zube 1979). In personality research, the respondent is asked to place cards with personality descriptors into separate piles that relate to the applicability of the descriptor to that individual's personality. The number of cards allowed per pile is predetermined to force a statistically normal distribution, which is useful in subsequent statistical analysis. Adapting this technique for landscape perception research involves replacing the descriptor cards with photographs of landscape scenes. For example, in one study, Zube et al. had respondents place fifty-six scenes of the Connecticut River Valley into the following distribution (from lowest to highest scenic quality) (1974):

Pile	1	2	3	4	5	6	7
Number of Photos	3	7	11	14	11	7	3

The task can be carried out without difficulty if done sequentially: "place the three scenes with highest scenic quality in pile 7 and the three lowest in pile 1; of the remaining 50 scenes, place the seven with highest scenic quality in pile 6 and the seven lowest in pile 2;" and so on. Analysis of the ratings was carried out by measuring and correlating the landscape dimensions listed (ibid.). The results of the study suggested the importance of topographic relief, water, agricultural elements, natural elements, the context of cultural features, and such elements of land-use cover as shrubs, broadleaf trees, or the edges of clearings.

Cherem conducted an experiment that was particularly interesting in its simplicity: hikers were given cameras, and asked to photograph areas along their hikes that they felt were especially scenic (1973). Cherem's analysis suggests that perceived landscape quality relates to "senso-environmental change"; that is, a hiker in a forest area will find clearings especially attractive, while a hiker in an open area will prefer the forest edge—each representing something different than the usual.

Psychophysical researchers have been strongly interested in alternative methods of simulating or depicting landscapes. This extends beyond comparisons of photos and site visits to some quite sophisticated simulation techniques. No discussion of landscape simulation would be complete without mention of the Berkeley Environmental Simulator, formerly under the direction of the late Donald Appleyard. The simulator consists of scale models, constructed in minute detail, of landscapes; and a photographic boom, with light-transmission equipment, that allows "ground level" movies or still-photos to be taken within the landscape model. This combination of detailed modeling and photographic technique has proved to be so realistic that many respondents, after rating the landscapes depicted, have asked, "When are we going to see pictures of the model?" The Berkeley simulator represents an approach to the very difficult problem of how to assess the scenic quality of future landscapes—of landscapes that do not yet exist. Attention to this problem is critical to planners or resource managers, who need to get some idea of scenic impacts before they take actions rather than after, when it may be too late.

Wohlwill, in researching "fittingness" of man-made structures in natural settings also used scale models (1978). Models of a coastal area, a lodge, and a lumber mill were constructed and combinations of the following elements were photographed: the area without man-made structures; the area with the lodge included; and the area with the lumber mill included. The resulting photographs were shown in sets of three (three views of the lodge in situ, and so on) to respondents who judged the fittingness of the structures on a 7-point scale from −3 to +3. Although the fittingness criterion tends to lead into the search for the meaning of landscape quality—that is, into the cognitive paradigm, the simulation technique certainly has applicability within the psychophysical paradigm. A similar procedure has been developed by the BLM in which two-dimensional models of proposed developments are superimposed onto photos or slides of landscape settings (1980). Respondents can then rate fittingness of the development, or simply rate scenic quality of scenes with and without the proposed structures. These methods can help planners and resource managers estimate what the scenic effects of alternate development schemes might be. However, a word of caution should be introduced here: Zube found preliminary indications that, although designers and the lay public tend to rate landscape aesthetics quite similarly based on photographs, significant differences may occur between those groups in ratings based on renderings or drawings of landscapes (1973).

The Cognitive Paradigm

Origins and Assumptions. The central concept underlying the cognitive paradigm is that humans are thinking creatures who do not merely respond passively to environmental stimuli, but select aspects of the landscape that have value to them. Landscape quality is seen as a construct built up in the mind, usually on the basis of visual information. The meaning of that construct is the important focus of cognitive approaches to research. Because meaning is of primary importance, researchers in this paradigm are less concerned with *what* landscapes are valued than with *why* they are so valued. The pursuit of landscape meaning leads in diverse directions, from diverse underlying assumptions. These assumptions are often more explicitly stated in the cognitive approach, rather than only implied as is true for much of the expert and psychophysical paradigm research. There are, as well, more attempts to develop the theoretical aspects of landscape perception.

Several lines of cognitive research are based upon assumptions about the role of perception in human adaptation and evolution. One such approach is a psychobiological one, an adaptation of Berlyne's arousal theory (1971; 1960) to landscape aesthetics by Wohlwill and his colleagues (Wohlwill 1976; Wohlwill and Kohn 1976). In this arousal approach, there is assumed to be an optimal level of stimulus information from the landscape—too much information is stressful, and too little information is boring. Thus, the scenic landscape has to have enough features to be interesting, but not so many that it is confusing or oppressive. Wohlwill and Kohn "dimensionalized" landscape perception through the following set of postulates (1976):

1. Preference is inversely related to uncertainty or conflict offered by a given landscape.
2. Intermediate levels of stimulation are preferred—too much or too little stimulation is not preferred. This leads to the "inverted U" function relating landscape complexity and preference where medium levels of complexity yield maximum preference, and maximum and minimum complexity levels yield minimal preference.
3. Past experience provides the frame of reference for evaluating a given landscape. Thus, preference along a specific dimension reflects adaptation levels from past experience.

Appleton felt that the human experience of landscape is most closely connected with our evolutionary heritage (1975a, 1975b). Part of this connection is drawn from Searles, who stresses the importance of "a sense of relatedness to his total environment" in each person, a sense so important that ignoring it will cause "peril to his psychological well-being" (1961). Examining also the hunting heritage of humans, Appleton drew material from ethology, relying especially on Lorenz's statement about the significance of observation: "[W]e reconnoitre, seeking, before we leave our cover, to gain from it the advantage which it can offer alike to hunter and hunted—namely to see without being seen" (1964). From this notion of hiding and seeing as the key to human relatedness to environment, Appleton has developed a "prospect—refuge theory" in which human aesthetics are related to landscape elements symbolizing places from which "to see without being seen" (1975a).

Also grounded in an evolutionary approach is the work of Stephen and Rachel Kaplan (S. Kaplan 1979; R. Kaplan 1979). Using an information-processing model of the human mind, the Kaplans have stressed the role of information in human evolution. Their approach also draws from Gibson's theory of affordances, in which perception is related to the needs of the perceiver (1977), and Charlesworth's notion that species prefer environments to which they are best adapted (1976). To the Kaplans landscape preference is an expression of adaptational suitability and is inextricably connected with the basic human purpose of gathering and organizing information. S. Kaplan identified two pervasive underlying human goals in perception (1979). One is "making sense," a concern with comprehension and maintenance of proper orientation in landscapes. The other is "involvement," a concern with stimulation and challenge. By crossing these two central goals with two levels of landscape interpretation—"visual array" (the two-dimensional view one sees) and "dimensional space" (the three-dimensional space one operates in), Kaplan developed a matrix of components significant in landscape perception:

Human Goals	Making Sense	Involvement
Visual Array	Coherence	Complexity
Dimensional Space	Legibility	Mystery

In this way, Kaplan established a parallel between perception space and action space. "Making sense" can be seen in two dimensions in terms of coherence (perceptual organization of patterns) and in three dimensions as legibility (the ability to create a cognitive map and know an environment well enough to act in it). "Involvement" in visual terms is related to complexity (the amount of information there is to perceive) and three dimensionally to mystery (the promise of, or inducement to obtain new information by acting in the environment). Mystery can be related to what is hidden in the landscape, and the opportunity to see new things if one goes over the next hill, or looks behind the trees blocking the view.

A few researchers in the cognitive paradigm have been especially interested in cross-cultural, or social or professional group differences in landscape perception. An early study of cross-cultural relationships was that of Sonnenfeld, who compared "home area preferences" of residents of Delaware and Alaskan natives and nonnatives (1967). Although Sonnenfeld found significant differences in his population groups, these differences tended to diminish with increased experience outside the home area. Shafer and Tooby found a very high correspondence in campground preferences between American and Scottish campers, although there may be some question that the cultural differences between Scottish and American campers may not be great enough to expect significant differences (1973). Zube and his colleagues have done some preliminary comparisons of landscape perceptions across cultures. Zube and Mills also found high correlation in landscape preference between Lorne, Australia residents, visitors, and University of Massachusetts students (1976). However, Zube and Pitt reported significant differences between Connecticut River Valley residents, Yugoslav students and University of Massachusetts students on the one hand, and inner-city residents (blacks and Italian-Americans) and Virgin Islanders on the other (1981). Preferences for man-made structures in natural landscapes had reverse patterns between these two groups (inner-city residents and Virgin Islanders preferred structures, while the others did not). In another study of sociocultural effects, it was found that landscape architects adopted stated client preferences and in fact proved themselves capable of being sensitive to client perceptions (Buhyoff et al. 1978).

On an individual level, some researchers have been investigating the relationship between personality and landscape perception. In an extensive study, Craik used a number of personality and landscape preference tests, including the Gottschaldt figures test, Barron-Welsh art scale leisure activities blank, Environmental Response Inventory, Rotter's social attitude scale, adjective checklists for personality and landscape and questionnaires about personal and environmental background, familiarity with the study area and environmental attitudes (1975). By using a cluster analysis, Craik was able to identify fourteen personality types that affected landscape perception.

In another approach, Little focused on the two personality dimensions of "thing" or "person" orientation in a four-fold classification scheme (1975). According to Little, Non-Specialists had little interest in persons or things other than self; Person-Specialists showed little interest in physical objects, construed things in person terms, rated high in "femininity" scores, and tended to follow literary or social science pursuits; Thing-Specialists showed little interest in persons, construed persons in "thing" terms, rated high in "masculinity" scores, and tended to follow scientific or practical fields. Generalists, on the other hand, tended to overload in information; construed both persons and things in appropriate terms; were open to both masculine and feminine aspects of self; tended to choose synoptic professions such as anthropology, geography, or planning; and placed high value on a balance between rigor and relevance. These personality traits, in turn, were thought to greatly affect the way in which people perceive their environments or surrounding landscapes. Frankly, self-avowed generalists such as the authors of this chapter find this categorization of personalities so highly flattering as to be difficult to dispute.

It is in the area of the natural/man-made dichotomy that the cognitive research paradigm has contributed research that can be related to a specific landscape "area of application." Researchers concerned with arousal theory have concentrated their research in this area. Ulrich considered the role of natural versus urban scenery in reducing stress (1979), Wohlwill and Harris studied the fittingness of man-made structures in natural settings (1980), Wohlwill and Heft examined differences in attitudes towards development in parks (1977), and Acking and Sorte studied the relationship of landscape complexity and unity to the number of elements in a scene and their degree of permanence (1973). R. Kaplan related stress potentials of landscapes to voluntary and involuntary attention (1975). Elements that receive involuntary human attention need no effort to perceive, whereas elements that require voluntary or forced conscious attention take effort and are stressing. Kaplan found a significant correlation between natural landscapes and involuntary attention, thus suggesting why natural landscapes may tend to be more relaxing than man-made landscapes.

At this point it is appropriate to summarize the general concepts of the human–landscape interaction in the cognitive paradigm. On the *human* side, there is an emphasis on cognitive processes, in which people process environmental information and make aesthetic choices. There is also a greater awareness of the context of human thought, in terms of evolution, social and cultural group, education, personality, professional role, and level of arousal. For the *landscape,* there is a stress on the meaning and information available, often depicted by such human-defined expressions as complexity, unity, coherence, mystery, or degree of naturalism. Although others have also studied such physical landscape measures as amount of relative relief, land-use diversity, or water, much of the cognitive research has been concerned with landscape meaning rather than manipulatable landscape dimensions, and is therefore harder to use in environmental design. References to outcome also reveal a tendency toward the human side, often involving emotional or aesthetic feelings, reduction in arousal levels, or feelings of personal satisfaction (Zube et al. 1982).

Applications and Examples. By the very nature of the landscape perception research paradigms outlined in this chapter, fewer methodological examples can be presented for the cognitive and experiential paradigms than for the expert and psychophysical paradigms. The latter two research approaches have been oriented specifically toward development of methods applicable to investigating perceived landscape quality, while cognitive research concentrates on meaning, and experiential on experience of landscape. Much of the cognitive work has been especially concerned with verbal evaluations of landscapes, using such techniques as survey questions, adjective checklists, or semantic differentials.

The simplest form of verbal response tool is the adjective checklist. Here a list of adjectives potentially useful for describing landscapes is compiled, and the respondents check all those terms which apply to the specific landscape under examination. Figure 12–10 provides an example of such a checklist, used by Craik in his study of personality and landscape preference in the San Francisco Bay Area (1975).

Although the adjective checklist is useful in examining overall descriptive traits, there is a more sensitive measure that allows respondents to choose finer shades of meaning. That measure is the semantic differential, in which pairs of terms with meanings that are polar opposites are arranged across a numerical range, usually seven or ten points. Subjects are asked to rate landscapes along the resulting continua. Figure 12–11 provides an example, the semantic scale used in the Zube et al. study of the Connecticut River Valley (1974). Penning-Rowsell has added an interesting dimension to semantic differentials for use in landscape research (1979). In addition to rating landscapes along semantic scales, respondents were also asked to rate the importance of each pair of terms to the overall preference for the landscape.

It is also possible to use survey questions in land-

1. active
2. alive
3. Alpine
4. angry
5. arid
6. artificial
7. autumnal
8. awesome
9. bare
10. barren
11. beautiful
12. black
13. bleak
14. blooming
15. blue
16. boggy
17. boring
18. bright
19. brisk
20. broad
21. brown
22. burned
23. bushy
24. calm
25. challenging
26. changing
27. clean
28. clear
29. close
30. cloudy
31. cold
32. colorful
33. colorless
34. comfortable
35. complex
36. contrasting
37. cool
38. craggy
39. crashing
40. creviced
41. crisp
42. cultivated
43. damp
44. dangerous
45. dank
46. dark
47. deep
48. dense
49. depressing
50. deserted
51. desolate
52. destroyed
53. dirty
54. distant
55. drab
56. dry
57. dull
58. eerie
59. empty
60. enclosed
61. eroded
62. external
63. exciting
64. expansive
65. extensive
66. falling
67. farmed
68. flat
69. flowery
70. flowing
71. foamy
72. foggy
73. forbidding
74. forceful
75. forested
76. free
77. fresh
78. friendly
79. frightening
80. gentle
81. glacial
82. gloomy
83. golden
84. grassy
85. gravelly
86. gray
87. green
88. happy
89. hard
90. harsh
91. hazardous
92. hazy
93. hidden
94. high
95. hilly
96. hot
97. humid
98. icy
99. imposing
100. impressive
101. inhabited
102. inspiring
103. intimate
104. invigorating
105. inviting
106. isolated
107. jagged
108. lazy
109. leafy
110. lifeless
111. light
112. living
113. lonely
114. lovely
115. low
116. lumpy
117. lush
118. majestic
119. marshy
120. massive
121. meadowy
122. misty
123. moist
124. monotonous
125. mossy
126. motionless
127. mountainous
128. muddy
129. mysterious
130. narrow
131. natural
132. nocturnal
133. noisy
134. open
135. orange
136. overpowering
137. pastoral
138. peaceful
139. picturesque
140. placid
141. plain
142. pleasant
143. pointed
144. polluted
145. powerful
146. pretty
147. pure
148. purple
149. quiet
150. rainy
151. rapid
152. reaching
153. red
154. reflecting
155. refreshing
156. relaxing
157. remote
158. restful
159. rich
160. rippled
161. rocky
162. rolling
163. romantic
164. rough
165. round
166. rugged
167. running
168. rushing
169. rustic
170. rusty
171. sad
172. sandy
173. scraggly
174. secluded

(continued)

12–10. Adjective checklist. From Craik, 1975, "Individual Variations in Landscape Description," pp. 138–39.

175. secure
176. serene
177. shadowy
178. shady
179. shallow
180. sharp
181. simple
182. sliding
183. slippery
184. sloping
185. slow
186. smoggy
187. smooth
188. snow-covered
189. soft
190. spacious
191. sparse
192. spring-like
193. stark
194. steep
195. still
196. stony
197. stormy
198. straight
199. strange
200. summery
201. sunny
202. swampy
203. swift
204. tall
205. terraced
206. terrifying
207. thicketed
208. threatening
209. timbered
210. towering
211. tranquil
212. tree-studded
213. tropical
214. ugly
215. undulating
216. unfriendly
217. uniform
218. uninspiring
219. uninteresting
220. uninviting
221. unspoiled
222. unusual
223. varied
224. vast
225. vegetated
226. violent
227. warm
228. watery
229. weedy
230. wet
231. white
232. wide
233. wild
234. winding
235. windswept
236. wintry
237. withered
238. wooded
239. worn
240. yellow

Figure 12–10 continued

scape evaluation, although this technique is not as common as the semantic differential or other rating methods. Survey questions, as in the example in figure 12–12, can go beyond aesthetic ratings and more effectively incorporate action type variables. In the example, preferences for residing, recreating, and traveling in the landscape, as well as scenic quality, were evaluated. Open-ended questions, such as What do you like about this landscape? can also be used to explore more deeply the cognitive basis for scenic judgments. Such questions have not been as common as other measures because analyzing an open-ended response requires more time and thus reduces the number of respondents that can be included. However, questions of that sort may be very useful at the beginning of a study or to add depth to a more numerically oriented analysis.

Other researchers have used more standard psychological tests to attempt to understand the meaning and importance of landscape. For example Ulrich used several different psychological measures to study the relationships between landscape scenery and emotional stress (1981). While subjects were shown a series of slides containing views of nature-with-water, natural vegetation, and urban landscapes, their heart rates and alpha rhythms were measured with an electrocardiograph (EKG) and electroencephalograph (EEG). In addition, they were given before-and-after measures of the Zuckerman Inventory of Personal Relations (ZIPERS), testing the five variables of fear arousal, positive affect, anger/aggression, attentiveness, and sadness, as well as a semantic differential treatment of the four variables of dominance, wakefulness, attention/interest, and stability. Ulrich found no association of the scenes with heart rate, but alpha rhythm was significantly higher when viewing natural vegetation (indicating lower arousal levels) than when viewing urban scenes. For the emotional scales, Ulrich found a significant increase in sadness after viewing urban scenes, and a decrease in fear arousal associated with nature-with-water scenes. He also found a significant sex difference in positive affect, which decreased for females after viewing urban landscapes, but was relatively unchanged for males. Overall, attentiveness was lowered following each eighty-eight-minute session,

Landscape Description and Evaluation Scales

1	Varied 1	:	2	:	3	:	4	:	5	:	6	:	7	Monotonous
2	Common 1	:	2	:	3	:	4	:	5	:	6	:	7	Unusual
3	Pleasant 1	:	2	:	3	:	4	:	5	:	6	:	7	Unpleasant
4	Beautiful 1	:	2	:	3	:	4	:	5	:	6	:	7	Ugly
5	Boring 1	:	2	:	3	:	4	:	5	:	6	:	7	Interesting
6	Tidy 1	:	2	:	3	:	4	:	5	:	6	:	7	Untidy
7	High Scenic Value 1	:	2	:	3	:	4	:	5	:	6	:	7	Low Scenic Value
8	Bright 1	:	2	:	3	:	4	:	5	:	6	:	7	Dull
9	Like 1	:	2	:	3	:	4	:	5	:	6	:	7	Dislike
10	Natural 1	:	2	:	3	:	4	:	5	:	6	:	7	Man-Made
11	Colorless 1	:	2	:	3	:	4	:	5	:	6	:	7	Colorful
12	Inviting 1	:	2	:	3	:	4	:	5	:	6	:	7	Uninviting
13	Obvious 1	:	2	:	3	:	4	:	5	:	6	:	7	Mysterious
14	Closed 1	:	2	:	3	:	4	:	5	:	6	:	7	Open
15	Hard 1	:	2	:	3	:	4	:	5	:	6	:	7	Soft
16	Smooth 1	:	2	:	3	:	4	:	5	:	6	:	7	Rough
17	Angular 1	:	2	:	3	:	4	:	5	:	6	:	7	Rounded
18	Light 1	:	2	:	3	:	4	:	5	:	6	:	7	Dark

12–11. Semantic scale. From Zube, Pitt, and Anderson, 1974.

While traveling between viewing stations, please look at the landscape on both sides of the road. The vehicle will pull off the road periodically, and you will be asked to evaluate the landscape you have traveled through since the preceding stop. At each stop, you will be asked to indicate:

1. How strongly you would like to have a permanent residence in the landscape you just traveled through.
2. How strongly you would like to participate in outdoor recreational activities in the landscape you just traveled through.
3. How strongly you would like to pass through the landscape and enjoy the scenery.
4. How you would rate the scenic quality of the landscape you just traveled through.

In answering these questions at each stop, please base your decision only on the physical attributes of the section of landscape you just traveled through. Disregard any socioeconomic considerations, such as distance to work, availability of land, taxes, etc., that might otherwise influence your decision.

Indicate your reaction by circling the number that corresponds with your feeling. The meaning associated with each number is:

Questions 1, 2, and 3	*Question 4*
1–strongly dislike	1–very low
2–dislike	2–low
3–neutral	3–moderate
4–like	4–high
5–strongly like	5–very high

12–12. Field survey questions. From Zube, Pitt, and Anderson, 1974.

which is not surprising; but attention was lowered somewhat less after viewing nature-with-water slides. Ulrich has shown that some standardized psychological tests offer promise as a basis for investigating the meaning of landscape; perhaps soon there will be more landscape-specific adaptations of these approaches.

Other methods have also been used. For example, one of the authors of this chapter (Taylor) experimented with a modification of Kelley's personal construct methodology to elicit meaning in landscape perception (Kelley 1955). In this experiment, pictures of landscapes are exhibited in groups of three, or triads. Respondents are asked to sort each triad into two subsets, one with two similar scenes and one other that is most different. They are then asked, "What makes the two landscapes alike?" (the construct); and, "What made the third landscape different?" (the opposite pole). After sorting ten sets of landscape triads, the respondents are asked to identify the three best and three worst scenes in the total set. This method may be able to lend insight into how people order their environment in terms of constructs and opposite poles, and what constructs can be most clearly associated with the landscapes identified as "best" or "worst."

The Experiential Paradigm

Origins and Assumptions. In the experiential paradigm, the focus of attention is not on human or landscape components as independent of one another, but on the experience of their interaction. Researchers using experiential methods have concentrated heavily on understanding the nature of the interaction and its outcomes, rather than identifying particular scenic landscape features. The experiential viewpoint also stresses the active nature of this interaction. In this view, people are not simply observers of landscapes but participants in them, and the way they participate has some influence on their landscape values:

> Judgments of landscape quality, even more than those of works of art, involve the beholder's active participation. Art and other objects of aesthetic appreciation are detached from the observer, framed in space and time, quite distinct from their milieus. But landscapes surround the observer, merging continuously with other landscapes to the horizon, and the absence of a set frame challenges the viewer to create his own perspectives. [Lowenthal, 1978, 5]

A useful way to explain the experiential approach would be as it relates to the components of our model. Humans are seen as active participants in the landscape, and human qualities such as intentions, needs, knowledge, abilities, and culture, affect judgments. The landscape is the landscape as experienced, whether it be the setting for everyday activities, scenic wonder, or creative inspiration. The landscape gains meaning and value through the situations in which it is experienced. As the nature of that experience changes—over time, between different groups, or among different individuals—so too does the attachment to landscape. Experiential researchers also are concerned with a variety of outcomes, mostly relating to the quality or process of the experience. For example, habitual behavior grows out of the long-term everyday experience of living in a particular place; the value of that place may not even be consciously known until that place is gone or damaged (Seamon 1979). On a more judgmental level, outcomes have been expressed as descriptions of landscape tastes (Lowenthal 1968; Lowenthal and Prince 1965), of particular experiences with landscapes (Wilkinson 1979), and change in landscape or human quality (Lewis et al. 1973; Relph 1979). Of special note is the emphasis on a broader definition of landscape value beyond scenic beauty: " . . . esthetic satisfaction is only one of the many pleasures taken in landscapes, our attachments have other roots as well, and these too must be identified and analyzed'' (Lowenthal, 1978, 2).

The roots of the experiential approach derive primarily from phenomenology, landscape study, and the history of art and literature. Use of this paradigm is most characteristic of geographers, who, in their long striving to understand the evolution of landscapes and human activity in the environment, have also been interested in landscape values. It also emphasizes the value of a subjective approach, of direct involvement with people and landscapes instead of objective detachment:

> . . . an experiential approach requires that, instead of remaining aloof and apart, the researcher endeavors to establish viable open relationships with those he studies. No attempt is made to minimize the contamination of intervention in an existential situation. Emphasis is placed on interpersonal knowing through dialog rather than observation. [Rowles, 1978, 184]

One approach, phenomenology, attempts to study things as they are experienced holistically without trying to define, categorize, or structure. It seeks to ''understand and describe the phenomenon as it is in itself before any prejudices or *a priori* theories have identified, labelled or explained it'' (Seamon 1979).

Seamon's phenomenological approach stresses the importance of ''body-subject,'' the not-wholly-conscious knowledge used in routine or habitual behavior in day-to-day living. Everyone has routines that are carried out with little thought—washing, eating, or driving to work. Such activities are done automatically, usually while the conscious mind is engaged with other topics. These sorts of ''unconscious'' routines can, over time, develop into a strong attachment to the places where they occur (ibid.). The strength of these attachments may not be apparent until places are removed from the landscape—when the corner store is torn down, the childhood swimming hole filled, or the nearby woodlot cut down.

A phenomenological approach strives for insights into the process of landscape encounter. Psychometric notions of validity or reliability embedded in the psychophysical and cognitive paradigms are not significant to these researchers. Instead, there is an assumption that the descriptions and insights are valid if they have meaning to other readers. The primary contribution of phenomenological work to landscape perception to date can be seen in terms of the human landscape interaction model. The notion of body-subject expands the concept of the human beyond the cognitive to include a prejudgmental element in the system. This may relate quite closely to the ''affective'' system postulated by Ittelson (1973) and Zajonc (1980) to underlie cognitive judgments. Landscape studies have also benefitted from the recognition of the value of the everyday landscape, seen perhaps as ordinary but of great importance to those who live in it. The outcome of habitual behavior patterns in these everyday landscapes gains its value from the constant recurrence of these place-person patterns over time to create intense attachments to places. Such landscape values are rarely articulated because people are seldom conscious of them, but change in these everyday landscapes can produce a strong sense of loss.

A related approach is the method of phenomenological experience of landscapes put forward by E. Relph (1979, 1984). Relph's concentration is on his own perception, describing what he thinks and feels about particular landscapes without attempting to examine other people's views. It is a concentration on seeing the ''inner character'' or ''genius loci'' of landscapes with a sensitive, creative vision:

> What I am concerned with is seeing as a faculty that can be made increasingly more sensitive in order to attain this understanding. By a

> deliberate effort of concentration and wonder about the nature of things it is possible to see in more detail, to discern hues and textures, literally to develop a greater acuity of vision. [1984, 4]

In terms of our model, Relph's approach concentrates on the human side, on improving the ability of the observer to see landscapes. The landscape need not necessarily be attractive, because landscape values encompass more than aesthetics. A significant outcome discussed by E. Relph (1979) is the "peak or transcendental experience," which is often triggered by landscapes. These are almost "religious" experiences,

> . . . in which the universe is lucidly perceived as an integrated whole, in which everything, including ugliness and evil, has its place, in which a sense of timelessness and spacelessness exist, in which life is given meaning and purpose. These experiences are so dramatic and overwhelming that they can only be understood as transcendental. [1979, 34]

Many geographers, stressing their discipline as the "science of observation," have advocated the necessity of direct study of the landscape, as well as its meanings, and its history (Sauer 1956). An important part of this approach is that sensitive appreciation of landscape beauty demands some knowledge. The English historian, Hoskins, emphasized such a view, noting:

> One may liken the English landscape . . . to a symphony, which it is possible to enjoy as an architectural mass of sound, beautiful or impressive as the case may be, without being able to analyze it in detail or to see the logical development of its structure. The enjoyment may be real, but it is limited in scope and in the last resort vaguely diffused in emotion. But if instead of hearing merely a symphonic mass of sound, we are able to isolate the themes as they enter, to see how one by one they are intricately woven together and by what magic new harmonies are produced, perceive the manifold subtle variations on a single theme, however disguised it may be, then the total effect is immeasurably enhanced. So it is with landscapes . . . Only when we know all the themes and harmonies can we begin to appreciate its full beauty and discover in it new subtleties every time we visit it. [1955, 197]

Perceiving a landscape, then, requires an eye for subtleties, which in turn requires some knowledge. Students of the landscape are also quick to point out that an aesthetic view is only one way of perceiving a landscape (Lewis 1976). Meinig, for example, listed ten ways to view the landscape, each with value connotations: as nature, habitat, artifact, system, problem, wealth, ideology, history, place, and aesthetic (1976).

This awareness of aesthetic as part of the total value of the landscape is exemplified in the writings of Jackson (Zube 1970; Jackson 1980). In Jackson's view, making a landscape pretty to look at is less desirable than making it livable. In his commentary "To Pity the Plumage and Forget the Dying Bird," he stressed a social aesthetic:

> . . . what is also essential is for every responsible American to add a new social dimension to his definition of landscape beauty. We will have to see that an inhabited landscape is neither beautiful nor sound unless it makes possible an unfolding of the individual in work and social relationships just as much as in health and recreation. [1967, 4]

Another way to study the experience of landscape is to examine art and literature. Tuan noted that "Actual experience can only be lived," and any attempt to describe it reduces it to generalities. Literature, however, is more particular than other forms of discourse, more able to describe experience specifically (Tuan 1977). The real advantage of art or literature in studying how people value landscapes is that these are active, creative processes:

> The significance of aesthetic value lies not in its identification, but in the action of its formulation and articulation . . . The art form provides concrete access to the complex web of relations by which each individual in society connects to others. This web of relations is established by actions instigated toward things on the basis of meanings those things hold for the individual. [Kobayashi, 1980, 6]

This idea was echoed by Matro who held that perception of landscape is a creative activity and ought therefore to be studied through creative expressions (1978). When thinking about Relph's statements about transcendental experience, it is easy to see the importance of inspirational landscapes, or as Lowenthal stressed, of uniquely valued landscapes (1978). In relation to our model, as the previous statement suggests the landscape element consists of inspirational landscapes, what might be referred to as the ''sublime'' (Lowenthal 1978; Zaring 1977). The human in this approach is an active, seeking, creative individual; and the outcome is a creative work—art, literature, music, architecture.

Applications and Examples. Techniques in the experiential approach are not as structured as in the other paradigms, tending to concentrate on holistic descriptions. This lack of structuring is deliberate and rests on the assumption that landscape value should be defined by the criteria used by the individuals experiencing that landscape rather than experts studying it. There is also an admission of the importance of the subjective element and an attempt to use it to understand the process of landscape experience rather than to attempt what seems to be the impossible task of ''objectification.'' Accordingly, in our description of techniques used in experiential landscape perception study, we start from the most subjective, phenomenology, and proceed through landscape study to examination of creative works.

Phenomenological techniques rest upon the unstructured experience of a situation. The primary approach is to elicit descriptions of personal experience as it happens, without attempting to be analytical, and to avoid preconceived notions that may distort the basic experience. Reflection on that experience can present insights that contribute to understanding. Naturally, a person can rely on his own experience as raw material, but more insights are possible if a group of people can share their experiences. Seamon appears to be the only researcher who has used group inquiry as a phenomenological approach to examining how people encounter landscapes (1979). In this method, the group members share descriptions of their experiences, which are recorded and used as material for reflection and subsequent generalization.

Relph's landscape study approach is a phenomenological method that involves ''seeing with the soul of the eye,'' using training and awareness to examine the depths of landscape experience (1979). There is some similarity to the expert viewpoint in Relph's advocation of knowledgeable, sensitive, creative seeing of landscapes, but there are major differences as well. Making no pretense of seeing landscapes as others see them, Relph records his own thoughts and assumes validity is found ''if what I describe makes sense and clarifies matters for others'' (1984). His approach is aimed more towards understanding and development of the ability to see what is in landscapes than toward manipulating the landscapes themselves. His emphasis is placed on education rather than landscape design:

> Landscapes are transcriptions of ourselves. If we cannot see well, if we lack a deep visual re-

> lationship with surroundings and awareness of possibility of experiencing landscapes transcendentally, we are not likely to inspire architects, developers, planners and property owners to make landscapes look aesthetically pleasing. If we want landscapes to appear better, we first have to see them better. [1979, 34]

The central approach to the study of creative efforts in landscape evaluation is content analysis of literature, art history, and travelers' descriptions or diaries, used in the pioneering works of Lowenthal (1968) and Lowenthal and Prince (1965) in their examination of English and American landscape tastes, as well as Zaring's (1977) research on romantic perceptions of scenery in Wales. Kobayashi concentrated on analysis of poetry as a means of expressing landscape aesthetics by Japanese immigrants to Canada (1980). Diaries, journals, and letters were employed by Wilkinson to describe the landscapes experienced by women on the Oregon Trail (1979) and by Zube to describe landscape images of residents and visitors to the post-Civil War Southwest (1982). In addition to these are studies of landscape itself as a statement of human values, examples of which are provided by Duncan's (1972) study of group identity in a suburban area and Riley's (1980) speculations on the new American landscape.

CHOOSING APPROACHES TO LANDSCAPE ASSESSMENT

Each of the four previously discussed paradigms takes a unique approach to landscape assessment. Each differs methodologically, substantively, and with respect to emphasis on applications or theory. However, each also strives to measure or learn something about landscape aesthetics and other values important to people. The differences seem to derive mainly from two major sources. One of these sources is the body of disciplinary information represented by these paradigms—artistic, scientific, experimental, cognitive, and experiential. The other is the purpose of the research. Expert and psychophysical paradigms emphasize landscape management applications, while cognitive and experiential seek to understand the importance of valued landscapes to people. We cannot afford to ignore any of these conceptual approaches or goals. Indeed, the focus of all these paradigms on the single theme of landscape assessment enables us to examine the possibilities for a synthesis of approaches (the authors have made some such suggestions) (Sell et al. 1984). In this concluding section, we summarize the contributions of each paradigm, discuss the strengths and weaknesses of each and suggest how paradigms might be combined to provide better answers and to advance the state of the art in landscape assessment.

PARADIGM CONTRIBUTIONS

The expert paradigm provides a description of the landscape from the viewpoint of the professional designer, planner, or manager. Descriptions are derived from artistic or ecological principles and tend to include those attributes of the landscape that (1) are within the technical training of the respective professions and that (2) can be manipulated through design, planning, and management decisions. It is generally assumed that at least some training in art or ecology is necessary for a person to appreciate landscape aesthetics fully, and there is some caution about incorporating the views of the general public, who may lack such training.

The psychophysical paradigm provides a means of predicting which landscape dimensions will be associated with public perceptions of scenic beauty.

These associations are derived from ratings by the general public obtained from controlled, experimental manipulations of landscape views, or landscape surrogates or simulations. There seems to be an assumption that the psychophysical techniques will be able to tap the underlying psychological processes behind perceptions of aesthetics, which are more basic than artistic or scientific training. The landscape variables, as in the expert paradigm, are usually selected with reference to specific planning or management needs such as species or size composition of forest cover or the areal amount of surface water, forest vegetation, and meadow within a specified landscape.

The cognitive paradigm provides an understanding of people's judgments of scenic beauty. It is similar to the psychophysical in that it draws upon statistical analyses of public responses. It differs, however, in that it does not usually emphasize physical landscape attributes or variables that are directly manipulatable by designers, planners, and managers. Rather, studies within this paradigm tend to search for meanings associated with landscapes. The qualities emphasized as important, such as complexity, mystery, degree of naturalness, and prospects and refuges, are decidedly influenced by human cognitive processing.

The experiential paradigm provides descriptions of the processes of interaction between and among individuals, groups, and landscapes. The unit of analysis for the experiential is the human–landscape interaction, unlike the cognitive, which focuses on the human, or the expert and psychophysical, which emphasize landscape features. Also, unlike the other approaches, experiential research emphasizes the importance of varying modes of experience, including the nature of activity, the degree of awareness of the landscape, the social and cultural context, and the purposes to be achieved. It also recognizes that there is a wider range of landscape values than merely the aesthetic, and seeks to place these values in balance.

Strengths and Weaknesses

Many of the strengths and weaknesses of the four paradigms are apparent from the detailed descriptions presented earlier in this chapter and from the preceding summaries. Several merit specific mention here, however, and provide reinforcement for the notion of combining paradigms in future studies. The discussion that follows is based on several recent review papers that the reader may wish to consult for further amplification (Penning-Roswell 1981; Porteous 1982; Zube et al. 1982; Daniel and Vining 1983; Sell et al. 1984).

The expert and psychophysical paradigms have been most used by environmental decision makers and managers. They rate high on utility because they specifically address those attributes and characteristics of the landscape that can be manipulated. In many cases, these techniques have been developed in close cooperation with environmental agencies (such as the U.S. Forest Service and Bureau of Land Management) and are couched in terms of interest to those organizations. The cognitive and especially the experiential paradigms, which have been of less interest to environmental managers, have tended to resist translation into landscape design or management. How does one, for example, design for mystery or transcendent experience?

In many of the psychophysical and cognitive studies, a great deal of care has been taken to demonstrate that the measures are valid and reliable. Procedures are usually consistent and the information is presented in ways that enable replication and generalization. The data provide decision makers with some indication of the amount of confidence they can have in the findings. The expert and experiential approaches, on the other hand, are more subjective and idiosyncratic, and are often not amenable to rigorous statistical analysis. As a result, reliability and validity cannot be measured in the usual psychological sense.

Sensitivity, in terms of the ability to detect real differences in meaning and value, is probably greatest in the experiential paradigm. This approach probes most deeply into individual interactions with the landscape. However, much of the information may be highly personal, making it difficult to generalize to values held by a larger public. Both the cognitive and psychophysical have "given up" some of that sensitivity in return for applicability to wider public or general human values. It is uncertain just how sensitive the expert paradigm is. Often the expert eye is apt to detect differences that are not perceptible to people without ecological or artistic training. On the other hand, many of the expert rating scales are ordinal (value ordered) and differences between valued landscapes may be difficult to clarify.

As we stated earlier, the psychophysical paradigm relies heavily on stimulus-response assumptions that originate in psychology, especially from the tradition of behaviorism. It is at this point that landscape perception research becomes involved in one of the oldest controversies in the social sciences: that of environmental determinism. This dispute rests upon the degree to which external environmental factors can cause specific types of human behavior (see Gold 1980 for a thoughtful discussion of behaviorism, determinism, and environmental perception research). It is not our intention to accuse the psychophysical researchers of advocating a simplistic cause (landscape) and effect (perception) relationship. There has been a tendency, however, to view the landscape as the source of value and ignore the decision making of people.

Finally, something should be said about whether a paradigm emphasizes theory or applications. It should come as no surprise that most of the really explicit theoretical views have been classified in the cognitive paradigm, with some other important contributions arising in experiential work, for these two approaches have been primarily concerned with understanding how values arise from the human-landscape interaction process. The expert and psychophysical have catered most to the needs of environmental decision makers and have paid more attention to applications. We see this split widening between the task of understanding how landscape values develop and that of discovering valued landscape elements for manipulation. This separation will soon lead to difficulty, if it has not already. For example, landscape evaluations are beginning to become more common in litigations, and researchers are often called as expert witnesses. It is not hard to imagine what can happen in cross examination if an expert is not well versed on the theoretical as well as methodological foundations of his or her assessment approach. Without a unified framework incorporating both theoretical and applied views, landscape assessment will choke on its own contradictions and come to be perceived as of little or no value in environmental decision making. It is important, then, to choose carefully and combine approaches whose strengths will complement each others' weaknesses.

COMBINING PARADIGMS

Although we have tended to emphasize the differences between paradigms in this presentation, there are some common relationships and consistent variations among the four approaches. Some landscape qualities have achieved salience in several paradigms, such as complexity or variety, views of water, or edges and perimeters—as, for example, in the boundaries between field and forest or land and water. The paradigms also vary consistently in concepts of the human and landscape elements in the interaction. On a continuum from expert to psychophysical through cognitive to experiential, the human component of the system can be seen to change from passive observer through selective information processor to active participant. In a similar way, the conceptualization of the landscape evolves from a dimensional outlook in the expert to a holistic one in the experiential paradigm. The methods concerned with isolating salient landscape features (such as stream size, form, or amount of vegetation) gradually give way to compositional qualities and then to undifferentiated holistic approaches to landscapes. These commonalities and consistencies can be used to combine approaches (Sell et al. 1984).

Some work already has shown some overlap between paradigms. An example is Wohlwill's research on the "fittingness" of man-made objects in natural landscapes that uses a psychophysical rating for a specific kind of human meaning. Similarly, Simpson et al. (1976) used a psychophysical rating scheme in what was essentially a cognitive investigation, to test social influences on scenic ratings. In this study, 120 female subjects were asked to rate slides of natural, two-thirds thinned, or clear-cut forest areas, after being given persuasive messages about the ecological effects of forest thinning, or told of scenic ratings by either prior groups or "experts." All of these treatments increased subjects' acceptance of the management practices. Another combination of paradigm approaches can be seen in a consulting report on the visual impact of power lines in the Pacific Northwest (Blair et al. 1976). In this case, expert ratings of landscapes based on the qualities of "vividness," "intactness," and "unity" were supplemented by psychophysical ratings by public groups of "compatibility" of transmission lines in certain landscapes. Blair and his colleagues found considerable agreement between the different approaches. There are other examples of combined research that also provide evidence for the usefulness of a multi-paradigm outlook (Zube et al. 1974; Acking and Sorte 1973).

We might also suggest that the paradigms may be most useful in different stages of a research project. An experiential approach, exploring landscape experience phenomenologically or through art and literature, might best be employed early in the study to provide directions for investigation. Cognitive and psychophysical techniques can then be used to isolate salient human values and landscape features in representative landscapes. Finally, armed with such knowledge, experts can go into the field and provide detailed maps of landscape values. In such a way, the paradigm strengths can serve to complement each other to create a program that is both useful for environmental management and publicly defensible from both theoretical and methodological standpoints.

REFERENCES

Acking, C. A., and Sorte, G. J. 1973. How do we verbalize what we see? *Landscape Architecture* 63:120–25.

Appleton, J. 1975a. *The Experience of Landscape.* New York: Wiley.

———. 1975b. Landscape evaluation: The theoretical vacuum. *Institute of British Geographers, Transactions* 66:120–23.

Berlyne, D. E. 1960. *Conflict, Arousal, and Curiosity.* New York: McGraw-Hill.

———. 1971. *Aesthetics and Psychobiology.* New York: Appleton-Century-Crofts.

Blair, W. G. E., B. A. Gray, J. A. Hebert, and G. R. Jones. 1976. *Visual Impact of High-Voltage Transmission Facilities in Northern Idaho and Northwestern Montana.* Final report for Bonneville Power Administration, United States Department of the terior. Seattle: Jones & Jones.

Brush, R. O., and E. L. Shafer, Jr. 1975. Application of a landscape-preference model to land management. In *Landscape Assessment: Value Perceptions and Resources,* ed. E. H. Zube, R. O. Brush, and J. G. Fabos, 168–82. Stroudsburg, Pa.: Dowden, Hutchinson & Ross.

Buhyoff, G. J., W. A. Leuschner, and J. D. Wellman. 1979. Aesthetic impacts of southern pine beetle damage. *Journal of Environmental Management* 8:261–67.

Buhyoff, G. J., J. D. Wellman, H. Harvey, and R. A. Fraser. 1978. Landscape architects' interpretations of people's landscape preferences. *Journal of Environmental Management* 6:255–62.

Bureau of Land Management (BLM). 1980. *Visual Resource Management Program.* Washington, D.C.: U.S. Department of the Interior.

Burke, R. E. 1975. National forest visual management: A blend of landscape and timber management. *Journal of Forestry* 73:767–70.

Carls, E. G. 1974. The effects of people and man-induced conditions on preference for outdoor recreation landscapes. *Journal of Leisure Research* 6(2):113–24.

Carlson, A. A. 1977. On the possibility of quantifying scenic beauty. *Landscape Planning* 4:131–72.

Charlesworth, W. R. 1976. Human intelligence as adaptation: An ethological approach. In *The Nature of Intelligence,* ed. L. B. Resnick, 147–68. Hillsdale, N.J.: Erlbaum.

Cherem, G. J. 1973. Looking through the eye of the public or public images as social indications of aesthetic opportunity. In *Toward a Technique for Quantifying Aesthetic Quality of Water Resources,* ed. P. J. Brown, PRWG-120-2, 52–64. Utah State University, Institute for Water Resources. Logan.

Craik, K. H. 1972a. Appraising the objectivity of landscape dimensions. In *Natural Environments,* ed. J. V. Krutilla, 292–346. Baltimore: Johns Hopkins Univ. Press.

———. 1972b. Psychological factors in landscape appraisal. *Environment and Behavior* 4(3):255–66.

———. 1975. Individual variations in landscape description. In *Landscape Assessment: Values, Perceptions, and Resources,* ed. E. H. Zube. R. O. Brush, and J. G. Fabos, 130–50. Stroudsburg, Pa.: Dowden, Hutchinson & Ross.

Craik, K. H., and E. H. Zube. 1975. *Issues in Perceived Environmental Quality Research.* Univ. of Massachusetts, Institute for Man and Environment. Amherst.

Daniel, T. C., L. M. Anderson, H. W. Schroeder, and L. Wheeler, III. 1977. Mapping the scenic beauty of forest landscapes. *Leisure Science* 1:35–52.

Daniel, T. C., and R. S. Boster. 1976. *Measuring Landscape Esthetics: The Scenic Beauty Estimation Method.* USDA Forest Service, Research Paper RM-167. Fort Collins, Colo.

Daniel, T. C., and W. H. Ittelson. 1981. Conditions for environmental perception research: Comment on the psychological representation of molar physical environments by Ward and Russell. *Journal of Experimental Psychology: General* 110:153–57.

Daniel, T. C., and J. Vining. 1983. Methodological issues in the assessment of visual landscape quality. In *Behavior and the Natural Environment,* ed. I. Altman and J. Wohlwill, 39–84. New York: Plenum.

Duncan, J. S., Jr. 1973. Landscape taste as a symbol of group identity: A Westchester County village. *The Geographical Review* 63:334–55.

Elsner, G., and R. C. Smardon. 1979. *Our National Landscape.* USDA Forest Service General Technical Report PSW-35. Berkeley.

Fines, K. D. 1968. Landscape evaluation: A research project in East Sussex. *Regional Studies* 2:41–55.

Foster, R. J., and E. L. Jackson. 1979. Factors associated with camping satisfaction in Alberta Provincial Park campgrounds. *Journal of Leisure Research* 11(4):292–306.

Gibson, J. J. 1977. The theory of affordances. In *Perceiving, Acting and Knowing: Toward an Ecological Psychology,* ed. R. Shaw and J. Bransford, 67–82. Hillsdale, N.J.: Erlbaum.

Gold, J. R. 1980. *An Introduction to Behavioral Geography.* New York and London: Oxford.

Hancock, H. K. 1973. Recreation preference: Its relation to user behavior. *Journal of Forestry* 71:336–37.

Heberlein, T. A., and P. Dunwiddie. 1979. Systematic observation of use levels, campsite selection and visitor characteristics at a high mountain lake. *Journal of Leisure Research* 11:306–16.

Hoskins, W. G. 1955. *The Making of the English Landscape.* London: Hodder & Stoughton.

Ittelson, W. H. 1973. Environmental perception and contemporary perceptual theory. In *Environment and Cognition,* ed. W. H. Ittelson, 1–19. New York: Seminar Press.

Jackson, J. B. 1967. To pity the plumage and forget the dying bird. *Landscape* 17:1–4.

———. 1980. *The Necessity for Ruins.* Amherst: Univ. of Massachusetts Press.

Kaplan, R. 1975. Some methods and strategies in the prediction of preference. In *Landscape Assessment: Values, Perceptions, and Resources,* ed. E. H. Zube, R. O. Brush and J. G. Fabos, 118–29. Stroudsburg, Pa.: Dowden, Hutchinson & Ross.

———. 1979. Visual resources and the public: An empirical approach. In *Our National Landscape,* ed. G. H. Elsner and R. C. Smardon, 209–16. USDA Forest Service, General Technical Report PSW-35. Berkeley.

Kaplan, S. 1979. Perception and landscape: Conceptions and misconceptions. In *Our National Landscape,* ed. G. H. Elsner and R. C. Smardon, 241–48. USDA Forest Service, General Technical Report PSW-35. Berkeley.

Kelley, G. A. 1955. *The Psychology of Personal Constructs.* New York: Norton.

Kobayashi, A. 1980a. Landscape Aesthetics in Geography: An Existential Perspective. Paper presented at the Association of American Geographers Annual Meeting, April 1980. Louisville, Ky.

———. 1980b. Landscape and the poetic act: The role of haiku clubs for the Issei. *Landscape* 24:42–47.

Latimer, D. A., T. C. Daniel, and H. Hogo. 1980. *Relationships between Air Quality and Human Perception of Scenic Areas.* Systems Applications, Inc., Publication no. 4323. San Rafael, Calif.

Laurie, I. C. 1975. Aesthetic factors in visual evaluation. In *Landscape Assessment: Values, Perceptions, and Resources,* ed. E. H. Zube, R. O. Brush, and J. G. Fabos, 102–17. Stroudsburg, Pa.: Dowden, Hutchinson & Ross.

Leopold, L. B. 1969. *Quantitative Comparisons of Some Aesthetic Factors among Rivers.* U.S. Department of the Interior. U.S. Geological Survey Circular 620. Washington, D.C.

———. 1970. Landscape Esthetics. *Ekistics* 29:271–77.

Lewis, P. F. 1976. Axioms of the landscape. *Journal of Architectural Education* 30:6–9.

Lewis, P. F., D. Lowenthal, and Y. F. Tuan. 1973. *Visual Blight in America.* Washington, D.C.: Association of American Geographers, Commission of College Geography Resource Paper no. 23.

Linton, D. 1968. The assessment of scenery as a natural resource. *Scottish Geographical Magazine* 84:219–93.

Little, B. R. 1975. Specialization and the varieties of environmental experience: Empirical studies within the personality paradigm. In *Experiencing the Environment,* ed. S. Wapner, S. B. Cohen, and B. Kaplan, 81–116. New York: Plenum.

Litton, R. B. 1968. *Forest Landscape Description and Inventories.* USDA Forest Service, Research Paper PSW-49. Berkeley.

———. 1972. Aesthetic dimensions of the landscape. In *Natural Environments: Studies in Theoretical and Applied Analysis,* ed. J. V. Krutilla, 262–91. Baltimore: Johns Hopkins Univ. Press.

Lorenz, K. Z. 1964. *King Solomon's Ring.* London: Methuen.

Lowenthal, D. 1968. The American scene. *Geographical Review* 58:61–88.

———. 1978. Finding valued landscapes. *Progress in Human Geography* 2:373–418.

Lowenthal, D., and H. C. Prince. 1965. English landscape tastes. *Geographical Review* 55:186–222.

Lucas, R. C. 1972. Wilderness perception and use. In *Politics, Policy, and Natural Resources,* ed. D. L. Thompson, 309–23. New York: Macmillan.

Matro, T. 1978. Poetry and the effort of perception. *Landscape* 22:14–18.

Meinig, D. W. 1976. The beholding eye. *Landscape Architecture* 66:47–54.

Penning-Roswell, E. C. 1975. Constraints on the application of landscape evaluations. *Institute of British Geographers, Transactions* 66:149–55.

———. 1979. The social value of English landscapes. In *Our National Landscape,* ed. G. H. Elsner and R. C. Smardon, 249–55. USDA Forest Service, General Technical Report PSW-35. Berkeley.

———. 1981. Fluctuating fortunes in gauging landscape value. *Progress in Human Geography* 5:25–41.

Peterson, G. L. 1974. A comparison of the sentiments and perception of wilderness managers and canoeists in the Boundary Waters canoe area. *Journal of Leisure Research* 6(3):194–206.

Pitt, D. G., and E. H. Zube. 1979. The Q-sort method: Use in landscape assessment research and landscape planning. In *Our National Landscape,* ed. G. H. Elsner and R. C. Smardon, 227–34. USDA Forest Service, General Technical Report, PSW-35. Berkeley.

Porteous, D. 1982. Approaches to environmental aesthetics. *Journal of Environmental Psychology* 2:53–66.

Rabinowitz, C. B., and R. E. Coughlin. 1970. *Analyses of Landscape Characteristics Relevant to Preference.* Regional Science Research Institute, Discussion Paper no. 38. Philadelphia.

Relph, E. T. 1979. To see with the soul of the eye. *Landscape* 23:28–34.

———. 1984. Seeing, thinking, and describing landscapes. In *Environmental Perception and Behavior: Inventory and Prospect,* ed. T. F. Saarinen, D. Seamon, and J. L. Sell, 209–23. University of Chicago, Department of Geography Research Paper. Chicago.

Riley, R. B. 1980. Speculations on the new American landscapes. *Landscape* 24:1–9.

Rowles, G. 1978. Reflections on experimental field work. In *Humanistic Geography: Prospects and Problems,* ed. D. Ley and M. Samuels, 173–93. Chicago: Maaroufa.

Sauer, C. O. 1956. The education of a geographer. *Association of American Geographers Annual* 46:287–99.

Seamon, D. 1979. *A Geography of the Lifeworld.* New York: St. Martin's.

Searles, H. F. 1961–62. The Role of Nonhuman Environment. *Landscape* 11:31–34.

Sell, J. L., J. G. Taylor, and E. H. Zube. 1984. Toward a theoretical framework for landscape perception. In *Environmental Perception: Inventory and Prospects,* ed. T. F. Saarinen, D. Seamon and J. L. Sell, 61–83. University of Chicago, Department of Geography Research Paper. Chicago.

Shafer, E. L., Jr. 1969. Perception of natural environments. *Environment and Behavior* 1:71–82.

Shafer, E. L., Jr., and T. A. Richards. 1974. *A Comparison of Viewer Reactions to Outdoor Scenes and Photographs of Those Scenes.* USDA Forest Service, Research Paper NE-302. Upper Darby, Pa.

Shafer, E. L., Jr., and M. Tooby. 1973. Landscape preferences and international replication. *Journal of Leisure Research* 5:60–65.

Shuttleworth, S. 1980. The use of photographs as an environment presentation medium in landscape studies. *Journal of Environmental Management* 11:61–76.

Simpson, C. J., T. L. Rosenthal, T. C. Daniel, and G. M. White. 1976. Social-influence variations in evaluating managed and unmanaged forest areas. *Journal of Applied Psychology* 61:759–63.

Smardon, R. C. 1975. Assessing visual-cultural values of inland wetlands in Massachusetts. In *Landscape Assessment: Values, Perceptions, and Resources,* ed. E. H. Zube, R. O. Brush, and J. G. Fabos, 289–318. Stroudsburg, Pa.: Dowden, Hutchinson & Ross.

Sonnenfeld, J. 1967. Environmental perception and adaptation level in the Arctic. In *Environmental Perception and Behavior,* ed. D. Lowenthal, 42–59. University of Chicago, Department of Geography Research Paper no. 109. Chicago.

Taylor, J. G., and T. C. Daniel. 1984. Prescribed fire: Public education and perception. *Journal of Forestry* 82:361–65.

Tuan, Y. F. 1977. *Space and Place: The Perspective of Experience.* Minneapolis: Univ. of Minnesota Press.

Ulrich, R. S. 1979. Visual landscapes and psychological well-being. *Landscape Research* 4:17–23.

———. 1981. Natural versus urban scenes: Some psychophysiological effects. *Environment and Behavior* 13:523–56.

United States Forest Service. 1973. *National Forest Landscape Management,* Vol. 1. U.S. Department of Agriculture, Agriculture Handbook no. 434. Washington, D.C.: U.S. Government Printing Office.

———. 1974. The visual management system. *National Forest Landscape Management,* U.S. Department of Agriculture, Agriculture Handbook no. 462. Washington, D.C.: U.S. Government Printing Office.

Wilkinson, M. L. 1979. Women on the Oregon Trail. *Landscape* 23:43–47.

Wilson-Hodges, C. 1978. *The measurement of landscape aesthetics.* Univ. of Toronto, Institute for Environmental Studies, Environmental Perception Research, Working Paper no. 2. Toronto.

Wohlwill, J. F. 1976. Environmental aesthetics: The environment as a source of affect. In *Human Behavior and Environment,* vol. 1, ed. I. Altman and J. F. Wohlwill, 37–86. New York: Plenum.

———. 1978. What belongs where: Research on the fittingness of man-made structures in natural settings. *Landscape Research* 3:3–5.

Wohlwill, J. F., and G. Harris. 1980. Response to congruity or contrast for man-made features in natural recreation settings. *Leisure Science* 3:349–65.

Wohlwill, J. F., and H. Heft. 1977. A comparative study of user attitudes towards development and facilities in two contrasting natural recreation areas. *Journal of Leisure Research* 9:264–80.

Wohlwill, J. F., and I. Kohn. 1976. Dimensionalizing the environmental manifold. In *Experiencing the Environment,* ed. S. Wapner, S. B. Cohen and B. Kaplan, 19–54. New York: Plenum.

Wright, G. 1974. Appraisal of visual landscape qualities in a region selected for accelerated growth. *Landscape Planning* 1:307–27.

Zajonc, R. B. 1980. Feeling and thinking: Preferences need no inference. *American Psychologist* 35:151–75.

Zaring, J. 1977. The romantic face of Wales. *Association of American Geographers, Annals* 67:397–418.

Zube, E. H. 1973. Rating every day rural landscapes of the Northeastern U.S. *Landscape Architecture* 63:92–97.

———. 1982. An exploration of Southwestern landscape images. *Landscape Journal* 1:31–40.

Zube, E. H., ed. 1970. *Landscapes: Selected Writings of J. B. Jackson.* Amherst: Univ. of Massachusetts Press.

Zube, E. H., R. O. Brush, and J. G. Fabos, eds. 1975. *Landscape Assessment: Values, Perceptions, and Resources.* Stroudsburg, Pa.: Dowden, Hutchinson & Ross.

Zube, E. H., and C. V. Mills, Jr. 1976. Cross-cultural explorations in landscape perception. In *Studies in Landscape Perception,* ed. E. H. Zube, 162–69. Univ. of Massachusetts, Institute for Man and Environment. Amherst.

Zube, E. H., and D. G. Pitt. 1981. Cross-cultural perceptions of scenic and heritage landscapes. *Landscape Planning* 8:69–87.

Zube, E. H., D. G. Pitt, and T. W. Anderson. 1974. *Perception and measurement of scenic resource values in the Southern Connecticut River Valley.* Univ. of Massachusetts, Institute for Man and Environment, Publication no. R-74-1. Amherst.

Zube, E. H., J. L. Sell, and J. G. Taylor. 1982. Landscape perception: Research, application and theory. *Landscape Planning* 9:1–33.

CONCLUSIONS

Robert B. Bechtel
Robert W. Marans
and William Michelson

In this chapter we shall attempt to summarize the important issues connected with each method described in the book and strive for a synthesis both from a theoretical approach to environment and behavior studies and from the practical viewpoint of the practitioner and student attempting to find methods that fit problems in the real world. Such an attempt is foolhardy, but given the evolved state of the art, enough of a pattern is emerging to at least begin describing the broad outlines of some guiding principles. The theoretical watchwords are *ecological validity,* the process of linking data from concepts in the head to facts in the environment. The practical motto is *multiple methods,* a process of learning how to match and mix methods that reinforce one another without having to declare bankruptcy and keeping within tight deadlines. Both practical and theoretical issues really work together because every practical solution involves ecological validity and even the most theoretical problem cannot avoid the practical problems that are inherent in studies that deal with environmental variables.

The book ends with a fitting crescendo, a methods chart, which is intended as a distillation in a small space of some of the main points that the collective authors could bring to bear. Its purpose is to provide a starting place *after* the book is read from which methods can be matched to problems and the main text can then be used to reinforce or change the decision. Thus it is hoped that the reader will find it a useful guide whenever research in environment and behavior is contemplated.

HOW THE TOOLS FIT INTO THE UNIVERSE OF THE FIELD OF STUDY

The physical sciences take seriously the concept of the paradigm (Kuhn 1970). A paradigm is only a fancy name for how things are customarily done—in this case, how research is carried out. For the social sciences, which include anthropology, geography, psychology, behavioral economics, and sociology, the accepted way of doing things has depended on custom within each discipline. Anthropology has heavily relied on participant observation. Geography uses a number of different methods in environmental perception studies. Psychology has probably overemphasized the experiment as a paradigm. Behavioral economics has relied on survey research, while sociology has used surveys, observations, and a variety of techniques.

If it can be said that environment and behavior research has developed a paradigm, many would suggest it approximates the POE (see Zimring's chapter 9). Certainly, POEs have been the ''way of doing things'' more than any other technique used. But a detractor can easily point out that the POE is not a consistent method, even of evaluation, for it often uses more than one method, borrowing from the various contributing disciplines, rarely tests hypotheses or uses control groups, and often produces contradictory findings and interpretations of those findings. Whatever its limitations, it is not likely the POE will just go away. It may, in fact, evolve into a more fixed paradigm some day, because the POE seems to be in a state of evolution. But in any case, it addresses only one of the many calls for research on the built environment.

Yet, it would be remiss to say that environment and behavior research has no paradigm. It has many. It should have, because practical design problems are multi-sided and unceasingly original. All the methods mentioned in this book, including surveys, time diaries, behavior settings, observation, and so forth, are very much part of the paradigm of environment and behavior research. The point of the book is that environment and behavior research is truly interdisciplinary in its nature, truly *eclectic,* borrowing from every social science discipline and professional field. In this sense, as the book illustrates, the environment and behavior field borrows from others and is busily developing its own paradigms. All methods are acceptable, relative to their proper context and limitations. There is no doctrine of accepted practice that says any one method is a priori the proper way to do things. For this reason, however, attention must be paid more closely than in the more conventional disciplines to the problems of internal and external validity.

In the more conventional disciplines a long history of research has developed that painstakingly parcels out causal variables for examination. In the field of environment and behavior, the studies are so new that ''the environment'' is often a vague totality in which aspects and dimensions are still being discovered. Many studies talk about environmental variables and their influence on behavior without measuring or specifying the nature of these variables. Operational definitions of environment are only just emerging.

The main methodological problem of environment and behavior research, as it exists today, is to specify and examine those variables and sets of variables existing in the environment that influence behavior.

Most of the methods in this book have focused on procedures for understanding the dependent variables—that is, the behaviors and attitudes that are influenced by the environment. This emphasis reflects the state of the art, and it is the direct result of borrowing from fields that have had more time to develop concepts for behavior.

The problem can be cast as shown in figure C–1. In situation A, the naive observer assumes that because a certain behavior seems to be linked to a particular environmental variable, there is a one-to-one relationship such that variable 1 causes behavior 1 in a simple, direct fashion. Take the case of a pedestrian who sees a car coming toward him and moves. Because the connection can rarely be accounted for in such simple terms, most people will recognize situation B as somewhat closer to reality. Here it is shown that *several* variables work together to cause behavior 1. For example, in the simple act of perceiving, the car is a figure that is always part of a background. The street and this combine to produce the total situation in which the car is a threat because of where it is in relation to the observer vis à vis the street. The background itself is always part of a larger environmental context (the street, crosswalk complex). In short, it is not possible to extract single variables from the environment because they are arranged together in a system. A car does not move in a vacuum. It is

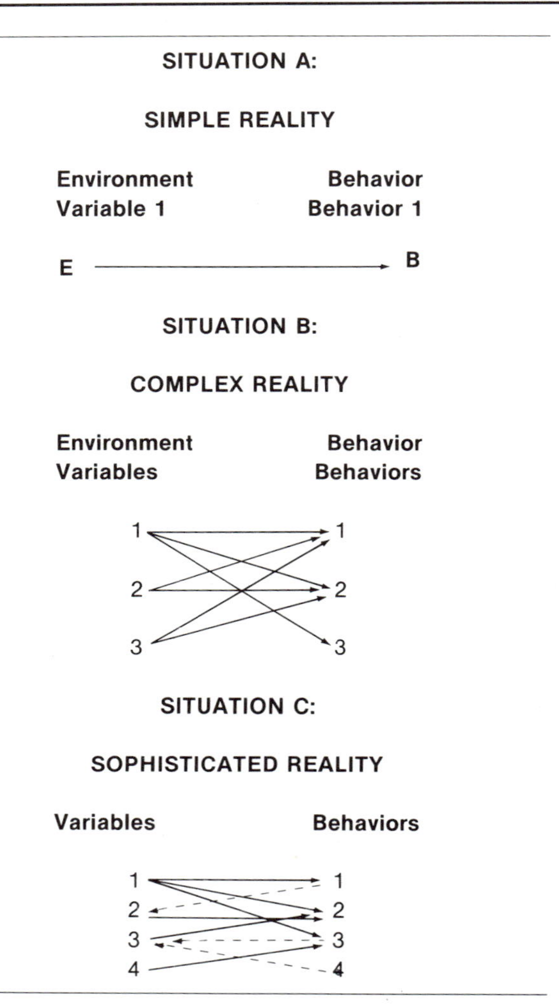

C–1. Three views of the relationship of independent and dependent variables in environment and behavior research.

usually on a street and only a threat to a person in front of it when it is moving. It is the whole set of circumstances that define the car as a threat. Were the pedestrian on the sidewalk, the moving car on the street would possibly not even be noticed.

Situation C, the more sophisticated view of reality, shows that many variables interact to cause several behaviors and these in turn then may influence the variables themselves.

For example, when the pedestrian sees a car bearing down while crossing the street, the pedestrian may move more quickly to avoid being hit. Therefore, the car changes from being background to being a figure, where it is seen as a threat but then returns to the background when quick movement makes it no longer a threat. In this short sequence the variables contained in the street, crosswalk, traffic, and a particular automobile interact to produce a threat. The behavior changes the situation by way of having the pedestrian move from the path of the auto. In this and many ways the complex of environment and behavior are constantly interacting to change and redefine situations and behaviors. The problem of environment and behavior research is to appraise how environmental variables interact to influence behavior and then to understand how the behavior interacts with the environment. Some abstract terms are necessary to provide a framework.

Every environment and behavior study requires evidence of *internal validity.* There is a striving to show that the elements of the environment directly influenced the elements of behavior in a clearly demonstrable way and without contrary interpretations.

External validity requires that the subjects and variables have been selected so that they are representative of populations at large and the results can be generalized. This is a research population to real-world population correspondence.

Ecological validity refers to finding the same relationship in the world outside the study that existed within the study. This is a research environment-to-real-world environment correspondence. It is possible to have both strict internal and external validity yet results that do not apply beyond the study group because the same configuration of variables that existed in the study cannot be found anywhere else. For example, research subjects may want to please researchers in an experiment, but the experiment may not reflect their behavior in the real world. This says that research studies sometimes create worlds of their own. Of all the methods presented, games exhibit this tendency most clearly, but every method that interferes with natural behavior in any way has the potential for creating its own world unrelated to the larger world.

According to the psychological perspective of Kurt Lewin, behavior is a function of the person and the environment, $B = f(P, E)$, but in many environment and behavior studies, each individual person is treated as an unknowable part of the equation. "Person" is assumed to represent a symbol that can be extrapolated for large numbers of persons. In this way, a significant number of environment and behavior studies ignore differences among individuals. A little reflection will show why individual differences are often not measured. First, an environmental variable that influences one person in a way that is peculiar to only that person is a finding that is too trivial to bother with. There is no way a study can be done to account for each individual's uniqueness in large populations. Environment and behavior studies are concerned only with variables across groups or classes of individuals. Of course, these may involve common individual differences because such individual qualities as introversion, blindness, tallness, and other traits are critical elements that interact with environmental variables and are common to many persons, not just a single individual. After all, whole classes of environmental variables must be modified to enable the handicapped to have a chance at approaching normal access. Even in this case, however, decisions are still made not to modify the environment, because the handicapped constitute too small a minority. Therefore, environment and behavior studies will often treat individual differences as a source of error unless they constitute a fairly large stable class of responses. This is a profound difference from, say, clinical psychology or psychiatry, where individual characteristics require a personally tailored therapy.

The situation is different, however, for what is called demographic characteristics. These are sets of variables that belong to a particular aggregate (or set) of individuals such as age, sex, family structure, and social and economic status (SES). Such variables are not tied to particular individuals but are seen as affecting large numbers of individuals as a whole. Thus, in this book we have chapters that deal with very large aggregates of the population such as the elderly and children because the variables operating within these groups cause special problems of measurement, as well as being highly salient to the persons involved.

AVOIDING THE PITFALLS

To continue with the rough concepts of figure C-1, consider that two major problems can arise that are peculiar to the field of environment and behavior studies. These have been pointed out in the literature as the failure to discriminate among environments (Danford and Willems 1975) and the confusion of a response to something in the environment with a response to a remembered word (Daniel and Ittelson 1981).

The failure to discriminate among environments is a very common problem. Danford and Willems (1975) pointed out this problem by showing that use of a self-report measure can appear to give agreement among behavioral responses that come from several environments because the self-report measure simply does not measure differences that discriminate among the environments. There appears to be an agreement or convergence of methods, but as Danford and Willems point out, a true convergence can only occur if it is first shown that the method can measure *differences* among the environments.

In fact, this requirement of discrimination is not just an obscure technical point, it can have highly significant practical value. For example, in the series of studies using the Scenic Beauty Estimate (SBE), Daniel and his associates (Daniel and Boster 1976) discerned which slides of forests had highest versus lowest scenic value. This was an exercise in discriminating among environments (Briggs 1980). If the SBE were not able to discriminate validly, the results would have wasted valuable timber, because decisions to cut (or not to cut) were based on these data. However, the research was carried further by then measuring which variables in the slide photographs *that could be manipulated by the forester* contributed most to the scenic beauty estimate (Schroeder and Daniel 1981). This was an exercise in separating out variables within the environmental arrays presented, an even finer distinction. If the SBE were not able to discriminate, the research could have misdirected the management of thousands of acres of forest land.

In another study (Buhyoff et al. 1982), it was shown that knowledge of how insect damage was caused lowered the SBE for forests, as opposed to the ratings by viewers who saw the same damage without knowledge that it was caused by insects. This was an exercise in the interaction of the verbal concept with the visual stimulus in the environment. Far too few studies have attempted to separate out the meaning of visual stimuli from the mere visual impact itself. Daniel and Ittelson (1981) argue that it must be known how large the verbal influence is before the environmental impact can be measured. It is not easy to do, but consider the confusion that can result if one attempts to measure the behavioral response to a new hospital design when what may have happened is that the subjects only responded to the verbal stereotypes of hospitals they carry around in their heads. These confusions are represented in figure C-2.

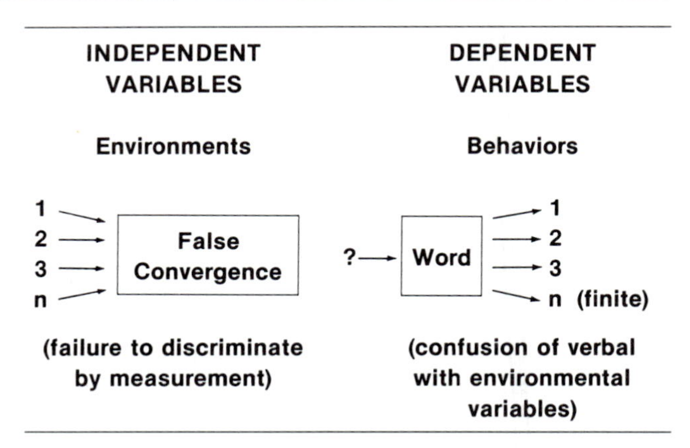

C-2. Two confusions in environment and behavior research.

Figure C-2 is similar to the figure C-1 in that the causal influence is assumed to flow from left to right—environment presumably influences behavior. In confusion 1, the three environments appear to be one because the instrument cannot discriminate among them. Thus, the instrument we used to measure *appears* to show that the environments were equal because we have only the measure that failed to discriminate among them. In confusion 2, the three behavioral responses are all stimulated by a single verbal concept and there is no contact at all with environmental variables. In this case the verbal concept we carry in our heads obscures any response to the environment and we falsely conclude that there are three behavioral responses to the environment when we have only measured responses to a word.

Another way to look at these confusions is to see that they both get in the way of measuring responses to the true environment. The failure of a method to discriminate among environments allows us falsely to conclude that they are equal, while the confusion of verbal with environmental responses does not let us measure anything environmental at all.

The two confusions can also overlap. A verbal stimulus, as in Danford's Law School example (1975), can obscure any distinction between actual parts of a law school environment or slides of a law school. As Danford found, using the words "law school" produced the same semantic differential scores as visiting the school or seeing slides of it.

Thus, environment and behavior studies must avoid the instrument's failure to discriminate among the specific environmental variables being studied and to eliminate the obfuscation caused by intruding verbal concepts. This is done by *pre-testing* instruments in an experimental fashion among the environmental variables to be studied and by being able to show contrasting results between the specific verbal concepts with the specific environment to be measured.

CHOOSING THE RIGHT TOOLS

Since it has now become common practice to use at least three methods (Bechtel and Srivastava, 1978) these must be chosen for compatibility and the ability to provide the data that will solve the problem. The following is a summary of cautions and admonitions about the use of each method treated in the chapters of this book.

Methods

Observation. Observation is a favorite "matching" method. It is almost never used by itself but will almost always precede or be accompanied by a questionnaire or interview. While it has the problem of causal inference, it is the one method that does not require independent confirmation to establish validity. More often than not, it is observation that establishes validity for other methods. Observation can be the loosest of methods, with no structure and no precision, or it can be the most precise method, employing highly structured categories and precisely sampled time intervals. Observation more nearly answers the question, What happened? than any other method. As soon as one wants to know *why* something happened, however, it becomes obvious why observation is almost never used alone.

Photography, which is recorded observation, has become a technological growth field in environment and behavior research. Time-lapse photography has developed into a separate method by itself and viewing the films provides a self-evident aspect of behavior to clients as well as a data source.

Zeisel's pioneering work in trace analysis has also become a separate branch in itself.

The three chief constraints to keep in mind when considering observation are: lack of causal inference, the possible intrusiveness of the observer, and the difficulty of obtaining a high reliability of observation categories. The lack of causal inference is usually overcome by accompanying observation with a method like an interview or questionnaire that asks directly about the behavior being observed. Intrusiveness can be overcome by either hiding the observer from view or allowing the observer to become a part of the surroundings so that the act of observation is not salient.

Obtaining reliable categories of behavior for observation is always a major effort. Often, filming the behavior to be studied helps train observers to a high degree of agreement. After reliability is established, it needs to be checked at mid-point and at the end of data collection.

Other problems with observation are determining the representativeness of the behavior observed and determining whether the time selected for observation biases the data in any way.

Survey Research. The survey usually involves face-to-face interviewing using a standardized questionnaire. Variations in data-gathering techniques include the mail or drop-off survey, which eliminates direct contact with the respondent, and the telephone survey, which relies on verbal contact only.

Actually the open or free response interview, followed by the structured interview, followed by the standardized questionnaire, and ultimately realized by the paper and pencil test can be seen as a continuum from least to most structured and least to most pre-tested and standardized. The most highly structured paper and pencil test began as an open-ended interview—many interviews have a way of ending up as more structured tests if they are to be used over a period of time. The survey questionnaire fits into this continuum at a point just before the paper and pencil test. On occasion, it is not standardized, but the instrument used is always pre-tested. The decision to standardize a survey questionnaire is a *conscious* attempt to gather comparable data from all respondents; this may be desirable for most surveys but not necessarily all.

The constraints to keep in mind when using a survey are the time and effort it takes to sample the population and to design, pre-test, and administer the questionnaire, and the size of the sample required.

Another problem of surveys is that many represent a situation at only one point in time, forcing retrospection for phenomena at earlier times. Panel studies help overcome problems of memory in assessing changes over time, but panels are costly and may have high attrition rates.

Nonetheless, survey research remains the most effective method of dealing with large numbers of people. Surveys, and the questions associated with them, have been perfected over decades of practice. It is the sampling technique that permits representative data collection that can be generalized accurately to large populations. Of course, other techniques can be embodied as part of surveys, such as the time diary or paper and pencil tests.

Observation-simulations and behavior setting techniques would be more difficult if not impractical to incorporate as part of a survey. On the other hand, survey methods can be used to develop paper and pencil tests (and paper and pencil tests can be embodied within surveys) and to do POEs, and can be embodied in other kinds of environment and behavior research.

A sample to be surveyed can be selected to represent not only many groups of people but also many types of environmental conditions, from workers at a single type of industry to people living in diverse geographical areas. And, like other methods, surveys are most effective when combined with other techniques, although a good survey would probably stand alone better than any other method covered in this volume.

A general problem with surveys, as with all methods, is that independent verification is needed to establish validity and this means, perhaps, a subsample for observation, an archival study, or some other means of measuring what the survey measures to demonstrate its validity.

Finally there is the problem of the high cost of conducting surveys, particularly those involving face-to-face interviews. Even the cheaper mail survey does not totally solve this problem, since it usually has a high attrition rate and must be pre-tested and validated.

Paper and Pencil Tests. The chief constraint in using paper and pencil tests is the high degree of specificity for which each test was created. Most tests have been created to measure some sort of internal or interpersonal variable (intelligence, values, or attitudes) and rarely are applicable to the measuring of behavioral response to environmental variables. Further, most tests are standardized on specific populations such as high school students and can be misleading or invalid when used on different populations. Few tests have been broadly enough standardized to have norms for most populations. The elderly and children may have difficulties with written tests.

The growth of environmental scales like the Social Climate Scales is the ''big news'' of paper and pencil instruments. While these do not yet go as far in measuring physical environmental qualities as many would like, they stand as the most standardized instruments in the field. Other instruments like the Internal-External scale continue to serve as workhorses.

The semantic differential continues in use despite the controversy it has spawned. Associated discriminant validity and verbal confusion problems may become the classical methodological dilemmas of the field. Such controversies are a sign of growth and sophistication, because they recognize and deal with increasing complexity.

Trade-off Games. The earlier edition of this volume touted trade-off games as a tool of research. That direction was not taken. Instead, they have become an extremely valuable and extensively used educational and training tool. The central experience around which trade-off games are built involves having to make decisions with limited resources. The game provides the player with the experience of making painful choices among various parts of a house, different services in a community, or even between such controversial items as defense versus social programs. The purpose of such games is to provide the player with the experience of having to decide among the same painful choices that a manager or policy maker must decide. The net result is to gain greater understanding and sympathy for the decision maker and the decision-making process. It is worthwhile noting that when it comes to cutting amenities in housing, the average subjects make the same cuts that housing managers typically find necessary—in areas such as landscaping. But it was also interesting to note that subjects were willing to cut services to residents more than professional planners anticipated.

The trade-off game can be used as part of a mailed questionnaire or telephone interview as well as a group session. This permits random selection and high generality. The data from a trade-off game can be projected graphically as a function. Trade-off games have wide applications across many populations and age ranges. They are an important tool for programming and planning and they can generate crucial variables as ideas for further research. However, the major problem of extrapolating to reality has not been overcome.

Simulation Studies. Both games and simulations must take great care to reproduce a real-life situation so that data can be generalized to some part of the environment. Simulations promise the savings of testing designs before actually building. The two constraints are the cost of the simulation and the difficulty of getting a valid simulation. While sophisticated simulators such as in-flight trainers work well and have high validity, their use for most research is too costly. On the other hand, cheaper simulations such as colored slides introduce validity problems.

With increasing sophistication in electronic technology and photographic techniques, simulation studies may become a more widely used method in environment and behavior research. Now that home video sets are available and techniques for simulating live situations through models have been perfected, simulations have begun to have a larger impact. As the cost of the hardware comes down and techniques become better known, simulations are reaching the classroom level as demonstrations. Reizenstein-Carpman's (1985) hospital entrance simulation is an example of the new video techniques that demonstrate such promise. It is now possible to arrange a convincing television simulation and reach a design decision in a matter of weeks.

Behavior Settings. The use of ecological psychological methods suffers falsely from the reputation of being too long and costly, and consequently few people have been trained in this technique. Yet in terms of fulfilling the broad perspective of design questions, the behavior setting survey remains the most comprehensive of all methods. Even so, it is best used with questionnaires asking about values and meaning. The new questionnaire methods, with practice, can yield the same completeness of global behavior as the old. Behavior settings are also effective in testing hypotheses and in POEs.

A limitation of behavior setting methods is that they become too unwieldy for very large populations, and sampling of settings will not solve the problem because one needs to know how many behavior settings exist before they can be sampled! Hence behavior setting surveys are limited (for the present) to relatively small communities or to known entities like organizations, buildings, or institutions. Karl Fox's work (1984), however, shows the promise of extrapolating behavior settings from economic data in large cities. At some future date it may be possible to do a behavior setting survey of a city through its economic archives. Furthermore, the language of behavior settings has crept into many of the other methods.

Time Budget and Time Geography. Time-budget measures are being put to practical use more often than some of the other methods considered. The many variations, such as questionnaires covering previous day activities, time diaries, and similar techniques, have now reached a stage of usefulness that is making them an increasingly important part of environment and behavior research. The importance of daily behavior is becoming recognized as both an objective and outcome of design, and the time budget is especially suitable for macro-level urban research topics. Time-budget methods offer a quick and relatively accurate way to measure the details of daily life in the context of environmental reference points. In addition, they have the advantage of wide use cross-culturally.

Disadvantages of the time diary are a loss of accuracy the longer the time span recorded, the small degree of intrusiveness required in recording activities, the problems of interchangeability of coding categories of time, and high costs. Usually time diaries are used for only a day or a week. Strategies such as telephone follow-ups to elicit longer diaries and increase accuracy have been developed to handle some of these difficulties. Another recently adopted strategy is to combine behavior settings with time diaries and to collect time data only on the behavior settings. The desire for varying degrees of subtlety in coding remains a significant problem of comparison among studies. Time budgets do not work well with children under ten or with the impaired elderly.

Time studies require explicit attention to evaluate the importance of various blocks of time in order to determine which amounts of time are most valuable to the respondent. Amounts of time alone cannot be assumed to be the indicator of meaningfulness.

Time geography promises to expand the concept and use of time studies to a much broader range combining the use of geographical space with the behavioral constraints imposed by time limitations. Time geography analyzes a given area to determine its behavioral potential, a concept remarkably similar to Barker's behavioral richness index. Time budgets and time geography remain an important tool of urban planning research.

Applications

Programming. It is appropriate that the second part of this book began with a chapter on programming because programming is nothing less than the information assembly upon which all design is based. Yet, as Spreckelmeyer states, (unfortunately) programming is currently seen as an additional, not a basic, service of design. Much has been written about this incongruity in the design professions, but at the least, it is a technological lag. Ironically, it is government and industry, not the design professions, that have taken the lead toward implementing the programming process (Bechtel and Zimring 1985).

As Spreckelmeyer points out, a decision-making

model of some kind must be involved in translating the information into the design process. But the programming concept goes beyond the design process and applies to any operation that utilizes information: public administration, policy making, legislation, and planning at any level. It is one of the ironies of our time that we live in a society that has produced the information explosion but at the same time has remained a society that has yet to learn how to use the vast amounts of information available—hence, the primary reason for programming in any endeavor that requires information use.

The Post-Occupancy Evaluation. POEs are evaluations of a physical environment, whether a building, a grouping of buildings, or a landscape. They use a combination of methods, and often suffer from a lack of focus. The best use of POEs is over a continuous series of evaluations so that each design can be an improvement over the last one. The constraints of the POE are the constraints of the various methods taken up—much the same as in programming.

Post-occupancy evaluation constitutes a mix of several of the above mentioned methods and is currently the most frequently applied vehicle for conducting research about behavior and the built environment. It is curious that both ends of the POE process are as important as any of the methods used. As Zimring points out in discussing the *entry* to a POE, it is absolutely critical that all persons who will be influenced by POE results become involved in the process. The POE is the most political of all the processes described in this book and must fit smoothly within the organization involved. Similarly, the presentation of data, the *endpoint,* really determines whether the POE information gets used. If an anatomical analogy may be permitted, the POE is like a muscle: it cannot function unless its origin and insertion are firmly anchored.

Children. Since the Cohen, Glass, and Singer study (1973) showed that noise can have harmful effects on the reading ability of children, the study of environmental influences on development has assumed a new importance. The Ziegler and Andrews chapter on methods to use when studying environmental influences on children shows a rough continuum from the most unobtrusive observation at the youngest age to the most sophisticated paper and pencil instruments in adolescence. Because of the time and expense that observation requires, there is a tendency to save time by such instruments as the Caldwell Inventory or the Environmental Response Inventory for Children (ERIC). However, observation should always be a blended part of any investigation of young children.

The use of parents as informants is not methodologically a sound practice when it comes to estimations of magnitude of environmental factors like noise or pollution. Parents are most useful when asked only to evaluate the presence or absence of a factor. The Bishop and Peterson (1971) study found that designers were remarkably poor in predicting children's preferences. This finding, with the general agreement that children are the most neglected age group in the field of design, further reinforces the need for more studies of children as a user group, keeping their special methodological requirements in mind.

The Elderly. Both the elderly and children require special methodological attention, because it is more difficult to apply many techniques to their situations.

Perhaps the most helpful distinction in dealing with an elderly population is to distinguish the impaired from the intact. The ''impaired elderly'' are those who have experienced the loss of some normal hearing, sight, or cognitive function. Generally, the ''intact elderly'' are not much different from the rest of the population. The fact that the elderly population also is generally less educated than younger age cohorts has been shown to have considerable effect on responses across many methods. Generally, the less educated use either middle or extreme ranges of response categories more. It has also been shown that the elderly in general often exhibit a favorable bias in responses to environmental questions. They appear to like the housing they live in and see fewer problems in the environment. These responses are seen as an environmental adaptation in themselves, a way of making life easier.

Interviewing is the preferred method of measuring an elderly population. Observation, especially of an ethnographic type, is a complementary method, while time diaries and more complex response modes often meet with difficulties in an elderly population. Lawton suggests ways to improve interviews with the elderly and cautions that most research has dealt with captive populations in nursing homes and age-segregated communities and is not representative. Studies of daily behavior of the typical elderly are lacking.

Environmental Perception. The four methods used in perception of environment studies are applicable to varying populations and problem situations. Experts are used, of course, when experts rather than average users are required. In every other respect the methods of assessment (scaling, for example) are the same. The expert method, then, is really just the use of a special population of subjects, and these special subjects can be ''experts'' even if they are trained for the job on the spot.

The psychophysical paradigm is adapted from experimental psychology, and landscapes are used as the principal stimulus. An example of the assessment method used is the Scenic Beauty Estimate (SBE), a simple ten-point scale that is used to rate slides taken at random from the environment to be assessed.

The cognitive paradigm attempts to assess meaning and importance as contrasted to preference and searches out responses to such variables as complexity, information load, and other cognitive aspects suspected to be inherent in any environment. Methods in this paradigm such as adjective check lists, survey questions, and the semantic differential are more often qualitative than quantitative.

The experiential paradigm attempts to understand the interaction between the environment and the organism. This paradigm measures values and feelings about landscapes and does not measure reliability of validity of instruments. It attempts to understand the true aesthetic experience.

According to Taylor et al., the expert paradigm provides a description of the environment, the psychophysical paradigm arrives at predictions about which dimensions are associated with public perceptions of beauty, the cognitive paradigm seeks an understanding of judgments of scenic beauty, and the experiential paradigm describes experiences of interactions between people and landscapes. The authors suggest combining paradigms to balance strengths and weaknesses.

Instruments in the psychophysical realm such as the SBE and various checklists have proved very useful in basic and applied research. The standardization of the SBE approaches that of a paper and pencil test.

CONCLUSION

Independent verification is the prime requirement for validity, and this phrase should be the watchword in the use of all methods. The results of one method should agree with the results of another, but care must be taken that the data are independent. For example, the presence of observers should not influence answers to a questionnaire and vice versa. The ultimate check is whether answers on one instrument correlate with answers on another. If both are administered at separate times and not connected by the respondents, the high correlation

SUMMARY CHART OF CONSTRAINTS FOR METHODS

	Biggest Advantage	*Biggest Disadvantage*
Observation	ecologically valid data	lack of causal inference
Survey	causal inference	cost/time
Tests	low cost, pretested	specificity
Perception of environment	low cost	validity
Ecological psychology	ecological validity	lack of causal inference
Time budgets	quantitative detail on daily behavior	cannot collect over long time, expense, amount of data
Games	education	validity
Simulation	cost	ecological validity
POE	environmental link	specificity

	Best Population	*Worst Population*
Observation	children	minorities
Survey	various	children
Tests	specific targets	children, elderly
Perception of environment	adults	children, elderly
Ecological psychology	various	minorities
Time budgets	adults	children
Games	various	children
Simulation	adults	children
POE	various	none

When you want to:

- Know how people use their time
  - Short term—time budgets
  - Long term—behavior settings
- Know what people do
  - Short term—observation, photography
  - Long term—survey research, behavior setting survey
- Educate or train
  - Short term—games
  - Long term—simulation
- Evaluate designs
  - Short term—POE, simulation (buildings—POE, out-of-doors perception paradigms)
  - Long term—POE
- Know what happened in the past
  - Short term—archives
  - Long term—literature search
- Know how people feel
  - Short term—questionnaires, paper and pencil tests
  - Long term—survey panels

confirms validity, but if respondents are aware of the connection, the association may be spurious.

The analysis in this book of many potentially fruitful research methods indicates that their applicability is a function of the research and design problems at hand. A method that is splendid at one level of specificity, for one setting, or with one age cohort may be inadequate at another. All methods have their strong and weak points.

Therefore, it is paramount that those applying research to the built environment not ride their favorite technique toward every potential topic or situation. Choice of method follows the problem in every research situation whether applied or basic. Those who wish to provide useful research for more than one very specific type of design problem will need to master a variety of techniques, as well as to be aware of what to use for particular needs.

Moreover, as the chapters on programming, POE, and applications for the young and the old indicate, the most fruitful results usually follow from a combination of research methods. These both complement and validate each other.

REFERENCES

Bechtel, R., and R. Srivastava. 1978. *Post Occupancy Evaluation of Housing.* Washington, D.C.: Department of Housing and Urban Development.

Bechtel, R., and C. Zimring. 1985. Successful use of POEs in large organizations. Symposium at EDRA 16.

Bishop, R., and G. Peterson. 1971. *A Synthesis of Environmental Design Recommendation, from the Visual Preferences of Children.* Northwestern Univ., Department of Civil Engineering. Evanston, Ill.

Briggs, D. 1980. Landscape evaluation: A comparative study. *Journal of Environmental Management* 10:263–75.

Buhyoff, G., J. Wellman, and T. Daniel. 1982. Predicting scenic quality for mountain pine beetle and western spruce budworm damaged forest vistas. *Forest Science* 28(4):827–38.

Campbell, D., and J. Stanley. 1963. *Experimental and Quasi-experimental Designs for Research.* Skokie, Ill.: Rand McNally.

Cohen, S., D. Glass, and J. Singer. 1973. Apartment noise, auditory discrimination, and reading ability in children. *Journal of Experimental Social Psychology* 9:407–22.

Danford, S., and E. Willems. 1975. Subjective responses to architecture displays: A question of validity. *Environment and Behavior* 7:486–516.

Daniel, T., and R. Boster. 1976. *Measuring Landscape Aesthetics: The Scenic Beauty Method.* U.S. Dept. of Agriculture Forest Research Paper RM-167, Rocky Mountain Forest and Range Experiment Station. Fort Collins, Colo.

Daniel, T., and W. Ittelson. 1981. Conditions for environmental research: Reactions to Ward and Russell. *Journal of Experimental Psychology: General* 110:153–57.

Festinger, L., S. Schachter, and K. Back. 1950. *Social Pressures in Informal Groups.* New York: Harper & Row.

Fox, K. 1984. Behavior settings and eco-behavioral science: A new arena for mathematical social science permitting a richer and more coherent view of human social systems. Part I. *Mathematical Social Sciences* 7:117–38.

Kuhn, T. 1970. *The Structure of Scientific Revolutions.* 2d ed. Chicago: Univ. of Chicago Press.

Petty, R., and A. Wicker. 1974. Degree of manning and degree of success of a group as determinants of members' subjective experiences and their acceptance of a new group member: A laboratory study of Barker's theory. *JSAS Catalogue of Selected Documents in Psychology* 4:43. Ms. no. 616.

Reizenstein-Carpman, J., M. Grant, and D. Simmons. 1985. Hospital design and wayfinding. *Environment and Behavior* 17:296–314.

Schroeder, H., and T. Daniel. 1981. Progress in predicting the perceived scenic beauty of forest landscapes. *Forest Science* 27(1):71–80.

Sommer, R. 1969. *Personal Space.* Englewood Cliffs, N.J.: Prentice-Hall.

Wicker, A., J. McGrath, and G. Armstrong. 1972. Organizational size and behavior setting capacity as determinants of member participation. *Behavioral Science* 17:499–513.

INDEX

Numbers in *italic* indicate figure numbers.